Springer Series in Information Sciences   12

Editor: King-sun Fu

Springer Series in Information Sciences

Editors: King-sun Fu   Thomas S. Huang   Manfred R. Schroeder

Multiresolution Image Processing and Analysis

Editor: A. Rosenfeld

With 198 Figures

Springer-Verlag
Berlin Heidelberg New York Tokyo 1984

Professor Azriel Rosenfeld

Center for Automation Research, University of Maryland,
College Park, MD 20742, USA

Series Editors:

Professor King-sun Fu

School of Electrical Engineering, Purdue University,
West Lafayette, IN 47907, USA

Professor Thomas S. Huang

Department of Electrical Engineering and Coordinated Science Laboratory,
University of Illinois, Urbana, IL 61801, USA

Professor Dr. Manfred R. Schroeder

Drittes Physikalisches Institut, Universität Göttingen, Bürgerstraße 42–44,
D-3400 Göttingen, Fed. Rep. of Germany

ISBN 3-540-13006-3 Springer-Verlag Berlin Heidelberg New York Tokyo
ISBN 0-387-13006-3 Springer-Verlag New York Heidelberg Berlin Tokyo

Library of Congress Cataloging in Publication Data. Main entry under title: Multiresolution image processing and analysis. (Springer series in information sciences ; v. 12). Based on a workshop held in Leesburg, Va., July 19–21, 1982. Includes indexes. 1. Image processing–Congresses. I. Rosenfeld, Azriel, 1931-. II. Series. TA1632.M85 1984   621.36'7   83-20074

Offset printing: Beltz Offsetdruck, 6944 Hemsbach/Bergstr. Bookbinding: J. Schäffer OHG, 6718 Grünstadt
2153/3130-543210

Preface

This book results from a Workshop on Multiresolution Image Processing and Analysis, held in Leesburg, VA on July 19-21, 1982. It contains updated versions of most of the papers that were presented at the Workshop, as well as new material added by the authors.

Four of the presented papers were not available for inclusion in the book: D. Sabbah, A computing with connections approach to visual recognition; R. M. Haralick, Fitting the gray tone intensity surface as a function of neighborhood size; E. M. Riseman, Hierarchical boundary formation; and W. L. Mahaffey, L. S. Davis, and J. K. Aggarwal, Region correspondence in multi-resolution images taken from dynamic scenes.

The number and variety of papers indicates the timeliness of the Workshop. Multiresolution methods are rapidly gaining recognition as an important theme in image processing and analysis.

I would like to express my thanks to the National Science Foundation for their support of the Workshop under Grant MCS-82-05942; to Barbara Hope for organizing and administering the Workshop; to Janet Salzman and Fran Cohen, for retyping the papers; and above all, to the speakers and other participants, for making the Workshop possible.

College Park, MD   *A. Rosenfeld*
September,1983

Contents

VIII

Part I

Image Pyramids and Their Uses

1. Some Useful Properties of Pyramids

A. Rosenfeld

Center for Automation Research, University of Maryland
College Park, MD 20742, USA

As the Table of Contents of this book demonstrates, multiresolution representations have many uses in image processing and analysis. This paper will not
attempt to classify, or even to list, all of these uses. Rather, it will concentrate on certain specific types of "pyramid-like" representations and will
describe some of their potential uses in image analysis.

Pyramids, in general, are data structures that provide successively condensed representations of the information in the input image. What is condensed may be simply image intensity, so that the successive levels of the
pyramid are reduced-resolution versions of the input image; but it may also
be descriptive information about features in the image, so that successive
levels represent increasingly coarse approximations to these features. Section
1.1 briefly discusses some of the different ways of constructing pyramids.

The most obvious advantage of pyramid representations is that they provide
a possibility for reducing the computational cost of various image operations
using divide-and-conquer principles. For example, intensity-based pyramids
can be used efficiently to perform coarse feature-detection operations on an
image (at a coarse grid of positions) by applying fine feature-detection operators to each level of the pyramid. Section 1.2 gives a few simple examples
of divide-and-conquer using pyramids.

Pyramids have the useful property of converting global image features into
local features. In particular, they permit local interactions between features
that are far apart in the original image. Some of these action-at-a-distance
properties of pyramids are described in Section 1.3.

Another important way that pyramids can be used is based on establishing
links between nodes at successive levels that represent information derived
from approximately the same position in the image. This allows us to construct subtrees of the pyramid whose leaves are pixels (or local features) in
the image, and whose roots represent global features of various types. As
discussed in Section 1.4, this provides some interesting possibilities for
cooperative computation involving both local and global information - e.g.,
pixel values and region properties. Thus pyramids provide a possible means
of bridging the gap between pixel-level and region-level image analysis processes.

1.1 Some Varieties of Pyramids

The simplest type of image pyramid is constructed by repeatedly averaging
the image intensities in nonoverlapping 2-by-2 blocks of pixels. Given
an input image of size 2^n by 2^n, applying this process yields a reduced im-

2

age of size 2^{n-1} by 2^{n-1}. Applying the process again to the reduced image yields a still smaller image of size 2^{n-2} by 2^{n-2}; and so on. We thus obtain a sequence of images of exponentially decreasing size: 2^n by 2^n, 2^{n-1} by 2^{n-1}, ... , 2 by 2, 1 by 1. If we imagine these images stacked on top of one another, they constitute an exponentially tapering "pyramid" of images.

In this simple method of pyramid construction, each node in the pyramid, say k levels above the base, represents the average of a square block of the base of size 2^k by 2^k. For most purposes, it would be preferable to use averages over regions that were more isotropic, i.e.,(approximately) circular rather than square. The sharp cutoff characteristic of unweighted averaging would also usually be undesirable; weighted averages, peaked at the center of the averaging region and falling off to zero at its border, would be preferable, and the regions represented by adjacent nodes should overlap. On methods of defining pyramids using overlapped weighted averaging, with isotropically varying weights, see the paper by BURT in this volume.

The nodes of a pyramid need not represent (weighted) averages of the gray levels in regions of the input image; they could also represent other types of information about these regions -- for example, various types of textural properties. As a more interesting example, we might represent information about lines or curves that are present in the image; here each node of the pyramid would store parameters that describe the curve(s) crossing its region of the image, and it would in general compute the values of these parameters on the basis of information provided by the nodes on the level below it. Such pyramid methods of curve encoding are described in the paper by SHNEIER in this volume.

These remarks suggest that many different types of pyramid representations might be useful in the analysis of a given image. In the following sections we will illustrate some of the ways in which such representations can be used.

1.2 Divide and Conquer

The process of pyramid construction is an application of the divide-and-conquer principle. The information at a given node is computed from the information at a small number of nodes on the level below; each of these in turn computes its information from that at a small number of nodes on the next lower level; and so on. If we could assign a processor to each node, and provide it with inputs from the appropriate nodes on the level below, the nodes on each level could compute their information in parallel. The total number of time steps required to compute the information at all levels of the pyramid would then be proportional to the pyramid height, which is the logarithm of the image diameter.

Multiresolution methods can be used to speed up many different types of image operations. An economical way to apply coarse feature detection operators (spot detectors, bar detectors, etc.) to an image at a coarse grid of positions is to apply the corresponding fine operators to the appropriate level(s) of the pyramid obtained by repeated averaging of the image. An efficient way to solve boundary value problems on an image is to use a multigrid approach in which we first perform relaxation on a coarse grid, then locally interpolate the results to a finer grid and use them as the new initial solution, and so on using successively finer grids; this yields rapid convergence even for the low-frequency components of the solution. Similarly, an efficient way to generate textures having significant low-frequency compon-

ents is to begin with a coarse-grid Markov model (using a small neighbor set),
then locally interpolate the results to a finer grid, use another model on
that grid, and so on. Various examples of such coarse-fine computational
methods are described in some of the papers in this volume.

1.3 Action at a Distance

The use of pyramids to encode image features makes it possible for the features to interact locally at higher levels of the pyramid, even though the
features themselves are far apart in the image. In this section we give a
few illustrations of this concept of "action at a distance"; for further
details see the paper by SHNEIER in this volume.

One method that has been used by SKLANSKY and his colleagues to detect
"blobs" in an image is to search outward from each pixel in various directions,
up to some maximum distance (the maximum expected blob radius), looking for
edges that are approximately perpendicular to the direction of search. If
such edges are found in enough directions, the given pixel is "surrounded"
by edges, we way that a blob has been detected.[1] A pyramid-based alternative scheme that does not require searching out to long distances is to
do a local search for edges, say out to distance 2, at each level of the
pyramid (up to some highest level, the log of the maximum expected blob diameter). This scheme capitalizes on the fact that any blob becomes a spot-
like local feature at some level of the pyramid.

As pointed out in Section 1.1, pyramid structures can be used to encode
increasingly coarse approximations to the curves (or edges) in an image. This
type of encoding can be used to bridge the gaps in broken curves; even if two
fragments of a curve are far apart, the nodes representing them will eventually become adjacent, and the common parent of these nodes will then discover whether or not the fragments are in alignment. Angles at any scale
can be detected without the need for extensive searches along the curve,
since eventually they give rise to pairs of adjacent nodes representing
relatively straight curve segments that have different slopes. Parallel
(or more generally, symmetric) pairs of curve segments can also be discovered,
even if they are far apart, since their nodes too will eventually become adjacent. The resulting local axes of symmetry can then in turn be merged into
increasingly global segments; by encoding both the axis and the local width, we
obtain an encoding of the "generalized ribbons" that occur in the image. These
types of processes for encoding blobs, curves, and ribbons are potentially useful for the multiresolution representation of information about the shapes
of regions in an image. (Compare the paper by CROWLEY in this volume.)

1.4 Bridging the Pixel-Region Gap

When pryamids are used to build up global features (blobs, curves, etc.) out
of local features, the node representing a global feature will generally contain
the values of various global properties of that feature, computed by merging
information about its parts. We can transmit these property values back down
through the pyramid, thus "informing" the pixels (or local features) about the

---

1. Strictly speaking, we need not search out to the maximum distance from every
   pixel; the longer the distance searched, the coarser the grid of pixels at
   which the search needs to be done.

global feature to which they belong. If we wish, we can then use the transmitted information to adjust the criteria that are used to combine the local
feature. In this way, for example, we can eliminate local features whose
properties do not conform closely enough to the global property values, thus
refining the definition of the global feature.[2]

By using vertical transmission of information in a pyramid in this way, we can
allow global (textural or geometrical) properties of a feature or region to directly influence the process of extracting that region from the image. [Infor-
mation about relationships between regions can also be used, in principle; note
that at the high levels of the pyramid, such information becomes local, and so
can be discovered by the nodes representing the regions and transmitted to their
constituent pixels.] Conventional methods of image analysis do not permit this
type of direct influence, since they do not provide a smooth transition between
the pixel level and the region level of image representation. In the conventional
approach, we first extract regions and measure their properties and relationships,
and if these are unsatisfactory, we must backtrack and repeat the extraction process. Pyramid methods now provide a potential means of bridging the gap between
pixel-level and region-level image analysis processes.

---

2. A similar idea can be used for pyramids based on (average) gray level or
   textural properties; see the papers by BURT and DYER in this volume. Here
   each node P contributes to the values of several nodes on the level above;
   we link P to any such node Q if the values of P and Q are sufficiently similar, and we then eliminate (from the averages) nodes that are not thus linked.

2. The Pyramid as a Structure for Efficient Computation

P.J. Burt

Electrical Computer & Systems Engineering Department
Rensselaer Polytechnique Institute, Troy, NY 12181, USA

Many basic image operations may be performed efficiently within pyramid structures. Pyramid algorithms can generate sets of low- and band-pass filtered
images at a fraction of the cost of the FFT. Local image properties such as
texture statistics can be estimated with equal efficiency within Gaussian-
like windows of many sizes. Pyramids support fast "coarse-fine" search strategies. Pyramids also provide a neural-like image representation which is
robust, compact and appropriate for a variety of higher level tasks including motion analysis. Through "linking," pyramids may be used to isolate and
represent image segments of arbitrary size and shape. Here the pyramid will
be viewed primarily as a computational tool. However, interesting similarities will be noted between pyramid processing and processing within the human
visual system.

2.1 Introduction

Several considerations have led to the present interest in pyramid structures
for image processing [e.g., 2.1-3]. Because they are hierarchically organized
and locally interconnected, pyramids support relatively simple yet highly efficient processing algorithms. Through level-to-level interconnections they
provide a bridge between pixel-level processing and more global object-level
processing. The pyramid may also be regarded as a model of certain types of
early processing in natural vision. For example, pyramid processing, like
vision, can be both spatially organized and organized into more or less independent spatial frequency tuned channels.

   Here I shall examine pyramids from the first of these perspectives, computational efficiency. A set of elementary pyramid operations will be described. These operations may serve a variety of image analysis tasks and
so are proposed as basic "computational tools." To illustrate their use and
generality, the pyramid operations will then be applied to image data compression and to texture and motion analysis.

   A particularly important property of natural vision, not shared by most
computer vision systems, is that analysis is essentially independent of image
scale. In order to identify mechanisms which underlie this property, I shall
begin the discussion by examining the role of image scale in human perception
of texture. Scale independence in this case can be understood in terms of
neural processing mechanisms which are analogous to the basic pyramid computations described here.

2.1.1 The Role of Scale in Texture Perception

Textures can often be described in terms of a two-level pattern hierarchy.
At a low, or microscopic level, this consists of the patterns formed by in-

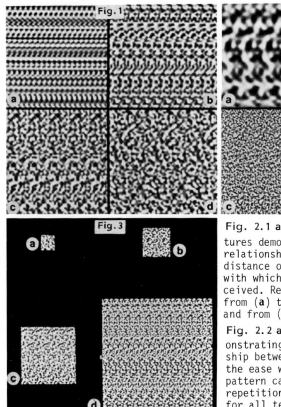

Fig. 2.1 a–d. Four artificial textures demonstrating the inverse relationship between the repetition distance or period λ_p, and the ease with which repetition can be perceived. Repetition distance doubles from (**a**) to (**b**), from (**b**) to (**c**), and from (**c**) to (**d**)

Fig. 2.2 a–d. Four textures demonstrating the direct relationship between grain size λ_g, and the ease with which a repeated pattern can be perceived. The repetition distance is the same for all textures, but the grain size is reduced by 1/2 from (**a**) to (**b**), from (**b**) to (**c**), and again from (**c**) to (**d**)

Fig. 2.3. Four textures demonstrating the direct relationship between texture area and the ease with which a repeated pattern can be perceived. Period length and grain size are the same in all textures

dividual texture grain elements, and at a higher, macroscopic level it consists of patterns formed by the distribution of these grain elements. Both grain and distribution patterns may be highly regular or more or less random. In order to distinguish one texture from another it is only necessary to measure appropriate characteristics of either of these patterns. Textures may then be used to segment the image into regions which ultimately will correspond to objects of interest. Unfortunately, computer procedures designed to obtain such measures must resolve a tree-forest scale dilemma. The system must select the scale at which to look for grain characteristics and another larger scale at which to look for distribution characteristics. An inappropriate choice may mean that texture elements are treated as objects of interest or that objects of interest are treated as texture grain. In general, different scales will be appropriate for different images and for different textured regions within a given image. These scales will not be known a priori.

The role of texture scale in human perception may be demonstrated with textures such as those shown in Figs.2.1-3. Each is constructed by bandpass filtering a random grain pattern which itself is repeated horizontally at regular intervals. Thus, two scale parameters characterize these textures: λ_g, the grain size (proportional to the wavelength at the center of the pass-band), and λ_p, the repetition distance or period.

The four textures in Fig.2.1 differ in the repetition distance only, so that λ_g is constant while λ_p doubles from Fig.2.1a to 2.1b and again from Fig. 2.1b to 2.1c and from Fig.2.1c to 2.1d. The reader may confirm that the repetitive pattern within these textures becomes more difficult to perceive as the repetition distance becomes longer. TYLER and CHANG [2.4] have quantified this effect by measuring the ability of human observers to perceive periodicity in textures. In effect, they determined the maximum period length, λ_p max, at which briefly presented periodic textures can be discriminated reliably from nonperiodic textures having the same grain structure. λ_p max may be regarded as a basic parameter of human vision: the spatial (angular) distance over which a texture is examined for repetition.

An intriguing observation made by TYLER is that a change in the overall scale of the texture image results in an equal scale change in the measured λ_p max. This may be appreciated qualitatively by the reader: changing the viewing distance to Fig.2.1, and hence image scale on the retina, does not significantly affect the detectability of texture repetition. If the repetition can be perceived in a given texture, it will remain perceptible if the texture is doubled or quadrupled in scale. This is true even though the new λ_p may be far larger than the period in other textures where repetition is not perceptible. Thus, the distance λ_p max which we interpreted above as a parameter of the visual system is found to depend systematically on the image itself. This observation is an example of a Perceptual Scaling Principle[1]:

Perception does not depend on the scale of the retinal image.

A corollary of perceptual scaling is the result described above:

Perception does not change with viewing distance.

Stated in this way, the scaling property is hardly surprising. It simply reflects the fact that the way we perceive objects does not change as we move towards or away from them[2]. Nonetheless, the property is worth emphasis because it is not shared by many computer image processing procedures. Too often, these are fixed in scale to the image sampling distance and yield different results when the image scale is changed relative to the sampling distance.

2.1.2 The Grain Size Effect

By what mechanism does the visual system match its processing to image scale? In the textures considered here, grain size λ_g, repetition distance λ_p, and image area change in proportion to any changes in image scale. It can be

---

1. Perceptual scaling has been found to hold in several "early" visual functions, including stereopsis [2.5-7] and motion perception [2.8,9], as well as in texture perception.

2. There are limits to the range of scales over which the scaling principle can hold: clearly a pattern cannot be so small (distant) that it becomes difficult to resolve, or so large (close) that it extends beyond the limits of the visual field.

shown that both grain size and texture area play critical roles in scale-independent texture perception in these examples.

The four textures in Fig.2.2 differ in grain size, λ_g, but all have exactly the same repetition period, λ_p. Again, the grain is random and bandpass filtered, but now the passband of each texture is an octave below that of its predecessor. Thus, λ_g is reduced by half from Fig. 2.2a to 2.2b and again from Fig. 2.2b to 2.2c and Fig. 2.2c to 2.2d. The reader may observe that repetition is most easily perceived in textures which have large grain size, Figs. 2.2c,d, while it can be difficult to detect in textures with small grain, Fig. 2.2b and particularly Fig. 2.2a. This dependence of the perception on grain size is summarized by the expression λ_p max = $H(\lambda_g)$ where H is a monotonically increasing function.

2.1.3 The Area Effect

The four textures in Fig.2.3 differ only in their area while grain size λ_g and period λ_p are identical. Now the periodicity is readily perceived only in the larger patterns (Fig.2.3c,d) while periodicity can be difficult to discover in the smaller patterns (Fig.2.3a,b). This result is not altogether surprising. Larger patterns contain more cycles of the periodic texture (horizontal direction) and more pattern elements per cycle (vertical direction) and thus a greater amount of repeated information on which the perception may be based. Indeed, it is found that λ_p max = $G(A)$, where G is a monotonically increasing function of the texture area A. This area effect demonstrates the ability of the visual system to take advantage of all available information, to "integrate evidence" over the entire area of the texture.

Neither the grain size nor the texture area alone is sufficient to account for perceptual scaling. Rather, it is the two taken together which yields an increase in λ_p max in exact proportion to texture scale. For scale factor s, it is found that H and G have the property[3]

$$\lambda_p \text{ max} = H(s\lambda_g) \ G(s^2 A)$$

$$= sH(\lambda_g) \ G(A).$$

We can account for scale-independent texture perception with a fairly simple model. Suppose that textures are analyzed in the visual system within a set of spatial frequency "tuned" spatially organized channels. Suppose also that neural processes responsible for detecting pattern repetition are localized in each channel to regions proportional in size to the spatial wavelengths handled by that channel. Then the observed λ_p max for a given texture would be proportional to the wavelengths in the particular channel analyzing the texture and that in turn would be determined by the frequency content (grain size) of the texture itself.

In a similar way, scale-independent processing can at least be approximated in computer image analysis through use of pyramid structures. Pyramid levels correspond to frequency-tuned channels. When a local operation is applied to a given level, the effective range of the operation in the image is proportional to the wavelengths processed by that level. This analogy will be made more explicit in the next sections as a set of elementary pyramid operations is developed. It will be found that some of these basic com-

---

3. This result was not stated by TYLER but appears consistent with his results. An analogous expression has been found to hold in stereopsis by BURT and JULESZ (unpublished).

putations embody a grain-size effect, others embody an area effect, and the net effect is scale-independent analysis. (See [2.10] for an alternative approach to scale-independent image processing.)

2.2 Pyramid Tools

Here I shall define four pyramid-based "computational tools." These basic operations will be applied in later sections to image coding and to motion and texture analysis. The operations include highly efficient multi-resolution low and bandpass filters and window functions. A fifth technique, for image segmentation, will be developed in Sect. 2.7.

2.2.1 The Gaussian Pyramid (Multi-Resolution Low-Pass Filter)

The Gaussian pyramid is a sequence of images in which each is a low-pass filtered copy of its predecessor. Let array G_0 be the original image; this becomes the bottom, or zero, level of the pyramid. Each node of the next pyramid level, image G_1, is obtained as a weighted average of G_0 nodes within a 5 by 5 window. Each node of G_2 is then obtained from G_1 by applying the same pattern of weights. A graphical representation of this process in one dimension is given in Fig.2.4. Note that the sample distance in each level is double that in the previous level. As a result, each image in the sequence is represented by an array which is half as large as its predecessor. If we imagine these arrays stacked one above another, the result is the tapering pyramid data structure[4]. Figure 2.5 shows the contents of the first five levels of a pyramid constructed from the 257 by 257 Lady image, G_0. Higher levels measure 129 by 129, 65 by 65, and so on[5].

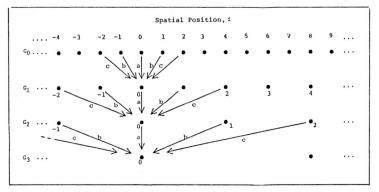

Fig. 2.4. A graphical representation of the repeated local averaging or REDUCE process used to construct the Gaussian pyramid

---

4. The weighting function used in pyramid generation may have a width other than 5 and the image-to-image sample reduction may be a factor other than 2[2.11]. Here these values have been selected for computational convenience.

5. The type of pyramid described here can be constructed from an image measuring $M_c 2^N+1$ columns by $M_r 2^N+1$ rows, where M_c, M_r and N are integers. The pyramid will contain $N+1$ levels and the ℓth level will measure $M_c 2^{N-\ell}+1$ by $M_r 2^{N-\ell}+1$.

GAUSSIAN PYRAMID

0   1   2   3 4 5

Fig. 2.5. The first six levels of the Gaussian pyramid obtained from the Lady image. Level 0, the original image, measures 257 by 257 pixels, level 1 measures 129 by 129, level 2 measures 65 by 65, and so on

The process which generates each image from its predecessor will be called a REDUCE operation since both resolution and sample density are decreased. Let G_0 be the original image and let G_N be the top level of the pyramid. Then for $0 < \ell \leq N$ we say

$$G_\ell = \text{REDUCE } [G_{\ell-1}]$$

which means

$$G_\ell(i,j) = \sum_{m,n=-2}^{+2} w(m,n) \, G_{\ell-1} \, (2i+m, 2j+n).$$

The weighting function w is called the generating kernel. This is chosen subject to four constraints. It is

    (i)   Separable: $w(m,n) = \hat{w}(m) \, \hat{w}(n)$

    (ii) Normalized: $\sum \hat{w}(m) = 1$, and

    (iii) Symmetric: $\hat{w}(m) = \hat{w}(-m)$.

The fourth constraint, "equal contribution", stipulates that each node at level ℓ contributes the same total weight to the nodes at level $\ell+1$. Let $\hat{w}(0) = a$, $\hat{w}(-1) = \hat{w}(1) = b$ and $\hat{w}(-2) = \hat{w}(2) = c$ as shown in Fig.2.4. Then

    (iv) Equal contribution: $a + 2c = 2b$.

Combining constraints we have

   a = free variable

   b = 1/4, and

   c = 1/4 - a/2.

Each node at pyramid level ℓ in Fig.2.4 is a weighted average of five nodes at level $\ell-1$, and each of these in turn represents an average of five (overlapping) nodes at level $\ell-2$. If we trace the pattern of weights from any level ℓ node to the original image, we find that there is always an "equivalent weighting function" W_ℓ which could have been applied directly to the image to obtain the G_ℓ values. That is, ℓ iterations of REDUCE are equivalent to convolving W_ℓ with the original image, followed by appropriate subsampling. It will often be useful to discuss pyramid operations in terms of convolutions with these equivalent weighting functions, although computations will always be performed through repeated application of REDUCE. As will be shown in a later section, the iterative procedure offers considerable advantages both in computation complexity and efficiency.

The set of equivalent weighting functions W_ℓ for $\ell=0$ to N exhibit several interesting properties. It is found that the shape of these functions depends on the value of the parameter a in the generating kernel, but that for a given generating kernel, all the W_ℓ have virtually identical shape. The functions differ in scale, however, and this doubles with each iteration. When a is about 0.4, the functions closely approximate the Gaussian probability density function as shown in Fig.2.6. (Note that axis scales have been adjusted by factors of 2 from level to level to aid in shape comparison.) It is this observation which has led to the name "Gaussian pyramid."

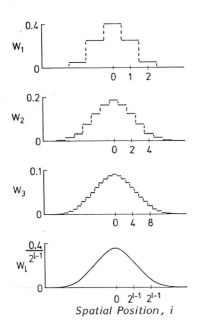

Fig. 2.6. Equivalent weighting functions obtained with a = 0.4 in the generating kernel. Note that scales have been adjusted by factors of two to aid in comparison. The shape of the functions converges rapidly to the Gaussian-like form shown at the bottom

Convolving an image with a Gaussian weighting function is equivalent to applying a low-pass filter to the image. Gaussian pyramid construction generates a set of low-pass filtered copies of the image, each with a band limit one octave lower than its predecessor. Sample rate reduction in the pyramid is in proportion to the band limit reduction, and remains above the NYQUIST rate. The Gaussian pyramid may, therefore, be viewed as a multiresolution low-pass filter.

2.2.2 Recursive Interpolation

A second pyramid operation, EXPAND, is defined as the inverse of REDUCE. Its function is to expand an image of size M+1 into an image of size 2M+1 by interpolating sample values between the given values. This is done, in effect, by reversing the direction of arrows in Fig.2.4. Let $G_{\ell,k}$ be the image obtained by applying EXPAND to G_ℓ k times. Then

$$G_{\ell,0} = G_\ell$$

and

$$G_{\ell,k} = \text{EXPAND} \left[G_{\ell,k-1} \right].$$

By this, we mean

$$G_{\ell,k}(i,j) = 4 \sum_{m,n=-2}^{2} w(m,n)\, G_{\ell,k=1}\left(\frac{i+m}{2}, \frac{j+n}{2}\right).$$

Here only terms for which (i+m)/2 and (j+n)/2 are integers contribute to the sum. Note that $G_{\ell,1}$ is the same size as image $G_{\ell-1}$, and that $G_{\ell,\ell}$ is the same size as the original image. Images G_{00}, G_{11}, G_{22} and G_{33}, obtained by expanding the first four levels of the Gaussian pyramid, Fig.2.5, are shown in the top row of Fig.2.7.

GAUSSIAN PYRAMID

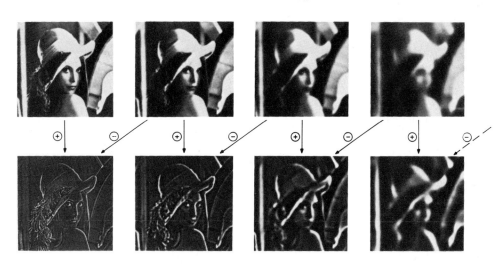

LAPLACIAN PYRAMID

Fig. 2.7. (*Above*) first four levels of the Gaussian pyramid expanded to the size of the original image. (*Below*) the corresponding levels of the Laplacian pyramid. While levels of the Gaussian pyramid represent low-pass filtered copies of the image, levels of the Laplacian represent convolutions with differences of Gaussian functions, or bandpass copies of the image

When EXPAND is applied to any image ℓ times, $2^{\ell}-1$ points are interpolated between each pair of neighboring image samples. In this process, the equivalent weighting function W_{ℓ} plays the role of an interpolation function. If a in the generating kernel is 0.5 then W is triangular and interpolation is linear. If a=.4, the interpolation function is Gaussian-like and resembles the cubic B spline [6].

2.2.3 The Laplacian Pyramid (Multiresolution Bandpass Filter)

A set of bandpass filtered images $L_0, L_1, \ldots, L_{N-1}$ may be defined simply as the differences between the low-pass images at successive levels of the Gaussian pyramid:

for $\ell < N$

$$L_{\ell} = G_{\ell} - \text{EXPAND } [G_{\ell+1}]$$

$$= G_{\ell} - G_{\ell+1,1}$$

and

$$L_N = G_N .$$

Image $G_{\ell+1}$ must be expanded to the size of G_{ℓ} before the difference is computed. Just as each node in the Gaussian pyramid represents the result of applying a Gaussian-like weighting function to the image, each node in image L_{ℓ} represents the result of applying a difference of two Gaussian functions to the original image. The difference of Gaussians resembles the Laplacian operators commonly used in image processing to enhance such image features as edges [2.12]. For this reason, we refer to the sequence of bandpass ima es $L_0, L_1, \ldots$ as the Laplacian pyramid.

Let $L_{\ell k}$ be the image obtained by expanding L_{ℓ} k times. Then $L_{\ell \ell}$ is the same size as the original image. The bottom row of images shown in Fig. 2.7 is the result of expanding the first four levels of the Laplacian pyramid for the Lady image. Note again that each level represents the difference of two levels of the Gaussian pyramid, and that this tends to enhance image features such as edges. Enhanced features are segregated by size with fine detail in L_0 and progressively coarser detail in each higher level.

An important property of the Laplacian pyramid is that the original image can be exactly recovered by summing pyramid levels:

$$G_0 = \sum_{\ell=0}^{N} L_{\ell \ell} .$$

Thus, the pyramid can be viewed as a reversible image code.

The zero crossings of bandpass images are being used by a number of researchers for such tasks as motion and stereo analysis [2.13,14]. These

---

6. Recursive interpolation does not strictly preserve the values at the original sample points unless c=0 in the generating kernel. A width-7 generating kernel with c=0 may be used to obtain smooth interpolation without altering the original samples, although this is not necessary for any of the applications described here.

Fig. 2.8 a–d. Zero crossings of the first four Laplacian pyramid levels for the Lady image

filtered images may be obtained particularly efficiently when the pyramid computation is used to perform the bandpass filtering. An example using the Lady image is shown in Fig. 2.8. Here, white pixels indicate positions of zero crossings at which the image gradient is positive to the right or bottom. Black pixels indicate zeros where the gradient is positive to the top or left. All nonzero-crossing points are represented by gray.

2.2.4 Hierarchical Discrete Correlation (Multiscale Window Function)

We now define a variant of the REDUCE operation in which sample density is not changed with each iteration. This process will be called the hierarchical discrete correlation [2.11] or, for the present discussion, the HDC window function. It is shown graphically in Fig. 2.9. Again, a sequence of images g_1, g_2,... is generated from an original image g_0. As in REDUCE, each node value in g_ℓ is obtained from a 5 by 5 weighted average of the values in $g_{\ell-1}$. However, the $g_{\ell-1}$ nodes which contribute to a given g_ℓ node are separated by a distance $2^{\ell-1}$ which doubles with each iteration.

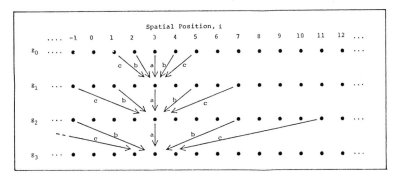

Fig. 2.9. Graphical representation of the HDC window function. This differs from Gaussian pyramid generation in that sample density is not reduced with each iteration

The HDC process is defined as follows:

$g_0 = f$, the original image, and

$$g_\ell(i,j) = \sum_{m,n=-2}^{2} w(m,n) g_{\ell-1} (i+m2^{\ell-1}, j+n2^{\ell-1}).$$

As with the Gaussian pyramid, each node represents an average value of the image computed within an equivalent weighting function W_ℓ. Nodes deleted in the REDUCE process are just those which are skipped in the HDC process. As a result, exactly the same equivalent weight functions contribute to nodes in both processes. Here, we regard W_ℓ as a local window. To simplify notation, we introduce the "average value" operator $A_\ell[\ ]$. Again, let $g_0 = f$, the original image. Then we define

$$A_\ell[f(i,j)] = g_\ell(i,j)$$

or simply

$$A_\ell[f] = g_\ell.$$

Thus, $A_\ell[f(i,j)]$ represents a local average of f obtained within the window W_ℓ centered at point (i,j).

In the above discussion, it has been assumed that f is a standard image so that $A_\ell[f]$ represents an average gray level. Alternatively, f could be some other two-dimensional function derived from an image. For example, if f is a binary "feature map" obtained by applying a feature "detector" to an image, then $A_\ell[f]$ represents the local feature density. More complex image properties may be computed efficiently by combining several HDC window operations. This will be the case in the motion analysis procedures defined below.

Unlike commonly used rectangular windows, HDC windows are Gaussian-like and circularly symmetric, so that the greatest weight is given to image points close to the window center. Through the HDC and pyramid procedures, many local image properties may be computed efficiently within windows of many sizes [2.15].

2.3 Image Representation

The form in which information is represented is a critical factor in any image analysis task. This representation, or image code, should be one in which the most salient information is also the most directly available. For the initial stages in the processing of complex scenes this seems to mean that relatively simple details such as edges should be enhanced. The code should be robust: changes in the viewing conditions or the presence of system noise should not greatly influence the image representation. The code should also be compact: it should not require excessive storage space. Finally, if it is to be a general code, suitable for a variety of analysis tasks, it should be complete: it should be possible to recover the original image from its representation within the vision system.

The Laplacian pyramid has many of these properties. As has been observed, edge features are enhanced in this code and furthermore are segregated by size. Changes in image scale correspond to simple shifts in the representation to higher or lower pyramid levels. The representation is complete:

by summing pyramid levels the original image is recovered exactly. We will now show that the Laplacian pyramid is a compact representation and one which is robust in the presence of noise.

2.3.1 A Compact Code

Each node value in the Laplacian pyramid is obtained from the corresponding Gaussian node by subtracting an average of neighboring node values. This has the effect of compressing image data by removing pixel to pixel correlations and shifting node values toward zero. The shift in values is evident in the histograms shown in Fig.2.10 of the Lady image and the bottom level of the corresponding Laplacian pyramid. Each pixel in the original Lady image is represented by 8 bits so pixel values in its histogram are distributed over a range from 0 to 255. The Laplacian pyramid, on the other hand, includes both positive and negative values, but these are clustered near zero. Since the range of values has been reduced, each sample may be represented with fewer than 8 bits. Furthermore, the values are not uniformly distributed, so that HUFFMAN or other variable word length encoding may be used to reduce the bit rate further. The entropy of the sample value distribution then provides an estimate of the average number of bits required per sample. In this case, it is roughly 4.5 or half that of the original image. Higher levels of the Laplacian pyramid must also be encoded, but their contribution to the effective bit rate is much less than that of the bottom level due to greatly reduced sample density.

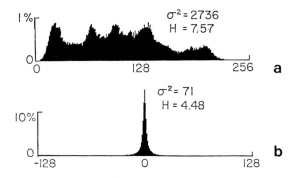

Fig. 2.10 a,b. Histograms of the Lady image (**a**) and first level of the corresponding Laplacian pyramid (**b**). The fact that node values are concentrated near zero means that fewer bits are required to represent node values in the latter case than in the former

In the technique outlined above the image is encoded without error. Considerably greater image compression can be achieved when a degree of degradation is permitted in the reconstructed image. Suppose, for example, that the number of discrete node values at level 0 of the pyramid is reduced by quantizing values into bins of size n: all samples between -n/2 and n/2 are set to zero, all between n/2 and 3n/2 are set to n, and so on. As n is made larger there will be fewer quantization levels and hence fewer bits will be required in the code. At the same time, increased n will result in increased image degradation. If image data compression is performed simply to achieve efficient storage or transmission and ultimately the image will be reconstructed for human viewing, e.g., for television, then the largest n should be found which just begins to produce noticeable degrada-

Fig. 2.11 a,b. Laplacian pyramid coding of the Lady image (**a**) yields little degradation at 1.58 bits per pixel (**b**)

tion. Humans are relatively insensitive to errors in high-frequency image components and are more sensitive to errors in low-frequency components. This means n in L_0 may be large, while in higher pyramid levels it must become progressively smaller. Figure2.11 shows the results of applying this technique to the Lady image. Here bin sizes of 19, 9, 5 and 3 have been used in the first four pyramid levels to obtain a rate of 1.57 bits per pixel of the reconstructed image. Degradation is just noticeable [2.16].

It seems likely that substantially greater image degradation can be tolerated if the encoded image is to be used for tasks such as motion or texture analysis. On the other hand, variable length HUFFMAN coding of node values is inappropriate for analysis applications, and each pyramid node must be allocated a fixed number of bits. Experiments have shown that 4 bits per node is quite adequate for motion analysis using the procedures to be outlined in Sect.2.5. The fact that substantial quantization does not degrade image appearance nor the results of image analysis demonstrates that the Laplacian code is indeed robust. It also means that arithmetic operations performed in the pyramid can be on very short data words.

2.3.2 An Analogy to Natural Vision

If very different images are presented to the two eyes, the resulting binocular perception will be a curious combination of features from the two monocular images. We may hope to discover the form of neural image coding at the level of binocular combination by carefully observing these perceived features. Suppose, for example, that a horizontal black bar is presented to the left eye at the same time that a similar vertical bar is presented to the right, as shown in Figs.2.12a,b. The resulting perception is somewhat unstable but often seems to consist of a central black square where the bars cross, flanked on all four sides by outlines of the end portions of the bars [2.17]. As might be expected, points in the central square region appear just as black in the binocular perception as they do in each of the monocular views. More surprising is the fact that the ends of the bars also appear black even though each is present in only one of the monocular images. Immediately around the central square is a halo of white and this is surrounded by a transition zone in which the white changes gradually to gray, then to the black at the ends of the bars.

If neural coding at the level of binocular combination is in terms of "high level" constructs such as "bars", we might expect to perceive both the right and left bars in their entireties. If, on the other hand, the representation is in terms of simple gray level samples, or pixels, then the combined image should be an average of the monocular images. We would expect its appearance to resemble a photographic double exposure with the central square black and bar ends a uniform gray (Fig.2.12c). Both of these explanations are contrary to observation.

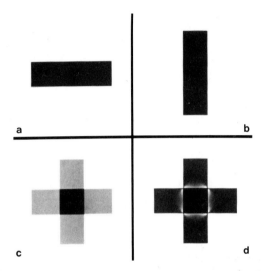

Fig. 2.12 a-d. When horizontal and vertical bars are presented to the left and right eyes respectively (a,b), the binocular perception retains all edge features from the monocular images, along with the gray level contrast across these edges. (c) shows the perception that would be expected if the visual system simply averaged the two images. (d) was obtained by combining the Laplacian pyramids for the left and right images and is similar to the actual perception

A more likely suggestion is that images are coded in terms of edge elements, with orientation and contrast specified in the code for each element. This suggestion is consistent with the observations, since all edges in the two monocular images are present in the perceived binocular image and each edge carries with it a region of black and white on either side. According to this hypothesis, the gray level in any uniform region of an image is not represented in the code at all but is perceptually inferred from the edge transitions surrounding the region. Thus, the central square appears uniformly black because it is surrounded by edges which specify black along their interior sides. Bar ends grade from white to black in rubber-sheet fashion because their edges specify both black and white along interior sides.

Although the edge coding hypothesis accounts at least qualitatively for the perceived binocular image, a still simpler explanation may suffice:

that code elements represent convolutions with Laplacian operations of many scales, as in the Laplacian pyramid code. To test this hypothesis, suppose the left and right bar images are separately encoded as Laplacian pyramids LL and LR, respectively. Suppose binocular combination is then achieved simply by constructing a third binocular pyramid LB, in which each node is set equal to the corresponding left or right monocular pyramid node with the largest absolute value. That is, for all i, j and ℓ

$$LB_\ell(i,j) = \begin{cases} LL_\ell(i,j) \text{ if } |LL_\ell(i,j)| > |LR_\ell(i,j)| \\ LR_\ell(i,j) \text{ otherwise} \end{cases}.$$

Figure 2.12d shows the reconstructed image obtained by following this rule. Note that ridges from both images are preserved in the binocular image even though they are not specifically encoded. The central square and bar ends are black as required. The shape and extent of the halo surrounding the central square represents the cumulative contribution of Laplacian functions of many scales. Thus, the Laplacian pyramid code along with the maximum-amplitude selection rule seems to account for the principal aspects of the binocular perception described above.

2.3.3 Multiresolution Spline

The Laplacian pyramid provides an elegant solution to a more practical problem in image combination, namely that of avoiding edge discontinuities in image mosaics. This problem is illustrated in Fig.2.13a where the left and right halves of a LANDSAT image of San Francisco have been separately distorted by adding low-frequency gray level functions. This simulates a mismatch that might have arisen if the two half images had actually been taken at different times under different cloud cover or lighting conditions. Even slight differences of this type will give rise to readily perceived edges in image mosaics. These edges cannot be removed through local blurring since this will also remove image detail. In principle, one would like to model the lighting conditions and correct for their effects before images are combined. However, sufficiently accurate models are generally not available.

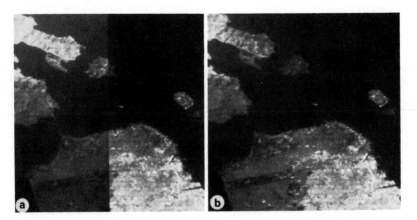

Fig. 2.13 a,b. Multiresolution spline: the boundary between the left and right halves of the Landsat image in (a) may be removed by merging their Laplacian pyramids and then reconstructing, as in (b)

20

The mosaic problem may be solved through use of a "multiresolution spline" [2.18]. In this technique, each image is first separated into a set of band-pass filtered component images, and the component images in each frequency band are then separately splined. Finally, the components are summed to obtain the desired mosaic. To spline a given pair of bandpass images, a new image is constructed in which pixels in a transition zone along the image boundary are a weighted average of the images on either side of the boundary. The width of this transition zone is proportional to the center wavelength of the bandpass filter. Thus, the zone is narrow for high-frequency image components and wide for low-frequency components.

The steps of the multiresolution spline are easily performed within the Laplacian pyramid structure. For the case shown in Fig.2.13a, Laplacian pyramids LL and LR are first constructed for the left and right half-images. Pyramid construction divides the images into the appropriate bandpass components. Next, a new Laplacian pyramid, LM, is constructed simply by copying values in its left half from LL and values in its right half from LR. Nodes which are positioned directly on the boundary between the two half-images are set equal to a simple (unweighted) average of the corresponding nodes in LL and LR. Finally, the mosaic is generated by summing the levels of LM. The appropriate degree of averaging for each passband is achieved automatically in the reconstruction process since node values represent scaled weighting functions which overlap along the boundary. The result of the process applied to Fig.2.13a is shown in Fig.2.13b. Note that the edge between the two half-images has been completely removed, that image details remain intact, and that this result has been obtained without any specific knowledge of the difference in lighting which gave rise to the original edge discontinuity.

2.4 Texture Analysis

2.4.1 Multiresolution Edge Density

It has been suggested that the density of edge elements may be a useful statistic for characterizing certain textures [2.19]. Here we extend the technique to edge detection and density estimation at multiple levels of resolution. Let f be the original textured image. The computation then proceeds in three steps:

Step 1: Let G_0 = f and construct a Gaussian pyramid $G_0, G_1, \ldots, G_N$ through repeated REDUCE operations.

Step 2: At each level G_ℓ of the Gaussian pyramid obtain an edge map E_ℓ by applying an edge operator. For example, for threshold T, let

$$E(i,j) = \begin{cases} 1 \text{ if } |G_\ell(i,j)+G_\ell(i+1,j)-G_\ell(i,j+1)-G_\ell(i+1,j+1)| > T \\ 0 \text{ otherwise} \end{cases} .$$

Step 3: Compute a set of local density functions for each edge map using the HDC process. Let $D_{\ell k}$ be the edge density function obtained by applying window W_k to edge map E_ℓ. Then

$$D_{\ell k} = A_k[E_\ell] .$$

The simple 2 by 2 vertical edge operator used in Step 2 is equivalent to the weighting function $W_\ell(i,j) + W_\ell(i+2^\ell,j) - W_\ell(i,j+2^\ell) - W_\ell(i+2^\ell,j+2^\ell)$ applied to the original image. This is a smoothly varying bimodal function as shown in Fig.2.14. Many other edge operators could be used in this step.

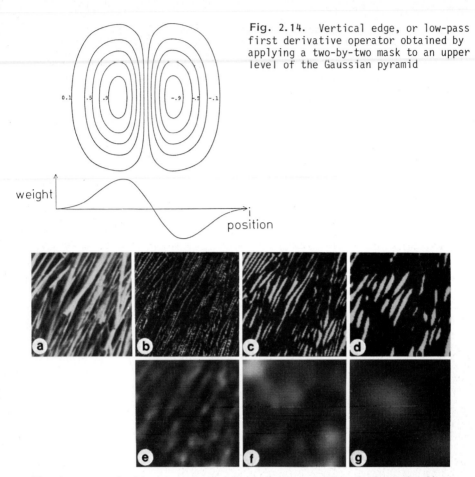

Fig. 2.14. Vertical edge, or low-pass first derivative operator obtained by applying a two-by-two mask to an upper level of the Gaussian pyramid

Fig. 2.15 a-g. Application of the edge operator of Fig. 2.14 to the first three levels of the Gaussian pyramid for the straw image (a) yields the edge maps shown in (b-d). (These have been expanded to the size of the original image.) The corresponding edge density functions obtained through a second application of the pyramid algorithm are shown in (e-g)

Edge maps E_0, E_1, and E_2 for the image in Fig.2.15a are shown in Figs.2.15b, c,d (expanded to the size of the original image). Edge density functions D_{02}, D_{12} and D_{22} are shown in Figs.2.15e,f,g. These and other pyramid-generated edge density functions are passed to other processes which perform actual texture classification.

2.4.2 Local Spectral Estimates

Estimates of the local power spectrum may also be used to classify textures. Again, it is desirable to obtain such estimates within windows of various sizes. The FFT may be used for this purpose provided Gaussian-like weighting functions are applied before the transform in order to avoid introducing spurious high-frequency components due to effective edge discontinuities. As a result of these two requirements, the computation is expensive.

The full spectrum provided by the FOURIER transform is not needed nor even desirable for texture discrimination. A set of energy estimates within relatively broad frequency bands are readily obtained from the Laplacian pyramid. The energy within a frequency band represented by a given level of the pyramid may be computed directly by squaring and summing the sample values at that level. The HDC window operation is applied to the squared values to obtain spatially localized spectral estimates.

Again, let f be the textured image. Estimates are computed in four steps:

Step 1: Let G_0 = f and generate the Gaussian pyramid $G_0, G_1, \ldots, G_N$ through repeated applications of REDUCE.

Step 2: The Laplacian pyramid is obtained as the difference of Gaussian levels: $L_\ell = G_\ell - \text{EXPAND } [G_{\ell+1}]$.

Step 3: Values in the Laplacian pyramid are squared to obtain arrays L_ℓ^2.

Step 4: The HDC window function is applied to each of the L_ℓ^2 arrays from Step 3 to obtain energy estimates $E_{\ell k} = A_k[L_\ell^2]$.

These sets of energy estimates are then passed on to another process which performs the discrimination task. The spectral estimates obtained from the Laplacian pyramid above are not sensitive to any prominent texture directionality. To compute orientation-selective estimates, various oriented opera-

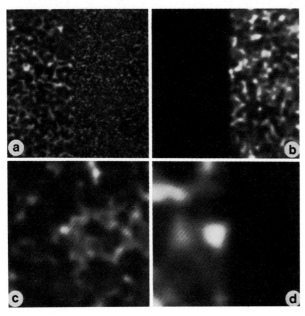

Fig. 2.16 a-d. Local spectral estimates for the texture in (**a**) may be obtained by (1) constructing its Laplacian pyramid, (2) squaring pyramid node values, and (3) integrating these values within local windows through a second application of the pyramid algorithm. This yields the energy estimates E_{02}, E_{12}, and E_{22} shown in (**b-d**), respectively. Note that E_{02} and E_{22} could be used to discriminate the coarse and fine textured regions of the original image

tors may be applied to each level of the Gaussian pyramid (Step 2). Operator outputs are squared (Step 3) and integrated (Step 4) as before. LAWS [2.20] has identified several operators of this type which yield good discrimination when applied at a single level of resolution. LARKIN and BURT [2.21] have used these and other operators for texture discrimination using multiple pyramid levels.

An example of pyramid-generated spectral estimates is shown in Fig.2.16. In this case, the original image Fig.2.16a consists of a relatively fine texture on the right and a coarser texture on the left. Figures 2.16b,c,d show energy arrays E_{02}, E_{12}, and E_{22}. Again, each spectral estimate array has been expanded to the size of the original image to aid in comparison. We see that only the fine texture in the right half of the original image has appreciable energy in L_0 while only the texture on the left has appreciable energy in L_2. The two textures have comparable energy in L_1. In this case, estimates from L_0 and L_2 could be used for texture discrimination.

2.5 Motion Analysis

2.5.1 Correlation Method

Suppose f and g are successive images in sequence depicting image motion. We wish to compute the optical flow field, or displacement vector field, between f and g by using correlation to identify matching image regions. Correlation matching tends to be computationally costly, so in developing the present pyramid-based approach, particular attention has been given to minimizing this cost.

To begin, a window function is used to subdivide the first image into a set of overlapping regions. An attempt is then made to locate the pattern contained in each of these windows within the second image. A priori knowledge of the possible magnitudes of the image velocities is used to limit the size of the search area in which a match is sought.

The overall cost of performing the match for a given window is proportional to $(D/\Delta_i)^2 (M/\Delta_c)^2$, where D is the diameter of the window, Δ_i is the sample distance used to define the pattern within the window, M is the diameter of the search area, and Δ_c is the sample distance of the correlation function. To minimize cost, we must make D small and Δ_i large. However, it has been found that the ratio D/Δ_i cannot be less than about 10 or the pattern contained in the window will not have sufficient detail to permit a reliable match. The sample distance in the correlation function, Δ_c, should approximately equal that of the pattern itself, $\Delta_c \simeq \Delta_i$. The frequency content of the pattern limits the rate at which the correlation function will change, so a smaller Δ_c will be redundant while a larger Δ_c may miss the correlation peak.

Finally, a coarse-fine search strategy is used in order to minimize the size of the search area, M. In this approach, a coarse estimate of the displacement is first found using low-pass filtered, coarsely sampled images. The estimate is then refined progressively with higher resolution images [2.22]. Estimates at each step are used to restrict the search area for the next step. In the procedure outlined here M/Δ_c has been reduced to just 3.

Suppose at the beginning of a particular iteration of the coarse-fine search it is known that the image displacement d is within an interval of size $\pm 2^k$. This a priori knowledge may be provided by known camera motion, by previous frames of the motion sequence, or, more generally, by previous iterations of the coarse-fine search procedure. The objective of this iteration is to obtain an estimate d_k of the displacement such that $|d-d_k|$ $<2^{k-1}$. That is, uncertainty in the actual displacement should be cut in half at this and each iteration. Thus, rather weak requirements are placed on the accuracy of the matching process at each iteration. The coarse-fine search is terminated when a desired level of resolution has been achieved.

Each iteration of the correlation matching process consists of four steps. To simplify notation, these steps will be outlined for the horizontal component of displacement only (see Fig.2.17). The vertical component is obtained in an analogous fashion.

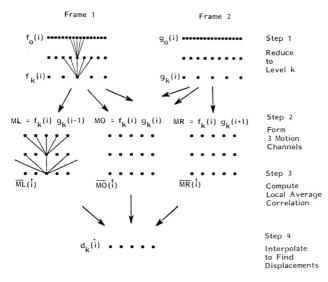

Fig. 2.17. Outline of a correlation approach to motion analysis in which pyramid procedures are used to minimize the cost of computation

Step 1: Let $Gf_0=f$ and $Gg_0=g$. Gaussian pyramids Gf_0, Gf_1,...,Gf_k and Gg_0, Gg_1,...,Gg_k are constructed to level k for f and g respectively. This reduces the search interval from $\pm 2^k$ in the original images to only ± 1 sample interval at level k.

Step 2: Three "motion channels" are formed by shifting and multiplying images Gf_k and Gg_k:

$ML(i) = Gf_k(i)\ Gg_k(i-1)$ Motion left

$MO(i) = Gf_k(i)\ Gg_k(i)$ Zero motion, and

$MR(i) = Gf_k(i)\ Gg_k(i+1)$ Motion right.

(Certain other quantities may also be computed, depending on the type of correlation to be used, as discussed below).

Step 3: A local correlation is computed within each channel by applying the HDC window function:

$\overline{ML}(i) = A_2[ML(i)]$, etc.

Just two iterations of this process are used to obtain correlation estimates which are reliable yet low in cost.

Step 4: Correlation values obtained in the three motion channels constitute "evidence" for motion in the respective directions. A single estimate of the displacement d_k is obtained at each sample position by interpolating between values in the three channels. For example, if a parabola is fit to the three data points and d_k is taken to be the position of the maximum of the parabola, then

$$d_k(i) = \frac{\overline{MR}(i) - \overline{ML}(i)}{\overline{MO}(i) - \frac{1}{2}[\overline{MR}(i) + \overline{ML}(i)]} .$$

In fact, a modified parabolic interpolation is used [2.23]. Again, d_k is only required to be correct to within $\pm 1/2$ sample distance at level k, or $\pm 2^{k-1}$ at the image level.

Having obtained estimates d_k, one of the original images is shifted by this amount and the matching process is repeated with d now known to be in the interval $\pm 2^{k-1}$.

In preliminary studies, two types of correlation have been found to yield reliable matches. These are normalized correlation of the Gaussian images

$$\overline{M} = \frac{\Sigma W_2(Gf_k - \overline{Gf}_k)(Gg_k - \overline{Gg}_k)}{[\Sigma W_2(Gf_k - \overline{Gf}_k)^2 \ \Sigma W_2(Gg_k - \overline{Gg}_k)^2]^{1/2}}$$

$$= \frac{A_2[Gf_k \ Gg_k] - A_2[Gf_k] \ A_2[Gg_k]}{(A_2[Gf_k^2] - A_2^2 \ [Gf_k])^{1/2} \ (A_2[Gg_k^2] - A_2^2 \ [Gg_k])^{1/2}}$$

and direct correlation of the Laplacian images

$$\overline{M} = \Sigma W_2 \ Lf_k Lg_k$$

$$= A_2[Lf_k \ Lg_k] .$$

Here the notation Gf_k and Lf_k has been used to represent the kth levels of the Gaussian and Laplacian pyramids constructed from image f. $\overline{Gf}_k$ is the local average computed in the window W_2, so is equal to $A_2[Gf]$.

2.5.2 Gradient Method

The temporal and spatial gradients of image gray level may also be used to compute pattern displacement [2.24]. In this "nonmatching" approach, an estimate of the displacement at each point is given by the ratio

$$d(i) = \frac{-\frac{df(i)}{dt}}{\frac{df(i)}{dx}} .$$

Here, the temporal derivative at point i (i,j in two dimensions) is approximated by the image intensity change between frames, g(i)-f(i), while the spatial derivative is given by its difference approximation $(f(i+1) - f(i-1))/2$. The resulting displacement estimates are reliable only if the displacement is small compared to image detail or to the wavelengths of prominent image frequency components[7]. When displacements are larger than this limit, high frequencies must be removed through low-pass filtering prior to performing the motion analysis. Still, such point-based motion estimates tend to be highly sensitive to sampling or other image noise, particularly when the spatial derivative is small. The estimates may be improved by computing a local average of the point measures.

LUCAS and KANADE [2.26] have proposed another form of the gradient-based approach. The problem is posed as one of finding that displacement which minimizes the squared error between local patches of the two image frames. The result can be expressed as follows:

$$d = \frac{\sum W(\frac{df}{dt})(\frac{df}{dx})}{\sum W(\frac{df}{dx})^2} \quad .$$

Note that this is a region measure, with numerator and denominator terms computed as averages within local windows before the division. As a result, these estimates are far more reliable than the simple point gradient measures or even the local average of such measures. Performance is further improved by applying the analysis to bandpass filtered images.

As with the correlation measures, the cost of computing the gradient measure may be minimized by performing required filter and window operations in the pyramid, by appropriately reducing the sample density, and by following a coarse-fine search strategy. Each iteration of the search may be formulated as a four-step process. Again, we assume it is known at the beginning of a particular iteration that the displacement is within the interval $-2^k < d < 2^k$. The objective of the iteration is then to obtain an estimate d_k such that $|d - d_k| < 2^{k-1}$.

Step 1: Let $Gf_0 = f$ and $Gf_0 = g$. Gaussian pyramids Gf_0, Gf_1,..., Gf_k and Gg_0, Gg_1,..., Gg_k are built to level k for each image. Again, this step reduces the displacement to just ± 1 sample interval at level k.

Step 2: Arrays are computed at level k for the products of temporal-spatial and spatial-spatial derivatives $XT_k(i)$ and $XX_k(i)$ respectively.

Step 3: Local averages are obtained for each array through two iterations of the HDC window function: $XT_{k2} = A_2[XT_k]$, $XX_{k2} = A_2[XX_k]$.

Step 4: Displacements are computed for each sample point as the quotient $d_k(i) = XT_{k2}(i)/XX_{k2}(i)$.

Each estimate of the displacement in the gradient method is based on exactly the same image sample points as in the correlation estimates. The methods differ in the way this information is manipulated and, hence, in their computational cost and possibly in their performance. A systematic study of es-

---

7. In two dimensions, this technique provides only an estimate of that component of the displacement vector which is in the direction of the image intensity gradient. Further steps are required to recover the component of displacement perpendicular to this gradient [2.25].

timation errors under a range of image and noise conditions has shown that
the three measures give comparable performance and that they are substantially better than other correlation and gradient measures tested [2.23].
In these studies, the gradient analysis was applied to Laplacian bandpass
filtered images. The cost of the computations depends largely on the number
of HDC operations required. This is roughly the same for the gradient and
Laplacian correlation measures and about twice as large for the normalized
correlation.

2.6 Computation

2.6.1 Cost

The computational cost of pyramid-based procedures such as those described
above for texture and motion is determined for the most part by the number
of times pyramid and HDC operations are performed in the procedure and the
cost of each such operation. The pyramid and HDC operations are themselves
highly efficient as a result of their hierarchical organization and in the
pyramid as a result of reduced sample density. In either case a basic operation, the application of the 5 by 5 generating kernel $w(i,j)$ is repeated
for each node at and above level 1. Overall cost is determined by the number of steps needed to compute this elementary convolution and the number
of nodes for which it is computed.

   Direct computation of a 5 by 5 weighted average requires 25 multiplies
and 24 adds. However, $w(i,j)$ is separable (constraint 1) so the computation can be performed in two steps by applying the one-dimensional width-5
weighting function $\hat{w}(i)$ first horizontally and then vertically. The fact
that $\hat{w}$ is symmetric (constraint 3) means that it requires only 4 adds and 3
multiplies, or seven basic arithmetic operations.

   In the HDC process two width-5 convolutions must be performed for each
node. Thus, if the process is iterated N times a total of 14N basic operations are required per pixel of the original image. Again, this produces
a set of N low-pass filtered images with bandwidths descending in one-octave
intervals, or equivalently, a set of local averages within Gaussian-like
windows which increase in size by factors of 2.

   In order to construct level $G_{\ell+1}$ of a Gaussian pyramid, $\hat{w}$ is first oriented horizontally and the weighted average is computed for all nodes in
every other column of G_ℓ, then it is oriented vertically and the average is
computed for every other row within the previously computed column averages.
This results in a total of three applications of $\hat{w}$ for each $G_{\ell+1}$ node, or
21 elementary arithmetic operations. However, G_1 has 1/4 as many nodes as
the original image, G_2 has 1/16, and so on. The total number of nodes in
pyramid level 1 and above is 1/3 of the number of nodes in G_0. Thus, an
entire Gaussian pyramid is constructed with just seven operations per node
of the original image. The pyramid computation requires one or two orders
of magnitude fewer steps than equivalent direct convolution or convolution
in the frequency domain using the FFT [2.15].

2.6.2 Complexity

The complexity of the pyramid algorithms is determined by the number of bits
that must be used to represent the data and the number of bits that must be
retained in each arithmetic operation. These factors may be as important as
the number of operations when we wish to design special purpose digital hardware to perform the pyramid computations.

28

The number of bits required for each arithmetic operation in a standard convolution can be excessively large due to a need to represent both very small numbers formed by the product of individual small kernel weights with possibly small image sample values, and very large numbers formed by the sum of the hundreds or thousands of such product terms which contribute to a single convolution sample. Conversely, the number of bits allocated to arithmetic operations sets a limit on the size of the convolutions which can be computed. Still, it is possible to perform large convolutions while using only short data words if the convolutions are broken into a number of small convolutions, with their results appropriately weighted and combined. The HDC and pyramid processes may be regarded as techniques for systematically dividing large convolutions into smaller convolutions and these into still smaller convolutions in an iterative fashion. As a result, the number of bits needed in arithmetic operations is independent of convolution size and is held to a minimum.

Since the pyramid and HDC-generated equivalent weighting functions are normalized, their convolution with a constant value image should produce exactly the same constant value as the output. We now wish to determine the number of bits required in convolution arithmetic to ensure that this is indeed the case and the output does not change due to roundoff. Suppose, for example, that the input image is represented in 8 bits. Weights of the generating kernel w can be represented in as few as three bits (e.g., a=6/16, b=4/16, and c=1/16). When the individual weights are multiplied by any 8-bit value and the resulting terms are summed, the same 8-bit value should be obtained. Thus, computations performed in evaluating the width-5 convolution require 11 bits while the final result may be rounded back to 8 bits without error. Once the constraint is satisfied for one iteration of a pyramid or HDC process, then it will be satisfied for all iterations. Just 11 bits are sufficient for computing convolutions of arbitrarily large size.

Now suppose the same computation is to be performed through direct convolution of the (constant-valued) image with the equivalent weighting function W rather than repeated convolutions with w. To do this $W_\ell(i,j)$ is first decomposed into a product of one-dimensional functions $\hat{W}_\ell(i)\hat{W}_\ell(j)$. (The equivalent weighting functions are separable because the generating kernel is separable.) If a 3-bit generating kernel is used, then 3ℓ bits will be required to represent W_ℓ exactly. Inexact representation would result in roundoff errors in the convolution. Therefore, the computations require $3\ell + 8$ bits. Values of ℓ of 6 and larger will be typical when processing images of size 256 by 256 pixels. In this case, direct computation requires 26 or more bits to achieve the same accuracy as is obtained with 11 bits in the pyramid computation.

2.7 Pyramid Linking

Local statistics for texture analysis and local correlation for motion analysis are examples of area-based image properties; each property estimate must be computed from image pixels within a local region or window. Such properties are often computed as an aid to image segmentation since image regions of homogeneous property value may correspond to physical objects of interest. However, the use of area measures in image segmentation inevitably presents a dilemma. Even as property estimates are being computed in order to locate segment boundaries, the windows in which these estimates are obtained must be constrained not to cross the segment boundaries. Otherwise, the estimates will confound properties of neighboring regions and obscure the boundary itself.

A possible resolution of this chicken-egg problem is to iterate the property estimation and segmentation steps. Initial estimates of the area properties are obtained within local but otherwise unconstrained windows. These are used to compute initial estimates of the segment boundary positions. The property estimates are then recomputed, now subject to the constraint that windows should not cross the estimated segment boundaries. Segment boundaries are then refined on the basis of the new property estimates. In order to implement this interactive approach, procedures must be found for computing area properties efficiently, for constraining the windows in which the properties are measured, and for the representing of the image segments derived from the properties. A pyramid-linking system will now be defined in which links serve both to represent image segments and to constrain window shapes. By performing computations within the pyramid structure property estimates are obtained efficiently.

The linking technique will be described in terms of an "even" pyramid since this is the form in which it was originally defined [2.27]. Figure 2.18 shows the pyramid and width-4 generating kernel in one dimension[8]. To begin, we consider a node at level ℓ. The generating kernel defines a father-son relationship between this node and nodes at other pyramid levels. In particular, the 16 nodes at level $\ell-1$ (4 in one dimension) which contribute to the level-ℓ node will be called its sons, while the 4 nodes (2 in one dimension) at level $\ell+1$ to which the level-ℓ node contributes will be called its fathers.

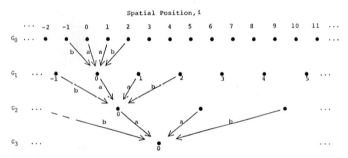

Fig. 2.18. Graphical representation of Gaussian pyramid generation with a width-4 generating kernel. Note that pyramid nodes at level ℓ are positioned midway between nodes at level $\ell-1$ in this "even" pyramid

Suppose each node in a pyramid is assigned an initial value though repeated applications of the REDUCE operation (now defined in terms of the width-4 kernel). In the pyramid-linking process each node is then linked to that single father of its four which has a value closest to its own. In this way, each node at level 0 is linked to just one node at level 1 and through it to just one node at level 2, and so on to level N. Thus, son-father links define tree structures within the pyramid. Nodes at any pyramid level L may be regarded as the roots of a "forest" of trees which have branches to lower-level nodes and leaf nodes on level 0. We call the

8. An even pyramid is defined in [2.11] to be one constructed from a generating kernel which has even width. In this case, each pyramid node is positioned midway between nodes on the next lower level as shown in Fig. 2.18.

30

leaf nodes of a given tree its support. Now observe that the support areas
for all trees rooted at level L partition the image into disjoint regions.
Through the most-similar linking rule, the support of each tree will tend
to include leaf nodes with similar property values. As a result, the tree-
support areas represent estimated image segments. The number of image segments defined through linking depends on the choice of the root level. If
L=N, the height of the pyramid, there will be just one root node and one
segment. If L=N-1, there will be four nodes (two in one dimension) and
four segments, and so on.

Once son-father links have been assigned and a pyramid level L has been
selected at which to root the resulting trees (e.g., on the basis of the
expected number of segments), the value of each node from level 1 to level
L is recomputed from just the son nodes linked to it. In this way, the links
serve to constrain property estimates to the respective segments. Next,
the father-son links are themselves reassigned on the basis of the new node
values. These property computation and relinking steps may be repeated
until the process converges to a stable image segmentation.

The steps in pyramid linking are illustrated in Fig.2.19. Here the original is a one-dimensional "image" of a step edge in a noisy environment.
Suppose this is to be segmented into two regions; let L=N-1=3.

Step 0: Let G_0, the bottom pyramid level, be the original image, and
generate values for higher levels using a width-4 generating kernel,
Fig.2.19a. (Here uniform kernel weights are assumed, a=b=1/4.)

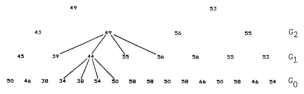

Fig. 2.19a. Steps in pyramid linking. In each case G_0, the original image,
represents a step edge in a noisy environment. The initial values of upper
level pyramid nodes are computed through iterative application of the width-
4 generating kernel

Step 1: Each node is linked to that father which has a value closest
to its own value, Fig.2.19b. (After the first iteration, the link can be
either to the father with a value closest to the node's value, or, as in
the present example, to the father which belongs to the tree in which
the root node value is closest to the node's value.)

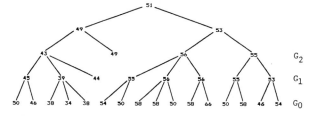

Fig. 2.19b. Each node is linked to that "father" node which has b value
closest to its own value

Step 2: Node values are recomputed from level 1 to L, now with the value of each node set equal to a weighted average of the sons which are linked to it, Fig.2.19c. The weight given to each son is proportional to the size of its support area.

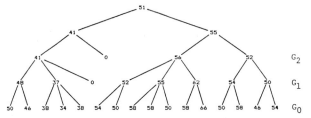

Fig. 2.19c. The value of each upper level node is recomputed using only the "son" nodes which are linked to it

Steps 1 and 2 are alternated several times until convergence is reached. In our example, this is after three iterations, Fig.2.19d.

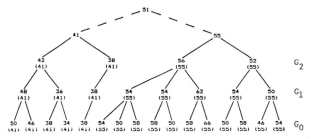

Fig. 2.19d. Final node values and links after the linking and node evaluation steps have been repeated several times. Values in brackets are region averages for the "trees" rooted at level 3. At level 0 these constitute a step edge fitted by the linking process to the original noisy image

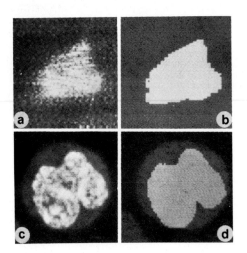

Fig. 2.20 a–d. Tank (**a**) and blood cell (**c**) images are segmented into two (**b**) and three (**d**) regions respectively by the pyramid-linking process

Figure 2.20 shows the results of applying the linking process to two two-dimensional images (from [2.27]). In the first case, a FLIR tank image, Fig.2.20a, is segmented into two regions, Fig.2.20b. Here, the final segmentation is shown by resetting the value of each pixel to the value of the root node to which it is linked. This corresponds to the average gray level value for the segment. In the second example, Fig.2.20c, a blood cell is segmented into three regions, Fig.2.20d. As this example demonstrates, segments represented through pyramid linking can be of almost arbitrary shape. Here, segments actually surround one another, and their respective tree structures are interwined within the pyramid.

In the examples given here, segmentation has been based on image gray level. Linking may be based on other properties, such as texture statistics [2.28]. (CHEN and PAVLIDIS [2.29] report application of a related split-and-merge technique to textures.) A number of variations on the linking process have also been investigated, e.g., [2.30]. The power of the technique lies in the fact that links provide a structure for representing image segments which is general and which may also be combined directly with the efficient pyramid procedures for computing image properties.

2.8 Discussion

A number of basic pyramid procedures, or "computational tools," have now been described along with possible applications of these procedures to image analysis. It has been suggested that the pyramid constitutes an image code which is both robust and compact. It is a structure in which local image properties can be computed efficiently and within windows of many sizes. It is also a structure in which images may be segmented into regions of almost arbitrary shape and size. Perhaps the most noteworthy aspect of this variety of techniques and applications is the fact that there is such a variety, the fact that the pyramid may serve as a unifying structure in which to perform many computer image analysis tasks.

Pyramid processing also bears interesting similarities to natural vision. As an image code, it represents images in terms of "Laplacian" weighting functions which resemble the receptive fields of ganglion cells in the retina and optic nerve, processing within the spatially organized but frequency-tuned channels which have been postulated in human vision (e.g., [2.31]). A local operation performed on a given level of the pyramid has an effective scale in the image which is proportional to the wavelengths processed by that level. In this way, pyramid processing exhibits an operator-scale to image-frequency content relationship similar to the grain-size effect for texture perception described in the introduction. Use of the HDC or pyramid procedures to compute image properties within windows of many sizes permits efficient "integration of evidence" similar to the area effect in texture perception. The net result of performing the same processing steps and windowing operations at all pyramid levels is analysis that is substantially independent of pattern scale in the image. This is comparable to the scale-independent property of human texture perception.

Pyramid processing is particularly well suited for computing local area-based image characteristics such as the statistical and correlation measures described here for texture and motion analysis. These are examples of "early" and computation-bound analysis tasks. The challenge presented by such tasks is not that analysis must be subtle or deep but that it must be performed efficiently on a vast amount of data. The cost inherent in computing area properties is compounded by the window size problem. Windows must be sufficiently large to yield reliable property estimates, yet not so large that they overlap regions having different properties. In general, the correct window size is not known a priori and different sizes are re-quired for different images and in different regions within a given image.

Two approaches to the window-size problem may be contemplated. In the first, a search is made for the appropriate window at each sample point, guided in part by trial and error, in part by already analyzed neighboring regions, and in the case of time-varying imagery, by analysis of previous frames of the sequence. This approach is essentially sequential. The second approach is to compute property estimates at all image positions of all images within a complete set of window sizes. The estimates best matched to individual images are then selected a posteriori as that subset which yields the most internally consistent interpretation of the image. This approach requires a great deal more computation, but computation that may be performed in parallel. We refer to this as a "flow-through" system be-cause processing is uniform over each image and constant from image to image. As images enter the system standard sets of property estimates are generated.

A flow-through system for performing these early computation-bound steps in analysis may be regarded as an image preprocessor. The pyramid offers an attractive structure for such a system since property estimates can be computed efficiently and within a full set of windows without significant cost beyond that of computing properties in just one window. It is inter-esting to note that a general pyramid preprocessor might be implemented as a hardware device. This is true because processing requires only local communication between nodes, relatively simple arithmetic, and if the flow-through strategy is followed, a relatively simple control structure.

Acknowledgment

Preparation of this paper has been supported in part by the National Science Foundation under Grant No. ECS82-05321. Portions appear in the Proceedings of the SPIE Conference on Robotics and Industrial Inspection, San Diego, CA, August 1982.

The author wishes to thank Ted Adelson of RCA, David Sarnoff Research Center, and Azriel Rosenfeld of the University of Maryland for their col-laboration in aspects of the research summarized here, and Sharon Sorell for help in preparation of this paper.

References

2.1 E. M. Riseman, A. R. Hanson: "Design of a Semantically-Directed Vi-sion Processor", Technical Report 74C-1, Department of Computer and Information Sciences, University of Massachusetts (1974)

2.2 P. S. Schenker, E. G. Cande, K. M. Wong, W. R. Patterson III: "New sensor geometries for image processing: computer vision in the polar exponential grid", Proc. IEEE Int'l. Conf. on Acoustics, Speech and Signal Processing, Atlanta, GA, 1981, 1144-1148

2.3 S. L. Tanimoto, T. Pavlidis: A hierarchical data structure for pic-ture processing, Computer Graphics Image Processing $\underline{4}$, 104-119 (1975)

2.4 C. W. Tyler, J. J. Chang: Visual echoes: the perception of repeti-tion in quasi-random patterns, Vision Research $\underline{17}$, 109-116 (1977)

2.5 C. W. Tyler: Stereoscopic vision: cortical limitations and a dis-parity scaling effect, Science $\underline{181}$, 276-278 (1973)

2.6 C. W. Tyler: Spatial organization of binocular disparity sensitivity, Vision Research $\underline{15}$, 583-590 (1975)

2.7 P. J. Burt, B. Julesz: A disparity gradient limit for binocular fusion, Science 208, 615-617 (1980)

2.8 J. S. Lappin, H. H. Bell: The detection of coherence in moving random-dot patterns, Vision Research 16, 161-168 (1976)

2.9 P. J. Burt, G. Sperling: Time, distance, and feature trade-offs in visual apparent motion, Psychological Review 88, 171-195 (1981)

2.10 C. R. Carlson, R. W. Klopfenstein, C. H. Anderson: Spatially inhomogeneous scaled transforms for vision and pattern recognition, Optics Letters 6, 386-388 (1981)

2.11 P. J. Burt: Fast filter transforms for image processing, Computer Graphics Image Processing 16, 20-51 (1981)

2.12 A. Rosenfeld, A. C. Kak: Digital Picture Processing (Academic Press, New York, 1976)

2.13 J. Batali, S. Ullman: "Motion detection and analysis", in Proc. Image Understanding Workshop, Los Angeles, CA, 1979, pp. 69-75

2.14 W. E. L. Grimson: "Aspects of a computational theory of human stereo vision", in Proc. Image Understanding Workshop, College Park, MD, 1980, pp. 128-149

2.15 P. J. Burt: Fast algorithms for estimating local image properties, Computer Graphics Image Processing 21, 368-382 (1983)

2.16 P. J. Burt, E. Adelson: The Laplacian pyramid as a compact image code, IEEE Trans. Communications COMM-31, 532-540 (1983)

2.17 H. von Helmoltz: Handbook of Physiological Optics, ed. by J. Southall (Optical Society of America, 1925)

2.18 P. J. Burt, E. Adelson: A multiresolution spline with applications to image mosaics, submitted

2.19 A. Rosenfeld, M. Thurston: Edge and curve detection for visual scene analysis, IEEE Trans. Computers C-20, 562-569 (1971)

2.20 K. Laws: "Texture energy measures", in Proc. Image Understanding Workshop, Los Angeles, CA, 1979, pp. 47-51

2.21 L. Larkin, P. J. Burt: Multiresolution texture energy measures, in Proc. Computer Vision and Pattern Recognition Conf., Arlington, VA, 1983

2.22 R. Y. Wong, E. L. Hall, J. Rouge: "Hierarchical search for image matching", in Proc. IEEE Conf. on Decision and Control, Clearwater, FL, 1977

2.23 P. J. Burt, C. Yen, X. Xu: "Local correlation measures for motion analysis, a comparative study", in Proc. Pattern Recognition and Image Processing Conf., Las Vegas, NV, 1982, pp. 269-274

2.24 J. O. Limb, J. A. Murphy: Estimating the velocity of moving images in television signals, Computer Graphics Image Processing 4, 311-327 (1975)

2.25 C. L. Fennema, W. B. Thompson: Velocity determination in scenes containing several moving objects, Computer Graphics Image Processing 9, 301-315 (1979)

2.26 B. D. Lucas, T. Kanade: "An iterative image registration technique with an application to stereo vision", in Proc. Image Understanidng Workshop, Washington, DC, 1981, pp. 121-130

2.27 P. J. Burt, T. H. Hong, A. Rosenfeld: Segmentation and estimation of image region properties through cooperative hierarchical computation, IEEE Trans. Systems, Man, Cybernetics SMC-11, 802-809 (1981)

2.28 M. Pietikainen, A. Rosenfeld: Image segmentation by texture using pyramid node linking, IEEE Trans. Systems, Man, Cybernetics SMC-11, 822-825 (1981)

2.29 P. C. Chen, T. Pavlidis: Image segmentation as an estimation problem, Computer Graphics Image Processing 12, 153-172 (1980)

2.30 M. Pietikainen, A. Rosenfeld: Gray level pyramid linking as an aid in texture analysis, IEEE Trans. Systems, Man, Cybernetics SMC-12, 422-429 (1982)

2.31 F. W. Campbell, J. G. Robson: Application of Fourier analysis to the visibility of gratings, J. Physiology (London) 197, 551-566 (1968)

Part II

Architectures and Systems

3. Multiprocessor Pyramid Architectures for Bottom-Up Image Analysis *

N. Ahuja and S. Swamy

Coordinated Science Laboratory, University of Illinois at Urbana-Champaign
Urbana, IL 61801, USA

This paper describes three hierarchical organizations of small processors for bottom-up image analysis: pyramids, interleaved pyramids, and pyramid trees. Progressively lower levels in the hierarchies process image windows of decreasing size. Bottom-up analysis is made feasible by transmitting up the levels quadrant borders and border-related information that captures quadrant interaction of interest for a given computation. The operation of the pyramid is illustrated by examples of standard algorithms for interior-based computations (e.g., area) and border-based computations of local properties (e.g., perimeter). A connected component-counting algorithm is described that illustrates the role of border-related information in representing quadrant interaction. Interleaved pyramids are obtained by sharing processors among several pyramids. They increase processor utilization and throughput rate at the cost of increased hardware. Trees of shallow interleaved pyramids, called pyramid trees, are introduced to reduce the hardware requirements of large interleaved pyramids at the expense of increased processing time, without sacrificing processor utilization. The three organizations are compared with respect to several performance measures.

3.1 Introduction

This paper explores the use of hierarchical organization of processors to perform strictly bottom-up computations. Three architectures are described: pyramids, interleaved pyramids, and pyramid trees. These architectures perform computations that result in a small number of output bits (small compared to the number of bits necessary to represent the entire image). The architectures are thus intended to compute image properties or to perform image analysis. They are not suitable for performing image transformations, such as segmentation or enhancement, which provide a whole image as output.

The central feature of the architectures described is a hierarchy imposed on the image by a recursive square decomposition of the image. This hierarchy has formed the basis of various pyramid approaches (to be reviewed later in this section) and of the quadtree representation of images. To obtain its quadtree, the image is overlaid with a sequence of increasingly fine tessellations that defines a recursive embedding of quadrants and thus a hierarchy over image windows. The hierarchy is described by a tree whose root node is associated with the entire image. Each node in the tree represents a square window. A node has four children unless it corresponds to a window that is of the smallest allowed size. Each child node is associated with a quadrant

---

*This research was supported by the Joint Services Electronics Program (U.S. Army, Navy and Air Force) under Contract N00014-79-C-0424.

of the parent window. Leaf nodes correspond to pixels or to windows of the smallest size.

Consider a set of images and the set of nodes in their tree representations. Different mappings from the nodes (windows) of possibly more than one tree (image) to a set of processors define different processor hierarchies. The processors perform computations on their corresponding windows. A single tree (image) is processed a level at a time starting at the bottom and progressing up the levels. The results of computations on the images are obtained at the processors corresponding to the root nodes. We will use the terms node and processor interchangeably. A nonleaf node receives the results of computation from its children nodes and combines them, making use of the way in which the children quadrants interact, to obtain the result for its own window. Information about quadrant interaction is necessary to make strictly bottom-up computation possible. Clearly, it would be desirable to minimize the volume of such information flow up the hierarchy. For such simple computations as area, no information about quadrant interaction is necessary. For more involved computations such as perimeter, quadrant borders completely specify quadrant interaction. For complex computations such as connected component counting, connectivity properties of quadrant interiors constitute quadrant interaction and can be represented by borders and certain border-related structures (Sect.3.3.2.2). A variety of image analysis tasks can be carried out efficiently on such hierarchies. Bottom-up algorithms can be adapted from the literature to perform simple computations such as area and perimeter. More complex computations that can be implemented efficiently include connected component counting and transformation of point sets into graphs.

The choice of the mapping, possibly many to one, from the tree nodes to the processors determines the different architectures discussed in this paper. The first choice assigns one processor to each node in the tree, yielding the standard multiprocessor pyramid organization proposed by UHR in 1971 [3.1] (see also [3.2-4]) and called a "recognition cone." A similar organization, called a cellular pyramid acceptor, was considered by DYER [3.5]. There, the processors are organized as a complete quadtree with additional interconnections between neighboring processors at the same level. Each node has a finite set of states. A node changes its state depending upon its current state and the states of its parent, children and siblings, and in parallel with all other nodes. The special case of a bottom-up cellular pyramid acceptor has also been considered [3.6], where each node changes its state based upon its current state and the states of its children. The interconnections among the processors in bottom-up cellular pyramids and in our first hierarchy are similar. However, each nonleaf node in our case receives from its children the results of their computations and explicit information about quadrant interaction, which cannot be naturally described in terms of states and state transitions. We assume a small general-purpose processor at each node. An algorithm for counting the number of connected components is given that highlights the need for a general processor and complex border-related information from quadrants, and distinguishes the use of our first hierarchy from the bottom-up pyramids described in [3.6]. In [3.7] DYER discusses a pyramid machine where each node has a small processor. He considers the node interconnections and chip layout aspects with respect to VLSI design. We discuss the data flow aspects and implementation of bottom-up algorithms.

The remaining two choices of the node-to-processor mapping are many-to-one. Both can be viewed as hierarchies using different interconnections among pyramids. The first of the two choices involves interleaving of pyramids where processors at a single level of the hierarchy may simultaneously process windows from several images. Interleaved pyramids achieve high through-put at the cost of increased hardware. The second choice involves a hier-archy of pyramids interconnected as a tree, with each pyramid capable of pro-cessing a subimage. A large image is divided into sets of subimages which are processed in parallel by the nodes of the pyramid tree. Pyramid trees reduce the input bandwidth and hardware costs of the interleaved pyramids at the expense of increased computation time.

The pyramid organization of processing elements has received the attention of several researchers, as we have noted earlier. ROSENFELD [3.8] presents an enlightening treatment of cellular pyramids, cellular arrays, other related machines, and their performance with respect to commonly used image opera-tions. Some of the work is motivated by the quadtree representation of images [3.9,10], which uses recursive decomposition [3.11] of an image for the pur-pose of compact representation rather than multiprocessing. Pyramids have also been used to obtain a hierarchical representation of an image at several resolutions, not necessarily to be processed by more than one processor; see [3.2,9,12-16]. The coarser resolutions are obtained by, for example, apply-ing averaging Boolean operators to the pixels of a window. The analysis at higher levels is approximate but quick and is used to "plan" the more de-tailed analysis at lower levels. Multiresolution pyramids may have overlap between the windows of adjacent nodes [3.17]. Multiresolution pyramids to represent edges at different resolutions [3.18] have also been investigated.

A hierarchical architecture called active quadtree networks, which is an adaptation of the quadtree representation to multiprocessing, has been de-scribed by DUBITZKI et al. [3.19]. They assign a processor to each block in the quadtree representation of the image. The number of and interconnections among processors are thus image dependent.

Among the nonhierarchical architectures, a common approach is to assign a processor to each pixel or to each neighborhood of pixels, with local in-terconnections among processors. Examples of such mesh architectures are MPP [3.20], CLIP4 [3.21], and DAP [3.22]. Other architectures establish dynamic interconnections among processors (ZMOB [3.23], PASM [3.24]).

Section 3.2 describes the architectural details of the multiprocessor pyra-mid. Section 3.3 briefly describes standard algorithms for interior-based com-putations (e.g., area) and border-based computations (e.g., perimeter). Sec-tion 3.3 further describes a connected component-counting algorithm to illus-trate the role of border-based information in making bottom-up analysis fea-sible. The computational complexity and memory requirements are also dis-cussed. Section 3.4 describes performance measures that are used to evaluate the architectures described in this paper. Interleaved pyramids and pyramid trees are described in Sects. 3.5 and 3.6, respectively, as architectures for achieving increased processor utilization. The pyramid algorithms of Sect. 3.3 may be used on interleaved pyramids and pyramid trees. Section 3.7 presents concluding remarks.

3.2 The Pyramid Architecture

In this section we describe the pyramid architecture, the first and the most basic of the three hierarchical organizations of PEs to be discussed in this paper.

3.2.1 Processor Hierarchy

We will assume that the windows of the finest tessellation contain single pixels. If such is not the case, only trivial modifications to our description need to be made. To describe the pyramid architecture, we will use a notation similar to that used by BURT et al. [3.17]. Consider a 2^L by 2^L image. A pyramid to process this image is a layered arrangement of L + 1 square arrays of processing elements (PEs) A(0), A(1),...,A(L). The bottom array is at level 0 and is of size $2^L \times 2^L$. Arrays at higher levels have their dimensions reduced by half from level to level. Thus, A(1) measures $2^{L-1} \times 2^{L-1}$ and any A(ℓ), $0 \le \ell \le L$, measures $2^{L-\ell}$ $2^{L-\ell}$. The number of PEs is reduced by a factor of four from level to level. The number of PEs in A(ℓ), $0 \le \ell \le L$, is $2^{2(L-\ell)}$. A(L) has a single PE which is the apex of the pyramid (Fig.3.1).

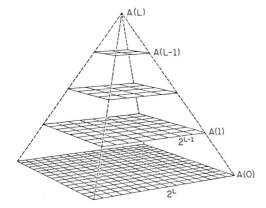

Fig. 3.1. Arrays in an L + 1 level pyramid that can process a 2^L x 2^L image

Each PE in the pyramid is indexed by a triple (i,j,ℓ), where ℓ is its array level and i and j are its row and column numbers within that array. Rows and columns in an array A(ℓ) are numbered $0,1,...,2^{L-\ell}-1$, from bottom to top and from left to right, respectively. The interconnections among various PEs in the pyramid are given by their i, j, and ℓ coordinates, viewing the pyramid as a three-dimensional structure. Each PE (i,j,ℓ) has a position $(x(i,\ell), y(j,\ell))$ relative to the image. Let the pixels be placed at the centers of the square windows of the finest tessellation. If the origin of the x-y plane is assumed to coincide with the bottom left corner of the Euclidean image, then the continuous coordinates of the bottom left pixel are given by

$$x(0,0) = y(0,0) = 1/2$$

where the North and East directions are labelled as positive x and y axes, respectively. Then

$$x(i,0) = i + 1/2, \qquad 0 \le i \le 2^L - 1$$

$$y(j,0) = j + 1/2, \qquad 0 \le j \le 2^L - 1.$$

At any level $\ell > 0$

$$x(0,\ell) = y(0,\ell) = 2^{\ell-1}$$

and

$$x(i,\ell) = x(0,\ell) + i2^{\ell} = 2^{\ell-1}(1 + 2i), \qquad 0 < i \le 2^{L-\ell}-1$$

$$y(j,\ell) = 2^{\ell-1}(1 + 2j) \qquad\qquad , \qquad 0 < j \le 2^{L-\ell}-1.$$

Each PE indexed (i,j,ℓ) corresponds to the $2^{\ell}\times2^{\ell}$ window centered at $(x(i,\ell)$, $y(j,\ell))$. The total length of the border of this window is $4(2^{\ell}-1)$ since each corner pixel is shared by two edges. The PEs corresponding to the quadrants of (i,j,ℓ)'s window constitute (i,j,ℓ)'s children at level $(\ell-1)$. The children PEs have indices $(2i+1,2j,\ell-1)$, $(2i+1,2j+1,\ell-1)$, $(2i,2j+1,\ell-1)$, and $(2i,2j,\ell-1)$, respectively. A PE at level $\ell = 0$ corresponds to a single pixel which also constitutes its four border segments. (See Fig.3.2.)

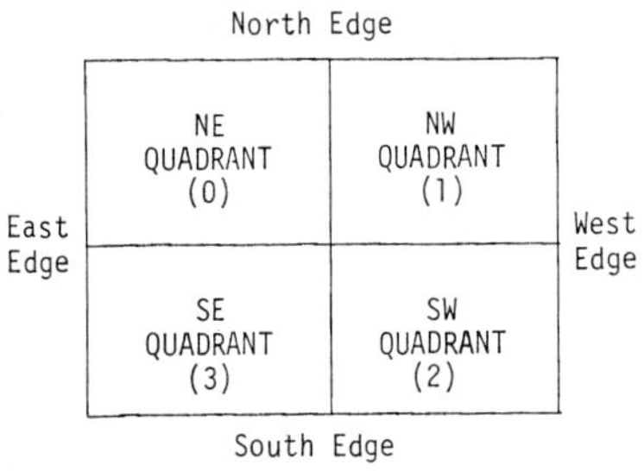

North Edge

East Edge / West Edge

| | NE QUADRANT (0) | NW QUADRANT (1) | |
| | SE QUADRANT (3) | SW QUADRANT (2) | |

South Edge

Fig. 3.2. The window corresponding to a node (i, j, ℓ) and its four quadrants. The four edges of the parent window are also shown

3.2.2 Data Flow

As pointed out in Sect.3.1, the architecture to be described performs bottom-up computations on the image. In order to compute a given property on a window, its PE must receive data from its children. The data transmitted by a PE to its parent consists of the results of computation performed by the PE on its corresponding window, and border-related information. The latter is used by the parent PE to determine the interaction among its window's quadrants. In all three architectures discussed in this paper, the image data is loaded into the PEs at the base of the hierarchy in a manner determined by the architecture. Data paths are provided between each PE and its four children along which it receives, in parallel, data from its children. The hierarchical manner of computation necessitates limited information flow from bottom to top; otherwise the data transmission time may dominate the overall computation time.

Now, given a window, the structural relationships among its quadrants must depend upon their adjacent borders. Therefore, the quadrant interaction necessary for computing various properties may be expressed by borders and the relationships of quadrant interiors to their borders. For example, borders are required for perimeter computation (Sect.3.3.1), and connected-ness properties of border runs must be known in order to count the number of connected componetns (Sect.3.3.2). The total volume of data to be transmitted from a PE to its parent is proportional to the length of the borders of its corresponding window -- O(n) for an n×n window. It is assumed that the data transmission rate is fixed for all data paths between PEs at adjacent levels. Thus, data transmission time per PE corresponding to an n×n window is O(n). The total volume of data transmitted per PE doubles with level. However, since the number of PEs decreases by a factor of four per level, the overall data flow up the pyramid halves with level.

3. 2. 3 Processor Element Hardware

The PEs are small general-purpose processors with identical CPUs and variable memory size. This is in contrast with the finite-state machine model
of a processor used in bottom-up cellular pyramid acceptors, as pointed out
in Sect.3.1. PEs at different levels of the pyramid execute the same set
of instructions on windows of different sizes, and hence on different data.
The execution of most algorithms is data dependent. This suggests that the
PEs operate in a MIMD mode and that the instruction and data memories be
segregated. The total size of the data memory for a PE at level k is $O(2^k)$.
The data word size at all levels is fixed and is sufficiently large to hold
the results ($O(\log N)$ bits) for the largest ($N \times N$) images of interest.

3.3 Image Analysis

In this section we consider several image-analysis algorithms for the pyramid architecture described in Sect.3.2. These algorithms are also valid
for the interleaved pyramids and pyramid trees discussed in Sects.3.5 and
3.6. The chosen algorithms are illustrative of the range of complexity of
commonly performed image operations. We consider binary images in which 0
and 1 denote the (white) background and (black) foreground, respectively.
The algorithms are divided into two classes: interior-based algorithms,
whose computations on a window involve only the results on the quadrants;
and border-based algorithms, whose computations on a window involve
results on the quadrants, as well as the quadrant borders. We will
only outline the interior-based and the simple border-based algorithms (e.g.,
local property counting), since they are straightforward adaptations of algorithms that have appeared in the literature. We will describe the connected component counting algorithm in detail.

3. 3. 1 Interior-Based Algorithms

These algorithms compute properties of images that depend upon the numbers
and coordinates of the black pixels, but not on the relative positions of
the black and white pixels. Bottom-up algorithms for the computation of
total black area and centroid in quadtree networks, outlined in [3.19], can
be used for pyramids. The leaves of the pyramid are assigned an area measure
of 0 or 1, the same as their color. Each nonleaf node then computes its
area by adding the areas of its four children nodes. The area computed at
the root is the total black area in the image. To compute the centroid of
an image, the south-west corner pixel in any window is given the coordinates
$(1/2,1/2)$. Each black leaf is given the centroid coordinates of $(1/2,1/2)$.
The centroid of an interior node is computed as an area-weighted mean of
the centroids of the four quadrant nodes, whose coordinates are expressed
with respect to the origin of the parent window.

3. 3. 2 Border-Based Algorithms

The properties computed by the algorithms described in this section are determined by the number of black pixels and their neighborhood configurations.
The neighborhood information is accumulated by processing border segments of
adjacent quadrants of increasing size, unlike the situation for quadtrees
[3.9] and quadtree networks [3.19], where such information is extracted from
blocks and their neighbors. Examples of border-based properties are perimeter, which is a local property, and number of connected components, which
involves global connectivity among black pixels. Thus, additional information about which pixels along the borders of a quadrant are connected via
black pixels in the quadrant's interior must be carried up the pyramid, along

with the borders themselves. In this sense, the algorithms for such properties are more complex.

3.3.2.1 Local Property Counting

These algorithms are based upon the frequencies of various local configurations of 1s and 0s. The   frequencies are computed from the adjacent border
segments of quadrants of increasing sizes as computation progresses up the
pyramid. Two examples of such computations are perimeter and genus.

The total perimeter of an image may be defined as the number of black-
white pairs of neighbors in the image [3.25]. Leaves (pixels) are assigned
a perimeter value of 0. The perimeter at an interior node has two components:
(a) that due to the black-white pairs of pixels within the node's quadrants,
which is the sum of the perimeter values assigned to its children nodes,
and (b) that due to the black-white pairs of pixels belonging to adjacent
quadrants, which must be computed from the pairs of border segments of quadrants which are adjacent in the image. Computation at the root yields the
total perimeter value for the image.

The genus of an image is defined as the number of components minus the
number of holes. It can be computed from the histogram of the image defined
over distinct classes of configurations of its 2×2 neighborhoods [3.25].
Each node carries the histogram for its window, which is initialized to a
vector of zeroes for leaves. The genus at a node is computed as a linear
sum of the histogram bin counts. An interior node at level $\ell > 0$ contains
$(2^\ell - 1)^2$ 2×2 neighborhoods formed by (a) the interiors of its four quadrants, each contributing $((2^\ell-1)^2-1)/4$ neighborhoods; (b) four pairs of adjacent quadrant border segments, each pair contributing $(2^{\ell-1}-1)$ neighborhoods; and (c) the interior corner pixels of the quadrants, contributing
the central neighborhood. The histogram for the node is obtained by computing the histograms of (b) and (c) and adding to them the four already
known histograms for (a). DYER [3.26] gives a genus algorithm for quadtrees that uses a similar approach. However, as mentioned earlier, the
neighborhood information is gathered differently in quadtrees than in pyramids.

3.3.2.2 Connected Component Counting

Connected components of a binary image refer to the black regions in the
image. In the algorithm to count the connected components described below,
each node carries (a) the number of components within its window that do not
reach its border; and (b) for each component in the window that touches the
border of that window, a doubly-linked list linking the component's border
intercepts (runs) in the same order as they are encountered along a border
scan (Fig.3.3a). Leaves are assigned a component count of 0. The linked
list of a leaf node is empty if it is white, and contains exactly one black
run of unit length if the leaf is black. Each interior node receives from
its children their counts and linked lists, and obtains its own count and
linked list in three steps. First, the NW and NE quadrants are merged to obtain the count and linked lists for the northern half of the window. The
same procedure is then repeated on the SW and SE quadrants. Finally, a
third application of the procedure merges the northern and southern halves.
We will now illustrate the merge procedure for the NW and NE quadrants. Let
L(R) denote the east (west) border of the NW (NE) quadrant (Fig. 3.3b). The
remaining six border segments will be termed external border segments. Let
LLINK and RLINK denote the linked lists of runs in L and R, respectively.

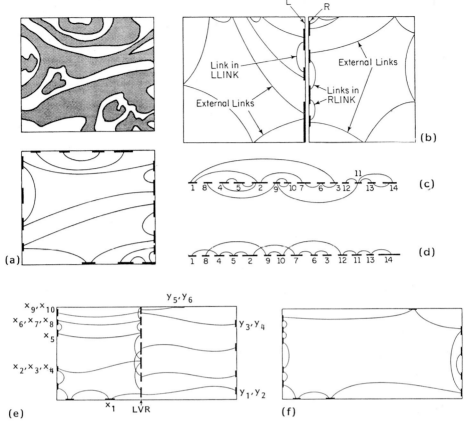

Fig. 3.3. (a) Components in an image window and the corresponding set of doubly-linked lists. Each list links successive border intercepts of a single component that reaches the window border. Links are shown by arcs joining pairs of border runs. (b) Merging the NW and NE quadrants of a window. The sets LLINK and RLINK are shown before the merger takes place. These are used to obtain two-way linked chains for LVR. (c) An example of the sets LLINK and RLINK on LVR. Two runs connected by either LLINK or RLINK belong to the same congruence class. Two congruence classes are shown in the figure. (d) A single linear linked list identifies each congruence class (see procedure CLOSR). (e) External links of the congruence classes of runs of LVR. (f) Linked lists of the merged window (see procedure RELOC)

We replace both L and R by LVR, the pixelwise OR of L and R. Every run in L and R is contained in some run in LVR. Therefore, there is a many-to-one correspondence between runs in L(R) and their parent runs in LVR. For each link in LLINK (RLINK) between two runs in L(R), a link is established between the parents of the runs in LVR. If a run in L(R) is linked to a run RUN on an external border segment, the corresponding run in LVR is also linked to RUN. Such links are termed external links. LLINK and RLINK now denote the set of links obtained on LVR as above.

The black runs in LVR represent the components that straddle or touch L and R. To find the number of such components two-way linked chains of

black runs are constructed. Each list connects black runs on LVR that be-
long to a single component situated in, possibly, both NW and NE quadrants.
The predecessor and successor of a run in the chain are the closest neigh-
boring runs in LVR that belong to the same component as the original run.
All the chains in LVR can be constructed from LLINK and RLINK by procedure
CLOSR described below.

The procedure traverses LVR examining each run. When a run
is encountered that has no predecessors in LLINK or RLINK, the traversal
is suspended temporarily to identify all runs on LVR that will form a chain
with the run just encountered. This is done by a process called "marking"
whereby a pointer is set up from every run in the chain to a common address
with each chain having a unique address. First, the run encountered in the
traversal is marked along with all its successors in LLINK and RLINK, and
the locations of the successor and predecessor runs are put on a queue. Subsequently (LLINK and RLINK) successors and predecessors of every run on the
queue that have not been marked as yet are marked and their locations entered
on the queue. Since all runs in the chain are connected to the original run
by LLINK or RLINK, they will eventually be marked by the above process. The
traversal of LVR is then resumed and the marking process continued until LVR
is completely traversed. During the marking process the number of times a
run is accessed is the number of predecessor and successor links it has in
LLINK and RLINK. Hence the total number of run accesses in CLOSR is equal
to the number of links in LLINK and RLINK, which is linear in the number of
runs in LVR.

To establish the two-way chains mentioned earlier, LVR is traversed once
again. The locations pointed to by the various runs are used to build successive links in the chains. When the first run in a chain is encountered,
its address is stored in the location to which the run points. When later
runs pointing to the same location are encountered, successor and predecessor links between the current run and the contents of the common location
are established, and the contents of the common location are replaced by the
address of the current run. With a single scan all chains on LVR can be
constructed simultaneously. In the example of Fig.3.3c,d, the numbers on the
runs indicate the order in which they are marked. A and B denote the common
location for each chain. Each chain represents a congruence class of runs
on LVR, all of whose elements can be accessed in time proportional to the
length of the list.

Next, we count those components intersecting L or R that do not reach the
external border segments, i.e., the border of the merged window. LVR is
scanned in one direction, say from south to north. Each congruence class of
runs is examined for external links. If none of the runs has external links,
the class represents a component that does not reach the border of the merged
window. For each such component found, the desired count is incremented by
1.

Finally, we must obtain the linked list of the remaining components for
the new window formed by merging NW and NE (procedure RELOC). This is done
by performing a scan (say south to north) of each congruence class of runs
on LVR. A sequence of successive runs along a chain having external links
is identified. Let the corresponding sequences of external runs that are
linked to the above sequence of runs be $x_1,x_3,x_5,\ldots$ (along the external
borders of NW) and $y_1,y_3,y_5,\ldots$ (along the external borders of NE). Let
$x_2,x_4,x_6,\ldots$ be the farthest successors, along the external borders of NW,
of runs $x_1,x_3,x_5,\ldots$ .Similarly, let $y_2,y_4,y_6,\ldots$ be the farthest successors,
along the external borders of NE, of runs $y_1,y_3,y_5,\ldots$ .Then x_3 and x_2 belong

to the same component and x_3 is the closest successor of x_2 along the border of the merged window. Runs x_2 and x_3 are therefore a successor-predecessor pair in the linked list of the merged window. Similar remarks hold for the pairs (x_4,x_5), (x_6,x_7), etc. In the same manner, pairs of runs (y_2,y_3), (y_4,y_5), (y_6,y_7) form successor-predecessor pairs in the merged window. Links are established for each pair. Finally, we are left with four runs, x_1, x_ℓ and y_1, y_m. Runs $x_1,x_\ell(y_1,y_m)$ denote the extreme runs along the external borders of the NW (NE) quadrants of a single component. Successor-predecessor links are therefore established between x_1 and y_1 and between x_ℓ and y_m. The above procedure is repeated for all congruence classes in LVR. All four sequences of runs can be obtained in time proportional to the sum of the number of runs in the congruence class being examined, and the number of external runs that belong to the same component as the runs in the congruence class. Thus, over all congruence classes, the total number of (run) accesses is proportional to the number of runs in NW and NE, and is thus linear in the lengths of the border segments of NW and NE. Figures 3.3e,f show the external links of two congruence classes. For one of the congruence classes, the runs $x_1,x_2,x_3,\ldots,x_{10}$ and $y_1,y_2,\ldots,y_6$ are shown. Note that these runs are not all distinct. The final connections are made between x_1 and y_1 and x_{10} and y_6.

3.3.3 Complexity Issues

We will estimate the RAM storage and computation time required by the pyramid to execute the representative algorithms described in Sects.3.3.1 and 3.3.2.

3.3.3.1 Memory Requirements

The total amount of local random access memory required by all the PEs depends on the type of computations to be performed. The interior-based algorithms do not involve any cross-border computations. Consequently, the amount of memory required at a PE at any level reflects the requirements of a fixed number of arithmetic operations on numbers representing area, centroid, etc. Since a fixed memory word length of $O(\log N)$ bits is used in the PEs at all levels, the total memory required by each PE for the interior-based algorithms is $O(1)$ words.

The local property-counting algorithms perform Boolean operations on cross-border bit pairs while the connected component-counting algorithm generates and processes linked lists representing run and component connectivities. Let $C_m n$ be the memory required to store border information for an $n \times n$ window; the constant C_m does not depend on the window size but depends on the algorithm. Since the memory required for arithmetic operations is small ($O(1)$) and border information is restricted to $O(n)$, the above two algorithms have memory requirements approaching the maximum for any algorithm. The total memory required by the pyramid is

$$= \sum_{\ell=0}^{\log N} 4^{\log N-\ell} \cdot C_m \cdot 2^\ell$$

$$= O(N^2) \text{ words.}$$

3.3.3.2 Computation Time

The total computation time for an $N \times N$ image is the sum of the computation times at all $\log N + 1$ levels of the pyramid and the sum of the transmission times between all $\log N$ pairs of adjacent levels.

Interior-based algorithms perform a fixed number of arithmetic operations at each PE in the pyramid and transmit a fixed number of data words per PE. Hence the total number of parallel arithmetic operations and parallel data transfers executed is proportional to the number of levels, i.e., O(log N). Border-based algorithms that count local properties perform a fixed number of arithmetic operations at each PE plus a Boolean operation on the edges, requiring O(n) time for an n×n window. Thus the total number of arithmetic/ logical operations executed is O(n). The connected component counting algorithm has procedures that scan linked lists of length O(n) for an n×n window. As pointed out in Sect.3.3, for each of the procedures the total number of run accesses and logical operations required is proportional to the number of border runs. Scanning a linked list of length O(n) and relocating pointers in the list requires O(n) arithmetic operations and predicate evaluations. The time required by border-based algorithms to transmit data for an n×n window is O(n). Thus, the sum of the computation and data transmission times for border-based algorithms for an n×n window is $C_t n$, where the constant C_t depends on the algorithm but not on the window size. The total computation time for an N×N image is therefore

$$O \left(\sum_{\ell=0}^{\log N} C_t \cdot 2^\ell \right) = O(N) .$$

3.4 Performance Measures

In this section we evaluate the number of PEs and the total memory requirement of the basic (pipelined) pyramid, and evaluate its performance with respect to (i) the output latency (reciprocal of the throughput), (ii) the input bandwidth, and (iii) the image turnaround time. Since border-based algorithms require the most memory and time, the expressions given below will be for the execution of such algorithms.

(a) Number of processors = $\displaystyle\sum_{\ell=0}^{\log N} 4^\ell \approx \frac{4N^2}{3}$

(b) Total memory = $\displaystyle\sum_{\ell=0}^{\log N} 4^{\log N - \ell} \cdot C_m \cdot 2^\ell$

   = $C_m N(2N-1)$

(c) The PE at the root of the pyramid takes the longest time to process its window. Therefore the delay between two consecutive input (output) images is the time taken by the PE at the root of the pyramid. Therefore,

   Output latency = $C_t N$

(d) The input bandwidth is the number of parallel pixel inputs to the PEs at the bottom level of the pyramid. Since there are as many PEs at the bottom level as the number of pixels, and all pixels are loaded in parallel, we have

   Input bandwidth = $4^{\log N} = N^2$

(e) The image turnaround time is the time required to process an entire image. This is simply the sum of the processing times required at all the levels of the pyramid. Therefore,

$$\text{Image turnaround time} = \sum_{\ell=0}^{\log N} C_t \cdot 2^{\ell}$$

$$= C_t \cdot (2N - 1) .$$

As we will see in Sects.3.5 and 3.6, the interleaved pyramids and the pyramid trees achieve reduced output latencies partly at the expense of increased PE and memory requirements. To compare the three architectures with respect to the effective PE and memory utilization, we will normalize (a) and (b) with respect to (c) to obtain two additional measures. The first of these measures, PE_T, is the number of PEs used per unit output latency (or throughput time). This measure reflects overall processor utilization -- the smaller its value, the better the utilization. A deficiency of this measure is that it assigns the same weight to PEs at all levels and does not take into account their different memory sizes. To remedy this, we compute M_T, the total memory required per unit output latency (or throughput time). Taking their weighted sum in some technology-dependent proportion, PE_T and M_T together measure the overall efficiency of a design. For the basic pyramid

(f) $PE_T = C_t N \cdot (4N^2/3) = \frac{4}{3} C_t N^3$

(g) $M_T = C_m N(2N - 1)C_t N = C_t C_m N^2(2N - 1) .$

3.5 Interleaved Pyramids

The pyramid architecture described in Sect.3.2 is a natural candidate for pipelining [3.4] since at any given time an image is processed at a single level. Progressively higher levels define successive segments in the pipeline. For interior-based algorithms the PEs at every level execute the same number of arithmetic operations, requiring the same amount of time. Pipelining, therefore, results in simultaneous utilization of all the processors in the pyramid. For the border-based algorithms, on the other hand, each PE corresponding to an n×n window must process a volume O(n) of data. The actual processing time is data dependent and, in general, is proportional to n. The PE at the root of the pyramid has the largest volume of data, and hence takes the longest time to process its window. The delay between the inputs (outputs) of two consecutive images is equal to the time taken by the PE at the root of the pyramid, and is O(N). Pipelining therefore results in high utilization of the PE at the root and progressively lower utilization of PEs at lower levels, the utilization halving with each level down.

A simple method to utilize the nonapex PEs better is to share them among several pyramids. This approach characterizes our second hierarchy, called interleaved pyramids, which achieves the high utilization of the apex processor at all levels. To describe interleaved pyramids, first let $C_t n$ denote, as before, the time required to execute a border-based algorithm on an n×n window, where C_t is a constant that depends on the algorithm and can be interpreted as the worst-case execution time. A PE cannot process windows at intervals less than $C_t n$. This restriction is imposed in order to synchronize data transfer between levels. In case a PE completes its execution in time less than $C_t n$, it idles for the remaining time. The lower the level, the lower the processor utilization, and hence the larger number of pyramids that can share that level.

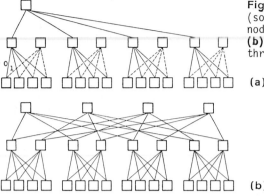

Fig. 3.4. (a) The basic pyramid (solid lines) with additional nodes (dotted lines) at level 1. **(b)** Interleaved pyramid with three levels

(a)

(b)

Figure 3.4a shows the basic pyramid, drawn in solid lines. Since a PE at level ℓ has half the workload of its parent at level $\ell + 1$, and hence is half as busy, it can be time-shared by two parents. Consider the leaf nodes. Let us insert additional nodes at level 1 to double their number. Each leaf now sends data to two different parents alternately (Fig.3.4a). Let us say that a leaf initially inputs data to its left parent (position 0), then switches to its right parent (position 1), and then back again. If the leaf nodes transmit data to their parents every C_t time units, then the left and right parents receive data at times 0 and C_t (modulo $2C_t$) respectively. The two sets of parents process different data, received at level 0 at different times. The nodes at level 1 are in turn shared by two parents at level 2 (Fig.3.4b). Thus, level 2 has four sets of nodes, each set synchronously transmitting and receiving data every $4C_t$ time units. The different sets receive data in a round-robin fashion. The order in which this happens is given by the integers represented by the sequences of position bits along the paths from different sets leading to level 0, level 0 positions representing the least significant bits. Figure 3.4b shows interleaved pyramids containing three levels. In general, an (L+1)-level interleaved pyramid has 2^{2L} input PEs and 2^L output PEs. Nodes at any level ℓ belong to 2^ℓ different sets. The sets time-share the levels below, each set transmitting and receiving data every $2^\ell C_t$ time units. For an N×N image the root level has 2^{logN} (= N) nodes each of which outputs its data every NC_t time units, the outputs being interleaved in time and appearing at times $0, C_t,..., (N-1)C_t$. The N nodes represent the roots of N interleaved pyramids, which output results at the same rate at which images are fed in.

The image window to PE mapping used by the interleaved pyramids may be obtained by considering the PEs at a given level in an interleaved pyramid and the nodes at the same level in the complete quadtree representations of the input images. The number of PEs at level ℓ of an interleaved pyramid is $2^{2logN-\ell}$. The number of nodes at level ℓ in a single complete quadtree is $4^{logN-\ell}$. Thus, nodes at level ℓ in $(2^{2logN-\ell})/(4^{logN-\ell}) = 2^\ell$ successive trees map onto different PEs at level ℓ in the interleaved pyramid. Alternately, a node in a given position at level ℓ in every $(2^\ell+1)$st tree maps onto the same PE at level ℓ. In contrast, the basic pyramid architecture employs a one-to-one mapping between image windows (quadtree nodes) and PEs. Each node in the tree maps onto the PE in the corresponding position in the pyramid.

Since the same computations on tree nodes are performed both by the basic and the interleaved pyramids, and only the PE assignment to the nodes changes, the algorithms for the basic pyramids are also valid for the interleaved pyramids.

3.5.1 Performance Measures

The interleaved pyramid conceptually provides the same kind of improvement in performance over the basic pipelined pyramid for processing border-based algorithms, as pipelining provides over the basic pyramid for processing interior-based algorithms; both increase utilization of lower-level PEs and the throughput rate. However, the interleaved pyramid uses many more PEs than the basic pyramid, although the computation time and memory size required at a single PE corresponding to an $n \times n$ window remain $C_t n$ and $C_m n$, respectively, as in the basic pyramid. We will now compute the performance measures described in Sect. 3.4 for the interleaved pyramids.

(a) Number of processors = $\displaystyle\sum_{\ell=0}^{\log N} 2^{2\log N - \ell} = N(2N-1)$

(b) Total memory = $\displaystyle\sum_{\ell=0}^{\log N}$ (number of nodes at level ℓ) $\cdot$

(memory required per node at level ℓ)

$\displaystyle = \sum_{\ell=0}^{\log N} 2^{2\log N - \ell} \cdot C_m 2^\ell$

$= C_m N^2 \log 2N$

(c) Output latency = C_t

(d) Input bandwidth = N^2 (same as for the basic pyramid)

(e) Image turnaround time = $C_t(2N - 1)$ (same as for the basic pyramid)

(f) $PE_T = C_t \cdot (2N^2 - N)$

(g) $M_T = C_t C_m \cdot N^2 \log 2N$.

Note that the output latency is equal to the processing time of a PE at the base of the pyramid. The expressions for PE_T and M_T indicate that the interleaved pyramid achieves a factor of N improvement in processor utilization and a factor of $N/\log N$ improvement in memory utilization over the pipelined basic pyramid. This is achieved by approximately a 3/2 increase in the number of processors and a $\log N$ increase in the amount of memory.

3.6 Pyramid Trees

Despite its high throughput rate, the interleaved pyramid presents severe implementation problems, chiefly due to its size. (The same is also true of the basic pyramid.) For example, to process a 512×512 image, an interleaved pyramid requires about half a million PEs at ten different levels. Moreover, for maximum speed, the entire image must be input in parallel. We will now describe our third hierarchy, called a pyramid tree, which provides a way of reducing the required number of PEs and the input memory bandwidth at the cost of a decrease in the throughput rate.

Since the number of PEs in interleaved pyramids grows very fast with the number of levels, shallow interleaved pyramids are desirable. However, interleaved pyramids with fewer than $\log N + 1$ levels can only process images smaller than $N \times N$. Let us consider interleaved pyramids with k levels. Let $N = 2^L$ and

$L = pk$, where p and k are positive integers. The image array of $2^L \times 2^L$ pixels may be represented as a $2^k \times 2^k$ array of $2^{k(p-1)} \times 2^{k(p-1)}$ windows of pixels. If the results of computation and border-related information pertaining to these windows are available, they may be processed by a k-level interleaved pyramid, each of whose bottom-level PEs receives data corresponding to four windows. Since a $2^{k(p-1)} \times 2^{k(p-1)}$ window may still be too large to be processed by a single k-level interleaved pyramid, it can be further divided into a $2^k \times 2^k$ array of $2^{k(p-2)} \times 2^{k(p-2)}$ windows of pixels. If such a recursive division is continued for $(p-1)$ steps, $2^k \times 2^k$ arrays of $2^{k[p-(p-1)]} \times 2^{k[p-(p-1)]}$, i.e., $2^k \times 2^k$, windows of pixels are obtained. The final set of $2^k \times 2^k$ windows requires a $(k + 1)$-level interleaved pyramid. The required interconnection of interleaved pyramids is a tree (Fig. 3.5). For a $2^L \times 2^L$ image, where $L = pk$, the tree has p levels. The leaf nodes are $(k+1)$-level interleaved pyramids and accept pixel inputs. Such a two-step hierarchy (tree of interleaved pyramids) of PEs, called a pyramid tree, defines our third organization. We will now discuss the branching factor of the tree.

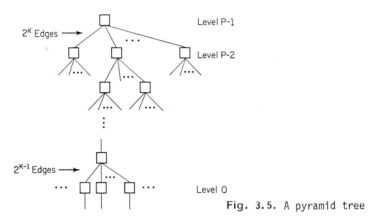

Fig. 3.5. A pyramid tree

Let a PE in the pyramid tree have the index (ℓ_t, ℓ_p), meaning that the PE is located at level ℓ_p of an interleaved pyramid that is itself located at level ℓ_t of the tree. Consider a nonleaf interleaved pyramid at level ℓ_t, $2 \le \ell_t \le p-1$. It has $2^{2(k-1)}$ PEs at level 0 (index$(\ell_t, 0)$) and 2^{k-1} PEs at level $k-1$ (index $(\ell_t, k-1)$). Each PE with index $(\ell_t, 0)$, $\ell_t \ge 2$, receives data for four windows, each of size $2^{k(\ell_t-1)} \times 2^{k(\ell_t-1)}$, processed by PEs indexed $(\ell_t-1, k-1)$. Thus data for 2^{2k} windows is received from interleaved pyramids each of which has 2^{k-1} output PEs. This requires $(2^{2k})/(2^{k-1}) = 2^{k+1}$ children interleaved pyramids at level ℓ_t-1. However, as will be seen later, for synchronization purposes we will allow only 2^k children (Fig.3.5). Thus each child PE indexed $(\ell_t-1, k-1)$ sends data for two windows in the $2^k \times 2^k$ array of windows.

Now consider the pyramids at level $\ell_t = 1$. Each such interleaved pyramid must receive data from the output PEs of $(k+1)$-level interleaved pyramids at level $\ell_t = 0$. Since level-0 pyramids have 2^k output PEs each, where each output PE supplies data for two windows serially, the number of children interleaved pyramids per interleaved pyramid at level $\ell_t = 1$ is $(2^{2k})/(2^k \cdot 2) = 2^{k-1}$ (Fig.3.5). PEs indexed $(\ell_t, 0)$, $\ell_t \ge 1$, receive four (window) inputs each, whereas PEs with index $(0,0)$ receive single pixel inputs. Figure 3.6a shows a schematic of a pyramid tree for a 512×512 image with $k = p = 3$. The root node and its $2^k = 8$ children nodes constitute the top $p-1 = 2$ levels of the

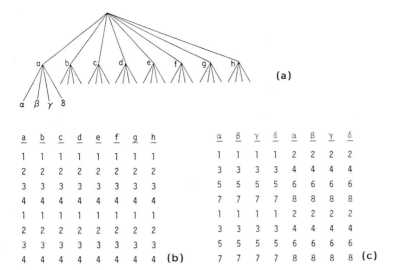

(a)

a	b	c	d	e	f	g	h
1	1	1	1	1	1	1	1
2	2	2	2	2	2	2	2
3	3	3	3	3	3	3	3
4	4	4	4	4	4	4	4
1	1	1	1	1	1	1	1
2	2	2	2	2	2	2	2
3	3	3	3	3	3	3	3
4	4	4	4	4	4	4	4	(b)

α	β	γ	δ	α	β	γ	δ
1	1	1	1	2	2	2	2
3	3	3	3	4	4	4	4
5	5	5	5	6	6	6	6
7	7	7	7	8	8	8	8
1	1	1	1	2	2	2	2
3	3	3	3	4	4	4	4
5	5	5	5	6	6	6	6
7	7	7	7	8	8	8	8	(c)

Fig. 3.6. (a) A schematic for a pyramid tree with k = p = 3. Each node represents an interleaved pyramid. (b) An 8 x 8 array of 64 x 64 windows of a
512 x 512 image to be processed by the interleaved pyramids at level 1. (c)
An 8 x 8 array of 8 x 8 windows to be processed by a set of four level-0
interleaved pyramids

pyramid tree. Thus each of these nodes represents a 3-level interleaved
pyramid. Each of the level-1 nodes has 2^{k-1} = 4 children nodes, each representing a k+1 = 4-level interleaved pyramid.

Figure 3.6b shows a 512×512 pixel image divided into an 8×8 (2^k×2^k) array
of 64×64 windows. These windows are processed in two batches (for synchronization) by the level-1 pyramids to provide inputs to the root node. The division of the windows into two batches and the order in which the windows within each batch are processed is not unique; one way is shown in Fig. 3.6b. In
this example an 8×8 array is divided into its northern and southern halves.
The windows in the northern half are processed prior to those in the southern
half. In either half, each of the 2^k = 8 level-1 interleaved pyramids processes all windows from a single column in the order shown by the integer
labels.

Figure 3.6c represents one of the 64×64 windows divided into an 8×8
array of subwindows to be processed by 2^{k-1} = 4 of the bottom level interleaved pyramids that have a common parent. As in Fig. 3.6b, the array is
divided into its northern and southern halves. In either half each of the
four interleaved pyramids processes all the windows from two columns with
the same column header and in the order shown by the integer labels.

We will now see that such a serial-parallel mode of data flow does not
render any node idle due to lack of data. This is because the time required
by a node to process current data is also the time required to receive the
data for the following computation. In the following we will denote ℓ_t by
ℓ for short. An interleaved pyramid represented by a node at level ℓ, $1 \le \ell \le$
p-1, of the tree has inputs that correspond to windows of size $2^{k\ell} \times 2^{k\ell}$. The
processing time in a PE at the base of that pyramid is $C_t \cdot 2^{k\ell+1}$, and there-

fore the output latency of that pyramid is $C_t \cdot 2^{k\ell+1}$, provided the inputs arrive at the same rate (Sect.3.5). The node's 2^{2k} inputs are divided into 2^k groups each of size 2^k with inputs within a group arriving serially since they are the interleaved outputs (each output being used twice) of a single interleaved pyramid one level below. Thus all the inputs arrive in the time required to produce 2^k interleaved outputs serially in an interleaved pyramid at level $\ell-1$. Using an inductive argument on ℓ for $\ell \geq 1$, the output latency of such a pyramid at level $\ell-1$ is $C_t \cdot 2^{k(\ell-1)+1}$, and hence the total time to produce all 2^k outputs within a group is $C_t \cdot 2^{k\ell+1}$, as is required.

3.6.1 Performance Measures

The performance of the pyramid tree is a function of the parameters p and k.

a) Let PE(p,k) be the total number of PEs in the pyramid tree required to process an N×N image ($N=2^{pk}$). Recall that each of the level-1 nodes has 2^{k-1} children nodes, and all higher level nodes have 2^k children each. The number of k-level interleaved pyramids at level ℓ, $1 \leq \ell \leq p-1$, is thus $2^{k(p-1-\ell)}$. The number of level-1 nodes is $2^{k(p-2)}$, and hence the number of leaf nodes (each of which is a (k+1)-level interleaved pyramid) is $2^{k(p-2)} \cdot 2^{k-1}$. If H(k) denotes the number of PEs in a k-level interleaved pyramid, we have

$$
PE(p,k) = \begin{cases} H(k+1) \cdot 2^{k(p-2)+k-1} + H(k) \cdot \displaystyle\sum_{\ell=1}^{p-1} 2^{k(p-1-\ell)} & \text{for } p \geq 2 \\[3ex] H(k+1) & \text{for } p=1 \ . \end{cases}
$$

In the previous section we derived $H(k) = 2^{k-1}(2^k-1)$. Values of PE(p,k) for several small values of p and k are given below.

k	1	2	3	4
			p	
2	28	62	254	1022
3	120	508	4092	32,764
4	496	4088	65,528	1.049×10^6

The number of PEs in the $p = \dfrac{\log N}{k}$ -level tree as a function of k and N is

$$
= \begin{cases} N \cdot 2^k - 2^{k-1} & \text{for } p \geq 2 \\[2ex] N(2N-1) & \text{for } p = 1 \ . \end{cases}
$$

The mapping between image windows and PEs in a pyramid tree may be obtained in two steps. First, the mapping between image windows and interleaved pyramids in the tree is given by the recursive division of the image into a $2^k \times 2^k$ subarray of windows, as described earlier in this section. Next, within an interleaved pyramid, the image window to PE mapping is the same as described in Sect.3.5. Together, the two steps determine the general image window to PE mapping in pyramid tree. Algorithms designed for the basic pyramid may also be used for pyramid trees.

b) Let $M(p,k)$ be the total memory required by the pyramid tree. To compute $M(p,k)$, we will compute the memory requirements of a non-leaf node and a leaf node separately. A non-leaf node at level ℓ, $\ell \geq 1$, of the tree is a k-level interleaved pyramid which, according to the result of the previous section, requires a memory of $C_m \cdot 2^{2(k-1)} \cdot k \cdot 2^{\ell k+1}$. Here the factor $2^{\ell k+1}$ occurs because of the fact that the inputs are windows of size $2^{\ell k} \times 2^{\ell k}$ rather than single pixels. However, unlike the interleaved pyramid of Sect.3.5, the interleaved pyramid at level ℓ of the tree does not receive all its inputs in parallel and therefore must use extra memory in the PEs at its base to store serially arriving inputs of size $2^{\ell k}$. There are $2^{2(k-1)}$ PEs at the base and each PE needs extra memory of $C_m 2^{\ell k+1}$. The total memory requirement of a nonleaf node at level ℓ is therefore

$$C_m \cdot 2^{2(k-1)} \cdot k \cdot 2^{\ell k+1} + C_m \cdot 2^{2(k-1)} 2^{\ell k}$$

$$= \frac{C_m}{2} \cdot 2^{k(\ell+2)}(k+1).$$

There are $2^{k \cdot (p-1-\ell)}$ such nodes at level ℓ, $1 \leq \ell \leq p-1$. Among the $2^{k(p-2)+(k-1)}$ leaf nodes, each is a $(k+1)$ level interleaved pyramid requiring memory of $C_m \cdot 2^{2k} \cdot (k+1)$. Thus the memory required by the pyramid tree to process an $N \times N$ image, $M(p,k)$, is obtained by adding the memory requirements of the non-leaf and leaf nodes. For the case $p>1$, we have

$$M(p,k) = \frac{C_m}{2}(k+1) \sum_{\ell=1}^{p-1} 2^{k(p-1-\ell)} \cdot 2^{k(\ell+2)}$$

$$+ C_m \cdot 2^{k(p-2) + (k-1)} \cdot 2^{2k}(k+1)$$

$$= C_m 2^{k(p+1)} \left(\frac{(k+1)(p-1)}{2} + \frac{(k+1)}{2} \right)$$

$$= \frac{C_m}{2} \cdot (k+1) \cdot p \cdot 2^{k(p+1)}.$$

For the case $p=1$, we have

$$M(1,k) = C_m 2^{2k}(k+1).$$

Normalized values of $M(p,k)$ for several small values of p and k are

			p	
k	1	2	3	4
2	48	176	104	5376
3	256	1920	22,528	237,568
4	1280	19,456	448×2^{10}	37×2^{18}

c) To compute the output latency of the pyramid tree we observe that the outputs of pyramids at any given level of the tree occur in synchronism. Therefore, the entire tree may be viewed as a segmented pipeline with the delay at a given segment equal to the output latency of an interleaved pyramid at that level. The maximum such delay occurs at the interleaved pyramid at the root of the tree.

The PEs comprising the base of the interleaved pyramid at the root of the tree process borders of size $2^{k(p-1)+1} \times 2^{k(p-1)+1}$, and hence require processing time $C_t \cdot 2^{k(p-1)+1}$. The interleaved pyramid is thus able to accept new inputs at a maximum rate of $C_t \cdot 2^{k(p-1)+1}$. Such an input rate is actually achieved because the output latency of an interleaved pyramid one level down (whose 2^{k-1} outputs are fed serially to the pyramid at the root) is $C_t \cdot 2^{k(p-2)+1}$. Hence, 2^k output values (with each output PE used twice) are available at the rate of $C_t \cdot 2^{k(p-1)+1}$, the maximum rate at which inputs are accepted by the interleaved pyramid at the root. From Sect. 3.5 it follows that the output latency of the interleaved pyramid at the root is $C_t \cdot 2^{k(p-1)+1}$. Thus

Output latency = Output latency of the interleaved pyramid at the root
of the tree

$$= C_t \cdot 2^{k(p-1)+1}$$

$$= 2C_t \cdot N/2^k .$$

d) The input bandwidth is the number of parallel pixel inputs. Since the interleaved pyramids corresponding to the leaf nodes of the tree accept single pixel inputs, the total number of PEs at the base of the $2^{k(p-2)+k-1}$ level-0 pyramids in the tree must equal the bandwidth. Thus

Input bandwidth = (number of interleaved pyramids at level 0 of the
pyramid tree) $\cdot 2^{2k}$

$$= 2^{k(p-2)+k-1} \cdot 2^{2k}$$

$$= 2^{kp+k-1} = \frac{N}{2} \cdot 2^k .$$

e) The turnaround time is the total time required to process an image. Let us first compute the time taken by a nonleaf node at level ℓ, $1 \le \ell \le p-1$, to process a set of 2^{2k} input windows, each of size $2^{k\ell} \times 2^{k\ell}$, that arrive in parallel in batches of size 2^k. From the discussion at the beginning of this section, the output latency of nodes one level down, i.e., at level $\ell-1$, is $C_t \cdot 2^{k(\ell-1)+1}$. Hence, 2^k batches of inputs to nodes at level ℓ arrive serially in time $C_t \cdot 2^{k(\ell-1)+1} \cdot 2^k$. These inputs are then processed by the k-level interleaved pyramid with the PEs at level j, $0 \le j \le k-1$, taking time $C_t \cdot 2^{k\ell+1+j}$. The total time required by the node is thus the sum of the time required to collect all the inputs and the time required to process these inputs through the k levels. Thus, the total time is

$$= C_t \cdot 2^{k\ell+1} + C_t \cdot \sum_{j=0}^{k-1} 2^{k\ell+1+j}$$

$$= C_t \cdot 2^{k+1} \cdot 2^{k\ell} .$$

The single pixel inputs to a leaf in the pyramid tree arrive in parallel and are processed by the k+1 levels of the interleaved pyramid in total time $C_t \cdot (2^{k+1}-1)$. Since the input bandwidth of the pyramid tree is $(N/2)2^k$, the processing time for a single set of $(N/2)2^k$ pixel inputs is

$$= C_t \cdot (2^{k+1} - 1) + C_t \cdot 2^{k+1} \cdot \sum_{\ell=1}^{p-1} 2^{k\ell}$$

$$< 2C_t \cdot N .$$

There are $2N^2/N2^k$ sets of pixel inputs per image occurring at time intervals of C_t. The turnaround time for the entire image is therefore given by

$$\text{Turnaround time} \approx C_t \cdot 2N/2^k + 2C_t \cdot N$$

$$= 2C_t \cdot (N + N^{1-1/P}) \quad .$$

f) $PE_T = (2N - 1)2^{k-1} \cdot 2C_t \cdot N/2^k$

$$= C_t \cdot N(2N - 1) = O(N^2) \quad .$$

g) $M_T < \frac{C_m}{2} \cdot N \cdot 2^k \cdot p \cdot (k+1) \cdot 2C_t \cdot N/2^k$

$$< C_m \cdot C_t \cdot p(k+1) \cdot N^2$$

$$= O(N^2 \log N) \quad .$$

3.7 Conclusions

We have described three multiprocessor pyramid architectures for bottom-up image analysis: pyramids, interleaved pyramids, and pyramid trees. Bottom-up analysis is made feasible by transmitting up the pyramid levels quadrant borders and border-related information that captures quadrant interaction of interest for a given computation. We use a small general-purpose processor as the processing element (PE).

Since output is available only at the apex PEs, the only time-efficient computations are those which provide small numbers of result bits, to keep the data output operation from dominating the overall processing time. The algorithms described in the paper compute $O(\log N)$-bit results on an N×N image. However, other computations can be performed if the time required for outputting the results from apex PE(s) is acceptable (e.g., when the basic pyramid is not pipelined, or when slow loading of the input image makes the outputting time at the apex irrelevant). Certain transformations on point patterns constitute one class of such computations. For instance, the Voronoi tessellation of the plane defined by a set of points (nuclei) is the partition of the plane into cells in which each cell contains exactly one nucleus, and all points within the cell are closer to the cell's nucleus than to any other nucleus. Similarly, the minimal spanning tree defined by a set of points is a tree that connects all points and has a minimal cost, say the sum of edge lengths. Such transformations on point patterns are useful in a wide variety of applications [3.27], and involve specifying $O(N \log N)$ bits for a pattern consisting of N points ($O(\log N)$ bits for each of the line segments defining the desired graph). The architectures described in this paper also offer the possibility of using 4-way divide-and-conquer based algorithms, instead of the often used 2-way divide-and-conquer paradigm, thus reducing the computation time requirements of the above transformations from $O(N \log_2 N)$ to $O(N \log_4 N)$.

Interleaved pyramids result in high utilization of PEs at all levels, unlike the basic pyramids where the PEs at lower levels are increasingly idle. The pyramid tree offers a solution to the problems of large input bandwidth and large number of PEs required for a purely interleaved pyramid. The designer is provided with parameters that can be manipulated to achieve suitable tradeoffs between hardware cost and processing time.

Table 3.1 summarizes performance measures (a) through (g) for all three architectures described in this paper. One note of caution must, however, be

Table 3.1. Comparison of performance of multiprocessor pyramid architectures

	# of PEs	Total memory size	Output latency	Input Bandwidth	Turnaround time	PE_T	M_T
Basic Pyramid	$\approx \dfrac{4N^2}{3}$	$O(N^2)$	$O(N)$	$O(N^2)$	$O(N)$	$O(N^3)$	$O(N^3)$
Interleaved Pyramid	$2N^2-N$	$O(N^2\log N)$	$O(1)$	$O(N^2)$	$O(N)$	$O(N^2)$	$O(N^2\log N)$
Pyramid Tree $(p > 1)$	$\approx N^{1+1/p}$	$O(N^{1+1/p}\log N)$	$O(N^{1-1/p})$	$O(N^{1+1/p})$	$O(N+N^{1-1/p})$	$O(N^2)$	$O(N^2\log N)$

added. The implementation of pipelining and interleaving assumes that images can be loaded in parallel and at as fast a rate as desired. This is not possible if, for example, one does not have parallel access to the input image pixels (e.g., outputs of individual sensors). In such cases the input image loading time may dominate the processing time, and hence may make fast processing capabilities superfluous. Parallel optical transmission of the sensor outputs using fiber optics is one solution to designing the focal plane architectures [3.17] which will make parallel loading of images possible.

References

3.1 L. Uhr: Layered "recognition cone" networks that preprocess, classify, and describe, IEEE Trans. Computers C-21, 758-768 (1972)

3.2 A. R. Hanson, E. M. Riseman (eds.): Computer Vision Systems (Academic Press, New York, 1978)

3.3 L. Uhr, M. Thompson, J. Lackey: "A 2-layered SIMD/MIMD parallel pyramidal array/net", in Proc. Workshop on Computer Architecture for Pattern Analysis and Image Database Management, Hot Springs, VA, 1981, pp. 209-216

3.4 L. Uhr: "Converging pyramids of arrays", in Proc. Workshop on Computer Architecture for Pattern Analysis and Image Database Management, Hot Springs, VA, 1981, pp. 31-34

3.5 C. R. Dyer: "Augmented Cellular Automata for Image Analysis", Ph.D. dissertation, Department of Computer Science, University of Maryland (1978)

3.6 A. Nakamura, C. R. Dyer: "Bottom-up cellular pyramids for image analysis", in Proc. 4th Int'l. Joint Conf. on Pattern Recognition, Kyoto, Japan, 1978, pp. 474-496

3.7 C. R. Dyer: "A VLSI pyramid machine for hierarchical parallel image processing", in Proc. Pattern Recognition and Image Processing Conf., Dallas, TX, 1981, pp. 381-386

3.8 A. Rosenfeld: Picture Languages (Academic Press, New York, 1979)

3.9   A. Rosenfeld: "Quadtrees and pyramids for pattern recognition and image processing", in Proc. 5th Int'l. Conf. on Pattern Recognition, Miami Beach, FL, 1980, pp. 802-811

3.10 H. Samet, A. Rosenfeld: "Quadtree representations of binary images", in Proc. 5th Int'l. Conf. on Pattern Recognition, Miami Beach, FL, 1980, pp. 815-818

3.11 N. Ahuja: "Approaches to recursive image decomposition", in Proc. Pattern Recognition and Image Processing Conf., Dallas, TX, 1981, pp. 75-80

3.12 M. D. Kelly: "Edge detection in pictures by computer using planning", in Machine Intelligence 6, ed. by B. Meltzer, D. Michie (University of Edinburgh Press, Edinburgh, UK, 1971), pp. 379-409

3.13 M. D. Levine: "A knowledge based computer vision system", in Computer Vision Systems, ed. by A. Hanson, E. Riseman (Academic Press, New York, 1978), pp. 335-352

3.14 K. Price, R. Reddy: "Change detection and analysis in multispectral images", in Proc. 5th Int'l. Joint Conf. on Artificial Intelligence, Cambridge, MA, 1977, pp. 619-625

3.15 S. L. Tanimoto: Pictorial feature distortion in a pyramid, Computer Graphics Image Processing 5, 333-352 (1976)

3.16 S. L. Tanimoto, T. Pavlidis: A hierarchical data structure for picture processing, Computer Graphics Image Processing 4, 104-119 (1975)

3.17 P. J. Burt, T. H. Hong, A. Rosenfeld: Segmentation and estimation of image region properties through cooperative hierarchical computation, IEEE Trans. Systems, Man, Cybernetics SMC-11, 802-809 (1981)

3.18 M. Shneier: Two hierarchical linear feature representations: edge pyramids and edge quadtrees, Computer Graphics Image Proceeding 17, 211-224 (1981)

3.19 T. Dubitzki, A. Wu, A. Rosenfeld: Parallel region property computation by active quadtree networks, IEEE Trans. Pattern Analysis Machine Intelligence PAMI-3, 626-633 (1981)

3.20 K. Batcher: Bit-serial parallel processing systems, IEEE Trans. Computers C-31, 377-384 (1982)

3.21 M. J. B. Duff: "CLIP 4: a large scale integrated circuit array parallel processor", in Proc. Third Int'l. Joint Conf. on Pattern Recognition, Coronado, CA, 1976, pp. 728-733

3.22 S. F. Reddaway: "DAP--a flexible number cruncher", in Proc. Workshop on Vector and Parallel Processors, Los Alamos, NM, 1978, pp. 233-234

3.23 C. Rieger: "ZMOB: doing it in parallel", in Proc. Workshop on Computer Architecture for Pattern Analysis and Image Database Management, Hot Springs, VA, 1981, pp. 119-124

3.24 H. J. Siegel, L. J. Siegel, F. C. Kemmerer, P. T. Mueller Jr., H. E. Smalley Jr., S. D. Smith: PASM: a partitionable SIMD/MIMD system for image processing and pattern recognition, IEEE Trans. Computers C-30, 934-947 (1981)

3.25 A. Rosenfeld, A. C. Kak: Digital Picture Processing (Academic Press, New York, 1976)

3.26 C. R. Dyer: Computing the Euler number of an image from its quadtree, Computer Graphics Image Processing 13, 270-276 (1980)

3.27 N. Ahuja: Dot pattern processing using Voronoi neighborhoods, IEEE Trans. Pattern Analysis Machine Intelligence PAMI-4, 336-343 (1982)

4. Visual and Conceptual Hierarchy – A Paradigm for Studies of Automated Generation of Recognition Strategies *

D.A. Rosenthal

Datacor, Inc., Bernardsville, NJ 07924, USA

R. Bajcsy

Department of Computer & Information Science, University of Pennsylvania
Philadelphia, PA 19104, USA

The purpose of this paper is to discuss design considerations in the choice
of mechanisms when a flexible query system dealing with visual scenes is being
constructed. More concretely, the issues are:

- Flexibility in adding new information to the knowledge base
- Power of inferencing
- Avoiding unnecessary generation of hypotheses where a great deal of
  image processing has to be perfected in order to test them
- Automatic generation of recognition strategies .

4.1 Introduction

In the past most of the research in computer vision has concentrated on the
development of image processing routines, such as finding edges and regions,
outlines, shapes and their descriptions. This process is usually called
feature extraction and/or image (scene) segmentation and its main purpose is
to reduce the data but preserve the most characteristic invariant or semi-
invariant features. The recognition process then takes these features and
descriptions and matches them to some model(s). This process by and large
is explicitly embedded in the recognition program and frequently very dependent on the application.

Recently, there have been attempts to make this process more systematic
and at the same time flexible [4.1-3]. Rule-based systems, in particular,
have turned out to be very useful for this purpose. The goal, however,
should be to discover the right structure of the rules which in turn will
allow automatic data- and/or query-driven generation of recognition strategies. This is the subject of this paper.

We start with a query which restricts the areas of analysis to highly
probable places and also suggests a range of expected sizes and shapes. In
turn the size expectation is translated into the necessary spatial resolution
which will make the sought object visible. This naturally will reduce the
number of pixels used in the analysis. From there on the strategy is data-
driven, i.e., dependent on the local contrast, noise, continuity of boundaries, etc.

The domain consists of aerial images of an urban area (Washington, DC).
The rationale behind this choice was that:

---

*This work was supported by NSF grant MCS-81-96176.

a) an aerial image is an orthogonal projection of a three-dimensional world without any perspective distortion, hence the image processing part is simplified;

b) an urban area as opposed to a nonurban area was chosen because of the regular shapes available in urban areas which are used as features during the recognition process.

Currently, the system is capable of locating different types of motor vehicles, various street markings, buildings, objects which appear on the tops of buildings, and other objects.

In an earlier paper [4.4], we described the motivation behind the conceptual and visual hierarchy. Our notion of conceptual hierarchies is that visual concepts or objects can be ordered with respect to some criteria, such as part-whole relationships, class inclusion, contextual relations, etc.

Visual hierarchy has received a fair amount of attention in image processing in the past [4.5-8]. It has been called the "pyramid" data structure or "processing cone." In practice, a visual hierarchy is a set of different sized images of the original input image, usually organized in descending or ascending order with respect to spatial resolution.

It is the interaction between the conceptual hierarchy and visual hierarchy which is important in this paper and this interaction produces a recognition strategy in response to a query.

The body of the paper is divided into three parts:

Section 4.2:   the formalism for knowledge representation;
Section 4.3:   the implementation;
Section 4.4:   the results.

The overall scheme is shown in Fig. 4.1.

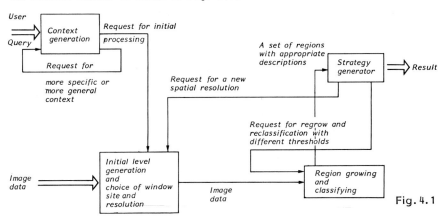

Fig. 4.1

4.2 The Formalism for Knowledge Representation

There have been various attempts to develop a formal structure for representation of knowledge in various AI systems. Among the more successful ones are:

- Production systems
- First-order predicate calculus
- Procedural systems
- State-space representation.

Each of these structures has been used in the pure classical form as well as in various extensions required by the application problems. In computer vision, we can formulate the following requirements:

1) the flexibility and consistency of a knowledge representation scheme to which one can add or delete needed pieces of knowledge in a systematic fashion;

2) a facility for representing factual information (predicates, functions or relations) and procedures which can extract information on request from the sensory data;

3) an inferencing scheme which can generate recognition strategies.

It is not our purpose to evaluate each of these structures; rather, we wish to report our experience with one of them, namely with production systems.

4.2.1 Production Systems

Production systems are a general class of computation mechanisms. They have been applied to a variety of problems. Although there is no standard production system, there are some unifying themes that embody each implementation. (See [4.9] for an excellent overview.)

A production system is composed of three elements: a data base, a set of rules, and an interpreter. Implementations vary in the performance of the interpreter and the structure of the rules.

The production system that we used was initially developed as a tool for natural language processing [4.10]. It was later used by SLOAN [4.11] for sequencing operations in a computer vision experiment. Before we describe in detail each element of our production system we need to establish some notation:

Let CONS and VARS be sets of constants and variables, respectively. FORMS are

1) A CONS ⇒ A FORMS;(A) FORMS
2) ?X VARS ⇒ ?X FORMS
3) A CONS & F1,F2,..Fn FORMS ⇒ (A F1 F2 .....Fn)
4) Nothing else.

Examples of FORMS are:

1) (SPATIAL-RELATION CAR ON STREET)
2) (REGION ? NUMBER CAR) .

The data base can be viewed in a number of different ways; in the most general form, as a set of strings. Intuitively, it represents the state of the world or a set of assertions which encode the knowledge at hand. In our application, a set of elements of the data base at any one time might be a description of an object, descriptions of a grown region, or the manner in

which a region was labelled as an object. In our case it consists of an unordered set of assertions called FACTS. FACTS are formally described in
terms of FORMS without variables. Example (1) above is a FACT.

The rules are composed of two parts: a set of conditions known as the
left-hand side (LHS), and a set of actions associated with the conditions,
known as the right-hand side (RHS). The rules are used to encode what transitions should be made, based on what is known. Both LHS and RHS are composed
of a set of FORMS. While in natural language applications the system has to
infer from propositions and predicates only, in computer vision we needed in
addition a vehicle for accessing and processing the visual sensory data. For
this purpose we added two special FORMS: the MUST FORM and the EXEC FORM.

The MUST FORM may appear in the RHS of a rule in the form (MUST[x]). Its
semantics are such that the corresponding FORM[x] must appear in FACTS for
this rule to fire. The facility is used to prevent undesirable inferences.

The EXEC FORM similarly appears in the RHS of a rule in the form of
EXEC[x]. The elements of [x] are LISP function calls. This FORM allows us
to invoke image processing routines.

The interpreter compares elements of the data base to the LHSs of the
rules in order to determine which rules to match or fire. In constructing
an interpreter to accomplish this task, the designer has to address the following issues:

1) The order in which rules are compared. Should the rule set be an
   ordered or unordered set?
2) The resolution of conflict of multiple rule firings. If more than one
   rule matches the data base, which of the RHSs should be invoked?
3) The determination of an acceptable match. Should a total match (i.e.,
   every condition of a rule must be matched) be the criterion for a rule
   to be considered matched, or should matches of only some of the conditions be considered as matches?

The interpreter is implemented in our system as a function called REWRITE,
and we use:

1) An unordered set of rules, i.e., the order in which the matching takes
   place is irrelevant.
2) If more than one rule matches the same subset of FACTS, then the minimal
   rule is the one which fires. Here an explanation of what we mean by
   "minimal" is in order: rule (i) is less than rule (j) if LHS(rule
   (i)) is a subset of LHS (rule (j)). In addition, if two rules are
   identical with respect to the above definition then the one that has
   a constant is less than the one that has a variable.
3) Partial matches are allowed. For example, an object will be recognized
   even if only some but not all of its features are present in the data.

The intuition of using a minimal rule is that the system wants to use the
rule with the fewest unmatched items and hence take those actions for which
it has the best evidence.

Our selection of a production system with partial matching capabilities
was motivated by the work of Tidhar [4.12]. In that system a lattice structure was used for representing knowledge about 2-D complex shapes. The lattice structure modelled the observation that for recognition of an object one
needs to extract only those features that uniquely discriminate the object

from everything else in the world. The greatest lower bound of the lattice was computed, which in turn identified the shape only from partial information. It was shown that by structuring the objects and their characteristics into a lattice, the best description would always be obtained. Unfortunately, it was also found that structuring the objects and their characteristics into a lattice was very cumbersome. In order to adhere to the lattice restriction that every pair of nodes has a unique greatest lower bound and least upper bound, intermediate nodes had to be added. These intermediate nodes had no intuitive value (they were mostly conjunctions of descriptors) and just generated large data structures. All the knowledge was explicitly encoded and static (no procedures were allowed). Attempting to avoid this problem led to the next implementation of a production system with partial matching as described above. Within this system in addition to a priori FACTS we were able to generate new FACTS by applying image processing routines and dynamically computing properties such as color, shape, texture, and spatial relationship [4.11]. While we succeeded in building a flexible system that could acquire knowledge during the recognition process, we encountered another difficulty. In a flexible recognition system one is driven by the principle of "least commitment"; hence one has to allow for the generation of many plausible explanations until there is sufficient contrary evidence. In our system this was implemented in such a way that the interpreter tried to cover as many FACTS as possible. Naturally this led to a combinatorial explosion of generated new FACTS.

These new FACTS triggered different rules which in turn invoked different image processing operations. The problem with the multiple rule firing was that it would invoke a parallel computation of the image processing operations in the RHS. This was not the desired effect. For example, consider a region growing process. A set of rules was set up to compute the thresholds desirable at that point. FACTS made that decision from characteristics of the object plus results of previous analysis. Now imagine that due to previous analysis two thresholds are simultaneously generated and hence two different regions are delineated. This of course causes confusion and reduces our ability to use newly found results in future computation. Even with the overused MUST FORM, this problem could not be overcome since the MUST checks only for the appearance of the FORM in FACTS but it does not check for the equivalence of two FORMS. Another solution available would be to restrict the assertions that were put into FACTS at each iteration. It was felt that this answer was totally contrary to the spirit of production systems.

A natural way to solve the problem of combinatorial explosion is to impose an order on the set of rules. This has been implemented by augmenting the RHS of each rule by a LISP function ARBITRATE. ARBITRATE is a function with two parameters: a priority value and a list of actions. The list of actions consists of the image processing operations that are associated with the rule. The priority value is a number that ranks the rule with respect to the other rules in the rule set (the smaller the priority value the higher the position of the rule in the set). The priority values are set by us during system design. The effect of this is to order the rule set. Now, whenever a RHS is invokved, ARBITRATE compares the priority of that rule to the priority of the highest-order rule matched previously. If the priority is lower (indicating a higher position in the order) then a global variable, ACTIONS, is set to the actions of the rule. Otherwise it does nothing. After the interpreter has completed matching, ACTIONS contains the actions of the rule with the highest priority that was matched.

One additional mechanism was needed to deactivate rules. Namely, at a particular instance in an iteration, a mechanism was needed to prevent a particular rule from firing. The need for this mechanism comes up in the following situation. A rule will fire on an assertion and this assertion will always be in FACTS. (It can't be purged from FACTS because other rules fire off it.) Thus, the rule will fire each time a REWRITE is done. If this rule has a high priority, then other rules which should fire will not.

The solution is to add a clause to the LHS of the rule we want to deactivate. This clause will essentially be a flag which indicates whether the assertion which causes the rule to fire has already been used. If it has not, then the rule will fire. If it has, then this clause will prevent it from firing again. This clause will be a MUST FORM. The RHS of the rule is the place where the rule is turned on and off. This effect is achieved by inserting and deleting assertions from FACTS.

4.2.2 Object Description Notation

In quest of developing a more systematic approach to presentation of knowledge about the expected world rather than just having a set of feature extraction procedures, we have constructed an object description notation. The goal of this notation is to provide an ample set of descriptors so that the user of this system will be able to describe an object in the scene.

At present, our object description notation is divided into three parts: visual, contextual, and regularity-in-spatial-relations. Naturally the notation can be extended to many more parts. The visual part encompasses descriptions of the visual properties of the object, such as shape, reflectance, size, and texture. The contextual description represents the contextual proximity relationship. It embodies our expectations of finding certain objects in a certain context. For example, cars are usually found either on roads or in a garage, but not in a living room unless the car is a toy. The "regularity-in-spatial-relations" category was chosen because

a) regularity in spatial arrangement in general is an important recognition feature;

b) in particular, in our domain it is an important characteristic of some objects, such as lane markers, which appear as broken lines arranged in a sequential manner, and cars in a parking lot, which usually are parked parallel to each other.

In our implementation the form of the object description notation will be a LISP list where the first element is the name of the descriptor and the others are parameters.

Instead of further theorizing, we present an example of an object description for the object "CAR":

CONTEXTUAL
```
(ON STREET ((POSITION VARIABLE)
            (ORIENTATION VARIABLE)
)           )
```

VISUAL
```
(RELATIVE-REFLECTANCE LIGHTER-OR-DARKER STREET)
(WIDTH (14 26))
(LENGTH (32 50))
(SHAPE RECT-SOLID)
(HOMOGENEITY HOMOGENEOUS)
```

To elaborate, a CAR is defined as lying on a STREET with no specification as
to its position or orientation on the street. Visually, its reflectance
could be lighter or darker than the STREET. (One might ask how to describe
an object that has the same reflectance as the object it lies on. The answer
is that this is not needed, since the described object would be indistinguishable from the contextual object and therefore could not be extracted.) Its
width and length are specified as a minimum and maximum size. Its shape is
a solid rectangle and it is homogeneous. As far as having a fixed, repetitive
spatial relationship with any other object, or itself, it doesn't have any.
Therefore, we have the (UNIT) description for REGULARITY-IN-SPATIAL-RELATIONS.

4.3 Implementation

Figure 4.1 gives the basic structure of the system. The names of the modules
in this diagram refer to the separate stages of the analysis. The first
three modules are simple and straightforward. Each has a set of rules to
either compute a final value or compute a set of thresholds. The following
is a summary of the aim of each:

1) Contextual: find the contextual area for the queried object. To achieve
   this, elements from the concept hierarchy have to be extracted. The
   elements extracted are the contextual object(s) and their relations to
   the queried object.

   Input to this phase is the name of the queried object. All other
   data will come from the description of the queried object. In particular, the contextual description will be accessed, and will be put
   into FACTS.

   The result of this phase will be

   a) Updating IP-FACTS (a global data-base of facts found during the
      analysis) with the gray level statistics of the object found.

   b) Returning the coordinates of the contextual areas.

2) Initial Level: given the visual characteristics of the object, what
   is the best level at which to start the search? We wish to calculate
   the coarsest spatial resolution to which we can shrink the data and
   still retain enough of the characteristics of the queried object so
   that it can be distinguished. The characteristics we are interested
   in are shape, size, and a sufficient contrast in gray level from the
   background.

3) Region Growing/Classification

   The goal of this phase is to grow and classify regions in a specific
   window in an image. The image, the coordinates of the window, the region growing thresholds, and the classification thresholds are set
   upon entry into this phase. The routines that invoke this part of the
   analysis are required to set these values.   There are presently two
   ways to enter this phase: initially from the initial level phase or
   from the strategy generator. The rest of this section will discuss
   how the required values get set when entry is from the initial level
   phase.

Inputs to calculate the region growing thresholds come from two sources: IP-FACTS and the reflectance entry in the object's description. From IP-FACTS comes the gray level statistics of the contextual (nearby) object. This part represents the bottom-up information. From the description (the a priori information) comes the spatial relation between the queried object and the contextual object which determines the relative reflectance, and the range of absolute reflectance. Once the thresholds are set up the region growing proceeds following the standard algorithm. Finally, the regions are classified, based on the expected size of an object, into three categories:

a) WHOLE -- regions whose size and reflectance are within the range of a whole object.

b) PART -- regions whose size and reflectance are within the range of a fragment or part of an object.

c) ATTACHED -- regions that possibly include more than one object.

One additional fact should be noted. The system is initialized with a data base containing the coordinates of most of the streets in the image. In addition to the coordinates, the mean and standard deviation of the gray level of the streets is also given. This information was computed by a method developed earlier [4.13]. The reason why the street-finding routine was not incorporated was the size limitation on the programs. If this restriction were not present, streets would have been found like any other objects.

4.3.1 Strategy Generator

This module is the heart of the system. Its aim is to combine the description of the object with the region growing results and decide on a sequence of actions to take.

The module is divided into two parts; the first works for homogeneous (coherent) objects and the other works for heterogeneous (made of parts) objects. This division was made for the sake of programming ease.

The strategy generator loops through a fixed sequence of actions to produce its results. This sequence is the same for homogeneous or heterogeneous objects. The loop can be summarized as follows:

1) Set RULES to the appropriate rule set:

   a) current set of WHOLE, PART and ATTACHED

   b) the REGULARITY-IN-SPATIAL-RELATIONS descriptor for the queried object.

2) REWRITE.

3) Evaluate all the actions in ACTIONS.

4) If END-LOOP is an element of ACTIONS then STOP else go to (2).

The result of evaluating ACTIONS causes functions to be invoked. These functions alter WHOLE, PART and ATTACHED. They also update FACTS with additional assertions. The functions that get invoked and the results of the steps taken cause the dynamic effect of actions. For the sake of brevity we shall only present the sequence of actions for the strategy generator if the object is homogeneous. The input data for setting both the RULES and the FACTS are classified sets, WHOLE, PART, ATTACHED and REGULARITY-IN-SPATIAL-RELATIONS.

Before the first iteration, FACTS consists of:

1. (WHOLE object list-of-region-params) for each element in WHOLE.

2. (ATTACHED object list-of-region-params) for each element in ATTACHED.

3. (PARTS-AVAILABLE object) if PARTS is not null. The actual list of PARTS is kept on a global variable called PART-LIST.

4. The REGULARITY-IN-SPATIAL-RELATIONS descriptor is input.

The rules prescribe a set of actions, listed below, to perform if the region is a WHOLE or PART or ATTACHED and has a REGULARITY-IN-SPATIAL-RELATIONS descriptor. The corresponding set of actions is:

CHECK-OUT-FINE, i.e., find out if the region classified as a WHOLE in the coarser resolution image is really the queried object in the finest resolution image.
CHECK-OUT-REST-SEQUENTIAL, i.e., check the rest of the objects which are possible composite wholes which meet sequential criteria.
CHECK-OUT-REST-PARALLEL, i.e., check the rest of the objects which are in parallel to the currently examined object.
CHECK-OUT-ATTACHED, i.e., the attached routines try to split merged regions into meaningful subregions.
FIND-OTHER-PART : the goal of this function is to invoke a procedure to find combinations of parts which form possible wholes.

If the queried object is HETEROGENEOUS (composed of components), then the strategy generator could call on the following additional routines:

ADD-COMPONENT: this procedure will try to find the components which make up the queried object.
DISMEMBER-COMPONENT-ATTACHED: this function will split attached regions into meaningful subregions.
ADD-COMPONENT-PART: this routine is very similar to ADD-COMPONENT except that no WHOLEs have been found. Instead, composite wholes are formed from the part list and used in the same manner as the WHOLEs in ADD-COMPONENT.

The result of these routines is to alter the state of FACTS. This will cause other rules to fire on subsequent REWRITES.

4.3.2 Methodology Used in Implementation

This section will discuss three rules we adhered to while constructing this system. While these rules were arrived at independently, the last two are similar to a current image processing technique called relaxation [4.14].

1) No Absolute Gray Levels as Descriptors

There are two reasons why this rule is important: one is general and the other is specific to the pyramid.

In general, it is absurd to build a general computer vision system and use absolute gray levels as descriptors. By a general computer vision system we mean one that will work on images in different domains and for different sensory inputs. Clearly, the reflectance of an object in one image will be different in another. In addition, most real-world objects do not have a strict range of colors and this will be reflected in the image. What is constant is the relative reflectances of objects. If the specification of a reflectance is made in terms of another, then the type of image is of no consequence, as long as the gray level restriction holds. The latter method is the one we use to describe an object's reflectance.

2) Use Knowledge from Previous Analysis to Aid the Present One

The use of this rule is motivated by the following situation. At some point in the analysis, a threshold has to be set. How does one do it?

Typically, in the past, this problem was solved by building the threshold values into the procedure. This solution lacks generality. That is, it seems improbable that the thresholds used for one object would be effective for another.

Our solution would be to take the following approach: use the information acquired from the analysis up to this point to guide in the threshold selection. This guide could take the form of range limits or tolerances. In any event, it would be more accurate and general than the former method as the values are based on the image being used.

3) Avoid Making Irreversible Decisions

This idea can be broken down into two parts:

a) in the initial stages of the analysis, use conservative thresholds;

b) carry around sufficient information so that re-evaluations can be made.

Point (a) seems to be contradict rule (2), as we are imposing a fixed discipline on the threshold selection instead of letting the system figure it out from previous analysis. However, this is not a contradiction because there are times in an analysis where there is no relevant information from the past analysis available. At these points, an ad hoc method must be used. Point (a) states that at these times, conservative estimates should be made. Obviously, these selections will not be optimal. However, refinements on these results can be made as the analysis goes along. As the system progresses further into the analysis, tighter thresholds can be set. We have more confidence in setting these tighter thresholds, at this point, because more is known about the image and the particular characteristics of the queried object.

4.4 Results

The complete description of all the details of the implementation is beyond the scope of this paper. The great power of this system is that one can try it on numerous examples and follow the recognition process step by step. We have tested the system on twenty objects [4.15], including a car, a bus, a truck, a crosswalk, lane markers, air conditioners, buildings, a street,

street intersections, a median, a sidewalk, a parking lot, and a street access.

An example of such a step by step recognition of a crosswalk is presented
below:

CROSSWALK

Loosely speaking, a crosswalk in this model is described as a part of an
intersection. The expected visual properties as they are observed from a
"bird's eye view" are: two parallel solid rectangular stripes. The intersection is similarly described as a right angular cross section of two streets.
In addition there is in the memory information about expected size ranges
and relative reflectances of the sought object with respect to its surround-
ings.

More formally we have:

```
CROSSWALK
    CONTEXTUAL
        (ON INTERSECTION ((POSITION VARIABLE)
                          (ORIENTATION VARIABLE)
        )                 )
    VISUAL
        (HOMOGENEITY HETEROGENEOUS)
        (COMPONENTS ((RECT1 RECT2)
                     (PARALLEL RECT1 RECT2 (8 20))
        )            )
    REGULARITY-IN-SPATIAL-RELATIONS
        (UNIT)
RECT1
    VISUAL
        (WIDTH (4 12))
        (LENGTH * (WIDTH INTERSECTION MINUS 0.50))
        (RELATIVE-REFLECTANCE LIGHTER INTERSECTION)
RECT2
    VISUAL
        (WIDTH (4 12))
        (LENGTH * (WIDTH INTERSECTION MINUS 0.50))
        (RELATIVE-REFLECTANCE LIGHTER INTERSECTION)
INTERSECTION
    CONTEXTUAL
        (ON STREET ((POSITION VARIABLE)
                    (ORIENTATION STREET)
        )           )

    VISUAL
        (HOMOGENEITY HETEROGENEOUS)
        (COMPONENTS ((STREET STREET)
                     (INTERSECTS STREET STREET 90)
        )            )
    REGULARITY-IN SPATIAL-RELATIONS
        (UNIT)
```

Figure 4.2 shows the window on which the search will be carried out. The
contextual object for CROSSWALK is INTERSECTION (Fig. 4.3). The context generation generates the query FIND INTERSECTION (Fig. 4.3). The contextual object for INTERSECTION is STREET so the context generator generates the query

FIND STREET (Fig. 4.4). The system retrieves and returns the fact that two STREETs occur in that window. In Figs. 4.5-9 and 4.15-17 the format of the display is as follows: The left figure shows the original image and the right figure displays the processed image at the appropriate level.

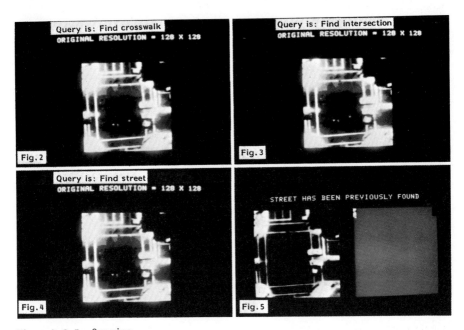

Figs. 4.2-5. Queries

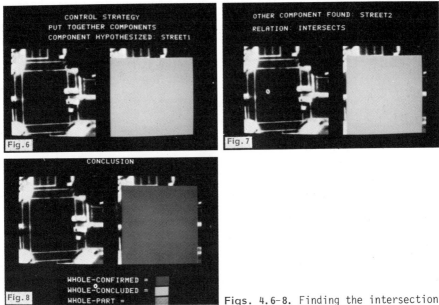

Figs. 4.6-8. Finding the intersection

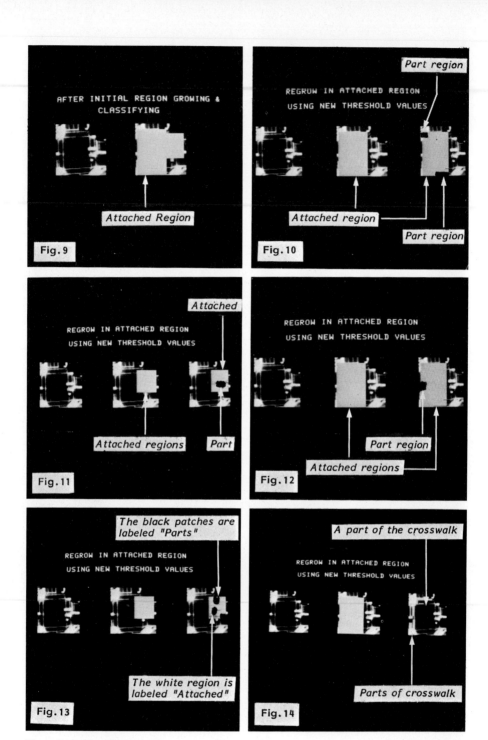

Figs. 4.9–14. Finding the crosswalk

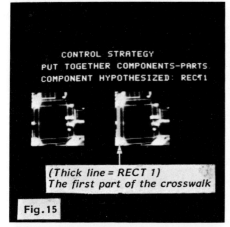

CONTROL STRATEGY
PUT TOGETHER COMPONENTS-PARTS
COMPONENT HYPOTHESIZED: RECT1

(Thick line = RECT 1)
The first part of the crosswalk

Fig.15

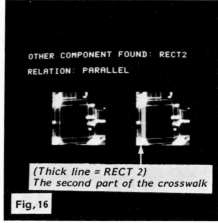

OTHER COMPONENT FOUND: RECT2
RELATION: PARALLEL

(Thick line = RECT 2)
The second part of the crosswalk

Fig.16

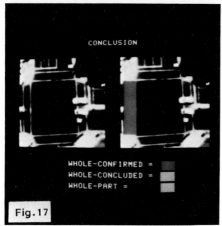

CONCLUSION

WHOLE-CONFIRMED =
WHOLE-CONCLUDED =
WHOLE-PART =

Fig.17

Figs. 4.15-17. Finding the crosswalk

Popping up a level to the INTERSECTION query, the system notes that INTER-SECTION is a HETEROGENEOUS object composed of two STREETs that intersect each other at a 90 degree angle. The system would now normally calculate the level to shrink to in order to locate the largest component of INTERSEC-TION. Since the component is STREET, and STREET has been found already, this task and the region growing/classification are skipped.

The strategy generator is the next module used. Its first action will be to swap in the heterogeneous rule set. The FACTS are that two WHOLEs have been found (the two STREETs) during the context generation. Rule: R1 (whole rule) fires and invokes a function which will hypothesize that the WHOLE is the largest component and will look for the other component (Fig. 4.6). The search will be restricted by the spatial relationship be-tween the two components. For INTERSECTION, the spatial relationship is INTERSECT. This search is cut short, in this case, as another STREET had been previously found. The two regions are tested to see if they are at right angles. Since they are, the function is satisfied that it has found the other component (Fig. 4.7). The function deletes the WHOLE entries from FACTS.

As there are no regions in FACTS, the system returns the result of the INTERSECTION computation to the function which invoked it (Fig. 4.8).

At this point, the system goes back to looking for CROSSWALK. The result of the previous context establishment calculation was to narrow down the search area to the dark part of the left picture in Fig. 4.8.

The system continues its normal sequence by calculating the initial level to search in. Since CROSSWALK is HETEROGENEOUS, the calculation is based on the largest component, RECT1.

Region growing/classification is the next operation to be performed on the shrunken image. Figure 4.9 shows the result of this operation: two large merged (ATTACHED) regions and some PARTs which are not visible in the picture were found.

From the strategy generator, using the heterogeneous rule set, rule R2 (attached rule) will fire. The function it invokes will try to split the ATTACHED region by region growing. The gray level of the ATTACHED area will guide the function in threshold selection. Figures 4.10,11 show the result of this operation. (The format of Figs.4.10-14 displays three pictures: the leftmost is the original window, the center picture represents the previous stage of the processing and the rightmost shows the final processing at that point.) In both cases, a few PARTs were broken away but the thresholds were not precise enough to destroy completely the ATTACHED region. So the system does the operation over again, this time using the gray level statistics from the last region growing as a guide. Figures 4.12,13 are the results. Notice that in Figs. 4.10,11 (as consequently in Figs. 4.12,13) the system is pursuing two different crosswalks; one is at the right side and the other at the left side of the intersection. Again the ATTACHED regions were grown. The system tries this process over again with Fig.4.14 resulting, but here we pursue only the left crosswalk. This time the ATTACHED regions are completely broken into PARTs.

Now that there are only PARTs left, the part rule fires. The function which combines PARTs into composite wholes is invoked. It finds that it can form a RECT1, the largest component of CROSSWALK (Fig. 4.15). The other component, RECT2, is searched for. Again the function which makes composite wholes from PARTs is called. It finds it can form a number of RECT2s, one of which is PARALLEL to RECT1, and spaced the correct distance apart (as specified in the COMPONENTS descriptor). Figure 4.16 shows this. Now that both components are found, the system computes the encompassing area around both regions and labels it a CROSSWALK.

On the next REWRITE, FACTS will be nil and the system halts. Figure 4.17 is the conclusion. Note that only one CROSSWALK was found. The other ones in the image did not have a sufficient number of PARTs broken away so that a composite whole could be formed.

4.5 Discussion

In this paper we have tried to present some design considerations of our automatically generated recognition system. The basic framework that we set up was the pyramid data structure for the pictorial data as well as the hierarchical data structure of the knowledge base. The foundation chosen for the representation of the knowledge is the production schema with some modifications.

74

The contributions of this work as we see them are:

a) Expandability of the system -- Although we have tested the system only on 12 different objects, due to the use of a rule-based system and the development of notation for describing objects, one can easily add other objects.

b) Improved usage of the pyramid data structure through interaction with a conceptual hierarchy.

In the course of locating an object, the system avoided much useless computation. This effect was a result of:

1) searching for a queried object only in highly probable areas, and

2) carrying out searches in small images.

c) At the design stage of this system, we decided to follow three principles for implementing system tasks. They are:

1) use no absolute gray levels,

2) use previous results to guide the present analysis,

3) try to avoid making irreversible decisions.

We feel that it is necessary to adhere to these rules when constructing a general computer vision system.

d) A conceptualization of rules for building a general computer vision system.

Although most of our experiments proved successful, there are areas in our system that are weak.

1) Shape description -- The shape operator implemented was very crude. The reason this was not apparent in our results was that urban areas have mostly rectilinear objects. These shapes are easy to discern. However, our system would fail to recognize more complex shapes.

The reason why a more complex shape identifier could not be implemented was that all the analysis was done in terms of the statistics returned by the region grower. Since these were only estimates of the true structure of the region, only crude shape descriptors could be used.

2) Texture -- As stated, we solved this problem by ignoring it. Again, this deficiency was not apparent in our results because of the images used. If rural scenes were examined, we think that the absence of a texture description would be extremely visible.

3) Production systems -- Although rule-based systems give the designer a certain framework to represent knowledge, we have to be careful in the choice of the interpreter. Our experience taught us that partial matching requiring image processing operations is futile.

Clearly, in the future, the interpreter must be such that it will match the parts to rules instead of the other way around.

Overall, we believe that this work is a successful contribution toward a more systematic design of query-driven recognition systems.

References

4.1 R. A. Brooks: Model based three dimensional interpretations of two-dimensional images, IEEE Trans. Pattern Analysis Machine Intelligence PAMI-5, 140-150 (1983)

4.2 D. H. Ballard, C. M. Brown, J. A. Feldman: "An approach to knowledge directed image analysis", in Proc. 5th Int'l Joint Conf. on Artificial Intelligence, Cambridge, MA, 1977, pp. 664-670

4.3 A. Hanson, E. Riseman: "The Design of a Semantically Directed Vision Processor", Computer and Information Sciences Department Report 75C-1, University of Massachusetts (1975)

4.4 R. Bajcsy, D. Rosenthal: "Visual and conceptual focus of attention", in Structured Computer Vision, ed. by S. Tanimoto, A. Klinger (Academic Press, New York, 1980), pp. 133-149

4.5 P. J. Burt, T. H. Hong, A. Rosenfeld: Segmentation and estimation of image region properties through cooperative hierarchical computation, IEEE Trans. Systems, Man, Cybernetics SMC-11, 802-809 (1981)

4.6 M. D. Kelly: "Edge detection in pictures by computer using planning", in Machine Intelligence 6, ed. by B. Meltzer, D. Michie (University of Edinburgh Press, Edinburgh, UK, 1971), pp. 379-409

4.7 M. D. Levine: "Region analysis using a pyramid data structure", in Structured Computer Vision, ed. by S. Tanimoto, A. Klinger (Academic Press, New York, 1980), pp. 57-100

4.8 S. Tanimoto: "Image data structures", in Structured Computer Vision, ed. by S. Tanimoto, A. Klinger (Academic Press, New York, 1980), pp. 31-55

4.9 R. Davis, J. King: "An Overview of Production Systems", Artificial Intelligence Laboratory Memo AIM-271, Stanford University (1975)

4.10 A. K. Joshi: "Some Extensions of a System for Inferencing on Partial Information", Computer and Information Sciences Department, University of Pennsylvania (1977)

4.11 K. R. Sloan, Jr.: "World Model Driven Recognition of Natural Scenes", Ph.D. dissertation, Computer and Information Sciences Department, University of Pennsylvania (1977)

4.12 A. Tidhar: "Using a Structural World Model in Flexible Recognition of 2-D Patterns", Ph.D. dissertation, Computer and Information Sciences Department, University of Pennsylvania (1974)

4.13 D. A. Rosenthal: "Strip Finding in Fourier Space", Computer and Information Sciences Department, University of Pennsylvania (1978)

4.14 A. Rosenfeld, R. Hummel, S. Zucker: Scene labeling by relaxation operations, IEEE Trans. Systems, Man, Cybernetics SMC-6, 420-433 (1976)

4.15 D. A. Rosenthal: An Inquiry Driven Vision System Based on Visual and Conceptual Hierarchies (UMI Research Press, Ann Arbor, MI, 1981)

5. Multiresolution Processing

A. Klinger

Computer Science Department, University of California at Los Angeles
Los Angeles, CA 90024, USA

5.1 Introduction

This paper concerns a method for processing large two-dimensional arrays of
data. The multiresolution method views condensed versions of the original
array to enable global decisions that otherwise would be impeded by the
amount of data present. The concept is applicable to image data processing
and scanning (i.e., digitization or acquisition by computer). Because the
process of extracting global information from local information involves associating elementary data units with one another, the data structures needed
are similar to those used in displaying of images on computer graphic con-
soles.

Some multiresolution-processing references are [5.1-4]. The first two
involve display: [5.1] partitions space to obtain an efficient method to
decide whether a line is in front of or behind another (WARNOCK's hidden-
line elimination algorithm). The last two involve analysis: reasoning
about picture analysis, in [5.4] using information at one level to plan
search at a more detailed one. Refs. [5.5-7] independently developed ideas
of regular partitioning of space for autonomous and interactive analysis of
pictorial data, including the use of different partitioning modes, formali-
zation of heuristic search based on sample statistics, the equivalence to
tree data structures, the use of DEWEY decimal system notation for both data
structure position and actual image/display location, and the essential unity
of image analysis and graphics display algorithms through their common dependence on similar data structures.

Advances in computer technology make practical a much broader class of
applications of multiresolution processing than were envisioned in the above-
mentioned references. In the past, multiresolution was a vehicle for saving
space in the computer. Today, with inexpensive computing elements, special-
purpose processors have been designed that can be used to implement real-time
image handling capability for interpretation or design/manufacturing.

This paper presents the initial analysis of practical aspects of developing
a multiresolution image processing computer. The paper consists of four sections. The first is an overview of computer architecture, discussing the capabilities of current commercial configurations and describing the evolution of
computers from single-instruction-stream single-data-stream devices to complex
systems that include high-speed special-purpose processors. The second section
concerns the capabilities and potential of multiresolution. Some applications
and techniques enabled by multiresolution concepts are described along
with the notations and methods for regular decomposition. This section also
discusses indexing by symmetry as a useful method for maintaining, and improving access to, large files of digitzed images. The third section deals
with regular refinement with overlaps. In order to avoid object segmentation,

77

the partition refinement method must retain parts of the higher-level data. The fourth section is a preliminary discussion of a three-level system architecture for the multiresolution processor design with the overall system configuration.

5.2 Computer Architecture

The basic digital computer architecture, due to VON NEUMANN, involves five units: input, output, memory, an arithmetic unit, and a control unit. The memory unit involves registers and buffers which enable the arithmetic unit to make varied types of accesses. The arithmetic unit accomplishes most of its operations via an accumulator, i.e., by repeated addition. The control unit decodes the sequential instructions read from memory, i.e., it senses which of the different possible operating codes is present in each program instruction step: hence the use of the term "stored program device" for "digital computer".

Today a wide variety of other forms of digital computing systems are available. In most of these there is a host computer and a peripheral processor. The host performs general computing, and such functions as data acquisition and data transfer; in many cases, the peripheral processor is able to perform special computations, such as vector multiplication, vector addition, and fast FOURIER transformation, at a very high speed.

Many image processing operations are very simple but must be performed on many data elements (the number of picture elements, pixels, per image is on the order of a million). For example, a frequently used algorithm performs thresholding, to eliminate noise (yielding image filtering) by retaining only picture values above a chosen level. The simplicity of the thresholding operation is also characteristic of the other image processing algorithms such as that for calculating the pseudogradient for line finding. (Line finding is essential to structure detection, itself a basic module for picture analysis.) Another necessary algorithm, shrinking, enables object detection, and involves simple comparisons of picture elements with their neighbors. The same types of comparisons are involved in neighbor-restriction algorithms, in which nearby pixels with certain properties are required; such procedures are good for performing corner detection.

In most cases where image or sensor data has to be handled there are also significant problems due to the high volume of data, in addition to the large size of individual data records. Furthermore there are many individual records; fast data acquisition frequently occurs, both from earth satellites and medical scanners. Because each record is of large size, there are many picture elements even at low resolution. However, today, images with extremely high resolution and a correspondingly large number of data points are available. Efficient algorithms for detection and description of objects and extraction of relationships are needed for effective image and sensor data handling in high-resolution imaging, and from sequences of images of any resolution. Effective comparison mechanisms for relating current images to those previously stored, i.e., registration, change detection, and template matching, are also needed. In all these cases multiresolution offers significant advantages. It is particularly well suited to processing large numbers of digital images. Use of time history and records in military, industrial, and medical applications (industrial assembly, medical record comparisons, and detection and tracking of space and aircraft vehicles) all require comparisons of time history data. Some of the approaches to image and sensor data handling use a general-purpose or VON NEUMANN digital computer; recently, special image-processing computers have become commercially available; finally, a method based on distribution of simple computing elements over the data array, cellular processing, is a possibility. This paper emphasizes the capabilities obtainable from the latter two approaches, and a generalization: a general-purpose host computer with a peripheral array processor.

To begin, in considering computer architectures for multiresolution image data handling, the general-purpose digital computer is too slow to be effective in processing and reprocessing segments of image data. Image processing computers are relatively inflexible; without the special hardware discussed below a standard host-computer/peripheral-array-processor system may also be too slow. The key idea in the host/peripheral case, distributed processing, is also present in cellular processing, and both approaches have significant potential. This paper provides a preliminary investigation regarding building a multiresolution computer. The general approach involves combining distributed computing and special-purpose peripheral processors with cellular logic. The end goal is a high-speed flexible device. In the final section of this paper we discuss a simulation analysis and some approaches to design techniques useful for building a multiresolution computer.

5.3 Multiresolution Functions

In this section we consider the reasons for multiresolution. The basic use of multiresolution is the search of images for structure--that is, the efficient implementation of object detection, registration, tracking, and analysis functions on large digital arrays. Changes in the technology market, that have seen small, inexpensive, digital circuitry become widely available, enable replication of first the arithmetic and later the control units, so that many other kinds of computing systems became possible. (The general-purpose digital computer has but one arithmetic and one control unit so a single instruction stream processes a single data stream there.) With more than one arithmetic unit available a single instruction stream, multiple data stream computer becomes a possible configuration. Replication of both control and arithmetic units enables creation of multiple-instruction, multiple-data-stream structures, an array of processors, or, to use the most general term, distributed computing. For example, today fast and powerful computers with several processors, including Texas Instruments' Advanced Scientific Computer, are commercially available. The lower cost and size of digital elements has made widespread computing feasible and enabled peripheral array processors, such as those made by Floating Point Systems, Applied Dynamics, and CSPI, systems capable of implementing functions on entire arrays of data at highly cost-effective rates compared with the most powerful stand-alone scientific computer, the CRAY-1. The result of a cursory examination of the computer system market reveals numerous devices suitable for specific functions on arrays (as are the above-mentioned peripheral array processors), such as fast FOURIER transformation; scaling, rotation, and translation; convolution with a mask or template; but none capable of the multilevel partitioning/analysis needed for structure detection. Let us now consider the hardware implications of this proposed idea.

The multiresolution concept involves coarse resolution models and fine image domains. Aggregation of elementary data, the averages, sums and derived measures obtained from that data, and algorithms over different data domains are to be used to detect objects. In this paper we also discuss tests for symmetry on subordinate data domains that can be used for indexing and storage/retrieval of image data. The technique of hidden-line elimina-

tion for image display used in graphic design is based on a multiresolution
concept. It is also closely related to capabilities needed in automation
(manufacture by computer-controlled machine, or robotics) where location-
grid simplification is necessary to speed flow of parts. Since the multiresolution data structure enables rapid location-finding, a computer built
along such principles should have major benefits in manufacturing. Benefits
should also accrue due to increases in speed and accuracy of search both for
picture analysis (structure/object detection) and part-assembly tasks through
data reduction obtained from multiresolution. Since multiresolution creates
the ability to scan and store imagery more effectively and more efficiently,
indexing pictorial records by such a device should be a significant asset for
handling digitized imagery from space, medical, and other domains.

5.4 Some Techniques of Multiresolution

In [5.5] methods of alternately using quarter and ninth regular decomposition was discussed; [5.6] presented use of quartering alone. Both papers
involve use of hypothesis generation and test, and image condensation. In
[5.8] algorithms which involve functions of only neighbor pixel values are
described. Cellular or neighborhood logic relates to the multiresolution
computer concept since it is clear that algorithms based on adjacency in
level [5.4-6] are essential for rapid structure detection. On the other
hand, speed is obtained at a cost: loss of accuracy (i.e., representation
of fine-structure detail). By overlapping the multilevel structures (sometimes called pyramids) or by the algorithmic procedures in [5.7] (zone-
extension at finer levels when high-level adjacent regions show information
content), needed accuracy improvement can be obtained at the cost of a reduction in speed. Ref. [5.9] gives a sketch of one-dimensional overlapping; below we analyze in detail some properties of overlapping two-dimensional multiresolution structures.

5.5 Three-Level Decomposition

The argument in favor of three-level decomposition is based on the effectiveness of the algorithms in [5.4-8] for finding structures within a picture
(digitized array). From the viewpoint of designing a special-purpose peripheral processor to do three-level processing there are two basic questions:

1) Should the three levels be adjacent? (This in the sense that the
   image viewed by each is obtainable from that at a higher level (hence
   coarser resolution) by one refinement stage: presumably quartering.)
2) How much detail should be present at any one level? Equivalently,
   what number of picture elements should there be at the finest of the
   three levels?

Figure 5.1 shows three alternative answers for question (2). (Question
(1) has been answered "yes", by assumption, throughout the following.) The
first is an averaged image, its four quarters after one successive level of
refinement, and the 16 quarters after one further step. The second begins
at the coarsest level with four subimages and proceeds to the finest level
of 64. The third begins with 16, proceeds to 64, and at the finest level,
has 256 subimages. The quantitative aspects of this are expressed in Figs.
5.2,3.

Figure 5.2 tabulates the effect of using a fixed-size three-level multiresolution processor (tlmp) with quartering (quaternary image partitions).

80

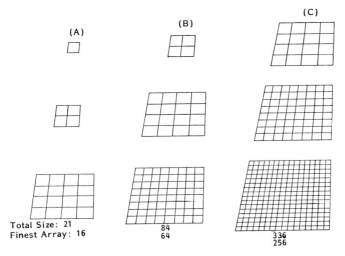

Fig. 5.1. Three-level quaternary multiresolution

Total Size: 21
Finest Array: 16

84
64

336
256

PROCESSING WITH THREE RESOLUTION LEVELS

QUATERNARY IMAGE PARTITIONS		PROCESSOR DESIGN CONSIDERATIONS
Total Number of Elements	Image Dimension (Finest Resolution)	Total Number of Inputs
1	1×1	21
4	2×2	84
16	4×4	335
64	8×8	1,344
256	16×16	5,376
1,024	32×32	21,504
4,096	64×64	86,016
16,384	128×128	344,064
65,536	256×256	1,376,256
262,144	512×512	5,505,024
1,048,576	1024×1024	22,020,096
4,194,304	2048×2048	
16,777,216	4096×4096	

Fig. 5.2. Tabulation of the total number of inputs to a three-resolution processor as its minimum fineness increases for various image resolutions

MAXIMUM TOTAL TOP-DOWN ITERATIONS NEEDED WITH THREE ADJACENT LEVELS

IMAGE SIDE s	PROCESSOR TOTAL SIZE:	21	84	336
	FINEST ARRAY SIZE:	16	64	256
512		4096	1024	256
1024		16384	4096	1024
2048		65536	16384	4096
4096		262144	65536	16384

Fig. 5.3. Maximum iterations in three-resolution processing. (Processing involves applying the fixed-size three-level multiresolution processor (tlmp) top down, beginning at the coarsest level of the tlmp and proceeding to the finest level in the digitized image.)

There, as in Fig. 5.3, we show the total number of inputs to such a tlmp. (For the above-described cases, depicted in Fig. 5.1, the respective numbers are 21, 84, and 336.)

5.6 Multiresolution Processing

Two viewpoints are possible for multiresolution:

1) a fixed-sized array of processors (which contains processors operating on aggregates of the pixels, the constituent/elementary input elements seen by the array at its lowest or finest level) is passed over the finest refinement level of an image; or

2) the same (processor-array) entity is passed down a tree which creates groups of elements: sets that fit the lowest (finest refinement) level array in the multiresolution processor.

The number of passes (iterations) needed in the first case is just the number of finest-array sized (a) entities that fit inside an $s \times s$ image (side with s elements) or s^2/a. Let us call this number n; it becomes an upper bound to the actual outcome if the following (second viewpoint) actually occurs.

In the second case, a top-down approach is used in which at each stage three adjacent picture levels are available. Based on the relative values within them, one of ten possible successor actions is established with a 21-element multiresolution processor, one of 26 possible with an 84-element one. Each successor action (except "stop") involves examining only a restricted portion of the entire array on a three-level basis. Were it not for the restriction, four times as many elements would appear at the finest resolution level after every successor action; as it is, each element there is one-quarter the size of analogous finest elements in the preceding stage.

Assuming a picture or sensor array of size b (where $b = s^2$), the number of iterations m until the finest level of a three-level (tlmp) multiresolution processor has inputs which are at the level where there are b elements is given, under quaternary decomposition, by:

$$a \times 4^m = b$$

$$m = (\log_2 (b/a))/2 .$$

This function is tabulated in Fig. 5.4.

s	b	16	64	256	1024	4096
16	256	2	1	0	-	-
32	1024	3	2	1	0	-
64	4096	4	3	2	1	0
128	16384	5	4	3	2	1
256	65536	6	5	4	3	2
512	262144	7	6	5	4	3
1024	1048576	8	7	6	5	4
2048	4194304	9	8	7	6	5
4096	16777216	10	9	8	7	6

Fig. 5.4. Number of top-down iterations for various picture sides s and sizes $b = s^2$ with different three-level multiresolution processor finest level array sizes a

Figure 5.5 shows the number n of nonoverlapping arrays of finest size a that fit in an image of size b for various finest-sized three-level multiresolution processors. We now investigate the case of refinement under host-computer control allowing reorientation of the tlmp so that overlapping arrays are involved. We note that there are five basic operations at a finer resolution in the 21-element case: upper left, upper right, lower left, lower right, and overlap all; to this must be added four where the middle cells of two adjacent regions are combined (e.g.,upper and lower left) and where no further action occurs, for a total of ten outcomes. There are 25 partitions in the 84-element case: the above five, the four "overlap mid-" (i.e., upper, left, lower, and right), plus four shifted one element diagonally from the corner, eight shifted one row or column from an "overlap mid- (e.g., upper)" location, and four shifted one row or column from "overlap all."

s	b	n=b/a:	16	64	256	1024	4096
16	256		16	4	1	-	-
32	1024		64	16	4	1	-
64	4096		256	64	16	4	1
128	16384		1024	256	64	16	4
256	65536		4096	1024	256	64	16
512	262144		16384	4096	1024	256	64
1024	1048576		65536	16384	4096	1024	256
2048	4194304		262144	65536	16384	4096	1024
4096	16777216		1048576	262144	65536	16384	4096

Fig. 5.5. Table of packing numbers: number of nonoverlapping arrays of finest size a that fit in image of size b for various finest-sized three-level multiresolution processors

a	k/a	TOTAL OUTCOMES	NUMBER OF LOCATIONS (FINER PARTITIONS)
16	0.625	10	9
64	0.40625	26	25
256	0.3203125	82	81
1024	0.2832031	290	289
4096	0.2661132	1090	1089
16384	0.2579345	4226	4225
65536	0.2539367	16642	16641
262144	0.2519607	66050	66049
1048576	0.2509784	263170	263169

Fig. 5.6. Table of outcomes: number of possible locations for a three-level multiresolution processor when overlapping positioning at the finest level is allowed

In the 336-element case, the finest array has 256 elements, for 16 on a side, and we must fit 8×8 arrays within 16×16 ones. There are nine column locations where the central point of an 8×8 array can be placed in any acceptable row of a 16×16. Since there are just nine of these rows the number of partitions is 81, and of total outcomes, exactly 82. Similar reasoning for a finest array of size 1024, where acceptable locations total 17, yields 290 outcomes. The rule for outcomes k in terms of finest array size a is: square the quantity "fitted subarray side" plus one, and add one (for no successor), or analytically,

$$k = [(a/4)^{1/2}+1]^2 + 1 .$$

The ratio of outcomes to array size is therefore given by $k/a = 2a^{-1} + a^{-1/2}$ + 0.25. A table of k/a versus a is given as Fig.5.6. We see that

$$\lim_{a\to\infty} k/a = 0.25 .$$

For 4096-element finest size arrays the ratio k/a of outcomes to array size is within 6.5% (0.0644528) of the limiting value of 0.25.

5 .7 Conclusion

We have investigated some of the quantitative aspects of designing a multiresolution processor. A reasonable view of the system organization we envision
is given by Fig. 5 .7.

DATA ACQUISITION	CONTROL AND SEQUENCING	MULTIRESOLUTION PROCESSOR	
CONVENTIONAL IMAGE SCANNER	LOGIC AND BUFFERS	HOST COMPUTER	QUATERNARY TRI-LEVEL
		ALGORITHMS IN SOFTWARE	HARDWIRED ALGORITHMS
PHOTO-DIODE ARRAY	MASS STORAGE	LEVEL ADAPTATION	
SPECIAL-PURPOSE MULTICHANNEL SCANNER		SYMMETRY TEST	SYMMETRY FUNCTION
		EDGE DETECTION	CONTROL
		INDEXING	REGULARITY CODE
		RETRIEVAL	

Fig. 5.7. Possible organizations of a multiresolution system

   Much remains to be done to complete the design, yet it is clear that an
experimental multiresolution processor is feasible and potentially highly
useful.

Acknowledgment

Thanks are due to A. Rosenfeld for organizing the meeting where this work was
presented, to H. Samet and S. Tanimoto for their interest in multiresolution,
and to G. Estrin, S. Perry, the UCLA Computer Science Department, the IBM
Corporation, and the National Science Foundation for encouragement and support; IBM and NSF INT 79 16919 grants to UCLA partially supported this work.

References

5.1 J. E. Warnock: "The hidden line problem and the use of halftone dis-
      plays", in Pertinent Concepts in Computer Graphics, ed. by J.
      Nievergelt (University of Illinois Press, Urbana, IL, 1969), 154-163

5.2 C. M. Eastman: Representation for space planning, Comm. ACM 13, 242-250 (1970)

5.3 C. A. Rosen, N. J. Nilsson: "Application of Intelligent Automata to Reconnaissance", Report on Project 5953, Stanford Research Institute, Menlo Park, CA (1967)

5.4 M. D. Kelly: "Edge detection in pictures by computer using planning", in Machine Intelligence 6, ed. by B. Meltzer, D. Michie (University of Edinburgh Press, Edinburgh, UK, 1971), pp. 379-409

5.5 A. Klinger: "Patterns and search statistics", in Optimizing Methods in Statistics, ed. by J. S. Rustagi (Academic Press, New York, 1972), pp. 303-339

5.6 A. Klinger: "Regular decomposition and picture structure", in Proc. Int'l Conf. on Systems, Man, and Cybernetics, 1974, pp. 207-310

5.7 A. Klinger, M. Rhodes: Organization and access of image data by areas, IEEE Trans. Pattern Analysis Machine Intelligence PAMI-1, 50-60 (1979)

5.8 K. Preston, Jr., M. J. B. Duff, S. Levialdi, P. E. Norgren, J. I. Toriwaki: Basics of cellular logic with applications in medical image processing, Proc. IEEE 67, 826-856 (1979)

5.9 A. Rosenfeld: "Some uses of pyramids in image processing and segmentation", in Proc. Image Understanding Workshop, College Park, MD, 1980, pp. 112-120

6. The Several Steps from Icon to Symbol Using Structured Cone/Pyramids

L. Uhr and L. Schmitt

Computer Science Department, University of Wisconsin, Madison, WI 53706, USA

Layered pyramids, cones and quad-trees have been developed almost always with emphasis on only one of their several possibilities. Either:

1) They are used to reduce information, usually by some simple function like averaging or differencing, so that successively less detailed representations of the original raw image are obtained.

2) They are used to converge, collect, organize, and broadcast information, as when building successively more global histograms from which a threshold is computed and then broadcast back down the pyramid.

3) They are used to effect step-by-step transformations that interpret quantitatively encoded images into qualitative identifying "features," "compound characteristics" and other types of "labels," with sets of lower-level "meaningless" labels successively combining into higher-level "meaningful" "external labels" such as "vertical", "L-angle", "enclosure", "house", "chair", "Einstein".

This paper explores how these different uses can be combined, with emphasis on the development of successively higher-level descriptive labellings of the scene. It indicates how "models" of objects to be recognized can be decomposed into overlapping trees of relatively simple local transforms that are embedded into the layers of a pyramid, and executed efficiently in a hardware pyramid. It examines how the successive transformation from iconic-quantitative to symbolic-qualitative can be effected (as the programmer desires) in several small steps, so that there is a gradual transition, one where the very efficiently represented iconic-structural-geometric information implicit in the two-dimensional retinal image is kept so long as it is useful.

6.1 Introduction

Layered pyramids (e.g., [6.1-4], cones (e.g., [6.5-8]), and quad-trees (e.g., [6.9-10]) have, as this paper shows, the ability to transform from iconic raw image to symbolic representations in a gradual small-step manner that throws light on the "iconic-symbolic" issue. (See also [6.11,12] for additional related systems.)

The "raw" image input to the computer (e.g., via a TV camera) is the classic example of an "iconic" representation. It consists of a two-dimensional array of integer numbers that represent the intensity of the image at each picture element ("pixel") of the array.

a) It has the structure, the texture, the color, and the other qualities of the objects it represents; it "looks like" them.

b) It is spread out in the two spatial dimensions of a picture, with this geometric information stored implicitly in the array structure used to store this image. Again, it "looks like" the two-dimensional projection of the three-dimensional world that impinges upon the sensing medium.

c) Each individual pixel cell contains numbers (usually integers) that quantitatively represent the intensity of the image at that point.

The names and descriptions of objects, which are generated at the relatively much higher levels of the perceptual system, are, in contrast, symbolic. Thus an output like "house, tree, auto" or "2-story red brick house with green shingled eaves; tall oak tree to the left of the front door; green convertible entering the garage" is usually considered to be "symbolic." [Note that today's vision programs are just beginning to reach the point where they can achieve the unrelated symbols "house", "tree", "auto" when input a TV picture of a real-world street scene; they are far from achieving the symbolic representation needed for a full description.]

The following examines simple examples of data structures and operations (called "transforms") that process these data structures in a "recognition cone" system for perceptual recognition, starting with the iconic information in the raw sensed image as input by a TV camera and ending with the symbolic names and descriptions of objects in that image.

There are several closely related issues of interest:

A) Is the information output by (sets of) transforms iconic, symbolic, or one or another mixture of both?

B) Is the transformation from input to output iconic, symbolic, or one or another mixture of both?

C) What is the most useful combination of iconic and symbolic information, from the point of view of achieving fast and efficient perceptual recognition?

6.2 The Structure of a Multilayered Converging Perceptual System

"Recognition cones" [[6.7,8,13-19] are parallel-serial structures of converging layers of transforms sandwiched between input memories into which they look and output memories into which they merge implications.

6.2.1 The Structure of an Individual Transform

A "transform" (Fig. 6.1) is a specification of:

a) a structured set of entities to search for;

b) a rule for determining whether this structure has been found with sufficient assurance to consider that the transform has succeeded on this image;

c) a set of actions to be effected contingent upon success;

d) weights can be associated with the entities to be looked for and the actions to effect.

```
┌─────────────────────────────────────────────────────────────────┐
│ A) Description of Entities to be Searched for:                    │
│    Relation(Entity1,weight1;Entity2,weight2;...EntityN,weightN)   │
│ B) Rule for Determining Success or Failure:                       │
│    Combining Rule; Threshold                                      │
│ C) Actions to be Effected Contingent Upon Success:                │
│    Action(Entity,Location-Result-Stored)                          │
└─────────────────────────────────────────────────────────────────┘
```

Fig. 6.1. The general structure of a "transform"

For example, an edge feature-detecting transform might be coded to look for a continuing gradient of intensity values, in a 3 by 7 window, outputting "SVE" (for "short vertical edge") when successful. A much higher-level compound characterizer transform might look for "LEAF"s, "BRANCH"es, "BARK" texture,"GREEN"patches, and one "VTT" (for "vertical tree trunk"), outputting "TREE" if "VTT" and at least a few of the other features are found.

These are just two simple examples from the wide variety of transforms that can be specified for a "recognition cone" or pyramid system of the sort being examined. To make this examination completely precise and concrete, we will give examples of transforms built when using the interactive ICON system [6.18], a system that prompts and helps a relatively naive user build recognition cone programs for object and scene description.

6.2.2 The Overall Structure of a Recognition Cone Perceptual System

A recognition cone (Fig. 6.2) starts with a "retina" array R into which the "sensed image" is input (e.g., by a TV camera). This array forms the "base" of the cone (actually a pyramid when rectangular arrays are used).

Ret	T1	I1	T2	I2	T3	I3	T4	Apex
0	>							
0	>	0	>					
0	>	0	>	0	>			
0	>	0	>	0	>	0	>	
0	>	0	>	0	>	0	>	0
0	>	0	>	0	>	0	>	
0	>	0	>	0	>			
0	>	0	>					
0	>							

Fig. 6.2. The overall structure of a recognition cone

An array of transforms T1 is sandwiched between the retina array and an internal buffer array I1 (into which these transforms output their implications, that is, the transformed image). The transform array might contain one, two, or up to several hundred transforms. Each transform is positioned at each and every cell in the array (in a parallel-serial multi-computer structure; alternately, such a system is simulated on the serial computer by iterating each transform over the entire array). Retinal transforms output their implications to array I1, which contains the first internal image.

A second transform array T2 looks at and interprets the internal image in I1, and outputs to I2. Each buffer is (usually, but not necessarily) smaller than the previous buffer (so that usually several outputs will be merged into the same cell). This gives the overall cone/pyramid shape to the structure. The converging process continues until an image buffer IL, with only one single cell,is reached. This forms the "apex" of the L-layer cone. Actions can also imply entities into a "LOOKFOR" list, which results in the application of "dynamic" transforms (that gather, in a top-down manner, additional information.)

6.3 Model Trees of Transforms Embedded into Pyramid Structrues

Individual transforms can be combined within the cone/pyramid structure in any way that a user chooses. But a simple and efficient approach is to build trees of transforms that contain the "knowledge" about the different object classes that the system must recognize dispersed among the trees' nodes.

Consider a more traditional vision program, one that tries to effect a serial match of a graph "model" of "house" or "auto" with a subgraph of the image graph into which "lower-level" processes have transformed the raw input image. Rather than try to effect this potentially explosive match (subgraph isomorphism is NP complete) one can decompose the single complex model graph into a tree whose root node represents the object class (e.g., "house", "chair", "auto", "Einstein"). Now each successively lower ply of the tree contains nodes that are transforms appropriate to that level of decomposition and detail. Thus, for example, "house" might have "roof", "wall", "porch", ...; then (moving down the leftmost branches of the tree) "eave", "chimney",...; "shingle",..,"roofing", ...; "diagonal edge", "pebbled", ...; "gradient", ...; (continuing in this way to form the complete tree).

Many different trees will have nodes in common, especially at the levels nearer the raw input--the so-called lower levels. For example, almost all nameable objects have edges; many have horizontal or vertical edges, simple curves and identifying angles, colors and textures. Higher-level parts, like legs, enclosures, assemblages of legs, and supported horizontal planes, are also held in common by many still higher-level objects.

All the different model trees can be superimposed into a single tree of trees, and these embedded in a pyramid of arrays. The object-model nodes will reside at higher layers in the pyramid, and their successively more detailed and local parts, subparts, characteristics, and qualities at successively lower layers. Now, rather than make a potentially explosive serial search for a match of each complex object-model stored in memory, the system need only apply the transforms at each layer/ply of the tree-of-model-trees in turn.

Thus if each layer has T transforms, each with P parts (in the sense that a "part" is something that takes one instruction to examine, so that a P-part transform takes P instructions), and the pyramid has L (= log (N)) layers, with an N by N array at its base, then a recognition cone/pyramid will (when executed on a parallel hardware pyramid) take PTL (PTlog (N)) instructions (that is, time) to apply all models, plus a few more instructions to choose the best match. This can be further speeded up by placing T processors at each layer, rather than just one, to take only Plog(N) time. And if each processor is given a parallel window capability, so that it can examine all P parts in parallel, only log(N) time.

In contrast, a serial model-matching program will, at least in the worst cases, need extremely large amounts of time. Each model can be assumed to have $O(PTlog(N))$ nodes. That is, the number of nodes in the entire tree-of-model-trees is only a small constant times the number of nodes in each single model tree (this is increasingly true to the extent that each node is shared among many model trees). But even in the extremely bizarre case where each node was used in only one model tree each object model has only PTlog(N)/M nodes, where M is the number of different object models. Now M such PTlog(N) graphs must be matched as subgraphs of the larger image graph. A variety of heuristics can be used that take advantage of facts about real-world objects to try to cut down this explosively large search; but since subgraph isomorphism is NP complete this is potentially an extremely long process. The pyramid serves as a global heuristic that makes use of the geometric structure of its arrays and the converging tree structure that links and organizes them together.

6.4 Hardware Multicomputer Embodiments of Cones and Pyramids

This suggests a multicomputer pyramid structure embodied in hardware into which such a system can be embedded rather directly, one that will execute recognition cone programs with important increases in speed. In a hardware pyramid each transform node is executed in parallel by the entire array of processors in the layer at which that transform is embedded. This imposes the additional restriction that for efficiency each transform "looks at," that is, input as its arguments, only locally available information. But that fits closely with the spirit of the pyramid, which decomposes very complex functions like "Einstein" or "house" into a tree of cascading functions where the decomposition continues until each function can be executed in minimal time with minimal hardware.

A pyramid is, essentially, a two-dimensional N by N array of processors (like DUFF's CLIP4 [6.20], REDDAWAY's DAP [6.21], BATCHER's MPP [6.22]), each directly linked to its 4, 6 or 8 nearest neighbors, and also to the N^2 buds of a tree of processors. An alternate construction would build successively smaller arrays (N/2, N/4, ..., 1; or N/3, N/9, ..., 1) linking each cell in the smaller array with the corresponding 4 or 9 cells in the larger array. There are a number of interesting variants in terms of details of linkages, convergence and overlap -- e.g., processors might be linked only to their offspring and parents, or to siblings as well; linkage might be to only one parent, or to several parents (giving overlap). (See [6.23-27] for proposals and examinations of hardware pyramids.)

Such a system has the very good local interconnection topology of a grid, one that reflects well the physical forces of nature, where the closer together are several entities the more likely it is that they will interact. In addition, the tree/pyramid structure gives surprisingly good global interconnections. Essentially, the diameter of the array, which is O(N), is reduced to O(logN) in the corresponding pyramid. This is crucially important for making a global assessment and interpretation of a large object, as when combining the several parts of a transform into a larger whole. For example, when using an array alone to recognize a house one must at some point shift the various parts together in order to compute a transform like "step", "pane", "window", "wall", or "house". A large house might cover a region several hundred pixels in diameter; a small window might cover a region at least 8 or 16 pixels in diameter. The array would need the same number of instructions as a pyramid of arrays to actually compute T transforms. But whereas in a pyramid this need be multiplied only by log(N) (for the pyramid's processes of converging the parts together for the next-level computation), in an array it must be multiplied by N to shift the parts together. With a 1,024 by 1,024 array the pyramid is 100 times faster.

6.5 The ICON System for Constructing Transforms and Recognition Cones

We will now look at a few transforms from a total set built with ICON [6.18].
The ICON program development system builds a cone/pyramid perceptual system as
follows: it asks a user to specify the number of layers in the system and the
size (number of rows, number of columns) of each layer. It also asks the user:

1) to name transforms to be placed at each layer (using names of transforms
that have previously been stored in files that can be accessed by descriptors),
and
2) to construct new transforms (when desired), file them away under appropriate user-designated descriptor names, and assign them to layers of the
system presently being constructed.

The system helps the user construct a transform by specifying the types
of information needed, displaying a two-dimensional grid into which the transform can (to some extent iconically) be drawn, and displaying the finished
transform, for verification, correction, and filing. Thus a user can build
a system of (potentially) any size, in terms of image buffers, number of
layers, and number of transforms at each layer.

The system can then be executed (in either interpreted or compiled form)
on images input to it (either stored on disk or directly via a TV camera).
The results of each layer of transforms, and of each transform at each layer,
can be displayed for examination, so that transforms can be modified,
discarded, or added, as appropriate.

6.6 Examples of "Low-Level" "Iconic" Transforms Using the ICON System

One of the simplest and most iconic of operations is a straightforward
averaging of the intensity values of several neighboring pixels, e.g., within
a 2 by 2 window. This kind of operation is frequently used to eliminate noise,
smooth the image, and/or reduce unnecessarily large images.

Figure 6.3 shows a 2 by 2 averaging transform, as displayed by ICON after
construction has been completed.

```
                        TRANSFORM average

    THRESHOLD = 0
    TYPE = numeric    FUNCTION = average

              REF CELL             2
          0         :10    0         :10

                 3                4
          0         :10    0         :10


    TRANSFORM HAS NO IMPLIEDS

    NOTE:  The transform is displayed in a two-dimensional grid.  Each cell
    of the grid contains (to the left of the colon) the object being looked
    for (in this case an integer) at that relative location, and (to the
    right of the colon) the weight of that object.  In the case of an aver-
    aging transform, the object being looked for in each cell is a 0 (which
    means "don't care").  The weights, being all equal, will cause each cell
    to contribute equally to the transform function.  This is an example of
    what is called, in the ICON system, an "absolute, numeric transform."
```

Fig. 6.3. A transform that averages a 2 by 2 subarray

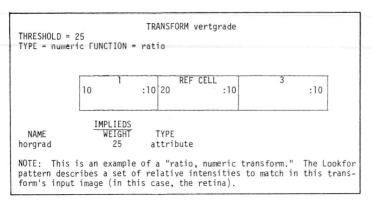

```
                          TRANSFORM vertgrade
THRESHOLD = 25
TYPE = numeric FUNCTION = ratio


                   1            REF CELL          3
         10            :10 20           :10            :10


              IMPLIEDS
   NAME       WEIGHT     TYPE
   horgrad      25       attribute

NOTE:  This is an example of a "ratio, numeric transform."  The Lookfor
pattern describes a set of relative intensities to match in this trans-
form's input image (in this case, the retina).
```

Fig. 6.4. A simple gradient-detecting transform

A second transformation that is often effected on the raw image is one that detects gradients. Figure 6.4 shows a simple (vertical) gradient detector that was constructed using ICON, as displayed by ICON.

Note that whereas the averaging transform shown in Fig. 6.3 outputs an array of (averaged) numbers reflecting average intensities, and that intensities are stored in the input array, the gradient transform of Fig. 6.4 outputs numbers reflecting a new dimension, "gradient." Here is the first aspect in which we begin to move away from the iconic.

The TV camera "transduces" the sensed image; if the transducer is of high enough quality it makes little or no change. Its result is a "good picture" almost indistinguishable from the image as directly viewed by the eye, and as "iconic" (in a common sense of the word) as it can be.

Averaging reduces the image and summarizes, hence loses, information, but its output is still in the same intensity domain. Since an "icon" is commonly thought of as a reduced, albeit often stylized, representation of the original, the averaged result (at least until it destroys most vestiges of the image) is usually considered among the most iconic of icons.

But when we move from the intensity domain to an array of gradient elements, things begin to change. To the extent that one defines and thinks of an icon as a stylized representation in which the essential qualities of the object are heightened one might assert that this new representation is actually more iconic.

6.6.1 Examples of Simple Edge and Feature Detectors

Figures 6.5-8 give simple examples of the kinds of lowish-level edge and feature detectors most vision programs use. Note that these transforms use symbols to define their Lookfor patterns. Such "symbolic" transforms should not be interpreted as necessarily being noniconic.

These are very simple examples of transforms. But they are rather interesting in the way they suggest, and can help us begin to ease out, some of the aspects of the icon-to-symbol sequence of transformations.

The edge and the gradient are closely related. The edge asserts a qualitative change at a certain point in the gradient. Both "gradient" and "edge" are new attributes. But somehow edge is farther away from the intensity domain.

92

```
                              TRANSFORM vertedge
THRESHOLD = 25
TYPE = symbolic
```

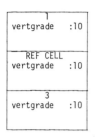

```
           ┌──────1──────┐
           │ vertgrade  :10│
           │             │
           ├──REF CELL───┤
           │ vertgrade  :10│
           │             │
           ├──────3──────┤
           │ vertgrade  :10│
           └─────────────┘
```

```
              IMPLIEDS
    NAME      WEIGHT    TYPE
  vertedge      25    attribute
```

Fig. 6.5. A simple vertical edge detector

```
                              TRANSFORM vertedge2
THRESHOLD = 40
TYPE = symbolic
```

```
           ┌──────1──────┐
           │ grad20deg :2 │
           │ grad10deg :5 │
           │ grad00deg :10│
           ├──REF CELL───┤
           │ grad20deg :2 │
           │ grad10deg :5 │
           │ grad00deg :10│
           ├──────3──────┤
           │ grad20deg :2 │
           │ grad10deg :5 │
           │ grad00deg :10│
           └─────────────┘
```

```
              IMPLIEDS
    NAME      WEIGHT      TYPE
  edge100deg    15      attribute
  edge80deg     15      attribute
  edge90deg     40      attribute
```

Fig. 6.6. A simple (but slightly more general and robust) edge detector

```
                              TRANSFORM Langle
THRESHOLD = 40
TYPE = symbolic
```

```
    ┌──────1──────┬──────2──────┬──────3──────┐
    │ edge90deg :10│             │             │
    │              │             │             │
    ├──────4──────┼──────5──────┼──────6──────┤
    │ edge90deg :10│  REF CELL   │             │
    │              │             │             │
    ├──────7──────┼──────8──────┼──────9──────┤
    │              │ edge00deg :10│ edge00deg :10│
    │              │             │             │
    └─────────────┴─────────────┴─────────────┘
```

```
              IMPLIEDS
    NAME      WEIGHT    TYPE
    Langle      40    attribute
```

Fig. 6.7. A very simple detector for a near-perfect "L angle"

```
                        TRANSFORM Langle2
THRESHOLD = 40
TYPE = symbolic
```

1 edge90deg :10	2	3
4 edge90deg :10	REF CELL edge00deg :5 edge90deg :5	6
7 edge90deg :10 edge00deg :10	8 edge00deg :10	9 edge00deg :5

```
              IMPLIEDS
   NAME       WEGIHT     TYPE
   Langle     40         attribute
```

Fig. 6.8. A slightly more robust detector for an "L angle"

A gradient is a change in intensities; an edge is a statement that such a change makes something qualitatively different and new, the "edge".

It is important to emphasize that these distinctions hold only to the extent that they are subsequently made use of by the transforms that examine these implied entities as part of their input and interpret their significance. We might say that these distinctions lie in the eyes of their beholders, and that their beholders are just those transforms that interpret them.

The L angle is (as in Fig. 6.7) simply a compound of edges or (as in Fig. 6.8) a new label implied when enough of the expected subelements of an L angle are present. But the L-angle label (especially in the second case) appears to be taking on more of the qualities of a symbol. There is an increasingly arbitrary relation between the label implied by the transform and merged into its output buffer and the information the transform examined and assessed in deciding whether to output that label.

One might conjecture that the iconic transformation is one where the output is computed as a function of the input, whereas the symbolic transformation is one where a table is used to store arbitrarily connected labels. But this does not seem nearly so simple as the commonly suggested analogy to a code book that arbitrarily associates and transforms between sets of symbols (e.g., between letters in English and Morse code, or between words in English and words in French). Whether the transform computes or uses table information is an implementation detail, of importance for reasons of efficiency in space for storage or time for processing, but scarcely related to the iconic/symbolic aspects of either transform or transformation.

Still, translation from English to Pig Latin suggests that some transformations can be effected by a very simple transform rule, whereas others need a code book or a dictionary. Translations from English to Pidgin English suggest that sometimes a simple transform rule must be augmented by a more or less simple mixture of code book plus additional rules. And of course from English to French we must add very deep and complex contextual syntactic and especially semantic rules to move beyond the very poor word-by-word translation.

6.6.2 Examples of "Higher-Level" More Symbolic Transforms

Figures 6.9,10 illustrate how transforms at deeper levels of the cone/pyramid can work with symbolic labels, sometimes in combination with numeric and more or less iconic information, to produce new (often more, sometimes less) symbolic labels.

TRANSFORM door

THRESHOLD = 60
TYPE = symbolic

1 gamma :10	2 edge00deg :7	3 revgamma :10
4 edge90deg :7 gamma :6	5 constarea :3	6 edge90deg :7 bgamma :6
7 Langle :2 edge90deg :7	REF CELL constarea :3	9 edge90deg :7 bgamma :2
10 Langle :6 edge90deg :7	11 constarea :3	12 edge90deg :7 revLangle :6
13 Langle :10	14 edge00deg :7	15 revLangle :10

	IMPLIEDS	
NAME	WEIGHT	TYPE
window	20	attribute
doorframe	40	attribute

Fig. 6.9. A simple "door" built from angles and edges

TRANSFORM house

THRESHOLD = 60
TYPE = symbolic

1 roof :4 chimney :8	2 roof :8	3 roof :8	4 roof :8	5 roof :4 chimney :8
6	7 roof :4	8 roof :4	9 roof :4	10
11 vertedge :4	12 window :6 vertedge :4 wall :5	REF CELL window :6 wall :5	14 window :6 vertedge :4 wall :5	15 vertedge :4
16 vertedge :4	17 horedge :4 vertedge :4 wall :5	18 window :6 door :8 horedge :4 wall :5	19 horedge :4 vertedge :4 wall :5	20 vertedge :4
21 vertedge :4	22 Langle :8 horedge :4 vertedge :4 wall :5	23 door :8 horedge :4 wall :5	24 revLangle :8 horedge :4 vertedge :4 wall :5	25 vertedge :4

	IMPLIEDS	
NAME	WEIGHT	TYPE
building	35	attribute
house	25	attribute

Fig. 6.10. The implication of house by subsets of symbols and icons

The transforms shown, plus all the additional transforms specified in their Lookfors, were input using ICON and build into a simple 4-layer pyramid (Figs. 6.3-10 are the actual transform displays ICON generates). These transforms succeeded at finding edges, L angles, doors, roofs, houses, etc., in the very simple line drawings used to check them out. A much larger set of transforms, albeit of the same general types, must be used to make tests on a larger variety of real-world images.

These examples suggest two important points:

a) There are several aspects or dimensions on which "icons" differ from "symbols."

b) It is fruitful to move gradually from the iconic raw sensed retinal image to the fully symbolic naming and description of the objects in a scene.

Indeed it appears to be preferable to consider five major stepping-stones in the transition from raw input image to completed perceptual recognition:

1) picture,

2) icon,

3) sign,

4) symbol,

5) semantic understanding.

The many-layered structure of a cone or pyramid appears to be a convenient system for controlling this gradual movement, so that the various kinds of information needed to achieve recognition are assessed, efficiently.

The original input is a (minimal) transduction; it is maximally iconic, or pictorial. It might best be called a "picture." It reflects the two-dimensional aspect of the array of energy being sensed, and also the quantitative amount of energy at each region in that array.

Some transformations, like simple averages, output similarly quantitative information in the same two-dimensional intensity domain. These are usually thought of as the most iconic, or pictorial. But as averaging becomes increasingly global, so that it destroys the details needed to resolve and recognize the object, it gives less iconic results from the point of view of reflecting the objects rather than the raw image. (Note that the convergence to smaller output arrays is itself a type of averaging, as is the coarsening of the range of values over which intensity, or any other quantitative attribute, can vary.)

If a picture is input in color, even the raw sensed image is to some extent symbolic, for the primary red, green, blue colors must be labeled. This gives three arrays of intensity, instead of the single gray-scale intensity array for black-gray-white pictures. But note what this reveals: even the raw gray-scale intensity array is to some extent symbolic, with the labelling-attribute "gray-scale" implicit as the name of the single array. It is only because there is but one possibility, that is, only one attribute, that this need not be made explicit.

From the very beginning, images are transformed into new symbols/labels. Some of these symbols seem more iconic, e.g., "gradient", "purple" (the result of a transform that combines primary colors), "hair-textured" (the result of a texture-detecting transform), or even "short-vertical-edge". Some seem more symbolic. But can we draw a sharp line between, e.g., "S curve" and "L angle" and the symbols "S", "L", "{", "+"?

Between icons and symbols we should consider still another distinction, a "sign." And there appear to be several dimensions, each with several steps, along which entities can be placed, rather than a single path from icon to symbol.

To the extent that the symbol is more arbitrarily related to the region of information assessed by the transforms that implied it we tend to think of it as more symbolic. Thus we can consider the implied label from the point of view of the raw input image, or of the abstracted image in the layer at which it is implied, where it will be relatively more iconic.

To the extent that the symbol is "higher-level" it tends to take on a richer association of meanings, and therefore to appear more symbolic. For example, "L angle", "board", "window", "house" seem successively more symbolic. But this is simply a function of their symbolic/semantic import to us, that is, of the richness of associations and meanings they invoke in the "cognitive networks" of our mind. For the computer program they are all simply labels, or pointers. Those generated at a deeper level of the pyramid/cone will be the function of a deeper, probably larger, structure of transforms, and we might for this reason say they are indeed more "symbolic" and/or "semantic."

6.8 Toward Integrating Perceptual and Cognitive Subsystems

Alternately, we might consider that only after we have integrated the perceptual recognition program into a larger perceptual/cognitive system, where labels take on much richer meanings because they point to larger associated structures, can we begin to achieve the full "meaningful" "semantic" "symbol."

The typical current conception appears to be that of the "iconic" vision system and the "symbolic" semantic memory net. This leads to the misconception that information stored in arrays, with their implicit two-dimensional structure, and in quantitative attribute dimensions, like gray-scale intensity or gradient strength, is wholly iconic, whereas labels like "dog", "mammal", "above", and "is-a" are wholly symbolic. But these kinds of symbolic labels are necessary for perception programs, and are often found stored in arrays of symbols. And structural, quantitative, relational information, although rarely stored and used in today's semantic networks, would be very useful if not essential information in many situations.

It seems best, and simplest, to think of the array of spatial and other quantitative dimensions simply as a structure that can often be used in very powerful ways to access and handle quantitative information. Whereas graphs (list structures) are often convenient, e.g., when there are no simple orderings that can be computed, or when the nonzero entries in large arrays are rare (as they will be in "higher levels" of perceptual systems that do not, as do the cones and pyramids, push them together toward the center).

Symbols like "bright", "very bright", "above", and "slightly above" might best be thought of as very coarse quantitative, hence to some extent iconic, intervals. A semantic memory graph might store, in addition to such symbols, little pieces of more precise quantitative information, including computational procedures, that define, explain, and replace such coarse and vague concepts, as needed.

Thus it seems of interest to consider combining the more iconic aspects of the pictorial arrays used in perception programs with the more symbolic aspects of the networks of symbols used in semantic memory systems. The perceptual array-oriented structure and the memorial graph-represented structure are each chosen (or evolved) because of their efficiencies in storage space and processing time (to transform and to access).

Symbols, and structures of symbols, can usefully be implied and stored in the perceptual system. Arrays and icons can be stored and used as nodes in the semantic memory network. The perceptual and the semantic/cognitive system must, of course, be connected. But they can both, potentially, gain greatly in power if they are intimately interconnected so that each can make use of the other, as needed.

6.9 Summary

Layered converging cones and pyramids allow a user to build pattern recognition and scene description systems whose "knowledge" of the object-classes they must identify is embedded into a hardware pyramid of arrays as follows: each object is represented as a "model" in the form of a tree, starting with the root node that represents that object (e.g., "house"), with the successive plies of offspring nodes representing successively lower-level parts, qualities and other characteristics (e.g., "roof", "wall", ... ; then "window", "door", ...; then "pane", "panel", ...; then "vertical edge",... ; "L angle",...; then "gradient",...; and so on).

All such model trees are combined into a tree-of-trees, where each node (e.g., "window" or "L angle") need be computed only once, even though it may be a part of many different model trees (e.g., "house", "auto", "store").

This tree-of-model-trees is then embedded into a pyramid of arrays, with the root model-nodes embedded into the higher layers of the pyramid and the nodes that compute lowest-level features like gradients, short edges, and local textures toward the base of the pyramid.

The pyramid architecture essentially superimposes the relatively good (diameter = $O(logN)$) interconnection topology of a tree over the near-neighbor topology of an array (which is especially useful for computing local interactions in images). An $N \times N$ array can speed up processing of an individual transform from $O(N \times N)$ to $O(1)$, and a pyramid of such arrays, by eliminating the need to do $O(N)$ shifts to move information together into the local window where successively higher-level transforms can be effected, can reduce the time needed to compute the transforms used by an entire model tree from $O(N)$ to $O(logN)$.

Each transform node in this structure can look at and interpret any type of information, and output any type of information (which will then be input by the next-higher-level transform nodes). The raw input image is iconic, and therefore the lowest-level transforms must input and deal with iconic information. The identifying, descriptive information the system must output is symbolic. The movement from "icon" to "symbol" can usefully and naturally be effected (as the user chooses) in a gradual small-step manner. This paper gives examples of transforms taken from several different levels in one model tree of a program with many model trees that illustrate a variety of different steps in this process.

References

6.1 M. D. Levine, J. Leemet: "A method for nonpurposive picture segmentation", in Proc. 3rd Int'l. Joint Conf. on Pattern Recognition, Coronado, CA, 1976, pp. 494-498

6.2 M. D. Levine: "A knowledge-based computer vision system", in Computer Vision Systems, ed. by A. R. Hanson, E. M. Riseman (Academic Press, New York, 1978), pp. 335-352

6.3 S. L. Tanimoto: Pictorial feature distortion in a pyramid, Computer Graphics Image Processing 5, 333-352 (1976)

6.4 S. L. Tanimoto: "Regular hierarchical image and processing structures in machine vision", in Computer Vision Systems, ed. by A. R. Hanson, E. M. Riseman (Academic Press, New York, 1978), pp. 165-174

6.5 A. R. Hanson, E. M. Riseman: "Pre-processing Cones: a Computational Structure for Scene Analysis", Computer and Information Sciences Technical Report 74-7, University of Massachusetts (1974)

6.6 A. R. Hanson, E. M. Riseman: "VISIONS: a computer system for interpreting scenes", in Computer Vision Systems, ed. by A. R. Hanson, E. M. Riseman (Academic Press, New York, 1978), pp. 303-334

6.7 L. Uhr: Layered "recognition cone" networks that preprocess, classify and describe, IEEE Trans. Computers C-21, 758-768 (1972)

6.8 L. Uhr: "'Recognition cones' and some test results", in Computer Vision Systems, ed. by A. R. Hanson, E. M. Riseman (Academic Press, New York, 1978), pp. 363-372

6.9 A. Klinger, C. R. Dyer: Experiments on picture representation using regular decomposition, Computer Graphics Image Processing 5, 68-105 (1976)

6.10 A. Rosenfeld: "Quadtrees and pyramids for pattern recognition and image processing", in Proc. 5th Int'l. Conf. on Pattern Recognition, Miami Beach, FL, 1980, pp. 802-811

6.11 A. R. Hanson, E. M. Riseman (eds.): Computer Vision Systems (Academic Press, New York, 1978)

6.12 S. L. Tanimoto, A. Klinger (eds.): Structured Computer Vision: Machine Perception Through Hierarchical Computation Structures (Academic Press, New York, 1980)

6.13 L. Uhr: "A Model of Form Perception and Scene Description", Computer Sciences Department Technical Report 176, University of Wisconsin (1974)

6.14 L. Uhr: "'Recognition cones' that perceive and describe scenes that move and change over time", in Proc. 3rd Int'l. Joint Conf. on Pattern Recognition, Coronado, CA, 1976, pp. 287-293

6.15 L. Uhr, R. Douglass: A parallel-serial recognition cone system for perception, Pattern Recognition 11, 29-40 (1979)

6.16 R. J. Douglass: "Recognition and depth perception of objects in real world scenes", in Proc. 5th Int'l. Joint Conf. on Artificial Intelligence, Pittsburgh, PA, 1977, p. 657

6.17 R. J. Douglass: "A Computer Vision Model for Recognition, Description, and Depth Perception in Outdoor Scenes", Ph.D. dissertation, Computer Sciences Department, University of Wisconsin (1978)

6.18 L. Schmitt: "The ICON Perception Laboratory User Manual and Reference Guide", Computer Sciences Department Technical Report 421, University of Wisconsin (1981)

6.19 L. Schmitt: "The Use of a Network Representation of Visual Knowledge in a Hierarchically Structured Vision System", Computer Sciences Department Technical Report, University of Wisconsin (1981)

6.20 M. J. B. Duff: "Review of the CLIP image processing system", in Proc. Nat'l Computer Conf., 1978, pp. 1055-1060

6.21 S. F. Reddaway: "DAP--a flexible number cruncher," in Proc. Workshop on Vector and Parallel Processors, Los Alamos, NM, 1978, pp. 233-234

6.22 K. E. Batcher: Design of a massively parallel processor, IEEE Trans. Computers C-29, 836-840 (1980)

6.23 C. R. Dyer: "Pyramid algorithms and machines", in <u>Multi-Computers</u>
      <u>and Image Processing</u>, ed. by K. Preston, Jr., L. Uhr (Academic Press,
      New York, 1982), pp. 409-420
6.24 S. L. Tanimoto, J. J. Pfeiffer, Jr.: "An image processor based on
      an array of pipelines", in Proc. Workshop on Computer Architecture
      for Pattern Analysis and Image Database Management, Hot Springs, VA,
      1981, pp. 201-208
6.25 S. L. Tanimoto: "Programming techniques for hierarchical parallel
      image processors", in <u>Multi-Computers and Image Processing</u>, ed. by
      K. Preston, Jr., L. Uhr (Academic Press, New York, 1982), pp. 421-429
6.26 L. Uhr: "Converging pyramids of arrays", in Proc. Workshop on Com-
      puter Architecture for Pattern Analysis and Image Database Management,
      Hot Springs, VA, 1981, pp. 31-24
6.27 L. Uhr: <u>Algorithm-Structured Computer Arrays and Networks: Parallel</u>
      <u>Architectures for Perception and Modelling</u> (Academic Press, New York,
      to appear)

Part III

Modelling, Processing, and Segmentation

7. Time Series Models for Multiresolution Images

R. Chellappa

Department of EE-Systems, University of Southern California
Los Angeles, CA 90089, USA

This paper is concerned with representing multiresolution images using 1-D time series models. We assume that the given high resolution image $\{y_0(t)\}$ obeys an autoregressive model of order p and analyzes the structure of the models obeyed by low resolution copies of $\{y_0(t)\}$. The problem of estimating the parameters of the model generating $\{y_0(t)\}$ given its low-resolution sequence is also considered. Applications to spectral feature extraction and image synthesis are indicated.

7.1 Introduction

Analysis and processing of multiresolution (MR) images is a topic of current interest in image processing [7.1]. Since the appropriate resolution at which the given image should be processed is not known a priori, it is useful to process the image at different resolutions and extract information of different kinds. Much of the reported research on MR image processing and analysis is concerned with segmentation [7.2,3], linear feature extraction [7.4], and related problems. The only work using MR images for classical image processing problems such as coding is [7.5]. The usefulness of MR representations of images for other problems such as restoration and synthesis of images has not been investigated. In addition, not much is known regarding the statistical modeling of MR images. The purpose of this paper is to explore the possibility of using time series models for synthesis, coding, and classification of MR images. One-dimensional time series models have been used for the synthesis and coding of single-resolution images and textures [7.6] and it is useful to look into generalizations to MR images. In order to keep the details simple we consider the one-dimensional case.

Let $\{y_0(t), t=1,\ldots,N\}$ represent 1-D data extracted from an image. Suppose we create a new set of data $\{y_1(\tau(m+1))\}$, $\tau=0,1,\ldots$, where

$$y_1(t) = \sum_{i=0}^{m-1} y_0(t-i) . \tag{7.1}$$

The new data, consisting of averages or sums over nonoverlapping intervals of "length" m+1, is a low-resolution copy of the original sequence $\{y_0(t)\}$. The above operation corresponds to the simplest pyramid operation of unweighted averaging over nonoverlapping intervals [7.1]. The averaging transformation cuts down the information present from $\{y_0(t)\}$ to $\{y_1(t)\}$ but does not do this uniformly to each frequency component in $\{y_0(t)\}$. The averaging transformation acts as a low-pass filter which suppresses fine details in the picture corresponding to $\{y_0(t)\}$. One can repeat the averaging transformation on $\{y_1(t)\}$ and produce another low-resolution copy of the given image $\{y_2(t)\}$. Thus in the 1-D case, instead of generating a pyramid of

102

images, we generate a triangle of 1-D images. Suppose we assume that the base of the triangle corresponding to $\{y_0(t)\}$ obeys a time series autoregressive (AR) model of order p. The following basic issues are of interest:

a) What is the model obeyed by the observation set $\{y_1(t)\}$, related to $\{y_0(t)\}$ as in (7.1)?

b) Given the observation set from the low-resolution sequence $\{y_1(t)\}$, can we identify the parameters of the AR model generating $\{y_0(t)\}$?

Issues (a) and (b) correspond to the analysis of reduction and expand operations [7.3], known in the pyramid literature.

Satisfactory answers to problems (a) and (b) can be useful in designing algorithms involving MR images. Consider for instance the problem of extracting spectral features for classification purposes. The knowledge of the particular model obeyed by $\{y_0(t)\}$ and $\{y_1(t)\}$ and their lower-resolution copies is vital, as the expression for the power spectrum is different for different time-series models. Likewise, the solution to (b) can be used for designing image synthesis and coding algorithms, as will be explained later.

The organization of the paper is as follows: Section 7.2 discusses the changes induced in the model structure due to the simple pyramid operation in (7.1). In Sect.7.3, methods of estimating the parameters of the AR model generating $\{y_0(t)\}$, given $\{y_1(t)\}$, and applications to image synthesis are discussed.

7.2 Structure of the Low-Resolution Image Sequences

For the sake of simplicity, suppose the image sequence corresponding to $\{y_0(t)\}$ obeys the first-order AR model

$$y_0(t) = \theta \, y_0(t-1) + \omega_0(t) \tag{7.2}$$

where the $\omega_0(t)$ are zero-mean, mutually uncorrelated noise variables with finite variance σ_0^2 and

$$E(y_0(t-1) \, \omega_0(t)) = 0 \ .$$

Define

$$y_1(t) = \sum_{i=1}^{2} y_0(t-i)$$
$$\omega_1(t) = \sum_{i=0}^{2} \omega_0(t-i) \ . \tag{7.3}$$

The sequence $\{y_1(t)\}$ obeys the model

$$y_1(t) = \theta y_1(t-1) + \omega_1(t) \ . \tag{7.4}$$

Suppose that we observe only $y_1(0)$, $y_1(3)$, $y_1(6)$, and so on; by successively substituting the observed $y_1(.)$ in (7.4) one gets the model

$$y_1(t) = \theta^3 y_1(t-1) + \omega_1(t) + \theta\omega_1(t-1) + \theta^2\omega_1(t-2)$$

for $\{y_1(3\tau), \ \tau=0,1,\ldots\}$. \tag{7.5}

Thus the low-resolution sequence $y_1(.)$ obeys an autoregressive and moving average (ARMA) model. One can generalize this result to the case when $\{y_0(t)\}$ obeys a higher-order AR model:

Theorem 1 [7.7]: Let $y_0(t)$ obey the pth order AR model

$$y_0(t) = \sum_{j=1}^{p} \theta_j\, y_0(t-j) + \omega_0(t) \tag{7.6}$$

where the $\{\omega_0(.)\}$ are mutually correlated random variables with $E(\omega_0(t))=0$, $E(\omega_0^2(t))=\sigma_0^2$, $E(y_0(t-j)\omega_0(t))=0$ for $j\geq 1$ and the θ_js are constants such that the roots of $(1- \sum_{j=1}^{p} \theta_j\, z^j$) lie outside the unit circle to ensure stability.

Let $y_1(t) = \sum_{j=0}^{m-1} y_0(t-j)$. Then $\{y_1(t),\ y_1(t-m),\ y_1(t-2m),...\}$ obeys the ARMA model

$$y_1(t) = \sum_{j=1}^{p} \alpha_j\, y_1(t-j) + \sum_{j=1}^{q} \beta_j\, \omega_1(t-j) + \omega_1(t) \tag{7.7}$$

where $\{\omega_1(t)\}$ is a mutually uncorrelated random sequence with $E(\omega_1(t))=0$, $E(\omega_1^2(t))=\sigma_1^2$, the α_js and β_js are functions of θ_j and σ_0^2, and q is the largest integer satisfying $qm<(p+1)(m-1)+1$; i.e., q is at most$=p$ and if $m>p+1$, then $q=p$. The coefficients α_j are related to the reciprocals of the roots $r_1,...,r_p$ of $(1- \sum_{j=1}^{p} \theta_j z^j)$.

An important point to note is that the order of the AR part in the ARMA model for $\{y_1(t)\}$ is p, the order of the AR model generating $\{y_0(t)\}$. One can further generalize Theorem 1 to derive the structure of the model obeyed by $\{y_2(t)\}$ where

$$y_2(t) = \sum_{j=0}^{m-1} y_1(t-j)\ .$$

It can be shown that the nonoverlapping sequence $\{y_2(t)\}$ is generated by an ARMA model whose AR part is of order p and whose MA part is $(p+1)(m-1)+q$. For large m this reduces to p+1 if q>p+1 or p if q$\leq$p+1. Thus if $y_0(t)$ obeys an AR model of known order p, the low-resolution sequences $\{y_1(t),\ y_2(t),...\}$ obey an ARMA model whose AR part is of order p and whose MA part depends on p and m. In some practical cases one may approximate the model structure for $\{y_1(t)\}$ and its low-resolution copies to be AR of order p. But this may be a very crude approximation, as very high order AR models are required to approximate an ARMA model. (See [7.8].)

One can use the knowledge regarding the model structures of $y_0(.)$, $y_1(.)$, $y_2(.)$,... to extract spectral features for classification of textures. Such features have been considered in the image processing literature [7.9,10]. For instance, the features corresponding to the high-resolution sequence $y_0(t)$ can be obtained from the spectral density function $S_0(\lambda)$ of $y_0(t)$, which is

$$S_0(\lambda) = \frac{\sigma_0^2}{\left\| 1 - \sum\limits_{j=1}^{p} \theta_j\, \exp\,(\sqrt{-1}\ \lambda\ j)\ \right\|^2}\ .$$

104

Likewise, the features corresponding to $y_1(t)$ may be obtained from the spectral density function $S_1(\lambda)$ of $y_1(t)$, which is

$$S_1(\lambda) = \sigma_1^2 \; (\|1 + \beta_j \; \exp \; (\sqrt{-1} \; \lambda \; j)\|^2 \; / \; \| \; 1 \; - \; \alpha_j \; \exp \; (\sqrt{-1} \; \lambda \; j)\|^2)$$

and so on. The relevant features for texture classification [7.9,10] may then be extracted from $S_0(\lambda)$ and $S_1(\lambda)$. It may be expected that classification results will be better when features from sequences of different resolutions can be used. If the θ_js (or their consistent estimates) are known, the α_js and β_js can be computed directly. Alternatively, one can fit an ARMA model of order (p,q) to $\{y_1(t)\}$ by any one of the estimation methods in [7.11] and identify the α_js and β_js and compute $S_1(\lambda)$.

Another problem of interest which has applications in MR image synthesis and coding is to predict the values of $y_1(t)$. Suppose one wishes to predict $y_1(t)$ given the observations $y_1(t-jm)$, $j=1,2,\ldots$ The optimal predictor is obtained [7.10] by inverting the moving average part of the model obeyed by $\{y_1(t)\}$ in (7.7) and representing $y_1(t)$ as an infinite AR system with the residual $y_1(t)$. Due to the computations involved in this method, two alternate predictor structures can be conisdered. The first of these is the so-called linear least squares predictor of $y_1(t)$ on $y_1(t-jm)$, $j=1,2,\ldots$. It is given by [7.7]

$$\underset{\sim}{z}_1(t-m)^T \begin{bmatrix} R_0 & R_1 \ldots R_{p-1} \\ R_1 & \\ \ldots & \\ R_{p-1} & R_0 \end{bmatrix} \begin{bmatrix} R_1 \\ \vdots \\ R_p \end{bmatrix}$$

where $\underset{\sim}{z}_1(t-m) = \mathrm{Col.}[y_1(t-m),\ldots,y_1(t-pm)]$ and $R_j = \mathrm{Cov}(y_1(j),y_1(t-jm))$. The third predictor simply ignores the MA part of the model obeyed by $y_1(t)$. The predictor structure is given by

$$y_1(t) = \sum_{j=1}^{p} \alpha_j \; y_1(t-j) \; . \tag{7.8}$$

In (7.7), the α_js are the true parameters; in practice they are replaced by consistent estimates, which can be obtained by using $y_1(t-(p+k)m)$, $k=1,2,\ldots$, p as instrumental variables. Similarly, one can derive predictor structures for $y_0(t)$ given the observations $y_0(t-m-j)$, $j=0,1,2,\ldots$ This is obtained by writing $y_0(t-j)$ in terms of $\omega_0(t-j-n)$, $n=0,m-1-j$ and $y_0(t-j-n)$, $n=m-j,\ldots$ and summing $y_0(t-j)$ over $j=0$ to $m-1$ to obtain $y_1(t)$. The details of this scheme may be found in [7.7].

7.3 Estimation of Parameters

Suppose we are given the sequence $\{y_1(t)\}$ and the fact that $\{y_0(t)\}$ is generated by an AR model of order p characterized by $\{\theta_j, j=1,\ldots,p\}$. The problem is to estimate the parameters $\{\theta_j, j=1,\ldots,p\}$.

Let $C_1(k) = \mathrm{Cov}(y_1(t), y_1(t-k))$ be the autocovariance of the low-resolution sequence $\{y_1(t)\}$. Given $\{y_1(\tau(m+1))\}$ for $\tau=0,1,2,\ldots$, one can obtain consistent estimates of the covariances $C_1(\tau(m+1))$ for $\tau=0,1,2,\ldots$. Let the high-resolution sequence $\{y_1(t)\}$ obey the AR model

$$y_0(t) = \sum_{j=1}^{p} \theta_j \; y_0(t-j) + \omega_0(t) \; . \tag{7.9}$$

105

Define

$$A(L) = 1 - \sum_{j=1}^{p} \theta_j L^j$$

where

$$L \, y_0(t) = y_0(t-1) .$$

If $s_1, s_2,...,s_p$ are the roots of $A(z^{-1}) = \prod_{j=1}^{p} (1-s_j z^{-1})$ then it can be shown [7.12] that the autocovariance $\{C_1(\tau(m+1))\}$ obeys the difference equation

$$\prod_{j=1}^{p} (1-(s_j L)^{m+1}) \, C_1(\tau(m+1)) = 0, \text{ if } \tau > p(m+1) . \qquad (7.10)$$

Equivalently one can write (7.10) as

$$(1 + q_1 L^{m+1} + ... + q_p L^{p+1}) \, C_1(\tau(m+1)) = 0, \ \tau > p(m+1) \qquad (7.11)$$

where

$$\prod_{j=1}^{p} (1 - (s_j L)^{m+1}) = 1 + \sum_{j=1}^{p} q_j \, L^{j(m+1)} . \qquad (7.12)$$

Likewise it can be shown [7.12] that $\{y(\tau(m+1))\}$ satisfies the difference equation

$$\left[1 + \sum_{j=1}^{p} q_j \, L^{j(m+1)}\right] y_1(\tau(m+1)) = n_1(\tau(m+1)), \ \tau = 0,1,2,... \ .$$

The basic idea in estimating the parameters of the AR model obeyed by $\{y_0(t)\}$ is to obtain consistent estimates of the qs and the variance of $n_1(t)$ and to obtain estimates of $\{\theta_j\}$. To appreciate this method consider the simple case of p=2 and m=2. For this situation, (7.11) reduces to

$$C_1(9) + q_1 \, C_1(6) + q_2 \, C_1(3) = 0$$
$$C_1(12) + q_1 \, C_1(9) + q_2 \, C_1(6) = 0 . \qquad (7.13)$$

Substituting the sample moments of $C_1(.)$, which can be computed given $\{y_1(.)\}$, and solving for the qs, one can obtain consistent estimators for the qs. Note that q_1 and q_2 determine the roots s_1 and s_2 which determine θ_1 and θ_2, the parameters of the second-order AR model generating $y_0(t)$. However, the roots s_1 and s_2 are not single-valued functions of q_1 and q_2; for the case under consideration,

$$q_1 = - (s_1^3 + s_2^3) \qquad (7.14)$$
$$q_2 = s_1^3 s_2^3 .$$

Hence, it is not possible to obtain consistent estimates of s_1 and s_2 from consistent estimates of q_1 and q_2. It is necessary to use the information contained in the residuals n_t. For the example under discussion,

$$\eta_t = \omega_1(t) + (s_1 + s_2)\,\omega_1\,(t-1) + (s_1^2 + s_2^2)\,\omega_1(t-2)$$
$$- s_1 s_2\,(s_1^2 + s_2^2)\,\omega_1(t-4)$$
$$- s_1^2\,s_2^2\,(s_1 + s_2)\,\omega_1(t-5)\ .$$

Defining

$$\lambda = \text{var}\,(\eta_t)\,/\,C_1(0) \tag{7.15}$$

where var (η_t) denotes the variance of η_t, one can obtain a consistent estimate of λ by using the estimate of var (η_t) from the variance of the sample residuals; thus var (η_t) is also a function of q_1 and q_2. Using the estimates of q_1, q_2, and λ, from the three possible pairs of s_1 and s_2 compatible with (7.14), one can identify the only pair that also satisfies (7.15) for large samples.

This method can be extended to arbitrary values m and p, as summarized in [7.12]. Thus given the low-resolution sequence $\{y_1(t)\}$ one can identify the parameters of the AR model generating $\{y_0(t)\}$.

One can use the estimation scheme discussed above for the synthesis of high-resolution images. Suppose we are given $y_1(\tau(m+1))$, $\tau=0,1,2,\ldots$, and that $\{y_0(t)\}$ can be generated by an AR model of known order. Then by using the estimation scheme discussed above one can identify the parameters corresponding to the AR model generating $\{y_0(t)\}$ and generate a sequence close to $\{y_0(t)\}$ by using a pseudo-random number sequence. Similarly, one can develop algorithms for synthesis of MR images. Assume that the given image sequence $\{y_0(t)\}$ is represented by an AR model of order p. We generate the low-resolution sequence $\{y_0(t)\}$ using (7.1) and fit an ARMA model whose AR part is of order p and whose MA part is of order q as given in Theorem 1. The parameters that characterize $\{y_1(t)\}$ are the parameters of the ARMA model and the quantized residuals of $\omega_1(t)$. Experience indicates [7.5] that fewer bits are required to represent the quantized residuals of $\{\omega_1(t)\}$ compared to the quantized residuals of $\{\omega_0(t)\}$. At any time when synthesis of $\{y_0(t)\}$ is required, one can generate a close approximation to $y_1(.)$ by using the fitted ARMA model and quantized residuals of $\{\omega_1(t)\}$ and then generate a sequence close to $\{y_0(t)\}$ as described in the previous paragraph. The advantage of this method over the direct method of fitting an AR model to $\{y_0(t)\}$ and resynthesizing a close approximation to $\{y_0(t)\}$ using the AR model is not clear due to lack of experimental results.

7.4 Conclusions

In conclusion, we have explored the possibility of using 1-D time-series models to represent MR images. The discussion has been primarily focussed on the 1-D case. Possible applications in spectral feature extraction and image synthesis have been considered. We are currently testing the theory discussed in this paper on real images. Extensions to the case where $\{y_0(t)\}$ obeys a 2-D random field model from the class of models discussed in [7.13-15] are under study, as are also extensions to more general reduction operations than (7.1).

Acknowledgment

The partial support of the National Science Foundation under Grant ECS-82-04181 is gratefully acknowledged.

References

7.1 A. Rosenfeld: "Quadtrees and pyramids for pattern recognition and image processing," in Proc. 5th Intl. Conf. on Pattern Recognition, Miami Beach, FL, 1980, pp. 802-811

7.2 S. L. Tanimoto, T. Pavlidis: A hierarchical data structure for picture processing, Computer Graphics Image Processing 4, 104-119 (1975)

7.3 A. R. Hanson, E. M. Riseman: "Segmentation of natural scenes," in Computer Vision Systems, ed. by A. R. Hanson, E. M. Riseman (Academic Press, New York, 1978), pp. 129-163

7.4 M. Shneier: Extracting linear feaures from images using pyramids, IEEE Trans. Systems, Man, Cybernetics SMC-12,569-572 (1982)

7.5 E. H. Adelson, P. J. Burt: "Image data compression with the Laplacian pyramid," in Proc. Pattern Recognition and Image Processing Conf., Dallas, TX, 1981, pp. 218-223

7.6 B. H. McCormick, S. N. Jayaramamurthy: Time series model for texture synthesis, Intl. J. Computer Information Sciences 3, 329-343 (1974)

7.7 T. Amemiya, R. Y. We: The effect of aggregation on prediction in the autoregressive model, J. American Statistical Assoc. 67, 628-632 (1972)

7.8 K. R. W. Brewer: Some consequences of temporal aggregation and systematic sampling for ARMA models, J. Econometrics 1, 133-154 (1973)

7.9 J. S. Weszka, C. R. Dyer, A. Rosenfeld: A comparative study of texture measures for terrain classification, IEEE Trans. Systems, Man, Cybernetics SMC-6, 269-285 (1976)

7.10 P. J. Burt: "Fast algorithms for estimating local image properties," in Proc. Pattern Recognition and Image Processing Conf., Las Vegas, NV, 1982, pp. 669-671

7.11 R. L. Kashyap, A. R. Rao: Dynamic Stochastic Models from Empirical Data (Academic Press, New York, 1976)

7.12 L. G. Telser: Discrete samples and moving sums in stationary stochastic processes, J. American Statistical Assoc. 62, 484-499 (1967)

7.13 R. L. Kashyap: "Analysis and synthesis of image patterns by spatial interaction models," in Progress in Pattern Recognition, ed., by L. N. Kanal, A. Rosenfeld (North Holland, Amsterdam, 1981), pp. 149-186

7.14 R. Chellappa, R. L. Kashyap: Digital image restoration using spatial interaction models, IEEE Trans. Acoustics, Speech, Signal Processing ASSP-30, 461-472 (1982)

7.15 R. L. Kashyap, R. Chellappa: Estimation and choice of neighbors in spatial interaction models of images, IEEE Trans. Information Theory IT-29, 60-72 (1983)

8. Node Linking Strategies in Pyramids for Image Segmentation

J. Cibulskis

Department of Mathematics, Northeastern Illinois University
Chicago, IL 60625, USA

C.R. Dyer

Computer Sciences Department, University of Wisconsin
Madison, WI 53706, USA

A one-pass, bottom-up overlapped pyramid-linking algorithm is described. This algorithm differs from other pyramid-linking methods in (a) the ordering of node linking, (b) pyramid initialization, and (c) root and leaf marking schemes for determining region segmentation trees. A proof of the convergence of the algorithm is also given.

8.1 Introduction

A new class of image segmentation algorithms has recently been proposed which attempts to partition an image into regions using evidence gathered at many levels of resolution [8.1-6]. These algorithms iteratively refine segmentations alternately with updating property measurements taken over the current partition. The interdependence of these two processes leads to a final segmentation which is guided by property measurements taken over many scales and combined by their similarity at adjacent levels of resolution.

An overlapped pyramid data structure is used in which at each level is stored an image which is half the resolution of the image at the level below it. Pixels are grouped into regions by a procedure which defines "links" between nodes (pixels) at adjacent levels of the pyramid. (Of course this grouping process could easily be generalized to include neighboring nodes at the same level or even at an arbitrary level in the pyramid but this would quickly lead to a combinatorial explosion in the ways in which pixels could be combined; hence in this work we restrict the grouping process to the simple scheme just outlined.) Our method may be loosely described as a hierarchical region growing method which uses a hill-climbing technique to iteratively update segmentations a level at a time in a one-pass bottom-up (fine to coarse resolution) procedure. The focus of our attention in this paper is on new node linking control strategies for merging nodes at many resolutions into homogeneous, connected regions. This includes experiments on improving the speed of the linking process, and various decision methods for linking/not-linking nodes so that final "segmentation trees" are defined. Also included is an analysis of how the process is guaranteed to converge to a final segmentation.

8.2 Overlapped Pyramid Linking

The overlapped pyramid representation used here was originally proposed by BURT et al. [8.1]. A 2^n by 2^n image defines the bottom level (level 0) of the pyramid. Above this level are defined successively reduced-resolution versions of size 2^{n-1} by 2^{n-1},..., 2 by 2, and 1 by 1. The neighborhood of a node is specified so that a node at level k > 0 has sixteen "children" at level k-1 (the level below it) corresponding to a 4 by 4 block of nodes. (A node which is on the border of an array at any level has its missing children defined by reflecting the top and bottom rows and the left and right columns of the image outward.) A pair of horizontally or vertically adjacent nodes at level k have child neighborhoods overlapping by 50% (i.e., eight nodes); a pair of nodes which are diagonally adjacent have four common children representing a 25% overlap. Each node at level k < n also has four "parent" nodes at level k+1 so that the parent and child relations are inverses (i.e., node x is a parent of node y if and only if node y is a child of x). Finally, each node has eight "siblings" at its own level, defined as the eight nearest neighbors of the node.

Associated with each node is a set of property values; in this paper average gray level of selected children is used as the single feature value stored at a node. Image segmentation is defined by a grouping process which merges nodes at a given level by having each node select a single best parent node from its four candidate parent neighbors. "Best" is defined as the parent with the most similar gray level to the given node's gray level. We say that each node is now "linked" to its most similar parent. The gray level representing a node may now be updated using the node's current subset of children which are linked to it. This process of alternately updating property values and reselecting most similar parents is iterated, allowing nodes to merge into a set of trees based on gray level similarity. The set of leaf nodes (at level 0) in each such tree constitutes a homogeneous subpopulation of image pixels. More precisely, one form of the basic procedure defined by BURT, HONG, and ROSENFELD is as follows:

```
procedure BHR(Image)
begin
    /* Initialize entire pyramid by setting node i's integral property
    value, f(i), to the (rounded) average of its sixteen children's
    values */
    Pyramid := INITIALIZE_PYRAMID(Image);
    /* Iteratively link each node to its best parent, updating the
    parent's property value based on these links */
    LINK(Pyramid);
    /* Obtain final segmentation by tracing trees of linked nodes down
    pyramid starting from level Top-1 (containing a 2 by 2 array) */
    SEGMENT(Pyramid);
end;


procedure LINK(Pyramid)
do begin
    for each node i in Pyramid do
        /* Phase I:  Update best parent link */
        begin
            j := MOST_SIMILAR_PARENT(i);
            if j ≠ Parent(i) then Parent(i) := j;
        end
    for each node i in Pyramid do
        /* Phase II:  Update property value using
        children linked to the current node i */
        f(i) := [AVERAGE{f(j) | Parent(j)=i}];
        /*  square brackets represent the rounding function */
    end; until no_parents_updated;
```

8.3 Convergence of Pyramid Linking

To motivate the alternative algorithm presented below, we now analyze the behavior of algorithm BHR. Specifically, we are concerned with the convergence behavior of the algorithm and how we can speed it up without sacrificing the stabilization guarantee. For an alternative proof of the convergence of BHR, see [8 .7].

   Theorem: Procedure BHR is guaranteed to converge to a final solution.

   Proof: First, observe that all of the gray levels at level 0 are never updated by BHR. Second, the property value at a node at level k, $0 < k \leq$ Top_level, can never depend on the property value of any node at a level greater than or equal to k. Now consider nodes at level 1 of the pyramid. By the above two observations we know (1) all children at level 0 have fixed property values, and (2) the property value of a node at level 1 can only depend on the property values of (at most) its sixteen children.

   Now consider the behavior of procedure LINK during a single iteration at level 1. At the beginning of Phase I say the current best parent of node i at level 0 is node j at level 1. After updating all parent links, say the new best parent of node i is node j'. Since procedure MOST_SIMILAR_PARENT is defined to return the parent node whose gray level is closest to the given node's gray level, we know

$$(f(i) - f(j'))^2 \leq (f(i) - f(j))^2 .$$

Therefore, letting

$$V = \Sigma \ (f(i) - f(j))^2 \qquad \text{and} \quad V' = \Sigma \ (f(i) - f(j'))^2$$
all nodes i $\qquad\qquad\qquad\qquad$ all nodes i
   at level 0 $\qquad\qquad\qquad\qquad\quad$ at level 0

we immediately have $V' \leq V$. Furthermore, if we assume that ties are always broken in favor of the current parent, then clearly $V = V'$ if and only if no links were updated during this phase.

   At the beginning of Phase II, consider the sum-squared error of each node at level 0 with its current best parent at level 1, i.e.,

$$V = \Sigma \ (f(i) - f(\text{Parent}(i)))^2$$
   all nodes i
   at level 0 .

After recomputing the gray level property value for each node at level 1 using those children which are currently linked to it, say the new value is f'(j), for each node j at level 1. Then

$$V' = \Sigma \ (f(i) - f'(\text{Parent}(i)))^2 \qquad\qquad = \Sigma \ (f(i) - f'(n_1))^2 + ...$$
   all nodes i $\qquad\qquad\qquad\qquad\qquad\qquad$ all nodes i
      at level 0 $\qquad\qquad\qquad\qquad\qquad\qquad$ at level 0 which
                                                          are linked to
$$+ \Sigma \ (f(i) - f'(n_k))^2 \qquad\qquad\qquad \text{node } n_1 \text{ at level 1}$$
   all nodes i
   at level 0 which
   are linked to
node n_k at level 1

where $n_1, n_2, \ldots, n_k$ are all the nodes at level 1. Each term is of the form

$$\sum_i (f(i) - A_j)^2 .$$

It is easily shown that the integer which minimizes this value is precisely the rounded value of the average of the $f(i)$'s in which $Parent(i) = j$ -- that is, when $A_j = f'(j)$. Therefore, for all j at level 1

$$\sum_{\substack{\text{all nodes } i \\ \text{such that} \\ Parent(i)=j}} (f(i) - f'(j))^2 \leq \sum_{\substack{\text{all nodes } i \\ \text{such that} \\ Parent(i)=j}} (f(i) - f(j))^2$$

Thus, $V' < V$. Furthermore, equality holds if and only if no links were up-dated at the previous phase. Thus if V0 is the initial sum squared error value and Phases I and II cannot increase V, V must eventually stabilize ($V > 0$). When stabilization occurs, all parent links must also have sta-bilized.

Finally, once the gray level property values at level 1 have stabilized, the same argument applies to level 2, etc. Q.E.D.

8.4 An Alternative Pyramid-Linking Algorithm

From the proof of convergence given above, it is clear that a node need not begin to compute its property value or best parent link until after all of its descendants have stabilized to their final values. Thus for this form of the linking process, a strictly one-pass, bottom-up procedure is all that is needed. Beginning at level 1, each level is processed until all of its nodes attain stable property values and all of the nodes at the next lower level attain stable best parent links. More specifically, the algo-rithm can be revised as follows:

```
procedure CD (Image)
begin
    Pyramid := INITIALIZE_PYRAMID_LEVEL_0(Image);
    LINK2(Pyramid);
    SEGMENT2(Pyramid);
end;

procedure LINK2(Pyramid)
for k := 1 to Top_level do
    begin
        if k ≠ 1 then
            for each node i at level k-1 do
                /* Mark those nodes at level k-1 which are either roots (have
                   no parents) or leaves (have no children linked to them). */
                if ROOT(i) or LEAF(i) then MARK(i);
        for each node j at level k do
            INITIALIZE_PROPERTY_VALUE(j);
        do begin
            for each unmarked node i at level k-1 do
                UPDATE_PARENT_POINTER(i);
            for each node j at level k do
                UPDATE_PROPERTY_VALUE(j);
        end; until no_links_updated;
    end;
```

```
procedure SEGMENT2(Pyramid)
for each root node i in Pyramid do
    LABEL_ALL_DESCENDANTS(i);
```

In the remainder of this section we describe the details of this algorithm
and present experimental results on several versions that were implemented.

8.4.1 Node-Linking Sequence

One of the principal changes in procedure CD from BHR is in the iterative
process of updating node properties and links. In CD, level by level processing is enforced since a node's final property value and best parent link
depend only on properties and links of its descendants. We have removed
all previous iterations from BHR since they are just busy work. Furthermore,
this form of the algorithm makes explicit the bottom-up nature of processing.
Clearly, this form of node sequencing does not affect the guarantee of convergence -- algorithm CD must also stabilize. It does not guarantee, however, that CD and BHR will converge to the same final values or segmentation.
In the experiments that we have done, these differences are minor and rarely
noticeable.

This form of node sequencing makes algorithm CD similar in many respects
to HOROWITZ and PAVLIDIS' split-and-merge algorithm [8.8]. Algorithm CD
differs from split-and-merge (SM) in the following ways: (a) In CD splitting
and merging are iterated at a given level of resolution via the repeated updating of parent links; once a level is completed, however, the last partition is permanent -- at coarser resolutions only merging of the results obtained from below is allowed. On the other hand, SM makes one pass up to
merge and one pass down to split. (b) SM uses a "nonoverlapped" pyramid as
the basic data structure, whereas CD uses an overlapped pyramid. (c) SM's
merging process is a one-shot yes/no procedure which uses the fixed nonoverlapped pyramid structure for considering which quadruples of nodes may
be merged; algorithm CD iteratively considers the ways in which a node may
be merged to one of four nodes at the next higher level. Also,(d) SM uses a
final grouping step to merge adjacent regions into a region adjacency graph;
CD's overlapped child neighborhoods allow this grouping process to be partially contained within the merging step itself.

8.4.2 Pyramid Initialization

In previous work, each node's initial property value has been computed by a
simple (weighted or unweighted) averaging process using a subset of the node's
sixteen children [8.1-6]. In an effort to speed up processing and to evaluate
the effects of the iterative updating process, we have experimented with variations on the method of assigning each node's initial property value. Rather
than make one pass up the pyramid initially to create a complete "gray scale"
pyramid (procedure INITIALIZE_PYRAMID in BHR), we have used a simple average
of the stabilized property values of all the children of a node. In this
way we need only initialize the bottom level of the pyramid before initiating
the node linking process (procedure LINK2). Since the final stabilized
values at a given level k represent the algorithm's best estimate of the
property values for the nodes at that level, the initialization of property
values at level k+1 will in general be closer to their final values than they
would have been if we had used the average value of all of its descendant
pixels (at level 0).

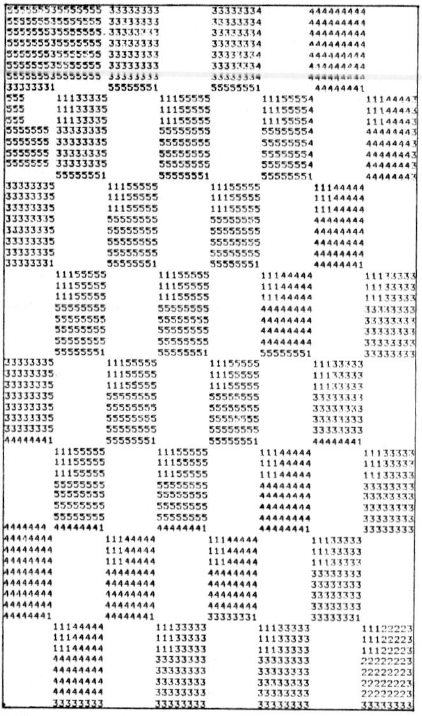

(a)

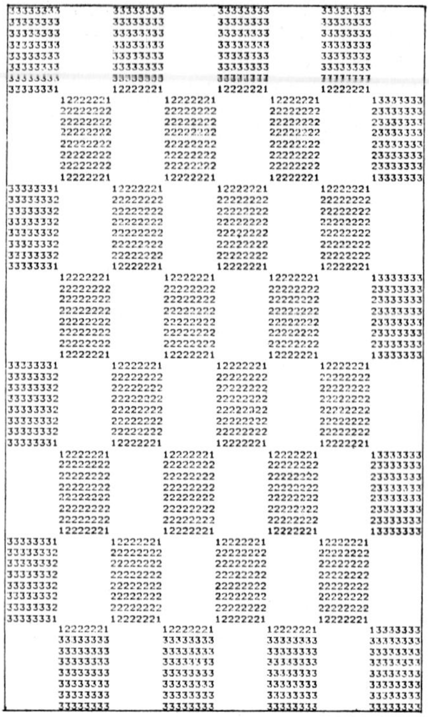

(b)

Fig. 8.1. (a) Final segmentation of a binary checkerboard image using the zero-initialization method. Each pixel is assigned a label equal to the height of the segmentation tree in which it is contained; pixels linked to the pyramid apex node (at level 6) are labelled as blanks. **(b)** Final segmentation of a binary checkerboard image using algorithm CD's pyramid initialization scheme. (Results using BHR's initialization method were identical for this image.)

Table 8.1. Comparison of pyramid initialization methods

Image	Total number of iterations		Percent speedup	Average number of iterations per node		Percent speedup
	BHR	CD		BHR	CD	
Chrom1	19	18	5%	4.03	3.99	1.0%
Chrom2	18	16	11%	3.60	3.26	9.4%
Num32	22	20	9%	4.98	4.92	1.2%
GMrods	22	18	18%	5.16	4.87	5.6%
Ckrbrd	8	5	38%	1.14	1.00	12.3%

114

It was conjectured that an initialization scheme which used information about the input image would perform better than an unstructured scheme which did not. To verify this, the above two methods were run on a checkerboard image and compared with a third approach which merely initialized all the nodes above the base to the value 0. BHR required about half the number of iterations as the zero-initialization method; CD needed only a third as many iterations. In addition, the zero-initialization approach created artifacts whereas the others produced identical and accurate final segmentations of the checkerboard (see Fig.8 .1).

The BHR and CD initialization methods were then compared using five test images. The overall quality of the resultant segmentations was roughly the same in each case. The method in CD, however, always required fewer total iterations and fewer iterations per level. Table 8.1 compares the speeds of convergence of these two approaches.

8.4.3 Root and Leaf Marking

In earlier work, it has been observed that if we force each node in the pyramid (up to a prespecified level) to link to its best parent, then in many cases a node which has no "good" parents is forced to merge with a region that has vastly different properties from those of the given node. Other problems with forced linking include: (a) final segmentation trees exist for each node at the designated last level no matter how many pixel populations exist in the image, (b) the height of the segmentation tree is dependent on the image size, not the size of the region being represented, and (c) small regions will be merged with other regions of the same type into one conglomerate segmentation tree for all the pixels in a given population. To overcome these kinds of artifacts, methods have been developed which associate a weight with each node's parent link [8.3,4]. By adjusting these weights a node could be partially linked to each of its four parents, or not be linked to any of its parents at all (all weights approximately equal to zero). If a node is not linked to any of its parents, then we say that this node is a root node of a segmentation tree in the pyramid.

The root marking technique is crucial to the success of all pyramid linking algorithms for two reasons. First, forced linking methods require that no more than a fixed number of regions be present in the image, and each of these regions is forced to contain a segmentation tree with its root at a prespecified level. Initial experiments have shown many artifacts are introduced when using this method [8.2,4]. Second, marking a node corresponds to making a decision about what the best level of resolution is for a particular image "patch." We would like to define an operator which marks a node as the root of a segmentation tree whenever it detects that a particular image property becomes local. That is, at the level where a part of a region becomes line- or spot-like, that feature is locally detected by a node in the pyramid which is then made the root of a tree for that patch of the region. Care must be taken, however, since marking roots too liberally means regions will be fragmented into many pieces, while marking roots too conservatively will cause separate regions to be merged into a single segmentation tree.

Rather than adjust link weights we have tried to define operators which can be applied to each level of resolution in order to detect spot- and line-like features. A node is marked as a root if after its level has stabilized, its final property value is significantly different from most of its eight siblings' values. In our experiments we assume that the image contains exactly two populations of pixels -- dark objects on a light background. We then designed a number of operators which detected dark spots and lines for use with the root marking step. More specifically, the following operators were among those tested (in reverse order of overall performance):

(1) A 3 by 3 Laplacian operator with a prespecified threshold. This method proved to be too sensitive to edges, resulting in roots being marked near all object borders instead of forcing linking to a higher level where lines and spots could be detected.

(2) If no more than two neighbors have a gray level similar to the given node's gray level and all of its dissimilar neighbors are lighter than it is, then mark the node as a root. Results using this technique are given in Fig. 8.2; each pixel is labelled with the height of the segmentation tree in which it is located (except nodes linked to the pyramid's apex are printed as blanks). Notice that parts of the checkerboard are missing. In addition, the rooting pattern is very sporadic. It was felt that the chief reason for the poor performance of this technique was due to its failure to take into account the presence of leaf nodes (see below).

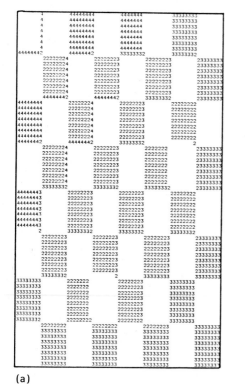
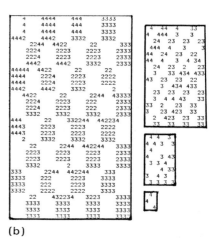

(a)   (b)

Fig. 8.2 a,b. Final segmentation trees for a checkerboard image. Each node is labelled with the height of the segmentation tree in which it is contained (except nodes rooting at level 6 are printed as blanks.) **(a)** Level 0. **(b)** Levels 1-4

116

(3) If a node has no children linked to it, then mark the node as a "leaf" since it can never become part of any segmentation tree. If no more than x of a node's nonleaf neighbors have a gray level similar to the given node's gray level, and all of its dissimilar neighbors are lighter than it is, then mark the node as a root. The (number of neighbors, maximum number of similar neighbors) pairs were developed to (a) improve marking of corners and (b) improve reliability of the property values by ignoring property values at leaf nodes. The pairs used were: (8,3), (7,3), (6,3), (5,3), (4,3), (3,1), (2,0), and (1,0). If a node has no nonleaf neighbors but its gray level is greater than a specified threshold, then we also mark the node as a root. A problem with this approach was that it did not allow a thin line bordered by leaf nodes to be marked as a root, forcing linking up to the next higher level. This resulted in inconsistencies when root marking did occur and so was rejected in favor of the following method.

(4) If a node has at least four nonleaf neighbors, no more than three of which have a gray level similar to the given node's gray level, and all dissimilar neighbors are lighter, then mark the node as a root. If the node has less than four nonleaf neighbors but its gray level is greater than a specified threshold, then mark the node as a root. It is interesting to note that it was crucial to use four as the cut-off number of nonleaf neighbors. Originally we used three and found that artifacts were being introduced where light (background) corners were surrounded by leaf nodes, causing erroneous root marking. In the remainder of this section we will use this method for root marking.

With all of these methods the goal was to force all pixels associated with the background to be merged into a single segmentation tree with its root marked at the apex of the pyramid. Every other region would build one or more segmentation trees (depending on its shape) with roots at levels below the apex. The final part of algorithm CD (called SEGMENT2) makes one pass down the pyramid starting at a specified level below the apex and marks each pixel in the base with a label corresponding to the height of the segmentation tree in which it is contained. Due to uneven illumination and noise, however, background pixels sometimes merge into regions below the top level. For this reason, it has proven practical to begin the final downward pass at a level below the next to highest one. In our experiments where 64 by 64 images were used resulting in pyramids with the apex node at level 6, we have found that initiating the SEGMENT2 procedure at either level 3, 4, or 5 gives good results in which, for the most part, only trees representing background regions have been ignored. Figure 8.3 illustrates the effects of starting the downward pass at levels 3, 4, and 5. Roots at levels 4 and 5 contribute mainly artifacts whereas ignoring the roots at level 3 would cause many object pixels to be missed.

Two other aspects of the root marking step that proved important were (a) threshold selection, and (b) leaf node identification. Initially, we selected a global threshold for each of the methods 1-4 described above. This proved to be a sensitive process of trial and error, so we developed automatic threshold selection techniques. Two thresholds were selected: TO, to decide whether two gray levels were "similar," and SO, to decide whether a gray level was dark enough to be an object pixel. TO was chosen to be some multiple of the standard deviation, either of the original image, the current level of processing, or the 3 by 3 neighborhood surrounding the current node. In the first case, SO was chosen to be the average gray level in the original image; in the second and third cases, the average gray level for all nodes at the current level was used. Of the three methods, the first (using the

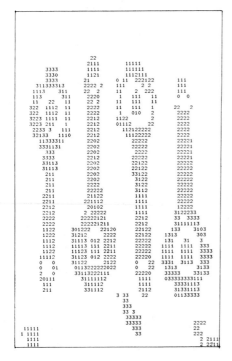

Fig. 8.3 a–c. Effects of starting level on procedure SEGMENT2 using an image containing four piston rods. **(a)** Starting level 5. **(b)** Starting level 4. **(c)** Starting level 3

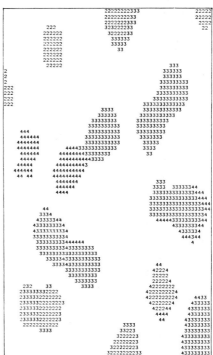

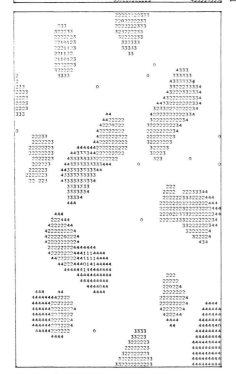

Fig. 8.4 a–c. Effects of threshold selection on segmenting a chromosome image. **(a)** Threshold equal to 1.25 times the standard deviation of gray levels in the original image. **(b)** Threshold equal to 1.25 times the standard deviation of the stabilized gray level values at the current level of the pyramid. **(c)** Threshold equal to 1.25 times the standard deviation of the gray levels in the 3 by 3 neighborhood surrounding the given node

119

original image) gave the best results. Once object pixels became part of a rooted tree, it made no sense to decide if a pixel was dark by comparing its value to other pixels on that level. On the other hand, the pixel by pixel method proved too sensitive to noise. Figure 8.4 illustrates the effects of these three methods. A threshold value of 1.25 times the standard deviation was used.

The identification of leaf nodes significantly improved the performance of our algorithm in the following ways. During initialization of a node, only those children which were not roots or leaves were used in the averaging process. This improved the initial property values since the values stored at leaf nodes represented some intermediate state of processing this node at the previous level. During the updating procedure, only a node's nonleaf children were used again to prevent "meaningless" property values stored at leaf nodes from being interpreted as representative of a collection of pixels in the image.

8.5 Concluding Remarks

In this paper we have shown that a one-pass, bottom-up pyramid linking algorithm can be used for segmentation. Unlike previous pyramid-linking procedures, the algorithm presented iteratively computes pixel property values for all nodes at one level of resolution using the property values for pixels at twice the resolution. Once property values and links have stabilized at the given level, its values are fixed and processing proceeds at the next higher level. Final segmentation is obtained during a single top-down traversal of the pyramid. Although considerable improvement may be possible by using a combined top-down/bottom-up linking method, the current method is (a) easier to implement as a special-purpose hardware device, (b) converges faster to a stable state, and (c) provides a clearer initial analysis of the utility of hierarchical linking techniques.

References

8.1 P. Burt, T. H. Hong, A. Rosenfeld: Segmentation and estimation of image region properties through cooperative hierarchical computation, IEEE Trans. Systems, Man, Cybernetics SMC-11, 802-809 (1981)
8.2 T. Silberberg, S. Peleg, A. Rosenfeld: "Multiresolution Pixel Linking for Image Smoothing and Segmentation", Computer Science Technical Report TR-977, University of Maryland (1980)
8.3 K. Narayanan, S. Peleg, A. Rosenfeld, T. Silberberg: "Iterative Image Smoothing and Segmentation by Weighted Pyramid Linking", Computer Science Technical Report TR-989, University of Maryland (1980)
8.4 H. J. Antonisse: Image segmentation in pyramids, Computer Graphics Image Processing 19, 367-383 (1982)
8.5 M. Pietikainen, A. Rosenfeld: Image segmentation by texture using pyramid node linking, IEEE Trans. Systems, Man, Cybernetics SMC-11, 822-825 (1981)
8.6 T. H. Hong: "Pyramid Methods in Image Analysis", Ph.D. dissertation, Department of Computer Science, University of Maryland (1982)
8.7 S. Kasif, A. Rosenfeld: Pyramid linking is a special case of ISODATA, IEEE Trans. Systems, Man, Cybernetics SMC-13, 84-85 (1983)
8.8 S. L. Horowitz, T. Pavlidis: Picture segmentation by a tree traversal algorithm, J. ACM 23, 368-388 (1976)

9. Multilevel Image Reconstruction

G.T. Herman, H. Levkowitz, and H.K. Tuy

Department of Radiology, Hospital of the University of Pennsylvania
3400 Spruce Street, Philadelphia, PA 19104, USA

S. McCormick

Department of Mathematics, Colorado State University
Fort Collins, CO 80523, USA

In image reconstruction from projections, one attempts to estimate values of
an unknown function f of two variables at points of a finite grid (usually
uniformly spaced in two orthogonal directions) from a finite number of (measured) line integrals of f. Lines can be characterized by two variables,
typically a distance ℓ and an angle θ. Usually the lines along which integrals of f are measured correspond to a grid of sample points in the
(ℓ,θ) space. Thus, both the input (the line integrals) and the output
(values of f) can be thought of as samples of a function on a grid. The
problem then translates into solving a system of linear equations, the size
of which depends on the sizes of the grids associated with the input and
the output.

For accurate solution usually fine grids are required, and we end up with
a very large, but sparse, system of equations. Typically, iterative methods
have been used to solve the equations. These tend to be slow because (i)
the system is large, and (ii) initially large reductions in the residual
error quickly become small. Repeatedly changing the size of one or both of
the grids and/or the organization of the equations during the iterative procedure has the potential of overcoming both these problems.

We discuss both the theory and implementation of such multilevel image
reconstruction methods, and illustrate their use on reconstructions from
(simulated) x-ray projections.

9.1 Image Reconstruction from Projections

The problem of image reconstruction from projections has arisen independently
in a large number of scientific fields. An important version of the problem
in medicine is that of obtaining the density distribution within the human
body from multiple x-ray projections. This process is referred to as computerized tomography (CT); it has revolutionized diagnostic radiology over
the past decade. The 1979 Nobel prize in medicine was awarded for work on
computerized tomography. The 1982 Nobel prize in chemistry was also awarded
for work on image reconstruction: this time for the reconstruction of vir-
uses and macromolecules from electron micrographs.

There is a large literature on image reconstruction from projections; we
refer to [9.1] for a general discussion. In this paper we concentrate our
attention on a rather specific group of approaches to solving the image reconstruction problem.

Following the terminology and notation of [9.1], we define a picture
function f to be a function of two polar variables (r,ϕ) which is zero-

Fig. 9.1. The line $L(\ell,\theta)$ is the one whose distance from the origin O is ℓ and the perpendicular to which makes an angle θ with the base line OB

valued outside a square-shaped picture region whose center is at the origin of the coordinate system. In what follows we assume that f has additional properties, so that all integrals used below are defined.

The mathematical idealization of the image reconstruction problem is: "recover the picture function f from its line integrals." More precisely, we use the pair (ℓ,θ) to parametrize a line (see Fig.9.1) and we define the RADON transform Rf of f by

$$[Rf](\ell,\theta) = \int_{-\infty}^{\infty} f(\sqrt{\ell^2 + z^2}, \theta + \tan^{-1}(z/\ell))dz, \text{ if } \ell \neq 0$$

$$(9.1)$$

$$[Rf](0,\theta) = \int_{-\infty}^{\infty} f(z, \theta + \pi/2)dz.$$

The input data to a reconstruction algorithm are estimates (based on physical measurements) of the values of $[Rf](\ell,\theta)$ for a finite number of pairs (ℓ_i,θ_i), $1 \leq i \leq I$, and its output is an estimate, in some sense, of f. For $1 \leq i \leq I$, define

$$R_i f = [Rf](\ell_i,\theta_i) \qquad (9.2)$$

and let y denote the I-dimensional column vector whose ith component y_i is the available estimate of $R_i f$. We refer to y as the measurement vector.

We now discuss one of the common modes of data collection in x-ray computerized tomography. The x-ray source and the detector strip are on either side of the object to be reconstructed and they move in unison around a common center of rotation, denoted by 0 in Fig.9.2. The data collection takes place in P distinct steps. The source (which is assumed to be a point) and detector strip are rotated between two steps of the data collection by a small angle, but are assumed to be stationary while the measurement is taken. The P distinct positions of the source during the P steps of the data collection are indicated by the points $S_0,\ldots,Sp_{-1}$ in Fig.9.2. The detector strip consists of $2Q + 1$ detectors, also assumed to be points, spaced equally on an arc whose center is the source position. The line from the source to the center of rotation goes through the central detector. Thus in this case $I = P(2Q + 1)$.

When designing a reconstruction algorithm we assume that the method of data collection, and hence the set $\{(\ell_1,\theta_1),\ldots,(\ell_I,\theta_I)\}$, is fixed and known. Roughly stated the problem is

GIVEN measurement vector y,

ESTIMATE picture f.

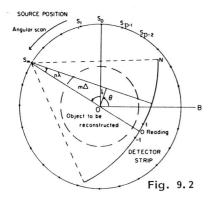

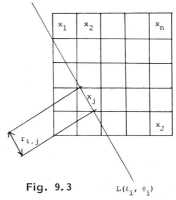

$L(\ell_i, \theta_i)$

Fig. 9.2. Schematic of our standard method of data collection (divergent beam)

Fig. 9.3. In an n x n digitization the picture region is subdivided into $J = n^2$ small equal-sized square-shaped pixels. The average value of the picture function in the jth pixel is x_j. The length of intersection of the ith line $L(\ell_i, \theta_i)$ with the jth pixel is $r_{i,j}$

One way of making this statement precise is by the so-called <u>series expansion</u> approach in which we make use of a fixed set of J <u>basis pictures</u> $\{b_1, \ldots, b_J\}$. It is assumed that any picture f which we may wish to reconstruct can be adequately approximated by a linear combination of the b_js.

An example of such an approach is n×n digitization, in which the picture region is subdivided into an n×n array of small squares, called <u>pixels</u> (for picture elements, see Fig.9.3). We number the pixels from 1 to $J = n^2$, and define

$$b_j(r,\phi) = \begin{cases} 1, & \text{if } (r,\phi) \text{ is inside the jth pixel} \\ 0, & \text{otherwise.} \end{cases} \tag{9.3}$$

Then the n×n digitization of the picture f is the picture $\hat{f}$ defined by

$$\hat{f} = \sum_{j=1}^{J} x_j \, b_j \tag{9.4}$$

where x_j is the average value of f inside the jth pixel.

There are other ways of choosing the basis pictures, but once they are chosen, any picture $\hat{f}$ that can be represented as a linear combination of the basis pictures $\{b_j\}$ is uniquely determined by the choice of the coefficients x_j as shown in (9.4). The column vector x whose jth component is x_j is referred to as <u>image vector</u>. In this environment the problem "estimate the picture f" becomes the problem "find the image vector x" such that the $\hat{f}$ defined by (9.4) is a good approximation to f.

The functionals R_i defined in (9.2) are clearly linear. Assuming that they are continuous (an assumption which may well be violated when we make precise the underlying function spaces and hence the notion of continuity), it follows that if $\hat{f}$ approximates f, then

$$R_i f \simeq \sum_{j=1}^{J} x_j \ R_i b_j \ . \tag{9.5}$$

Since the b_js are user-defined functions, $R_i b_j$ is usually easily calculated. (In our digitization example it denotes the length of intersection of the ith line $L(\ell_i, \theta_i)$ with the jth pixel; see Fig.9.3). Denoting the calculated value of $R_i b_j$ by $r_{i,j}$ and recalling that y_i is an estimate of $R_i f$, it follows that

$$y_i \simeq \sum_{j=1}^{J} r_{i,j} \ x_j, \qquad 1 \le i \le I \ . \tag{9.6}$$

We refer to the matrix R whose (i,j)th element is $r_{i,j}$ as the <u>projection matrix</u>. Let e denote the I-dimensional <u>error vector</u> defined by

$$y = Rx + e \ . \tag{9.7}$$

The series expansion approach leads us to the following <u>discrete reconstruction problem</u>: based on (9.7),

GIVEN measurement vector y,

ESTIMATE image vector x.

The estimation is usually performed using an optimization criterion which defines the image vector of choice for a given measurement vector.

Often such an optimization is equivalent to solving a system of consistent equations, which are usually solved iteratively.

For example (for details see [9.1], Chapters 11 and 12), one possible optimization criterion is of the form:

FIND the x which minimizes $\|D^{-1} x\|$ among all the minimizers of

$$(y - Rx)^T \ W_1 (y - Rx) + (x - x_0)^T \ W_2 (x - x_0) \ . \tag{9.8}$$

Here D is a given symmetric positive definite matrix, W_1 and W_2 are given symmetric nonnegative definite matrices, x_0 is a given vector, and $\| \ \|$ denotes the Euclidean norm (i.e., $\|x\|^2 = \sum_{j=1}^{J} x_j^2$). This formulation is called the <u>regularized weighted least squares problem with weighted norm</u>. It is equivalent to the problem:

FIND the x which minimizes $\|D^{-1} x\|$ subject to

$$(R^T W_1 R + W_2) \ x = R^T W_1 y + W_2 x_0 \tag{9.9}$$

where R^T denotes the transpose of the matrix R. The important point here is that (9.9) always has a solution, while the original system y = Rx may not be consistent. However, it has also been found that iterative procedures which ignore the error vector (i.e., they are based on the assumption that y = Rx is consistent and we need to find a solution of it) often produce acceptable estimates of the image vector in surprisingly few iterations.

In this paper we investigate whether notions motivated by the so-called multigrid approach can be used to improve further the performance of iterative procedures in image reconstruction from projections.

9.2 Iterative Algorithms for Linear Systems

EGGERMONT, HERMAN and LENT [9.2] presented a unifying framework for a wide class of iterative methods in numerical linear algebra. In particular, the class of algorithms contains KACZMARZ's [9.3] and RICHARDSON's [9.4] methods for the regularized weighted least squares problem with weighted norm. The convergence theory in [9.2] yields as corollaries the usual conditions for KACZMARZ's and RICHARDSON's methods. The algorithms in the class may be characterized as being group-iterative, and incorporate relaxation matrices. EGGERMONT, HERMAN and LENT [9.2] showed that some standard iterative methods in image reconstruction fall into their class of algorithms and described, in particular, an application to truly three-dimensional image reconstruction.

The class of algorithms in [9.2] form the basis of the work we carried out for this paper. We therefore state the algorithm schema of [9.2] in its general form and quote the main convergence result. Afterwards, we discuss two special cases that we have actually used.

Consider the system of linear equations

$$Az = Y \tag{9.10}$$

where A is an $LM \times N$ matrix and z is an N-dimensional vector. We do not necessarily assume that the system is consistent. Partition the matrix A and the vector Y as

$$A = \begin{bmatrix} A_1 \\ \overline{A_2} \\ \vdots \\ A_M \end{bmatrix} , \qquad Y = \begin{bmatrix} Y_1 \\ \overline{Y_2} \\ \vdots \\ Y_M \end{bmatrix} \tag{9.11}$$

where the A_m are $L \times N$ matrices and the Y_m are L-dimensional vectors, for $1 \leq m \leq M$.

Algorithm Schema

$z^{(0)}$ is an arbitrary N-dimensional vector

$$z^{(n+1)} = z^{(n)} + A_{m_n}^T \Sigma^{(n)} (Y_{m_n} - A_{m_n} z^{(n)}) \tag{9.12}$$

for $m_n = n \pmod{M} + 1$, $n = 0,1,\ldots$, and $\Sigma^{(n)}$ is an $L \times L$ relaxation matrix.

Theorem [9.2]

Let $\{\Sigma^{(n)}\}_n$ be a bounded sequence of relaxation matrices, satisfying

$$\lim_{n \to \infty} \sup \| A_{m_n}^+ (I_L - A_{m_n} A_{m_n}^T \Sigma^{(n)}) A_{m_n} \| < 1 \tag{9.13}$$

125

where I_L denotes the L×L identity matrix and S^+ denotes the MOORE-PENROSE pseudoinverse of the matrix S (see, e.g., [9.5]), and $\|S\|$ denotes the norm of the matrix S. If $Az = Y$ is consistent, then the sequence $\{z^{(n)}\}_n$ generated by (9.12) converges to a solution of $Az = Y$. If in addition $z^{(0)}$ is in the range of A^T, then

$$\lim_{n\to\infty} z^{(n)} = A^+Y . \tag{9.14}$$

If the method (9.12) is periodic (i.e., $\Sigma^{(n)} = \Sigma^{(m_n-1)}$), then every subsequence $\{z^{(nM+m)}\}_n$, $0 \le m < M$, converges even if $Az = Y$ is not consistent.

We shall not make use of the algorithm schema in its greatest generality, but restrict our attention to the case when the $\Sigma^{(n)}$ are diagonal. For convenience of expression we introduce a new partitioning of A and Y as

$$A = \begin{bmatrix} a_1^T \\ a_2^T \\ \vdots \\ a_{LM}^T \end{bmatrix} , \qquad Y = \begin{bmatrix} y_1 \\ y_2 \\ \vdots \\ y_{LM} \end{bmatrix} \tag{9.15}$$

where the a_i are N-dimensional vectors and the y_i are real numbers for $1 \le i \le LM$. In this notation (9.10) can be rewritten as

$$<a_i,z> = y_i, \qquad 1 \le i \le LM \tag{9.16}$$

where $<a_i,z>$ denotes the inner product of the vectors a_i and z. Using this notation, our special $\Sigma^{(n)}$ is of the form

$$\Sigma^{(n)} = \lambda \begin{bmatrix} W_1^{(n)} & & & 0 \\ & W_2^{(n)} & & \\ & & \ddots & \\ 0 & & & W_L^{(n)} \end{bmatrix} \tag{9.17}$$

where

$$W_\ell^{(n)} = \frac{1}{\|a_{m_n-1+\ell}\|^2} \tag{9.18}$$

and λ is called the relaxation parameter.

With this choice of $\Sigma^{(n)}$, the iterative step (9.12) of the algorithm schema becomes

$$z^{(n+1)} = z^{(n)} + \lambda \sum_{\ell=1}^{L} \frac{y_{m_n-1+\ell} - <a_{m_n-1+\ell}, z^{(n)}>}{\|a_{m_n-1+\ell}\|^2} a_{m_n-1+\ell} . \tag{9.19}$$

An important property of these algorithms in the environment of image reconstruction from projections is the following. The matrix A tends to be extremely large, very sparse, and without any apparent structure. On the other hand, based on the underlying data collection and digitization, it is easy to write a subroutine which, for any index i, returns the locations and sizes of the nonzero components of the vector a_i. Using such a subroutine the step in (9.19) can be efficiently implemented, in spite of the large size of the vector z.

The notation considerably simplifies in two special cases, which we now discuss.

In the first case L=1. Then (9.19) can be rewritten as

$$z^{(n+1)} = z^n + \lambda \frac{y_{m_n} - <a_{m_n}, z^{(n)}>}{\|a_{m_n}\|^2} a_{m_n} . \qquad (9.20)$$

The convergence condition in (9.13) translates into

$$|1-\lambda| < 2 . \qquad (9.21)$$

If $\lambda=1$, (9.20) is the classical algorithm of KACZMARZ [9.3] for solving (9.16). A geometrical interpretation of KACZMARZ's algorithm is the following. Take the equations in (9.16) one by one. $z^{(n+1)}$ is obtained from $z^{(n)}$ by orthogonal projection of $z^{(n)}$ onto the hyperplane determined by the m_nth equation. In image reconstruction literature the KACZMARZ method is usually referred to as ART (for Algebraic Reconstruction Techniques; see, e.g., [9.1], Chapter 11).

In the second case M=1. Then (9.19) can be rewritten as

$$z^{(n+1)} = z^{(n)} + \lambda \sum_{\ell=1}^{L} \frac{y_\ell - <a_\ell, z^{(n)}>}{\|a_\ell\|^2} a_\ell . \qquad (9.22)$$

If $\lambda = 2/L$, (9.22) is the classical algorithm of CIMMINO [9.6] for solving (9.16). A geometrical interpretation of CIMMINO's algorithm is the following. Consider all equations in (9.16) simultaneously and take mirror images of $z^{(n)}$ in each of the hyperplanes determined by the equations. Then $z^{(n+1)}$ is the mean of these mirror images.

9.3 Multilevel Approaches

Procedures of the type described in (9.19) have been applied to image reconstruction from projections [9.1,2,7,8]. There are a number of difficulties associated with them, three of which we now discuss.

One difficulty is the choice of the relaxation parameter λ. If this is chosen too large, the convergence criterion (9.13) may be violated. Even if the convergence criterion is satisfied, larger values of λ tend to introduce features (such as streaks) during the early stages of the iterative process, which may then require many iterations before they are removed. On the other hand, too low a choice of λ will result in hardly any change during one iteration. While there is a lot of ad hoc practical experience with different choices of λ (see, e.g., [9.1,8]), and there are some theoretical results on limiting behavior [9.9], there are no generally applicable guidelines on exactly how λ should be chosen in a special case. The main result of this uncertainty is that we may have to do many more iterations than we would require with the optimal λ to achieve the same quality reconstruction.

This brings us to the second difficulty. Iterative methods have been found to be significantly more expensive (in terms of computer time) than alternative techniques that have been used in image reconstruction. An example of a less time-consuming technique is the so-called convolution method (see, e.g., [9.1]), which has become the standard in the medical application area.

The third difficulty is with the choice of $z^{(0)}$ in the Algorithm Schema. If it is already a good approximation to the sought after solution, we may not have to do much work in getting to an acceptable iterate. This implies that we need a preliminary procedure to estimate $z^{(0)}$. In some applications [9.1,2,7], this procedure has been the convolution method itself, causing the iterative approach to be unavoidably more expensive than the convolution method.

We are investigating multilevel approaches, since we hope that they have the potential to speed up iterative reconstruction procedures so that they become competitive with the convolution method. By multilevel approaches we mean methods in which we repeatedly change during the iterative process the system of equations (9.10) to be solved and/or the way the system is organized into blocks(9.11).

One of the multilevel approaches is the so-called multigrid approach. This has been found useful in other application areas, such as boundary value problems (see, e.g., [9.10]). The idea here is that we can change either one or both of the picture digitization (i.e., the size of J in eqs. (9.3) and (9.4)) and the data sampling (i.e., the size of I in eq. (9.2)). Since we have found that in image reconstruction the overhead associated with changing picture digitization outweighs any potential savings, we discuss in a precise fashion only the special case in which the data sampling is variable but the picture digitization does not change. This is the so-called unigrid approach which we first describe for the general case of a system of equations (9.10), and assume that A has an even number of rows.

Suppose that an iterative procedure has given us a sequence $z^{(0)}, z^{(1)}$, ...,$z^{(n)}$ of estimates for solving (9.10). We could now use the procedure once more to obtain further iterates. An alternative is the following. If we had a solution z_c to the system of equations

$$Az_c = Y - Az^{(n)} \qquad (9.23)$$

then $z^{(n)} + z_c$ would be a solution to (9.10). Suppose that there are two matrices S and T such that solutions z'_c of

$$(S\,A)z'_c = T(Y - Az^{(n)}) \qquad (9.24)$$

are "approximately" the same as z_c. If S and T are chosen so that the iterative procedure applied to (9.24) is less expensive than that applied to (9.10), then for the same cost we can do many more iterations on (9.24) to approximate z'_c (and hence z_c) than we can do on the original system. Furthermore, the process is recursive; at some point the iterative procedure to approximate z'_c can be abandoned in favor of the alternative procedure of

128

finding a correction term to the current estimate of z_c' by using yet an even simpler system of equations.

We now make this general approach concrete for the case of image reconstruction from projections and the iterative schema depicted in (9.19). We consider the case when each row a_i^T of A is a row of the projection matrix R. As mentioned immediately after eq. (9.19), one makes essential use of an algorithm which for any i returns the locations and sizes of the nonzero entries of a_i. One way of retaining the use of this subroutine and yet reducing the size of the system of equations is to choose S so that SA is a submatrix of A. Typically we may aim at retaining, say, half the rows of A.

In deciding which half to retain we are guided by the underlying physical problem. We consider the mode of data collection which is depicted in Fig. 9.2 and the digitization which is depicted in Fig.9.3. The unigrid approach implies that the digitization does not change. The number of detectors (2Q+ 1) is related to the digitization. This is because the iterative methods discussed in the last section do not produce good reconstructions if the data sampling in each view is too sparse as compared to the digitization [9.11]. On the other hand, too dense data sampling as compared to the digitization implies that equations associated with two neighboring rays give rise to essentially the same information, and so collecting and processing them separately is just a waste of time. For these reasons, we do not change the number of rays per view in the unigrid approach. In other words, if we retain one row of A (or R), then all the rows associated with rays from the same source position are retained. Under these circumstances, the most logical way of reducing the size of the matrix A by half is to retain rows associated with every second source position. (We assume that the number of source positions P is even. We shall in fact use a P which is a power of 2, thereby making it easier to do the unigrid step recursively.)

This defines S of eq. (9.24) to be a 0-1 matrix with half as many rows as A. We could of course choose T to be the same matrix. The physical interpretation of that choice would be that the unigrid step consists of simply ignoring half our data. There is an alternative approach; we can choose T to be an averaging matrix, and thus retain to some extent the higher resolution information at the lower level. To be more precise, if the rows associated with the pth source position are to be retained, the matrix T provides the right-hand side of (9.24) by weighted averaging appropriate elements of the right-hand side of (9.23). A reasonable process is where the new value for the qth ray in the pth projection is obtained from the old values of the qth rays in the (p-1)st, pth, and (p+1)st projection with weights 1/4, 1/2, and 1/4, respectively.

Note that making S the same as T is desirable from the point of view of getting a good approximation z_c' to z_c. We have decided against this, since T would alter the rows of A (in particular, would make A less sparse).

This unigrid approach allows us to move up and down different levels of resolution. Moving down to lower resolution speeds things up in two ways. (i) A single cycle through all the equations takes half the time, since only half of the rows are retained. (ii) It is possible for iterative procedures of the type depicted in (9.19) to get "stuck" in the sense that a single cycle through the equations causes very little change in the iterate $z^{(n)}$. This has to do with the iterate aligning itself in the direction of the eigenvector associated with the largest eigenvalue of a matrix underlying the procedure; the nature of the problem and specific examples have been reported for special cases similar to those depicted by (9.20) and by (9.22)

in [9.12] and [9.13], respectively. By changing the system of equations in
the unigrid step we also change this underlying matrix and may achieve more
rapid changes in the iterate. Thus the unigrid approach may help us in
solving the second difficulty mentioned at the beginning of the section:
namely, the speed of the iterative procedure.

The ideas embedded in unigrid may also be useful in solving the third
difficulty: the choice of $z^{(0)}$. The process described by T in (9.24) averages the projection data while halving the number of projections. Repeated
applications of the process produce a small data set, each item in which
is the average of many items in the original data set. From this we can
produce, very inexpensively, a reconstruction that is likely to be very
blurry. Then we can move up to higher and higher resolution levels of
the averaged data, until we get back to the level of the original data set,
making iterative refinements to our current estimate at each step. This
can be combined with the unigrid concept with moves down, such as depicted
in (9.24), intermixed with the moves up. Specific examples will be given
in the next section.

As mentioned before, the use of different matrices on the two sides of
(9.24) introduces an inconsistency (or adds to the inconsistency at the
higher level). An alternative approach to unigrid, which is similar in
spirit, is to vary the block size L in (9.19): moving down one level in
unigrid corresponds to doubling the block size. This does not save computer cost as far as cycling through the data once is concerned, but it
does change the eigenvectors of the underlying matrix and can possibly
get the process unstuck if it was stuck at the other level. The extra
cost in cycling through the data may well be compensated by the greater
consistency of the systems of equations that are being solved, resulting
in fewer cycles through the data producing acceptable estimates. In
the next section we also illustrate the use of variable block size.

9.4 Experiments

We now demonstrate the ideas discussed in the previous section by report-
ing on a sequence of experiments.

A function f representing a cross section of a patient's head has been
mathematically described by superimposing ellipses, triangles, rectangles,
and segments and sectors of circles. For a precise description of the object, see [9.14]. Line integrals of the object have been calculated according to the geometry described in Fig.9.2 with P = 64 and Q = 98, and so
I = 12,608. Digitization was done according to Fig.9.3, with n = 65 and
so J = 4,225.

In what follows we use the notation R_5 and y_5 for the reconstruction
matrix and measurement vector associated with the whole data set, and R_4
and y_4 for those if every second source position is discarded with y_4
obtained from y_5 by using the averaging matrix T_5, and so on till R_1 and y_1,
which correspond to four source positions. If R and y are used without
subscript, they represent the original R_5 and y_5.

In order to compare different procedures fairly, we have plotted performance versus computer cost (as determined by the number of inner products
$<a_{m_n-1+\ell}, z^n>$ that are evaluated in using (9.19)). We have used two measures

of performance: one is the residual norm (reported in Fig.9.4)

130

$$\| y - Rx_e \| \qquad\qquad (9.25)$$

where x_e is the current estimate of x, and the error (reported in Fig.9.5)

$$\| x_d - x_e \| \qquad\qquad (9.26)$$

where x_d is the vector obtained by sampling the original function f at the centers of the pixels. (Note that since x_d is a sampled version of f and y is obtained by taking line integrals of the original f, x_d is unlikely to be a solution of Rx = y.)

We report on five experiments and their variants. In all experiments the initial iterate was taken to be the zero vector.

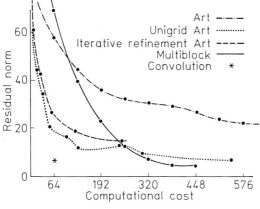

Fig. 9.4. Curves of the residual norm (see (9.25)). The computational cost is measured in terms of the cumulative number of processed equations

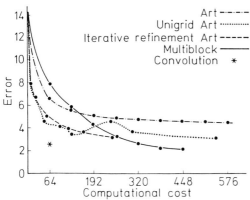

Fig. 9.5. Curves of the image error (see (9.26)). The computational cost is measured in terms of the cumulative number of processed equations

Experiment 1.   ART

This is the classical KACZMARZ [9.3] method, eq. (9.20) with $\lambda=1$, applied to the (inconsistent) system

$$Rx = y . \qquad\qquad (9.27)$$

Slightly, but not significantly better performance than reported in Figs. 9.4,5 has been obtained with $\lambda = 0.5$ and with $\lambda = 0.15$.

Experiment 2.   Unigrid ART

To describe what happens here conceptually, it is easiest to think of having five iterates of size I, $x_1^{(n)}$, $x_4^{(n)}$, $x_3^{(n)}$, $x_2^{(n)}$, and $x_1^{(n)}$. All these are altered by the algorithm as it progresses. The actual implementation is of course more efficient in storage. The final outcome is to be stored in x_5. Initially all $x_t^{(0)}$ ($1 \leq t \leq 5$) are set to be the zero vector. Also, for conceptual understanding only, we introduce for each level t a variable vector $Y_t^{(n)}$, which is initially set to y.

The progress of the algorithm is described by Fig.9.6. We refer to the circles in the figure as stages. Within a stage at level t, we use the ART algorithm (9.20) with $\lambda=1$ to alter $x_t^{(n)}$. During this time $x_{t'}^{(n)}$ for $t' \neq t$ and $Y_{t'}^{(n)}$ for all t' do not change.

Level

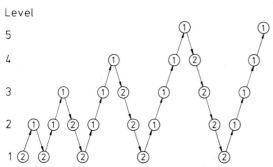

Fig. 9.6. Schema representing the progress of the Unigrid ART algorithm. The numbers inside the circles indicate the number of cycles of ART reconstruction at that level

Let n denote the iteration when we enter a stage at level t. We define the values of $x_t^{(n)}$ and $Y_t^{(n)}$ as follows. If the stage is entered from above

$$\begin{cases} x_t^{(n)} \text{ is the zero vector} \\ Y_t^{(n)} = T_{t+1} (Y_{t+1}^{(n)} - R_{t+1} x_{t+1}^{(n)}) \end{cases} \qquad (9.28)$$

If the stage is entered from below

$$\begin{cases} x_t^{(n)} = x_t^{(n-1)} + x_{t-1}^{(n)} \\ Y_t^{(n)} = Y_t^{(n-1)} \end{cases} \qquad (9.29)$$

Within the stage the value of x_t is altered by the ART method applied to the system

$$R_t \, x_t = Y_t^{(n)} \, . \qquad (9.30)$$

The number of iterates for which we stay within a stage is the number of equations in (9.30) if we entered from below and twice the number of equations in (9.30) otherwise.

Figures 9.4,5 show a considerable improvement of unigrid ART over ordinary ART.

Experiment 3. Iterative refinement ART

The question arises whether the improvement of unigrid ART over ordinary ART is at all due to the more complicated step (9.28), or whether it is really the consequence of the iterative refinements in (9.29). We have carried out a purely iterative refinement procedure shown in Fig.9.7. For this, we need to have only one iterating image vector $x^{(n)}$, which is initially the zero vector. At the beginning of the stage at level t, $x^{(n)}$ is just taken over from the previous stage unaltered, and the ART algorithm is applied to the system

$$R_t \, x = y_t \, . \qquad\qquad (9.31)$$

The number of iterates for which we stayed within a stage here is twice the number of equations in (9.31).

Level

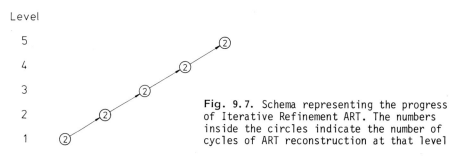

Fig. 9.7. Schema representing the progress of Iterative Refinement ART. The numbers inside the circles indicate the number of cycles of ART reconstruction at that level

Figures 9.4,5 show that iterative refinement ART is superior to ordinary ART, but is somewhat inferior to unigrid ART.

Experiment 4. Multiblock

In this method we match the general outline of iterative refinement, but, as explained at the end of Sect.9.3, we use a variable block size in (9.19) in place of changing the data resolution. We used M iterative steps successively for each of $M = 2^0, 2^1, \dots, 2^6$ (and $L = P(2Q + 1)/M$). We found that λ in (9.19) had to be carefully selected for good convergence. The value $92/L$ was selected, since it is inversely proportional to L (as suggested by CIMMINO) and is such that the average value in the first iterate matches the average value of the phantom. (The average value of the phantom can be estimated from the measurement vector, as explained for example in [9.1], p. 106.)

As can be seen from Figs.9.4,5, multiblock outperforms all the variants of ART reported here, if it is run long enough.

Experiment 5. Convolution

As has been mentioned earlier, the convolution methods are commonly used in most applications of image reconstruction. These are noniterative procedures, all costing the same. We have applied some variants (different filters) of the divergent beam convolution method [9.1, Chapter 10] to the measurement vector y. The cost and performance of the best of these are indicated by the * in Figs.9.4,5.

9.5 Conclusions

We have shown that some multilevel approaches can significantly improve the performance of iterative methods of image reconstruction. In the rather limited experiments that we have performed, multiblock produced reconstructions somewhat superior in quality (as measured by the residual norm and the error) to the convolution method. However, it is superior to convolution only after a number of iterative steps which makes it approximately five times as expensive as the convolution method. Whether the improvement is worth the extra cost can only be determined by more realistic (i.e., larger) experiments, in which both the digitization and the data sampling are much finer. (A typical digitization in CT today is 320×320, making the image vector 25 times larger than what we have used in our experiments.)

Irrespective of their eventual usefulness to CT, multilevel image reconstruction approaches are of interest in themselves. This article demonstrates that such approaches can be used to improve the rate of convergence of iterative methods for solving not only discretized differential equations [9.10], but also discretized integral equations (9.1). It may well be that multiresolution approaches are useful in all areas where iterative techniques have been used to solve a discretized version of a continuous problem.

Acknowledgments

The research work of the authors is supported by NSF grant ECS-81-17908 and NIH grants HL28438 and RRO1372. We would like to thank Dr. Yair Censor for many useful discussions and Mrs. Mary A. Blue for preparing the manuscript.

References

9.1 G. T. Herman: Image Reconstruction from Projections, the Fundamentals of Computerized Tomography (Academic Press, New York, 1980)

9.2 P. P. B. Eggermont, G. T. Herman, A. Lent: Iterative algorithms for large partitioned linear systems, with applications to image reconstruction, Linear Algebra and its Applications 40, 37-67 (1981)

9.3 S. Kaczmarz: Angenaherte Auflosung von Systemen linearer Gleichungen, Bull. Acad. Polon. Sci. Lett. A35, 355-357 (1937)

9.4 L. F. Richardson: The approximate arithmetical solution by finite differences of physical problems involving differential equations with an application to the stresses in a masonry dam, Phil. Trans. Royal Society (London) A210, 307-357 (1910)

9.5 A. Ben-Israel, T. N. E. Greville: Generalized Inverses: Theory and Applications (Wiley-Interscience, New York, 1974)

9.6 G. Cimmino: Calcolo approssimato per le soluzioni dei sistemi di equazioni lineari, La Ricerca Scientifica (Roma) XVI, Serie II, Anno IX, Vol. 1, 326-333 (1938)

9.7 G. T. Herman, R. A. Robb, J. E. Gray, R. M. Lewitt, R. A. Reynolds, B. Smith, H. Tuy, D. P. Hanson, C. M. Kratz: "Reconstruction algorithms for dose reduction in x-ray computed tomography", in Proc. MEDCOMP '82, Philadelphia, PA, 1982, pp. 448-455

9.8 G. T. Herman, H. Hurwitz, A. Lent: A storage efficient algorithm for finding the regularized solution of a large inconsistent system of equations, J. Inst. Maths. Applics. 25, 361-366 (1980)

9.9 Y. Censor, P. P. B. Eggermont, D. Gordon: Strong underrelaxation in Kaczmarz's method for inconsistent systems, Numerische Mathematik 40, to appear

9.10 A. Brandt: Multilevel adaptive solutions to boundary value problems,
      Math. Comp. 31, 333-390 (1977)
9.11 K. Kouris, H. Tuy, A. Lent, G. T. Herman, R. M. Lewitt: Reconstruction
      from sparsely sampled data by ART with interpolated rays, IEEE Trans.
      Medical Imaging, to appear
9.12 G. T. Herman, A. Lent, S. W. Rowland: ART: mathematics and applica-
      tions, a report on the mathematical foundations and on the applicability
      to real data of the algebraic reconstruction techniques, J. Theor. Biol.
      42, 1-32 (1973)
9.13 G. T. Herman, A. Lent: Quadratic optimization for image reconstruc-
      tion I, Computer Graphics Image Processing 5, 319-332 (1976)
9.14 J. E. Gray, D. P. Hanson, G. T. Herman, R. M. Lewitt, R. A. Reynolds,
      R. A. Robb, B. Smith, H. Tuy: "Reconstruction Algorithms for Dose Re-
      duction in X-Ray Computed Tomography", Technical Report MIPG63, Medical
      Image Processing Group, Dept. of Radiology, University of Pennsylvania
      (1982)

10. Sorting, Histogramming, and Other Statistical Operations on a Pyramid Machine

S.L. Tanimoto

Department of Computer Science, University of Washington
Seattle, WA 98195, USA

We define a pyramid machine to consist of an SIMD cellular array having pyramid interconnections, together with a controller consisting of a conventional microcomputer augmented with hardware to communicate with the cellular array. Primarily intended for graphics and image analysis applications, pyramid machines may also be used for more general data processing. Many operations can be performed in O(log N) time with this architecture; finding maxima, areas, and centroids are typical of such operations. Here algorithms are given for sorting, for finding the kth largest element, for local order statistics, for median filtering of image data, for computing the histogram of a set of numbers, and for computing the mean and standard deviation. Most of these algorithms run as fast as or faster than the best known algorithms for any SISD or flat array SIMD computer. Others offer simpler programs than those for the optimal algorithms.

10.1 Introduction

10.1.1 Background

The pyramid machine architecture is motivated by several considerations: (a) the hierarchical structure of the mammalian visual pathway starting at the retina and ending in the deepest layers of the visual cortex: (b) the possibility of computing many functions of N^2 variables in O(log N) time; (c) the ease with which tree algorithms may be implemented; and (d) the ease of image noise suppression. For an introduction to hierarchical image processing see [10.1].

Several related structures have been discussed in the literature: tree machines [10.2], quad trees [10.3-6], and overlapped pyramids [10.7-9]. One of the more theoretically interesting models of a hierarchical machine was the pyramid cellular acceptor described by DYER [10.10]. There each node in the pyramid structure was an automaton (finite state machine in one case, Turing machine in another case). The model used in our work is somewhat different, motivated by economical considerations related to VLSI design. Our model may be called an SIMD pyramid machine because the nodes of the pyramid structure have almost no control ability of their own, but operate in lockstep from the instructions of a single controller processor.

10.1.2 The SIMD Pyramid Machine Model

The SIMD pyramid machine model is based on the pyramid data structure first used for image processing in 1973-74 [10.11], being a variation of the "regular decomposition" structure used previously [10.12]. A pyramid may be defined as follows. It is a set P of nodes called cells, each of which contains a set of slots for data. The set P is of the form

P = {(k,i,j) such that $0 \leq k \leq L$, $0 \leq i, j \leq 2^k - 1$} .

Here k is the level index of a cell, i is the latitude (row), and j is the longitude (column).

Each cell is related in important ways to 13 others (except those at the borders, roots or leaves of the pyramid). These 13 cells we call the pyramid neighbors of the cell. The pyramid neighborhood of the cell includes the cell itself and thus has 14 members. They are: the father of the cell, the nine cells of the cell's 3 by 3 lateral neighborhood, and the four (quad-tree) sons of the cell.

Our SIMD pyramid machine consists of a pyramidal array of processing elements (PEs) connected to a controller which consists of a general-purpose processor with additional instructions for controlling the pyramidal array.

Each PE contains the logic to perform any of a set of elementary operations (described later) and has enough memory to store several thousand bit values. These bits can in turn represent flags, gray values, integers, etc., by logical groupings established in software. No program code is stored in PE memories; it is stored in the controller's memory. Memory addresses for the PE memories are generated by the controller and are not affected by the state of each PE. However, write operations may be selectively disabled at each PE by a one-bit flag register at each PE. A special register in each PE is its accumulator (AC). The AC stores one bit. This bit can be accessed by neighboring PEs during match operations (described later).

We may assume that there are connections between the pyramidal array and an image data channel for input and output of images. However, our discussion of algorithms need not be concerned with this input/output means.

10.1.3 Elementary Operations

The elementary operations for our pyramid machine model fall into four categories: (1) pure SIMD Operations, (2) controller/array communications, (3) controller-only operations, and (4) image input/output.

Pure SIMD operations are those in which the states of the PEs' memories or registers change but the controller's memory (other than the program counter) does not change. These operations are:

- Load memory value into AC (bit).
- Store AC value into memory.
- Compute OR of AC with memory, result in AC.
- Compute AND of AC with memory, result in AC.
- Compute NOT of AC, result in AC.
- Load disabling flag from memory.
- Clear all disabling flags.
- Load a constant into AC (value is broadcast by controller).
- Match the values of the 14 ACs of the pyramid neighborhood to a pattern broadcast by the controller and write a 1 into the home cell's AC if the match is successful and 0 otherwise. The pattern consists of a string of 14 symbols each of which may be 0, 1, or D. The meaning of D is " don't care." The result of this operation (0 or 1) is the logical AND of the 14 comparisons, where each comparison yields a 1 if either

the pattern symbol is D or if it equals the value of the AC of the corresponding neighbor. This elementary operation is referred to as ANDNB ("AND NeighBorhood").

- Match as above, except that comparisons with D yield 0 and the overall result is the logical OR of the 14 comparisons. This is the ORNB ("OR NeighBorhood") operation.

It is easy to see that special cases of the ANDNB and ORNB operations allow one PE to load its AC with the AC value of any neighbor, thus effecting communication within the pyramidal array. In addition, a wide variety of cellular-logic image processing operations can be built from sequences of these two instructions and other elementary operations. For studies of cellular logic see [10.13-15].

Controller/array communication operations include those in which the controller senses a local or global condition in the pyramidal array, and also those in which the controller can selectively enable or disable a subset of the PEs.

- Controller read value from root PE's AC; CAC :=AC[0,0,0].
- Controller test for all ACs equal to zero.
- Controller enable a set of levels.
- Controller disable a set of levels.
- Controller enable a set of son types (subsets of {NE,NW,SE,SW}).
- Controller disable a set of son types.

Controller-only operations are typical instructions of a conventional minicomputer. CAC and cmem[k] represent the controller accumulator and controller memory location k, respectively.

- Add integers; CAC :=CAC + cmem[k].
- Subtract integers; CAC :=CAC - cmem[k].
- Multiply integers; CAC :=CAC * cmem[k].
- Divide integers; CAC :=CAC / cmem[k].
- Clear CAC; CAC :=0.
- Load CAC; CAC :=cmem[k].
- Store; cmem[k] :=CAC.
- Test for 0 and branch; if CAC = 0 then PC :=address.
- Call subroutine.
- Return from subroutine.
- Logical AND bitwise; CAC :=AND(CAC, cmem[k]).
- Logical OR bitwise; CAC :=OR(CAC, cmem[k]).
- Shift CAC by n (n can be a memory argument, contents + or -).
- Input from terminal or file system.
- Output to terminal or file system.

Image I/O operations are needed to load and output image data to and from the pyramidal array:

- Load bitplane into level L PE ACs from data channel
- Unload bitplane from level L PE ACs to data channel .

For purposes of algorithm analysis we shall assume that each of the above instructions (except for I/O) requires one time unit to complete and that only one instruction is being executed at a time, albeit often by every PE in the pyramid simultaneously. We shall not be concerned with input or output of data into or out of the pyramid machine in this paper.

10.2 Algorithms Based on Bit Counting

10.2.1 Bit Counting, Area, Perimeter

Algorithms for counting the number of pixels in a given subset of an image
contained in a given level of the pyramid have been developed by DYER [10.10]
and by REEVES [10.16]. The general scheme is to have each cell perform a bit-
serial operation to compute the sum of its sons' values. By suitably stag-
gering the beginnings of the addition operations at each level of the pyramid in pipelined fashion, it is possible to get one bit of the global sum
popping out of the root of the pyramid at each bit-serial step (after log
L steps).

The area of a binary image is then easily computed by counting the "1"
bits in that image. The perimeter of a binary image is found by first transforming the binary image into a binary edge image and then counting the 1s
in the edge image. The edge image is easily computed by using the ORNB elementary operation to determine if any lateral neighbors of each cell are 0,
and then ANDing this result with the original value of the cell, so that the
edge image contains a 1 at a cell if and only if the original image contained
a 1 there, and at least one of the lateral neighbors contained a 0.

10.2.2 Histogramming

In order to compute a histogram of an image, the following procedure is used:
the grayscale range is divided by the number of bins desired in order to derive a "bin width." The bin width can later be used to determine a sequence
of threshold values. The image is thresholded using the upper limit on intensity for the first bin. The threshold operation is easily implemented as
a sequence of elementary operations; a bit-serial comparison is performed between PE memory and bit values broadcast by the controller. The subset of
pixels that are at or below the threshold are counted using the counting procedure above. This results in the first component of the histogram. Subsequent components are computed in a pipeline; as soon as the cells in level L
have been counted, a new thresholding operation is commenced in level L to
determine the subset of points that contribute to the count for the second
bin. This new subset is obtained by first thresholding the image with the
value which is the upper limit for the new bin, and then subtracting out the
pixels already counted (which is the union of all previously counted subsets, or more simply the result of the previous thresholding operation).
The selection of each new subset is synchronized with the summation so that
sums flow smoothly up the pyramid, without colliding. On an SIMD machine,
the subset selection and the counting must be performed alternately in order
to keep the pipe full and moving. If separate instructions can be executed
by level L cells, then subset selection can be truly overlapped with summation. However, the gain from this overlapping is insignificant, because the
time taken to compute each new subset is small in comparison with the time
required for the longest bit-serial addition operation (which takes place
at the root).

10.2.3 Euler Numbers

Euler numbers are computed by computing four sets of pixels, counting the
pixels in each of them, and adding or subtracting the counts. The method is
similar to those proposed by other researchers [10.17,18], but is somewhat
simpler on the SIMD pyramid machine because the lateral interconnections of

the pyramidal array permit the four sets of pixels to be determined more easily.

The four sets of pixels and the methods for computing them are the following:

1. Cells containing 1: no work is needed to compute this since it is given as input.
2. Cells whose value is 1 and whose neighbor to the east also has value 1: the ANDB operation computes this in one step.
3. Cells whose value is 1 and whose neighbor to the south also has value 1: this is similar to the previous computation.
4. Cells whose value is 1 and whose neighbors to the east, south, and southeast all have value 1: once again, a single ANDNB operation does the job.

The Euler number is computed as N1 - N2 - N3 + N4, where Ni is the count of cells in set i.

10.2.4 Mean, Standard Deviation

The mean value of an array of b-bit integers is easily computed using bit-serial addition in bottom-up fashion in the pyramid. Extending the integers' representations to b+2L bits allows addition without roundoff error. The controller has the responsibility for dividing the sum by N^2 and setting the degree of precision for the computed mean. Once computed, all PEs at level L can subtract the mean (directed by the controller) from their AC values. These values can be squared by bit-serial multiplication, and the squares summed up the pyramid. The controller may then compute the standard deviation from this sum with a conventional normalization and square-root algorithm.

10.2.5 Centroid

The centroid is computed using a variation of the algorithm described by DUBITZKI et al. [10.18]. The algorithm proceeds in three steps.

1. In the first step, the area is computed as above.
2. In the second step, the X and Y moments at each PE are computed. For a binary image, these moments are 0 if the pixel value is 0; otherwise, they are the X and Y coordinates of the cell. The X moments are summed up the pyramid as are the Y values.
3. In the third step, the X sum is divided by the area, and so is the Y sum. The resulting pair of values is the centroid of the binary image.

The coordinate information can either be preloaded, hardwired, or computed in software (as discussed subsequently). The computational effort required to compute the centroid by this method is O(log N) elementary operations, since the computation is dominated by step 2 in which two sums each requiring $\log_2(N^3)=3\log_2 N$ bits must be computed bit-serially up the pyramid.

A simple way to compute the coordinates of each PE is as follows: Clear all ACs. Disable all but PEs which are east sons. Load these ACs with 1. Enable all PEs again. Load a b-bit register X (at each PE) with the contents of the AC (b is chosen to be the least integer greater than or equal to $\log_2 N$). Set k=1. Disable all but level k PEs. Enter a loop in which first each PE adds its X value to twice that of its father (storing the re-

sult back in X), and then k is incremented by 1. The loop continues until
the PEs in level L have performed the operation. The resulting X values
are the correct X coordinates for the PEs in level L. A similar procedure
computes Y coordinates.

10.3 Algorithms Based on Hierarchical Comparison

10.3.1 Computing the Maximum

Let us assume that an N by N array of integers has been input into level L
of the SIMD pyramid machine, using b bits per value. Let the b bits make
up a register in each PE's memory called VAL. The maximum value in the array is computed as follows:

```
For k := L-1 to 0 Do
begin
    Enable only the PEs  in level k.
    Load each PE's memory (in a slot called TEMP) with the
        value (in VAL) of its NW son.
    Compare this to the value of the NE son and if less, copy the NE son
        data up to replace the NW data in TEMP.
    Compare current value to value of SW son and if less, copy the SW
        data up.
    Compare current value to value of SE son and if less, copy the SE
        data up.
end.
```

Note that after each execution of this instruction (by all PEs in parallel), meaningful data moves up from one level to the next. After L iterations (equal to the number of levels minus one), the maximum over the entire pyramid is placed in the TEMP memory location belonging to the root
node.

10.3.2 Finding the kth Largest Element

The procedure above obtains the maximum value in an image using a number of
comparison steps proportional to L. By continuing to iterate the loop above
even after the root has received a value, the root receives additional values
which are also relatively large, though not maxima. The procedure can be
modified slightly so that after the kth additional iteration, the (k-1)st
largest element appears at the root. This is accomplished by the following
program which repeatedly finds the kth largest element for k=1 to N^2.

Algorithm Pyramid Sort

```
procedure CEX;
    (* Compare and EXchange operation, performed first at even-level
        nodes, then at odd-level nodes. Each node ends up with the
        maximum value of its four sons.*)

    procedure half_CEX;
    begin
      for r :=0 to 1 do begin
        for s :=0 to 1 do begin
          if V[Son(r,s)] > V[Self]
            then begin
                  temp := V[Self];
```

```
                V[Self] := V[SON(r,s)];
                V[Son(r,s)] := temp;
        end;
    end;
  end;
 end; (* half_CEX *)

begin (* CEX *)
 enable_even_levels_only;
 half_CEX;
 enable_odd_levels_only;
 half_CEX;
end; (* CEX *)

begin (* Main routine *)

   (* Establish induction basis: *)
   for iter :=0 to L/2 do begin
        CEX;
   end;

   (* Now for the main loop: *)
   for iter :=0 to (2**L)**2 -1 do begin
                (* Pump out the sorted data *)
        output(V[0,0,0]);
                (* Output root as next largest element *)
        V[0,0,0] := MINIMUM
                (* Remove root value,
                    replacing with minus infinity *)
        CEX; CEX; (* Performed twice for worst case *)
   end;
end.
```

Notice that in order to guarantee that after each iteration of the main
loop the maximum value in the pyramid is at the root, the CEX operation is
performed twice. By induction we can prove that during execution of the
main loop, the kth largest of the remaining values in the pyramid can be found
among the levels 0 to 2k. This implies that the largest element resides in
levels 0, 1 or 2. After executing CEX twice, we may be sure that the largest
is at the root, and that other high values have moved up, if necessary.

Pyramid Sort, like Heapsort [10.19], works by repeatedly selecting the
maximum element and adjusting the pyramid (like the heap) to make it easy
to find the next maximum. However, the pyramid contents seldom form an actual heap, because the "minus infinity" values trickle down from the root
and prevent the heap property from being satisfied. In theory, a true Heapsort could be implemented on the pyramid machine. However, such an implementation would be inelegant and offer no advantages over Pyramid Sort.

10.4 Median Filtering

10.4.1 Hierarchical Method

An interesting application of the method above for finding the kth largest
element of an image is in median filtering. Our goal is to take an input
image and produce an output image such that at every pixel P (except those
within a short distance of the border of the image), the output value is

the median over the neighborhood of P (where the dimensions of the neighborhood are given ahead of time). Let us assume that the neighborhood of P is defined to be the d by d block of pixels whose northwest corner is at P.

The pyramid machine algorithm for computing the median-filtered image works by repeatedly partitioning the image into a set of nonoverlapping windows that can be processed independently in parallel. The steps of the algorithm are as follows:

1. Let $m = round(d^2/2)$. Thus m is the rank order of the median.

2. Determine L1 such that $2^{(L1-1)} < d < 2^{L1} + 1$. This is the height of the subpyramids used to perform counting over local windows.

3. Let L2 = L-L1. We may consider each node at level L2 to be the root of a pyramid consisting of all its descendant cells.

4. Compute the mth largest value, where $m = (k^2)/2$, over these d by d blocks by taking z by z blocks where $z=2^{L1}$, and temporarily zeroing out all but the d by d subblocks in their upper left corners. Apply the parallel pyramid heapsort to find the mth largest values over these blocks. The sorts need not be completed once the values of rank m are found.

The computational effort for this method is of order bd^4 elementary operations where b is the maximum number of bits used to represent each pixel value and the medians are computed over d by d neighborhoods   This is easily seen by first noting that $(N/z)^2$ sorting operations are done in parallel using $O(bz^2)$ elementary operations, but that the filtering requires a total of N^2 local sorts (one for each pixel). Thus the parallel sorting operations must be executed z^2 times. Since d^2 is less than or equal to z^2 which is in turn less than $4d^2$, we have our result.

10.4.2 Other Methods

Another technique for computing local medians is to use the method of REEVES which employs a mesh-connected SIMD cellular array (the upper levels of the pyramid are not needed for this method). The method has a good growth rate, but is somewhat complicated to program.

Yet another method for computing local medians is to use a method of DANIELSSON [10.20], modified for the pyramid machine. The bit counting needed in refinement of the median can be made hierarchical. This results in the PEs on level L being freed up most of the time for possible concurrent operations (with a slightly modified control scheme in the hardware), with a similar running time.

Sorting N^2 numbers on a cellular array of N^2 processors can be accomplished in $O(N)$ comparison-exchange step times, using a method of THOMPSON and KUNG [10.21]. A program for their algorithm would be elaborate, but it also could serve as the basis for a median-filtering method. A detailed comparison of median filtering on flat and pyramidal array computers is the subject of a forthcoming paper.

10.5 Summary

The SIMD pyramid machine is a cellular array computer architecture which combines features of two-dimensional cellular logic array machines with those of tree machines. It can perform statistical operations on images very efficiently, usually requiring on the order of log N elementary steps for an N by N image. Algorithms have been described here for computing features via bit counting and for order statistics via hierarchical comparisons. A pyramid-sorting algorithm was described and its application to median filtering of images explained.

Acknowledgments

The author thanks J. J. Pfeiffer, Jr. for constructive discussions related to this paper.

References

10.1 S. L. Tanimoto, A. Klinger (eds.): Structured Computer Vision: Machine Perception Through Hierarchical Computation Structures (Academic Press, New York, 1980)

10.2 J. L. Bentley, H. T. Kung: "A Tree Machine for Searching Problems", Department of Computer Science Technical Report 79-142, Carnegie-Mellon University (1979)

10.3 A. Klinger, C. R. Dyer: Experiments on picture representation using regular decomposition, Computer Graphics Image Processing $\underline{5}$, 68-105 (1976)

10.4 G. M. Hunter, K. Steiglitz: Operations on images using quad trees, IEEE Trans. Pattern Analysis Machine Intelligence $\underline{PAMI-1}$, 145-153 (1979)

10.5 C. R. Dyer, A. Rosenfeld, H. Samet: Region representation: boundary codes from quadtrees, Comm. ACM $\underline{23}$, 171-179 (1980)

10.6 H. Samet: Region representation: quadtrees from boundary codes, Comm. ACM $\underline{23}$, 163-170 (1980)

10.7 A. R. Hanson, E. M. Riseman: "Design of a Semantically-Directed Vision Processor", Computer and Information Sciences Technical Report 74-1, University of Massachusetts (1974)

10.8 A. R. Hanson, E. M. Riseman: "Processing cones: a computational structure for image analysis", in Structured Computer Vision: Machine Perception Through Hierarchical Computation Structures, ed. by S. L. Tanimoto, A. Klinger (Academic Press, New York, 1980), pp. 101-131

10.9 C. R. Dyer: "A Quadtree Machine for Parallel Image Processing", Knowledge Systems Laboratory Technical Report KSL 51, University of Illinois at Chicago Circle (1981)

10.10 C. R. Dyer: "Augmented Cellular Automata for Image Analysis", Ph.D. dissertation, Department of Computer Science, University of Maryland (1979)

10.11 S. L. Tanimoto, T. Pavlidis: A hierarchical data structure for picture processing, Computer Graphics Image Processing $\underline{4}$, 104-119 (1975)

10.12 A. Klinger: "Patterns and search statistics", in Optimizing Methods in Statistics, ed. by J. S. Rustagi (Academic Press, New York, 1972), pp. 303-339

10.13 M. J. B. Duff: "CLIP 4: a large scale integrated circuit array parallel processor", in Proc. 3rd Int'l. Joint Conf. on Pattern Recognition, Coronado, CA, 1976, pp. 728-733

10.14 K. Preston, Jr., M. J. B. Duff, S. Levialdi, P. Norgren, J. I. Toriwaki: Basics of cellular logic with some applications in medical image processing, Proc. IEEE $\underline{67}$, 826-856 (1979)

10.15 S. L. Tanimoto: "Programming techniques for hierarchical parellel image processors", in Multicomputers and Image Processing: Algorithms and Programs, ed. by K. Preston, Jr., L. Uhr (Academic Press, New York, 1982) pp. 421-429

10.16 A. Reeves: Personal communication (1981)

10.17 C. R. Dyer: Computing the Euler number of an image from its quadtree, Computer Graphics Image Processing 13, 270-276 (1980)
10.18 T. Dubitzki, A. Y. Wu, A. Rosenfeld: Parallel region property computation by active quadtree networks, IEEE Trans. Pattern Analysis Machine Intelligence PAMI-3, 626-633 (1981)
10.19 D. E. Knuth: The Art of Computer Programming, Vol. 3: Sorting and Searching (Addison-Wesley, Reading, MA, 1973)
10.20 P. E. Danielsson: Getting the median faster, Computer Graphics Image Processing 17, 71-78 (1981)
10.21 C. D. Thompson, H. T. Kung: Sorting on a mesh-connected parallel computer, Comm. ACM 20, 263-270 (1982)

Part IV

Features and Shape Analysis

11. A Hierarchical Image Analysis System Based Upon Oriented Zero Crossings of Bandpassed Images

J.J. Clark and P.D. Lawrence

Department of Electrical Engineering, University of British Columbia
Vancouver, B.C. Canada V6T 1W5

In this paper the use of oriented zero crossings of bandpassed images as representational primitives for hierarchical operations is discussed. Some theoretical properties of oriented zero crossings are presented and a hardware system for the production of a zero-crossing "pyramid" is proposed. The hardware processor utilizes a set of "systolic" array processors which implement two-dimensional digital lowpass and bandpass filters as well as zero-crossing detectors and zero-crossing orientation measurements. A multilevel interleaved system is described which allows concurrent processing of two sets of image descriptions and ensures that the component processing elements are utilized to the fullest. Results provided by simulations of the system applied to real imagery are described.

11.1 Introduction

There has been much interest recently in the use of multiple levels of image resolution in image analysis systems. A review of early work in the field of "hierarchical" image processing is provided in [11.1]. Description of more recent research in this area can be found elsewhere in this volume.

This paper describes briefly the nature of hierarchical operations and discusses the ways in which information can be represented in these processes. In particular, the use of zero crossings of bandpassed images as representational primitives is discussed, illustrating some of the properties of these elements. A system for producing a hierarchical image description based on oriented zero crossings (zero-crossing pyramid) is presented. The design of a "systolic" processor implementation of this system is described which promises rapid computation of a low level image representation to be used in a hierarchical image analysis system.

11.1.1 Hierarchical Operations

Hierarchical operations (in this paper the term "hierarchy" refers to a spatial frequency or resolution hierarchy) are a means by which "global" information at one resolution can be found by local operations at another, lower spatial resolution. In the context of this paper, the terms "global" and "local" refer to image areas whose sizes are arbitrarily different, the global region being the larger of the two. Use of global information allows one to add constraints to a local operation which may otherwise be ambiguous. That is, the local operation may produce a number of answers, all of which appear to the local operator to be equally valid. The global information may be able to decide between them. The success of a system that uses such global information to guide local operations depends on the strength of the global information that is available and on the nature of the problem.

In a hierarchical system, the global information (at a given level in the hierarchy) is derived from a local operation at a lower resolution level. Hence the amount of computation required to obtain the global information is ostensibly equal to the amount of computation required for the local operation. Thus for a hierarchical system containing N levels, each having L times the resolution of the previous, and with the ratio of the areas of the global and local regions equal to L^2, the amount of computation required for a global process at the highest level compared to the amount of computation required for the same process in a nonhierarchical system is N/L^{2N-2}. Thus hierarchical operations can be much more efficient than single resolution systems. Of course, the preceding analysis assumes that the "global" information supplied by the lower resolution levels contains the same information that is used by the equivalent global operation acting on the highest-resolution image.

An unavoidable by-product of the process of obtaining a low resolution image from a high-resolution image is the loss of information. If this lost information is actually required by an operation, then this operation cannot be done hierarchically. Thus, it is clear that only a subset of all image analysis operations can hope to benefit from a hierarchical approach. However, as evidenced by the amount of research going on in the field of multiresolution image analysis as well as the increasing evidence for hierarchical processes in biological vision systems (see [11.2,3]), there are many types of useful image analysis operations which can be done hierarchically.

Many of these operations are so-called "search" operations. In these operations a search is performed for an image primitive that satisfies some given set of constraints. For example, a segmentation algorithm that operates by labelling all white (high gray level) pixels as belonging to a given region can be thought of as a search for all pixels that satisfy the whiteness constraint. Constraints can be specified in a variety of ways, but are usually posed as constraints on point properties (intensity, texture, color, etc.) and spatial properties (spatial relationship to other primitives, i.e., the primitives are part of an object O, part of a uniform region, at least r units away from the nearest primitive, etc.). The constraints can either be part of the search algorithm explicitly (as in find all white pixels) or they can be implicit in the definition of the image primitives (for example the spatial structure of the primitives supplies some constraints, as we will see later in the case of zero crossings).

In general, a hierarchical search algorithm operates by attempting to find image primitives that satisfy a set of constraints in a local region, and using the result to guide the search in a higher resolution image. Thus we can perform a global search using only local searches. Many important image analysis operations such as stereopsis [11.4], motion detection [11.5], and boundary finding [11.6] can be formulated as hierarchical search operations.

11.1.2 Hierarchical Image Primitives

In the above discussion we have mentioned the term "image primitive." This refers to a structural element created from the fundamental image source (e.g., a camera's gray level image description) upon which the hierarchical searches are based. In a hierarchical search algorithm we are searching for image primitives which satisfy a certain set of constraints. Having accepted this role for image primitives, we are now faced with the problem of defining the nature of the image primitives to be used in a given system.

The simplest image primitive is the pixel (or point) which can be para-meterized by a number of point functions such as intensity and color. A pixel by itself has no implicit spatial constraints so that if an algorithm requires these constraints it has to supply them. This can lead to very complex algorithms in some cases (e.g., in stereopsis the inherent spatial ambiguity between pixels of similar intensity is enormous [11.7]). One would prefer to use image primitives which had implicit spatial constraints in order to simplify the search algorithms. For example, if one used object surfaces as the image primitives, parameterized by intensity, color, and normal vector, the stereopsis problem would be simpler, chiefly because there is less ambiguity between the image primitives and hence a search for a given image primitive would be relatively easy. The price paid for this reduction in the search algorithm complexity is, of course, an increase in the complexity of the image primitive production process. This is a classic tradeoff and just where to draw the line is somewhat unclear. It seems likely that one should not go to either extreme (i.e., gray levels are too ambiguous and object descriptions are the end and not the means), but rather draw the line somewhere between them. It has been noted [11.1] that hierar-chical systems are best suited to "low level" parts of a vision system, where no symbolic assertions have been made at the object level.

11.1.3 Zero Crossings of Bandpassed Images as Image Primitives

For the applications our group is working on (stereopsis, motion detection, and contour extraction) we have decided to use small edge segments as our image primitives. Small edge segments can be parameterized by their orienta-tion and contrast. Recent work in stereopsis [11.8,9] and motion detection [11.10] have utilized edge segments as their basic descriptive elements.

To provide a set of edge segments at varying resolutions we use the zero crossings of bandpassed images, for a number of different center frequencies. Zero crossings of bandpassed images have a number of properties which make them useful image primitives for hierarchical operations. A basic property is provided by LOGAN's theorem [11.11]. This theorem states that the posi-tions of the zero crossings of a bandpassed one-dimensional signal, when the signal bandwidth is less than or equal to one octave, contain enough infor-mation to specify the signal to within a constant scale factor. MARR et al. [11.12] discuss the extension of LOGAN's theorem to two-dimensional functions as well as the relaxation of the one-octave bandwidth constraint to include signals of larger bandwidth.

If the bandpass filtering is produced by concatenating a low-pass filter with a Gaussian frequency response and a Laplacian operator (to give a $\nabla^2 G$ filter), then, as MARR and HILDRETH [11.13] have shown, the bandpass filter will respond optimally to intensity changes (edges) over a range of scales set by the filter's center frequency. Thus this second property of zero crossings means that using a set of $\nabla^2 G$ filters, each having a different center frequency, one can optimally detect edges over a large range of scales. Also this results naturally in a hierarchical description of the image intensity changes (and, because of LOGAN's theorem, a hierarchical image intensity description as well).

A third property of zero crossings of two-dimensional bandpass signals is that they "repel" each other. That is, there exist implicit spatial constraints on the zero crossings which state that there is a region about a given zero crossing for which the probability of finding another zero crossing is arbitrarily small. If we add zero-crossing orientation and contrast sign information to this constraint, then this region is much larger for a given probability. This effect can be illustrated by a graph of the probability density or distribution of the interval between two zero crossings of the same contrast sign (up-crossing or down-crossing) and orientation. Two approximations of the probability density and distribution are shown in Figs.11.1,2 for the case of 0° orientation and Q(0°)=0.15, where Q(θ) is the probability density of zero-crossing orientation. The signal was assumed to be Gaussian white noise filtered by a $\nabla^2 G$ filter with frequency response $F(\omega_1,\omega_2)=k(\omega_1^2+\omega_2^2)\exp(-\sigma^2(\omega_1^2+\omega_2^2))$. Approximation 1 is the result of using the formula used in [11.4] by GRIMSON. Approximation 2 is a more accurate result found by analytically summing the series [11.14]

$$P(\theta,\tau)= \sum_{\substack{n=2 \\ \text{even}}}^{\infty} P_{n-1}(\tau)R(n,\theta)$$

where $P_{n-1}(\tau)$ is as defined by LONGUET-HIGGINS [11.15] to be the probability density of the distance τ between the ith and the $(i+n)$th zero crossings.

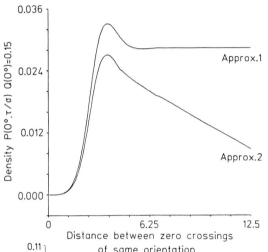

Fig. 11.1. Theoretical probability density function for the interval between successive zero crossings of same contrast sign and orientation (=0°)

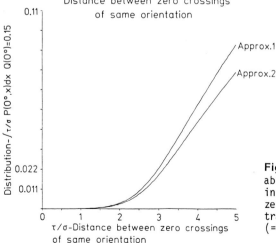

Fig. 11.2. Theoretical probability distribution for the interval between successive zero crossings of same contrast sign and orientation (=0°)

$R(n,\theta)$ is the probability that the ith and $(i+n)^{th}$ zero crossings have the same orientation θ while the $(i+1)st, (i+2)nd,...,(i+n-1)st$ zero crossings have angle $\theta\neq\theta_i$. If the zero-crossing orientations are assumed statistically independent then $R(n,\theta)$ is equal to $Q(\theta)(1-Q(\theta))^{n-1}$.

The probability distribution shown in Fig. 11.2 is an important parameter in stereopsis algorithms that use zero crossings as matching primitives as it gives the proportion of ambiguous matches that can be expected when searching in a region of given size.

11.2 A Hierarchical Zero-Crossing Extraction System

Based on the preceding discussion and on the inadequacy of hierarchical operations using other primitives for our applications, we decided to use oriented zero crossings of bandpassed images as the image primitives for our hierarchical system.

The specifications of our system were as follows:

- Four spatial frequency channels, having center frequencies ω_0, $2\omega_0$, $4\omega_0$ and $8\omega_0$.
- Basic low-level image primitives to be used are oriented zero crossings of the spatially bandpass filtered channels.
- The major analysis operations performed by the system are to be done hierarchically using the zero-crossing image representation.

In this section we discuss the implementation of the subsystem responsible for the production of the hierarchical zero-crossing image representation. This subsystem can be broken into two sections: the spatial filtering to produce the set of spatial frequency channels, and the zero-crossing detection and orientation calculation. The spatial filtering is performed as shown in Fig.11.3. The low-pass filter and subsampler sections form a two-dimensional decimator or sampling rate reducer. The low-pass filter restricts the maximum frequency of the image to one half its previous maximum, so that there will be no aliasing error when the filtered image is subsampled.

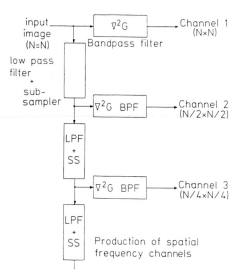

Production of spatial frequency channels

Fig. 11.3. Spatial filtering scheme to produce a spatial frequency image hierarchy

Each decimation stage reduces the number of image samples by a factor of 4 (2 in each of the horizontal and vertical directions). Each low-pass filter section has exactly the same set of filter coefficients. Each successive stage of the decimator is followed by a $\nabla^2 G$ bandpass filter. Even though the coefficients for each of these $\nabla^2 G$ filters are the same, the apparent frequency response of these filters with respect to the input have different values of σ due to the sampling rate reductions.

This scheme of spatial frequency channel production offers distinct advantages over the direct method in which the input signal is filtered by four separate bandpass filters, each having a different frequency response. The first, and probably least important advantage, is that only one set of filter coefficients is required for all the low-pass filters and for all the $\nabla^2 G$ filters. A more important advantage lies in the fact that the center frequency of the prototypical bandpass filter, with respect to the input, is fairly high, on the order of 1/4. In designing digital bandpass filters the number of coefficients required to approximate an ideal filter response to a given accuracy is inversely proportional to the center frequency. For example, in the direct method we would require a filter size on the order of 8N×8N for the lowest (fourth) spatial frequency channel filter (given that the highest frequency filter was of size N×N), compared to the N×N size filter required in the hierarchical scheme for all the channels. Of course, we must take into account the low-pass filters in the hierarchical case but these too will be of constant, not exponential, size. In addition, the structure of our hierarchical filtering system facilitates the pipelining of computation, as will be seen in a later section.

If we let the low-pass filter prototype have a frequency response $L(\omega_1,\omega_2)$ and the bandpass filter have a frequency response $B(\omega_1,\omega_2)$, then the frequency responses of the spatial frequency channels, referred to the input, are as follows:

$$H_1(\omega_1,\omega_2)=B(\omega_1,\omega_2)$$
$$H_2(\omega_1,\omega_2)=B(2\omega_1,2\omega_2)L(\omega_1,\omega_2)$$
$$H_3(\omega_1,\omega_2)=B(4\omega_1,4\omega_2)L(\omega_1,\omega_2)L(2\omega_1,2\omega_2)$$
$$H_4(\omega_1,\omega_2)=B(8\omega_1,8\omega_2)L(\omega_1,\omega_2)L(2\omega_1,2\omega_2)L(4\omega_1,4\omega_2) \ .$$

Also, due to the signal sampling, we have $B(\omega_1,\omega_2)=B(\omega_1+2\pi k,\omega_2+2\pi \ell)$ and $L(\omega_1,\omega_2)=L(\omega_1+2\omega k,\omega_2+2\pi \ell)$ for $k,\ell=\pm 1,2,3....$

The prototype two-dimensional low-pass filter was designed by transforming a one-dimensional low-pass filter using the MCCLELLAN transformation [11.16]. This transformation takes a one-dimensional filter with transfer function $F_1(\omega)$ and produces a two-dimensional filter with transfer function

$$F_2(\omega_1,\omega_2)=F_1(f(\omega_1,\omega_2))$$

where

$$f(\omega_1,\omega_2)=ARCOS[.5(COS(\omega_1)+COS(\omega_2)+COS(\omega_1)COS(\omega_2)-1)] \ .$$

This transformation preserves the optimality (if present) of the one-dimensional filter in the two-dimensional design. The one-dimensional filter was designed using the REMEZ exchange algorithm [11.17] to produce an optimal half-band low-pass filter (optimal in the sense that the peak approximation error to an ideal low-pass filter is minimized using a minimax criterion). The resulting one-dimensional filter, using 25 coefficients, is

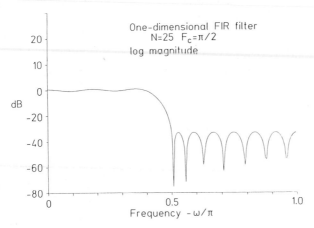

Fig. 11.4. One-dimensional prototype for the half-band low-pass filter: log magnitude frequency response

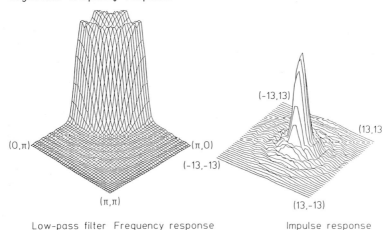

Low-pass filter Frequency response   Impulse response

Fig. 11.5. Impulse response and frequency response of the two-dimensional half-band low-pass filter

shown in Fig.11.4. The impulse and frequency response of the transformed two-dimensional filter is shown in Fig.11.5.

The peak sidelobe level of the low-pass filter is set by the number of coefficients used in the filter. For N=25 this level is about -33dB. One result of the MCCLELLAN transformation is that the resulting filter displays octant symmetry. Thus $L(\omega_1,\omega_2)=L(\omega_2,\omega_1)=L(\omega_1,-\omega_2)=L(-\omega_1,\omega_2)=L(\omega_2,-\omega_1)$ $=L(-\omega_2,\omega_1)=L(-\omega_1,-\omega_2)=L(-\omega_2,-\omega_1)$. This means that, for N odd, there are only $(N+1)^2/8+(N+1)/4$ unique filter coefficients instead of N^2. This can result in a large saving in computation and increased throughput if the symmetry is taken advantage of.

The prototype bandpass filter is, as mentioned earlier, a $\nabla^2 G$ filter with transfer function

$$B(\omega_1,\omega_2)=k(\omega_1^2+\omega_2^2)\exp(-\sigma^2(\omega_1^2+\omega_2^2)).$$

This type of filter has a bandwidth of about 1.2 octaves. Thus LOGAN's theorem does not hold exactly, but, as MARR et al. [11.12] have shown, the error induced is small. Frequently, one is not interested in obtaining image intensity reconstructions from the zero crossings, but only in using the zero crossings as edge indicators or structural descriptions. In such cases the loss of some image information may be allowed. In our system, the contrast across the zero crossing is also measured and this additional information may allow LOGAN's theorem to be extended to larger bandwidths [11.12].

The value of σ used in our prototype bandpass filter was $\sqrt{2}$. This value was chosen to trade off between high bandwidth (lower number of filter coefficients) and low aliasing error (due to the sampling of the ideal continuous filter).

The frequency response of the four spatial filters is shown in Figs. 11.6,7. One of the spatial frequency axes has been suppressed ($\omega_2=0$) for clarity. Figure 11.6 is a magnitude plot and Fig.11.7 is a log magnitude plot. Note that the peak sidelobe levels are less than -33dB in all cases.

Zero crossings are detected by scanning along horizontal lines (rasters) for the following occurrences:

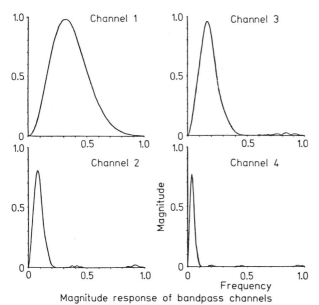

When one of these is found, a zero crossing is assigned to the position of the left pixel in cases 2 and 6, and to the zero pixel in the other cases.

Magnitude response of bandpass channels

Fig. 11.6. One-dimensional slice ($\omega_2=0$) of the two-dimensional half-band low-pass filter

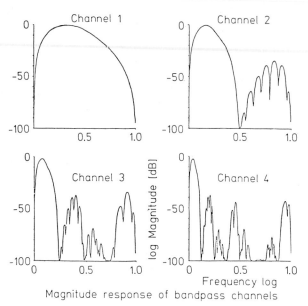

Magnitude response of bandpass channels

Fig. 11.7. One-dimensional slice ($\omega_2=0$) of the two-dimensional half-band low-pass filter: log magnitude

Note that this can introduce a "quantization" error into the zero-crossing position. In hierarchical systems this error will be only as large as the error in the highest spatial frequency channel, which may be small enough for many applications. If higher accuracy is needed interpolation may be performed at the highest spatial frequency level. To provide some measure of noise immunity, we ignore all zero crossings whose contrast falls below a given threshold. The threshold used will depend on the expected signal-to-noise ratio of the $\nabla^2 G$-filtered images (which in turn will depend on the processor word length and camera characteristics). In our 8-bit system we used a threshold of 20/255, as the majority of noise-like zero crossings fell below this threshold.

The zero-crossing orientation θ (measured with respect to the vertical) is found by determining the direction of zero gradient of the $\nabla^2 G$ output. If we let $\nabla(\nabla^2 G)=(f_x,f_y)$ then it can be shown that $\theta=\arctan(f_y,f_x)$. A note on the effects of spatial quantization on the distribution of zero crossings should be given here. The probability density shown in Fig.11.1 is for zero crossings along a straight line and assumes that arbitrarily close zero crossings can be resolved. When the zero-crossing position is quantized, as is the case in any digital system, only zero crossings whose orientations lie within 45° of the measurement axis will follow the predicted probability density. This can be seen in Fig.11.8. This shows that for $|\theta|$ greater than 45° there will be a large number of occurrences of zero crossings one unit apart, which are not predicted by the theory for continuous functions. Thus, if one is going to use the constraints implied by Figs.11.1,2 in a hierarchical algorithm, only those zero crossings with $|\theta|$ less than 45° can be used. If one does not use these constraints (as in boundary detection) then one can operate on all zero crossings that are detected.

156

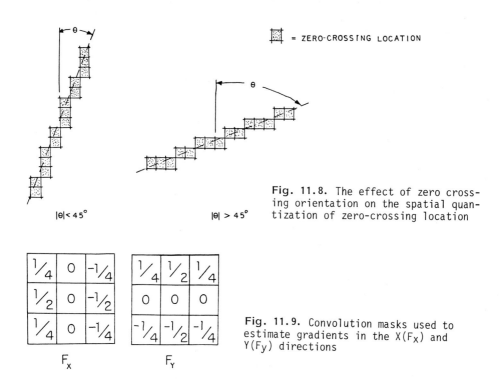

□ = ZERO-CROSSING LOCATION

$|\theta| < 45°$ $|\theta| > 45°$

Fig. 11.8. The effect of zero crossing orientation on the spatial quantization of zero-crossing location

$1/4$	0	$-1/4$
$1/2$	0	$-1/2$
$1/4$	0	$-1/4$

F_X

$1/4$	$1/2$	$1/4$
0	0	0
$-1/4$	$-1/2$	$-1/4$

F_Y

Fig. 11.9. Convolution masks used to
estimate gradients in the $X(F_X)$ and
$Y(F_Y)$ directions

The gradient values f_x and f_y are estimated in our system by convolving
the $\nabla^2 G$ images with a pair of 3×3 masks which are shown in Fig.11.9. The
masks are centered over the zero-crossing position.

11.2.1 Simulation Results

The hierarchical zero-crossing image description system described above was
simulated on an Amdahl 470 V/8 mainframe computer. Eight bits were used to
represent the filter coefficients and image data. The input test image is
shown in Fig.11.10a. This is a 256×256 pixel digitization of a scene containing highly textured, low contrast objects (logs). Figures 11.10b-d show
the decimator (low-pass filter and sub-sampler) output after each stage. The
pixel sizes are magnified for ease of viewing. Note the reduction of information at each level. Figure 11.11 shows the outputs of the $\nabla^2 G$ bandpass filters, and Fig.11.12 shows the outputs of the zero-crossing detectors for
each channel. The zero-crossing orientation is not shown. Black represents
negative contrasts, grey represents the absence of zero crossings, and white
represents positive contrast across the zero crossings. The measured probability density function for the zero-crossing interval is shown in Fig.11.13
(for $\theta=0°$). This graph contains data from four input images, each of which
were random dot binary images, with dot densities of 25 and 50 percent. Compare this to the theoretical densities shown in Fig.11.1. (Note: the zero-
crossing orientation calculation used in determining Fig.11.13 was a more
precise and computationally expensive method than the simple method described
here.)

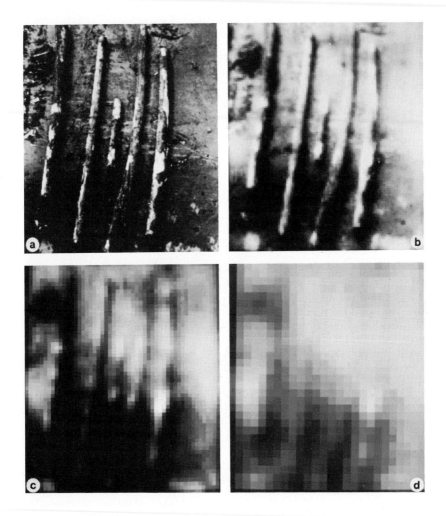

Fig. 11.10. (a) Input image (256 x 256 pixels)
(b) Output of first decimator stage (128 x 128 pixels)
(c) Output of second decimator stage (64 x 64 pixels)
(d) Output of third decimator stage (32 x 32 pixels)

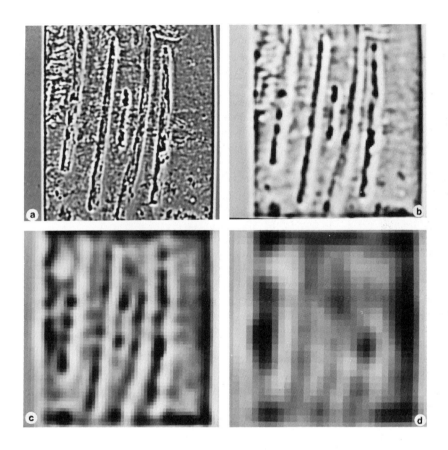

Fig. 11.11. **(a)** Output of first $\nabla^2 G$ filter stage (256 x 256 pixels)
(b) Output of second $\nabla^2 G$ filter stage (128 x 128 pixels)
(c) Output of third $\nabla^2 G$ filter stage (64 x 64 pixels)
(d) Output of fourth $\nabla^2 G$ filter stage (32 x 32 pixels)

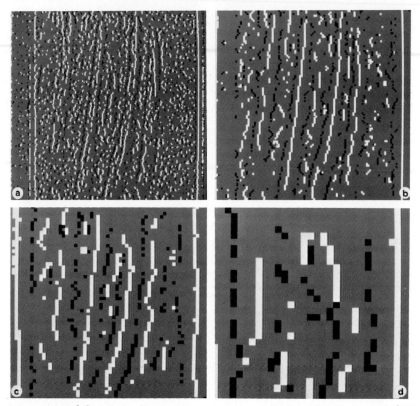

Fig. 11.12. **(a)** Output of the first zero-crossing detector channel (256 x 256 pixels)
(b) Output of the second zero-crossing detector channel (128 x 128 pixels)
(c) Output of the third zero-crossing detector channel (64 x 64 pixels)
(d) Output of the fourth zero-crossing detector channel (32 x 32 pixels)

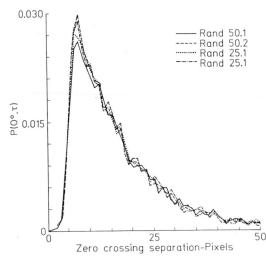

——— Rand 50.1
- - - - Rand 50.2
·········· Rand 25.1
-··-··- Rand 25.1

Fig. 11.13. Experimental probability density function of the interval between zero crossings having the same contrast sign and orientation (0°) measured for four different binary random dot images

11.3 A Proposed Hardware Implementation Using Systolic Processors

In designing vision systems for industrial applications, one is faced with two somewhat conflicting requirements. These are the need for high through-put and the need for small, economical systems. The first requirement is commonly dealt with by using large mainframe computing systems and the second requirement is satisfied by using small computing systems such as minicom-puters. Using mainframe computers is very expensive and is an inefficient use of computing resources, since they are usually not designed for dedi-cated applications. Mini- and micro-computers are economical but are much too slow for complex low-level vision processing.

The most efficient means of implementing industrial vision systems is in special-purpose dedicated hardware. These systems can be made as fast as,or faster than, a mainframe computer, and yet have a cost and size com-parable to a minicomputer. Drawbacks to using special-purpose hardware include large development costs (since one is not using predesigned compo-nents such as a minicomputer) and lack of computational flexibility.

A hardware structure that is special purpose, but can have low design cost and relative computational flexibility, is the so-called systolic array processor proposed by KUNG [11.18]. Systolic array processors are com-putational engines which consist of regular arrays of simple computational building blocks. Data and results flow through the array in a serial fashion through the "cells," much like the flow of blood in a human body (hence the term "systolic").

We will now describe a systolic implementation of the hierarchical zero-crossing extraction system described earlier. Throughout the design a word length of eight bits is used for the filter coefficients and image data (some intermediate results may have longer word lengths). Using eight bits for the $\nabla^2 G$ filter coefficients means that for $\sigma=\sqrt{2}$ the filter will have a size of 11×11 coefficients. All other coefficients, outside this 11×11 region, will be zero. The size of the low-pass filter is largely insensitive to the word length, and is mainly dependent on the required sidelobe attenuation. We took, as a design criterion, a peak sidelobe level of less than -30 dB. For a filter size of 25×25 the peak sidelobe level is -33 dB. A systolic array processor implementation of a two-dimensional convolver (for implementing the digital filters) is shown in Fig.11.14. The case shown is that of the $\nabla^2 G$ bandpass filter. The systolic convolver consists of an array of 121 computational elements or cells. There are four different types of cells (all based on a single cell type). Input data flows in one direction through the cells and results flow in the other direction. The filter coefficients do not move and each cell is associated with a certain filter coefficient. The shift registers buffer intermediate results and allow the convolution "window" to overlay the proper region of the image (this, in effect, trans-forms the linear parallel processor into a neighborhood parallel processor). The size of the shift register, in data words, is $S=M-N+Z$ where M is the size of one input image line (i.e., 256 pixels), N^2 is the number of filter coefficients, and Z is the number of zeros added to each line of the image. The zeros must be added to the end of each image line to prevent wraparound errors from occurring in the convolution near the edges of the image. Z must be at least $(N-1)/2$. The convolution is produced by each cell multiplying its input $x(n)$ by its resident filter coefficient $w(n)$, adding the result to the output $y(n)$ from the previous stage, and passing this sum along to the next cell in the array. By the time the first input value $x(1)$ has perco-lated to the last cell of the array, the first valid output $y(1)$ is available at the output of the first cell in the array. The total delay between data

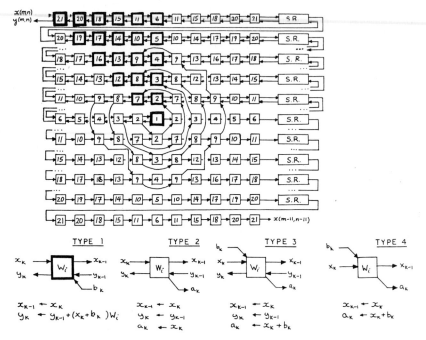

Fig. 11.14. A systolic array processor implementation of an 11 x 11 coefficient digital filter with octant symmetry

first entering the array and the first valid output is thus $N^2+(N-1)S$ cycles. However, because of the pipelined nature of the computation, after this delay time a valid output is generated every cycle.

Because the filter has octal symmetry, not all cells are required to perform multiplications. Only those cells bordered in black in Fig.11.14 are needed to do multiplications. There are $(N+1)^2/8+(N+1)/4$ of these "type 1" cells. Input values from every cell having the same coefficient (denoted by the numbers on the cells in Fig.11.14) are ripple-summed (i.e., asynchronously) in a cyclical manner (illustrated by the arrows in Fig.11.14) into the cell containing the multiplier where the sum is multiplied by the filter coefficient. Due to this use of symmetry, not all cells in the array are identical. There are four different types as shown in Fig.11.14. The internal structure of each cell is shown in Fig.11.15. Note that the computation, in this design, occurs in two stages. During clock phase ϕ_1 (ϕ_1 and ϕ_2 are nonoverlapping clock signals) the multiplier in the first cell is active and produces y_{k-1}. On the trailing edge of ϕ_1, the input data x_k and the result of computation y_{k-1} are strobed into the latches of the first cell. The second cell remains passive during ϕ_1 and becomes active during ϕ_2 (and the first cell becomes passive). In this manner valid outputs are generated every two cycles (a cycle being the time in which one of the two clock phases is active). The output stream is of the form aabbccdd... where a given output is repeated for two clock cycles. Note that the multipliers are active for only half of the time. To enable the multipliers to work al-

162

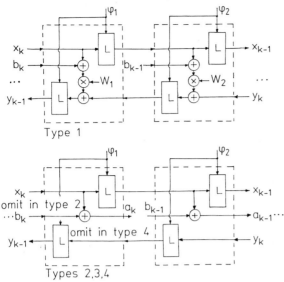

Type 1

Types 2,3,4

*Cell design*1*

Fig. 11.15. Internal structure of a systolic convolver computational element

most continuously we can use an interleaved structure, in which two data streams are interleaved into a single data stream and processed with a multiplexed cell. In this structure, data and results are clocked into one set of latches during ϕ_1 and into another set of latches during ϕ_2. Outputs are passed to adjacent cells from those latches that are not being strobed during a given cycle. This ensures that no race conditions are set up and that the data is stable when processed. The output data stream is now of the form $a_1b_1a_2b_2...$ where $a_1a_2...$ belongs to one data stream and $b_1b_2...$ belongs to the other. Notice that a valid output value is available every clock cycle, although for a given data stream a valid output value is available every second cycle. The multiplier in each cell now is active during each clock cycle. An interleaved scheme such as this allows the processing of stereo images concurrently, which minimizes the distortions induced by the motion of objects during the time between the processing of the two stereo images.

This interleaving provides a constraint on the length of the shift register. In order for each cell having the same coefficient to be operating on the same data stream (note that alternate cells operate on alternate data streams) at the same time, the shift register length must be even (for N odd).

We could implement the system shown in Fig.11.3 with a systolic processor for each of the filter blocks. However, the processors for the lower levels (lower spatial frequency) would be under-utilized since, due to the subsampling and the synchronous serial flow of data, the lower-level processors would only be active a fraction of the time. To reduce the processor idle time we can use a single systolic processor for all levels of each of the low-pass filter, bandpass filter, and zero-crossing detector. This is done by multiplexing the computation between each level. Due to the subsampling we need only compute on level 2 once for every four computations at level 1,

163

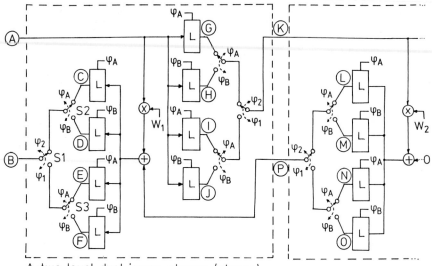

A two level-dual image stream (stereo)
systolic convolver processing element

Fig. 11.16. The internal structure of a two-level interleaved systolic
convolver computational element

once on level 3 for every four computations on level 2, and so on. Thus
the data stream would have the form $a_{11}b_{11}a_{12}b_{12}a_{13}b_{13}a_{14}b_{14}a_{21}b_{21}...$, where
a_{ij} is the jth data word of the first (of the two stereo images) data stream
on level i. The internal structure of a two-level interleaved processor is
shown in Fig.11.16. The circled letters represent points at which data values
are tabulated in Table 11.1 for sixteen successive clock cycles. Table 11.1 traces
the data flow and illustrates how the convolution operation is performed.
The clock phases used in our four-level system, which is a straightforward
extension of Fig.11.16, are shown in Fig.11.17. One can see how a given
processor acts on data at a given level once for every four computations
at the next highest level.

The nature of the subsampling (which is implemented purely by the timing
of the clock phases), combined with the specification that the shift register
lengths be even, results in a filtered image being sampled as shown in
Fig.11.18. One sample is retained in each 2×2 neighborhood, albeit in different locations within the neighborhoods.

The zeros that were added to the image are also subsampled by a factor
of 4 at each level. Thus, in order to have at least (N-1)/2 zeros per line
in the lowest spatial frequency channel (level L) we require a total of at
least $(2^{L-1}$ (N-1)/2) zeros added to each input line at the highest level.
Thus the number of zeros for a four-level system whose largest N value
(over all filters in the system) is 25 is Z=96. Therefore the shift registers must have a length of at least 256-25+96=327. And since S must be
even we set S=328.

The overall operation of the hierarchical zero-crossing extraction system
is shown in Fig.11.19. The total delay from the time the first camera data

Table 11.1.

$\emptyset_1$	$\emptyset_2$	$\emptyset_A$	$\bar\emptyset_A$	$\emptyset_B$	$\bar\emptyset_B$	A	B	C	D	E	F	G	H	I	J	K	L	M	N	O	P
1	0	0	1	0	1	a	0	aw_1	0	0	0	a	0	0	0	0	0	0	0	0	0
0	1	0	1	0	1	b	aw_1	aw_1	0	bw_1	0	a	0	0	0	a	0	0	aw_2	0	0
1	0	1	0	0	1	c	0	aw_1	cw_1	bw_1	dw_1	a	c	b	0	b	0	0	aw_2	0	0
0	1	1	0	0	1	d	cw_1	aw_1	cw_1	bw_1	dw_1	a	c	b	d	c	0	0	aw_2	cw_2	0
1	0	0	1	0	1	e	dw_1	aw_1	(ew_1+cw_2)	bw_1	dw_1	a	e	b	d	d	0	dw_2	aw_2	cw_2	cw_2
0	1	0	1	0	1	f	(ew_1+cw_2)	aw_1	(ew_1+cw_2)	bw_1	(fw_1+dw_2)	a	e	b	f	e	0	dw_2	aw_2	ew_2	dw_2
1	0	0	1	0	1	g	(fw_1+dw_2)	aw_1	(gw_1+ew_2)	bw_1	(fw_1+dw_2)	a	g	b	f	f	0	fw_2	aw_2	ew_2	ew_2
0	1	0	1	0	1	h	(gw_1+ew_2)	aw_1	(gw_1+ew_2)	bw_1	(hw_1+fw_2)	a	g	b	h	g	0	fw_2	aw_2	gw_2	fw_2
1	0	0	1	0	1	i	(hw_1+fw_2)	aw_1	(iw_1+gw_2)	bw_1	(hw_1+fw_2)	a	i	b	h	h	0	hw_2	aw_2	gw_2	gw_2
0	1	0	1	0	1	j	(iw_1+gw_2)	aw_1	(iw_1+gw_2)	bw_1	(jw_1+hw_2)	a	i	b	j	i	0	hw_2	aw_2	iw_2	hw_2
1	0	0	1	1	0	k	bw_1	(kw_1+aw_2)	(iw_1+gw_2)	bw_1	(jw_1+hw_2)	k	k	∝	j	j	bw_2	hw_2	aw_2	iw_2	aw_2
0	1	0	1	1	0	ℓ	(kw_1+bw_2)	(kw_1+aw_2)	(iw_1+gw_2)	(ℓw_1+bw_2)	(jw_1+hw_2)	k	k	∝	j	k	bw_2	hw_2	kw_2	iw_2	bw_2
1	0	0	1	1	0	m	(jw_1+hw_2)	(kw_1+aw_2)	(mw_1+iw_2)	(ℓw_1+bw_2)	(jw_1+hw_2)	k	m	∝	m	ℓ	bw_2	jw_2	kw_2	iw_2	iw_2
0	1	0	1	1	0	n	(mw_1+iw_2)	(kw_1+aw_2)	(mw_1+iw_2)	(ℓw_1+bw_2)	(nw_1+jw_2)	k	m	∝	n	m	bw_2	nw_2	kw_2	mw_2	jw_2
1	0	0	1	1	0	o	(nw_1+jw_2)	(kw_1+aw_2)	(ow_1+mw_2)	(ℓw_1+bw_2)	(nw_1+jw_2)	k	o	∝	n	n	bw_2	nw_2	kw_2	mw_2	mw_2
0	1	0	1	1	0	p	(ow_1+mw_2)	(kw_1+aw_2)	(ow_1+mw_2)	(ℓw_1+bw_2)	(pw_1+nw_2)	k	0	∝	p	o	bw_2	nw_2	kw_2	ow_2	nw_2

165

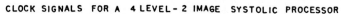
CLOCK SIGNALS FOR A 4 LEVEL-2 IMAGE SYSTOLIC PROCESSOR

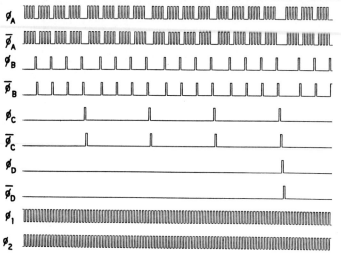

Fig. 11.17. Relation between clock phases in a four-level interleaved systolic convolver

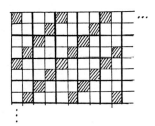

☒ = SAMPLED PIXEL

Fig. 11.18. The form of the subsampling process

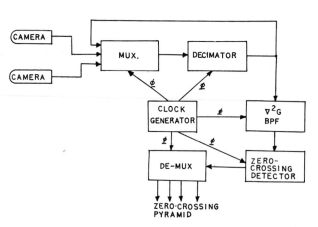

Fig. 11.19. Overview of the hierarchical zero-crossing extraction system

166

word is input to the low-pass filter to the time the first output from the lowest level on the zero-crossing detector is available is given by $\tau=(4N_L+N_B+N_Z)T$ where $N_L=25$, $N_B=11$, $N_Z=3$, and T is the number of clock cycles needed to process a single line of data (of length $N_L+S=353$). T is the number of clock cycles between fourth-level clock pulses times the number of fourth-level clock pulses that occur in processing a single image line. Thus T= 178*353/64=1068 (rounding up). Thus the total delay τ is about 121,752 clock cycles. After this initial delay a new output value is available every clock cycle. An entire zero-crossing pyramid is available in 2*353*(256+128+64+32+4*96)=609,984 clock cycles (not counting original delay). Thus at a cycle time of 100 nsec a stereo zero-crossing pyramid is available every 61 msec, or about 16 times a second. Cycle time is chiefly dependent on the multiplier speed and clever multiplier design (such as pipelining the multiplier itself) may bring down the cycle time.

11.4 Future Work and Summary

We are presently examining the design of computational elements, such as those that make up the systolic array processor, for implementation in VLSI circuitry (for which the regularity inherent in the systolic approach makes it well suited). We are also designing and evaluating hierarchical algorithms for depth and motion perception which utilize zero-crossing image descriptions. The resulting system will be tailored for industrial applications, particularly in materials-handling applications such as found in the forestry industry.

This paper illustrates some properties of oriented zero crossings of band-passed images which make them useful image primitives for hierarchical image analysis operations. Algorithms for the digital implementation of a system for the extraction of a zero-crossing image representation are detailed and simulations shown. A hardware system design of this system utilizing a pipelined, multilevel, interleaved systolic array processor is described.

Acknowledgments

The authors gratefully acknowledge the support and services provided by the Forest Engineering Research Institute of Canada (FERIC) in this study. Funding was also supplied by a grant from the Natural Sciences and Engineering Research Council of Canada (NSERC) (Grant A-9341). The authors also wish to thank Block Brothers Realty Co. for the use of their digitization equipment. The image processing experiments described herein were performed at the Laboratory for Computational Vision in the Computer Science Department of the University of British Columbia.

References

11.1 S. L. Tanimoto: "Regular hierarchical image and processing structures in machine vision", in Computer Vision Systems, ed. by A. R. Hanson, E. M. Riseman (Academic Press, New York, 1978), pp. 165-174
11.2 F. W. Campbell, G. F. Cooper, C. Enroth-Cugell: The spatial selectivity of the visual cells of the cat, J. Physiology (London) 203, 223-236 (1969)
11.3 C. Blakemore, F. W. Campbell: On the existence of neurons in the human visual system selectively sensitive to the orientation and size of retinal images, J. Physiology (London) 203, 237-260 (1969)

11.4 D. Marr, T. Poggio: A computational theory of human stereo vision, Proc. Royal Society (London) B204, 301-328 (1979)

11.5 D. Marr, S. Ullman: Directional selectivity and its use in early visual processing, Proc. Royal Society (London) B211, 151-180 (1981)

11.6 M. D. Kelly: "Edge detection in pictures by computer using planning" in Machine Intelligence 6, ed. by B. Meltzer, D. Michie (Edinburgh University Press, Edinburgh, UK, 1971), pp. 379-409

11.7 R. Nevatia: Depth measurement by motion stereo, Computer Graphics Image Processing 5, 203-214 (1976)

11.8 W. E. L. Grimson: A computer implementation of a theory of human stereo vision, Philosophical Trans. Royal Society (London) B292, 217-253 (1981)

11.9 H. H. Baker, T. O. Binford: "Depth from edge and intensity based stereo," in Proc. 7th Intl. Joint Conf. Artificial Intelligence, Vancouver, BC, 1981, pp. 631-636

11.10 S. Ullman: Analysis of visual motion by biological and computer systems, Computer 14 (8), 57-69 (1981)

11.11 B. F. Logan: Information in the zero crossings of bandpass signals, Bell System Technical J. 56, 487-510 (1977)

11.12 D. Marr, S. Ullman, T. Poggio: Bandpass channels, zero crossings, and early visual information processing, J. Optical Society America 69, 914-916 (1979)

11.13 D. Marr, E. Hildreth: Theory of edge detection, Proc. Royal Society (London) B207, 187-217 (1980)

11.14 J. Clark: Ph.D. dissertation, University of British Columbia, in preparation

11.15 M. S. Longuet-Higgins: The distribution of intervals between zeros of a stationary random function, Philosophical Trans. Royal Society (London) A254, 557-599 (1962)

11.16 J. H. McClellan: "The design of two-dimensional digital filters by transformations", in Proc. 7th Princeton Conf. on Information Sciences and Systems (1973)

11.17 J. H. McClellan, T. W. Parks, L. R. Rabiner: A complete program for designing optimum FIR linear phase digital filters, IEEE Trans. Audio Electroacoustics AU-21, 506-526 (1973)

11.18 H. T. Kung: Why systolic architectures?, Computer 15(1), 37-46 (1982)

12. A Multiresolution Representation for Shape

J.L. Crowley

C-MU Robotics Institute, Carnegie-Mellon University
Pittsburgh, PA 15213, USA

This paper defines a multiple-resolution representation for shape. The representation is constructed by detecting peaks and ridges in the Difference of Low-Pass (DOLP) transform. Descriptions of shape which are encoded in this representation may be matched efficiently despite changes in size, orientation, or position.

The concept of a representation is introduced first, followed by the definition of the DOLP transform. Techniques are then presented for encoding a symbolic structural description of shape from the DOLP transform. This process involves detecting local peaks and ridges in each bandpass image and in the entire three-dimensional space defined by the DOLP transform. Linking adjacent peaks in different bandpass images gives a multiple resolution tree which describes shape. Peaks which are local maxima in this tree provide landmarks for aligning, manipulating, and matching shapes. Detecting and linking the ridges in each DOLP bandpass image provides a graph which links peaks within a shape in a bandpass image and describes the positions of the boundaries of the shape at multiple resolutions. Detecting and linking the ridges in the DOLP three-space describes elongated forms and links the largest peaks in the tree.

Principles and techniques for finding the correspondence between symbols in two descriptions of shape are described. An example is presented in which the correspondence is shown for the descriptions of a stereo pair of paper wad images.

12.1 Introduction

A representation is a <u>formal system</u> for making explicit certain entities or types of information, and a specification of how the system does this [12.1]. Representation plays a crucial role in determining the computational complexity of an information-processing problem.

This paper describes a representation for two-dimensional shape which can be used for a variety of tasks in which the shapes (or gray-level forms) in an image must be manipulated. An important property of this representation is that it makes the task of comparing the structure of two shapes to determine the correspondence of their components computationally simple. However, this representation has other desirable properties as well. For example,

---

*This research was partially supported by the C-MU Robotics Institute, National Science Foundation Grant APR-75-08154, and Naval Electronics System Command (NELC) Grant N00039-79-Z-0169.

the network of symbols that describes a shape in this representation has a structure which, except for the effects of quantization, is invariant to the size, orientation, and position of a shape. Thus a shape can be compared to prototypes without having to normalize its size or orientation. An object can be tracked in a sequence of images by matching the largest peak(s) in its description in each image. This representation can also describe a shape when its boundaries are blurred or poorly defined or when the image has been corrupted by various sources of image noise.

This representation is based on a reversible transform referred to as the "Difference of Low-Pass" (DOLP) transform. From its definition, the DOLP transform of an image appears to be very costly to compute. However, several techniques can be used to reduce greatly the computational complexity and memory requirements for a DOLP transform. These techniques, together with the definition of the DOLP transform, are presented in [12.2].

The Difference of Low-Pass (DOLP) transform is a reversible transform which converts an image into a set of bandpass images. Each bandpass image is equivalent to a convolution of the original image with a bandpass filter b_k. Each bandpass filter is formed by a difference of two size-scaled copies of a low-pass filter, g_{k-1} and g_k:

$$b_k = g_{k-1} - g_k \; .$$

Each low-pass filter g_k is a copy of the low-pass filter g_{k-1} scaled larger in size. These bandpass images comprise a three-space (the DOLP space). The representation is constructed by detecting peaks and ridges in the DOLP space.

12.1.1 Motivation: A Multiresolution Structural Description of Images

Peaks and ridges in a DOLP transform provide a structural description of the gray-scale shapes in an image. Matching the structural descriptions of shapes in images is an efficient approach for determining the three-dimensional structure of objects from stereo pairs of images and from motion sequences of images [12.3]. Matching to a prototype description of an object class is also useful for recognizing shapes in both two-dimensional and three-dimensional image domains [12.4].

The motivation for computing a structural description is to spend a fixed computational cost to transform the information in each image into a representation in which searching and matching are more efficient. In many cases the computation involved in constructing a structural description is regular and local, making the computation amenable to fast implementation in special-purpose hardware.

Several researchers have shown that the efficiency of searching and matching processes can be dramatically improved by performing the search at multiple resolutions. MORAVEC [12.5] has demonstrated a multiresolution correspondence matching algorithm for object location in stereo images. MARR and POGGIO [12.3] have demonstrated correspondence matching using edges detected by a difference of Gaussian filters at four resolutions. ROSENFELD and VANDERBRUG [12.6] have described a two-stage hierarchical template-matching algorithm. HALL [12.7] has reported using a multiresolution pyramid to dramatically speed up correlation of aerial images.

There is also experimental evidence that the visual systems of humans and other mammals separate images into a set of "spatial frequency" channels as a first encoding of visual information. This "multi-channel theory" is based on measurements of the adaption of the threshold sensitivity to vertical sinusoidal functions of various frequencies [12.8,9]. Adaption to a sinusoid of a particular frequency affects only the threshold sensitivity for frequencies within one octave. This evidence suggests that mammalian visual systems employ a set of bandpass channels with a bandwidth of about one octave. Such a set of channels would carry information from different resolutions in the image. These studies, and physiological experiments supporting the concept of parallel spatial frequency analysis, are reviewed in [12.10,11].

12.1.2 Properties of the Representation

The patterns which are described by this representation are "gray-scale shapes" or "forms." We prefer the term "forms," because the term "shape" carries connotations of the outline of a uniform intensity region. It is not necessary for a pattern to have a uniform intensity for it to have a well-defined description in this representation. In this paper we will use the term "form" to refer to the patterns in an image.

In this representation, a form is described by a tree of symbols which represent the structure of the form at every resolution. There are four types of symbols {M,L,P,R}[1] which mark locations (x,y,k) in the DOLP three-space where a bandpass filter of radius R_k is a local "best fit" to the form.

Figure 12.1 shows an example of the use of peaks and ridges for representing a uniform intensity form. This figure shows the outline of a dark rhomboid on a light background. Circles illustrate the positions and radii of bandpass filters whose positive center lobes best fit the rhomboid. Below the rhomboid is part of the graph produced by detecting and linking peaks and ridges in the sampled DOLP transform. The meaning of the symbols in this graph is described below.

A description in this representation contains a small number of symbols at the root. These symbols describe the global (or low-frequency) structure of a form. At lower levels, this tree contains increasingly larger numbers of symbols which represent more local details. The correspondence between

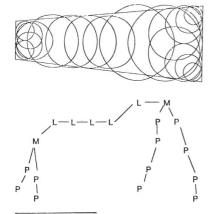

Fig. 12.1. A rhomboidal form and its representation . In the upper part of this figure the rhomboidal form is outlined in solid straight lines. The description is for a form which is dark on a light background. Circles indicate the locations and sizes where the bandpass filters from a sampled DOLP transform produced 3-space peaks (M nodes), 2-space peaks (P nodes), and 3-space ridges (L nodes). The structure of the resulting description is shown in the lower part of the figure. The description of the "negative shape" which surround this form is not presented

1. In previous writing about this representation, most notably in [12.12], these symbols were referred to by the names {M*,L,M,P}.

symbols at one level in the tree constrains the possible set of correspondences at the next higher resolution level.

The description is created by detecting local positive maxima and negative minima in one dimension (ridges) and two dimensions (peaks) in each
bandpass image of a DOLP transform. Local peaks in the DOLP three-space
define locations and sizes at which a DOLP bandpass filter best fits a gray-
scale pattern. These points are encoded as symbols which serve as landmarks
for matching the information in images. Peaks of the same sign which are in
adjacent positions in adjacent bandpass images are linked to form a tree.
During the linking process, the largest peak along each branch is detected.
The largest peak serves as a landmark which marks the position and size of
a gray-scale form. The paths of the other peaks which are attached to such
landmarks provide further description of the form, as well as continuity
with structure at other resolutions. Further information is encoded by
detecting and linking two-dimensional ridge points in each bandpass image
and three-dimensional ridge points within the DOLP three-space. The ridges
in each bandpass image link the peaks in that image which are part of the
same form. The three-dimensional ridges link the largest peaks that are part
of the same form and provide a description of elongated forms.

12.2   The Difference of Low-Pass Transform

This section defines the Difference of Low-Pass (DOLP) transform and demon-
states its reversibility. A fast algorithm is then described for computing
the DOLP transform.

12.2.1   The Purpose of the DOLP Transform

The DOLP transform expresses the image information at a discrete set of resolutions in a manner which preserves all of the image information. This transform separates local forms from more global forms in a manner that makes no
assumptions about the scales at which significant information occurs. The
DOLP filters overlap in the frequency domain; thus there is a smooth variation from each bandpass level to the next. This "smoothness" makes size-
independent matching of forms possible and makes it possible to use the symbols from one bandpass level to constrain the correspondence of symbols at
the next (higher resolution) level.

12.2.2   Definition of the DOLP Transform

The DOLP transform expands an $N=M \times M$ image signal $p(x,y)$ into $\text{Log}_S (N)$ bandpass
images $B_k(x,y)$. Each bandpass image is equivalent to a convolution of the
image $p(x,y)$ with a bandpass impulse response $b_k(x,y)$:

$$B_k(x,y) = p(x,y) * b_k(x,y) .$$

For $k=0$, the bandpass filter is formed by subtracting a circularly symmetric low-pass filter $g_0(x,y)$ from a unit sample positioned over the center
coefficient at the point $(0,0)$:

$$b_0(x,y) = \delta(x,y) - g_0(x,y) .$$

---

2. S is the square of the scale factor.

The filter $b_0(x,y)$ gives a high-pass image $B_0(x,y)$. This image is equivalent to the result produced by the edge detection technique known as "unsharp masking" [12.13]:

$$B_0(x,y) = p(x,y) * (1-g_0(x,y))$$

$$= p(x,y)-(p(x,y) * g_0(x,y)) .$$

For bandpass levels $1 \leq k < K$ the bandpass filter is formed as a difference of two size-scaled copies of the low-pass filter:

$$b_k(x,y) = g_{k-1}(x,y)-g_k(x,y) .$$

In order for the configuration of peaks in a DOLP transform of a form to be invariant to the size of the form, it is necessary that each low-pass filter $g_k(x,y)$ be a copy of the circularly symmetric low-pass filter $g_0(x,y)$ scaled larger in size by a scale factor raised to the kth power [12.12]. Thus for each k, the bandpass impulse response $b_k(x,y)$ is a size-scaled copy of the bandpass impulse responce $b_{k-1}(x,y)$.

The scale factor is an important parameter. For a two-dimensional DOLP transform, this scale factor, denoted S_2, has a typical value of $\sqrt{2}$. For two-dimensional circularly symmetric filters which are defined by sampling a continuous function, size scaling increases the density of sample points over a fixed domain of the function. In the Gaussian filter, this increases the standard deviation σ relative to the image sample rate by a factor of S_2^k.

It is possible to define a DOLP transform with any scale factor S_2 for which the difference of low-pass filter provides a useful pass band. MARR, for example, argues that a scale factor of $S_2=1.6$ is optimum for a difference of Gaussian filters [12.14]. We have found that a scale factor $S_2=\sqrt{2}$ yields effectively the same bandpass filter and provides two other interesting properties [12.12].

First, resampling each bandpass image at a sample distance which is a fixed fraction of the filter's size provides a configuration of peaks and ridges in each bandpass image which is invariant to the size of the object, except for the effects of quantization. The smallest distance at which a two-dimensional signal can be resampled is $\sqrt{2}$. Second, a DOLP transform can be computed using Gaussian low-pass filters. The convolution of a Gaussian filter with itself produces a new Gaussian filter which is scaled larger in size by a factor of $\sqrt{2}$. These two properties make S_2 a convenient value for the scale factor.

In principle the DOLP transform can be defined for any number of bandpass levels K. A convenient value of K is

$$K = Log_S(N)$$

where the value S is the square of the sample distance S_2:

$$S = S_2^2 .$$

This value of K is the number of bandpass images that result if each bandpass image B_k is resampled at a sampling distance of S_2^k. With this resampling, the Kth image contains only one sample.

The DOLP transform is reversible which proves that no information is lost. The original image may be recovered by adding all of the bandpass images, plus a low-pass residue. This low-pass residue, which has not been found to be useful for describing the image, is the convolution of the lowest frequency (largest) low-pass filter $g_K(x,y)$ with the image:

$$p(x,y) = (p(x,y) * g_K(x,y)) + \sum_{k=0}^{K-1} B_k(x,y) \ .$$

12.2.3 Fast Computation Techniques: Resampling and Cascade Convolution

A full DOLP transform of an image composed of N samples produces $K = Log_S(N)$ bandpass images of N samples each, and requires $O(N^2)$ multiplies and additions. Two techniques can be used to reduce the computational complexity of the DOLP transform: "resampling" and "cascaded convolution with expansion."

Resampling is based on the fact that the filters used in a DOLP transform are scaled copies of a band-limited filter. As the filter's impulse response becomes larger, its upper cutoff frequency decreases, and thus its output can be resampled with coarser spacing without loss of information. The exponential growth in the number of filter coefficients which results from the exponential scaling of size is offset by an exponential growth in distance between points at which the convolution is computed. The result is that each bandpass image may be computed with the same number of multiplications and additions. Resampling each bandpass image at a distance of $\sqrt{2}$ reduces the total number of points in the DOLP space from N $Log_S(N)$ samples to 3N samples.

Cascaded convolution exploits the fact that the convolution of a Gaussian function with itself produces a Gaussian scaled larger by $\sqrt{2}$. This method also employs "expansion," in which the coefficients of a filter are mapped into a larger sample grid, thereby expanding the size of the filter, at the cost of introducing reflections of the pass region about a new NYQUIST boundary in the transfer function of the filter. This operation does not introduce distortion, provided the filter is designed so that the reflections of the pass region fall on the stop region of the composite filter and are sufficiently attenuated so as to have a negligible effect on the composite filter.

Combining these two techniques gives an algorithm which will compute a DOLP transform of an N-sample signal in $O(N)$ multiplies, producing 3N sample points. This algorithm is described in [12.2]. In this algorithm, each low-pass image is resampled at $\sqrt{2}$ and then convolved with the low-pass filter g_0 to form the next low-pass image. Since each low-pass image has half the number of samples as the previous low-pass image, and the number of filter coefficients is constant, each low-pass image is computed from the previous low-pass image using half the number of multiplies and additions. Thus, if C_0 is the number of multiplies required to compute low-pass image 0, the total number of multiplies needed to compute K bandpass levels is given by

$$C_{Tot} = C_0(1 + 1 + 1/2 + 1/4 + 1/8 + 1/16 + \ldots + 1/K)$$

$$\approx 3C_0 \ .$$

Each low-pass image is then subtracted from the resampled version of the previous low-pass image to form the band-pass image. Thus each bandpass image has a sample density which is proportional to the size of its impulse response.

12.2.4 The Algorithm and Complexity Analysis

The algorithm for resampling and cascaded convolution with expansion is illustrated in the data flow graph shown in Fig.12.2. This algorithm runs

174

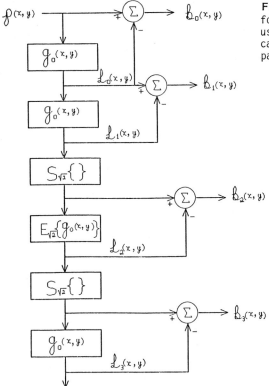

Fig. 12.2. Data flow graph for composite fast algorithm using resampling and cascaded convolution with expansion

as follows. Low-pass and bandpass levels 0 and 1 are computed as described above for cascaded convolution with expansion. That is, low-pass level 0 is constructed by convolving the picture with the low-pass filter $g_0(x,y)$:

$$L_0(x,y) = p(x,y) * g_0(x,y) .$$

Bandpass level 0, $B_0(x,y)$, is then produced by subtracting $L_0(x,y)$ from $p(x,y)$:

$$B_0(x,y) = p(x,y)-L_0(x,y) .$$

Thus the bandpass impulse response at level 0 is

$$b_0(x,y) = \delta(x,y)-g_0(x,y) .$$

Low-pass level 1 is then formed by convolving low-pass level 0 with the low-pass filter:

$$L_1(x,y) = L_0(x,y) * g_0(x,y) .$$

Bandpass level 1 is then formed by subtracting low-pass level 1 from low-pass level 0:

$$B_1(x,y) = L_0(x,y)-L_1(x,y) .$$

The impulse response at bandpass level 1 is

$$b_1(x,y) = g_0(x,y) - (g_0(x,y) * g_0(x,y)) .$$

Both bandpass level 0 and bandpass level 1 require $X_0 N$ multiplies and $(X_0+1)N$ additions. They each produce N bandpass samples.

For each bandpass level 2 through K-1, the low-pass image k-1 is first resampled at $\sqrt{2}$ by the operation $S_{\sqrt{2}}\{.\}$. This resampling reduces the number of sample points by a factor of 2 from the low-pass image at k-1. For odd levels, resampling leaves the data on a Cartesian grid, and thus no expansion is necessary. The low-pass image or level k is thus formed by simply convolving the filter with the low-pass image from level k-1:

$$L_k(x,y) = L_{k-1}(x,y) * g_0(x,y) .$$

On even levels, resampling places the data onto a $\sqrt{2}$ sample grid. To convolve an image on a $\sqrt{2}$ sample grid, the low-pass filter coefficients must be remapped to a $\sqrt{2}$ grid by the expansion operation:

$$L_k(x,y) = L_{k-1}(x,y) * E_{\sqrt{2}}\{g_0(x,y)\} .$$

In both cases the bandpass image is then formed by subtracting the result of the convolution from the previous low-pass image:

$$B_k(x,y) = L_{k-1}(x,y) - L_k(x,y) .$$

For $S_2 = \sqrt{2}$, each resampling reduces the number of sample points by 2, and thus reduces the number of multiplies and additions by a factor of 2. Thus the total number of multiplies and additions is given by

$$C = X_0 N(1 + 1 + 1/2 + 1/4 + 1/8 + ...)$$

$$= 3NX_0 \text{ multiplies}$$

and

$$3N(X_0 + 1) \text{ additions.}$$

As with the resampling algorithm described above, the total number of memory cells required is

$$M = 3N .$$

12.2.4.1 The Impulse Responses for Cascaded Convolution with Expansion and Resampling

In the cascaded filtering algorithms described above, the bandpass images are formed by subtracting adjacent low-pass images. The bandpass impulse responses are thus equal to a difference of low-pass impulse responses which are produced by cascaded filtering. Because a finite impulse response Gaussian filter is only an approximation of the Gaussian function, the low-pass impulse responses for levels 1 through K are only approximations of scaled copies of the level 0 low-pass impulse response.

The low-pass impulse response at level 1 is

$$g_1(x,y) = g_0(x,y) * g_0(x,y) .$$

176

Thus at low-pass level 1, a $\sqrt{2}$ scaling in size of $g_0(x,y)$ is approximated by the simple cascaded convolution of $g_0(x,y)$.

Low-pass level 2 is formed by resampling low-pass level 1 at a sample distance of $\sqrt{2}$ and then convolving with an expanded version of the low-pass filter $g_0(x,y)$:

$$g_2(x,y) = E_{\sqrt{2}}\{g_0(x,y)\} * S_{\sqrt{2}}\{g_0(x,y) * g_0(x,y)\} .$$

The low-pass image from level 2 is then resampled at a distance of $\sqrt{2}$ for a second time, which places it on a sample grid with a unit distance of 2. This low-pass image is then convolved with the low-pass filter $g_0(x,y)$. The resampling provides a remapping of the filter coefficients and so no expansion is needed at this level. Thus the size scaling of g_0 by a factor of $2\sqrt{2}$ is approximated by

$$g_3(x,y) = g_0(x,y) * S_{\sqrt{2}}\{E_{\sqrt{2}}\{g_0(x,y)\} * S_{\sqrt{2}}\{g_0(x,y) * g_0(x,y)\}\}.$$

In general, the impulse response at low-pass level k, from k=2 to K-1, is given by the following recursive relationships depending on whether k is even or odd:

For even k:

$$g_k(x,y) = E_{\sqrt{2}}\{g_0(x,y)\} * S_{\sqrt{2}}\{g_{k-1}(x,y)\} .$$

For odd k:

$$g_k(x,y) = g_0(x,y) * S_{\sqrt{2}}\{g_{k-1}(x,y)\} .$$

12.2.4.2   The Size of the Impulse Responses

Size-scaling the kernel low-pass impulse response by resampling the continuous Gaussian function at a denser sample rate would yield a sequence of radii R_k given by

$$R_k = R_0 2^{(k/2)} .$$

The sequence of radii is somewhat different with cascaded filtering. In this case, the expansion operation maps the furthest coefficient, at say (R,0), to a new point at (R,R). This gives an increase in radius of $\sqrt{2}$. Convolution with the composite low-pass filter then adds this new size to that of the composite filter.

That is, at level 0 the radius is R_0. At level 1 the composite filter is the auto-convolution of $g_0(x,y)$, and its radius is thus $2R_0-1$. The level 2 composite filter is formed by convolving the level 1 composite filter with a $\sqrt{2}$ expanded version of g_0. The radius of the level 2 composite filter is thus $2R_0 + \sqrt{2}R_0 - 2$. A general formula for the radius at any level k>0 is

$$R_k = R_0-k+R_0 \sum_{n=0}^{(k-1)} (\sqrt{2})^{n-1} .$$

12.2.5   An Example: The DOLP Transform of a Teapot Image

Figure 12.3 shows a DOLP transform of an image of a teapot that was produced using the fast computation techniques described above. In this figure the

Fig. 12.3. The resampled DOLP transform of a teapot image

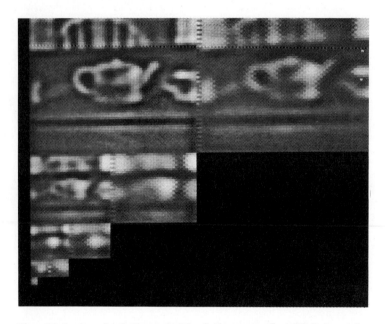

Fig. 12.4. Levels 5 through 13 of the resampled DOLP transform of a teapot image

image at the lower right is the high-frequency image, $B_0(x,y)$. The upper left corner shows the level 1 bandpass image, $B_1(x,y)$, while the upper right-hand corner contains the level 2 bandpass image, $B_2(x,y)$. Underneath the level 1 bandpass image are levels 3 and 4, then 5 and 6, etc. Figure 12.4 shows an enlarged view of bandpass levels 5 through 13. This enlargement illustrates the unique peaks in the low-frequency images that occur for each gray-scale form.

The use of $\sqrt{2}$ resampling is apparent from the reduction in size for each image from level 3 to 13. Each even numbered image is actually on a $\sqrt{2}$ sample grid. To display these $\sqrt{2}$ images, each pixel is printed twice, creating the interlocking brick texture evident in Fig.12.4.

12.3 Construction of the Representation from a DOLP Transform

The easiest method for determining the correspondence between the signals from DOLP transforms of a pair of images is to detect landmarks in the two signals and determine the correspondence of these landmarks. The peaks and ridges in a DOLP transform make excellent landmarks for such correspondence matching. When the DOLP transform is computed with a scale factor of $\sqrt{2}$, there is a continuity between peaks at different levels which provides a description which varies gradually from a few symbols which describe low resolution information to the much larger number of symbols that describe high resolution details. Finding the correspondence between any pair of peaks constrains the possible correspondences of peaks under them at higher resolutions.

The two-dimensional nature of images makes it possible for a DOLP band-pass filter to have a strong response to a form along a sequence of points. This occurs along elongated forms such as lines and bars as well as along the boundaries of a form. Elongated forms and boundaries result in a pattern of filter values referred to as a "ridge" or R path. A ridge path is a sequence of nodes such that the largest neighbor of each ridge node is also on the ridge.

12.3.0.1 The Approach

The "local neighborhood" of a DOLP sample is the nearest eight neighbors on the sample grid at its bandpass level. A "peak" (or P node) is a local positive maximum or negative minimum within a two-dimensional bandpass image. A "ridge node" (or R node) is a local one-dimensional positive maximum or negative minimum within a two-dimensional bandpass image. Peaks within a form are linked by paths of largest ridge nodes (R paths).

In order for a DOLP sample to be a local positive maximum or negative minimum in the DOLP three-space, it must also be a local peak within its bandpass level. Furthermore, for a sample to be a peak in its bandpass level, it must be a ridge node in the four directions given by opposite pairs of its eight neighbors. Peaks and ridge nodes are first detected within each bandpass image. Peaks are then linked to peaks at adjacent levels to form a tree of symbols (comprised of paths of peaks, or P paths). During this linking it is possible to detect the peaks which are local positive maxima and negative minima in the DOLP three-space. The three-space peaks are referred to as M nodes.

The ridge nodes are also linked to form ridge paths in each bandpass image (called R paths) and in the DOLP three-space (called L paths). The ridges in the DOLP three-space (L paths) describe elongated forms and connect the largest peaks (M nodes) which are part of the same form.

The process for constructing a description is composed of the following stages:

1) Detect ridge nodes (R nodes) and peaks (P nodes) at each bandpass level.

2) Link the largest adjacent ridge nodes with the same direction flags in a bandpass level to form ridges (R paths) which connect the P nodes on that level.

3) Link two-dimensional peaks (P nodes) at adjacent positions on adjacent levels to form P paths.

4) Detect local maxima along each P path (M nodes).

5) Detect the ridge nodes (R nodes) which have larger DOLP values than those at neighboring locations in adjacent images to detect L nodes.

6) Link the largest adjacent ridge points with the same direction among the bandpass levels to form three-dimensional ridge paths (L paths).

The result of this process is a tree-like graph which contains four classes of symbols:

- R nodes: DOLP samples which are on a ridge at a level.

- P nodes: DOLP samples which are local two-dimensional maxima at a level.

- L nodes: DOLP samples which are on a ridge across levels (i.e., in the three-space (x,y,k)).

- M nodes: Points which are local maxima in the three-space.

Every uniform (or approximately uniform) region will have one or more M nodes as a root in its description. These are connected to paths of Ls (L paths) which describe the general form of the region, and paths of P nodes (P paths) which branch into the concavities and convexities. L paths terminate at other M nodes which describe significant features at higher resolutions. The shapes of the boundaries are described at multiple resolutions by the ridges at each bandpass level (R paths). If a boundary is blurry, then the highest resolution (lowest-level) R paths are lost, but the boundary is still described by the lower-resolution R paths.

12. 3. 1 Detection of Peak Nodes and Ridge Nodes within Each Bandpass Image

Peak nodes and ridge nodes in each bandpass level are detected by comparing the magnitude and sign of each sample with the magnitude and sign of opposite pairs of its eight nearest neighbors. This comparison is made in four directions and can result in one of four "direction flags" being set. A direction flag is set when neither neighbor sample in a direction has a DOLP value of the same sign and a larger magnitude.

If any of the four direction flags are set, then the sample is encoded as an R node. If all four direction flags have been set then the sample is encoded as a P node. The direction flags are saved to be used to guide the processes for detecting two-dimensional ridges (R paths) and three-dimensional ridges (L paths).

Two possibilities complicate this rather simple process. When the amplitude of the signal is very small, it is possible to have a small region of adjacent samples with the same DOLP sample value. Such a plateau region may be avoided by not setting direction flags for samples with a magnitude less

180

than a small threshold. The value 5 has been found to work well for 8-bit DOLP samples. Also, it is possible to have two adjacent samples with equal DOLP values, while only one has a neighbor with a larger magnitude. Such cases may be easily detected and corrected by a local two-stage process. The correction involves turning off the direction flag for the neighbor without a larger neighbor.

Figure 12.5 shows the direction flags detected in a region from bandpass level 7 of the teapot image. Each direction flag which is set is represented as a pair of short line segments on both sides of a sample. These line segments point in the direction in which the sample is a one-dimensional maxima. Samples which are two-dimensional peaks (P nodes) are marked with a circle. It is possible to implement this detection in parallel or with a fast serial procedure.

Bandpass level 7   Teapot image   Direction flags

	73	81	89	97	105	113	121	129	137	145	153	161
73	-12	-19	-20	-24	-26	-28	(-29)	-28	-27	-31	(-36)	(-36)
81	-16	-18	-23	-26	(-29)	-24	-19	-16	-12	-19	-28	-34
89	-10	-9	-11	-12	-7	-4	4	9	9	4	0	-10
97	0	0	2	9	14	17	16	20	21	23	31	30
105	3	5	6	11	18	(19)	16	10	20	32	52	63
113	7	6	-4	-1	10	11	6	1	13	35	57	(73)
121	12	8	-8	(-10)	-1	5	1	0	10	29	49	60
129	(14)	12	2	-6	-2	-2	-4	-4	4	17	34	46
137	7	10	4	1	-1	-2	-5	(-9)	-5	8	24	37
145	-3	0	3	4	3	0	-1	-4	-3	8	24	35
153	-8	-8	-5	-3	1	4	2	-1	2	11	24	29
161	-7	-5	-8	-5	0	1	-2	-1	0	3	10	12

Fig. 12.5. This figure shows the direction flags detected in a region of bandpass level 7 of the teapot image. Each flag is represented by a pair of bars pointing toward the smaller valued neighbors. Ridges tend to run perpendicular to the flags. Peaks (P nodes) are marked which circles. Note that both the positive and negative peaks and ridges are shown. Note also that direction flags are not detected for nodes where the magnitude of the DOLP response is less than 5

12.3.2 Linking of Ridge Paths at a Bandpass Level

There are two purposes for which ridge paths in a two-dimensional bandpass level are detected:

1) to provide a link between P nodes at a given level which are part of the same form, and

2) to construct a description of the boundary of a form.

Linking P nodes of the same sign and bandpass level with ridges provides information about the connectivity of a form and provides attributes of distance and relative orientation which can be used in determining correspondences of P nodes across levels.

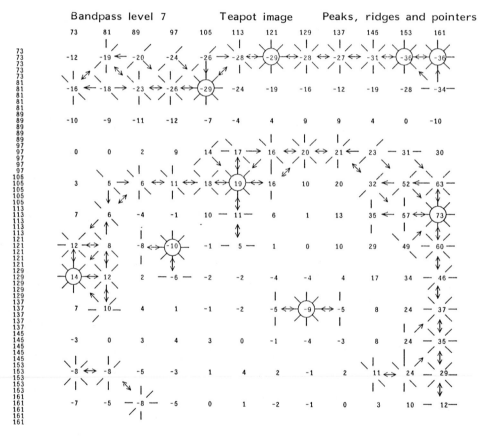

Fig. 12.6. The ridge paths connecting peaks (P nodes) in bandpass level 7 in the teapot image. This figure shows the pointers connecting adjacent DOLP samples along positive and negative ridges in the crop from bandpass level 7 of the teapot image. Each pointer is represented by an arrow pointing to a neighbor node. A pointer is made from a R node to a neighboring R node if it has a common direction flag and is a local maximum among the nearest eight neighbors. A ridge may be traced between peaks by following the pointers

182

In general, when a boundary is not a straight line, the convexities and concavities are described by a P path. However, when the curvature is very gradual P nodes may not occur for the concavities and convexities. In either case, a precise description of the location of the boundary is provided at multiple resolutions by the path of the ridge in a bandpass level.

A ridge is the path of largest R nodes between P nodes. This path can be formed by a local linking process which is executed independently at each R node. The ridge path can be detected by having each R node make a pointer to neighboring R nodes which meet two conditions:

1) the neighbor R node has the same sign and direction flags, and

2) the magnitude of the DOLP sample at the neighboring R node is a local maximum in a linear list of DOLP values of neighbors.

An earlier, more complex algorithm for the same purpose was described in [12.12]. The result of this process when applied to the level-7 bandpass image is shown in Fig.12.6.

12. 3. 3 Linking Peaks Between Levels and Detecting the Largest Peak

The bandpass filters which compose a DOLP transform are densely packed in the frequency domain. Each filter has a significant overlap in the pass-band of its transfer function with the bandpass filters from neighboring levels. As a result, when a form results in a two-dimensional peak (or P node) at one bandpass level the filters at adjacent levels will tend to cause a peak of the same sign to occur at the same or adjacent positions. Connecting P nodes of the same sign which are at adjacent locations in adjacent bandpass images yields a sequence of P nodes referred to as a P path. P paths tend to converge at lower resolutions, which gives the description the form of a tree. The branches at higher resolution of this tree describe the form of "roundish" blobs, bar ends, corners, and pointed protrusions, and the patterns of concavities and convexities along a boundary. Descending the tree of P paths in a description gives an increasingly more complex and higher-resolution description of the form.

The magnitudes of the DOLP filter responses of P nodes along a P path tend to rise monotonically to a largest magnitude, and then drop off monotonically. This largest value is encoded as an M node. Such nodes serve as landmarks for matching descriptions. An M node gives an estimate of the size and position of a form or a significant component of a form. Determining the correspondence of parts of forms in two descriptions is primarily a problem of finding the correspondence between M nodes and the L paths which connect them.

A simple technique may be used simultaneously to link P nodes into a P path and detect the M node (largest P node) along each P path. This technique is applied iteratively for each level, starting at the next-to-lowest resolution level of the DOLP transform (level K-2). The technique can be implemented in parallel within each level. This technique works as follows. Starting at each P node at level k, the nearest upper neighbors at level k+1 are examined to see if they are also P nodes of the same sign. If so, a two-way pointer is made between these two P nodes.

It is possible for P nodes that describe the same form at two adjacent levels to be separated by as much as two samples. Thus, if no P nodes are found among the nearest 4 or 8 neighbors[3] at level k+1 for a P node at level k, then the nodes in the larger neighborhood given by the neighbors of the neighbors are examined. A two-way pointer is made for any P nodes in this larger neighborhood.

During this linking process it is also possible to detect the largest P nodes on a P path by a process referred to as "flag stealing." This technique requires that P-node linking occur serially by level. In the flag stealing process, a P node with no upper neighbor or with a magnitude greater or equal to all of its upper neighbors sets a flag which indicates that it is an M node. Peaks which are adjacent to it at lower levels can "steal" this flag if they have an equal or larger magnitude. When the flag is stolen, the lower node sets its own flag as well as setting a second flag in the upper P node which is then used to cancel the flag. This two-stage process permits the M flag to propagate down multiple branches if the P path splits.

Figure 12.7 shows the P paths and the M node that occur at levels 6 through 1 for a uniform intensity square of 11×11 pixels, having gray level 96 on a background of 32. The reader can simulate the P-node linking and flag steal-ing process with this figure. This process starts at level 6, where the P node has a value of 19.

The P nodes for levels 12 through 6 of the teapot image are shown in Fig. 12.8. In levels 12 through 9 of Fig. 12.8 only a single P node occurs in the teapot. These P nodes all occur within a distance of two samples of the P node above them, and are thus linked into a single P path. The peak at level 8 has a larger DOLP sample than the peaks at adjacent levels and is thus marked as an M. The peaks at levels 7 and 6 are connected by a ridge of R nodes. These ridges are encoded as links between P nodes, with attri-butes of length and orientation. The circled number beside a link is a label and is also used to refer to a table of attributes.

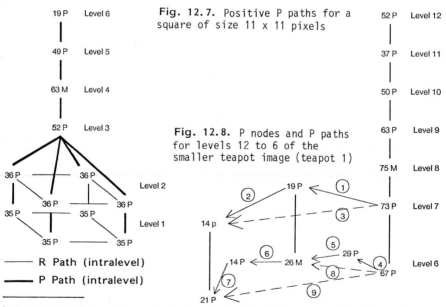

Fig. 12.7. Positive P paths for a square of size 11 x 11 pixels

Fig. 12.8. P nodes and P paths for levels 12 to 6 of the smaller teapot image (teapot 1)

———— R Path (intralevel)

——— P Path (intralevel)

3. The two possible upper neighborhoods in the DOLP space with $\sqrt{2}$ sampling.

184

12.3.4 Detecting the Largest Three-Dimensional Ridge Path

Three-dimensional ridges are essential for describing forms which are elongated. An elongated form almost always has an M node at each end, and a ridge of large DOLP values connecting the two M nodes. The DOLP values along this ridge tend to be larger than those along the ridges on the bandpass levels above and below, because the positive center coefficients of the bandpass for that level "fit" the width of the elongated form. Where the form grows wider, the largest ridge will move to a higher (coarser) bandpass level. Where the form grows thinner, the largest ridge will move to a lower (coarser resolution) bandpass level. This ridge of largest DOLP samples is called an L path and the nodes along it are called L nodes. L nodes are R nodes that are larger than their neighbors at adjacent band-pass levels.

L nodes may be detected by a process similar to the flag-stealing process used to detect the largest peak, or M node, along a P path. That is, starting at the bandpass level below the lowest resolution, each R node examines a neighborhood in the level above it. An R node is determined to be an L node if it has a larger value than the R nodes in approximately the same place in the ridges above and below it.

Thus each R node scans an area of the bandpass level above it. This area is above and to the sides of its ridge. The magnitudes of DOLP samples of the same sign found in the neighborhood in the upper ridge are compared to that of the R node, and a flag is set in the lower R node and cleared in the upper R node if the lower R node is smaller. In this way, the L flags propagate down to the level with the largest DOLP samples along the ridge. L nodes are linked to form L paths, by having each L node scan its three-dimensional neighborhood and link to L nodes which have the same sign and are local maxima in the three-dimensional DOLP space neighborhood.

12.4 Matching Descriptions of Shape

There are several problem domains where it is desirable to determine the correspondence between parts of two or more images, or between a shape in an image and a representation of a prototype shape. One such problem domain is the interpretation of pairs of stereo images to obtain depth information. Another domain is the interpretation of sequences of images in which the camera is moving, and in which the relative motion of points on surfaces provides information about the three-dimensional structure of a physical environment. Yet another such problem domain is the interpretation of sequences of images in which objects are moving, to construct and maintain a model of the scene.

The representation developed in the previous sections has properties which greatly simplify the process of determining the correspondence of patterns of pixels in two images.

1) Only peaks correspond to peaks. The existence of peaks or P nodes provides a set of landmarks which can be used as tokens in the matching process.

2) The multiresolution structure of the representation permits the correspondence process to commence with the most global M nodes for each form. Since very few such symbols exist at the coarsest resolution, the complexity of this process is kept small.

3) The connectivity of P paths permits the match information from a coarse resolution to constrain the possible set of matches at the next higher resolution level. Thus what could be a very large graph matching problem is repeatedly partitioned into several small problems.

Another important problem domain in image understanding is classifying two-dimensional gray-scale forms. The representation developed in this paper can be used for a structural pattern recognition approach to this problem. That is, a gray-scale form may be classified by measuring the similarity of its representation to a number of prototype representations for object classes.

The properties of the representation cited above also facilitate its use for constructing object class prototypes and for matching prototypes to object descriptions. An object class prototype may be formed by constructing the descriptions of objects in a training set. The configurations of P paths and L paths that occur for a given class of objects can be determined by matching the representations from this training set. The prototype description can be composed of the P paths and L paths that occur in all of the descriptions of training objects. This provides a simplified representation which can serve as an object class prototype. The multiresolution structure of the representation permits the set of possible matching prototypes to be reduced on the basis of the few coarsest-resolution symbols.

12.4.1 Some Principles for Matching Gray-Scale Forms

Matching is a problem of comparing a reference description to a measured description. In this process the reference description is transformed in size, orientation, and position so as to bring its components into correspondence with the measured data. The goal of this process is to determine:

- the overall relative position, orientation, and size of the forms represented in the two descriptions,
- which M nodes, P nodes, and L nodes in the reference description correspond to which M nodes, P nodes, and L nodes in the measured description (the correspondence mapping),
- local relative changes in position, orientation, and size between parts of the reference description and the corresponding parts of the measured description, and
- parts in either of the descriptions that do not occur in the other description.

Such matching consists of several steps:

1) Initial alignment: In this stage the most global M node(s) is(are) used to determine the relative positions and sizes of the two descriptions.

2) Orientation: Given the relative positions and sizes, the correspondence of P nodes and L nodes in the few levels below the most global M node(s) can be used to estimate the relative orientations of the two descriptions. This correspondence can be found by the same procedure used for the following task.

3) Correspondence of P nodes: Each level on which there is more than one P node in the description of a form yields a graph composed of P nodes connected by ridges (R paths). Each R path has the attributes of distance and orientation between the P nodes at either end. Techniques exist for determining the correspondence between nodes in such a pair of graphs. Indeed, when the number of nodes is small it is not unreasonable to examine exhaustively every possible correspondence. A similarity measure, such as the average difference in the lengths and orientations of the R paths, may be used to determine the correspondence

which is most likely. A fundamental principle in matching descriptions from a DOLP transform is to use the correspondence at a lower resolution level to constrain the set of possible correspondences at the next higher resolution level. This prevents the computational complexity of matching P nodes from growing exponentially as the number of P nodes grows exponentially with increasing resolution.

4) <u>Correspondence of L nodes</u>: Forms which are elongated can result in a description which contains few P nodes. The shape of such forms can be compared by comparing the L paths in their descriptions. Comparing L paths consists of two stages:

- alignment of the L paths by aligning the M nodes which terminate these L paths at each end, and

- computing the distance of each L node in the reference L path to the nearest L node in the measured L path.

Determining the correspondence of individual L nodes in two descriptions is not a reasonable approach because the distance between L nodes in an L path varies by as much as a factor of $\sqrt{2}$ with orientation. Measuring the distance from each L node in one description to the nearest L node in the second description allows the measures of maximum distance and average distance to be used to compare the entire L path. Examples of matching L paths are presented in [12.12].

12.4.2 Stereo Matching Example

A stereo pair of images of a paper wad was formed to test the use of the representation for determining the correspondence between structural components in a stereo pair of images. The scene was formed by placing the paper wad on a dark lab bench under a desk lamp. A vidicon camera, mounted on a tripod, was placed approximately 14 inches from the paper wad, and the left image was digitized. The camera was then moved to the right approximately 6 inches and tilted so that the paper wad was located in roughly the same part of the image. This tilt angle was approximately 20°. The right image was then digitized. The purpose of this experiment was to test the use of the representation for determining the correspondence of parts of the two images. No attempt was planned or made to use this correspondence to determine the actual distances to surface points on the paper wad.

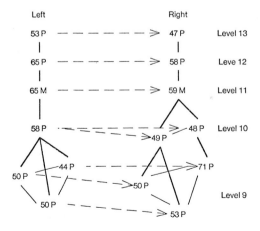

Fig. 12.9. Stereo correspondence of the P nodes for paper wads, levels 13 through 9

The P nodes for Levels 13 through 9 of the two paper wads are shown in Fig.12.9. The correspondence between P nodes was assigned by hand. This correspondence is illustrated by the dashed arrows in Fig.12.9. Assigning these correspondences was a relatively easy task because of the small number of P nodes at each level. Even when the number of P nodes increased at the levels below level 9, the correspondences at the previous level constrain the possible correspondences so that there is often no choice as to which P nodes correspond.

Note that at level 10, two P nodes occur in the right image, while only a single P node occurs in the left image. This difference in structure is the result of the parallax created by the difference in perspective. This illustrates one of the problems in determining stereo correspondence: shape changes when seen from different perspectives. Thus a stereo correspondence algorithm must be capable of assigning a sample from one image to more than one sample in the second.

12.5 Summary and Conclusion

The principal topic of this paper is a representation for gray-scale shape which is composed of peaks and ridges in the DOLP transform of an image. Descriptions of the shape of an object which are encoded in this representation may be matched efficiently despite changes in size, orientation or position by the object. Such descriptions can also be matched when the object is blurry or noisy.

The definition of the DOLP transform was presented, and the DOLP transform was shown to be reversible. A fast algorithm for computing the DOLP transform based on the techniques of resampling and cascaded convolution with expansion was then described. This fast algorithm is described in greater detail in [12.2]. This section concluded with an example of the DOLP transform of an image which contains a teapot.

A representation for gray-scale form based on the peaks and ridges in a DOLP transform was then described. This representation is composed of four types of symbols: {M,P,L,R}. The symbols R and P (Ridge and Peak) are detected within each DOLP bandpass image. R nodes are samples which are local positive maxima or negative minima among three contiguous DOLP samples in any of the four possible directions. P nodes are samples which are local positive maxima or negative minima in all four directions. P nodes within the same form in a bandpass level are connected by a path of largest R nodes, called an R path (or ridge). An R path is formed by having each R node make a pointer to members of its local neighborhood which are also R nodes and local maxima within a linear list of the neighborhood. P nodes are connected with nearby P nodes at adjacent bandpass levels to form P paths. The skeleton of the description of a form is a tree composed of P paths.

The DOLP values along each P path rise monotonically to a maximum in magnitude and then decrease. The maximum magnitude DOLP sample along a P path is marked as an M node. M nodes serve as landmarks for matching, and provide an estimate of the position and orientation of a form in an image. If the values along an R path are compared to the values along the R paths at nearby locations in adjacent bandpass images, an R path of largest DOLP samples can be detected. These samples are marked as L nodes, and these nodes form an L path. L paths begin and end at M nodes and describe elongated forms. Thus, descriptions in this representation have the structure of a tree composed of P paths, with a distinguished M node along each. The

P nodes in each level are connected by R paths, and the M nodes are connected by L paths which can travel among as well as within the levels. The teapot image was used to illustrate the construction of a description in this representation. In this illustration, the R nodes and P nodes from bandpass level 7 from the DOLP transform of the teapot and the pointers between these R nodes were displayed.

The problem of matching descriptions of shape in this representation was discussed, and the principles for such a matching algorithm were described. An example of matching for the lower resolution levels of a stereo pair of images was presented. This section addresses only a small part of the general problem of matching descriptions of objects. The problem of matching two descriptions of an object with large differences in image plane orientation was not illustrated. An example of such matching is provided in [12.12].

The more difficult problem of matching in the presence of motion of either the camera or the object is now being investigated. Such matching must be robust enough to accommodate the changes in two-dimensional shape that occur with a changing three-dimensional viewing angle. Similarly, the problems of forming and matching to a prototype for a class of objects were not discussed. We believe that this representation will provide a powerful structural pattern recognition technique for recognizing objects in a two-dimensional domain and for dynamically constructing a three-dimensional model of a three-dimensional scene.

References

12.1 D. Marr: Vision: A Computational Investigation into the Human Representation and Processing of Visual Information (Freeman, San Francisco, CA, 1982)
12.2 J. L. Crowley, R. M. Stern: Fast computation of the difference-of-low-pass transform, to appear
12.3 D. Marr, T. Poggio: A computational theory of human stereo vision, Proc. Royal Society (London) B204, 301-328 (1979)
12.4 T. O. Binford: Survey of model-based image analysis systems, Int'l. J. Robotics Research 1(1), 18-64 (1982)
12.5 H. P. Moravec: "Obstacle Avoidance and Navigation in the Real World by a Seeing Robot Rover", Ph.D. dissertation, Stanford University (1980)
12.6 A. Rosenfeld, G. J. Vanderbrug: Coarse-fine template matching, IEEE Trans. Systems, Man, Cybernetics SMC-7, 104-107 (1977)
12.7 E. L. Hall, J. D. Rouge, R. Y. Wong: "Hierarchical search for image matching", in Proc. Conf. on Decision and Control, 1976, pp. 791-796
12.8 F. W. Campbell, J. G. Robson: Applications of Fourier analysis to the visibility of gratings, J. Physiology (London) 197, 551-566 (1968)
12.9 M. Sachs, J. Nachmias, J. G. Robson: Spatial-frequency channels in human vision, J. Optical Society America 61, 1176-1186 (1971)
12.10 F. W. Campbell: The Transmission of Spatial Information through the Visual System (MIT Press, Cambridge, MA, 1974)
12.11 J. P. Thomas: Spatial Resolution and Spatial Interaction (Academic Press, New York, 1975)
12.12 J. L. Crowley: "A Representation for Visual Information", Ph.D. dissertation, Carnegie-Mellon University (1981)
12.13 W. K. Pratt: Digital Image Processing (Wiley, New York, 1978), p. 322
12.14 D. Marr, E. C. Hildreth: Theory of Edge Detection, Proc. Royal Society (London) B207, 187-217 (1980)

13. Multiresolution Feature Encodings

M. Shneier*

National Bureau of Standards, Building 220, Room A-123
Washington, DC 20234, USA

Multiresolution data structures require that information be summarized or encoded as the resolution decreases. Pyramids and quadtrees provide convenient
structures for representing this process, especially for intensity information
in images. Encodings are also possible for other image features, such as
lines and curves, and objects that are compact or elongated. Methods are described for representing such features at successively lower resolutions,
and for using the resulting structures to find objects or regions with particular properties. Advantages of the techniques include (1) their processing
speed, if suitable parallel hardware is available; (2) the fact that they
provide approximate representations of the features at a wide range of scales;
(3) the fact that they condense global information about features into local
labels, which can then interact with other such information, and can also
provide feedback to influence the condensation processes themselves.

13.1 Introduction

Multiresolution representations, especially pyramids and quadtrees, have been
used in many applications of region-based image processing. (ROSENFELD [13.1]
gives an overview of some of these applications.) The use of such representations for region boundaries, lines, curves, and edges provides more of a
challenge, because the pyramid is naturally better suited to storing region-
like information than curve-like information. Nevertheless, there are significant advantages to constructing multiresolution representations of such
information, and several techniques have been developed for summarizing and
encoding images containing curve-like information. This paper discusses some
of these techniques, and gives examples of their use in analyzing images.

A further challenge involves the detection of more complex features, such
as compact or elongated combinations of edges. By employing several different kinds of multiple-resolution structures, it is possible to extract such
features selectively in a much simpler manner than is possible using conventional single-resolution methods.

Advantages of multiresolution representations include their ability to
make operations that are global in the original image into truly local operations. Searching is also fast, because large regions can be spanned in a
single step. Objects of known sizes can be extracted selectively because
their size is related to the level in the representation at which they are
locally represented (i.e., just before they disappear). Multiresolution
representations also allow attention to be focused and complex operations
to be performed only on regions that are promising. As a side-effect, the
representations can also be used to remove noise from images.

---

*Present address: National Bureau of Standards, Gaithersburg, MD.

Multiresolution representations fall into two broad classes, exact representations and approximations. Exact representations, such as quadtrees, take advantage of structure or homogeneity in the image to group data into uniform regions that can be described completely by a small number of parameters. Such representations give rise to variable-sized regions, depending on the size of the homogeneous regions in the image. Inexact representations, such as pyramids, usually use a uniform subdivision rule that summarizes fixed-sized regions in the image, regardless of their contents. These representations tend to smooth out variations within regions, resulting in the loss of some information. Some representations, such as strip trees, may be exact or inexact, depending on the number of times that a region is subdivided.

The main emphasis in this paper is on pyramid-based representations. In the next section, other representations are briefly described.

13.2 Quadtrees and Strip Trees

A quadtree is obtained from a binary image by successive subdivision into quadrants. If the original image is homogeneous, a single leaf node is created. Otherwise, the image is divided into four quadrants, which become sons of the root node. This process is applied recursively until all terminal nodes are homogeneous. For gray-level images, a class of quadtrees can also be defined, based on the brightness characteristics of the image. The root node represents the whole image, and typically stores the average gray level. If the image is sufficiently homogeneous (i.e., if the variance in gray level is not too great) no subdivision is performed. Otherwise, the image is divided into four subimages, and four children of the root are constructed. As long as the variance in any quadrant is higher than a threshold, the process is repeated. The result is a tree that represents the image to a degree of accuracy dependent on the threshold. Quadtrees have traditionally been used to represent region-like information. It is, however, possible to devise quadtree representations for borders [13.2] or for curves [13.3].

SAMET and WEBBER [13.2] describe an exact quadtree representation for region boundaries, called a line quadtree. The representation is isomorphic to the corresponding region quadtree for the same image, but each terminal node in the tree stores information as to which of its sides are adjacent to boundaries. The choice of what information to store at nonterminal nodes affects the speeds of algorithms performed on the quadtree. By storing edge information in nonterminals, it is possible to perform operations such as border following without examining all the terminal nodes. SAMET and WEBBER illustrate the efficiency of their representation by defining an algorithm that superimposes one map on another, where both maps are represented as line quadtrees. Figure 13.1b shows the line quadtree for the image of Fig.13.1a.

A rather different quadtree representation for curve-like information is described by SHNEIER [13.3]. His representation, called an edge quadtree, is based on approximations to curves passing through square regions. The quadtree is constructed using overlapping 4 by 4 neighborhoods. Within each neighborhood, the best edge is sought, according to straightness criteria, and is represented at the next level by a straight-line approximation. The magnitude of the response (if appropriate) and a direction and direction error estimate are stored with each curve, and are used to decide whether or not to continue to merge lines at higher levels. The structure produced in this way is a quadtree, but differs from the tree of SAMET and WEBBER in that it stores approximations instead of exact boundaries, and in its ability to store curves that do not bound closed regions. Figure 13.2 shows the edge quadtree for an image of an airplane.

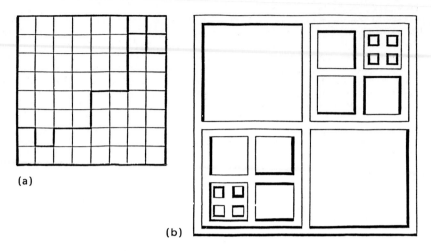

Fig. 13.1. **(a)** A map with six regions, outlined in bold lines.**(b)** The line quadtree for the map in (a). Bold lines show sides of quadrants that are adjacent to boundaries

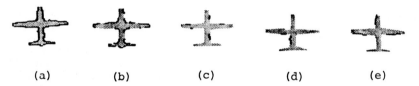

(a) (b) (c) (d) (e)

Fig. 13.2. The edge quadtree of an airplane image. **(a)** The edge magnitude image. **(b)** The lowest level of the edge quadtree (individual pixels). **(c)** The level having 2 by 2 blocks of pixels. **(d)** 4 by 4 blocks. **(e)** 8 by 8 blocks

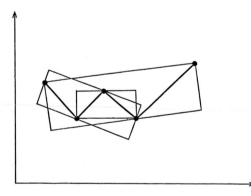

Fig. 13.3. The sequence of rectangles used to form the strip tree of a curve

Strip trees [13.4] are a different approach to the hierarchical representation of curves, based on a well-known algorithm for splitting a curve into piecewise linear approximations [13.5]. Unlike quadtrees and pyramids, strip trees represent individual curves instead of entire images. Each curve is represented as a set of successive approximations by rectangles. The line joining the end points of the curve defines the orientation and length of the rectangle, while the extrema in the direction normal to this line define the width. The curve is recursively split at extremal width points until its width is less than some threshold. The resulting set of nested rectangles forms the strip tree. The technique can be adapted to handle closed or broken curves, and is useful for finding intersections and unions of curves, distances between points and curves, and whether or not a point lies within a region. Figure 13.3 depicts a strip tree for a curve.

While the potential of the representations described in this section is still largely to be determined, a number of experiments have been performed using pyramid representations for curves. The next section introduces these pyramids and discusses some of their applications.

13.3 Edge and Curve Pyramids

A pyramid, like a quadtree, is constructed based on recursive subdivision of an image into quadrants. Unlike the quadtree, however, the pyramid construction process is always continued until all nodes represent individual pixels in the original image. Thus, the lowest level of the pyramid represents the original image at full resolution, the next level represents the image at a uniformly lower resolution (usually half the resolution in each dimension), and so on. The simplest way of constructing a pyramid is to start with the original image, and successively represent nonoverlapping 2 by 2 blocks by their average values at the next level. It is also possible to represent overlapping 4 by 4 blocks by their averages (or their medians, or some other function), also giving rise to a pyramid that tapers exponentially. If the lowest level has a size of 2^n by 2^n, the next level will have size 2^{n-1} by 2^{n-1}.

A further refinement to the pyramid construction process involves linking nodes across levels. A node at level L can link to a node at level L+1 (its father) if it is used in the process that calculates the value of that node. Thus, for simple averaging on 2 by 2 neighborhoods, each node at level L+1 links to 4 nodes at level L (sons), and each son links to one father. In the case in which 4 by 4 overlapped neighborhoods are used in the construction, each father has 16 sons, and each son has 4 fathers. The linking process can be iterated; for example, a son can link only to his most similar father, resulting in a new basis for calculating the value of that father, and a possibility that the new value will no longer be the most similar to that of the son.

Edge information is usually obtained from a gray-scale image. If so, there are two ways of constructing the edge pyramid. First, the gray-scale image can be processed to produce an edge image, from which the pyramid can be constructed. Alternatively, a gray-scale pyramid can be constructed and an edge operator applied at each level. Note that the two methods do not yield the same results. For information that is inherently curve-like, only the first of these methods is applicable. Both have been used in experiments, and each has its own advantages.

Two representative applications of the pyramid structures will be described. The first involves the extraction of curves and straight-line segments, perhaps broken or obscured, as single components. The second application concerns the extraction of compact objects from gray-scale imagery.

The goal of the first application [13.6] is to detect good continuation of curves, and hence to be able to join broken pieces and ignore segments that do not belong together. The method involves the construction of a single pyramid of curve information. The process involves a single pass from the bottom of the pyramid (the original image) to the top, where the components are extracted. The process uses position, direction, and curvature information to construct a linked pyramid.

The pyramid is based on 4 by 4 overlapping neighborhoods, so that each node has 4 fathers on the level above it, and 16 sons on the level below it, when these levels exist. Each node in the pyramid contains three kinds of information. First is a counter or flag that ensures that the capacity of the node to store curves is not exceeded. In the implementation, the maximum was set at 5 curves. Second, the coordinates of the end points are stored, at full resolution. If a curve extends outside the central 2 by 2 region of its 4 by 4 neighborhood, its extremal points within the borders of the 2 by 2 region are stored as its end points. Third, a measure of the direction of the curve at each end point is stored.

Only the central 2 by 2 region of a neighborhood is summarized by its father, although information from the whole neighborhood is used to compute the summary. The central 2 by 2 regions cover the image, so this does not result in a loss of information. The conditions for a curve to be passed up to the next level are that it lie in the central 2 by 2 region and that it receive support from some other curve in the 4 by 4 neighborhood. Support is measured by a merit function. This is based on fitting a circle with some given radius to the region between the endpoints of two adjacent curves. If the radius is large, the function will favor straight-line segments, while if it is small, curves will be preferred. By restricting the function in different ways, straight lines, curves, or arcs of circles can be extracted. The figure of merit is applied to each pair, consisting of a curve from the central 2 by 2 region and a curve in a compatible grid position (based on the direction of the curve) in the 4 by 4 neighborhood. When a curve receives support, it passes its end points up to its father, together with the directions of the curve at these end points. Information about the shape of the curve between the end points is not known at the next level, although it can be recovered by tracing links through the pyramid to the bottom level.

The process is repeated at each level of the pyramid until the top level is reached. At this stage, the remaining lines and curves can be displayed. Figure 13.4 shows examples of images that were processed, and Figs. 13.5,6 show the results of the processing.

A rather more complex application [13.7] involves the use of closure and similarity measures to extract compact objects from imagery. The method makes use of three different pyramids, a gray-scale pyramid to hypothesize regions, an edge pyramid to find region boundaries, and a "surroundedness" pyramid to select those regions that are compact and have more or less closed boundaries. The pyramids are built one upon the other. First, a gray-scale pyramid is constructed. Next an edge detector is applied at each level to produce an edge pyramid, and finally the edges at each level are used to construct the surroundedness pyramid.

The gray-scale pyramid is constructed using 4 by 4 overlapping neighborhoods, whose average is used as the value at the next level. The levels are linked together when each son chooses to be assigned to that father node that has the most similar gray level. Fathers then recompute their gray values,

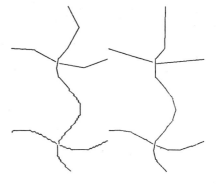

Fig. 13.4. Two images that were processed to detect good continuation

Fig. 13.5. The results of processing the first picture of Fig. 13.4 (*Bottom left:*) original picture. (*Bottom right:*) level 3 of the pyramid (8 by 8). (*Top left:*) level 4 (4 by 4). (*Top right:*) level 5 (2 by 2)

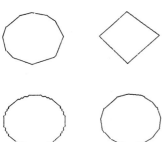

Fig. 13.6. The results of processing the second picture of Fig. 13.4, with the merit function tuned to favor circular arcs

based on the sons that chose them, and the process is iterated until it converges, usually in a small number of iterations.

The pyramid is constructed to the 2 by 2 level, where there are at most four different gray values. When these gray values are projected down the pyramid, they give rise to a segmentation of the scene. By forcing the segmentation into at most four categories, however, it is possible to merge separate objects into a single component, or to lose them in the background. The edge and surroundedness pyramids provide additional constraints that can assist in retaining the identities of objects.

The edge pyramid is built on the gray-scale pyramid, by applying an edge detector at each level, and suppressing nonmaxima. This is done immediately after the initial construction of the gray-scale pyramid, before the iteration has begun. Edges are linked across levels if the direction of a son is compatible with its father (i.e., within 45 degrees). Otherwise, the edge serves as the root of a subtree in the pyramid. The linking process is not iterated.

The edge pyramid forms the basis of the surroundedness pyramid, the last of the three, whose purpose is to locate those objects that are surrounded by edges (closed) and are compact. The surroundedness pyramid is constructed by marking each nonedge point based on the number of surrounding compatible edge points. This is a local operation in the pyramid, because interior

195

points eventually become adjacent to their surrounding edges at some level in the pyramid.

The points that are marked in the surroundedness pyramid form the basis for the process that extracts the compact regions. This process relies heavily on the existence of the registered edge and region pyramids. Simply projecting points with high compactness down through the gray-scale pyramid can fail for a number of reasons. The gray-scale pyramid could have given rise to a poor segmentation, or the edge or compactness data could be poor, with missing or extra edges or misshapen boundaries. A more informed process uses information from all three pyramids to extract the regions.

The edge and surroundedness pyramids guide the simultaneous addition and deletion of nodes in the gray-scale pyramid, on a level-by-level basis. The process works top-down. Nodes are added in if they are on the interior of an edge and adjacent to a compact point; they are deleted if they are outside an edge of the compact object. Gaps in the edges are bridged by interpolation at each level; thus the borders of the object approach those of the real object more and more closely as the resolution increases, without the region "leaking out" through holes in the boundary.

Fig. 13.7   Fig. 13.8

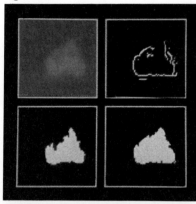

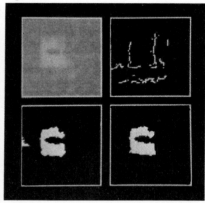

Fig. 13.7. (*Top left:*) original FLIR image of a tank. (*Top right:*) edge image projected from the 8 by 8 level. (*Bottom left:*) the compact object found at the 8 by 8 level. (*Bottom right:*) the results of adding points to fit the edge data

Fig. 13.8. (*Top left:*) original image. (*Top right:*) edge image projected from the 8 by 8 level. (*Bottom left:*) compact object without pruning. (*Bottom right:*) compact object after pruning

Fig. 13.9. Part of a suburban scene with a road and a house. The house is compact enough to be extracted, but the road is not

Table 13.1. Summary of results for the comparative segmentation study

Images	Targets	Method	Correctly detected	Extra detections	False alarms	Segmentation accuracy
2-10 (Navy, China Lake)	8	2-class relaxation	0	0	43	-
		3-class relaxation	2	0	67	0.70
		Pyramid linking	0	0	145	-
		Superspike	3	0	77	0.51
		Surroundedness pyramid	4	0	32	0.60
11-30 (NVL data)	80		40	0	92	0.73
			20	8	92	0.49
			72	32	392	0.67
			76	24	60	0.64
			76	0	16	0.73
31-36 (Air Force, TASVAL)	6		2	0	9	0.74
			3	1	27	0.73
			3	2	100	0.57
			6	1	63	0.60
			5	0	11	0.70
55-70 (NVL flight test)	32		2	0	6	0.67
			13	1	19	0.65
			4	0	38	0.80
			26	1	2	0.73
			26	0	7	0.60
Overall	126		44	0	150	0.73
			38	10	205	0.58
			79	34	675	0.68
			111	26	202	0.66
			111	0	67	0.69

Figures 13.7,8 show the results of applying the method to two gray-scale images. The method can be tuned to ignore elongated objects (Fig.13.9), and to detect only objects of a known range of sizes. In a comparative study [13.8] it was found that the pyramid method outperformed all the other tested methods, being particularly good at suppressing false detections (Table13.1).

13.4 Discussion and Conclusion

A vast amount of image data consists largely of lines or curves. This includes maps, circuit diagrams, and building plans. To store this information in a manner that allows quick and easy retrieval based on image content requires some means of rapidly finding salient features in images. Because of the large amounts of data, this strongly suggests the use of a multiresolution representation that allows large parts of the image to be ignored without risk. The representations discussed here represent attempts to develop such multiple resolution systems. The advent of parallel processors will enhance the viability of such techniques and make them practicable.

All pyramid-based methods share a number of advantages over single-resolution methods. These include the ability to make global information local, and to focus attention on small parts of the image, which can then be examined selectively at full resolution. The added power of representing curves and edges at multiple resolutions allows this information to be used in conjunction with region information to improve the performance of algorithms such as object extraction. It also extends the domain to which multiresolution representations can be applied.

Edges and curves provide a very significant set of image features, and there is evidence of multiresolution detectors in the human visual system. The study of various Gestalt processes such as similarity grouping, closure, and good continuation has shown that pyramids at least have the potential to utilize such information, and can do so using parallel local computations, that is, in real time on a parallel processor. Single resolution techniques must search arbitrarily large regions in order to achieve similar performance.

Popular algorithms have been devised that detect edges using a sequence of detectors whose sizes grow exponentially [13.9,10]. The method of first constructing a gray-scale pyramid and then applying an edge detector at each level provides an economical implementation of such detectors. It differs from them in that it computes edge values at fewer and fewer points as the resolution decreases, but this is not a serious handicap because values computed at adjacent points are largely redundant since they are based on overlapping regions in the original image.

A major advantage of the pyramid representation is the ability it provides to select the sizes of objects to be extracted. For example, extracting the major edges from an image involves finding those edges that survive to the highest levels of the pyramid and projecting them down. The results are the full resolution edges at the bottom level, without the smaller edges having been detected at all. It is also possible to detect features derived from edges, such as antiparallel pairs or the borders of closed objects [13.11]. This can be done using local operations because the edges are guaranteed to become close enough together at some level.

A fruitful cooperation could be established between region-based pyramids and edge and curve pyramids, to extract elongated thick objects (e.g., roads and rivers in high-resolution aerial photographs). Elongated objects would be reduced to curves or lines in the gray-scale pyramid, but, before being lost at higher levels, would be transferred to the appropriate level in a curve pyramid. This pyramid would complete the processing, and, on projecting down, would transfer back to the region pyramid at the appropriate level.

One-dimensional versions of pyramids and quadtrees can also be developed for representing individual lines and curves [13.12]. They give rise to piecewise approximations of the curves at successively lower resolutions. These representations are related to the strip trees described above, but use fixed-sized neighborhoods instead of variable regions based on the shape of the enclosed curves.

There are some difficulties with multiresolution representations for linear features. They arise because the features extend over large parts of an image relative to their width. This makes it hard to assign a single node in a representation to represent the whole curve (unless each curve is first extracted from the image and processed separately as in strip trees). The result is a collection of adjacent nodes that must be linked in some way. The alternative is to go on passing up the curves until they are represented by a single node. This, however, highlights another problem. As the level in the representation increases, there are fewer and fewer nodes available to represent the curves. Either curves must be discarded or nodes must be able to represent the many different curves that pass through them. One of the differences between such methods as those of [13.3] and [13.6] is in the way in which this problem is approached.

These problems notwithstanding, the success of the systems described in this paper and the continuing research in multiresolution representations indicates their growing importance in image processing. In addition, their potential for real-time implementation and their biological analogues strengthen their claim to legitimacy.

References

13.1 A. Rosenfeld: "Quadtrees and Pyramids: Hierarchical Representation of Images", Computer Science TR-1171, University of Maryland (1982)
13.2 H. Samet, R. E. Webber: "On Encoding Boundaries with Quadtrees", Computer Science TR-1162, University of Maryland (1982)
13.3 M. Shneier: Two hierarchical linear feature representations: edge pyramids and edge quadtrees, Computer Graphics Image Processing 17, 211-224 (1981)
13.4 D. H. Ballard: Strip trees: a hierarchical representation for curves, Comm. ACM 24, 310-321 (1981)
13.5 R. O. Duda, P. E. Hart: Pattern Recognition and Scene Analysis (Wiley, New York, 1973)
13.6 T. H. Hong, M. Shneier, R. Hartley, A. Rosenfeld: "Using Pyramids to Detect Good Continuation", Computer Science TR-1185, University of Maryland (1982)
13.7 T. H. Hong, M. Shneier: "Extracting compact objects using linked pyramids", in Proc. Image Understanding Workshop, Stanford, CA, 1982, pp. 58-71
13.8 R. L. Hartley, L. J. Kitchen, C. Y. Wang, A. Rosenfeld: Segmentation of FLIR images: a comparative study, IEEE Trans. Systems, Man, Cybernetics SMC-12, 553-566 (1982)
13.9 A. Rosenfeld, M. Thurston: Edge and curve detection for visual scene analysis, IEEE Trans. Computers C-20, 562-569 (1971)
13.10 D. Marr, E. Hildreth: Theory of edge detection, Proc. Royal Society (London) B207, 187-217 (1980)
13.11 T. H. Hong, M. Shneier, A. Rosenfeld: Border extraction using linked edge pyramids, IEEE Trans. Systems, Man, Cybernetics SMC-12, 660-668 (1982)
13.12 K. A. Narayanan, A. Rosenfeld: Approximation of waveforms and contours by one-dimensional pyramid linking, Pattern Recognition 15, 389-396 (1982)

14. Multiple-Size Operators and Optimal Curve Finding

S.W. Zucker and P. Parent

Department of Electrical Engineering, McGill University, 3480 University Street
Montreal, Quebec, Canada H3A 2A7

14.1 Introduction

The problem of locating lines and curves in digital imagery is a real problem
for many applications, as well as a generic example of the difficulties inherent in interpreting the response of local operators tuned, or designed,
to detect predetermined features. The difficulty with local operators, of
course, is that they do not respond uniquely to (a local portion of) the
selected pattern; they also respond to images that are similar to, but not,
an instance of the pattern. These problems are, furthermore, exacerbated in
the presence of noise.

Oriented second derivative operators, or so-called line detectors [14.1],
provide a classical example of these difficulties; when convolved with an
image, they provide a response that is strong when a line is present on a
perfect background, but is weaker in all other circumstances. The problem,
then, is how to interpret these responses. This is the problem with which
we shall be concerned in this paper, both literally and generically.

The solution to the operator response interpretation problem requires the
introduction of additional constraints on interpretation, as well as a framework within which these constraints can be applied. Perhaps the most attractive framework is optimization theory, and a number of researchers have attempted to apply it to this problem with limited success. MONTANARI [14.2],
for example, formulated a mathematical programming approach to line finding,
based on a functional that accumulated intensity differences in an additive
manner; for related, subsequent work see [14.3]. Whereas we believe that
this approach has many merits, the choice of functional and of mathematical
programming constrained the line finder in a way that is inappropriate for
general curve finding; these two choices introduced the implicit constraint
that there was, essentially, exactly one curve in the image, and that it
started at the top and ran to the bottom. While such an assumption may be
valid within very special problem formulations, such as when an image has
been partially matched to a model in a verification scenario, in general it
is not the case. Rather, the line finder must determine both where the
curve is, and where its end points are. A second, related problem with this
line finder is that it was globally homogeneous, in that it was evaluated
over all curves possibly in the image.

Another approach that is similar in intent was provided by the early work
of ZUCKER, HUMMEL, and ROSENFELD [14.4] in applying relaxation techniques to
the line-and curve-finding problem. Realizing that the individual operators
were too local to decide on the proper response interpretation, they attempted
to use constraints, or compatibilities, between the possible interpretations
of the line operators centered at neighboring spatial positions to modify

the response interpretations at each position. That is, they attempted to use the spatial context around each operator to refine its response. For example, if a line operator indicated the presence of a line in a particular direction, then, assuming the line did not end at that position, there should be compatible response indicators at the previous and the following positions (in the direction of the line). If this further support was found, then a measure of the likelihood for a line at that position was strengthened; if it was not found, then the measure was weakened. This process was repeated until a stable set of response interpretations was obtained.

The above approach was shown to work well in some cases, but not in all. These failures could be attributed to two main causes: (i) the relaxation algorithm, which was motivated primarily by ad hoc criteria [14.5], could not have been functioning properly for this problem; or (ii) the constraints between response interpretations, which were also chosen for heuristic reasons, may have been in error. (For a subsequent, but in practice equally poor, approach to selecting these constraints, or compatibilities, see [14.6]. Again, as we shall show, this scheme is still context-insensitive, although it does involve an explicit estimation step. The problem is that the estimation is global, and makes no use of the operator's structure. First attempts to use operator structure appear in the work of RISEMAN and HANSON and their students; see [14.7]. But, again, their work evolved in a different direction than that reported here.)

The immediate contribution of this paper is to correct both of these possible faults. In the next section we review a different, and more recent approach to relaxation, that is much more well-founded mathematically. This new approach makes the connection between relaxation and optimization explicit, and provides an optimal algorithm for implementing it. Following this, we present a new approach to selecting compatibilities for line-operator interpretation. These new compatibilities are based on operators of different sizes, in which the larger ones provide the context for interpreting the smaller ones. The new compatibilities also reveal the problem with the original ones; the original ones involved an implicit assumption that the underlying line pattern consisted only of straight, nonintersecting lines. The new system is equivalent to the old one when these circumstances hold, but is substantially more general in that it also allows for curved lines.

The considerations leading to the new line and curve compatibilities also have a much more general implication -- they provide a methodology for selecting compatibilities for the optimal interpretation of arbitrary operators, provided their structure is known. These considerations can have serious application in related areas, such as the computational modeling of human perception [14.8].

14.2 Relaxation Labeling, Variational Inequalities, and Optimization

Relaxation labeling provides an appropriate framework for interpreting the responses of nonunique local operators. Abstractly, suppose that we are given a graph $G(N,E)$, in which each node N corresponds to a pictorial position and in which edges (E) are defined between spatially proximate (8-connected) neighbors. Assume that there are n nodes and that attached to each node i is a set of labels $L_i = \{\ell\}$, $\ell = 1,2,\ldots,m$. Each label ℓ denotes a possible assertion to be associated with that position. In our application, for example, the labels will indicate the presence of an oriented unit line segment at that position, as well as a NO-LINE label. (More precisely, the labels will indicate that the associated pixel is part of a line, with an orientation as shown; or it will indicate that the pixel is not part of a line.)

Associated with each label is a measure of the certainty with which it is correct; we denote these $Pi(\ell)$. They are always positive, are bounded by 0 and 1, inclusive, and sum to 1 at each node (position). That is,

$$0 \leq Pi(\ell) \leq 1 \qquad \begin{array}{l} i = 1,2,\ldots,n \\ \ell = 1,2,\ldots,m \end{array} \tag{14.1}$$

$$\sum_{\ell} Pi(\ell) = 1 \qquad i = 1,2,\ldots,n \ .$$

The graph is further structured by the existence of constraints between the labels on neighboring nodes. These constraints are modeled as compatibility functions defined over n-tuples (usually pairs) of labels. Again they are numerically valued, are represented (in the pairwise case) as $Rij(\ell,\ell')$, and denote the compatibility between label ℓ at position i with label ℓ' at neighboring position j. They are bounded below by minus infinity, inclusive, and above by plus infinity.

We now have enough structure to specify the selection problem: select the label at each node that maximizes an appropriate measure of performance. Typical among these measures is one that maximizes an additive sum of the certainty factors weighted by their compatibilities ([14.9]; see also [14.10]):

$$A(P) = \sum_{i,\ell} \sum_{j,\ell'} Rij(\ell,\ell')*Pj(\ell')*Pi(\ell)$$

where the inner sum is evaluted over all neighbors j of i and each of their labels ℓ', while the outer sum is evaluated over all ℓs at i and all nodes i. In short, this functional is designed to find the label set which has, among all those possible, the largest compatibility. These compatibilties are, of course, problem dependent, and we discuss how to obtain them for the line-finding problem in the next section.

The above functional A(P) is typical, and can be maximized by techniques such as gradient ascent, provided the constraints (14.1) are not violated. This is the basis for the relaxation/optimization approaches in [14.9]. But problems arise when the $Rij(\ell,\ell')$ are not symmetric; the gradient computation, if carried out straightforwardly, introduces an explicit symmetricization of the compatibilities, destroying essential information in the process. (To see the need for asymmetric compatibilities, just consider the letters q and u in English!)

The main foundation for the theory of relaxation proposed by HUMMEL and ZUCKER [14.11] is a notion of support for a label, or, in other words, a measure of how consistent a label is with the labels in its neighborhood. Formalizing such a notion of support will allow us to pose the relaxation computation in more general terms than the optimization described above, thereby allowing nonsymmetric compatibilities. It also provides an explicit connection with differential equations and with discrete relaxation [14.12]. This formulation, which is posed in the variational calculus, provably reduces to the above case for symmetric compatibilties (provided the gradient ascent is performed correctly).

In the simplest case support is defined by the inner loop of the above sum:

$$Si(\ell) = \sum_{j} \sum_{\ell'} Rij(\ell,\ell')*Pj(\ell')$$

which shows the support for label ℓ at position i. Relaxation is really after consistent labelings, or assignments of labels to each node in G; we shall denote such a labeling by P*, which is the vector concatenation of the labeling vectors at each position, Pi. For example, when there is exactly one label for each node, P* has the form

P* = [0,0,...,1,0,...,1,...,0]

where, if there are m possible labels on n nodes, then P has dimension n*m, with precisely n 1s indicating the selected labels.

Consistency can now be defined as follows: a labeling P* is consistent if and only if:

$$\sum_{\ell} Pi(\ell)*Si(\ell) \geq \sum_{\ell} Vi(\ell)*Si(\ell) \qquad i = 1,2,...,n$$

for all other possible labelings V*. The components of V*, Vi( ), indicate possible labelings at node i; they are each of dimension m. This inequality must hold for all nodes. The search for consistent labelings can now be posed as the search for solutions to the following variational inequality:

Find a legal labeling P* such that

$$\sum_{i,\ell,j,\ell'} Rij(\ell,\ell')Pj(\ell')[Vi(\ell)-Pi(\ell)] \leq 0$$

for all legal labelings V.

HUMMEL and ZUCKER [14.11] prove that (i) the solution to this variational inequality can be obtained by the algorithm given in the Appendix to this paper; (ii) solutions to this variational inequality exist; (iii) the stopping points of the algorithm must be consistent labelings; (iv) when the compatibilities are symmetric, the algorithm becomes formally equivalent to a constrained gradient ascent; and (v) if the iterates enter a neighborhood around a strictly consistent labeling, then it will converge to that labeling. Furthermore, they show that the original nonlinear relaxation algorithm approximates this optimal one in the interior of the labeling space. We take this to imply that when the original algorithm was functioning properly, it should have been viewed as performing the computation indicated above.

Before closing this section, we should like to stress the difference between standard optimization theory and the variational techniques used above. In optimization theory, as it is typically applied to problems of the sort considered in this paper, functionals must be defined a priori. The naturalness, usefulness, and even existence of these functionals is the responsibility of the designer. The above variational approach provides, through the definitions of support and consistency, a much more general approach to structuring problem solutions. Consistent labelings imply large support locally, but all of these support functions overlap and hence interact. Consistency thus amounts to the solution of a system of coupled inequalities, which, under certain conditions, imply the existence of a suitable functional.

14.3 The Line Labeling Problem

The development of a relaxation process for labeling lines and curves must begin with a definition of a curve. We shall adopt a differential point of view, and shall aim for a specification of the tangent to the curve at every point along it--that is, the derivative of the curve with respect to an intrinsic parameter running along it.

Both the points and the tangents to the curve will be quantized. The points will be expressed in Cartesian image coordinates, and the curve will be taken to be exactly one pixel thick. The curve will be smooth, in these coordinates, and will be assumed to be continuous. It may end. The possible tangents to the curve will be quantized into eight directions, for simplicity, although nothing changes in principle if a finer quantization is adopted.

The above assumptions begin to define the label structure -- we shall attempt to label the points along the curve with the orientations of their tangents, and other points as not being part of the curve. The labels will be denoted LINE (orientation) or NO-LINE. This is the same labeling scheme used in [14.4]. Note that the primitive unit of length, here taken as one pixel, could also be changed without altering any of the arguments.

Asserting which of these possible labels is best for each pixel in a noisy image of lines and curves is our next problem. If an operator could be found whose output could be quantified precisely into these label classes, perhaps by a thresholding operation, then our task would be complete. But such an operator, if it existed, would be so complex that it would be practically impossible to evaluate it, because it would have to examine large sections of curves to be successful; locally, the structure is too ambiguous.

The solution that we shall adopt decomposes into two parts: (i) the selection of an operator that signals reasonable possibilities; and then (ii) the optimal selection among these possibilities. As we shall show, it is an analysis of the chosen operators that suggests criteria appropriate for the optimization. We shall use the theory of relaxation sketched in the previous section to perform the optimization, since it will turn out that the compatibilities are all symmetric.

The obvious choice for an operator is the second directional derivative, or "line detector" in common use. We shall use one with difference-of-Gaussians cross sections; see Fig. 14.1. An essential point about this operator is that it provides us with an explicit notion of orientation directly from its structure. There are many ways in which orientation can be expressed, e.g., as the ratio of axes of the operator. Given such an intrinsic notion of orientation, we can evaluate (i.e., convolve) the operator in several orientations at every point in an image. Each of these responses then gives an indication of how well the tangent to the curve corresponds to the orientation of the operator. Together they define a distribution over the possible tangents to the curve at a point; see Fig.14.2a.

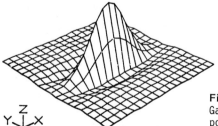

Z
Y⊥X

Fig. 14.1. Directional difference of Gaussians (DOG) mask with 3 x 13 central positive region

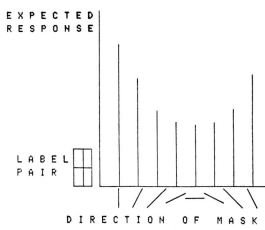

Fig. 14.2. (a) Directional response profile of a DOG mask when centered on a straight line. The response is strongest when the main axis of the mask is parallel to the line **(b)** Directional response profile of a DOG mask when centered near an angle in a line. Note that the presence of two peaks in the profile corresponds to the directions of the line on either side of the angle

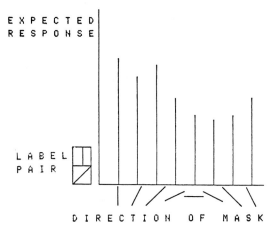

   The problem with the directional derivative operator is that it leads to distributions with symmetries; many underlying line configurations give equivalent responses. The problem with noise is that it alters this distribution. Thus, it would seem impossible to interpret the response of this operator purely locally, even if the rotated responses are allowed. Stated in other terms, even if one were to ask for an optimal interpretation of the operator's responses, the available constraints are too weak. For example, given only this single-point information, optimal interpretations would at best result in choosing the maximal response.

   Recalling the limiting process underlying differentiation, or, more precisely, a finite difference approximation to it, we note that at least two positions must be involved. Information obtained from this larger neighborhood can supply further constraints for the relaxation/optimization process. The simplest such constraint is one of good continuation for curves. Simply stated, if the tangent to the curve is in orientation i, then there should be strong indications of the curve at the next pixel in the direction i (or -i). Indeed, this was the thinking that was at the basis of the first relaxation system for line and curve enhancement [14.4]. Particular compatibilities were

defined from information analogous to that in Fig.14.2a: identically oriented
labels supported one another maximally, while perpendicular labels detracted
support. Intermediate cases took on intermediate values. Symbolically, such
compatibilities can be indicated by

$$Rij(-,-) = 1$$
$$Rij(-,/) = 0.5$$
$$Rij(-,|) = 0.0 \ .$$

There was little difference in performance whether the compatibilities dropped
off linearly or exponentially through these cases; the present point is that
they are derived from an implicit assumption that the line is straight. Thus
one would expect that they work less than optimally for curved lines, which
is exactly what was experienced.

The above notion of a slightly larger neighborhood can be used to relax
this dependence on straight lines. Given that we know the structure of our
operators, we can evaluate their performance over curved (as well as straight)
lines. From this evaluation explicit expectations can be accumulated about
how they will act in all possible circumstances. That is, we can actually
compute the expected response of our differential operator to all possible
underlying line configurations. Then we can base our interpretation process
on these expected response configurations. That there is substantially more
information in these operator response curves is shown in Fig.14.2b; note how
they differ from that for a straight line in Fig.14.2a.

The larger an operator becomes, the larger its support becomes in terms
of underlying patterns. For the above technique to work, at least one operator larger than the primitive pattern unit is necessary. Otherwise, none
of this contextual variation could be captured. Furthermore, since the response varies with size, if more than one size is used, more constraint is
possible. Combinations of small operators, for detailed fidelity, and larger
operators, for contextual constraint, thus seem most advisable. Such inter-
operator constraints may be (part of) the reason that certain multiple-size
operators are present in the human visual system [14.8].

We are now in a position to pose our optimal relaxation process for interpreting the responses of the differential operator. It is based on the
following

RESPONSE INTERPRETATION PROBLEM: Assume that we are given a description
of the operators whose responses we are to interpret. From these we can
compile expected response configurations to all possible underlying
image configurations (i.e., inverse images). Now, suppose that we are
given an observed response configuration from an unknown underlying
image. The problem is to find the image configuration which, if present,
would give a response configuration that most closely matches the given
observed one.

In terms of the line-labeling problem, we are given expected response curves
EXPECTED-RESPONSE (orientation, size), for at least two operator sizes. Furthermore, we are given OBSERVED-RESPONSE (orientation, size). Thus we wish
to find the line-label configuration that gives the EXPECTED-RESPONSE (.,.)
that minimizes

‖ EXPECTED-RESPONSE (orientation, size)
- OBSERVED-RESPONSE (orientation, size) ‖

under an appropriate norm ‖ ‖ .

206

14.4 The Relaxation Process

In this section we formulate a solution to the response interpretation problem using the theory of relaxation described in Sect.14.2. Our principal task is to obtain compatibility functions that lead to a suitable minimization of the line configuration whose response profile most closely matches the unknown, observed one. Since the expected and observed response profiles are given as curves, the most sensible class of norms are those that minimize the (pointwise) differences between these curves, i.e., those that are proportional to the area between the expected and the observed response profiles.

The particular compatibility between a label with orientation o at position i and another label with orientation o' at position j can be obtained by actually computing what the response profiles would be to this exact configuration. Note that this computation requires an operator whose size is at least as large as two underlying primitive units (in our case, two pixels). Thus it requires two labels to specify the configuration. The computation could either be done empirically, by creating an image of this line configuration and then convolving the various operators with it, or it could be computed analytically. Such techniques yield the EXPECTED-RESPONSE(o,o'; size) profiles. Then, the actual compatibility for this node/label pairing would be determined by the actual OBSERVED-RESPONSE(o,o'; size). In particular,

$$R_{ij}[o,o']=1-\|\text{EXP-RESPONSE}(o,o'; \text{size}) - \text{OBS-RESPONSE}(o,o'; \text{size})\| \quad .$$

Since the above norm involves the integral of the area between the two profiles, we make the additional simplifying assumption that the different size operator effects can be separated:

$$\|\text{EXP-RESPONSE}(o,o'; \text{size}) - \text{OBS-RESPONSE}(o,o'; \text{size})\|$$
$$= \|\text{EXP-RESPONSE}(o,o'; \text{large}) - \text{OBS-RESPONSE}(o,o'; \text{large})\|$$
$$+\|\text{EXP-RESPONSE}(o,o'; \text{small}) - \text{OBS-RESPONSE}(o,o'; \text{small})\| \quad .$$

That is, the small and the large masks (or any number of masks) are each treated separately, and the partial results are then combined additively. This approximation could be further improved by weighting the separate terms appropriately.

The interpretation of these compatibilities clearly depends on how well the expected and the observed response profiles match. When they are identical, the difference between them is 0, and the compatibility is 1. This is the most positive situation. As long as the profiles differ, the compatibility will be less than one. We further take the norm as having a maximal difference of 1, so that the minimal compatibility is 0.

Since the compatibility functions are symmetric, it is clear that the functional described in Sect.14.2 exists. Furthermore, the definition of the compatibilities is such that it makes sense for this problem. Finally, since the compatibilities are a function of the initial data, they are context sensitive to the kinds of patterns that may be present. In the special case of straight lines, they reduce to ones similar to those already proposed. However, they are much more general, in that they can handle curves as well. But perhaps the most important point is that they were derived from theoretical considerations about the task at hand -- the interpretation of operator responses -- and explicitly reflect this structure. The original ad hoc appeal to "good continuation" has been subsumed.

14.5 Experimental Results

In this section we describe a preliminary experiment with the above relaxation system. The label set consisted of nine possibilities for each position in the image: LINE(OR1),...,LINE(OR8), and NO-LINE. The second directional derivatives were roughly (3×13) and (7×27) for their positive centers.

Two examples were run. The first is a straight line on a noisy background (see Fig.14.3a), and is the sort of image that the original system could handle. The results are shown in Fig.14.3b. A second example of a curve (Fig.14.4a) on a noisy background was also run; see Fig.14.4b. It, too, has clearly been located, and is not the kind of curve that could be found and labeled using the straight-line assumption.

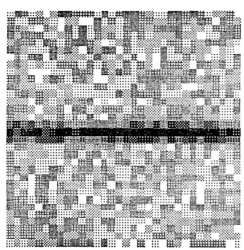

ITERATION: 07

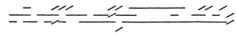

(b)

Fig. 14.3. **(a)** Straight line plus noise on a 32 x 32 grid **(b)** Labeling graph after 7 iterations of relaxation

(a)

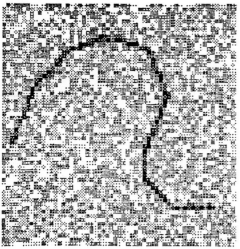

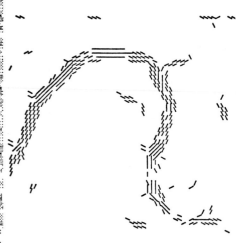

ITERATION: 06

Fig. 14.4 a,b. Caption see opposite page

14.6 Conclusions

Local operators provide a transduction of image properties into possible low-level feature spaces, and, as such, provide the first stage of processing for most vision systems. However, by their very nature, they respond ambiguously. In this paper, we developed an approach to interpreting optimally such operator responses. We concentrated on the line-and curve-finding problem, because it provided us with a concrete problem with which to pose our results.

The structure of the interpretation scheme was motivated by optimization theory, and was embodied in a relaxation process. Such processes are now becoming well-founded mathematically, and are becoming practical with VLSI technology.

Any optimization scheme requires constraints to be active, for it is from these constraints that functionals (or more generally variational inequalities) can be derived. Our principal contribution in this paper was to set out an approach to deriving these constraints from the structure of the operators themselves. In particular, for the line-and curve-finding problem, this involved using operators of different sizes. The smaller operators then provided the detailed spatial localization, while the larger operators provided the contextual constraint within which to perform the interpretation. The scheme was shown to work both for straight lines and for curves, and thus is an advance over previous work.

Appendix: The Relaxation Algorithm

Initialization: Start with an initial labeling P^0.
Set K = 0.

Iterate the following until STOP.

Compute Q^K = grad $A(P^K)$

Project Q^K onto the legal labeling space. (See [14.13] for algorithm and proof of correctness.)

Call this projection U^K.

If U^K = 0, STOP.

SET K = K+1.

Set $P^{K+1} = P^K + h * U^K$, where h is a small "step size."

References

14.1 A. Rosenfeld, A. C. Kak: Digital Picture Processing (Academic Press, New York, 1976)
14.2 U. Montanari: On the optimal detection of curves in noisy pictures, Comm. ACM 14, 335-345 (1971)

◄ Fig. 14.4. (a) Random curve plus noise on a 60 x 60 grid (b) Labeling graph after 6 iterations of relaxation

14.3 A. Martelli: An application of heuristic search methods to edge and contour detection, Comm. ACM 19, 73-83 (1976)

14.4 S. W. Zucker, R. A. Hummel, A. Rosenfeld: An application of relaxation to line and curve enhancement, IEEE Trans. Computers C-26, 393-403, 922-929 (1977)

14.5 A. Rosenfeld, R. A. Hummel, S. W. Zucker: Scene labeling by relaxation operations, IEEE Trans. Systems, Man, Cybernetics SMC-6, 420-433 (1976)

14.6 S. Peleg, A. Rosenfeld: Determining compatibility coefficients for curve enhancement relaxation processes, IEEE Trans. Systems, Man, Cybernetics SMC-8, 548-555 (1978)

14.7 J. M. Prager: Extracting and labeling boundary segments in natural images, IEEE Trans. Pattern Analysis Machine Intelligence PAMI-2, 16-26 (1980)

14.8 S. W. Zucker: "Computer vision and human perception: an essay on the discovery of constraints", in Proc. 7th Int'l. Joint Conf. on Artificial Intelligence, Vancouver, BC, 1981, pp. 1102-1116

14.9 O. Faugeras, M. Berthod: "Scene labeling: an optimization approach", in Proc. Pattern Recognition and Image Processing Conf., Chicago, IL, 1979, pp. 318-326

14.10 S. Ullman: Relaxation and constrained optimization by local processes, Computer Graphics Image Processing 10, 115-125 (1979)

14.11 R. A. Hummel, S. W. Zucker: "On the Foundations of Relaxation Labelling Processes", Computer Vision and Graphics Laboratory Technical Report 80-7, McGill University (1980)

14.12 D. Waltz: "Understanding line drawings of scenes with shadows", in The Psychology of Computer Vision, ed. by P. H. Winston (McGraw-Hill, New York, 1975), pp. 19-91

14.13 J. L. Mohammed, R. A. Hummel, S. W. Zucker: A feasible direction operator for relaxation labeling processes, IEEE Trans. Pattern Analysis Machine Intelligence, to appear

Part V

Region Representation and
Surface Interpolation

15. A Tutorial on Quadtree Research

H. Samet

Department of Computer Science, University of Maryland
College Park, MD 20742, USA

Region representation is an important issue in image processing, cartography, and computer graphics. A wide number of representations is currently in use. Recently, there has been much interest in a hierarchical data structure termed the quadtree. It is compact and depending on the nature of the region saves space as well as time and also facilitates operations such as search. In this section we give a brief overview of the quadtree data structure and related research results.

15.1 Introduction

In our discussion we assume that a region is a subset of a 2^n by 2^n array which is viewed as being composed of unit-square pixels. The most common region representations used in image processing are the binary array and the run length representation [15.1]. The binary array represents region pixels by 1s and nonregion pixels by 0s. The run length representation represents each row of the binary array as a sequence of runs of 1s alternating with runs of 0s.

Boundaries of regions are often specified as a sequence of unit vectors in the principal directions. This representation is termed a chain code [15.2]. For example, letting i represent $90° * i$ $(i=0,1,2,3)$, we have the following sequence as the chain code for the region in Fig.15.1a:

$$030^2 3^5 2^3 123^3 032^5 1^6 0101030101 \ .$$

Note that this is a clockwise code which starts at the leftmost of the uppermost border points. Chain codes yield a compact representation; however, they are somewhat inconvenient for performing operations such as set union and intersection. For an alternative boundary representation, see the strip trees of BALLARD [15.3].

Regions can also be represented by a collection of maximal blocks that are contained in the given region. One such trivial representation is the run length where the blocks are 1 by m rectangles. A more general representation treats the region as a union of maximal blocks (of 1s) of a given shape. The medial axis transform (MAT) [15.4,5] is the set of points serving as centers of these blocks and their corresponding radii.

The quadtree is a maximal block representation in which the blocks have standard sizes and positions (i.e., powers of two). It is an approach to region representation which is based on the successive subdivision of an image array into quadrants. If the array does not consist entirely of 1s or entirely of 0s, then we subdivide it into quadrants, subquadrants,...

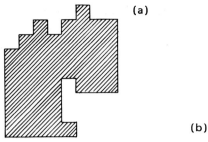

(a)

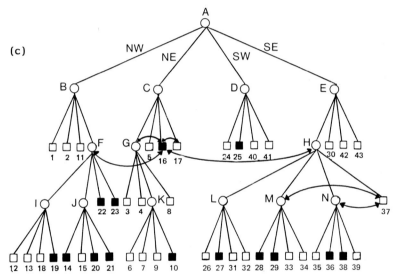

(b)

Fig. 15.1. A region, its maximal blocks, and the corresponding quadtree. Blocks in the region are shaded, background blocks are blank. **(a)** Region. **(b)** Blocks of decomposition of the region in (a). **(c)** Quadtree representation of the blocks in (b)

until we obtain blocks (possibly single pixels) that consist of 1s or of 0s, i.e., they are entirely contained in the region or entirely disjoint from it. This process is represented by a tree of out-degree 4 (i.e., each nonleaf node has four sons) in which the root node represents the entire array. The four sons of the root node represent the quadrants (labeled in order NW, NE, SW, SE), and the leaf nodes correspond to those blocks of the array for which no further subdivision is necessary. Leaf nodes are said to be "black" or "white" depending on whether their corresponding blocks are entirely within or outside of the region respectively. All nonleaf nodes are said to be "gray." Since the array was assumed to be 2^n by 2^n, the tree height is at most n. As an example, Fig.15.1b is a block decomposition of the region in Fig.15.1a while Fig.15.1c is the corresponding quadtree. Each quadtree node is implemented, storage-wise, as a record with six fields. Five fields contain pointers to the four sons and the father of a node. The sixth field contains type information such as color, etc. Note that the quadtree representation discussed here should not be confused with the quadtree representation of two-dimensional point space data introduced by FINKEL and BENTLEY [15.6] and also discussed in [15.7,8] and improved upon in [15.9].

The quadtree method of region representation is based on a regular decomposition. It has been employed in the domains of computer graphics, scene analysis, architectural design [15.10], and pattern recognition. In particular, WARNOCK's [15.11-13] algorithm for hidden surface elimination is based on such a principle--i.e., it successively subdivides the picture into smaller and smaller squares in the process of searching for areas to be displayed. Application of the quadtree to image representation was proposed by KLINGER [15.14] and further elaborated upon in [15.15-20]. It is relatively compact [15.15] and is well suited to operations such as union and intersection [15.21-23] and detecting various region properties [15.15,21,22,24]. HUNTER's Ph.D. thesis [15.21,22,24], in the domain of computer graphics, develops a variety of algorithms (including linear transformations) for the manipulation of a quadtree region representation. In [15.25-27] variations of the quadtree are applied in three dimensions to represent solid objects and in [15.28] to more dimensions.

There has been much work recently on the interchangeability between the quadtree and other traditional methods of region representation. Algorithms have been developed for converting a binary array to a quadtree [15.29], run lengths to a quadtree [15.30] and a quadtree to run lengths [15.31], as well as boundary codes to a quadtree [15.32] and a quadtree to boundary codes [15.33]. Work has also been done on computing geometric properties such as connected component labeling [15.34], perimeter [15.35], Euler number [15.36], areas and moments [15.23], as well as a distance transform [15.37,38]. In addition, the quadtree has been used in image processing applications such as shape approximation [15.39], edge enhancement [15.40], image segmentation [15.41], threshold selection [15.42], and smoothing [15.43].

15.2 Preliminaries

In the quadtree representation, by virtue of its tree-like nature, most operations are carried out by techniques which traverse the tree. In fact, many of the operations that we describe can be characterized as having two basic steps. The first step either traverses the quadtree in a specified order or constructs a quadtree. The second step performs a computation at each node which often makes use of its neighboring nodes, i.e., nodes representing image blocks that are adjacent to the given node's block. For examples, see [15.30-38]. Frequently, these two steps are performed in parallel.

In general, it is preferable to avoid having to use position (i.e., coordinates) and size information when making relative transitions (i.e., locating neighboring nodes) in the quadtree since they involve computation (rather than simply chasing links) and are clumsy when adjacent blocks are of different sizes (e.g., when a neighboring block is larger). Similarly, we do not assume that there are links from a node to its neighbors because we do not want to use links in excess of four links from a nonleaf node to its sons and the link from a nonroot node to its father. Such techniques, described in [15.44], are used in [15.30-38] and result in algorithms that only make use of the existing structure of the tree. This is in contrast with the methods of KLINGER and RHODES [15.19] which make use of size and position information, and those of HUNTER and STEIGLITZ [15.21,22,24] which locate neighbors through the use of explicit links (termed nets and ropes).

Locating neighbors in a given direction is quite straightforward. Given a node corresponding to a specific block in the image, its neighbor in a particular direction (horizontal or vertical) is determined by locating a common ancestor. For example, if we want to find an eastern neighbor, the common ancestor is the first ancestor node which is reached via its NW or SW son. Next, we retrace the path from the common ancestor, but making mirror image moves about the appropriate axis, e.g., to find an eastern or western neighbor, the mirror images of NE and SE are NW and SW, respectively. For example, the eastern neighbor of node 32 in Fig.15.1c is node 33. It is located by ascending the tree until the common ancestor H is found. This requires going through a SE link to reach L and a NW link to reach H. Node 33 is now reached by backtracking along the previous path with the appropriate mirror image moves (i.e., going through a NE link to reach M and a SW link to reach 33).

In general, adjacent neighbors need not be of the same size. If they are larger, then only a part of the path to the common ancestor is retraced. If they are smaller, then the retraced path ends at a "gray" node of equal size. Thus a "neighbor" is correctly defined as the smallest adjacent leaf whose corresponding block is of greater than or equal size. If no such node exists, then a gray node of equal size is returned. Note that similar techniques can be used to locate diagonal neighbors (i.e., nodes corresponding to blocks that touch the given node's block at a corner). For example, node 20 in Fig.15.1c is the NW neighbor of node 22. For more details, see [15.44].

In contrast with our neighbor-finding methods is the use of explicit links from a node to its adjacent neighbors in the horizontal and vertical directions reported in [15.21,22,24]. This is achieved through the use of adjacency trees, "ropes," and "nets." An adjacency tree exists whenever a leaf node, say X, has a GRAY neighbor, say Y, of equal size. In such a case, the adjacency tree of X is a binary tree rooted at Y whose nodes consist of all sons of Y (BLACK, WHITE, and GRAY) that are adjacent to X. For example, for node 16 in Fig.15.1, the western neighbor is GRAY node F with an adjacency tree as shown in Fig.15.2. A rope is a link between adjacent nodes of equal size at least one of which is a leaf node. For example, in Fig.15.1, there exists a rope between node 16 and nodes G, 17, H, and F. Similarly, there exists a rope between node 37 and nodes M and N; however, there does not exist a rope between node L and nodes M and N.

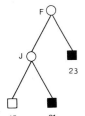

Fig. 15.2. Adjacency tree for the western neighbor of node 16 in Fig. 15.1.

The algorithm for finding a neighbor using a roped quadtree is quite simple. We want a neighbor, say Y, on a given side, say D, of a block, say X. If there is a rope from X on side D, then it leads to the desired neighbor. If no such rope exists, then the desired neighbor must be larger. In such a case, we ascend the tree until encountering a node having a rope on side D that leads to the desired neighbor. In effect, we have ascended the adjacency tree of Y. For example, to find the eastern neighbor of node 21 in Fig.15.1, we ascend through node J to node F, which has a rope along its eastern side leading to node 16.

At times it is not convenient to ascend nodes searching for ropes. A data structure named a net is used [15.21,22,24] to obviate this step by linking all leaf nodes to their neighbors regardless of their size. Thus in the previous example, there would be a direct link between nodes 21 and 16 along the eastern side of node 21. The advantage of ropes and nets is that the number of links that must be traversed is reduced. However, the disadvantage is that the storage requirements are considerably increased since many additional links are necessary. In contrast, our methods are implemented by algorithms that make use of the existing structure of the tree--i.e., four links from a nonleaf node to its sons, and a link from a nonroot node to its father.

15.3 Conversion

15.3.1 Quadtrees and Arrays

The definition of a quadtree leads naturally to a "top down" quadtree construction process. This may lead to excessive computation because the process of examining whether a quadrant contains all 1s or all 0s may cause certain parts of the region to be examined repeatedly by virtue of being composed of a mixture of 1s and 0s. Alternatively, a "bottom-up" method may be employed which scans the picture in the sequence

```
 1  2  5  6  17 18  21 22
 3  4  7  8  19 20  23 24
 9 10 13 14  25 26  29 30
11 12 15 16  27 28  31 32
33 ...
```

where the numbers indicate the sequence in which the pixels are examined. As maximal blocks of 0s or 1s are discovered, corresponding leaf nodes are added along with the necessary ancestor nodes. This is done in such a way that leaf nodes are never created until they are known to be maximal. Thus there is never a need to merge four leaves of the same color and change the color of their common parent from gray to white or black as is appropriate. See [15.29] for the details of such an algorithm whose execution time is proportional to the number of pixels in the image.

If it is necessary to scan the picture row by row (e.g., when the input is a run length coding) the quadtree construction process is somewhat more complex. We scan the picture a row at a time. For odd-numbered rows, nodes corresponding to the pixel or run values are added for the pixels and attempts are made to discover maximal blocks of 0s or 1s whose size depends on the row number (e.g., when processing the fourth row, maximal blocks of maximum size 4 by 4 can be discovered). In such a case merging is said to take place. See [15.30] for the details of an algorithm that constructs a quadtree from a row by row scan such that at any instant of time a valid quadtree exists. This algorithm has an execution time that is proportional to the number of pixels in the image.

Similarly, for a given quadtree we can output the corresponding binary picture by traversing the tree in such a way that for each row the appropriate blocks are visited and a row of 0s or 1s is output. In essence, we visit each quadtree node once for each row that intersects it (i.e., a node corresponding to a block of size 2^K by 2^K is visited 2^K times). For the

216

details see [15.31] where an algorithm is described whose execution time depends only on the number of blocks of each size that comprise the image-- not on their particular configuration.

15.3.2 Quadtrees and Borders

In order to determine, for a given leaf node M of a quadtree, whether the corresponding block is on the border, we must visit the leaf nodes that correspond to 4-adjacent blocks and check whether they are black or white. For example, to find M's right-hand neighbor in Fig.15.3, we use the neighbor-finding techniques outlined in Sect.15.2.2. If the neighbor is a leaf node, then its block is at least as large as that of M and so it is M's sole neighbor to the right. Otherwise, the neighbor is the root of a subtree whose leftmost leaf nodes correspond to M's right-hand neighbors. These nodes are found by traversing that subtree.

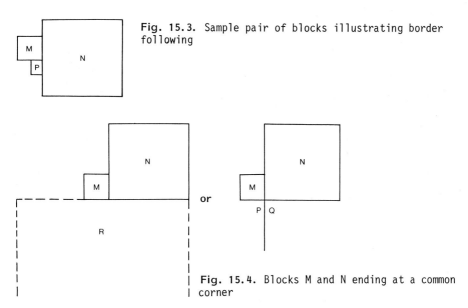

Fig. 15.3. Sample pair of blocks illustrating border following

Fig. 15.4. Blocks M and N ending at a common corner

Let M,N in Fig.15.3 be black and white leaf nodes whose associated blocks are 4-adjacent. Thus the pair M,N defines a common border segment of length 2^K (2^K is the minimum of the side lengths of M and N) which ends at a corner of the smaller of the two blocks (they may both end at a common point as in Fig.15.4). In order to produce a boundary code representation for a region in the image we must determine the next segment along the border whose previous segment lay between M and N. This is achieved by locating the other leaf P whose block touches the end of the segment between M and N. If the M,N segment ends at a corner of both M and N, then we must find the other leaf R or leaves P,Q whose blocks touch that corner (see Fig.15.4). Again, this can be accomplished by using neighbor-finding techniques as outlined in Sect.15.2.

For the noncommon corner case, the next border segment is the common border defined by M and P if P is white, or the common border defined by N and P if P is black. In the common corner case, the pair of blocks defining the next border segment is determined exactly as in the standard "crack following" algorithm [15 .45] for traversing region borders. This process is repeated until we re-encounter the block pair M,N. At this point the entire border has been traversed. The successive border segments constitute a 4-direction chain code, broken up into segments whose lengths are sums of powers of two. The time required for this process is on the order of the number of border nodes times the tree height. For more details see [15.33].

Using the methods described in the last two paragraphs, we can traverse the quadtree, find all borders, and generate their codes. During this process, we mark each border as we follow it, so that it will not be followed again from a different starting point. Note that the marking process is complicated by the fact that a node's block may be on many different borders.

In order to generate a quadtree from a set of 4-direction chain codes we use a two-step process. First, we trace the boundary in a clockwise direction and construct a quadtree whose black leaf nodes are of a size equal to the unit code length. All the black nodes correspond to blocks on the interior side of the boundary. All remaining nodes are left uncolored. Second, all uncolored nodes are set to black or white as appropriate. This is achieved by traversing the tree, and for each uncolored leaf node, examining its neighbors. The node is colored black unless any of its neighbors is white or is black with a border along the shared boundary. At any stage, merging occurs if the four sons of a nonleaf node are leaves having the same color. The details of the algorithm are given in [15.32]. The time required is proportional to the product of the perimeter (i.e., the 4-direction chain code length) and the tree height.

15.3.3 Quadtrees of Derived Sets

Let S be the set of 1s in a given binary array, and let $\overline{S}$ be the complement of S. The quadtree of the complement of S is the same as that of S, with black leaf nodes changed to white and vice versa. To get the quadtree of the union of S and T from those of S and T, we traverse the two trees simultaneously. Where they agree, the new tree is the same and if the two nodes are gray, then their subtrees are traversed. If S has a gray (=nonleaf) node where T has a black node, the new tree gets a black node; if T has a white node there, we copy the subtree of S at that gray node into the new tree. If S has a white node, we copy the subtree of T at the corresponding node. The algorithm for the intersection of S and T is exactly analogous with the roles of black and white reversed. The time required for these algorithms is proportional to the number of nodes in the smaller of the two trees [15.23].

15.3.4 Skeletons and Medial Axis Transforms

The medial axis of a region is a subset of its points each of which has a distance from the complement of the region (using a suitably defined distance metric) which is a local maximum. The medial axis transform (MAT) consists of the set of medial axis or "skeleton" points and their associated distance values. The quadtree representation may be rendered even more compact by the use of a skeleton-like representation. Recall that a quadtree is a set of disjoint maximal square blocks having sides whose lengths are powers of 2. We define a quadtree skeleton to be a set of maximal square blocks having sides whose lengths are sums of powers of two. The maximum value (i.e., "chessboard") distance metric [15.45] is the most appropriate for an image represented by a quadtree. See [15.37] for the details of its computation

218

for a quadtree; see also [15.38] for a different quadtree distance transform. A quadtree medial axis transform (QMAT) is a quadtree whose black nodes correspond to members of the quadtree skeleton while all remaining leaf nodes are white. The QMAT has several important properties. First, it results in a partition of the image into a set of possibly nondisjoint squares having sides whose lengths are sums of powers of two rather than, as is the case with quadtrees, a set of disjoint squares having sides of lengths which are powers of two. Second, the QMAT is more compact than the quadtree and has a decreased shift sensitivity. See [15.46] for the details of a quadtree-to-QMAT conversion algorithm whose execution time is on the order of the number of nodes in the tree.

15.4 Property Measurement

15.4.1 Connected Component Labeling

Traditionally, connected component labeling is achieved by scanning a binary array row by row from left to right and labeling adjacencies that are discovered to the right and downward. During this process equivalences will be generated. A subsequent pass merges these equivalences and updates the labels of the affected pixels. In the case of the quadtree representation, we also scan the image in a sequential manner. However, the sequence's order is dictated by the tree structure -- i.e., we traverse the tree in postorder. Whenever a black leaf node is encountered all black nodes that are adjacent to its south and east sides are also visited and are labeled accordingly. Again, equivalences generated during this traversal are subsequently merged and a tree traversal is used to update the labels. The interesting result is that the algorithm's execution time is proportional to the number of pixels. An analogous result is described in the next section. See [15.34] for the details of an algorithm that labels connected components in time on the order of the number of nodes in the tree plus the product B log B, where B is the number of black leaf nodes.

15.4.2 Component Counting and Genus Computation

Once the connected components have been labeled, it is trivial to count them, since their number is the same as the number of inequivalent labels. We will next describe a method of determining the number of components minus the number of holes by counting certain types of local patterns in the array; this number g is known as the genus or Euler number of the array.

Let V be the number of 1s, E the number of horizontally adjacent pairs of 1s (i.e., 11) and vertically adjacent pairs of 1s, and F the number of two-by-two arrays of 1s in the array; it is well known [15.45] that g=V-E+F.

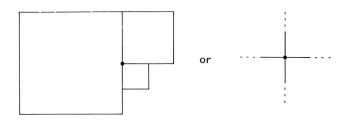

Fig. 15.5. Possible configurations of blocks that meet at and surround a common point

This result can be generalized to the case where the array is represented by a quadtree [15.36]. In fact, let V be the number of black leaf nodes; E the number of pairs of such nodes whose blocks are horizontally or vertically adjacent; and F the number of triples or quadruples of such nodes whose blocks meet at and surround a common point (see Fig.15.5). Then g=V-E+F. These adjacencies can be found (see Sect.15.3.2) by traversing the tree; the time required is on the order of the number of nodes in the tree.

15.4.3 Area and Moments

The area of a region represented by a quadtree can be obtained by summing the areas of the black leaf nodes, i.e., counting 4^h for each such node that represents a 2^h by 2^h block. Similarly, the first x and y moments of the region relative to a given origin can be computed by summing the first moments of these blocks; note that we know the position (and size) of each block from the coordinates of its leaf in the tree. Knowing the area and the first moments gives us the coordinates of the centroid, and we can then compute central moments relative to the centroid as the origin. The time required for any of these computations is proportional to the number of nodes in the tree. Further details on moment computation from quadtrees can be found in [15.23].

15.4.4 Perimeter

An obvious way of obtaining the perimeter of a region represented by a quadtree is simply to traverse its border and sum the number of steps. However, there is no need to traverse the border segments in order. Instead, we use a method which traverses the tree in postorder and for each black leaf node examines the colors of its neighbors on its four sides. For each white neighbor the length of the corresponding border segment is included in the perimeter. See [15.35] for the details of such an algorithm which has execution time proportional to the number of nodes in the tree. An even better formulation is reported in [15.47] which generalizes the concept of perimeter to n dimensions.

15.5 Concluding Remarks

We have briefly sketched algorithms for accomplishing traditional region processing operations by use of the quadtree representation. Many of the methods used on the pixel level carry over to the quadtree domain (e.g., connected component labeling, genus, etc.). Because of its compactness, the quadtree permits faster execution of these operations. Often the quadtree algorithms require time proportional to the number of blocks in the image, independent of their size.

The quadtree data structure requires storage for the various links. However, use of neighbor-finding techniques rather than ropes à la HUNTER [15.21, 22,24] is a compromise. In fact, experimental results show that the extra storage cost of ropes is not justified by the resulting minor decrease in execution time. This is because the average number of links traversed by neighbor finding methods is 3.5 in contrast with 1.5 for ropes. Nevertheless, there is a possibility that the quadtree may not be efficient spacewise. For example, a checkerboard-like region does not lead to economy of space. The space efficiency of the quadtree is analyzed in [15.48]. Some savings can be obtained by normalizing the quadtree [15.49,50] as is also possible by constructing a forest of quadtrees [15.51] to avoid large regions of WHITE. Storage can also be saved by using a locational code for all BLACK blocks [15.52]. Gray level quadtrees using a sequence of array codes to economize on storage are reported in [15.53].

The quadtree is especially useful for point-in-polygon operations as well as for query operations involving image overlays and set operations. Its hierarchical nature enables one to use image approximations. In particular, a breadth-first transmission of an image yields a successively finer image yet enabling the user to have a partial image. Thus the quadtree could be used in browsing through a large image database.

Quadtrees constitute an interesting alternative to the standard methods of digitally representing regions. Their chief disadvantage is that they are not shift invariant; two regions differing only by a translation may have quite different quadtrees (but see [15.46]). Thus shape matching from quadtrees is not straightforward. Nevertheless, in other respects, they have many potential advantages. They provide a compact and easily construct-ed representation from which standard region properties can be efficiently computed. In effect, they are "variable-resolution arrays" in which detail is represented only when it is available, without requiring excessive stor-age for parts of the image where detail is missing. Their variable-resolu-tion property is superior to trees based on a hexagonal decomposition [15.54] in that a square can be repeatedly decomposed into smaller squares (as can be done for triangles as well [15.55]), whereas once the smallest hexagon has been chosen it cannot be further decomposed into smaller hexagons. Note that the variance of resolution only applies to the area. For an appli-cation of the quadtree concept to borders, as well as area, see the line quadtree of [15.56].

References

15.1 D. Rutovitz: "Data structures for operations on digital images", in Pictorial Pattern Recognition, ed. by G. C. Cheng et al. (Thompson Book Co., Washington, DC, 1968), pp. 105-133

15.2 H. Freeman: Computer processing of line-drawing images, Computing Surveys 6, 57-97 (1974)

15.3 D. H. Ballard: Strip trees: a hierarchical representation for curves, Comm. ACM 24, 310-321 (1981)

15.4 H. Blum: "A transformation for extracting new descriptors of shape", in Models for the Perception of Speech and Visual Form, ed. by W. Wathen-Dunn (M.I.T. Press, Cambridge, MA, 1967), pp. 362-380

15.5 J. L. Pfaltz, A. Rosenfeld: Computer representation of planar regions by their skeletons, Comm. ACM 10, 119-122 (1967)

15.6 R. A. Finkel, J. L. Bentley: Quad trees: a data structure for re-trieval on composite keys, Acta Informatica 4, 1-9 (1974)

15.7 H. Samet: Deletion in two-dimensional quad trees, Comm. ACM 23, 703-710 (1980)

15.8 D. T. Lee, C. K. Wong: Worst-case analysis for region and partial region searches in multidimensional binary search trees and balanced quad trees, Acta Informatica 9, 23-29 (1977)

15.9 J. L. Bentley: Multidimensional binary search trees used for associa-tive searching, Comm. ACM 18, 509-517 (1975)

15.10 C. M. Eastman: Representations for space planning, Comm. ACM 13, 242-250 (1970)

15.11 J. E. Warnock: "A Hidden Surface Algorithm for Computer Generated Half Tone Pictures", Computer Science Department TR 4-15, University of Utah (1969)

15.12 I. E. Sutherland, R. F. Sproull, R. A. Schumacker: A characterization of ten hidden-surface algorithms, Computing Surveys 6, 1-55 (1974)

15.13 W. M. Newman, R. F. Sproull: Principles of Interactive Computer Graphics, 2nd ed. (McGraw-Hill, New York, 1971)

15.14 A. Klinger: "Patterns and search statistics", in <u>Optimizing Methods in Statistics</u>, ed. by J. S. Rustagi (Academic Press, New York, 1972) pp. 303-339

15.15 A. Klinger, C. R. Dyer: Experiments in picture representation using regular decomposition, Computer Graphics Image Processing 5, 68-105 (1975)

15.16 S. L. Tanimoto, T. Pavlidis: A hierarchical data structure for image processing, Computer Graphics Image Processing 4, 104-119 (1976)

15.17 S. L. Tanimoto: Pictorial feature distortion in a pyramid, Computer Graphics Image Processing 5, 333-352 (1976)

15.18 E. M. Riseman, M. A. Arbib: Computational techniques in the visual segmentation of static scenes, Computer Graphics Image Processing 6, 221-276 (1976)

15.19 A. Klinger, M. L. Rhodes: Organization and access of image data by areas, IEEE Trans. Pattern Analysis Machine Intelligence PAMI-1, 50-60 (1979)

15.20 N. Alexandridis, A. Klinger: Picture decomposition, tree data-structures, and identifying directional symmetries as node combinations, Computer Graphics Image Processing 8, 43-77 (1978)

15.21 G. M. Hunter: "Efficient Computation and Data Structures for Graphics", Ph.D. dissertation, Department of Electrical Engineering and Computer Science, Princeton University (1978)

15.22 G. M. Hunter, K. Steiglitz: Operations on images using quad trees, IEEE Trans. Pattern Analysis Machine Intelligence PAMI-1, 145-153 (1979)

15.23 M. Shneier: Calculations of geometric properties using quadtrees, Computer Graphics Image Processing 16, 296-302 (1981)

15.24 G. M. Hunter, K. Steiglitz: Linear transformation of pictures represented by quad trees, Computer Graphics Image Processing 10, 289-296 (1979)

15.25 D. R. Reddy, S. Rubin: "Representation of Three-Dimensional Objects", Department of Computer Science Technical Report 78-113, Carnegie-Mellon University (1978)

15.26 C. L. Jackins, S. L. Tanimoto: Oct-trees and their use in representing three-dimensional objects, Computer Graphics Image Processing 14, 249-270 (1980)

15.27 D. J. R. Meagher: "Octree Encoding: a New Technique for the Representation, Manipulation, and Display of Arbitrary 3-D Objects by Computer", TR 80-111, Rensselaer Polytechnic Institute (1980)

15.28 S. N. Srihari, M. Yau: "A Hierarchical Data Structure for Multidimensional Digital Images", Department of Computer Science Technical Report 185, State University of New York at Buffalo (1981)

15.29 H. Samet: Region representation: quadtrees from binary arrays, Computer Graphics Image Processing 13, 88-93 (1980)

15.30 H. Samet: An algorithm for converting rasters to quadtrees, IEEE Trans. Pattern Analysis Machine Intelligence PAMI-3, 93-95 (1981)

15.31 H. Samet: "Algorithms for the Conversion of Quadtrees to Rasters", Computer Graphics Image Processing, to appear

15.32 H. Samet: Region representation: quadtrees from boundary codes, Comm. ACM 23, 163-170 (1980)

15.33 C. R. Dyer, A. Rosenfeld, H. Samet: Region representation: boundary codes from quadtrees, Comm. ACM 23, 171-179 (1980)

15.34 H. Samet: Connected component labeling using quadtrees, J. ACM 28, 487-501 (1981)

15.35 H. Samet: Computing perimeters of images represented by quadtrees, IEEE Trans. Pattern Analysis Machine Intelligence PAMI-3, 683-687 (1981)

15.36 C. R. Dyer: Computing the Euler number of an image from its quadtree, Computer Graphics Image Processing 13, 270-276 (1980)

15.37 H. Samet: Distance transform for images represented by quadtrees, IEEE Trans. Pattern Analysis Machine Intelligence PAMI-4, 298-303 (1982)

15.38 M. Shneier: Path-length distances for quadtrees, Information Sciences 23, 49-67 (1981)

15.39 S. Ranade, A. Rosenfeld, H. Samet: Shape approximation using quadtrees, Pattern Recognition 15, 31-40 (1982)

15.40 S. Ranade: Use of quadtrees for edge enhancement, IEEE Trans. Systems, Man, Cybernetics SMC-11, 370-373 (1981)

15.41 S. Ranade, A. Rosenfeld, J. M. S. Prewitt: "Use of Quadtrees for Image Segmentation", Computer Science TR-878, University of Maryland (1980)

15.42 A. Y. Wu, T. H. Hong, A. Rosenfeld: Threshold selection using quadtrees, IEEE Trans. Pattern Analysis Machine Intelligence PAMI-4, 90-94 (1982)

15.43 S. Ranade M. Shneier: Using quadtrees to smooth images, IEEE Trans. Systems, Man, Cybernetics SMC-11, 373-376 (1981)

15.44 H. Samet: Neighbor finding techniques for images represented by quadtrees, Computer Graphics Image Processing 18, 37-57 (1982)

15.45 A. Rosenfeld, A. C. Kak: Digital Picture Processing (Academic Press, New York, 1976)

15.46 H. Samet: A quadtree medial axis transform, Comm. ACM, to appear.

15.47 C. Jackins, S. L. Tanimoto: "Quad-trees, Oct-trees, and K-trees: a Generalized Approach to Recursive Decomposition of Euclidean Space", IEEE Trans. Pattern Analysis Machine Intelligence, to appear.

15.48 C. R. Dyer: The space efficiency of quadtrees, Computer Graphics Image Processing 19, 335-348 (1982)

15.49 W. I. Grosky, R. Jain: "Optimal Quadtrees for Image Segments", IEEE Trans. Pattern Analysis Machine Intelligence PAMI-5, 1983, 77-83

15.50 M. Li, W. I. Grosky, R. Jain: Normalized quadtrees with respect to translations, Computer Graphics Image Processing 20, 72-81 (1982)

15.51 L. Jones, S. S. Iyengar: "Representation of regions as a forest of quadtrees", in Proc. Pattern Recognition and Image Processing Conf., Dallas, TX, 1981, pp. 57-59

15.52 I. Gargantini: An effective way to represent quadrees, Comm. ACM 25, 905-910 (1982)

15.53 E. Kawaguchi, T. Endo, J. Matsunaga: "DF-Expression Viewed from Digital Picture Processing", Department of Information Systems, Kyushu University (1982)

15.54 L. Gibson, D. Lucas: "Spatial data processing using generalized balanced ternary", in Proc. Pattern Recognition and Image Processing Conf., Los Vegas, NV, 1982, pp. 566-571

15.55 N. Ahuja: "Approaches to recursive image decomposition", in Proc. Pattern Recognition and Image Processing Conf., Dallas, TX, 1981, pp. 75-80

15.56 H. Samet, R. E. Webber: "On Encoding Boundaries with Quadtrees", Computer Science TR-1162, University of Maryland (1982)

16. Multiresolution 3-d Image Processing and Graphics

S.N. Srihari

Department of Computer Science, State University of New York at Buffalo
Amherst, NY 14226, USA

Hierarchical data structures for multiresolution processing of voxel-based
3-d images include the oct-tree and the dynamic binary tree. These data
structures can be used as pyramids for progressive refinement of gray-level
and binary 3-d images, analogous to pyramids of 2-d images. The paper develops the idea of 3-d pyramids considering each of the two data structures.
The concepts are illustrated by showing how a 3-d geometrical object can be
represented at varying levels of detail.

16.1 Introduction

Spatial information in the form of a 3-d array of values is encountered in
many applications including space planning for robot movement, display processing of reconstructions of internal organs of the human body computed
from projection images, geometrical modeling for computer-aided mechanical
design, and image processing of scanning electron microscope pictures of
serial sections of physical objects such as rocks and metals. Since the
amount of data in such arrays tends to be large, e.g., a coarse resolution
of 100 parts along each axis yields a million values, a number of data structures to exploit uniformities in the data have been proposed. In this paper
we examine the use of hierarchical data structures for the task of representing a given 3-d array at varying levels of resolution.

16.2 Terminology

The method of volume representation considered here is one based on a regu-
larly spaced array of points $(jd, kd, \ell d)$, where j, k, ℓ are integers between
0 and N-1 and d is a unit distance. A point $V \equiv (V1, V2, V3)$ of this array
is referred to as a <u>digital point</u>. Associating with each digital point V
those points $(x1, x2, x3)$ of continuous space satisfying $Vi - d/2 \leq xi < Vi +
d/2$ (for i=1,2,3), the resulting unit cube volume element is referred to as
<u>voxel</u> V.

A 3-d digital image is defined to be a mapping $F(V)$ that associates each
voxel V with a value (or color). The range of F is either a set of integers,
for a <u>gray-level image</u>, or binary valued, for a <u>binary image</u>. In the case
of a binary image the two values are equivalently referred to as {true, false},
{1,0}, {full, empty/void}, {black, white}, etc.; the set of voxels $S = \{V|
F(V)=1\}$ is referred to as the <u>object</u> and the set $\overline{S} = \{V|F(V)=0\}$ as the <u>back-
ground</u>.

A <u>hierarchical data structure</u> of a 2-d or 3-d image is a tree whose nodes
correspond to some portion (region, block) of the image. The image may be

224

reconstructed in its array form by traversing the tree. The principle of such a data structure was first described for 2-d pictures in the context of hidden line elimination in graphics, where the algorithm proceeds by recursively subdividing a square picture into four quadrants until each quadrant is simple according to some criterion [16.1]; the application of this idea to grey-level 2-d image processing was first proposed by KLINGER [16.2]. The principle of recursive subdivision of 3-d space is used for the data structures considered here with the termination criterion being that each block be uniform in color.

16.3 The Oct-Tree

Recursive subdivision of 2-d pictures into four quadrants, which has been referred to as the quad-tree, has been shown to be useful for certain image processing operations, e.g., segmentation and feature extraction. In the 3-d generalization of this method, the cubic block is subdivided into eight subcubes (or octants) of equal volume. Each of these octants will either be homogeneous (e.g., constant in color) or have some nonuniformity. The heterogeneous octants are further divided into suboctants. This procedure is repeated as long as necessary until we obtain blocks (possibly single voxels) of uniform color. The oct-tree data structure has a relatively long history, with the earliest references including [16.3-5].

Since the method can be modeled by a tree of degree 8, it is referred to as an oct-tree. Each nonterminal node of an oct-tree has eight successors and the leaves of an oct-tree correspond to data elements. In order to access a single point (X, Y, Z), the binary representations of X, Y, and Z are obtained as $x_0, x_1, \ldots, x_{M-1}, y_0, y_1, \ldots, y_{M-1}$, and $z_0, z_1, \ldots, z_{M-1}$, respectively, where $M = \log_2 N$. At the top level (level 0) of the tree is a table of eight elements, one for each octant. The index of this table, called son type, is obtained by concatenating the high bits of the X, Y, and Z coordinates. Thus $x_0 y_0 z_0$ selects an octant from the table. If that octant is to be further subdivided, then $x_1 y_1 z_1$ selects a suboctant, and so on. Thus a $N \times N \times N$ image is represented by a tree of at most $\log_2 N$ levels.

As an illustration of the oct-tree representation consider the polyhedral shown in Fig. 16.1a. This object can be regarded as a binary 3-d embedded in an $8 \times 8 \times 8$ voxel (or cellular) space. By concatenating the bits of the coordinates, the eight octants of this space are numbered own in Fig. 16.1b. The oct-tree representation of the object is given g. 16.1c, where the nonterminal nodes (which correspond to regions having empty voxels and some full voxels) are shown circular and terminal are shown square with black indicating full and white indicating empty. levels of the nodes (0-3), the son types (0-7), and the bits determining son types $(x_i y_i z_i)$ are also indicated in the figure (from [16.6]).

he maximum number of nodes in an oct-tree representation is

$$\sum_{k=0}^{\log_2 N} 8^k = \frac{8^{1+\log_2 N} - 1}{7} \simeq \frac{8}{7} N^3 .$$

s there can be up to 14 percent more nodes than voxels. Although this rhead can be large, the efficiency is higher than in the case of the quad-ee, where there can be 33% more nodes than pixels. The number of nodes in oct-tree representation of a binary image is proportional to the surface ea of the object (as measured by exposed voxel faces) rather than to the lume of the object (as measured by the number of voxels). The efficacy the oct-tree data structure for complex objects, such as those encountered

225

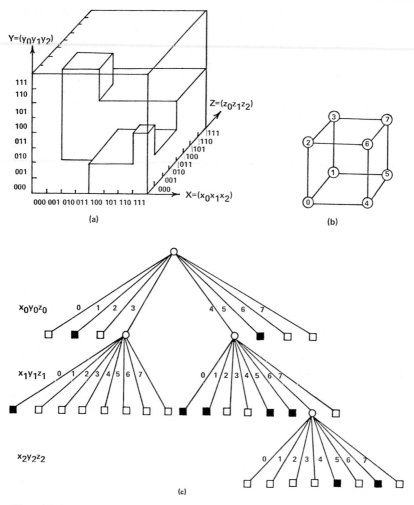

Fig. 16.1.

in reconstructions of medical objects from projection data, is demonstrated in [16.7]. A particular reconstructed human brain consisting of a 64×64×64 binary array was represented by an oct-tree with 2539 nonterminal nodes over six levels. Since the oct-tree can be completely represented using eight 12-bit fields per nonterminal node, the 243,744 bits (or 30,443 bytes) needed for the oct-tree represent a saving over the 262,144 bits (or 32,768 bytes) needed for the array.

The oct-tree data structure lends itself well to many geometrical operations. Particularly simple to implement are <u>rotation</u> by 90° (only the son types need to be permuted) and <u>scaling</u> by factors of 2 (e.g., delete the root node and make one of its sons the new root). <u>Translation</u> of an oct-tree

226

represented object involves converting a source tree to a target tree based on a movement vector. Such a translation algorithm only requires space proportional to the sum of the nodes in the two trees [16.8]. Interference between two oct-tree represented objects can be detected by traversing the two trees in parallel -- if A and B are corresponding nodes in the two trees, then we do not traverse their children if either of them is empty [16.9]. Computing the convex hull of an object from its oct-tree representation results in complexity proportional to the number of nodes rather than the number of voxels in the object, as with conventional methods [16.10].

The oct-tree data structure is also suitable for graphical display of 3-d objects on a 2-d screen with hidden surfaces eliminated. If octants are visited and displayed in the proper sequence, as determined by the location of the viewer, no octant can obscure the view of an octant later in the sequence. Thus if voxels are displayed such that later voxels overwrite earlier voxels in the sequence, a hidden surface eliminated view is generated [16.11-14]. For example, the view of the object in Fig. 16.1a is from octant 6; thus a possible sequence of visiting octants (son-types) is 1,3,5,7,0,2,4,6.

16.3.1 The Oct-Tree Pyramid

Utilization of the oct-tree data structure for multiresolution representation, in a manner analogous to planning [16.15] or pyramids [16.16,17] in 2-d picture processing, was first suggested in [16.18]. An oct-tree pyramid is obtained by associating a value with each nonterminal node of the oct-tree, so that the tree can be truncated at different levels to yield representations of the 3-d image at different resolutions. The value associated with a nonterminal node can be derived either from the values of its eight sons or from the values of the voxels in the block represented by the node. In the case of a gray-level image this value can be the mean value of the sons or, alternatively, of voxels in the block. The mean value is the best approximating constant in the least squared error sense and the mean squared error is the variance, and thus a method of deriving an approximate pyramid is to subdivide a block only if its variance exceeds a given threshold; this method is discussed for pyramids of 2-d pictures in [16.19].

In the case of a binary image the value associated with a nonterminal node can be derived using the mode rule, which assigns value 1 if more than half the sons (or voxels in the block) have value 1 and 0 otherwise. An alternative rule is to assign value 1 if more than a proportion, say one-third, of the sons or voxels are 1.

Based on the above considerations an oct-tree node, "octree," can be described as a variant record in Pascal as:

```
type
    octants = (0,1,2,3,4,5,6,7); (*eight octants*)
    colors  = (0,1,...,d-1); (*d gray levels*)
    region type = (uniform, mixed);
    octree  = record
                case region type of
                mixed: (son: array [octants]
                        of ↑octree;
                        value: colors);
                uniform: (value:colors);
                end;
```

According to the above definition the record octree represents a cubic block that is either mixed or uniform. When the record represents a mixed

227

cube, it contains a field called <u>son</u> which is an array of eight pointers to records representing each of the eight octants of the cube. The <u>value</u> field of the record contains, for a uniform cube, the value of the region, and for a mixed cube, a value that is functionally determined by the values of its descendants; note that a value is associated with a nonterminal node only in the case of a pyramid representation.

As an example of an oct-tree pyramid, consider the oct-tree of Fig.16.1c, which has four levels. If we apply the mode rule to the sons of each nonterminal node, every nonterminal node in the tree will have value empty. The set of objects in the pyramid, corresponding to levels 1, 2 and 3, is shown in Figs.16.2a-c respectively; the level 0 object is a cubic void. The graphic displays were obtained by applying a hidden surface removal algorithm that takes advantage of the implied sorting in the oct-tree. The displays correspond to the view from octant 7, where octant numbers are obtained by concatenating corresponding bits of X, Y and Z coordinates as shown in Fig.16.1b.

Some experiments were also conducted with oct-tree pyramids using different proportion rules applied to the voxels in the region represented by a nonterminal node (rather than deriving the value of a nonterminal node from the values of the sons of that node). A node was set to full if more than a fraction f of the volume was full. The results of these experiments for f corresponding to .2, .33 and .5 are shown in Figs.16.3a-c, respectively, using an orthogonal view from the octants corresponding to octants 0, 1, 2 and 3; the

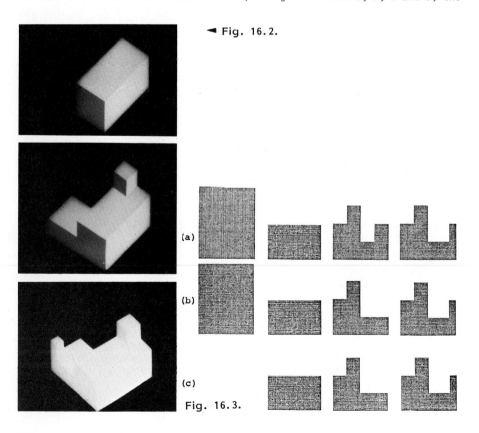

◄ Fig. 16.2.

(a)

(b)

(c)

Fig. 16.3.

228

displays were produced using an algorithm such as DISPLAY 1 of [16.14], which generates the display quad-tree given the oct-tree and a viewing direction. The case f=.5 shows a progressive increase in the surface area of the object (which is one measure of shape complexity). The cases f=.2 and f=.33 indicate the presence of material at an earlier stage of the process.

16.3.2 Asymmetric Oct-Trees

In the asymmetric oct-tree [16.4,6,20], the space to be subdivided is broken into rectangular parallelepipeds rather than into cubes. As with the (symmetric) oct-tree, subdivision is done with planes perpendicular to the X,Y, and Z axes, but the planes are not equally spaced. Because the subdivision is variable along the axes, storage can be saved by intelligent subdivision. For example, if a very small object is to be represented in the middle of a large empty volume, the equal subdivision (or symmetric) model will have to traverse many levels of the tree before it gets to the detail of the object. Using unequal subdivision, two closely spaced planes along each axis will exactly single out the object so that the next subdivision can begin at the proper level of detail.

Each nonterminal node of the asymmetric oct-tree requires three additional fields to indicate the location of the X, Y and Z planes which make up the subspaces. Let (X_{jk}, Y_{jk}, Z_{jk}) represent the indices of the partitioning planes at the kth nonterminal node of level j, where $0 \le k \le 7$, $0 \le j \le \log_2 N \le 1$. Then point (X, Y, Z) is accessed by selecting a branch at each nonterminal node by the concatenated bits $x_j y_j z_j$, where

$$x_j = \begin{cases} 1 & \text{if } X \ge X_{jk}, \\ 0 & \text{otherwise} \end{cases}$$

$$y_j = \begin{cases} 1 & \text{if } Y \ge Y_{jk}, \\ 0 & \text{otherwise} \end{cases}$$

$$z_j = \begin{cases} 1 & \text{if } Z \ge Z_{jk}, \\ 0 & \text{otherwise} \end{cases}$$

Analogous to the Pascal description of record octree, a node of the asymmetric oct-tree can be defined. In the following definition, the record a-octree represents a parallelepiped block that is either mixed or uniform. When the block is mixed, position is a field that specifies the location of the X,Y and Z planes. The fields son and value are defined as in octree.

```
type
  a-octree = record
               case region-type of
                 mixed:  (position: array
                          [0..2] of integer;
                          son: array[octants]
                          of ↑a-octree;
                          value: colors);
                 uniform: (value: colors);
               end;
```

An asymmetric oct-tree representation of the object in Fig.16.2a is given in Fig.16.4a. Values can be associated with nonterminal nodes, as before,

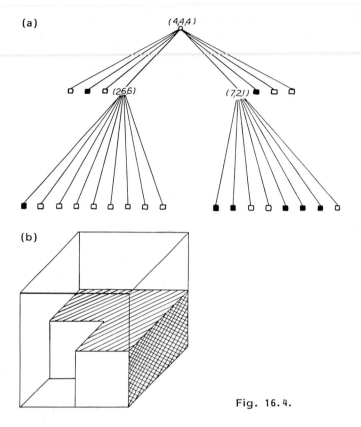

(a)

(4,4,4)

(2,6,6)

(7,2,1)

(b)

Fig. 16.4.

to get an asymmetric oct-tree pyramid. The object obtained by truncating the lowest level of the asymmetric oct-tree, after applying the mode rule to the sons, is shown in Fig.16.4b.

16.4 Dynamic Binary Trees

A data structure that has been proposed for searching high-dimensional spaces [16.21,22], and also has some advantages for multiresolution 2-d picture proces- sing [16.23], is known as the dynamic binary tree. In the 3-d version of the dynamic binary tree [16.6], blocks are rectangular parallelepipeds, unlike the oct-tree where blocks are necessarily cubes. A given rectangular parallele- piped is divided into two halves (upper and lower, or hi and lo) by means of a plane which is perpendicular to one of the axes and positioned midway along the extent of the parallelepiped along that axis. The two resulting paral- lelepipeds are divided recursively until each parallelepiped is uniform. The resulting data structure is in the form of a binary tree, where each nonterminal node has an axis field that specifies the direction of the plane as X, Y, or Z. The left subtree can be regarded as describing the upper half of the parallelepiped and the right subtree as describing the lower half.

The dynamic binary tree of a 3-d image can be made unique by eliminating the axis fields of nonterminal nodes and partitioning along a predetermined sequence of axes, e.g., X,Y,Z,X,Y,Z,..., until we have homogeneity. The advantage of not prespecifying the axes is that the partitioning planes can be judiciously chosen for a given image, so that the number of levels in the tree is minimized.

16.4.1 Dynamic Binary Tree Pyramids

The dynamic binary tree data structure can also be used for multiresolution representation of 3-d images. In the case of gray-level images, the value of a nonterminal node can be derived using the mean value of the two blocks represented by the sons of the node, or by using the mean value of all the voxels included in the block.

In the case of binary 3-d images the values of nonterminal nodes can be derived by applying the mode rule (or a proportion rule) to the voxel values in the region. The mode rule applied to the sons of a node in a bottom-up derivation will yield identical values for all the nonterminal nodes. Instead of assigning black (or white) to all nonterminal nodes, we can assign a third value, say gray or mixed.

The Pascal specification of a node of the binary tree pyramid, bitree, is given below. When the node is mixed, the axis field specifies the direction of the bisecting field and the son field specifies the two halves.

```
type
  half = (lo, hi); (*the two halves of a parallelepiped*)
  bitree = record
            case region-type of
            mixed: (axis:(X,Y,Z);
                    son: array[half]of ↑bitree;
                    value: colors);
            uniform: (value:colors);
            end;
```

A dynamic binary tree representation of the object in Fig.16.1a is given in Fig.16.5, where nonterminal nodes are assigned the value gray. The se-

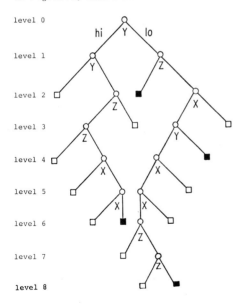

Fig. 16.5.

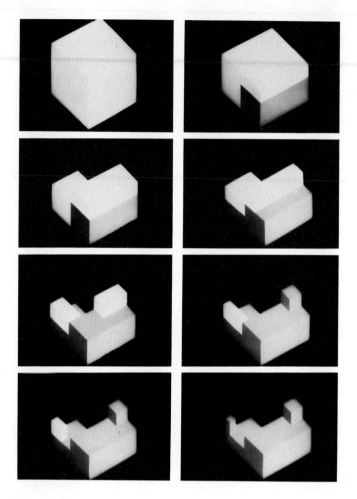

Fig. 16.6.

quence of objects in the dynamic binary tree pyramid is shown in Figs.16.6a-h, which correspond to levels 1-8 respectively. In the display, gray regions are allowed to obscure black regions. Note that the level-0 object is a transparent cube whereas the level-1 object is a gray cube.

The progression of objects in the binary tree pyramid of Fig.16.5, obtained by applying different proportion rules to the voxels in the region represented by a nonterminal node, is displayed in Figs. 16.7-9. Figs. 16.7-9 correspond to f=.2, .33, and .5 respectively. For each value of f the nine displays, which correspond to levels 0-8 of the tree in Fig.16.5, represent orthogonal views of the object, as in Fig.16.3.

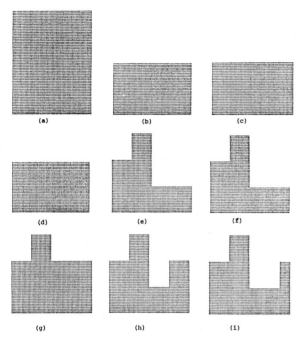

Fig. 16.7.

(a) (b) (c)

(d) (e) (f)

(g) (h) (i)

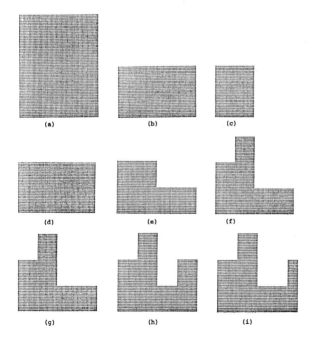

(a) (b) (c)

(d) (e) (f)

(g) (h) (i)

Fig. 16.8.

233

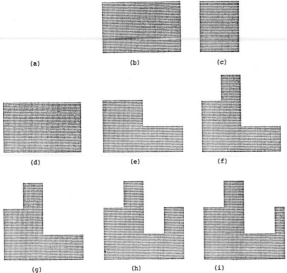

Fig. 16.9.

(a) (b) (c)

(d) (e) (f)

(g) (h) (i)

16.4.2 Asymmetric Binary Trees

Instead of positioning the partitioning planes at the midpoint along each axis, the planes can be positioned so that the object is represented with as few levels of the tree as possible. The definition of the asymmetric binary tree or a-bitree is similar to that of the bitree with an additional position field for mixed nodes.

16.5 Discussion

Tree data structures for 3-d images have been known to be suitable for efficient geometrical operations. They can also be used in the form of pyramids to provide a means for multiresolution representation of 3-d images. Such a representation allows a given image to be processed at progressively increasing levels of detail.

Pyramids based on the oct-tree and the dynamic binary tree are useful when 3-d images are transmitted over low-bandwidth channels and the receiver constructs progressively better approximations. In such a case the information in the tree is transmitted level by level (rather than in, say, post-order or preorder traversal of the tree) and the receiver can display improved approximations after each level is transmitted. By appropriate choice of values for nonterminal (and terminal) nodes it is possible to utilize the value of a father node in determining the values of its sons, thereby eliminating the need to transmit any more bits than are needed for transmitting the entire tree; this was shown for the 2-d case in [16.23].

While for oct-tree pyramids each level of the tree increases resolution (or object complexity) by a factor of 8, for dynamic binary pyramids resolution is only doubled at each level. Thus the dynamic binary tree pyramid provides a gentler way of improving the image; also, Gestalts of the image are formed earlier, since fewer nodes are included in the image at each level. The oct-tree pyramid has the advantage that each node represents a cube,

234

whereas a node of a dynamic binary tree represents a rectangular parallelepiped of arbitrary proportions. This makes graphics display algorithms --
those that perform hidden surface removal and shading -- much simpler for
the oct-tree. Although it is possible to generate displays directly from
dynamic binary trees, it may be simpler to map them into oct-trees for display purposes.

Representation of the shapes of 3-d objects by recursive models for the
purpose of recognition has been a goal of computer vision workers [16.24].
Such a representation allows us to view recognition as a gradual process
proceeding from the general to the specific. Pyramids based on tree data
structures are a formal means of specifying recursive models. Although it
may not be possible to justify the oct-tree and binary tree pyramids on
purely cognitive grounds, they provide a simple computational tool for 3-d
analysis whose potential needs further exploration.

Acknowledgments

The author wishes to thank Ron Lo and Jeffrey Tindall who produced the graphics displays. Thanks are also due to Eloise Benzel who cheerfully typed
the manuscript.

References

16.1 J. E. Warnock: "A Hidden Surface Algorithm for Computer Generated
     Half Tone Pictures", Computer Science Department TR-4-15, University
     of Utah (1969)
16.2 A. Klinger: "Patterns and search statistics", in Optimizing Methods
     in Statistics, ed. by J. S. Rustagi (Academic Press, New York, 1972),
     pp. 303-339
16.3 C. M. Eastman, Representations for space planning, Comm. ACM 13, 242-
     250 (1970)
16.4 D. R. Reddy, S. Rubin: "Representation of Three-Dimensional Objects",
     Department of Computer Science Technical Report 78-113, Carnegie-
     Mellon University (1978)
16.5 G. M. Hunter: "Efficient Computation and Data Structures for Graphics",
     Ph.D. dissertation, Department of Electrical Engineering and Computer
     Science, Princeton University (1978)
16.6 S. N. Srihari: Representation of three-dimensional images, Computing
     Surveys 13, 399-424 (1981)
16.7 M. Yau, S. N. Srihari: A hierarchical data structure for multidim-
     ensional digital images, Comm. ACM, to appear
16.8 C. L. Jackins, S. L. Tanimoto: Octrees and their use in representing
     three-dimensional objects, Computer Graphics Image Processing 14, 249-
     270 (1980)
16.9 N. Ahuja, R. T. Chien, R. Yen, N. Bridwell: "Interference detection
     and collision avoidance among three-dimensional objects", in Proc.
     Nat'l Conf. on Artificial Intelligence, Stanford, CA, 1980, pp. 44-48
16.10 M. Yau, S. N. Srihari: "Convex hulls from hierarchical data structures",
      in Proc. Canadian Man-Computer Communication Society Conf., Waterloo,
      ON, 1981, pp. 163-171
16.11 D. J. R. Meagher: "Octree Encoding: a New Technique for the Represen-
      tation, Manipulation, and Display of Arbitrary 3-D Objects by Computer",
      TR-80-111, Rensselaer Polytechnic Institute (1980)
16.12 D. J. Meagher: "Efficient synthetic image generation of arbitrary 3-d
      objects", in Proc. Pattern Recognition and Image Processing Conf., Las
      Vegas, NV, 1982, pp. 453-458

16.13 R. Gillespie, W. A. Davis: "Tree data structures for graphics and image processing", in Proc. Canadian Man-Computer Communication Society Conf., Waterloo, ON, 1981, pp. 155-162

16.14 L. J. Doctor, J. G. Torborg: Display techniques for octree-encoded objects, IEEE Computer Graphics Applications $\underline{1}$ (3), 29-38 (1981)

16.15 M. D. Kelly: "Edge detection by computer in pictures using planning", in Machine Intelligence 6, ed. by B. Meltzer, D. Michie (Edinburgh University Press, Edinburgh, UK, 1971), pp. 379-409

16.16 S. L. Tanimoto, T. Pavlidis: A hierarchical data structure for picture processing, Computer Graphics Image Processing $\underline{4}$, 104-119 (1975)

16.17 K. R. Sloan, Jr., S. L. Tanimoto: Progressive refinement of raster images, IEEE Trans. Computers $\underline{C-28}$, 871-874 (1979)

16.18 S. N. Srihari, "Hierarchical data structures and progressive refinement of 3-d images", in Proc. Pattern Recognition and Image Processing Conf., Las Vegas, NV, 1982, pp. 485-490

16.19 A. Rosenfeld: "Quadtrees and pyramids for pattern recognition and image processing", in Proc. 5th Int'l. Conf. on Pattern Recognition, Miami Beach, FL, 1980, pp. 802-807

16.20 S. N. Srihari: "Hierarchical representations for serial section images", in Proc. 5th Int'l. Conf. on Pattern Recognition, Miami Beach, FL, 1980, pp. 1075-1080

16.21 J. L. Bentley: Multidimensional binary search trees used for associative searching, Comm. ACM $\underline{18}$, 509-519 (1975)

16.22 J. O'Rourke: "Dynamically Quantized Spaces Applied to Motion Analysis", TR-EE-81-1, Johns Hopkins University (1981)

16.23 K. Knowlton: Progressive transmission of grey-scale and binary pictures by simple, efficient and lossless encoding schemes, Proc. IEEE $\underline{68}$, 885-896 (1980)

16.24 D. Marr, H. K. Nishihara: Representation and recognition of the spatial organization of three-dimensional shapes, Proc. Royal Society (London) $\underline{B200}$, 269-274 (1978)

17. Multilevel Reconstruction of Visual Surfaces: Variational Principles and Finite-Element Representations

D. Terzopoulos

Artificial Intelligence Laboratory, Massachusetts Institute of Technology
545 Technology Square, Cambridge, MA 02139, USA

Computational modules early in the human vision system typically generate
sparse information about the shapes of visible surfaces in the scene. Moreover, visual processes such as stereopsis can provide such information at
a number of levels spanning a range of resolutions. In this paper, we extend this multilevel structure to encompass the subsequent task of reconstructing full surface descriptions from the sparse information. The mathematical development proceeds in three steps. First, the surface most consistent with the sparse constraints is characterized as the solution to an
optimal approximation problem which is posed as a variational principle describing the constrained equilibrium state of a thin flexible plate. Second,
local, finite-element representations of surfaces are introduced, and by
applying the finite-element method, the continuous variational principle is
transformed into a discrete problem in the form of a large system of linear
algebraic equations whose solution is computable by local-support, cooperative mechanisms. Third, to exploit the information available at each level
of resolution, a hierarchy of discrete problems is formulated and a highly
efficient multilevel algorithm, involving both intralevel relaxation processes and bidirectional interlevel local interpolation processes, is applied
to their simultaneous solution. Examples of the generation of hierarchies
of surface representations from stereo constraints are given. Finally, the
basic surface approximation problem is revisited in a broader mathematical
context whose implications are of relevance to vision.

17.1 Introduction

A fundamental problem in early vision is that of inferring the three-dimensional geometry of visible surfaces in a scene from the intensity information available in the retinal images. This problem is surprisingly difficult. As a consequence, in advanced biological vision systems, there seem
to have evolved several specialized subsystems or modules which contribute
to the recovery of surface shape information through the interpretation of
specific classes of image cues. Examples of modules which have been identified include those responsible for stereo vision and the analysis of motion.

A particularly effective strategy for studying early vision is the one
described by MARR [17.1-3]. The strategy is to assume initially that, to a
first approximation, each module performs its analysis of the images independently of the others. A proper study of a particular module then requires that one first identify precisely the visual task which it performs,
and then model the module in terms of the representations and computational
processes through which it performs this task. According to this point of
view, the various computational processes in early vision are thought of as
transforming symbolic representations of images into symbolic representations
of surfaces, over several stages of analysis.

An understanding of some of the details of these processes and representations has evolved recently, especially at the earliest stages, closest to the image (e.g., [17.1,4-6]), where much of the work has been inspired by recent advances in neuroscience. On the other hand, insights into later stages closer to explicit surface and volumetric representations are meager. For example, these fundamental questions remain open: first, how is the information generated by the various modules amalgamated into retinocentric representations of surfaces (see, e.g., [17.7,8]), and, second, how do such representations give rise in turn to object-centered representations of the three-dimensional properties of objects in the scene [17.9-11]).

The work described in this paper is part of ongoing research into the problem of obtaining surface representations which will be useful to later processing stages in vision. Our goal is to analyze the computational process through which the information retrieved by, say, stereopsis or analysis of motion is combined and transformed into full, retinocentric descriptions of surface shape, consistent with our perception when we look around us. In particular, we argue that <u>hierarchies of full surface representations spanning a range of resolutions are desirable</u>. Moreover, we will demonstrate that <u>such representations may be generated by a highly efficient, multilevel surface reconstruction algorithm</u>. Our approach seems sufficiently general to allow eventually several classes of surface shape information (such as local depth or orientation measurements) provided by a number of vision modules to be merged in a meaningful way.

17.1.1 Motivation of the Multilevel Approach

Although it will become clear that the surface reconstruction problem may be formulated mathematically and solved in the abstract without any reference to vision, we intend to maintain close and explicit links to the underlying visual goal. Since our study of the problem has been motivated by considerations made in the context of MARR's framework of early vision, it is natural in our ensuing discussion of these motivating issues to make explicit reference to a number of relevant details within this framework.

MARR's framework is characterized by at least three major processing stages. Each of these stages transforms one retinocentric representation into another such representation, with the purpose of inferring, and making explicit, relevant information about the surfaces in a scene. The first stage transforms the intensity representations (or retinal images) into a primary representation, called the <u>primal sketch</u> [17.1]. Changes in the physical properties of surfaces almost always give rise to intensity changes in the images, and it is at the level of the primal sketch that the locations of these changes are made explicit. In the second processing stage, specialized processes, such as those concerned with stereo and analysis of motion, infer information about the shapes of surfaces from the contents of the primal sketch. Since inferences can typically be made only at those locations which have been marked in the primal sketch, the information generated is <u>sparse</u>, and it is collected into sparse representations of surface shape that are referred to as the <u>raw 2½-D sketch</u>. The final stage is one of <u>full surface reconstruction</u> in which the sparse representations are transformed into a <u>full 2½-D sketch</u> containing explicit information about surface shape at all points in the scene, consistent with our perception.

The goal of the first processing stage is the detection of intensity changes in the image. Recently, MARR and HILDRETH [17.6,12] proposed a theory of edge detection which was inspired by existing neurophysiological evidence and certain mathematical issues. An important aspect of this

theory is that intensity changes in the images must be isolated at several
scales of resolution. Indeed, there is evidence that the human visual system detects intensity changes over a range of resolutions through the use
of up to five independent, spatial-frequency-tuned, bandpass channels [17.13-
15]. The existence of these independent primal sketch representations is
a crucial factor which contributes to the success of some later computations such as stereopsis, as modeled by the MARR-POGGIO theory of stereo vision
[17.4](see also [17.16,17]). According to this model, the bandpass nature of
the channels leads to an almost trivial solution to the stereo correspondence
problem within the disparity range of each channel. Detailed depth information over a wide disparity range is obtained through a process by which the
coarser channels control vergence eye movements that bring the finer channels
into alignment (general studies of vergence eye movements include [17.18-20]).
On the other hand, computations such as motion correspondence [17.5], whose
function may not seem to depend critically on the existence of multiple representations, may nevertheless be operative at each of the levels. It is
likely in any case that multiple sparse representations of surface shape,
spanning a range of resolutions, are generated by most of these modules.

   In the context of stereopsis, GRIMSON [17.21,22] pioneered the mathematical theory of the subsequent visual surface reconstruction process which
transforms the sparse surface descriptions into full ones. He proposed that
before reconstruction begins, the multiple, sparse depth representations output through the different bandpass channels be combined into a single raw
2½-D sketch in a way which maintains consistency across all scales. The raw
2½-D sketch then contains sparse depth information at the finest resolution
possible. Next, a single reconstruction process operating at this finest

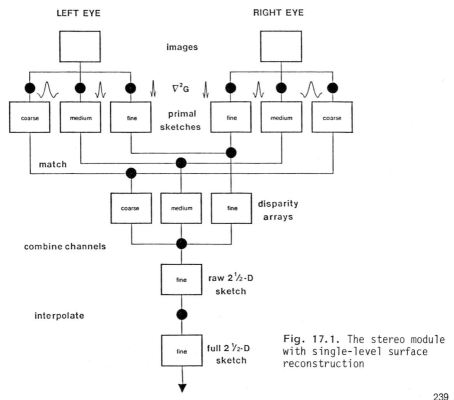

Fig. 17.1. The stereo module
with single-level surface
reconstruction

level generates a unique full 2½-D sketch representing depth information at high resolution. The steps are illustrated in Fig.17.1, in which only three bandpass channels are shown for simplicity.

A single full surface representation at the finest resolution possible certainly captures all of the information provided by the stereo module and it should, in principle, be sufficient input to later tasks. Unfortunately, a number of technical problems arise with this simple approach. First, in collapsing the multiple depth representations into one raw 2½-D sketch, information potentially useful in later processing stages which are concerned with object-centered surface descriptions, 3-D models of objects, and object recognition has been discarded prematurely. It now seems likely that in order for some of these later stages to succeed and work efficiently, surface representations at multiple scales will be necessary, just as they are necessary at earlier stages such as stereopsis. In accordance with MARR's princi-ple of least commitment [17.1], it would be wasteful to discard information, prior to surface reconstruction, which may have to be regenerated later. A second, and more immediately serious problem is a consequence of the great bulk of incoming information within the large raw 2½-D sketch which must be processed at the finest resolution. Biologically feasible surface recon-struction algorithms such as those developed by GRIMSON are extremely inef-ficient at generating full surface descriptions when faced with such large representations. This inefficiency is due primarily to the local nature of the algorithms in question.

The above problems may be avoided if the sparse representations are not collapsed into a single fine representation. We propose instead that mul-tiple full surface representations spanning a range of resolutions ought to be generated by the reconstruction process itself and made available to pro-cessing stages beyond. The multilevel surface reconstruction algorithm which we will develop in this paper accomplishes precisely this. Because the al-gorithm exploits information available at coarser resolutions, its speed efficiency is dramatically superior to that of single level reconstruction schemes. Order-of-magnitude improvements are typically observed for sur-faces reconstructed from information provided by stereopsis. On the other hand, the expense in space in maintaining all the coarser representations is very worthwhile, since it turns out to be only a fraction of that required to maintain the finest one.

Figure17.2 illustrates the multilevel surface reconstruction scheme and its incorporation into stereopsis. A fundamental point to realize about the multilevel approach in general is that information about surface depth or, for that matter, surface orientation is provided in each of the channels (i.e., sparse representations)by the various vision modules and, as will be shown, contributes in an optimal way to the generation of the hierarchy of full surface representations. The multilevel scheme involves both intra-level processes which propagate information within a representation, as well as interlevel processes which communicate between representations. The interlevel processes are further classified into those which transfer in-formation from coarser levels to finer ones, and those which transfer in-formation from finer levels to coarser ones. At this point, we emphasize that multiple representations of consistent accuracy can be achieved only if such a bidirectional flow of information is allowed to take place between the levels. This statement will be substantiated rigorously in a later section.

If the processes and representations envisioned are to be considered as models of the human visual system, their form is constrained from below by

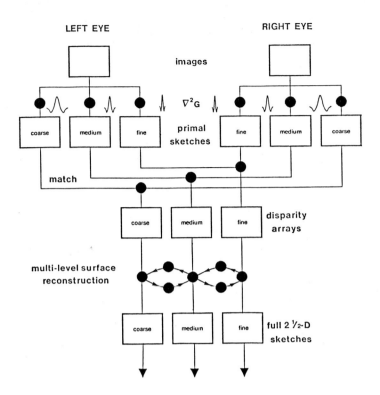

Fig. 17.2. Multilevel approach to surface reconstruction

what can be implemented in neuronal hardware. Although our incomplete knowledge renders premature the formulation of precise arguments along these
lines, some constraints which presently seem compelling, such as parallelism,
locality and simplicity of computation, efficiency, uniformity, and extensi-
bility [17.23] have been factors in the theoretical analysis of the surface
reconstruction problem and in the search for algorithms (similar constraints
apply when considering implementations within parallel, pipelined computer
architectures). Once a specific algorithm is selected based on these constraints, it can be implemented and its performance can be evaluated empirically in terms of the original computational goal. In our study of the surface reconstruction problem, we are ultimately striving for a theory which
is consistent with current psychophysical evidence.

17.1.2 Overview

In the remainder of this paper, we lay down the mathematical foundations of
a multilevel approach to visual surface reconstruction, primarily in the context of stereo vision. With the help of a physical model, the basic surface
approximation problem is interpreted intuitively. Although it is in general
a nontrivial matter to solve this problem, our model suggests the application
of potent methods which have arisen out of classical mathematical physics -
the calculus of variations, optimal approximation theory, and functional analysis. Aspects of the above formalisms are employed to render our problem
amenable to solution by numerical techniques. The development is as follows.

- In Sect.17.2, visual surface reconstruction is cast as an optimal approximation problem which involves finding the equilibrium position of a thin flexible plate undergoing bending. The problem is posed formally as a variational principle which we propose to solve by first converting it to discrete form using the finite-element method.

- In Sect.17.3, we prepare the way for applying this discrete approximation method by finding a set of minimal conditions for our continuous problem to have a unique solution. We show that these requirements will almost always be satisfied in practice, so that we can consider our surface approximation problem to be well posed, and can proceed to obtain the solution.

- In Sect.17.4, we turn to the task of converting our continuous problem into discrete form. To do so, we define a simple nonconforming finite element which will constitute the basis of our local, piecewise continuous representation of surfaces. Because the element is nonconforming, we first must prove that it leads to unique discrete approximations, and that these approximations converge to the exact solution as the elements decrease in size. Having done this, we derive the discrete surface approximation problem as a large system of linear equations.

- In Sect.17.5, we undertake the task of computing the solution to this linear system efficiently, using a biologically feasible algorithm. Here we formulate the multilevel approach for accomplishing this task. The approach involves setting up a hierarchy of discrete surface approximation problems which span a range of resolutions and exploit the information available at each scale. Subsequently, a multilevel algorithm is invoked to solve them simultaneously. Through a series of examples, we demonstrate the efficient performance of the multilevel surface reconstruction algorithm, and show that it generates useful hierarchies of full surface representations from constraints provided by stereopsis.

- In Sect.17.6, we reexamine our surface reconstruction problem and show that it is a special case within a general class of optimal interpolation problems involving arbitrary degrees of smoothness, in any number of dimensions. These general problems involve the minimization of functionals which possess a number of invariance properties making them attractive for application to problems in early vision whose solutions require the iterative propagation of smoothness constraints across retinocentric representations.

- In Sect.17.7, we conclude by discussing the overall implications of our approach to issues concerning the isolation of depth discontinuities, and the incorporation of other sources of information such as surface orientation. We discuss possible solutions to these problems in view of our finite-element representation of surfaces and the multilevel surface reconstruction algorithm.

- For convenience, we cover the relevant mathematical background of the finite element method and the iterative solution of large linear systems in two of the appendices.

17.2 The Most Consistent Surface

The sparse information about surface shape retrieved by the various vision modules is in general underconstraining. That is to say, it is insufficient to compel a unique inference of the physical properties of the surfaces in the scene. Yet, even when presented with impoverished stimuli (such as random dot stereograms [17.24] or kinetic depth effect displays (e.g., [17.5, 25-27]), the human visual system routinely arrives at unique interpretations and our typical perception is a stable one of full surfaces in depth. Clearly, the visual system must invoke certain assumptions which provide enough additional constraint to allow a unique full surface representation to be computed from the sparse information provided. However, these additional assumptions must be plausible in that they reflect certain domain-dependent expectations. For example, in stereo vision, the sparse information takes the form of depth constraints which reflect measurements of the distances from the viewer to the surfaces of objects in the scene. The additional assumptions should then be based on aspects of the optical and computational processes involved in the generation of these depth constraints, as well as general expectations about physical properties of surfaces in the visual world.

GRIMSON [17.21] explored a number of issues along these lines. Qualitatively, his thesis is as follows. A surface in the scene which varies radically in shape usually gives rise to intensity changes which are marked in the primal sketches as zero crossings of the Laplacian of the Gaussian-convolved images ($\nabla^2 G * I$ - see [17.6,12]). Moreover, it is only at the locations of zero crossings that the MARR-POGGIO stereo algorithm can generate measurements of the distance to the surface, in the form of explicit depth constraints. Therefore, the surface cannot in general be varying radically in depth between the constraints to which it gave rise. By introducing this additional surface smoothness assumption, the goal of accurately reconstructing the shapes of visible surfaces and thereby computing full surface representations consistent with our perception is attainable in principle. A theoretical proof of this statement lies in the domain of mathematics. In the next section, we take the first step by rigorously formulating the surface reconstruction problem as an optimal approximation problem. In our formulation, the smoothness assumption will be subject to a clear, intuitive interpretation.

17.2.1 A Physical Interpretation - The Bending of a Thin Plate

Visual surface reconstruction can be characterized formally as a constrained optimal approximation problem in two dimensions. In the context of stereo vision, where constraints embody depth measurements to surfaces in the scene, the goal is to reconstruct, as accurately as possible, the shape of the surface which gave rise to these measurements. Of course, it is necessary that we be able to deal with the complication due to arbitrarily placed constraints since, as we have noted, such constraints are generated naturally by, for instance, stereopsis. More rigorously, the problem can be stated as follows: given a finite set of arbitrarily located distinct point constraints within a planar region, each constraint having a real scalar value associated with it, find the unique optimal function of two variables which is most consistent with these constraints. Our notion of consistency will be defined shortly. We will consider the solution to our problem to be a full surface representation in that it makes explicit our best estimate of the distance to every visible point on the surface in the scene.

The constraints provided by the stereo computation are never completely reliable. Errors due to noise and errors in matching corresponding zero-crossings are bound to occur. This suggests that we should not try to interpolate the given data exactly, because a few "bad" constraints can have a detrimental effect on the shape of the recovered surface. Relaxing the interpolation requirement turns our problem into one of surface approximation in which we would like to maintain control over how closely the surface fits the data.

By thinking in terms of an optimal surface, we imply the choice of a suitable criterion that will allow us to measure the optimality of admissible functions. A suitable criterion for measuring the optimality of surfaces in the context of surface approximation in stereopsis translates into a precise mathematical statement which captures intuitive notions about the smoothness of admissible surfaces, as well as their closeness of fit to the known depth constraints. Perhaps the intuitively clearest treatment of our problem is in terms of the following physical model. Consider a planar region Ω, the region within which we wish to obtain an optimal approximating surface most consistent with a finite set of sparse constraints. Let us imagine that the constraints comprise a set of vertical pins scattered within Ω, the height of an individual pin being related to the distance from the viewer to the surface in the scene. Suppose that we take a thin flexible plate of elastic material that is planar in the absence of external forces, and constrain it to pass near the tips of the pins by attaching ideal springs between the pin tips and the surface of the plate as shown in Fig.17.3.

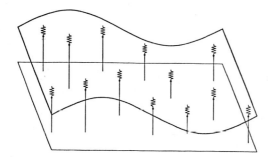

Fig. 17.3. The physical model for surface approximation

It is not difficult to imagine that in its equilibrium state the thin plate will generally trace out a "fair" approximating surface, and that this surface will be smooth in between constraints. But will it be sufficiently smooth? A partial answer to this question is provided by psychophysics. Experiments carried out by GRIMSON [17.21] seem to indicate that thin plate surfaces exhibit an appropriate degree of smoothness. Moreover, considerations of the imaging process provide some corroboration [17.28]. Now the characteristic degree of smoothness of thin plate surfaces can be quantified mathematically through the use of an ingenious formalism - the SOBOLEV spaces (see Appendix A). In particular, these spaces constitute a criterion by which we can compare surfaces generated by thin plates to less smooth ones, such as those generated by, say, rubber sheets. It seems that the latter do not exhibit sufficient smoothness for visual surface reconstruction in general. We postpone further discussion of these issues until Sect.17.6, where a number of formal generalizations will be made. Without further justification at this point, then, our claim is that we have a reasonable physical model for the class of desired approximating surfaces. Soon, we will see that this model suggests good strategies for solving our problem.

We emphasize, however, that the appropriateness of the model depends on two important issues. The first involves ensuring that a unique solution exists, and the second is to guarantee that the solution is meaningful in view of the constraints. Firstly, we should realize that the plate-spring system will be unstable for certain pin configurations. If we have but a single pin, then a stable equilibrium does not exist, as the plate has two unconstrained degrees of freedom (rotation about the axis of the pin is excluded). A similar degenerate situation arises for the case of any number of pins arranged linearly, the plate then having one unconstrained degree of freedom. Clearly at least three noncollinearly arranged pins are required to assure that a unique state of stable equilibrium exists. Secondly, a reasonable choice must be made for the stiffness of the springs. If the springs are too strong in relation to the rigidity of the plate material, then a pin whose height deviates significantly from that of its neighbors (i.e., an erroneous constraint) will place an abnormally large amount of strain on the plate locally and have undesirable effects on the shape of the surface. On the other hand, if the springs are too weak, the intrinsic rigidity of the plate can overwhelm them and the plate will remain nearly planar over large variations in the height of the pins. In the limit of a rigid plate, the resulting planar, least-squares approximation would be meaningless in that the solution will not in general lie close to constraints other than those arising from nearly flat surfaces.

We will now proceed to a mathematical characterization of the above physical model. To do so, we apply the well-known minimum <u>potential energy principle</u> from classical mechanics, which states that the potential energy of a physical system in a state of stable equilibrium is at a local minimum. For the model, the potential energy in question is that due to deformation of the plate and springs, as well as the energy imparted by any externally applied forces.

First, consider the plate itself. It is known (see, e.g., [17.29, p. 250; 17.30]) that the potential energy of a thin plate under deformation is given by an integral of a quadratic form in the <u>principal curvatures</u> of the plate. If the principal curvatures of the deformed plate are denoted by κ_1 and κ_2, the potential energy density is given by an expression of the form

$$\frac{A}{2}(\kappa_1^2+\kappa_2^2)+B\kappa_1\kappa_2=2A\left(\frac{\kappa_2+\kappa_2}{2}\right)^2-(A-B)\kappa_1\kappa_2$$

where A and B are constants determined by the plate material. The expression $\frac{1}{2}(\kappa_1+\kappa_2)$ is the <u>first</u> or <u>mean curvature</u> and $\kappa_1\kappa_2$ is the <u>second</u> or <u>Gaussian curvature</u> of the plate's surface (see, e.g., [17.31]).

Let the function $v(x,y)$ denote the deflection of the plate normal to the region Ω which can be taken to lie in the x-y plane. Assuming that the deflection function and its partial derivatives, $v, v_x, v_y, \ldots$ are small, it can be shown (see, e.g., [17.32, p. 368]) that

$$\frac{\kappa_1+\kappa_2}{2} \approx \tfrac{1}{2}\Delta v, \qquad \kappa_1\kappa_2 \approx v_{xx}v_{yy}-v_{xy}^2$$

where $\Delta = \dfrac{\partial^2}{\partial x^2} + \dfrac{\partial^2}{\partial y^2}$ denotes the Laplacian operator. Thus, the potential energy density can be written in any one of the following forms:

$$\begin{aligned}
e_1 &= \tfrac{1}{2}(\Delta v)^2-(1-\sigma)(v_{xx}v_{yy}-v_{xy}^2) \\
&= \tfrac{1}{2}(v_{xx}^2+2v_{xy}^2+v_{yy}^2)+\sigma(v_{xx}v_{yy}-v_{xy}^2) \\
&= \tfrac{1}{2}[\sigma(\Delta v)^2+(1-\sigma)(v_{xx}^2+2v_{xy}^2+v_{yy}^2)]
\end{aligned}$$
(17.1)

245

apart from a multiplicative constant which depends on the physical properties of the elastic material of the plate, and which has been set to unity
without loss of generality. The constant σ, called the <u>POISSON ratio</u>,
measures the change in width as the material is stretched lengthwise.[1] The
desired potential energy of deformation is obtained by integrating the energy
density over the domain in question, and is given by

$$E_1(v) = \int\int_\Omega \tfrac{1}{2}(\Delta v)^2 - (1-\sigma)(v_{xx}v_{yy} - v_{xy}^2)dx\ dy.$$

To the potential energy of deformation, we must add the potential energy
due to any external forces which may be present. The energy due to a force
density $g(x,y)$ applied to the surface of the plate (such as the effect of
gravity) is given by

$$E_2(v) = -\int\int_\Omega gv\ dx\ dy\ .$$

External forces and bending moments may also be applied around the boundary
$\partial\Omega$ of Ω. The energy due to a force density $p(s)$ on the boundary (s denotes
arc length along the boundary) is

$$E_3(v) = -\int_{\partial\Omega} p(s)v\ ds$$

while the energy due to bending moments applied around the boundary is

$$E_4(v) = -\int_{\partial\Omega} m(s)\frac{\partial v}{\partial n}\ ds$$

where $m(s)$ is the density of applied bending moments normal to the curve and
$\frac{\partial}{\partial n}$ denotes the directional derivative along the outward normal to $\partial\Omega$.

Finally, we must account for the potential energy of deformation of the
springs. Let C denote the set of points in Ω at which the imaginary pins
are located; that is, the sparse set of locations at which the surface is
constrained. Furthermore, denote the height of the pin (the value of the
constraint) by a real scalar $c_{(x_i,y_i)}$ and the stiffness of the spring attached
to it (influence of the constraint) by a positive constant $\beta_{(x_i,y_i)}$ for all
$(x_i,y_i) \in C$. According to HOOKE's law for an ideal spring, the total potential
energy of deformation in the springs is given by

$$E_5(v) = \tfrac{1}{2}\sum_{(x_i,y_i)\in C} \beta_{(x_i,y_i)}[v(x_i,y_i) - c_{(x_i,y_i)}]^2.$$

The equilibrium state of the mechanical system can be obtained as the
solution to the following minimization problem, which is referred to as a
<u>variational principle</u>:

The deflection of the plate at equilibrium is that function u from a
set V of admissible functions v, for which the total potential energy

$$E(v) = E_1(v) + E_2(v) + E_3(v) + E_4(v) + E_5(v) \tag{17.2}$$

is minimal.

---

1. From the last expression in (17.1), it is apparent that the potential
   energy density may be considered to be a <u>convex combination</u> with parameter σ of the square of the Laplacian and a quadratic term in second-
   order partial derivatives of the deflection function $(v_{xx}^2 + 2v_{xy}^2 + v_{yy}^2)$.
   This fact will be used in subsequent discussion.

Thus, quantitatively, the "most consistent" surface which we seek is the one having minimal energy E.

The visual surface approximation problem has been posed in integral form as a variational principle which is <u>quadratic</u> in that it involves terms that are at most quadratic in v and its derivatives. Through the formalism of the calculus of variations one can express the necessary condition for the minimum as the <u>EULER-LAGRANGE equation</u> which in this case can be shown to be a linear, self-adjoint partial differential equation. Much of classical mathematical physics is based on this duality, and it provides numerous techniques for solving our problem, those which are directed towards the variational principle, as well as those which are directed towards its EULER-LAGRANGE equation.

Whatever the strategy, although it is conceivable that the exact analytical solution u could be derived, it is normally impossible to do so for all but the simplest configurations of our system. Consequently, we are led to consider a numerical approach in which we somehow convert our continuous problem into a discrete problem whose numerical solution closely approximates the exact continuous solution u. We propose to employ what is probably the most potent tool for obtaining discrete approximations currently available - the <u>finite-element method</u>. The method is applied to the variational principle directly and, because the variational principle is quadratic, the resulting discrete problem will take the particularly simple form of a linear system of algebraic equations. The main advantage of the finite-element method is its generality. In the context of our surface approximation problem, it can be applied over domains Ω of comlicated shape, and it is <u>not</u> limited to uniform discretizations of these domains. The importance of the latter property in the context of vision is evident when one considers, for example, the nonuniform structure of the retina, where it is known that resolution decreases approximately linearly with eccentricity (see [17.14] for a quantitative model of this phenomenon in terms of the spatial-frequency channels in early vision). Moreover, the finite-element method leads to linear systems which are readily solvable in a parallel, iterative fashion by a sparsely interconnected network of simple processors, a mechanism which seems prevalent in early vision.

For several reasons, we have avoided the alternate route of using the well-known <u>finite difference method</u> to discretize the associated EULER-LAGRANGE equations (see, e.g., [17.33-35]). The finite difference method is much more restrictive in that it practically limits us to uniform discretizations, the underlying convergence theory is much less well developed, and, perhaps most importantly, it becomes very difficult to discretize the natural boundary conditions associated with our surface approximation problem, a task which is done trivially by the finite-element method.

The mathematical background of the finite-element method that is of relevance to our problem is included in Appendix A for convenience. The appendix introduces the required theory and lists the fundamental theorems which we will invoke in applying the method to the task at hand. The process will consist of several steps. First we pose the variational principle in an abstract form that is the basis of the mathematical machinery presented in Appendix A. Next, we determine formally the requirements on the boundary conditions that must be satisfied to ensure that our variational principle is <u>well-posed</u>, i.e., has a unique solution. Only then can we proceed to apply the finite-element method to approximate the solution.

17.3 The Variational Principle

In this section we analyze the continuous variational principle which embodies our visual surface approximation problem, in preparation for the application of the finite-element method. In view of the formalism presented in Appendix A, our first goal is to state the variational principle in the abstract form; that is, to isolate the energy inner product which characterizes our minimization problem. We then derive the associated EULER-LAGRANGE equation and, in the process, consider the various forms of boundary conditions that can be imposed. Finally, we choose the appropriate form of these conditions in view of our visual surface approximation problem and obtain formally the minimum requirements for our variational principle to be well posed.

17.3.1 The Energy Inner Product

According to (17.2), our variational principle asserting that the equilibrium state of thin plate is a minimal-energy configuration may be stated mathematically as the minimization of the expansion

$$E(v) = \int \int_\Omega \tfrac{1}{2}(\Delta v)^2 - (1-\sigma)(v_{xx}v_{yy} - v_{xy}) - gv \; dx \; dy$$
$$- \int_{\partial\Omega} p(s)v \; ds - \int_{\partial\Omega} m(s)\frac{\partial v}{\partial n} \; ds \tag{17.3}$$
$$+ \frac{\beta}{2} \sum_{(x_i,y_i)\in C} [v(x_i,y_i) - c_{(x_i,y_i)}]^2 \;.$$

Here we have assumed that the spring stiffnesses $\beta_{(x_i,y_i)} = \beta$ for all (x_i,y_i) $\in C$. The admissible space V for our variational principle is in general a subspace of the second-order SOBOLEV space $H^2(\Omega)$ over the region Ω (refer to the discussion in Appendix A). If $u \in V$ minimizes E, then $E(u) \leq E(u+\varepsilon v)$ for any $v \in V$. Therefore, to obtain the necessary condition for the minimum, we substitute for v the small variation $u+\varepsilon v$ about u and equate to zero the derivative with respect to ε for $\varepsilon=0$. Equivalently, we may perform the variation using the rules of differentiation:

$$\delta E(u) =$$
$$\int \int_\Omega \Delta u \delta(\Delta u) - (1-\sigma)[u_{xx}\delta(u_{yy}) + u_{yy}\delta(u_{xx}) - 2u_{xy}\delta(u_{xy})] - g\delta u \; dx \; dy$$
$$- \int_{\partial\Omega} p(s)\delta u \; ds - \int_{\partial\Omega} m(s)\delta(\frac{\partial u}{\partial n}) ds$$
$$+ \beta \sum_{(x_i,y_i)\in C} [u(x_i,y_i) - c_{(x_i,y_i)}]\delta u(x_i,y_i) \;.$$

Since variation commutes with differentiation, $\delta(\Delta u)=\Delta(\delta u)$, $\delta(\frac{\partial u}{\partial n})=\frac{\partial}{\partial n}(\delta u)$, $\delta(u_{yy})=(\delta u)_{yy}$, etc. If we now let $v=\delta u$, and set $\delta E=0$, we obtain

$$0 = \int \int_\Omega \Delta u \Delta v - (1-\sigma)(u_{xx}v_{yy} + u_{yy}v_{xx} - 2u_{xy}v_{xy}) - gv \; dx \; dy$$
$$- \int_{\partial\Omega} p(s)v \; ds - \int_{\partial\Omega} m(s)\frac{\partial v}{\partial n} \; ds \tag{17.4}$$
$$+ \beta \sum_{(x_i,y_i)\in C} [u(x_i,y_i) - c_{(x_i,y_i)}]v(x_i,y_i) \;.$$

Eqs. (17.3,4) may be cast in our abstract variational formulation of Appendix A. The key is in identifying the energy inner product as the bilinear form

$$a(u,v)=\int \int_\Omega \Delta u \Delta v - (1-\sigma)(u_{xx}v_{yy}+u_{yy}v_{xx}-2u_{xy}v_{xy})dx\ dy$$
$$+\beta \sum_{(x_i,y_i)\in C} u(x_i,y_i)v(x_i,y_i) \tag{17.5}$$

and in writing the linear form as

$$f(v)=\int \int_\Omega gv\ dx\ dy+\int_{\partial\Omega} p(s)v\ ds+\int_{\partial\Omega} m(s)\frac{\partial v}{\partial n}\ ds$$
$$+\beta \sum_{(x_i,y_i)\in C} [c_{(x_i,y_i)}v(x_i,y_i)-\tfrac{1}{2}c^2_{(x_i,y_i)}]\ . \tag{17.6}$$

Clearly then, (17.3) asserts that we are to minimize the quadratic functional $E(v)=\tfrac{1}{2}a(v,v)-f(v)$, as required in the definition of the abstract variational principle (Sect. A.2). On the other hand, (17.4), which expresses the necessary condition for the vanishing of the first variation, may be written as $a(u,v)=f(v)$, as expected from the discussion leading up to the variational equation (A.10).

Having obtained expressions for the bilinear and linear forms, we are in a position to bring the finite-element method to bear on the problem. Before doing so, however, it is imperative that we carry the analysis further so that we can express the necessary condition for a minimum as a partial differential equation, explore the issue of boundary conditions, and ensure that the problem is well posed.

17.3.2 The EULER-LAGRANGE Equation and Boundary Conditions

For the duration of this section, we will ignore the summation term arising from the (spring) constraints, since its presence will complicate the notation while making no significant contribution to the discussion. First, we will transform the energy inner product $a(\cdot,\cdot)$ given in (17.5) using integration by parts in two dimensions; i.e., GREEN's theorem. Let n be the outward normal vector to $\partial\Omega$, t be the usual tangent vector along $\partial\Omega$, and $\frac{\partial}{\partial n}$ and $\frac{\partial}{\partial t}$ denote partial differentiation along the normal and tangent respectively. Assuming that u is fourth-order differentiable, GREEN's identity (see, e.g., [17.36, p. 14; 17.32])

$$\int \int_\Omega u\Delta v-v\Delta u\ dx\ dy=\int_{\partial\Omega} u\frac{\partial v}{\partial n}-v\frac{\partial u}{\partial n}\ ds$$

may be used to transform the term $\Delta u\Delta v$ arising from the mean curvature of the surface:

$$\int \int_\Omega \Delta u\Delta v\ dx\ dy = \int \int_\Omega v\Delta^2 u\ dx\ dy+\int_{\partial\Omega} \Delta u\frac{\partial v}{\partial n}\ ds-\int_{\partial\Omega} v\frac{\partial}{\partial n}(\Delta u)ds \tag{17.7}$$

where $\Delta^2 u=\Delta\Delta u=u_{xxxx}+2u_{xxyy}+u_{yyyy}$. On the other hand, the Gaussian curvature term can be transformed using the identity [17.36, p. 15]

$$\int \int_\Omega u_{xx}v_{yy}+u_{yy}v_{xx}-2u_{xy}v_{xy}\ dx\ dy=\int_{\partial\Omega} \frac{\partial^2 u}{\partial t^2}\frac{\partial v}{\partial n}\ ds-\int_{\partial\Omega} \frac{\partial^2 u}{\partial n\partial t}\frac{\partial v}{\partial t}\ ds. \tag{17.8}$$

If the boundary is sufficiently smooth, it can be shown (see [17.37, pp. 268-269]) that the second boundary integral can be written as

$$\int_{\partial\Omega} \frac{\partial^2 u}{\partial n \partial t} \frac{\partial v}{\partial t} \, ds = \int_{\partial\Omega} \frac{d}{ds}\left(\frac{\partial^2 u}{\partial n \partial t}\right) v \, ds \ . \tag{17.9}$$

Substituting equations (17.7-9) into (17.5) (and ignoring the constraint term), we obtain

$$a(u,v) = \int \int_\Omega v \Delta^2 u \, dx \, dy + \int_{\partial\Omega} P(u) v \, ds + \int_{\partial\Omega} M(u) \frac{\partial v}{\partial n} \, ds$$

where

$$P(u) = -\frac{\partial}{\partial n}(\Delta u) + (1-\sigma)\frac{d}{ds}\left(\frac{\partial^2 u}{\partial n \partial t}\right)$$
$$M(u) = \Delta u - (1-\sigma)\frac{\partial^2 u}{\partial t^2} \ .$$

Thus, the necessary condition for the minimum (17.4) becomes

$$\int \int_\Omega (\Delta^2 u - g) v \, dx \, dy + \int_{\partial\Omega} [P(u) - p(s)] v \, ds + \int_{\partial\Omega} [M(u) - m(s)]\frac{\partial n}{\partial v} \, ds = 0 \ .$$

Now, since the above equation must hold and since v and $\frac{\partial v}{\partial n}$ are arbitrary on the closed region $\overline{\Omega}$, we must have

$$\Delta^2 u = g \quad \text{in } \Omega \ . \tag{17.10}$$

This is the fourth-order, linear, self-adjoint EULER-LAGRANGE equation that governs the small deflection of a thin plate at equilibrium, and it is satisfied by u inside Ω regardless of the boundary conditions on $\partial\Omega$. In its homogeneous form $\Delta^2 u = 0$, it is called the biharmonic equation. Furthermore, u must satisfy the natural boundary conditions

$$P(u) = p(s) \text{ and } M(u) = m(s) \quad \text{on } \partial\Omega \ . \tag{17.11}$$

According to (17.8), the integral over Ω of the Gaussian curvature approximation $(v_{xx} v_{yy} - 2v_{xy}^2)$ has no effect whatsoever on the EULER-LAGRANGE equation, but contributes only to the boundary conditions.[2] This reflects the fact that the Gaussian curvature of a surface patch is invariant as the surface is subjected to arbitrary bending, and that its average value over the patch depends only on the tangent planes of the surface around the periphery of the patch [17.31, pp. 193-204]. This invariance property of the Gaussian curvature renders it inappropriate as a measure of surface consistency. For example, it cannot distinguish two developable surfaces such as a wildly undulating sinusoidal surface and a planar surface, both of which are cylinders and therefore have zero Gaussian curvature everywhere. On the other hand, the mean curvature does not in general remain invariant under bending and therefore plays a vital role in our energy inner product. This is evident from (17.3) — no value of σ can make $(\Delta v)^2$, which approximates the mean curvature, vanish.[3]

Another consequence of the necessary condition for the minimum is that the form of the natural boundary conditions satisfied by u is determined

---

2. Expressions possessing this property are called divergence expressions [17.29].

3. BRADY and HORN [17.38, p. 29] state that "the choice of which performance index to use is reduced to the square Laplacian, the quadratic variation, and linear combinations of them." We stress that one should be careful not to choose that linear combination which results in a divergence expression (the Gaussian curvature) and therefore has an identically zero EULER-LAGRANGE equation. Recall from (17.1) that the small deflection theory of the thin plate allows only a convex combination so, fortunately, it can never reduce to a divergence expression and is thus free from danger.

by any essential boundary conditions which may be imposed on v. In general, we can impose up to two essential boundary conditions, one on v and the other on $\frac{\partial v}{\partial n}$. First, consider the case of a simply supported plate where the essential boundary condition v=0 is imposed on $\partial\Omega$ but $\frac{\partial v}{\partial n}$ is left unconstrained. The solution u must then still satisfy the second condition in (17.11). We therefore have the NEUMANN boundary conditions

u=0, M(u)=m(s)   on $\partial\Omega$

and, moreover, the first contour integral in (17.3) vanishes.

Next, suppose that we also set $\frac{\partial v}{\partial n}=0$ on $\partial\Omega$. Then

u = $\frac{\partial u}{\partial n}$ = 0   on $\partial\Omega$ (17.12)

which are the DIRICHLET boundary conditions for the clamped plate. In this case, both contour integrals in (17.3) vanish and, moreover, σ is arbitrary since it does not appear in the EULER-LAGRANGE equation (17.10), but only in the natural boundary conditions (17.11) which have now been replaced by (17.12). We can therefore greatly simplify the variational integral. In particular, the functional minimization problems involving

$$E(v)=\int\int_\Omega \tfrac{1}{2}(\Delta v)^2 -gv \; dx \; dy \qquad \text{for } \sigma=1$$

and

$$E(v)=\int\int_\Omega \tfrac{1}{2}(v_{xx}^2+2v_{xy}^2+v_{yy}^2)-gv \; dx \; dy \qquad \text{for } \sigma=0$$

are equivalent in the DIRICHLET case.

Finally, consider the case of a free boundary; that is, when the externally imposed force p(s) and moment m(s) on the boundary are zero. Then, there are no constraints on v, but according to (17.11), u must satisfy

P(u)=0   and   M(u)=0   on $\partial\Omega$.

These are the natural boundary conditions satisfied by the solution for the case of the free plate. Once again, the contour integrals in (17.3) vanish and the energy functional takes the simple form

$$E(v)= \int\int_\Omega \tfrac{1}{2}(\Delta v)^2-(1-\sigma)(v_{xx}v_{yy}-v_{xy}^2)-gv \; dx \; dy \; .$$

In general, the admissible space V is the subspace of the SOBOLEV space $H^2(\Omega)$ which satisfies the essential boundary conditions imposed on the plate. If, for example, a portion of the edge of the plate is simply supported, V will consist of functions which satisfy the essential condition v=0 on that portion of $\partial\Omega$. If part of the edge of the plate is clamped, then v=$\frac{\partial v}{\partial n}$=0 on that part of $\partial\Omega$. On the other hand, if part of the edge is free, then no constraints are imposed on v, over that portion of the boundary and, in the case of the free plate, $V\equiv H^2(\Omega)$. Of course, the plate cannot be "too free" on $\overline{\Omega}$, because then the physical system cannot achieve stable equilibrium and a unique solution would not exist. Precisely how much freedom can be allowed will be established formally in the next section.

17.3.3 When is the Problem Well Posed?

Turning to our visual surface approximation problem, we should at this point choose the appropriate form of boundary conditions on $\partial\Omega$. Since the only information about the surface that is provided by the stereo module, for example, is embodied in the sparse constraints, the strategy of least commitment is to "assume nothing" about the boundaries of the surface. In terms of our plate problem, this means that we should impose no essential boundary conditions on the plate; that is, we solve the <u>free-plate problem</u> whose admissible space $V \equiv H^2(\Omega)$.

If the boundary of the plate is free, it is clear that the constraints will play a critical role in assuring the existence of a unique state of stable equilibrium. Our goal in this section is to specify the existence and uniqueness requirements mathematically as conditions under which the surface approximation problem is <u>well posed</u>. To do this, we will invoke Theorem A.1, and satisfy its conditions by proving the following propositions.

Proposition 1. The energy inner product $a(\cdot,\cdot)$ is symmetric.

Proof. $a(u,v)=a(v,u)$ is evident by inspection of (17.5). $\square$

Proposition 2. If the set of constraints C contains (at least) three non-collinear points, then $a(\cdot,\cdot)$ is V elliptic for $0\le\sigma<1$.

Proof. We want to show that there exists an $\alpha>0$ such that $a(v,v)\ge\alpha\|v\|^2$, for all $v\in V$. To do so, it is sufficient to show that $a(v,v)=0$ only if $v=0$. We rewrite $a(v,v)$ as

$$a(v,v)=\int\int_{\Omega} \sigma(\Delta v)^2+(1-\sigma)(v_{xx}^2+2v_{xy}^2+v_{yy}^2)dx\,dy+\beta \sum_{(x_i,y_i)\in C} v(x_i,y_i)^2 \ .$$

Now, $\Delta v=0$ only if v is a <u>harmonic function</u>, while $(v_{xx}^2+2v_{xy}^2+v_{yy}^2)=0$ only if v is a first degree polynomial in x and y (as can easily be shown by integration), which is a subclass of the harmonic functions. Thus, the integral is ≥ 0 for $0\le\sigma<1$, and it is zero only if v is a linear function over Ω. On the other hand, since β is positive by definition the sum is also ≥ 0 and it is zero only if $v(x_i,y_i)=0$ for all $(x_i,y_i)\in C$. Therefore, if C contains three noncollinear points, then $a(v,v)=0$ only if $v\equiv 0$, implying that $a(\cdot,\cdot)$ is V elliptic. $\square$

By Propositions 1 and 2 and Theorem A.1, we are assured that the continuous approximation problem is well posed if $0\le\sigma<1$ and the set of constraints includes at least three noncollinear points. The condition on the constraints is not unexpected in view of the arguments made in Sect.17.2.1. Physically speaking, all unconstrained degrees of freedom of the plate must be precluded, and three noncollinear constraints is clearly the minimum requirement for this to be the case. In application to natural images, the stereo algorithm will almost always generate at least three noncollinear points, so we can, for all practical purposes, consider our surface approximation problem to be well posed so long as $0\le\sigma<1$.

17.4 Obtaining the Discrete Problem

So far, we have been dealing with the continuous form of our surface approximation problem. We formulated it in the required abstract form, selected appropriate boundary conditions, and showed that it is well posed in practice. In this section, we face the task of applying the finite-element method to transform the variational principle into an appropriate discrete problem whose discrete solution can be computed fairly easily. Our piecewise continuous representation of surfaces will be based on a very simple finite element which is, however, nonconforming. This will force us to introduce an approximate variational principle and to show that it has a unique solution which converges to the exact solution as the elements shrink in size. Only then can we undertake the next step which is to derive the discrete problem explicitly as a linear system of algebraic equations.

17.4.1 Conforming vs. Nonconforming Methods

Our well-posed variational principle satisfies all the necessary conditions to guarantee that any conforming finite-element method applied to it will converge. In principle, it is straightforward to apply a conforming finite-element method according to the steps in Appendix A. We generate a finite-element space S^h which is a subspace of our admissible space V, and apply the RITZ method to find that function $u^h \epsilon S^h$ which optimally approximates the exact solution $u \epsilon V$. The approximation is optimal in the sense that it is closest to u with respect to the strain energy norm $a(\cdot,\cdot)^{\frac{1}{2}}$, or equivalently, that the strain energy in the error $a(u-u^h, u-u^h)$ is minimal. To construct a conforming finite-element subspace, we must satisfy the completeness and conformity conditions given in Sect. A.4. Since the energy inner product $a(\cdot,\cdot)$ contains partial derivatives of order m=2, the completeness condition requires that the local polynomial defined within each element subdomain E must be at least a quadratic; $P^E \supset \Pi^2(E)$ for all $E \epsilon T^h$ ($\Pi^n(E)$ denotes the set of nth degree polynomials over E). On the other hand, the conformity condition states that the polynomials must be of class C^1 across interelement boundaries, and consequently $S^h \subset C^1(\bar{\Omega})$ globally. In satisfying both conditions, we are guaranteed that the finite element space is a subspace of the admissible space V, and that there exists a unique optimal approximation $u^h \epsilon S^h$.

If $\bar{\Omega}$ is a polygonal region, elements with straight sides will suffice. A number of such elements which are conforming for m=2 (i.e., problems characterized by fourth-order EULER-LAGRANGE equations) are available. Examples are the ARGYRIS triangle, BELL triangle, and BOGNER-FOX-SCHMIDT rectangle (see, e.g., [17.36,39,40] and the references therein). Unfortunately, we can expect serious computational difficulties to arise in the implementation of these conforming methods. The basic source of difficulty is the requirement of continuity of first partial derivatives across interelement boundaries - either the structure of the conforming element spaces P^E becomes complicated, or their dimension is large. For our problem, the simplest conforming polynomial element is the BELL triangle, in which we have a quintic polynomial uniquely determined by 18 nodal variables consisting of the approximation v^h, as well as its first and second partial derivatives at the three vertices.

As is described in Appendix A, the dimensions of the finite-element space can be reduced by the use of nonconforming elements. A popular nonconforming element for fourth-order problems is ADINI's rectangle, whose local function p^E is a 12-degree-of-freedom polynomial with nodal variables being the approximating function, as well as its first partial derivatives at the four vertices. The element is nonconforming since it is only of class C^0 across interelement boundaries. Many other nonconforming elements have been developed for fourth-order problems (see, e.g., [17.36,39,40]).

For this initial implementation, we have chosen to reduce the dimensions of the finite-element space as much as possible by defining what for our problem is probably the simplest successful nonconforming element imaginable. This element will be defined next.

17.4.2 A Simple Nonconforming Element

We will define a finite-element space by the standard procedure outlined in Sect. A.4. Suppose that $\bar{\Omega}$ is rectangular, and consider a uniform triangulation T^h of $\bar{\Omega}$ into identical square elements E, where the fundamental length h is the length of a side of E. By definition, we require that $\cup_{E \in T^h} E = \bar{\Omega}$ and that the elements be adjacent and overlap along their sides. A point in $\bar{\Omega}$ is a node of the triangulation if it is a vertex of an elemental square and, as usual, we consider the elements to be interconnected at the nodes. The nodal variables will simply be the node displacements, i.e., the values of the function $v^h \in S^h$ at the nodes.

The next step is to define a space P^E of polynomials p^E over the element domain. The polynomials must satisfy the completeness condition which states that $\Pi^2 \subset P^E$, since the energy inner product contains derivatives of order m=2. This is the requirement that the polynomials be able to reproduce exactly all states of constant strain which, in this case, are all polynomials up to degree 2. We will satisfy the requirement by choosing P^E to be the six-dimensional space of full second degree polynomials $p^E : E \to R$ such that

$$p^E(x,y) = ax^2 + by^2 + cxy + dx + ey + f \qquad (17.13)$$

where the six real parameters a to f are to be determined.

We must ensure that p^E is uniquely specified within E in terms of the node displacements. To do so, we isolate a representative element and set the origin of the x-y coordinate system at its lower left-hand corner, as illustrated in Fig.17.4. Our task is to choose a p^E-underline{unisolvent} set of nodes, the displacements at which uniquely determine p^E. An appropriate choice is the six nodes shown in the figure, whose node displacements are denoted by $v_{i,j} \in R$, for $(i,j) \in \{(-1,0),(0,0),(1,0),(0,-1),(0,1),(1,1)\}$. Expressing the six unknown parameters in terms of the node displacements is then a simple matter of substituting the displacements into (17.13) and solving the resulting nonsingular system of six equations. We obtain

$$a = \frac{1}{2h^2}(v_{1,0} - 2v_{0,0} + v_{-1,0}) \qquad\qquad d = \frac{1}{2h}(v_{1,0} - v_{-1,0})$$

$$b = \frac{1}{2h^2}(v_{0,1} - 2v_{0,0} + v_{0,-1}) \qquad\qquad e = \frac{1}{2h}(v_{0,1} - v_{0,-1}) \qquad (17.14)$$

$$c = \frac{1}{h^2}(v_{1,1} - v_{0,1} - v_{1,0} + v_{0,0}) \qquad\qquad f = v_{0,0} \ .$$

Of course, the six degrees of freedom of this element are insufficient to enforce C^1 continuity of v^h across interelement boundaries. Therefore, the element is nonconforming; $S^h \not\subset C^1(\Omega)$. It is a simple matter to show that the polynomials p^E are in general discontinuous across element boundaries, al-

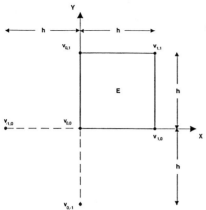

Fig. 17.4. Unisolvent nodes for the non-conforming element

though continuity is maintained at the nodes themselves because each poly-nomial interpolates its unisolvent set of nodal displacements. At this point, we acknowledge that our element is somewhat unorthodox in that the definition of p^E requires nodal variables associated with two nodes which lie outside the element domain E. The justification for this transgression is that our element, as defined, will yield a discrete system whose matrix is particularly simple and uniform in structure. This will simplify the eventual implementation considerably. On the other hand, alternate arrange-ments for the unisolvent set of nodes are clearly possible. Perhaps a more appropriate choice from a biological standpoint would be a hexagonal tri-angulation with the unisolvent set of nodes placed at the vertices of hexa-gonal element domains E having sides of common length h. Regardless of our particular choice, the quadratic elements must first be shown to be conver-gent since they will invariably be nonconforming. This we will do in the next subsection for the simple square element.

17.4.3 The Approximate Variational Principle

Due to the nonconformity of the elements, the finite element space is not a subspace of the admissible space V (i.e., $S^h \not\subset H^2(\Omega) \equiv V$). Therefore, in lieu of the energy inner product $a(\cdot, \cdot)$ of (17.5), we are forced to substitute the approximate energy inner product $a_h(\cdot, \cdot)$, given by (A.16), which can be written as

$$a_h(u^h, v^h) = \sum_{E \in T^h} \int \int_E \Delta u^h \Delta v^h - (1-\sigma)(u^h_{xx} v^h_{yy} + u^h_{yy} v^h_{xx} - 2u^h_{xy} v^h_{xy}) dx\, dy$$

$$+\beta \sum_{(x_i, y_i) \in C} u^h(x_i, y_i) v^h(x_i, y_i) \qquad (17.15)$$

$$= \sum_{E \in T^h} \int \int_E \sigma \Delta u^h \Delta v^h + (1-\sigma)(u^h_{xx} v^h_{xx} + 2u^h_{xy} v^h_{xy} + u^h_{yy} v^h_{yy}) dx\, dy$$

$$+\beta \sum_{(x_i, y_i) \in C} u^h(x_i, y_i) v^h(x_i, y_i)$$

where $0 \leq \sigma < 1$. The corresponding approximate variational principle and varia-tional equation are given by (A.17) and (A.18), respectively.

Does the approximate variational principle have a unique solution $u^h \in S^h$? To answer this question, we proceed in the spirit of Sect. A.5 by equipping

S^h with a norm which we will employ to show that $a_h(\cdot,\cdot)$ is uniformly S^h elliptic.

Proposition 3. The mapping $\|v^h\|_h : S^h \to \mathbb{R}$ defined by

$$\|v^h\|_h = \left(\sum_{E \in T^h} |v^h|^2_{2,E} + \sum_{(x_i,y_i) \in C} v^h(x_i,y_i)^2 \right)^{\frac{1}{2}},$$

where $|v^h|_{2,E} = (\int \int_E (v^h_{xx})^2 + (v^h_{xy})^2 + (v^h_{yy})^2 \, dx \, dy)^{\frac{1}{2}}$ is the second-order SOBOLEV seminorm (see (A.3)), is a norm over S^h.

Proof. $\|\cdot\|_h$ is a priori only a seminorm over S^h. Consider a $v^h \in S^h$ such that $\|v^h\|_h = 0$. Then it must be the case that (i) $|v^h|_{2,E} = 0$ for all $E \in T^h$, and that (ii) $v^h(x_i,y_i) = 0$ for all $(x_i,y_i) \in C$. Because of their interpolatory nature, the local polynomials p^E are continuous at all the nodes. Moreover, by condition (i), v^h must be a first-degree polynomial inside every E. With $a=b=c=0$ in (17.14), it is a simple matter to show that this implies that v^h is a continuous linear function over $\bar{\Omega}$. Now, by condition (ii), v^h is zero at all $(x_i,y_i) \in C$. Since the continuous problem is assumed to be well posed, C contains at least three noncollinear points. Consequently $v^h \equiv 0$, and $\|\cdot\|_h$ is therefore a norm. □

Proposition 4. The approximate energy inner product $a_h(\cdot,\cdot)$ is uniformly S^h elliptic.

Proof.

$$a_h(v^h,v^h) = \sum_{E \in T^h} \int \int_E \sigma(\Delta v^h)^2 + (1-\sigma)[(v^h_{xx})^2 + 2(v^h_{xy})^2 + (v^h_{yy})^2] \, dx \, dy$$

$$+ \beta \sum_{(x_i,y_i) \in C} v^h(x_i,y_i)^2$$

$$= (1-\sigma) \left(\sum_{E \in T^h} \int \int_E (v^h_{xx})^2 + (v^h_{xy})^2 + (v^h_{yy})^2 \, dx \, dy \right.$$

$$+ \sum_{(x_i,y_i) \in C} v^h(x_i,y_i)^2 \Big)$$

$$+ \sum_{E \in T^h} \int \int_E \sigma(\Delta v^h)^2 + (1-\sigma)(v^h_{xy})^2 \, dx \, dy$$

$$+ (\beta + \sigma - 1) \sum_{(x_i,y_i) \in C} v^h(x_i,y_i)^2$$

$$\geq (1-\sigma)\|v^h\|_h^2, \qquad \text{for } 0 \leq \sigma < 1 \text{ and } \beta \geq 1 - \sigma .$$

Since $1-\sigma$ is positive for $0 \leq \sigma < 1$, $a_h(\cdot,\cdot)$ is uniformly S^h elliptic. □

Therefore, the approximate variational principle has a unique solution $u^h \in S^h$. Moreover, because the ellipticity is uniform, STRANG's lemma (Theorem A.5) applies, and u^h will converge to the exact solution $u \in V$ as $h \to 0$, if the approximation is consistent in the sense of equation (A.21). To verify consistency, we apply the patch test, Theorem A.6.

256

Proposition 5. The square, nonconforming element whose local, quadratic function is defined by (17.13,14) passes the patch test.

Proof. Consider an arbitrary patch of four adjacent elements, all of which share a common node $v_{i,j}$ internal to the patch, as shown in Fig.17.5. Now, suppose that we impose a constant strain condition on the patch; that is, suppose that we constrain the displacements at all remaining nodes around the periphery of the patch by assigning to them values consistent with the function $\pi_2 \epsilon \Pi^2$, an arbitrary second-degree polynomial. Next, we solve the approximate variational principle (A.17) over the patch domain. This reduces to solving for the unknown displacement at the common unconstrained node $v_{i,j}$ such that it minimizes a quadratic equation. It is a matter of routine algebraic manipulation to show that the displacement obtained will also be consistent with π_2 (we omit the details). In fact, one can show that this is true for the internal, unconstrained nodes of an arbitrary patch of any number of elements whose boundary nodes are made consistent with π_2. Therefore, the element passes the patch test. □

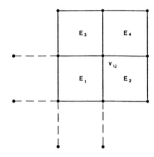

Fig. 17.5. Applying the patch test to four adjacent elements

Having proved the above propositions, we can now be secure in the fact that our approximate variational principle will provide unique discrete solutions which will converge to the exact solution of the continuous problem as the discretization is made increasingly fine. A limit to the order of convergence that we can expect from our approximation is given by (A.15) - since our element is complete only through quadratics (k=2), we are limited to a convergence rate of order h^2 in displacement (s=0). For a more precise statement, we should take into account the consistency error term in (A.20). Nevertheless, we will bypass this complicated analysis because the consistency error is not expected to be large for smooth u, which is normally the case when approximating smooth surfaces.

17.4.4 The Discrete Problem

We are finally ready to derive an explicit form of the discrete problem associated with our approximate variational principle. There are essentially two ways of proceeding. One possibility is to find the RITZ basis functions ϕ_i which are associated with our finite element and which span the space S^h. The basis functions are nonconforming piecewise quadratics with local support. A single basis function is associated with each node of the triangulation. We can then use the variational equation (A.18) directly, and write the discrete problem as the linear system of equations analogous to (A.13) by computing the matrix coefficients $a_h(\phi_i, \phi_j)$. Unfortunately, the piecewise continuous nature of the basis functions makes them tedious to manipulate, especially near the boundary. We will adopt an alternate approach which

257

altogether avoids the derivation and manipulation of the basis functions. The approach is to solve the approximate variational principle by minimizing the functional $E_h(\cdot)$ of (A.17). Before doing so, however, we make two additional simplifications.

The first simplification involves taking a conservative stance once more. There is no reason to believe that the human visual system is biased in the depth values it assigns such as, for example, making all of them too small or too large. That is to say, we have no reason to assume that there is an external influence on the surface other than that provided by the constraints C, and we should therefore nullify the externally applied surface force: $g(x,y) \equiv 0$. The linear form (17.6) for the free plate then reduces to

$$f(v^h) = \beta \sum_{(x_i,y_i) \in C} (c_{(x_i,y_i)} v^h(x_i,y_i) - \tfrac{1}{2} c^2_{(x_i,y_i)}) \; . \tag{17.16}$$

The second simplification involves the choice of a numerical value for the constant σ in our approximate energy inner product $a_h(\cdot,\cdot)$ given by (17.15). According to the proof of Proposition 4, we are at liberty to choose any value in the range $0 \le \sigma < 1$; therefore, the simplifying choice $\sigma = 0$ will be made.[4] Setting $\sigma = 0$ in (17.15), the energy inner product simplifies to

$$a_h(u^h,v^h) = \sum_{E \in Th} \int \int_E u^h_{xx} v^h_{xx} + 2u^h_{xy} v^h_{xy} + u^h_{yy} v^h_{yy} \; dx \; dy$$
$$+ \beta \sum_{(x_i,y_i) \in C} u^h(x_i,y_i) v^h(x_i,y_i) \; . \tag{17.17}$$

Thus, according to (A.17), we obtain the simplified energy functional

$$E_h(v^h) = \tfrac{1}{2} a_h(v^h,v^h) - f(v^h)$$
$$= \tfrac{1}{2} \sum_{E \in Th} \int \int_E (v^h_{xx})^2 + 2(v^h_{xy})^2 + (v^h_{yy})^2 \; dx \; dy \tag{17.18}$$
$$+ \frac{\beta}{2} \sum_{(x_i,y_i) \in C} [v^h(x_i,y_i) - c_{(x_i,y_i)}]^2 \; .$$

The expression inside the integral will be recognized as the "quadratic variation" expression used by GRIMSON [17.21].

Since the triangulation over the rectangular region $\bar{\Omega}$ is that of a uniform square grid, it is convenient to impose on the nodes the natural lexicographic indexing scheme implied by Fig.17.4. We index the nodes by (i,j) for $i=1,\ldots,N_x$ and $j=1,\ldots,N_y$, where N_x and N_y are the number of nodes along the x and y axis respectively. The total number of nodes is $N = N_x \times N_y$. The displacement at node (i,j) is denoted by the variable $v^h_{i,j}$, and all the displacements together are denoted by the vector $\underline{v}^h \in R^N$.

---

4. Recall that σ is the POISSON constant of the elastic material, so our choice implies that the material does not change in width as it stretches lengthwise. Although this value is not meaningful physically, it is perfectly acceptable mathematically. Aside from a question of convenience, there is further evidence that supports this choice in terms of the optical laws of image formation (see [17.28]).

The next step is to express the functional in terms of the node displacements with the help of our element. Inside each element domain E, v^h is a quadratic polynomial given by (17.13,14). Therefore, the second partial derivatives of p^E are constant within E, and are given by

$$v^h_{xx}|_E = p^E_{xx} = 2a = \frac{1}{h^2}(v^h_{i+1,j} - 2v^h_{i,j} + v^h_{i-1,j})$$

$$v^h_{yy}|_E = p^E_{yy} = 2b = \frac{1}{h^2}(v^h_{i,j+1} - 2v^h_{i,j} + v^h_{i,j-1})$$

$$v^h_{xy}|_E = p^E_{xy} = c = \frac{1}{h^2}(v^h_{i+1,j+1} - v^h_{i,j+1} - v^h_{i+1,j} + v^h_{i,j})$$

where it is assumed that i,j is the index of the lower left-hand node of E. The form of these second derivatives will be recognized as being simply the _finite difference_ approximations of order h^2 for the respective derivatives on a uniform, square mesh (see, e.g., [17.41, p. 884]). Of course, this result is a consequence of our particular choice of finite element, and it will lead to a particularly simple discrete problem. With other elements one cannot expect to obtain finite difference expressions, even for uniform triangulations. Substituting the expressions for the derivatives into $a_h(v^h, v^h)$ in (17.18) and noting that the area of each element is h^2, we obtain[5]

$$E_h(v^h) = \frac{1}{2} \sum_{E \in T^h} \int \int_E (p^E_{xx})^2 + 2(p^E_{xy})^2 + (p^E_{yy})^2 \ dx \ dy + \frac{\beta}{2} \sum_{(i,j) \in C} (v^h_{i,j} - c^h_{i,j})^2$$

$$= \frac{h^2}{2} \sum_{E \in T^h} [(2a)^2 + 2c^2 + (2b)^2] + \frac{\beta}{2} \sum_{(i,j) \in C} (v^h_{i,j} - c^h_{i,j})^2$$

$$= \frac{1}{2h^2} \sum_{E \in T^h} [(v^h_{i+1,j} - 2v^h_{i,j} + v^h_{i-1,j})^2$$

$$+ 2(v^h_{i+1,j+1} - v^h_{i,j+1} - v^h_{i+1,j} + v^h_{i,j})^2$$

$$+ (v^h_{i,j+1} - 2v^h_{i,j} + v^h_{i,j-1})^2] + \frac{\beta}{2} \sum_{(i,j) \in C} (v^h_{i,j} - c^h_{i,j})^2 \ .$$

We can write the above expression for the functional (aside from the additive constant term) in matrix form as

$$E_h(\underline{v}^h) = \tfrac{1}{2}(\underline{v}^h, \underline{A}^h \underline{v}^h) - (\underline{f}^h, \underline{v}^h) \tag{17.19}$$

where $(\cdot, \cdot): R^N \times R^N \to R$ denotes the familiar Euclidean inner product, and $\underline{A}^h \in R^{NN}$ is a matrix of coefficients. Clearly, (17.19) is the discrete equivalent of the functional (17.18). For the linear term, we have $\underline{f}^h = \beta \underline{c}^h$ where $\underline{c}^h \in R^N$ is a vector whose entries associated with constrained displacements are the constraint values $c^h_{i,j}$ and the rest are zero. On the other hand, the matrix $\underline{A}^h \in R^{NN}$, which forms the quadratic term, is a matrix of coefficients which can be broken down as the sum of two matrices: $\underline{A}^h = \underline{A}^h_\phi + \underline{B}^h$. The matrix $\underline{B}^h$ is a diagonal matrix whose diagonal entries associated with constrained displacements are equal to β, and the remainder are zero. As is clear from (A.13), the entries of the other component $\underline{A}^h_\phi$ can be interpreted as inner products between pairs of basis functions of the finite-element space S^h. Since the basis functions have local support, most of these inner products

---

5. We also assume for simplicity that all constraints $c(x_i, y_i)$ coincide with nodes (i,j) in T^h. Hence, we will denote the constraints by $c^h_{i,j}$.

will be zero, thereby making $\underline{A}^h$ sparse and banded. Moreover, since by Propositions 1 and 4, the energy inner product is symmetric and S^h elliptic, $\underline{A}_h$ is a positive definite, symmetric matrix. These are important properties from a computational point of view.

To obtain the minimum of $E_h(\underline{v}^h)$ we set to zero its partial derivatives with respect to each of the displacements $v^h_{i,j}$. The minimizing vector of displacements $\underline{u}^h$ satisfies the condition

$$\nabla E_h(\underline{u}^h) = \underline{A}^h \underline{u}^h - \underline{f}^h = \underline{0} \tag{17.20}$$

where the entries of $\underline{A}^h$ are given by

$$\underline{A}^h = [\frac{\partial^2 E_h(\underline{u}^h)}{\partial u_{i,j} \partial u_{k,\ell}}], \qquad 1 \le i, k \le N_x, \quad 1 \le j, \ell \le N_y .$$

From this expression, $\underline{A}^h$ will be recognized as the HESSIAN matrix of the functional E_h (see, e.g., [17.42]).

Although the evaluation of the Hessian matrix entries is routine for interior nodes, it is tedious due to the special cases for the elements around the boundaries of the region $\overline{\Omega}$. We omit the details and give the final result in terms of a set of computational molecules which are illustrated in Fig.17.6 in relation to the lower left-hand edge of $\overline{\Omega}$ whose boundary is indicated by bold links. Obviously, computational molecules for the remaining edges are appropriate rotations of those shown. The particular computational molecule associated with a node specifies the nonzero coefficients of the equation for that node. For example, the equation for the displacement at a node (i,j) in the interior of the region (indicated by the double circle in the topmost computational molecule in Fig.17.6) is

$$-\frac{8}{h^2}(v^h_{i-1,j} + v^h_{i+1,j} + v^h_{i,j-1} + v^h_{i,j+1})$$

$$+\frac{2}{h^2}(v^h_{i-1,j-1} + v^h_{i+1,j-1} + v^h_{i-1,j+1} + v^h_{i+1,j+1})$$

$$+\frac{1}{h^2}(v^h_{i-2,j} + v^h_{i+2,j} + v^h_{i,j-2} + v^h_{i,j+2}) \tag{17.21}$$

$$+\frac{20}{h^2}v^h_{i,j} + \beta v^h_{i,j} = \beta c_{i,j} .$$

The terms involving β are present only if there is a constraint $c_{i,j}$ at that node.

The sparseness of $\underline{A}^h$ is evident from the above equation - matrix rows associated with interior nodes have only 13 nonzero entries, while rows associated with nodes near the boundaries have even fewer. Also, note that the computational molecule for the center of the region is a factor of h^2 (due to the elemental area) times the finite difference approximation of order h^2 for the biharmonic operator [17.41, p. 885] that is associated with the EULER-LAGRANGE equation for our variational principle. This is an expected consequence of our particular choice of element which yielded finite difference approximations for the second partial derivatives of v^h. Moreover, aside from multiplicative constants, the same molecules were obtained by GRIMSON [17.21] in the specification of a (conjugate gradient) mathematical programming algorithm. As was previously argued, however, the finite-element method

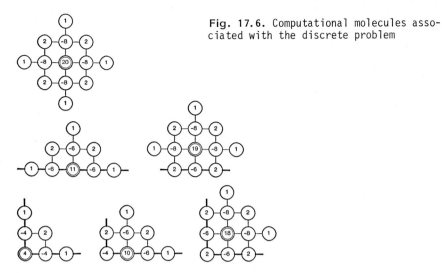

Fig. 17.6. Computational molecules associated with the discrete problem

is richer in that it systematically suggests many alternative, less restrictive triangulations, as well as more general local representations for surfaces.

17.5 Multilevel Surface Reconstruction

As we have seen, the application of the finite-element method to a well-posed quadratic variational principle, such as the one on which our surface approximation problem is based, inevitably leads to an equivalent discrete problem which takes the form of a linear system of algebraic equations. The matrix of coefficients of this nonsingular system is symmetric, positive definite, sparse, and banded. Computing the most consistent approximating surface now amounts to solving this system and, in this section, we adopt an efficient hierarchical algorithm to perform this task. We will proceed to develop the algorithm and to demonstrate its performance using constraints from stereopsis.

17.5.1 Possible Methodologies for Solving the Discrete Problem

The solution of linear systems is a very important problem in numerical analysis and the many techniques which have been developed fall into essentially two broad classes - direct methods, which yield the solution in a finite number of steps, and iterative methods, which typically converge asymptotically to the solution (see, e.g., [17.43] or [17.44]).

Direct methods include matrix inversion methods such as Gaussian elimination and LU decomposition. Although widely used for solving finite-element equations, they usually do not exploit the sparseness and bandedness of the system matrix because, during the inversion process, the sparse matrix is transformed into a full one.[6] Consequently, all the elements of the

6. For a positive definite symmetric matrix, the inverse matrix remains banded, but is no longer sparse within the band. The inverse matrix is the discrete GREEN's function for our problem, which in general has global support over $\bar{\Omega}$.

matrix must be stored. Moreover, direct methods are typically global and sequential algorithms, which makes them unsuitable models for neurally based visual processes.

On the other hand, the class of iterative methods readily gives rise to biologically feasible algorithms. Examples in this class are relaxation methods such as JACOBI relaxation, GAUSS-SEIDEL relaxation, and successive overrelaxation, as well as gradient methods such as gradient descent and the conjugate gradient method. Iterative methods exploit the sparseness of the matrix inasmuch as they do not modify its elements from one iteration to the next. Therefore, only the relatively few nonzero matrix elements need be stored. Owing to the sparseness and banded structure of the matrix, iterative methods require local-support computations only, and in certain forms such as JACOBI relaxation and gradient methods the computations can be performed in parallel. Because iterative methods in general and relaxation in particular are fundamental to the ensuing discussion, an introduction to some of the relevant mathematics of this class of techniques is included in Appendix B for convenience.

The algorithms we are contemplating are to be executed by computational mechanisms in the form of networks of many simple processors which are directly connected only to near neighbors; in other words, by mechanisms modeling current beliefs about neural nets. Due to the myopic nature of the processors, global interactions can take place only indirectly, through the iterative process, by an incremental propagation of information. Normally the network is large, and since this is reflected in the size of the linear system, we anticipate that a vast number of iterations will be required for any relaxation or gradient method to converge. Typically, the number of iterations will be on the order of N^m, where N is the dimension of the matrix, and m is the highest order of partial derivatives present in the energy inner product, which in our case is two. GRIMSON's [17.21] formulation of surface interpolation as a problem in mathematical programming naturally led him to the choice of a gradient method for its solution and, not unexpectedly, disappointingly slow convergence rates were observed due to the large size of the images typically encountered.

Recently, a class of iterative techniques called multigrid methods have seen increased application to the numerical solution of boundary value problems for which they achieve convergence in essentially order-N number of operations [17.45-47]. This spectacular improvement results from the use of a hierarchy of grids to increase the efficiency of the global propagation of information. Multigrid algorithms feature both intragrid and intergrid processes. Typically, the intragrid processes are relaxation iterations, while the intergrid processes are local polynomial interpolations. Therefore the multigrid algorithms are, in principle, biologically feasible. A final issue which speaks in favor of adopting them in vision is the intrinsic multilevel structure of the earliest stages of the visual system itself and, as we argued in Sect.17.1, the apparent need to maintain this structure at least to the level of the $2\frac{1}{2}$-D sketch.

We therefore advocate a hierarchical approach to surface reconstruction, and we will develop it initially in the context of the MARR-POGGIO stereo theory whose clear multilevel structure provides ample motivation. At the heart of the proposed scheme lies a multigrid algorithm adapted to the fast solution of a hierarchy of discrete, thin-plate surface approximation problems. In the following subsections, we present the underlying theory and build up a detailed description of the multilevel algorithm.

17.5.2 The Multilevel Equations

As we have stated, the stereo module generates sparse depth information over a range of resolutions. The information at any particular scale can be thought of as a set of constraints which, at that level, define a well-posed, discrete surface approximation problem. It is natural, then, to view our surface reconstruction problem as the solution of a hierarchy of such discrete problems. The discretizations are performed in the usual way by introducing a sequence of finite-element spaces $S^{h_1}, \ldots, S^{h_L}$ over the rectangular domain $\bar{\Omega}$, where L is the number of levels and $h_1 > \ldots > h_L$ are the fundamental lengths of the elements at each level. In the familiar notation, we will denote the functions which are members of the finite-element spaces by $v^{h_k} \in S^{h_k}$, and the parameters (i.e., the nodal displacements) which define these functions according to (A.11) by vectors $\underline{v}^{h_k} \in R^{N^{h_k}}$, where N^{h_k} is the dimension of S^{h_k}. The hierarchy of problems is then given by the sequence of L linear systems (see (17.20)) of the form

$$\underline{A}^{h_k}\underline{u}^{h_k} = \underline{f}^{h_k}, \quad 1 \le k \le L \tag{17.22}$$

whose discrete solutions $\underline{u}^{h_k} \in R^{N^{h_k}}$ for $1 \le k \le L$ define a sequence of functions $u^{h_k} \in S^k$ which constitute the hierarchy of full surface representations.

Although, in theory, there need be no restriction in the relationship of element sizes from one level to the next, a number of practical implementation-related issues point towards the subdivision of each square element domain on a given level S^{h_k} into four identical element domains on the next finer level $S^{h_{k+1}}$; that is, we choose $h_k = 2h_{k+1}$. Consequently, S^{h_k} will be a subspace of $S^{h_{k+1}}$, and the implementation of the interlevel processes is simplified substantially. Moreover, the 2:1 ratio is a natural one in view of the spatial-frequency bandpass channels in early vision whose center frequencies are spaced approximately one octave apart, the spatial resolution of a channel being about twice that of the immediately coarser one [17.14]. Finally, the choice can be shown to be near optimal in terms of the multigrid convergence rate [17.45, p. 353]. Since the triangulation of $\bar{\Omega}$ associated with our simple elements is a uniform grid of square-element domains, the 2:1 ratio implies that in scanning along the x or y direction, every second node of a grid coincides with a node of the next coarser grid and, furthermore, that the number of nodes is related from one level to the next by $N^{h_{k-1}} = \frac{1}{4}N^{h_k}$. Therefore, the total amount of space required to maintain all of the representations is bounded by $N^{h_L}(1 + \frac{1}{4} + \frac{1}{16} + \ldots) = \frac{4}{3}N^{h_L}$; i.e., it is only a small fraction more than that required for the finest grid.

One can think of several possibilities for exploiting the hierarchy of discrete problems to increase the convergence rate of the iterative process. Perhaps the first idea that comes to mind is to solve the system at the coarsest level, which can be done very quickly, and use the solution as an initial approximation in the iterative solution at the next finer level, proceeding in this manner to the finest level. This is an effective acceleration strategy which is almost as old as the idea of relaxation itself [17.48]. Although it is suitable for obtaining a single accurate solution at the finest level, it cannot generate solutions having the finest-level accuracy over the hierarchy of coarser levels, since the approximation error increases as the elements become larger. At the coarsest level, for instance, the accuracy may be poor. This is undesirable from the point of view of our surface reconstruction problem. Here we require that the accuracy of the finest-resolution surface be maintained throughout

263

the coarser surface descriptions. This will guarantee that the shape of the surface will be consistent over the hierarchy of representations.

The stipulation that accuracy be maintained is further motivated by psychophysical studies into the phenomenon of visual hyperacuity (see, e.g., [17.49-51]). Related computational studies indicate that, in principle, sharp, well-defined intensity edges can be localized to high (subreceptor separation) accuracies from the $\nabla^2 G$ convolution values through a process of spatiotemporal interpolation[17.12,15,52-54]. Consequently, it seems that although the depth constraints arising from the larger channels in stereopsis represent coarser spatial samplings of the scene, excluding erroneous matches, the samples may, in principle, provide measurements of high accuracy.

The only way that consistent accuracy can be maintained throughout the hierarchy of full surface representations is to allow the coarser levels access to the high-resolution information in the finer levels. The multigrid algorithm provides such a flow. The hierarchy of levels cooperate, through a bidirectional flow of information, to generate simultaneously multiple, equally accurate surface representations, and do so with much less computational effort than would be expended in solving the finest-level system in isolation. To see how this is accomplished, we will initially consider only two levels, a fine one and a coarse one, associated with the finite-element spaces S^h and S^{2h} respectively. Suppose that by some iterative process we obtain an approximate solution $\underline{v}^{2h}$ to the coarse level system $A^{2h}\underline{u}^{2h}=\underline{f}^{2h}$, which is then interpolated[7] to the fine level where it becomes the initial approximation $\underline{v}^h$:

$$\underline{v}^h \leftarrow I_{2h\Rightarrow h} \; \underline{v}^{2h} \; . \tag{17.23}$$

The mapping $I_{2h\Rightarrow h}:S^{2h}\to S^h$ denotes interpolation from the coarse space to the fine space. Normally, $\underline{v}_h$ will require substantial improvement.

Let $\underline{u}^h$ be the solution to the fine level system $A^h\underline{u}^h=\underline{f}^h$. Then we can define the error vector in a given approximation $\underline{v}^h$ by $\underline{e}^h=\underline{u}^h-\underline{v}^h$. Clearly, if $\underline{e}^h$ could be computed, it could be added as a correction to $\underline{v}^h$, thereby giving us the desired solution. But because the computation of $\underline{e}^h$ would take about as much effort as computing $\underline{u}^h$ itself, doing so would not be helpful. On the other hand, if we could somehow approximate the error function $\underline{e}^h$ by a function $\underline{e}^{2h}$ in the coarse space S^{2h}, such an approximation can be obtained quickly due to the fact that the coarse space has only one-quarter the dimensionality of the fine space. Such an approximation is generally not possible, however, because $\underline{e}^h$, having been generated by an interpolation from the coarse grid solution, is certain to have large fluctuations with wavelengths less than than 4h. These high-frequency FOURIER components could not be approximated on the coarse grid because there they would alias as lower-frequency components. Before a meaningful approximation to the error can be obtained on the coarse grid, the high-frequency components must be eliminated; that is to say, the error function $\underline{e}^h$ must be smoothed.

Since smoothing is inherently a local operation, it should not be surprising that local iterative methods, inefficient as they are in obtaining solutions, are very efficient at smoothing the error function. In particu-

---

7. LAGRANGE interpolation of a suitable order may be used.

lar, although relaxation generally requires very many iterations to eliminate the global, low-frequency components of the error, it only takes a few iterations to eliminate the local, high-frequency components. This behavior can be predicted mathematically by a local FOURIER analysis of the given iterative method [17.45]. The analysis involves a local FOURIER expansion of the error function followed by an examination of the effect that a single iteration has on the amplitudes of each component. An important quantity which is obtained through this analysis is the smoothing factor $\bar{\mu}$ of the iterative scheme, which is defined as the worst (i.e., the largest) amplification of a high-frequency component of the error from one iteration to the next. As an example, in Appendix C we carry out a local FOURIER analysis of the appropriate GAUSS-SEIDEL scheme for our discrete problem, and show that $\bar{\mu} \approx 0.8$. This implies that, for our problem, ten GAUSS-SEIDEL iterations on the fine grid are sufficient to reduce the high-frequency components of e^h by approximately an order of magnitude. A more effective weighted JACOBI relaxation scheme, which is also suitable for our problem and gives $\mu = 0.549$, is described in [17.45, p. 342].[8]

Once the error has been smoothed, it may be inexpensively approximated on the coarse grid. The equation for $\underline{e}^h$ on the fine grid is the residual equation

$$\underline{A}^h \underline{e}^h = \underline{r}^h, \quad \text{where} \quad \underline{r}^h = \underline{f}^h - \underline{A}^h \underline{v}^h \tag{17.24}$$

is called the residual of the approximation $\underline{v}^h$. The approximation to this equation on the coarser grid is

$$\underline{A}^{2h} \underline{e}^{2h} = I_{h \Rightarrow 2h} \underline{r}^h$$

where the mapping $I_{h \Rightarrow 2h} : S^h \to S^{2h}$ is an "interpolation" from the fine space to the coarse space. Because $S^{2h} \subset S^h$, the mapping can be a simple injection or some local averaging of node displacements from the fine grid to the coarse. After $\underline{e}^{2h}$ is computed, a better approximation to $\underline{v}^h$ may be obtained by interpolating the coarse-grid correction back to the fine grid; that is, by making the replacement:

$$\underline{v}^h \leftarrow \underline{v}^h + I_{2h \Rightarrow h} \underline{e}^{2h} \; .$$

This correction practically annihilates the smooth part of the error e^h.

BRANDT [17.45,46] calls the foregoing scheme a correction scheme in view of the fact that the function computed on the coarse grid is the error function - that is, the correction to the fine-grid approximation. The correction scheme is easy to implement, but it is unsuitable for our surface reconstruction problem because instead of an error function e^{2h}, we require that the function computed in the coarse space be a function u^{2h} which represents explicitly the distances to surfaces in the scene. This may be accomplished by a reformulation of the correction scheme equations which converts them into those of the related full approximation scheme.

First, we rewrite (17.24) in the equivalent form

$$\underline{A}^h(\underline{v}^h + \underline{e}^h) - \underline{A}^h \underline{v}^h = \underline{r}^h$$

---

8. BRANDT proposes this scheme for solving biharmonic boundary value problems. The scheme is also appropriate for our surface approximation problem, which is in essence a biharmonic problem in view of the associated EULER-LAGRANGE equation.

which may be approximated by the corresponding coarse-grid equation

$$\underline{A}^{2h}(\ \underset{h\rightarrow 2h}{I}\ \underline{v}^h+\underline{e}^{2h})-\underline{A}^{2h}(\ \underset{h\rightarrow 2h}{I}\ \underline{v}^h)=\ \underset{h\rightarrow 2h}{I}\ \underline{r}^h\ .$$

Defining a new function u^{2h} in S^{2h} by the nodal displacement vector $\underline{u}^{2h}=\underline{I}_{h\Rightarrow 2h}\underline{v}^h+\underline{e}^{2h}$, we obtain the coarse-level system

$$\underline{A}^{2h}\underline{u}^{2h}=\underline{g}^{2h}\qquad\text{where}\qquad \underline{g}^{2h}=\underline{A}^{2h}(\ \underset{h\Rightarrow 2h}{I}\ \underline{v}^h)+\ \underset{h\Rightarrow 2h}{I}\ \underline{r}^h\ .\qquad(17.25)$$

It is natural to interpret (17.25) as the original coarse-level system $\underline{A}^{2h}\underline{u}^{2h}=\underline{f}^{2h}$ but with a right-hand side which has been modified using information from the fine grid so as to maintain the fine-grid accuracy in the coarse-grid function u^{2h}. Thus, $\underline{g}^{2h}$ is an estimate of the local truncation error on the coarse level relative to the fine level (see [17.46, p. 284]).

Once the solution u^{2h} of (17.25) is available, we can write $\underline{e}^{2h}=\underline{u}^{2h}-\underline{I}_{h\Rightarrow 2h}\underline{v}^h$ as the desired coarse-grid approximation to the fine-grid error, and the approximation on the fine level can be corrected by the replacement

$$\underline{v}^h\leftarrow\underline{v}^h+\ \underset{2h\Rightarrow h}{I}\ (\underline{u}^{2h}-\ \underset{h\Rightarrow 2h}{I}\ \underline{v}^h)\ .\qquad(17.26)$$

Note that since $\underline{I}_{2h\Rightarrow h}\underline{I}_{h\Rightarrow 2h}\underline{v}^h\neq\underline{v}^h$ the replacements given by (17.23,26) are not equivalent. Since $\underline{u}^{2h}$ is a low-frequency correction, the replacement indicated by (17.21) would destroy the high-frequency components of v^h whereas the replacement indicated by (17.26) preserves them.

How do we solve the coarse-grid equation (17.25)? The obvious answer is: by relaxation iterations on the coarse grid, and with the help of corrections obtained from still coarser grids. Thus, in a straightforward recursive fashion, we can extend the above two-level equations to any number of levels. In view of (17.25) and the fact that the residual for the level k equations is given by

$$\underline{r}^{h_k}=\underline{g}^{h_k}-\underline{A}^{h_k}\underline{u}^{h_k}\ ,\qquad(17.27)$$

the multilevel equations for L levels are given by

$$\underline{A}^{h_k}\underline{u}^{h_k}=\underline{g}^{h_k}\qquad\text{for }1\leq k\leq L\qquad(17.28)$$

where

$$\underline{g}^{h_L}=\underline{f}^{h_L}\qquad\text{and}$$

$$\underline{g}^{h_k}=\underline{A}^{h_k}(\ \underset{h_{k+1}\Rightarrow h_k}{I}\ \underline{u}^{h_{k+1}})+\ \underset{h_{k+1}\Rightarrow h_k}{I}\ (\underline{g}^{h_{k+1}}-\underline{A}^{h_{k+1}}\underline{u}^{h_{k+1}})\qquad\text{for }1\leq k<L\ .\qquad(17.29)$$

Note that the original right-hand side $\underline{f}^{h_k}$ of the kth level problem occurs only on the finest level L. The right-hand sides of the coarser levels have been modified in order that the finest level accuracy be properly maintained throughout; that is to say, in order for the solutions u^{h_k} to coincide: $\underline{u}^{h_1}=\underline{I}_{h_2\Rightarrow h_1}\underline{u}^{h_2}=\ldots=\underline{I}_{h_2\Rightarrow h_1}\cdots\underline{I}_{h_L\Rightarrow h_{L-1}}\underline{u}^{h_L}$. Analogously to the two-grid case, we can interpret the difference of the original and the corrected right-hand sides, $\underline{f}^{h_k}-\underline{g}^{h_k}$, as an estimate of the local truncation error of level k relative to the finest level.

17.5.3 Multilevel Surface Reconstruction Algorithms

We have motivated the multilevel approach to surface reconstruction and described in a quantitative manner its basic components - the intralevel relaxation processes, and the interlevel interpolation processes. It now remains to show how to bring the components together into an algorithm for solving the multilevel equations (17.28, 29). Several schemes have been proposed [17.45-47]. We will describe one which is appropriate in terms of our surface approximation problem.[9] Before defining the full multilevel surface reconstruction algorithm, we will define its main procedure, the multilevel surface reconstruction cycle.

The multilevel surface reconstruction cycle starts at the (currently) finest level ℓ, making several cycles to the coarser levels $k=\ell-1,\ell-2,...,1$, until a hierarchy of surface representations which are as accurate as is possible in the S^{h_ℓ} space is obtained. Let ε_k denote a tolerance for solving the equations on level k. ξ and η are switching parameters which are given appropriate values below.

Algorithm 1: Multilevel Surface Reconstruction Cycle
    Step 1: initialize the finest level ℓ.
        Set the right-hand side of the level-ℓ problem $\underline{A}^{h_\ell}\underline{u}^{h_\ell}=\underline{g}^{h_\ell}$ to the original right-hand side: $\underline{g}^{h_\ell}\leftarrow\underline{f}^{h_\ell}$. Introduce the initial approximation $\underline{v}^{h_\ell}\leftarrow\underline{v}_0^{h_\ell}$. Set $\varepsilon_\ell\leftarrow 0$,[10] and $k\leftarrow\ell$.

    Step 2: start a new operation level k.
        Set $e_k^{old}\leftarrow\infty$.

    Step 3: perform a relaxation iteration.
        Perform a relaxation iteration for the equation $\underline{A}^{h_k}\underline{u}^{h_k}=\underline{g}^{h_k}$ and concurrently compute some norm of the residual given by (17.27), $e_k\leftarrow\|\underline{r}^{h_k}\|$.

    Step 4: test the convergence and its rate.
        If $e_k\leq\varepsilon_k$, then convergence has been obtained at the current operation level; go to Step 6. If $k=1$, go to Step 3. If $e_k\leq\eta e_k^{old}$ then the convergence rate is still satisfactory, set $e_k^{old}\leftarrow e_k$ and go to Step 3; otherwise the convergence rate is slow, so go to Step 5.

    Step 5: transfer to coarser level.
        Introduce as the first coarse-level approximation the function $v^{h_{k-1}}$ defined by the nodal displacements

$$\underline{v}^{h_{k-1}} \leftarrow \underset{h_k\Rightarrow h_{k-1}}{I} \underline{v}^{h_k}.$$

        Set the right-hand side of the coarser level problem $\underline{A}^{h_{k-1}}\underline{u}^{h_{k-1}}=\underline{g}^{h_{k-1}}$ to

$$\underline{g}^{h_{k-1}}\leftarrow\underline{A}^{h_{k-1}}\underline{v}^{h_{k-1}} + \underset{h_k\Rightarrow h_{k-1}}{I} (\underline{g}^{h_k}-\underline{A}^{h_k}\underline{v}^{h_k})$$

---

9. BRANDT refers to it as the accommodative, full multigrid, full approximation scheme algorithm [17.47].

10. This value for ε_ℓ is temporary. A realistic value is introduced in Step 5.

(in view of (17.29)). Set the tolerance $\varepsilon_{k-1} \leftarrow \xi \varepsilon_k$. Concurrently with the computation of $\underline{g}^{h_{k-1}}$, compute the norm of the local truncation error $\underline{f}^{h_{k-1}} - \underline{g}^{h_{k-1}}$ using the same norm as in Step 3. If $k = \ell$ set $\varepsilon_\ell \leftarrow \frac{1}{4} \| \underline{f}^{h_{k-1}} - \underline{g}^{h_{k-1}} \|$.[11] Finally, set $k \leftarrow k-1$ and go to Step 2.

Step 6: use the converged solution $\underline{u}^{h_k}$ to correct the finer level. If $k < \ell$, make the correction (in view of (17.26))

$$\underline{v}^{h_{k+1}} \leftarrow \underline{v}^{h_{k+1}} + \underset{h_k \Rightarrow h_{k+1}}{I} \ (\underline{u}^{h_k} - \underset{h_{k+1} \Rightarrow h_k}{I} \ \underline{v}^{h_{k+1}})$$

set $k \leftarrow k+1$ and go to Step 2. Otherwise, $k = \ell$ end.

The relaxation operation in Step 3 can be based on one of the iterative methods described in Appendix B. For example, in view of (17.21) and the discussion in Appendix B, the GAUSS-SEIDEL relaxation iteration in the interior of $\bar{\Omega}$ is given by

$$v_{i,j}^{(i+1)} = \frac{1}{\frac{20}{h^2} + \beta} \ [\frac{8}{h^2}(v_{i-1,j}^{(i+1)} + v_{i+1,j}^{(i)} + v_{i,j-1}^{(i+1)} + v_{i,j+1}^{(i)})$$

$$- \frac{2}{h^2} (v_{i-1,j-1}^{(i+1)} + v_{i+1,j-1}^{(i+1)} + v_{i-1,j+1}^{(i)} + v_{i+1,j+1}^{(i)}) \qquad (17.30)$$

$$- \frac{1}{h^2} (v_{i-2,j}^{(i+1)} + v_{i+2,j}^{(i)} + v_{i,j-2}^{(i+1)} + v_{i,j+2}^{(i)}) + \beta g_{i,j}]$$

where we have suppressed the superscripts h_k indicating the level, and have instead introduced the bracketed superscripts which indicate the iteration number. Analogous formulas for the boundary nodes can be derived from the computational molecules associated with them. Because the matrix of our discrete problem is symmetric and positive definite, the method is guaranteed to converge by Corollary 2 of Appendix B. Similar statements can be made about the SOR method in view of Theorem B.4. One must be more careful with the parallel schemes, however. Convergence cannot be taken for granted with the JACOBI method which is given by

$$v_{i,j}^{(i+1)} = \frac{1}{\frac{20}{h^2} + \beta} \ [\frac{8}{h^2}(v_{i-1,j}^{(i)} + v_{i+1,j}^{(i)} + v_{i,j-1}^{(i)} + v_{i,j+1}^{(i)})$$

$$- \frac{2}{h^2}(v_{i-1,j-1}^{(i)} + v_{i+1,j-1}^{(i)} + v_{i-1,j+1}^{(i)} + v_{i+1,j+1}^{(i)}) \qquad (17.31)$$

$$- \frac{1}{h^2}(v_{i-2,j}^{(i)} + v_{i+2,j}^{(i)} + v_{i,j-2}^{(i)} + v_{i,j+2}^{(i)}) + \beta g_{i,j}]$$

since, according to Theorem B.2, guaranteeing convergence of this method requires the stricter (weakly) diagonally dominant property which our matrix does not possess in general. On the other hand, one can use gradient descent (B.10), or, better yet, the weighted JACOBI scheme described by BRANDT [17.45, p. 342].

---

11. The constant $\frac{1}{4}$ is the value of 2^{-p} (see [17.47, p. 65]), where p=2 is the approximation order of the second partial derivatives of the energy inner product that is achieved by our quadratic element.

The norm computed in Steps 3 and 5 can be the discrete L_2 or L_∞ norm. In the case of GAUSS-SEIDEL relaxation, it is quicker to compute the <u>dynamic norm</u>, as the iteration progresses, rather than the static norm (see, e.g., [17.46, p. 286]).

An important feature of the multilevel algorithm is that the local FOURIER analysis, in addition to providing a prediction of the convergence rate, enables one to predict near-optimal values for the switching parameters. It turns out that the actual values assigned to the switching parameters are not critical, and that good values are $\xi=0.2$ and $\eta=\bar{\mu}$, where $\bar{\mu}$ is the smoothing factor of the relaxation method used in Step 3 of the algorithm (see [17.46, p. 290]). The order of the interpolation operators is determined by the problem itself; i.e., by the order of the derivatives in the energy inner product. For the coarse-to-fine interpolation $I_{h_k \Rightarrow h_{k+1}}$ in Step 6, the natural second-degree interpolation of the element polynomial p^E may be used. On the other hand, simple injections perform well for the fine-to-coarse transfers $I_{h_k \Rightarrow h_{k-1}}$ in Step 5 and $I_{h_{k+1} \Rightarrow h_k}$ in Step 6.

Having defined the multilevel cycle which starts at the finest level and cycles through the coarser levels, we will employ it as a procedure within a more general, full multilevel surface reconstruction algorithm. We now think of the level ℓ of the cycling algorithm as the <u>currently finest level</u>; i.e., the finest level for which an approximate solution has already been computed by the multilevel cycle. The full algorithm works in the opposite direction, the currently finest level progressing from the coarsest level $\ell=1$ to the finest level $\ell=L$.

Algorithm 2: Full Multilevel Surface Reconstruction Algorithm
Step 1: solve the coarsest-grid equation.
Compute by relaxation an approximate solution $\underline{u}^{h_1}$ to the coarsest-grid equation $\underline{A}^{h_1}\underline{u}^{h_1}=\underline{f}^{h_1}$. Set $\ell \leftarrow 1$.

Step 2: set a new finest level ℓ.
If $\ell=L$ stop. Otherwise increment the currently finest level $\ell \leftarrow \ell+1$, and set the first approximation on the new level to be the function $v_0^{h_\ell}$ defined by nodal displacements $\underline{v}_0^{h_\ell}=I_{h_{\ell-1} \Rightarrow h_\ell}\underline{u}^{h_{\ell-1}}$.

Step 3: perform a multilevel cycle.
Invoke Algorithm 1, and when it ends, go to Step 2.

Note that the solution in Step 1 will be performed quickly because S^{h_1} has relatively few dimensions. In Step 3, each time Algorithm 1 terminates at level ℓ, we have obtained a hierarchy of ℓ representations whose accuracy is the best possible on level ℓ. The currently finest approximation is then interpolated to the next finer level until the finest level L is reached. BRANDT recommends a somewhat higher-order interpolation for the initial interpolation $I_{h_{\ell-1} \Rightarrow h_\ell}$ in Step 2. Third-order Lagrangian interpolation seems adequate for our surface interpolation problem, as we will see from the demonstrations in the next subsection.

Algorithm 1 is <u>accommodative</u> in that it makes internal checks, based on the computation of norms, to determine when to switch levels. For many types of problems, accommodative algorithms behave in a fairly fixed manner, performing a similar number of iterations on each level before switching. It is then possible to avoid computing the dynamic-residual norm in Step 3 of Algorithm 1, and to preassign a fixed flow. A switch to the coarser level S^{h_k-1} is made after n_c iterations have been performed at level S^{h_k}.

Analogously, a switch to the finer level $S^h k+1$ is made after n_f iterations have been performed on level $S^h k$ since the last return from the finer level. n_c depends on the smoothing factor, a good choice being $n_c=\log.1/\log \bar{\mu}$. Sometimes n_f varies from level to level. For a more extensive discussion see [17.47, pp. 68-69]. Fixed algorithms are to be preferred for parallel implementations in general, and from a biological point of view in particular.

In order to evaluate the performance of the multilevel surface reconstruction algorithm, we define a unit of computation called a work unit which is the amount of computation required to perform one relaxation iteration on the finest level L. It is roughly equal to $wN^{h}L$ where w is the number of operations required to compute the residual at each node[12] and $N^{h}L$ is the number of nodes at the finest level. Since there are one quarter as many nodes on level k-1 as there are on level k, only $1/4^{1}$ work unit is required to perform a relaxation iteration on level L-i. The proportionate amount of computation done on coarser grids thus diminishes very rapidly. Although for accommodative algorithms it is difficult to predict the total number of operations consumed by the interlevel processes, it normally turns out to be considerably less than the total interlevel process computation, and is therefore usually ignored (see [17.45, Sect. 6.2]).

A final issue that we have not yet considered in quantitative terms is the choice of appropriate values for the (spring) constant β. In the mathematical and, in particular, in the finite-element literature, the constraint term $E_5(v)$ of (17.2) is known as a penalty function (see, e.g., [17.39, 55-57]). The incorporation of penalty functions into variational principles is a standard way of approximately satisfying essential boundary conditions by converting them into appropriate natural boundary conditions which may be handled straightforwardly by the finite-element method. Penalty functions are particularly useful when the essential boundary conditions in question are complicated, or when only their approximate satisfaction is desired, as in the case of visual surface approximation. An optimal value for β can be derived through the following considerations. Let w be the solution to our surface approximation problem, which interpolates the known depth points. As usual, $u \in H^2(\Omega)$ denotes the exact solution to the variational principle, including the penalty term E_5, and $u^h \in S^h$ denotes the finite-element approximation to u. Then, there will be a balance between the error w-u, which measures how closely the surface fits the constraints, and the error $u-u^h$, due to minimizing over a finite element subspace [17.39, pp. 132-133]. Analyzing this balance, BABUSKA [17.56] determined that the optimal value for β is dependent on h and is given by $\beta_h=\gamma h^{-k}$, where γ is a constant and k is the degree of the complete polynomial contained in S^h. Therefore, for our quadratic finite elements, k=2, and the best value for β at level j of the multilevel algorithm in $\beta_{h_j}=\gamma/h_j^2$.

17.5.4 Examples of Multilevel Surface Reconstruction

Figure 17.7 is a schematic diagram of the structure of the multilevel surface reconstruction algorithm, showing three levels of resolution. The diagram depicts the relaxation processes operating at each level, as well as the fine-to-coarse and coarse-to-fine processes which transfer information between levels. The algorithm transforms a hierarchy of sparse sur-

---

12. w is determined by the specific relaxation scheme used, but due to the size of the support of the central computational molecule, it is approximately equal to 13.

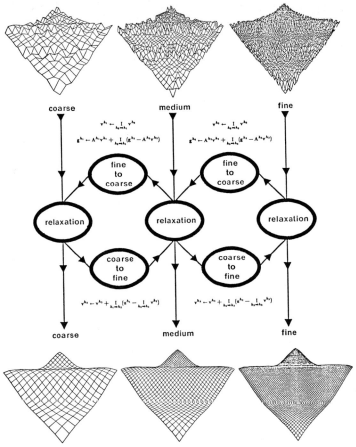

Fig. 17.7. The structure of the multilevel surface reconstruction algorithm

face depth representations, such as might be provided through the independent stereo bandpass channels, into a hierarchy of full surface representations which constitute the full 2½-D sketch. The constraints for the surfaces shown in the figure are random samples from a surface which varies sinusoidally in depth. It is evident that the multiple full representations output by the algorithm describe the sinusoidal surface over a range of scales, and that the accuracy of the finest representation is maintained in the coarser ones.

In this subsection, a number of examples of multilevel surface reconstruction are presented. We will consider the reconstruction of surfaces from artificially generated constraints, as well as constraints generated from natural images by an implementation of the MARR-POGGIO stereo theory. The performance of the multilevel algorithm is compared to that of single-level iterative algorithms. In the examples presented, the algorithm was started from identically zero initial approximations on all the levels.

In the first sequence of figures, we present synthetic examples of surface reconstructions with the purpose of illustrating the performance of the algorithm in reconstructing quadric surfaces having zero, positive, and

271

negative Gaussian curvatures. Constraints on each level were synthesized by sampling depth along arcs on the surface. The examples involved four levels whose grids had dimensions $N_x^{h_1}=N_y^{h_1}=17$, $N_x^{h_2}=N_y^{h_2}=33$, $N_x^{h_3}=N_y^{h_3}=65$, and $N_x^{h_4}=N_y^{h_4}=129$, with corresponding grid spacings $h_1=0.8$, $h_2=0.4$, $h_3=0.2$, and $h_4=0.1$. The relaxation method employed was the GAUSS-SEIDEL method of (17.30), and a value of 2.0 was chosen for γ, giving $\beta_{h_j}=2.0/h_j^2$.

Figure 17.8 shows depth constraints whose values are consistent with a cylindrical surface viewed at four resolutions. The constraints lie along arcs of greatest curvature. Figure 17.9 illustrates the hierarchy of full surface descriptions reconstructed by the four-level algorithm. Since the constraints on all the levels sample the same ideal cylindrical surface, the full surface representations coincide to a high degree of accuracy. Convergence was obtained after 12.0 work units. For comparison purposes, the finest-level problem was isolated from the coarser levels and the same GAUSS-SEIDEL relaxation algorithm was applied to it. Figure 17.10 shows the (single level) approximation obtained after 800 work units (i.e., iterations). It is clear that we are still very far from convergence. Although the approimxation is generally smooth, it has large low-frequency error components and the approximate surface lies far below its final value between constraints which are separated by fairly large distances. As predicted by the local FOURIER analysis, it is precisely such low-frequency error components that local iterative algorithms have difficulty liquidating. In fact, the following characteristic phenomenon was observed. During the initial iterations, the corrections made to the approximation decreased rapidly, so that by the 800th iteration they are minute, even though the error norm is still very large. Since there are 17,361 nodes in the grid, it may take on the order of $(17,361)^2$ work units to obtain the solution without the help of the coarser levels. Thus, the multilevel algorithm is vastly superior when the constraints are far apart.

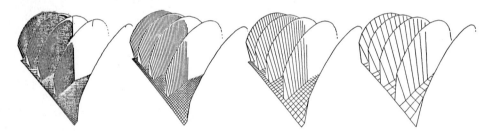

Fig. 17.8. Constraints at four scales consistent with a cylindrical surface

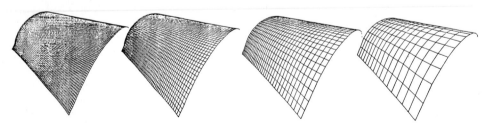

Fig. 17.9. Hierarchy of full surface descriptions reconstructed by multi-level algorithm

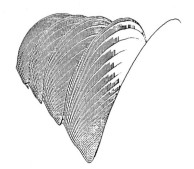

Fig. 17.10. Single-level approximation of cylinder after 800 work units

Figures 17.11,12 illustrate a synthetic example of the reconstruction of a hemispherical surface from constraints which form latitudinal circles. The hierarchy of full surface representations was obtained after 4.25 work units. Figures 17.13,14 show an analogous example involving a hyperbolic paraboloid (saddle surface), where the constraints form parallel parabolic arcs. Convergence was achieved after only 2.5 work units (only a single iteration was performed on the finest level). Single-level algorithms applied to the above surfaces exhibited poor convergence properties similar to the case of the cylinder.

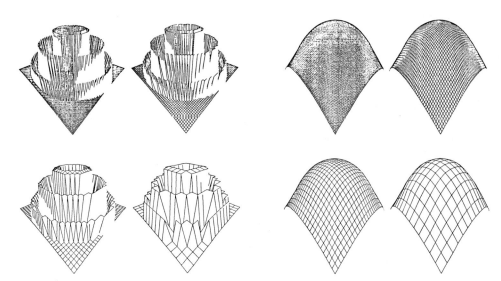

Fig. 17.11. Constraints at four scales consistent with a hemispherical surface

Fig. 17.12. Hierarchy of full surface descriptions reconstructed by multilevel algorithm for Fig. 17.11

The above examples simulate a visual situation where the surface in the scene has reflectance changes in the form of widely spaced rulings but is otherwise free of intensity changes. This is an unlikely situation in view of the fact that the visual world is full of textures, which often arise from surface material and pigment changes. Such textures generally result in relatively densely spaced zero crossings forming, to a certain extent,

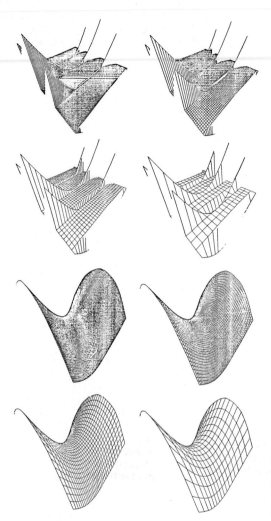

Fig. 17.13. Constraints at four scales consistent with a hyperbolic paraboloid

Fig. 17.14. Hierarchy of full surface descriptions reconstructed by multi-level algorithm for Fig. 17.13

random patterns. In turn, these zero crossings give rise to constraints having similar properties. Figure17.15 illustrates a simulation of this situation using a surface varying sinusoidally in depth. A three-level surface reconstruction algorithm was used. The constraints input on each level were 30%-density randomly located samples of the surface depth. In addition, to simulate the effects of possible inaccuracies in the constraint values, each sample was corrupted by zero-mean, uniformly distributed, additive noise whose magnitude was one-tenth the sample value. The algorithm generated the full surface representation hierarchy in 18.75 work units. Evidently, our spring model for the influence of the constraints, with $\beta_{h_j} = 2/h_j^2$, is adequate for this case in that the additive noise has not adversely affected the quality of the reconstructed surfaces. The results after 19 work units (iterations) with single-level GAUSS-SEIDEL relaxation on the isolated finest grid are shown in Fig.17.16 for comparison. It is evident that the approximation is still far from the true solution. In fact, a total

Fig. 17.15. Surface reconstruction from randomly placed depth constraints

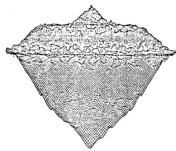

Fig. 17.16. Single-level approximation of sinusoid after 19 work units

of 71 work units was required to reduce the error norm to the magnitude obtained after 18.75 work units by the three-level algorithm. The saving in computation is less in this example than in the ones above because, first, only three levels were used, and second, the density of the constraints is greater. In general, the greater the density of the known depth values, the tighter the surface is constrained, and the convergence is expected to be faster. Another way to think of this is that as the average distance between constraints decreases, the efficiency of relaxation in liquidating the low-frequency FOURIER components in the error increases and, therefore, the relative advantage of the multilevel algorithm is correspondingly diminished.

The next examples illustrate the performance of the multilevel algorithm using disparity constraints generated by GRIMSON's implementation of the MARR-POGGIO stereo algorithm [17.21,58], which includes some of the modifications suggested by MAYHEW and FRISBY [17.16,17] for exploiting disparity gradient constraints along zero-crossing contours. The stereo algorithm was run on three stereo pairs of images, shown in Fig.17.17, which was digitized to 320×320 pixels using 256 gray levels. The pairs from top to bottom are a synthesized random dot stereogram of a "wedding cake" of stacked planes; natural images of a portion of a coffee jar sprayed with "random dot" paint; and an aerial view of a set of buildings on the University of British Columbia campus. A three-channel version of the stereo algorithm was used. The resulting sparse disparity representations were reduced spatially by a factor of 2, and input to a three-level surface reconstruction algorithm whose grids had dimensions $N_x^{h1}=N_y^{h1}=41$, $N_x^{h2}=N_y^{h2}=81$, $N_x^{h3}=N_y^{h3}=161$, with corresponding grid spacings $h_1=0.4$, $h_2=0.2$, and $h_3=0.1$. The surface reconstructions in the examples are based on the raw disparities whose relation to depth is through a nonlinear transformation. Consequently, the shapes of the reconstructed surfaces are distorted to a certain extent.

The sparse disparity constraints provided by the stereo algorithm and the hierarchy of full surface representations generated by the three-level reconstruction algorithm for the "wedding cake" stereogram are shown in Fig.17.18.

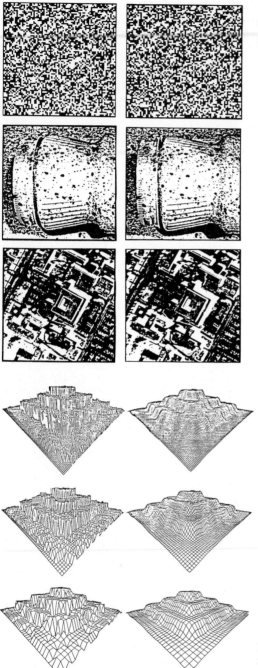

Fig. 17.17. Stereo images on which the multilevel reconstruction algorithm was tested

Fig. 17.18. Multilevel reconstruction of "wedding cake" stereogram

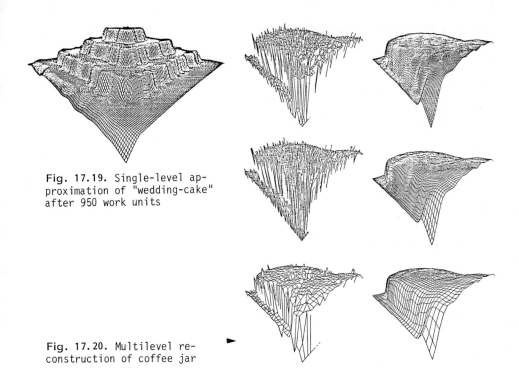

Fig. 17.19. Single-level approximation of "wedding-cake" after 950 work units

Fig. 17.20. Multilevel reconstruction of coffee jar

The value $\gamma=0.5$ was used in the algorithm, and the representations shown were generated after 16.75 work units. The three-dimensional structure of the planar surfaces is clearly evident at the three resolutions. The results can be compared to Fig.17.19 which shows the approximation obtained by a single-grid algorithm on the finest grid, after more than 900 work units.

Figure17.20 illustrates the sparse constraints and the full surface representations obtained (with $\gamma=0.1$) from the images of the coffee jar.[13] The reconstruction required 16.0 work units. Finally, Fig.17.21 shows the sparse constraints and the reconstruction obtained from the aerial view (with $\gamma=8.0$), after 21.875 work units. The representations are displayed as gray-level images, in which darkness is proportional to disparity.

It should be noted from the above examples that the multilevel surface reconstruction algorithm, in its present form, attempts to reconstruct a single surface over the entire grid. As a consequence, serious problems arise near sharp changes in depth such as those due to partial occlusions of surfaces in the scene. The reconstructed surface gives the undesirable impression of a tablecloth thrown over a 3-D model of the scene. The source of this difficulty is discussed further in Sect.17.7, where possible ways of overcoming it are suggested.

---

13. In this example, the constraints for the coarser channels were generated by averaging down the finest-channel disparities.

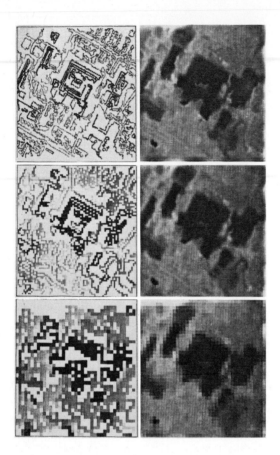

Fig. 17.21. Multilevel reconstruction of aerialview

17.6 Generalized Interpolation Problems in Vision

The key to the solution of many problems in early vision is the imposition
of constraints based upon assumptions about the visual world which are almost always true. A common assumption is that matter is cohesive, i.e.,
that surfaces are continuous over most of the scene. The assumption is usually introduced in the form of smoothness constraints, such as those characterizing the most consistent surface in visual surface reconstruction.
From our study of this problem, we have seen that it is appropriate to formulate smoothness constraints within variational principles. In this section,
we study a general class of variational principles, and we propose that the
functionals characterizing these variational principles are appropriate semi-
norms for formulating smoothness constraints because they possess several
invariance properties which become important in applications to early vision.
In order to simplify the discussion, the analysis will be in terms of inter-
polatory constraints and domains of infinite extent. Our visual surface re-
construction·problem will be shown to be a special case of this generalized,
optimal interpolation problem which is a natural generalization of the familiar curve-fitting problem involving splines.

The classical spline problem involves the minimization of the quadratic
functional

$$|v|_m^2 = \int_a^b \left|\frac{d^m v(x)}{dx^m}\right|^2 dx \qquad (17.32)$$

under the interpolatory constraints $v(x_i)=c_i$, $1 \le i \le N_c$ with $N_c \ge m \ge 1$, where the x_i are given distinct points in $[a,b]$ and the c_i are given real scalars. The natural setting for this problem is a vector space V formed by the class of functions whose (distributional) derivatives up to order m are $L_2(a,b)$; that is, the class of functions which are elements of the SOBOLEV space of order m over $[a,b]$, $H^m([a,b])$, defined in Sect. A.1. $|\cdot|_m$ is a seminorm which is derived from a semi-inner product and, equipped with it, V becomes a semi-HILBERT space. The conditions imposed on the constraints ensure the existence of a unique solution $u \in S$, where S is the convex subset of V whose elements interpolate the constraints. The characterization of u as an odd-degree polynomial spline and various intrinsic properties such as the minimum norm and best approximation properties follow from the orthogonal projection theorem [17.59] (see also the proof of Theorem A.1).

DUCHON [17.60,61] and MEINGUET [17.62,63] describe an n-dimensional generalization of the optimal, univariate spline interpolation problem. The generalized optimal interpolation problem involves the minimization of the functional $|\cdot|_m^2$, where

$$|v|_m = \left(\sum_{i_1,\dots,i_m=1} \int_{R^n} \left|\frac{\partial^m v(x)}{\partial x_{i_1}\cdots\partial x_{i_m}}\right|^2 dx \right)^{\frac{1}{2}} \qquad (17.33)$$

and m and n are given positive integers. The generalized interpolation problem is naturally set in a space V of functions which are elements of the SOBOLEV space $H^m(R^n)$.[14] $|\cdot|_m$ is a seminorm whose null space[15] is the $M=\binom{n+m-1}{n}$ dimensional space of all polynomials over R^n of degree less than or equal to $m-1$: $N \equiv \Pi^{m-1}(R^n)$ [17.64, p. 60]. Equipped with the semi-inner product corresponding to $|\cdot|_m$, V becomes a semi-Hilbert space.[16]

Let the finite set of distinct constraints $C = \{(x_i,c_i)|1 \le i \le N_c, \ x_i \in R^n, \ c_i \in R\}$ contain a subset of M members such that there exists a unique element $p \in \Pi^{m-1}(R^n)$ of the null space of $|\cdot|_m$ which interpolates the M constraints in the subset; that is, such that there exists a unique polynomial of degree $m-1$ which satisfies the conditions $p(x_j)=c_j$ for each j which indexes a constraint of the above subset. We call such a subset an N-unisolvent subset.

We can pose the generalized optimal interpolation problem in the following way. Given a set of constraints C which contain an N-unisolvent subset, find that element $u \in S$ such that

---

14. More precisely, the space V is the BEPPO LEVI space [17.61-63] of order m over R^n defined by $BL^m(R^n)=\{v \mid \partial^\alpha v \in L_2 \text{ for } |\alpha|=m\}$, where $\alpha=(\alpha_1,\dots,\alpha_n)$ is a "vector" of positive integers and $|\alpha|=\alpha_1+\dots+\alpha_n$; that is, it is the vector space of functions for which all the partial derivatives of (total) order m are square integrable in R^n. The BEPPO LEVI spaces are related to the SOBOLEV spaces.

15. The null space of a seminorm is the space of functions which the seminorm maps to zero.

16. According to the SOBOLEV inequality (see Sect. A.1), when $m>n/2$, V is a semi-Hilbert function space of continuous functions [17.62,63].

$$|u|_m^2 = \inf_{v \in S} |v|_m^2$$

where once again S is the set of functions in V which interpolate the constraints. The problem is well posed because we are minimizing a seminorm within a convex subset S of a semi-HILBERT space and, furthermore, the existence of an N-unisolvent subset of constraints reduces the null space of the functional to at most a single nonzero element of S. A solution u is then guaranteed to exist and be unique by the orthogonal projection theorem (see the proof of Theorem A.1).[17]

Why is the class of seminorms defined in (17.33) important in the context of vision? As was argued recently by BRADY and HORN [17.38], many processes in early vision are approximately isotropic and, therefore, it seems that operators which model these processes ought to be rotationally symmetric. An example of such an operator is the $\nabla^2 G$ edge operator proposed for computing the primal sketch [17.6,12]. The class of seminorms defined in (17.33) is of interest, since all its members $|v|_m$ are invariant under rotation and translation transformations and, moreover, if a dilation or contraction $\underline{x} \to \lambda \underline{x}$ is applied to v, they are multiplied by some power of $|\lambda|$ [17.61, p. 86]. Therefore, corresponding interpolation methods will commute with any similarity transformations applied to the constraints. Clearly, these properties are essential for interpolation processes which contribute to the generation of the 2½-D sketch; the surfaces generated by surface reconstruction algorithms should not change shape as the objects in the scene undergo translations or rotations parallel to the image plane, or undergo displacements directly towards or away from the viewer.

For certain instances of $m \geq 1$ and $n \geq 1$, the general interpolation problem has familiar physical interpretations which are most often encountered in a differential form through the associated EULER-LAGRANGE equations. Consider first the one-dimensional case, n=1. The generalized interpolation problem then reduces to the common univariate spline problem. The particular value chosen for m determines the order of continuity of the optimal curve - as m increases, the smoothness of the solutions increases. In particular, for the case m=1, $|v|_1^2 = \int_R v_x^2\, dx$ measures the energy in a string of infinite extent, and leads to interpolants having C^0 continuity. The associated EULER-LAGRANGE equation is $u_{xx}=0$. C^1 continuity may be imposed on the interpolant by choosing m=2. In this case, $|v|_2^2 = \int_R v_{xx}^2\, dx$ measures the strain energy of bending in a thin beam of infinite extent, and the EULER-LAGRANGE equation is $u_{xxxx}=0$. This class of univariate seminorms seems to be appropriate for imposing continuity constraints in the computation of optical flow along zero-crossing contours in the primal sketch (E. C. Hildreth, personal communication).

Next, consider the generalized interpolation problem in two dimensions. For n=2, the seminorms become

$$|v|_m^2 = \int \int_{R^2} \sum_{i=0}^{m} \binom{m}{i} \left(\frac{\partial^m v}{\partial x^i \partial y^{m-i}} \right)^2 dx\; dy$$

m, once again, determining the degree of smoothness of the solution. For m=1, $|v|_1^2 = \int \int_{R^2} (v_x^2 + v_x^2)\, dx\; dy$ measures the potential energy related to the

---

17. Moreover, as a consequence of the SOBOLEV inequality given in Sect. A.1, u will be continuous if m>n/2.

statics of a membrane (rubber sheet), and the associated EULER-LAGRANGE equation can be shown to be LAPLACE's equation, $\Delta u=0$ [17.29, p. 247]. A seminorm of this order implicitly imposes the smoothness constraints in algorithms proposed for computing lightness [17.65], shape from shading [17.66], optical flow [17.67], photometric stereo [17.68], etc. With m=2, the smoothness of the interpolating surface is increased to C^1, the functional taking the form $|v|_2^2 = \int \int_R 2(v_{xx}^2 + 2v_{xy}^2 + v_{yy}^2) dx\, dy$. This will be recognized as being our familiar functional representing the strain energy of the thin plate E_1 with POISSON constant $\sigma=0$ (refer to (17.1)$_2$ whose EULER-LAGRANGE equation was shown to be the biharmonic equation, $\Delta^2 u=0$.)[18] As we have demonstrated, this order of smoothness seems to be most appropriate in visual surface reconstruction from, e.g., stereo information (refer also to the discussion on the "quadratic variation" in [17.21]).

It becomes clear that we are dealing with a class of quadratic variational problems, the order of whose EULER equations is determined by the degree of smoothness demanded of the solutions. For m=1 we obtain LAPLACE's equation in n dimensions, for m=2 the biharmonic equation, and so on. In general, the EULER equation is an n-dimensional, linear, elliptic partial differential equation of order 2m. Moreover, the general interpolation problems have straightforward formulations as analogous approximation problems. For example, we can define appropriate constraint terms analogous to the term E_5 (17.2) for our surface approximation problem.

Hence, there exists a general framework in which to solve functional approximation problems, of the type arising naturally when smoothness constraints must be imposed within visual processing tasks. Meaningful problems can be formulated in any number of dimensions, and the degree of smoothness that the solutions are to possess may be specified a priori through the choice of m. Equivalently, this amounts to selecting the order of SOBOLEV space in which the admissible space for our problem is to be embedded. In this sense, then, the SOBOLEV spaces can be viewed as ingenious formalizations of the notion of the "degree of smoothness" of admissible functions and therefore are ideal domains in which to pose and solve such problems. By specifying the (order of the) SOBOLEV space to which the solution should belong, we designate its position in the wide spectrum from very smooth functions to singular distributions. Satisfaction of the requirements, that the admissible space be a semi-HILBERT space and that the constraints include an N-unisolvent subset, will guarantee uniqueness.

Needless to say, the theory of the finite-element method is applicable to either the interpolation or approximation formulations, and it will dictate appropriate finite-element discretization schemes for the associated variational principles. When solving these variational principles using local, iterative algorithms such as the ones described in this paper, smoothness constraints are imposed globally over retinocentric representations by a process of constraint propagation. Inspired by the work of WALTZ [17.70], a class of algorithms called relaxation labeling algorithms were introduced as cooperative constraint propagation techniques in vision and image processing by ROSENFELD, HUMMEL, and ZUCKER [17.71]. Although they have seen extensive use [17.72], their generality has made them difficult to understand and, unlike the techniques and algorithms which are the subject of this paper, the foundations of most relaxation labeling schemes are unfortunately poorly developed mathematically.

---

18. DUCHON [17.60] understandably refers to the solutions as thin plate splines, which also reflects the fact that they are natural two-dimensional generalizations of commonly used univariate splines. In the engineering literature they are called surface splines [17.69].

Recently, some theoretical understanding has been achieved by viewing relaxation algorithms as techniques for solving constrained optimization problems (see, e.g., [17.23,73,74]). From this new point of view, the relationships between relaxation labeling techniques and iterative solution of finite element equations arising from variational formulations become clearer - relaxation labeling schemes can be viewed as iterative algorithms for solving optimal approximation problems over closed convex subsets (of possible labelings) [17.74]. Necessary conditions for solutions (fixed points) are then expressed as sets of variational inequalities [17.36] and appropriate updating rules are natural generalizations of the classical local iterative methods for solving large systems of linear [17.75] or nonlinear [17.76] equations. Moreover, if the compatibility functions among neighboring nodes are symmetric, then there exist associated variational principles defining equivalent formulations as minimization problems. Fortunately, it is possible to apply the finite element method to nonlinear problems stemming from variational inequalities [17.36]. In a certain sense, then, finite elements can be viewed as systematically derived, physically based compatibility relationships among neighboring nodes. In view of the relationships between the two techniques, it is hoped that aspects of our multilevel approach to solving the discrete finite element equations for the surface reconstruction problem may contribute to the theory of hierarchical relaxation labeling (see, e.g., [17.72,77,78]).

17.7 Summary and Extensions

Information about the shapes of visual surfaces that is inferred from the retinal images in the early computational stages of vision is sparse. Nevertheless, our perception is that of full (piecewise) continuous surfaces. In this paper, we have proposed a hierarchical approach to the reconstruction of full surface representations, consistent with our perception of the visual world. The foundations of our paradigm are embedded in a tight mathematical formalism which at the same time seems sufficiently general to encompass many aspects of the complex information processing task which is the generation of the full 2½-D sketch.

Visual surface reconstruction was formulated as an optimal approximation problem having an intuitively simple physical interpretation - a thin flexible plate which is allowed to achieve an energy-minimizing state of stable equilibrium under the influence of externally imposed constraints. This physical model led directly to an analysis in terms of the calculus of variations, and a proof that the problem is well posed in practice. The model also suggested a class of techniques for optimally approximating the continuous solution by an equivalent discrete problem which is amenable to computational solution. We chose to apply the finite-element method for reasons which include its generality, the availability of a tight theory governing its use, the simple discrete problem to which it gives rise, and its promise in vision as a systematic methodology for constructing local representations of surfaces.[19] At each step, the underlying mathematical theory assured us that, ultimately, our problem would have a unique solution that, in principle, could be computed by biologically based mechanisms. Our search for efficient algorithms and our insights into the multilevel structure of the early processing stages in vision led us to a multilevel algorithm

---

19. On the latter point we should mention again that the finite-element method allows us to handle domains of complex shape, natural boundary conditions, and to set up nonuniform discretizations of the domain - e.g., to vary the resolution across the domain.

which solves simultaneously a hierarchy of surface approximation problems
spanning a range of resolutions. The local-support processes comprising the
algorithm include iterative intralevel relaxation processes, and interlevel
processes which serve to communicate information between levels. The interlevel processes include injections from fine grids to coarse and polynomial
interpolations from coarse grids to fine. Tests on stereo data verified
that our multilevel surface reconstruction algorithm meets theoretical
expectations of increased speed and, moreover, generates a potentially
useful hierarchy of consistent surface representations. Finally, we examined our basic surface approximation problem in a more general setting,
and related it to a broader class of optimal approximation problems based
on seminorms that commute with similarity transformations applied to the
constraints, a property which is important in the context of vision.

Although we have laid down the foundations of our approach primarily in
terms of stereopsis, the methodology is by no means limited to the type of
information produced by this particular module. Indeed, our point of view
speaks to the broader issue of how to combine the information about the
shapes of visible surfaces generated by various vision modules into a self-
consistent whole. Several possibilities arise, some of which we will now
consider briefly.

The simultaneous assimilation of information from different sources can
be realized by defining more sophisticated penalty functions to replace E_5
in Sect.17.2. For example, in the case of depth constraints from, say,
stereo and motion, we can straightforwardly introduce additional terms of
the same form as E_5 for each process. In terms of our plate model, we introduce two sets of imaginary pins with attached springs, and allow the
possibility of a constraint generated by stereo to coincide with one provided by motion. Imperfections in the retinal images are likely to affect
the two processes in different ways, and moreover each will in its own way
sporadically fall prey to gross misinterpretations of the information in
the primal sketches. Whatever the situation, our physical model assumes an
energy-minimizing state, and the resulting surface is an optimal compromise
in view of the constraints provided. In places where the information is
consistent, the final interpretation is reinforced. In places where there
is a conflict, it is resolved by competition with nearby constraints from
both processes.

The influence of each constraint may be controlled, possibly dynamically
by the processes themselves, by assigning different values to each spring
constant. For example, different confidence values may be given to individual constraints generated by the stereo matcher, according to regional
statistics of the rate of successfully matched zero crossings, which may
have to be computed anyway [17.4; 17.21, Sects. 2.5, 3.4]. The extent of
the constraint's influence on the surface may also be varied by extending
our model to that of an inhomogeneous plate whose flexibility varies over
the domain. Numerous possibilities exist for defining weighting functions
to apply to the strain energy density of the plate. All such proposals
for modifying the form of the functional must first be shown to lead to
well-posed problems, by extensions of the analysis carried out in Sects.
17.3,4.

Another important issue is how to incorporate information other than
measurements of the distance to the surface. An important class of processes generate cues about visual surfaces in the form of local orientation
measurements. Examples in this class are the analysis of occluding contours [17.79], as well as "shape-from" processes such as shape from shading

[17.80], contours and texture [17.81-83], regular patterns [17.84], etc.
The finite-element method provides a general way of handling orientation
constraints through the use of elements with degrees of freedom which include
the first partial derivatives of the surface. An appealing example is
ADINI's rectangle, which was described in Sect.17.4.1. Surface representation based on this element would make explicit the information about the
local slopes of surfaces, as well as their distances from the viewer. Discrete problems derived by applying this element would correspond to a
coupled system of two discrete EULER-LAGRANGE equations for the plate, a
fourth-order equation for the displacements at the nodes, and a second-
order equation for the slopes. On the other hand, we pay a price for this
added capability - the dimension of the finite element space is tripled,
making the resulting discrete system even larger. Nevertheless, the price
may turn out to be worth paying in order to obtain useful surface representations and, moreover, it may not be too high when massively parallel computational mechanisms are contemplated.

A different way of handling orientation constraints which can be used
with our simple quadratic elements is, once again, by the use of appropriate penalty functions. In terms of our model, we can imagine the situation for a single constraint and a surface patch as illustrated in Fig.17.22.

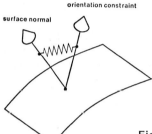

Fig. 17.22. Physical model of the effect of an
orientation constraint

Here, we attach a spring between the surface normal, an imaginary quill
rigidly fixed to the plate's surface at a particular point, and the orientation constraint, another quill emanating from the same point, but having
a fixed orientation in space. Given this arrangement, the surface is "pulled"
locally so that its orientation tends to align with that of the constraint.
The appropriate penalty term is the potential energy in the spring. This
energy can be expressed straightforwardly in terms of the first partial
derivatives of the quadratic surface patch within the element, and ultimately
in terms of the node displacements.

A more immediately important issue, one that was raised in reference to
the examples of surface reconstruction presented earlier, is that of dealing with depth discontinuities. In its present form, the surface approximation algorithm can deal in a meaningful way with scenes containing only
a single surface. This is due to the fact that it does not incorporate
the notion of an occluding contour; that is to say, it attempts to fit a
single surface over the whole sparse 2½-D sketch, interpolating indiscri-
minately across contours which correspond to places where surfaces in the
scene occlude one another from the viewer. Clearly, this action is inappropriate since the surfaces on either side of the occluding boundary ought
to have no influence on one another. Moreover, the variational principle

284

for surface approximation was based on the <u>small deflection</u> theory of the plate[20] and, consequently, we expect our surface to behave strangely in the vicinity of a large change in depth, resulting in, for example, a GIBBS phenomenon similar to that observed when approximating discontinuous functions with FOURIER series.

How can these depth discontinuities be detected and how do we prevent interpolation across them? GRIMSON [17.21, Sect. 9.4] noted the importance of this question and made some speculations about possible answers to the first of its two parts. The feasibility of his suggestions remains an open question. Here, we would like to propose another approach that is again suggested by our physical model. In places of sharp changes in depth (or surface orientation), the strain energy in the plate will be locally high. Measuring this energy locally is a simple matter - we use the energy inner product to compute the strain energy norm $a_h(v^h,v^h)^{\frac{1}{2}}$ over the element domains. Points of high strain energy are likely candidates for inferring the presence of discontinuities in depth. We can also exploit our expectations about the world for added constraints, and assert that since most of the retinal image is made up of coherent surfaces, occlusions in depth are likely to form contours in the image and not be sparsely occurring points. Hence, we look for <u>contours</u> along the surface of the plate, where the strain energy is high. Having located the occluding contours, the answer to the second part of the question is simple, in principle. To prevent interpolation across different surfaces, we "break" the plate along occluding contours. Mathematically speaking, this is done by removing plate elements along the occluding contour, thereby introducing free boundaries.

Our multilevel approach to surface reconstruction constitutes a computational paradigm which has contributed toward a more complete understanding of the generation of the 2½-D sketch. Many details such as the combination of information from the various modules in early vision and the isolation of depth discontinuities remain to be worked out rigorously within the paradigm. In addition, a number of exciting issues are raised. For example, how can the hierarchy of surface representations generated by the algorithm be used to advantage during later computational stages in which three-dimensional, object-centered representations are generated and objects are recognized? Similar implications directed to the related field of robotics and manipulation also suggest themselves. Research addressing some of these issues is currently in progress.

Acknowledgments

I would like to thank Shimon Ullman for pointing out the literature on multigrid methods and suggesting the possibility of their application to visual surface interpolation. Mike Brady, Eric Grimson, Tomaso Poggio, Whitman Richards, and Shimon Ullman contributed to the work through numerous valuable discussions. In addition, Eric Grimson's technical assistance with his stereo vision software for the LISP Machine is appreciated. Valuable comments on drafts of this paper were provided by Mike Brady, Eric Grimson, Ellen Hildreth, Berthold Horn, Yvan Leclerc, Shimon Ullman, and Steve Zucker.

---

20. The large-deflection plate bending theory is considerably more complicated and leads to an EULER-LAGRANGE equation in the form of two coupled, nonlinear, fourth-order partial differential equations known as <u>VON KARMANN's equations</u> (see, e.g., [17.30] or [17.85]).

This report describes research done at the Artificial Intelligence Laboratory of the Massachusetts Institute of Technology. Support for the laboratory's artificial intelligence research is provided in part by the Advanced Research Projects Agency of the Department of Defense under Office of Naval Research contract N00014-80-C-0505 and in part by National Science Foundation Grant MCS-79-23110. The author was supported by postgraduate scholarships from the Natural Sciences and Engineering Research Council of Canada and from Fonds F.C.A.C. pour l'aide et le soutien à la recherche, Québéc, Canada.

Appendix A. The Finite-Element Method

When it is impossible to derive an analytical solution to a continuous variational principle, it is usual to attempt an approximation by defining a discrete problem which is similar to the continuous one and which leads to a discrete solution. To this end, we will first state an abstract variational principle which will lead us to an optimal approximation to the exact solution. The variational principle is called abstract inasmuch as it represents a formulation which is common to a variety of physical problems, such as the physical model for our surface reconstruction problem. We will also state theorems which give conditions guaranteeing the existence and uniqueness of the approximate solution and, in addition, we will discuss the optimal properties of the proposed approximation.

The abstract variational principle and the associated theorems are stated in a form which is convenient for the application of the finite-element method, a powerful technique for obtaining, by numerical means, discrete solutions to variational problems.[21] The following sections develop the mathematical machinery which we will require to apply the method successfully. Key mathematical ideas include a set of HILBERT spaces (the SOBOLEV spaces) and their norms, a bilinear form (the energy inner product) which is naturally associated with the specific problem, and certain optimal properties of the (RITZ) approximation over finite-dimensional subspaces. These ideas lead to a clean and precise theory governing the application of the finite-element method, even for complicated geometries. Comparatively tight theories are unavailable for alternate approximation techniques which naturally arise from non-variational problem statements, e.g., the finite-difference method, which can be applied to equivalent formulations in terms of differential operator equations (such as EULER-LAGRANGE equations). Excellent accounts of the mathematical theory of the finite-element method are [17.36,39,86]. An extensive development from an engineering point of view is presented in [17.40].

A.1. The SOBOLEV Spaces

Fundamental to finite-element analysis are a set of spaces called the SOBOLEV spaces (see, e.g., [17.87,88]. They are a generalization of the familiar L_2 space which consists of all functions $v:\Omega \subset R^n \to R$ (where Ω is a bounded domain) whose L_2 norm over Ω

$$\|v\|_{L_2,\Omega} = (\int_\Omega |v(\underline{x})|^2 d\underline{x})^{\frac{1}{2}}$$

is finite. We denote the partial derivatives of v by the notation

$$\partial^\alpha v(\underline{x}) = (\frac{\partial}{\partial x_1})^{\alpha_1} \ldots (\frac{\partial}{\partial x_n})^{\alpha_n} v(\underline{x})$$

---

21. The finite-element method was conceived by COURANT [17.55].

where $\alpha = (\alpha_1, \ldots, \alpha_n)$ is a multi-index of positive integers α_i.[22] The SOBOLEV norm of order m over Ω combines the L_2 norms of all partial derivatives of v up to order m:

$$\|v\|_{m,\Omega} = \left(\sum_{|\alpha| \leq m} \int_\Omega |\partial^\alpha v|^2 d\underline{x} \right)^{\frac{1}{2}} \tag{A.1}$$

where $|\alpha| = \alpha_1 + \ldots + \alpha_n$. The SOBOLEV space of order m over Ω is then defined by

$$H^m(\Omega) = \{v \mid \|v\|_{m,\Omega} < \infty\} . \tag{A.2}$$

Clearly, $H^0 \equiv L_2$.

We will also require the associated seminorm

$$|v|_{m,\Omega} = \left(\sum_{|\alpha|=m} \int_\Omega |\partial^\alpha v|^2 dx \right)^{\frac{1}{2}} \tag{A.3}$$

which includes only the derivatives of order m exactly. It is a seminorm because it is zero if $v = \pi_{m-1} \in \Pi^{m-1}(\Omega)$, where Π^{m-1} is the space of polynomials of degree m-1 defined in Ω [17.39, p. 298].

Since the SOBOLEV norms are sums of L_2 norms, they have associated inner products and, therefore, the SOBOLEV spaces are HILBERT spaces[23]. Let $C^q(\Omega)$ denote the class functions which have continuous partial derivatives of all orders up to order q. A fundamental embedding property of the SOBOLEV spaces is given by the SOBOLEV inequality which states that $C^q \subset H^m$ if and only if m-q>n/2, where n is the dimension of R^n.

A.2. An Abstract Variational Principle

Let V be a normed vector space with norm $\|\cdot\|$, and S be a nonempty subset of V. Moreoever, let $a(\cdot,\cdot): V \times V \to R$ be a continuous bilinear form and f: $V \to R$ be a continuous linear form.

Definition 1: abstract (quadratic)variational principle

The problem:

Find an element u^S such that

$$u^S \in S \text{ and } E(u^S) = \inf_{v^S \in S} E(v^S) \tag{A.4}$$

where the functional $E: V \to R$ is defined by

$$E(v) = \tfrac{1}{2} a(v,v) - f(v) \tag{A.5}$$

will be referred to as the abstract variational principle.

---

22. The derivatives are to be interpreted in the generalized (distributional) sense, but when a derivative exists in the classical sense, it is equal to the generalized derivative (see, e.g., [17.64]).

23. Extensions of the definition of SOBOLEV spaces and norms have been made to negative and nonintegral order m (see, e.g., [17.87,88]).

Theorem A.1: existence and uniqueness

Assume in addition that

(i) the space V is complete,[24]

(ii) S is a closed convex subset of V,

(iii) the bilinear form $(\cdot,\cdot)$ is symmetric,

(iv) $(\cdot,\cdot)$ is V elliptic,[25] i.e., there exists a constant $\alpha > 0$ such that

$$\forall v \in V, \quad a(v,v) \geq \alpha \|v\|^2 . \tag{A.6}$$

Then the abstract variational principle has a unique solution $u^S \in S$.[26]

Proof. (Ref. [17.36], p. 3.) The bilinear form $(\cdot,\cdot)$ is an inner product over the space V. Since it is continuous, it is bounded,[27] and because it is also V elliptic, there exist constants α and μ such that $\alpha\|v\|^2 \leq a(v,v) \leq \mu\|v\|^2$.[28] Therefore, the norm associated with the inner product is equivalent to the given norm $\|\cdot\|$, and V becomes a HILBERT space when it is equipped with this inner product. According to the <u>REISZ representation theorem</u> (see, e.g., [17.89,90]), there exists an element $u \in V$ such that

$$\forall v \in V, \quad f(v) = a(u,v) \tag{A.7}$$

and because $a(\cdot,\cdot)$ is symmetric,

$$E(v^S) = \tfrac{1}{2}a(v^S,v^S) - a(u,v^S) = \tfrac{1}{2}a(v^S-u,v^S-u) - \tfrac{1}{2}a(u,u) .$$

Therefore, the minimum of $E(v^S)$ and the minimum of $a(v^S-u,v^S-u)$ as v^S ranges over the set S are achieved by the same element $u^S \in S$. In other words, solving the abstract variational principle is equivalent to finding an element $u^S \in S$ which is closest to u with respect to the norm $a(\cdot,\cdot)^{1/2}$:

$$a(u-u^S,u-u^S)^{1/2} = \inf_{v^S \in S} a(u-v^S,u-v^S)^{1/2} . \tag{A.8}$$

By the <u>projection theorem</u> (see, e.g., [17.89,90]), the solution is the projection of u onto S with respect to the inner product $a(\cdot,\cdot)$, and its exis-

---

24. That is to say, it is a <u>BANACH space</u>.

25. V ellipticity means that the bilinear form is <u>positive definite</u>; i.e., $a(v,v)=0$ if and only if $v=0$.

26. Theorem A.1 is a generalization of the familiar theorem for the existence of a unique solution to a (quadratic) minimization problem in mathematical programming (see, e.g., [17.42]).

27. A bilinear form is continuous if and only if it is bounded; i.e., there exists a constant μ such that $|a(u,v)| \leq \mu\|u\|\|v\|$ [17.37, p. 111].

28. Two norms $\|\cdot\|$ and $\|\cdot\|'$ on a linear vector space V are called <u>equivalent</u> if the corresponding metrics are equivalent. This amounts to the existence of two positive constants C_1 and C_2 such that $C_1\|v\| \leq \|v\|' \leq C_2\|v\|$.

tence and uniqueness is assured by the fact that S is a closed convex subset of V. □

The abstract formulation encompasses linear variational problems which
are posed classicially in terms of variational principles involving the
minimization of quadratic functionals $E(v) = \frac{1}{2}a(v,v)-f(v)$ over an admissible
space of functions $v \in V$. Such functionals often represent the potential
energy of a physical system, $a(v,v)$ being the second-degree term which is
the strain energy in the function v ($f(v)$ is a first-degree term). The
associated inner product $a(v,w)$ is the energy inner product which is intrinsic to the particular variational principle, and is defined for all admissible functions v and w.

It is clear from the above discussion that the admissible space V must be
complete and that $E(v)$ must be well defined for all $v \in V$ (i.e., that V must
be a space of finite energy). The SOBOLEV spaces fulfill these conditions.
Their use as generalized energy spaces is natural in the sense that, for a
given variational principle, the energy inner product is well defined over
a SOBOLEV space H^m, where m is the highest order of partial derivative of
v which occurs in $a(v,v)$. In general then, V is the space H^m whose natural
norm is the SOBOLEV norm $\|\cdot\|_m$.

The role of the subset S is in approximating the exact solution u. Although u is usually impossible to obtain over the full admissible space V,
it may be relatively straightforward to approximate it optimally by an element $u^S \in S$, especially if S is taken to be a closed subspace of V. The approximation is optimal in the sense of (A.8). In the ensuing discussion,
we will restrict ourselves to the special case where S is a closed subspace of V. The approximate solution of the abstract variational principle
may then be characterized by the following theorem.

Theorem A.2: variational equation

If S is a closed subspace of V, then $u^S \in S$ is a solution of the abstract
variational principle if and only if it satisfies the variational equation

$$\forall v^S \in S, \quad a(u^S,v^S) = f(v^S) .$$
(A.9)

Proof. If u^S minimizes E over S, then for any ε and $v^S \in S$,

$$E(u^S) \leq E(u^S+\varepsilon v^S) = \frac{1}{2}a(u^S+\varepsilon v^S,u^S+\varepsilon v^S)-f(u^S+\varepsilon v^S)$$

$$= E(u^S)+\varepsilon[a(u^S,v^S)-f(v^S)]+\frac{1}{2}\varepsilon^2 a(v^S,v^S) .$$

Therefore,

$$0 \leq \varepsilon[a(u^S,v^S)-f(v^S)]+\frac{1}{2}\varepsilon^2 a(v^S,v^S)$$

and since this must be true for small ε, both positive and negative, it
follows that $a(u^S,v^S)=f(v^S)$.[29] □

---

29. In the general case where S is not a closed subspace, but is only a closed
    convex subset of v as required by condition (ii) of Theorem 1, the solu-
    tion u^S must satisfy the variational inequality $a(u^S,v^S-u^S) \, f(v^S-u^S)$
    [7.36, p. 3].

We will now discuss some important properties of the solution of the abstract variational principle. First, from the proof of the theorem, it is clear that (A.9) is the well-known condition for the vanishing of the first variation of ε at u^S, in the direction of v^S. In particular, if S is the whole space V, then the solution satisfies

$$a(u,v) = f(v) \tag{A.10}$$

and the first variation at u vanishes in every direction v. Setting u=v, we have $a(u,u)=f(u)$ and hence

$$E(u) = \tfrac{1}{2}a(u,u)-f(u) = -\tfrac{1}{2}a(u,u) \ ,$$

i.e., at the minimum, the strain energy is the negative of the potential energy. Now, $E(u) \leq E(u^S)$ since u is minimal over a wider class of functions. Then

$$a(u^S,u^S) \leq a(u,u)$$

and so the strain energy in u^S always underestimates the strain energy in u. Moreover, since u^S is the projection of u onto the subspace S, the error $e^S=u-u^S$ is orthogonal to S:

$$a(e^S,v^S) = 0 \quad \forall v^S \in S \ .$$

In particular, $a(e^S,u^S)=0$ or $a(u,u^S)=a(u^S,u^S)$ and

$$a(e^S,e^S)=a(u,u)-a(u^S,u^S) \ ,$$

i.e., the energy in the error equals the error in the energy (the Pythagorean theorem holds).

A.3. The RITZ Approximation

The key condition in the hypothesis of Theorem A.2 is that the subspace S be closed. How can we ensure this? One possibility arises from the fact that finite-dimensional subspaces are always closed. A number of classical methods for solving variational problems, called direct methods, are based on this.[30] One of these, the (RAYLEIGH-)RITZ method [17.37,92,93], is of fundamental importance when a variational principle is involved. In the RITZ method, we choose a finite-dimensional subspace

$$S = S^h \equiv \{v^h \mid v^h = \sum_{i=1}^{N} v_i \phi_i\} \tag{A.11}$$

where $\phi_1,\ldots,\phi_N$ are independent basis functions which span S^h and $v_1,\ldots,v_N$ are unknown real parameters.

By Theorem A.1, the approximate solution to the variational principle is the unique element $u^h \in S^h$ which is the projection of u onto S^h. This amounts to choosing parameters v_i which satisfy the discrete variational principle

---

30. Direct methods include the method of weighted residuals, whose special cases include collocation methods and the GALERKIN method, the method of orthonormal(e.g., FOURIER) series, and the least squares method (see, e.g., [17.37,40,91,92]).

$$E(u^h) = \inf_{v^h \in S^h} E(v^h) = \inf_{v_1,\ldots,v_N \in R} \tfrac{1}{2} \sum_{i=1}^{N} \sum_{j=1}^{N} a(\phi_i,\phi_j)v_i v_j$$

$$- \sum_{i=1}^{N} f(\phi_i)v_i \qquad\qquad \text{(A.12)}$$

or, by Theorem A.2, the associated variational equation

$$\forall v^h \in S^h, \qquad a(u^h,v^h) = f(v^h)$$

which is, in fact, a linear system of algebraic equations

$$\sum_{j=1}^{N} a(\phi_i,\phi_j)u_j = f(\phi_i), \qquad 1 \le i \le N.$$

These equations can be written in the compact matrix form

$$\underline{A}\underline{u} = \underline{f} \qquad\qquad \text{(A.13)}$$

where $\underline{A} \in R^{NN} = [a(\phi_i,\phi_j)]$ and where $\underline{f} \in R^N = [f(\phi_i)]$ and $\underline{u} \in R^N = [u_i]$, called the discrete variational equation. Since the matrix of coefficients $\underline{A}$ is non-singular, the discrete solution is given by $\underline{u} = \underline{A}^{-1}\underline{f}$, although for the problem at hand $\underline{A}$ is huge, so it is usually impractical to compute $\underline{A}^{-1}$ directly. In the next subsection, we describe special types of basis functions which ultimately lead to practical iterative solutions.

A.4. Finite-Element Spaces

The RITZ method has given us a discrete solution $u^h = \sum_{i=1}^{N} u_i \phi_i$ which is optimal in the sense that the energy in the error, as measured in the natural energy norm $a(u-u^h,u-u^h)^{\frac{1}{2}}$, is as small as possible. In the classical RITZ method, the basis functions ϕ_i are generally chosen to be fairly complicated functions which have global support over the domain in question (e.g., trigonometric functions)[17.37,92]. Although this choice may be beneficial for analytic purposes, it renders the method unsuitable for numerical computation. The problem is overcome by the finite-element method which is a systematic procedure for constructing finite-dimensional approximating subspaces S^h, called finite-element spaces, which are very convenient for numerical computation. In certain forms, the method may be considered to be a special instance of the RITZ method in which the basis functions are simple functions having local support. In the ensuing discussion, we will restrict ourselves to a domain $\overline{\Omega}$ which is a polygon in R^2 with boundary $\partial\Omega$[31]. The following are basic characteristics of the construction in its simplest form:

(i) A "triangulation" T^h is established over the domain: $\overline{\Omega} = \cup_{E \in T^h} E$; that is, the domain is partitioned into the union of subdomains $E \in T^h$, called finite elements, such that the E are closed sets with nonempty interiors and polygonal boundaries. The elements are usually adjacently placed triangles or rectangles which overlap only at the inter-

---

31. The theory has been extended to domains with curved boundaries in any number of dimensions.

element boundaries. Associated with the triangulation is its funda-mental length h.[32]

(ii) The elements are considered to be interconnected at a discrete number of points on the interelement boundaries, which are called the nodes of the triangulation. The unknown real parameters of the discrete problem are the nodal variables, the values of the solution (and/or possibly of its derivatives) at the nodes.

(iii) Associated with the triangulation is a space of functions S^h defined over $\bar{\Omega}$. Defined within each element E is a finite-dimensional space $p^E=\{v^h|_E \mid v^h \in S^h\}$ consisting of functions which are polynomials (or ratios of polynomials). The polynomials $p^E \in p^E$ represent a local approximation of the solution within E, and are uniquely determined by the nodal variables associated with the element.

(iv) In certain elements, the functions p^E may have to satisfy the essential boundary conditions of the problem.

   While the classical RITZ method is limited to geometrically simple domains $\bar{\Omega}$, in the finite-element method this limitation occurs only within the element itself. Consequently, it is possible to "assemble" complicated configurations from simple element shapes. Several factors contribute to the success of the finite-element method from a computational point of view. Firstly, due to the fact that in the element interiors the solution is approximated by a low-order polynomial in x and y, the computations required to compute the dis-crete functional in (A.12) or, equivalently, to compute the entries of matrix A of the discrete variational equation (A.13), are often simple. Secondly, it can be shown that associated with the local polynomial functions, there exists a canonical set of basis functions ϕ_i spanning S^h which are also piece-wise polynomials and which have local support. A will therefore be sparse and banded; that is, most of its relatively few nonzero entries will lie near the main diagonal. Thirdly, when the problem is well posed in terms of a variational principle, $a(\cdot,\cdot)$ will be symmetric and S^h elliptic, which guarantees that A will be nonsingular, symmetric, and positive definite. In addition to these clear merits, piecewise polynomials are remarkable in that they are optimal in terms of their approximation properties and in that these properties are essential for proving convergence of the method [17.39, p. 153].

   The convergence properties of the finite-element method are an important issue. The object of the RITZ method is to find optimal values for the nodal variables (which are the parameters of the discrete solution) by minimizing the discrete functional $E(v^h)$. This suggests immediately the possibility of approximating the exact solution u by a minimizing sequence of discrete solutions to discrete problems associated with a family of subspaces S^h whose fundamental length h has limit zero. Although the approximation is known by (A.8) to be optimal in terms of the norm $a(\cdot,\cdot)^{\frac{1}{2}}$, is is more convenient to analyze the error in terms of the natural SOBOLEV norm $\|\cdot\|_m$ of $V \subset H^m$. The following theorem gives a sufficient condition for the convergence of such a sequence.

---

32. The fundamental length h of the triangulation T^h is the maximum "radius" of the elements. As the subdivision is made finer, the number of ele-ments increases and $h \to 0$.

Theorem A.3: CÉA's Lemma

Since there exists a constant C independent upon the subspace S^h such that

$$\|u-u^h\| \leq C \inf_{v^h \in S^h} \|u-v^h\| \qquad (A.14)$$

then a sufficient condition for convergence is that there exists a family S^h of subspaces of the space V such that, for each u∈V, $\lim_{h\to 0}\|u-u^h\|=0$; i.e.,

$$\lim_{h\to 0} \inf_{v^h \in S^h} \|u-v^h\|=0 \ .$$

Proof. Eq. (A.14) follows from (A.8) due to the continuity and V ellipticity of a(·,·). Moreover, $C=\sqrt{\frac{\mu}{\alpha}}$ is a constant independent of the subspace S^h. □

We see, then, that an estimation of the error reduces to finding the distance between the exact solution u and the subspace S^h -- a problem in <u>approximation theory</u>. The basic hypothesis about the finite-element space S^h was that the finite-dimensional space P^E within each element E is a space of polynomials. If we assume that the space contains the complete polynomials of degree k (i.e., $\Pi^k \subset P^E$), it can be shown in general that the approximation error in the sth derivative, where s≠m, is of the form

$$\|u-u^h\|_s = 0(h^{k+1-s}+h^{2(k+1-m)}) \qquad (A.15)$$

[7.39, p. 107]. On the other hand, because the approximation minimizes the strain energy, the order of convergence of the mth derivative is better. It is order $h^{2(k+1-m)}$.

The convergence properties implied by CÉA's lemma are contingent upon the finite-element spaces S^h being subspaces of the admissible space V. In view of this, if the energy inner product a(v,v) involves partial derivatives of v of order m so that $V \subset H^m(\Omega)$, ensuring convergence amounts to imposing the following two requirements on the local functions p^E:

(i) Completeness condition: As the size of any element tends to zero, the function p^E must be such that a constant value of the mth derivative will be attainable in the element subdomain; i.e., we must have k≥m so that $P^E \subset H^m(E)$, $\forall E \in T^h$.

(ii) Conformity condition: All derivatives of p^E of order less than m must be continuous across interelement boundaries; that is, $S^h \subset C^{m-1}(\overline{\Omega})$.

The two requirements are necessary and sufficient for $S^h \subset H^m(\Omega)$ when the p^E are polynomials (or ratios of polynomials). Another way of stating the completeness condition is that the local polynomials must be able to reproduce a <u>state of constant strain</u> -- any solution which is a polynomial of degree m. When the local polynomials satisfy the conformity condition, the elements are called <u>conforming finite elements</u>, and their use yields what are referred to as <u>conforming finite-element methods</u>.

A.5. Nonconforming Elements

In the above discussion, we assumed that the conforming finite-element methods approximate the solution u of $E(u)=\inf_{v \in S} E(v)$ by the solution u^h of $E(u^h)=\inf_{v^h \in S^h} E(v^h)$ where S^h is a <u>subspace</u> of S. This is a global condition on the approximation which is often violated for reasons of computational convenience. For instance, it may be violated by dropping the element conformity conditions.[33] Elements which do so are called <u>nonconforming elements</u>. They are often used in practice for higher-order problems because conforming elements for such problems are unnecessarily complicated or must have a large number of degrees of freedom in order to satisfy the interelement conformity conditions.

If nonconforming elements are used, it is clearly impossible to evaluate the true energy functional $E(v^h)$, due to the singularities in the mth derivatives of v^h which occur at the element boundaries. To avoid this problem, we can simply ignore the discontinuities between elements by computing the strain energies within each element and then summing the individual contributions; that is, for the original energy inner product $a(\cdot,\cdot)$, we substitute the <u>approximate energy inner product</u> $a_h(\cdot,\cdot)$ defined by the bilinear form

$$a_h(\cdot,\cdot) = \sum_{E \in T^h} a(\cdot,\cdot)|_E \qquad (A.16)$$

where the notation $|_E$ means a restriction to the element domain. The <u>approximate variational principle</u> is then the problem of finding a $u^h \in S^h$ which minimizes the functional

$$E_h(v^h) = \tfrac{1}{2} a_h(v^h,v^h) - f(v^h) \qquad (A.17)$$

and the necessary condition for the vanishing of the first variation becomes

$$\forall v^h \in S^h, \quad a_h(u^h,v^h) = f(v^h) . \qquad (A.18)$$

Following in the spirit of the conforming case, we must determine sufficient conditions for the existence and uniqueness of the solution u^h to the approximate variational principle, as well as under what conditions this approximate solution converges to the exact solution u as $h \to 0$. The conditions are natural extensions of Theorem A.1 and CÉA's lemma, and are given in the following theorem.

Theorem A.4: existence and uniqueness (nonconforming case)

If

    (i) there exists a mapping $\|\cdot\|_h$: $S^h \to R$ which is a norm over S^h

    (ii) $a_h(\cdot,\cdot)$ is bounded and S^h elliptic, in that there exists a constant $\alpha_h > 0$ such that

$$\forall v^h \in S^h, \quad a_h(v^h,v^h) \geq \alpha_h \|v^h\|_h^2$$

then the approximate variational principle has a unique solution $u^h \in S^h$.

---

33. This violation is an example of a so-called <u>variational crime</u> [17.35, Chapt. 4]. Besides violation of the element conformity condition, variational crimes also include inexact evaluation of the functional $E(v^h)$ (i.e., of the quadratic form $a(u^h,v^h)$ and linear form $f(v^h)$) such as by numerical integration, as well as various techniques for the approximation of essential boundary conditions.

Proof. Refer to the discussion in [17.36, Chapt. 4]. □

On the other hand, to obtain convergence, we impose a stronger condition, uniform S^h ellipticity, which requires that there exist a constant $\tilde{\alpha}>0$, independent of h, such that

$$\forall S^h, \ \forall v^h \epsilon S^h, \ a_h(v^h,v^h) \geq \tilde{\alpha} \|v^h\|_h^2 \ . \tag{A.19}$$

Convergence is then guaranteed by the following theorem.

Theorem A.5: STRANG's lemma

Given a family of discrete problems for which the associated approximate energy inner products are uniformly S^h elliptic, then there exists a constant C, independent of S^h, such that

$$\|u-u^h\|_h \leq C(\inf_{v^h \epsilon S^h} \|u-v^h\|_h + \sup_{w^h \epsilon S^h} \frac{|a_h(u,w^h)-f(w^h)|}{\|w^h\|_h})^{\frac{1}{2}} \ . \tag{A.20}$$

Proof. See [17.36, p. 210]. □

STRANG's lemma is a generalization of CÉA's lemma for conforming elements - in addition to the usual approximation error term, we have the (inf) term which measures the consistency error of the nonconforming space. Since the difference $a_h(u,w^h)-f(w^h)$ is zero for all $w^h \epsilon S^h$ when $S^h \subset V$, the consistency error for conforming spaces is identically zero and STRANG's lemma reduces to CÉA's lemma. However, for the nonconforming case, convergence is obtained if the consistency condition

$$\lim_{h \to 0} \sup_{w^h \epsilon S^h} \frac{a_h(u,w^h)-f(w^h)|}{\|w^h\|_h} = 0, \ \forall v^h \epsilon S^h \tag{A.21}$$

is satisfied.

The consistency condition was first recognized empirically and was stated in the form of a simple test known as the patch test. Subsequently, STRANG proved mathematically that the patch test was indeed a test for consistency and, by essentially making the above arguments, that nonconforming elements which pass it will yield convergence (see [17.34, Chapt. 4]). The test remains a convenient one to apply.

Theorem A.6: the patch test

Suppose that the energy inner product $a_h(u,v)$ contains derivatives of order at most m and the nonconforming space S^h contains all polynomials π_m of degree at most m. If the nonconforming finite-element method recovers all solutions which are polynomials of degree at most m, then the patch test is passed, and $\lim_{h \to 0}\|u-u^h\|_h=0$.

In other words, suppose that we put an arbitrary patch of nonconforming elements associated with the nonconforming space S^h in a state of constant strain; that is, we impose $v^h = \pi_m \epsilon \Pi^m$ on the displacements at nodes around the patch boundary. Because the completeness condition of the previous subsection is still binding on nonconforming elements, this polynomial is both an element of S^h and an element of V, hence its consistency error is zero. The conforming (RITZ) solution to (A.12) or (A.13) and the nonconforming, discrete solution of the approximate variational principle ought then to be identical and equal to π_m. The test is to determine whether this is indeed the case.

Appendix B. Iterative Solution of Large Linear Systems

The approximation of a variational principle by direct methods such as the finite-element method (or the approximation of a boundary value problem by finite differences) gives rise to a system of simultaneous algebraic equations. For quadratic functionals (or linear boundary value problems), the system will be linear. In this appendix, we consider the problem of solving, by iterative means, systems of linear equations of the form

$$\sum_{j=1}^{N} a_{ij}u_j = f_i \qquad 1 \leq i \leq N \tag{B.1}$$

where the coefficients a_{ij} and the values f_i are known. The system may also be written as the matrix equation

$$\underline{A}\underline{u}=\underline{f} \tag{B.2}$$

where $\underline{A} \epsilon R^{NN}=[a_{ij}]$ is a nonsingular matrix and where $\underline{f} \epsilon R^N=[f_i]$ is a column vector. We wish to solve the system for the column vector $\underline{u} \epsilon R^N=[u_i]=\underline{A}^{-1}\underline{f}$. In applying the finite-element method to our visual surface reconstruction problem, we will obtain large sparse matrices $\underline{A}$. In this appendix we will be concerned with numerical methods which are capable of solving such systems where N is in the range of, say, 10^3-10^6 or larger.

An _iterative method_ for solving equations (B.2) computes a sequence of approximations $\underline{u}^{(1)},\underline{u}^{(2)},\ldots$, to the exact solution $\underline{u}$. A new, and hopefully better, approximation is computed at each iteration, but, in general, the exact solution cannot be obtained in a finite number of iterations. If, regardless of the initial approximation $\underline{u}^{(0)},$[34] the _approximation error_ (i.e., the difference between the exact solution and the approximations, measured in some appropriate norm) tends to zero as the number of iterations increases, the iterative method is said to be _convergent_, and the rate at which the approximation error tends to zero is called its _rate of convergence_. In order that an iterative method be of practical use, it is important that it be convergent, and that it exhibit a sufficiently large rate of convergence to an approximation of prespecified accuracy. In this appendix, we review a number of the most common iterative methods, and examine their convergence properties and their rates of convergence. References for this material are [17,34,35,75,94,95].

B.1. Basic Relaxation Methods

Let us assume that $\underline{A}$ has nonzero diagonal elements. It will be convenient to express $\underline{A}$ as the sum

$$\underline{A}=\underline{D}-\underline{L}-\underline{U}$$

---

34. The trivial initial approximation $\underline{u}^{(0)}=\underline{0}$ is usually chosen.

where $\underline{D} \in R^{NN}$ is diagonal, $\underline{L} \in R^{NN}$ is strictly lower triangular, and $\underline{U} \in R^{NN}$ is strictly upper triangular. Clearly, the equations in (B.1) can be rewritten in the following form:

$$a_{ii}u_i = - \sum_{\substack{1 \le j \le N \\ j \ne i}} a_{ij}u_j + f_i, \qquad 1 \le i \le N.$$

Next, we will define three basic iterative methods for solving (B.2), popularly known as relaxation methods in the context of the numerical solution of partial differential equations.

B.1.1. JACOBI Relaxation

The JACOBI method (or the method of simultaneous displacements) is defined by

$$a_{ii}u_i^{(k+1)} = - \sum_{\substack{1 \le j \le N \\ j \ne i}} a_{ij}u_j^{(k)} + f_i \qquad 1 \le i \le N$$

which can be written in matrix form as

$$\underline{D}u^{(k+1)} = (\underline{L} + \underline{U})\underline{u}^{(k)} + \underline{f}$$

thus giving us the iterative scheme

$$\underline{u}^{(k+1)} = \underline{D}^{-1}(\underline{L} + \underline{U})\underline{u}^{(k)} + \underline{D}^{-1}\underline{f} \quad . \tag{B.3}$$

The matrix

$$\underline{G}_J = \underline{D}^{-1}(\underline{L} + \underline{U})$$

is called the JACOBI iteration matrix associated with matrix $\underline{A}$.

Clearly, the JACOBI method is a parallel method because the elements of the new approximation $\underline{u}^{(k+1)}$ may be computed simultaneously and in parallel by a network of processors whose inputs are elements of the old approximation $\underline{u}^{(k)}$. As such, it requires the storage of both the old and the new approximations.

B.1.2. GAUSS-SEIDEL Relaxation

Convergence of the JACOBI method is usually very slow. In a closely related method, the so-called GAUSS-SEIDEL method (or the method of immediate displacements), the elements of the new approximation are used in subsequent computations immediately after they become available. This increases the rate of convergence somewhat, but typically less than an order of magnitude. The equations are written as

$$a_{ii}u_i^{(k+1)} = - \sum_{j=1}^{i-1} a_{ij}u_j^{(k+1)} - \sum_{j=i+1}^{N} a_{ij}u_j^{(k)} + f_i \qquad 1 \le i \le N,$$

which, in matrix form, becomes

$$\underline{D}u^{(k+1)} = \underline{L}u^{(k+1)} + \underline{U}\underline{u}^{(k)} + \underline{f} \tag{B.4}$$

from which we obtain the iterative scheme defined by

$$\underline{u}^{(k+1)} = (\underline{D}-\underline{L})^{-1}\underline{U}\underline{u}^{(k)}+(\underline{D}-\underline{L})^{-1}\underline{f} \ . \tag{B.5}$$

The <u>GAUSS-SEIDEL iteration matrix</u> associated with matrix A is therefore given by

$$\underline{G}_{GS} = (\underline{D}-\underline{L})^{-1}\underline{U} \ .$$

In the GAUSS-SEIDEL method, we no longer need to store simultaneously the old and new approximations. As they are computed, the new elements can simply displace the old ones. Moreover, since the new values are exploited immediately in subsequent computations we can intuitively expect a higher rate of convergence compared with the JACOBI method. On the other hand, it can easily be seen that the GAUSS-SEIDEL method is inherently a <u>sequential</u> method which renders it unsuitable for implementation as a parallel network.

B.1.3. The Successive Overrelaxation (SOR) Method

The convergence of the GAUSS-SEIDEL method may be accelerated by a simple modification. Let us define the <u>dynamic residual vector</u>[35] at the kth iteration of the GAUSS-SEIDEL relaxation method as

$$\underline{r}^{(k)} = \underline{u}^{(k+1)}-\underline{u}^{(k)}$$
$$= \underline{D}^{-1}(\underline{L}\underline{u}^{(k+1)}+\underline{U}\underline{u}^{(k)}+\underline{f})-\underline{u}^{(k)}$$

(see (B.4)). Then, it is evident that the GAUSS-SEIDEL scheme can be written in the form

$$\underline{u}^{(k+1)} = \underline{u}^{(k)}+\underline{r}^{(k)} \ .$$

If the elements of all successive residual vectors are one-signed (as they usually are when approximating elliptic problems), then it is reasonable to anticipate an acceleration in the convergence of the GAUSS-SEIDEL scheme if the residual vector is scaled by a fixed real number $\omega>1$ before it is added to $\underline{u}^{(k)}$ in each GAUSS-SEIDEL iteration. ω is called the <u>relaxation parameter.</u> This idea leads to one of the most successful iterative methods for solving systems of linear equations currently available, the <u>successive overrelaxation method.</u> The method may be defined by

$$\underline{u}^{(k+1)} = \underline{u}^{(k)}+\omega\underline{r}^{(k)}$$
$$= \underline{u}^{(k)}+\omega[\underline{D}^{-1}(\underline{L}\underline{u}^{(k+1)}+\underline{U}\underline{u}^{(k)}+\underline{f})-\underline{u}^{(k)}]$$

which we can manipulate into the form

$$\underline{u}^{(k+1)} = (\underline{I}-\omega\underline{D}^{-1}\underline{L})^{-1}[(1-\omega)\underline{I}+\omega\underline{D}^{-1}\underline{U}]\underline{u}^{(k)}+(\underline{I}-\omega\underline{D}^{-1}\underline{L})^{-1}\omega\underline{D}^{-1}\underline{f} \ . \tag{B.6}$$

The <u>successive overrelaxation iteration matrix</u> is therefore given by

$$\underline{G}_{\omega} = (\underline{I}-\omega\underline{D}^{-1}\underline{L})^{-1}[(1-\omega)\underline{I}+\omega\underline{D}^{-1}\underline{U}] \ .$$

---

35. The residual vector is also called the <u>correction</u> or <u>displacement vector.</u> Note that the <u>residual</u> of an equation is the amount by which the equation fails to be satisfied.

Three cases arise:

   (i) if $\omega > 1$ the scheme is called overrelaxation,[36]

   (ii) if $\omega = 1$ we obtain the GAUSS-SEIDEL method, and

   (iii) if $0 < \omega < 1$ the scheme is termed underrelaxation.

B.1.4. Conditions for Convergence

The JACOBI, GAUSS-SEIDEL, and successive overrelaxation methods are particular instances of the general stationary iterative method

$$\underline{u}^{(k+1)} = \underline{G}\underline{u}^{(k)} + \underline{c} \tag{B.7}$$

where the iteration matrix $\underline{G}$ is taken to be $\underline{G}_J$, $\underline{G}_{GS}$, and $\underline{G}_\omega$, respectively, and $\underline{c}$ is a known column vector.[37] By subtracting $\underline{u} = \underline{G}\underline{u} + \underline{c}$ from (B.7), we can obtain an expression for the errors $\underline{e}^{(k)} = \underline{u}^{(k)} - \underline{u}$ of successive approximations,

$$\underline{e}^{(k+1)} = \underline{G}\underline{e}^{(k)}$$
$$= \underline{G}^{k+1}\underline{e}^{(0)} . \tag{B.8}$$

The sequence of approximations converges to the solution $\underline{u}$ if $\lim_{k \to \infty} \underline{e}^{(k)} = \underline{0}$, which will clearly be the case if and only if $\lim_{k \to \infty} \underline{G}^k = \underline{0}$, since $\underline{u}^{(0)}$ (and hence $\underline{e}^{(0)}$) is arbitrary. Let $\underline{G}$ have eigenvalues $\lambda_1, \lambda_2, \ldots, \lambda_N$, and assume that the corresponding eigenvectors $\underline{v}_1, \underline{v}_2, \ldots, \underline{v}_N$ are linearly independent. Then the initial error vector can be expressed uniquely as the linear combination

$$\underline{e}^{(0)} = \sum_{i=1}^{N} c_i \underline{v}_i .$$

But, by (B.8),

$$\underline{e}^{(k)} = \underline{G}^k \underline{e}^{(0)}$$
$$= \sum_{i=1}^{N} c_i \underline{G}^k \underline{v}_i$$
$$= \sum_{i=1}^{N} c_i \lambda_i^k \underline{v}_i .$$

---

36. It should be noted that there exist classes of matrices (which arise from many first- and second-order partial differential equations) for which the optimal value of ω, yielding the largest rate of convergence, may be determined analytically (see, e.g., [17.75,95]). Often, the convergence may be adequately accelerated by not necessarily optimal values of ω chosen empirically. Of course, it is possible to vary ω from iteration to iteration or from one equation to the next. A number of these modified methods have been studied in the literature (see, e.g., [17.75,94,95]).

37. The method is obtained by writing the original system $\underline{A}\underline{u} = \underline{f}$ as $\underline{u} = \underline{G}\underline{u} + \underline{c}$, and is referred to as being stationary because $\underline{G}$ is fixed for all iterations.

It follows that in the limit, $e^{(k)}$ will be zero for an arbitrary initial approximation if and only if $|\lambda_i|<1$, for $1 \le i \le N$. Thus, we have the following theorem.

Theorem B.1: convergence of the stationary iterative method

The stationary iterative method (B.7) is convergent if and only if

$$\rho(\underline{G}) = \max_{i=1}^{N} |\lambda_i(\underline{G})| < 1$$

where $\rho(\underline{G})$ is called the <u>spectral radius</u> of $\underline{G}$.[38]

Theorem 1 is mainly of theoretical value because, in practice, it is difficult to determine the eigenvalues of $\underline{G}$. Fortunately, we have a useful corollary giving sufficient conditions for convergence. The corollary results from the observation that for some matrix norm $\|\underline{G}\|$ which is consistent[39] with a vector norm $\|\underline{v}_i\|$,

$$\|\underline{e}^{(k)}\| \le \|\underline{G}^k\| \|\underline{e}^{(0)}\| \le \|\underline{G}\|^k \|\underline{e}^{(0)}\| \quad . \tag{B.9}$$

Hence we obtain the following corollary to Theorem B.1:

Corollary B.1: convergence of the stationary iterative method

If $\|\underline{G}\|<1$, then the stationary iterative method (B.7) is convergent.[40]

Suppose that the stationary iterative method is convergent. It can be shown (see [17.75,94]) that

$$\lim_{k \to \infty} \|\underline{G}^k\|_{L_2}^{1/k} = \rho(\underline{G}) \quad .$$

Hence, from (B.9) we have that, for large k,

$$\|\underline{e}^{(k)}\|_{L_2} \approx \rho(\underline{G})^k \|\underline{e}^{(0)}\|_{L_2} .$$

Thus, in a certain sense, $\rho(\underline{G})$ is a measure of the rate of convergence of the iterative method and therefore, like convergence itself, depends on the eigenvalues of $\underline{G}$.

We illustrate an application of Corollary B.1 in obtaining a simple but important sufficient condition for the convergence of JACOBI relaxation. The JACOBI iteration matrix $\underline{G}_J$ consists of the elements

$$g_{ij} = \frac{a_{ij}}{a_{ii}} \quad (i \ne j) \qquad g_{ii} = 0 \quad .$$

---

38. It can be shown (see, e.g., [17.94]) that the theorem holds without the independence assumption on the eigenvectors.

39. If a matrix norm and a vector norm satisfy the relation $\|A\underline{u}\| \le \|A\| \|\underline{u}\|$ for any $\underline{A}$ and $\underline{u}$, then the two norms are said to be <u>consistent</u> [17.43, p. 175].

40. The condition is not a necessary one because we can have $\|\underline{G}\|>1$ when $\rho(\underline{G})<1$.

Therefore the L_∞ norm of $\underline{G}_J$ is given by

$$\|\underline{G}_J\|_\infty = \max_{i=1}^{N} \sum_{\substack{1 \le j \le N \\ j \ne i}} \frac{|a_{ij}|}{|a_{ii}|} \quad .$$

Clearly, if $|a_{ii}| > \sum\limits_{\substack{i \le j \le N \\ j \ne i}} |a_{ij}|$, $\|\underline{G}_J\|_\infty < 1$, and JACOBI relaxation will converge by Corollary B.1. A much more general result may be obtained. We begin by defining two important properties that $\underline{A}$ may possess.

Definition B.1: (weakly) diagonally dominant matrix

A matrix $\underline{A}$ of order N is said to be <u>diagonally dominant</u> if

$$|a_{ii}| > \sum_{\substack{1 \le j \le N \\ j \ne i}} |a_{ij}| \quad (1 \le i \le N) \quad .$$

The matrix is said to be <u>weakly diagonally dominant</u> if the $>$ relation in the above inequality can be replaced by $\ge$ in some, but not all, of the equations.

Definition B.2: irreducible matrix

A matrix $\underline{A}$ of order N is irreducible if and only if N=1, or if N>1 and for any i and j such that $1 \le i$, $j \le N$ and $i \ne j$ either $a_{ij}=0$, or there exist $i_1, i_2, \ldots, i_k$ such that $a_{i,i_1} a_{i_1,i_2} \ldots a_{i_k,j} \ne 0$.[41]

It can be shown that if $\underline{A}$ is irreducible and has weak diagonal dominance, then it is nonsingular, and if in addition it is symmetric and has non-negative diagonal elements, then it is positive definite. The general theorem is given next (for a proof see [7.94, p. 73]).

Theorem B.2: convergence of JACOBI and GAUSS-SEIDEL relaxation

Let A be either a diagonally dominant or an irreducible and weakly diagonally dominant matrix. Then both the associated JACOBI and GAUSS-SEIDEL relaxation methods of (B.4) and (B.5) are convergent.

   Next, we turn our attention to the successive overrelaxation method. Since the inverse of a triangular matrix is also a triangular matrix, and its determinant is equal to the product of its diagonal elements, we have

$$\det(\underline{G}_\omega) = \det[(\underline{I} - \omega\underline{D}^{-1}\underline{L})^{-1}] \det[(1-\omega)\underline{I} + \omega\underline{D}^{-1}\underline{U}] = (1-\omega)^N \quad .$$

Since $\det(\underline{G}_\omega) = \Pi_{i=1}^{N} \lambda_i$, it follows that

$$\max_{i=1}^{N} |\lambda_i| \ge |1-\omega|$$

---

41. The term <u>irreducible matrix</u> was introduced by FROBENIUS for matrices
    which (informally speaking) correspond to systems of equations whose
    solutions cannot be reduced to the solution of two systems of lower
    order. One generally obtains irreducible matrices when discretizing
    boundary value problems over connected domains.

which, by Theorem B.1, leads to

Theorem B.3: convergence of the SOR method

$$\rho(\underline{G}_\omega) \geq |\omega-1| \quad ,$$

therefore the successive overrelaxation method (B.6) can converge only if $0<\omega<2$.

A set of necessary and sufficient conditions for convergence for the successive overrelaxation method is stated in the following theorem:

Theorem B.4: convergence of the SOR method for symmetric, positive definite $\underline{A}$

If $\underline{A}$ is a real, symmetric matrix with positive diagonal elements, then the successive overrelaxation method (B.5) is convergent if and only if $0<\omega<2$ and $\underline{A}$ is positive definite.

The same conditions for convergence hold for the GAUSS-SEIDEL method since, by definition, it is a special case of successive overrelaxation.

Corollary B.2: convergence of the GS method for symmetric, positive definite $\underline{A}$

If $\underline{A}$ is a symmetric matrix with positive diagonal elements, the the GAUSS-SEIDEL method is convergent if and only if $\underline{A}$ is positive definite.

It is important to note that the same statement cannot be made about the JACOBI method.

B.2. Basic Gradient Methods

In this section we investigate a class of iterative methods which are naturally associated with optimization theory. These are the so-called gradient methods which, in their full generality, are iterative techniques for minimizing nonlinear functionals. They may also be thought of as methods for solving systems of linear equations for the special case where the functional to be minimized is a quadratic form.

Assume that $\underline{A} \in R^{NN}$ is symmetric. Now suppose that we attempt to solve the following unconstrained minimization problem involving the quadratic form $E(\underline{v})$:

$$E(\underline{u}) = \inf_{\underline{v} \in R^N} E(\underline{v}) = \tfrac{1}{2}(\underline{v},\underline{Av})-(\underline{f},\underline{v})$$

where $(\cdot,\cdot): R^N \times R^N \to R$ denotes the familiar Euclidean inner product. From the well-known theorem of optimization theory (see, e.g., [7.42]), the gradient vector of $E(\underline{u})$

$$\nabla E(\underline{u})=\underline{Au}-\underline{f}$$

vanishes at a minimum $\underline{u}$ and, moreover, the minimum exists and is unique if the Hessian matrix

$$\left[\frac{\partial^2 E(\underline{u})}{\partial u_i \, \partial u_j}\right] = \underline{A}$$

is positive definite.

Thus, for symmetric, positive definite $\underline{A}$, solving the minimization problem is equivalent to solving the system of linear equations $\underline{Au}=\underline{f}$ and, consequently, relaxation methods can be thought of as being methods for descending to the minimum $\underline{u}$ of a quadratic functional.

B.2.1. Gradient Descent

Consider the iterative method $\underline{u}^{(k+1)}=\underline{u}^{(k)}+\alpha^{(k)}\underline{d}^{(k)}$, where at each iteration, we take a step in the direction of the vector $\underline{d}^{(k)}$. To minimize $E(\underline{u})$ quickly, we should move in the direction of steepest descent, which is given by the negative gradient; that is, $\underline{d}^{(k)}=-\nabla E(\underline{u}^{(k)})=\underline{f}-\underline{Au}^{(k)}=\underline{r}^{(k)}$, where $\underline{r}^{(k)}$ is the familiar residual vector. Thus we obtain the nonstationary iterative method defined by

$$\underline{u}^{(k+1)} = \underline{u}^{(k)}+\alpha^{(k)}\underline{r}^{(k)} \quad . \tag{B.10}$$

It seems reasonable to choose the step size at each iteration $\alpha^{(k)}$ so as to minimize $E(\underline{u}^{(k)}+\alpha^{(k)}\underline{r}^{(k)})$. The appropriate value can easily be shown to be

$$\alpha^{(k)} = \frac{(\underline{r}^{(k)},\underline{r}^{(k)})}{(\underline{r}^{(k)},\underline{Ar}^{(k)})} \quad . \tag{B.11}$$

On the other hand, if we fix $\alpha^{(k)}=$ for all iterations, then (B.10) becomes

$$\underline{u}^{(k+1)}=(\underline{I}-\alpha\underline{A})\underline{u}^{(k)}+\alpha\underline{f} \tag{B.12}$$

which can be identified as a stationary iterative method with iteration matrix $\underline{G}=\underline{I}-\alpha\underline{A}$.

B.2.2. The Conjugate Gradient Method

HESTENES and STIEFEL [17.96] introduced the conjugate gradient method, a modification of the method of gradient descent. The method is based on determining vectors $\underline{d}^{(0)},\underline{d}^{(1)},\ldots,\underline{d}^{(n-1)}$ which are pairwise conjugate in the sense that $(\underline{d}^{(i)},\underline{Ad}^{(j)})=0$ for $i\neq j$. The ease in applying the method derives from the fact that these vectors may also be determined iteratively. With the residual vector at the kth iteration given by $\underline{r}^{(k)}=\underline{f}-\underline{Au}^{(k)}$ and with $\underline{d}^{(0)}=\underline{r}^{(0)}$, the algorithm for determining the $\underline{d}^{(k)}$ and $\underline{u}^{(k)}$ is as follows.

$$\underline{u}^{(k+1)}=\underline{u}^{(k)}+ \frac{(\underline{r}^{(k)},\underline{d}^{(k)})}{(\underline{d}^{(k)},\underline{Ad}^{(k)})} \, \underline{d}^{(k)} \qquad 0\leq k\leq N-1$$

$$\underline{d}^{(k)}=\underline{r}^{(k)}- \frac{(\underline{r}^{(k)},\underline{Ad}^{(k-1)})}{(\underline{d}^{(k-1)},\underline{Ad}^{(k-1)})} \underline{d}^{(k-1)} \qquad 1\leq k\leq N-1.$$

Conjugacy of the vectors can be verified along with the fact that $(\underline{r}^{(i)},\underline{r}^{(j)})$ $=0$ for $i\neq j$. This implies that $\underline{r}^{(k)}=0$ for some $k\leq N$. Therefore, in the absence of roundoff errors, the method converges in at most N iterations. Of course, this property is of no real value to us because we must deal with cases where N is very large. Nevertheless, for N large, typically $u^{(k)} \simeq u$ for $k \ll N$ and the algorithm may be used in the iterative spirit. The conjugate gradient method is certainly the most expensive of the algorithms discussed both in terms of space (since the vectors $\underline{u}^{(k)}, \underline{d}^{(k)}, \underline{r}^{(k)}$, and $\underline{Ad}^{(k)}$ must be stored) and in terms of the number of operations to complete one iteration. While it is true that for model problems the number of iterations required to reduce the error by a specified amount is usually considerably less than for the other methods, the conjugate gradient method seems to exceed at least the successive overrelaxation method (with optimal ω) in total number of operations required (see, e.g., [17.95, p. 1071]).

B.2.3. Convergence and Comparisons to Relaxation

It is easy to show [17.42] that gradient descent (B.10) with (B.11) is convergent for a positive definite matrix $\underline{A}$ to the solution $\underline{u}=\underline{A}^{-1}\underline{f}$ where the quadratic form E is minimized. On the other hand, we must be a little more careful with the fixed-α descent algorithm (B.12). The eigenvalues λ_i of its iteration matrix $\underline{G}$ are related to the eigenvalues λ_i of $\underline{A}$, all of which are positive (since $\underline{A}$ is positive definite), by $\lambda_i = 1 - \alpha\lambda_i$. Therefore, according to Theorem B.1, we obtain

Theorem B.5: necessary and sufficient condition for convergence

For a positive definite matrix $\underline{A}$, the fixed-α method of (B.12) is convergent if and only if $0 < \alpha < \dfrac{2}{\rho(\underline{A})}$.

Of course, convergence is quickest for that α which minimizes ($\underline{G}$), which often cannot be determined in practice.

By comparing (B.12) with the JACOBI method (B.3), we can convince ourselves that the two methods become identical when $\underline{A}$ is positive definite, has identical elements on its main diagonal (i.e., $\underline{D}=a\underline{I}$), and $\alpha=1/a$. Moreover, FORSYTHE and WASOW [17.34] (see also [17.97]) show that the GAUSS-SEIDEL and successive overrelaxation methods are also subject to interpretations as descent methods. In these cases, however, we have not one, but a set of direction vectors which turn out to be $\underline{x}_i$, the coordinate unit vectors of R^N. During each iteration, we take a sequence of steps of different sizes in each of these directions. The step sizes are such that $E(\underline{u}^{(k)} + \alpha_i^{(k)}\underline{x}_i)$ is minimized, and are given by $\alpha_i^{(k)} = r_i^{(k)}/a_{ii}$ for the GAUSS-SEIDEL method and $\alpha_i^{(k)} = \omega r_i^{(k)}/a_{ii}$ for the successive overrelaxation method, where $r_i^{(k)}$ is the ith element of the residual vector at iteration k.

The computation of an optimal $\alpha^{(k)}$ at each iteration according to (B.11) requires that $\underline{r}^{(k)}$ be stored and that $\underline{Ar}^{(k)}$ be evaluated. This doubles the amount of work required per iteration in comparison with a fixed-α algorithm or JACOBI relaxation. This raises the question: which is better in the long run; N iterations of gradient descent, or 2N iterations of the fixed or JACOBI relaxation? To decide the issue quantitatively, a convergence analysis ought to be attempted. This is problem dependent and is generally difficult to do, so we will simply note that FORSYTHE and WASOW [17.34, p. 225] do not recommend the optimization of α and, moreover, refer to a result by STIEFEL [17.98] indicating that it is, at best, a short-sighted strategy. Interestingly enough, GRIMSON [17.21] used the optimal-α algorithm in his implementation of the surface interpolation algorithm (with a minor modification to make certain that the fixed constraints are never modified, thus, in effect, treating them as essential boundary conditions). Considering the statements of FORSYTHE and WASOW, it is not surprising that extremely slow convergence was observed in spite of the extra work expended at each iteration to compute the optimal α.

Appendix C. Local FOURIER Analysis of Relaxation

In this appendix, we present the details of a local FOURIER analysis of GAUSS-SEIDEL relaxation and obtain the smoothing factor for this method. The analysis involves studying separately the convergence of the high-frequency FOURIER components. Since these components have short coupling ranges, we can perform the analysis in the interior of $\overline{\Omega}$, ignoring the effects of the boundary and the constraints.

According to (17.21) the minimizing displacement $u_{i,j}$ at an interior node (i,j) is related to the other nodes by

$$20u_{i,j}-8(u_{i-1,j}+u_{i+1,j}+u_{i,j-1}+u_{i,j+1})$$
$$+2(u_{i-1,j-1}+u_{i+1,j-1}+u_{i-1,j+1}+u_{i+1,j+1}) \qquad (C.1)$$
$$+1(u_{i-2,j}+u_{i+2,j}+u_{i,j-2}+u_{i,j+2})=0$$

(for convenience, we have suppressed the superscripts h). According to the discussion in Appendix B, at iteration k of the GAUSS-SEIDEL relaxation method, $v_{i,j}^{(k)}$ is replaced by a new value $v_{i,j}^{(k+1)}$ such that

$$20v_{i,j}^{(k+1)}-8(v_{i-1,j}^{(k+1)}+v_{i+1,j}^{(k)}+v_{i,j-1}^{(k+1)}+v_{i,j+1}^{(k)})$$
$$+2(v_{i-1,j-1}^{(k+1)}+v_{i+1,j-1}^{(k+1)}+v_{i-1,j+1}^{(k)}+v_{i+1,j+1}^{(k)}) \qquad (C.2)$$
$$+1(v_{i-2,j}^{(k+1)}+v_{i+2,j}^{(k)}+v_{i,j-2}^{(k+1)}+v_{i,j+2}^{(k)})=0 \quad .$$

The errors of the approximation at iteration k and iteration k+1 are given by

$$e_{i,j}^{(k)} = u_{i,j}-v_{i,j}^{(k)} \qquad \text{and} \qquad e_{i,j}^{(k+1)}=u_{i,j}-v_{i,j}^{(k+1)}$$

respectively. Subtracting (C.2) from (C.1), we obtain

$$20e_{i,j}^{(k+1)}-8(e_{i-1,j}^{(k+1)}+e_{i+1,j}^{(k)}+e_{i,j-1}^{(k+1)}+e_{i,j+1}^{(k)})$$
$$+2(e_{i-1,j-1}^{(k+1)}+e_{i+1,j-1}^{(k+1)}+e_{i-1,j+1}^{(k)}+e_{i+1,j+1}^{(k)}) \qquad (C.3)$$
$$+1(e_{i-2,j}^{(k+1)}+e_{i+2,j}^{(k)}+e_{i,j-2}^{(k+1)}+e_{i,j+2}^{(k)})=0 \quad .$$

Suppose that the error consists of only a single spatial FOURIER component $\vec{\omega} =[\omega_1,\omega_2]$. Then the errors at node (i,j) before and after the kth iteration are given by

$$e_{i,j}^{(k)}=A_{\vec{\omega}}^{(k)} e^{\iota(\omega_1 i+\omega_2 j)} \qquad \text{and} \qquad e_{i,j}^{(k+1)}=A_{\vec{\omega}}^{(k+1)} e^{\iota(\omega_1 i+\omega_2 j)} \qquad (C.4)$$

respectively, where $\iota = \sqrt{-1}$.

Substituting (C.4) and (C.3), dividing through by $e^{\iota(\omega_1 i + \omega_2 j)}$, and collecting terms pertaining to the same iteration, we obtain

$$A_{\vec{\omega}}^{(k)}(-8(e^{\iota\omega_1}+e^{\iota\omega_2})+2(e^{\iota(\omega_1+\omega_2)}+e^{\iota(-\omega_1+\omega_2)})+(e^{2\iota\omega_1}+e^{2\iota\omega_2}))$$

$$+A_{\vec{\omega}}^{(k+1)}(20-8(e^{-\iota\omega_1}+e^{-\iota\omega_2})$$

$$+2(e^{\iota(\omega_1-\omega_2)}+e^{\iota(-\omega_1-\omega_2)})+(e^{-2\iota\omega_1}+e^{-2\iota\omega_2}))=0 \ .$$

The amplification of the $\vec{\omega}$ component is then given by

$$\mu_{GS}(\vec{\omega}) = \left| \frac{A_{\vec{\omega}}^{(k+1)}}{A_{\vec{\omega}}^{(k)}} \right|$$

$$= \left| \frac{8(e^{\iota\omega_1}+e^{\iota\omega_2})-2(e^{\iota(\omega_1+\omega_2)}+e^{\iota(-\omega_1+\omega_2)})-(e^{2\iota\omega_1}+e^{2\iota\omega_2})}{20-8(e^{-\iota\omega_1}+e^{-\iota\omega_2})+2(e^{\iota(\omega_1-\omega_2)}+e^{\iota(-\omega_1-\omega_2)})+(e^{-2\iota\omega_1}+e^{-2\iota\omega_2})} \right| \ .$$

Let $|\vec{\omega}| = \max(|\omega_1|,|\omega_2|)$. The GAUSS-SEIDEL smoothing factor is defined as the smallest amplification attained for a high-frequency component of the error; that is, a component which is visible on the find grid, but is aliased on the coarse grid:

$$\bar{\mu}_{GS} = \max_{\frac{\pi}{4} \leq |\vec{\omega}| \leq \pi} \mu_{GS}(\vec{\omega}) \ .$$

Evaluating this expression numerically, we obtain $\bar{\mu}_{GS} \approx 0.8$ (for $\omega_1 = 1.6$ and $\omega_2 = 0.3$).

References

17.1 D. Marr: Early processing of visual information, Philosophical Trans. Royal Society (London) B275, 483-534 (1976)
17.2 D. Marr, T. Poggio: From understanding computation to understanding neural circuitry , Neurosciences Research Program Bulletin 15, Neuronal Mechanisms in Visual Perception, ed. by E. Poppe et al., 470-488 (1977)
17.3 D. Marr: Vision: A Computational Investigation into the Human Representation and Processing of Visual Information (Freeman, San Francisco, CA, 1982)
17.4 D. Marr, T. Poggio: A computational theory of human stereo vision, Proc. Royal Society (London) B204, 301-328 (1979)
17.5 S. Ullman: The Interpretation of Visual Motion (MIT Press, Cambridge, MA, 1979)
17.6 D. Marr, E. C. Hildreth: Theory of edge detection, Proc. Royal Society (London) B207, 187-217 (1980)
17.7 H. G. Barrow, J. M. Tenenbaum: "Recovering intrinsic scene characteristics from images", in Computer Vision Systems, ed. by A. R. Hanson, E. M. Riseman (Academic Press, New York, 1978) pp. 3-26
17.8 H. K. Nishihara: Intensity, visible surface, and volumetric representations, Artificial Intelligence 17, 265-284 (1981)
17.9 R. Nevatia, T. O. Binford: Description and recognition of curved objects, Artificial Intelligence 8, 77-98 (1977)

17.10 D. Marr, H. K. Nishihara: Representation and recognition of the spatial organization of three-dimensional shapes, Proc. Royal Society (London) B200, 269-294 (1978)

17.11 R. A. Brooks: Symbolic reasoning among 3-D models and 2-D images, Artificial Intelligence 17, 285-348 (1981)

17.12 E. C. Hildreth: "Implementation of a Theory of Edge Detection", Artificial Intelligence Laboratory TR-579, MIT (1980)

17.13 F. W. Campbell, J. G. Robson: Application of Fourier analysis to the visibility of gratings, J. Physiology (London) 197, 551-566 (1968)

17.14 H. R. Wilson, S. C. Giese: Threshold visibility of frequency grating patterns, Vision Research 17, 1177-1190 (1977)

17.15 D. Marr, T. Poggio, E. C. Hildreth: The smallest channel in early human vision, J. Optical Society America 70, 868-870 (1980)

17.16 J. E. W. Mayhew, J. P. Frisby: The computation of binocular edges, Perception 9, 69-86 (1980)

17.17 J. E. W. Mayhew, J. P. Frisby: Psychophysical and computational studies toward a theory of human steropsis, Artificial Intelligence 17, 349-385 (1981)

17.18 L. A. Riggs, E. W. Niehl: Eye movements recorded during convergence and divergence, J. Optical Society America 50, 913-920 (1960)

17.19 C. Rashbass, G. Westheimer: Disjunctive eye movements, J. Physiology (London) 159, 339-360 (1961)

17.20 R. H. S. Carpenter: Movements of the Eyes (Pion, London, 1977)

17.21 W. E. L. Grimson: From Images to Surfaces: A Computational Study of the Human Early Visual System (MIT Press, Cambridge, MA, 1981)

17.22 W. E. L. Grimson: A computational theory of visual surface interpolation, Philosophical Trans. Royal Society (London), to appear

17.23 S. Ullman: Relaxation and constrained optimization by local processes, Computer Graphics Image Processing 10, 115-125 (1979)

17.24 B. Julesz: Foundations of Cyclopean Perception (University of Chicago Press, Chicago, IL, 1971)

17.25 H. Wallach, D. N. O'Connell: The kinetic depth effect, J. Experimental Psychology 52, 571-578 (1953)

17.26 H. Wallach: The perception of motion, Scientific American 210 ( ), 56-60 (1959)

17.27 G. Johansson: Visual motion perception, Scientific American 232 (6), 76-88 (1975)

17.28 W. E. L. Grimson: "The Implicit Constraints of the Primal Sketch", Artificial Intelligence Laboratory Memo 663, MIT, to appear

17.29 R. Courant, D. Hilbert: Methods of Mathematical Physics Vol. 1 (Interscience, New York, 1953)

17.30 L. Landau, E. Lifshitz: Theory of Elasticity (Pergamon Press, Oxford, UK, 1970)

17.31 D. Hilbert, S. Cohn-Vossen: Geometry and the Imagination (Chelsea, New York, 1952)

17.32 K. Rektorys (ed.): Survey of Applicable Mathematics (Iliffe, London, 1969)

17.33 L. Collatz: The Numerical Treatment of Differential Equations, 3rd ed. (Springer, Berlin, 1966)

17.34 G. E. Forsythe, W. R. Wasow: Finite Difference Methods for Partial Differential Equations (Wiley, New York, 1960)

17.35 G. D. Smith: Numerical Solution of Partial Differential Equations, 2nd ed. (Clarendon Press, Oxford, UK, 1977)

17.36 P. G. Ciarlet: The Finite Element Method for Elliptic Problems (North Holland, Amsterdam, 1978)

17.37 K. Rektorys: Variational Methods in Mathematics, Science, and Engineering, 2nd ed. (Reidel, Dordrecht, Holland, 1980)

17.38 J. M. Brady, B. K. P. Horn: "Rotationally Symmetric Operators for Surface Interpolation," Artificial Intelligence Laboratory Memo 654, MIT (1981)

17.39 G. Strang, G. J. Fix: An Analysis of the Finite Element Method (Prentice-Hall, Englewood Cliffs, NJ, 1973)

17.40 O. C. Zienkiewicz: The Finite Element Method, 3rd ed. (McGraw-Hill, New York, 1977)

17.41 M. Abramowitz, I. A. Stegun (eds.): Handbook of Mathematical Functions (Dover, New York, 1965)

17.42 D. G. Luenberger: Introduction to Linear and Nonlinear Programming (Addison-Wesley, Reading, MA, 1973)

17.43 G. Dahlquist, A. Björck: Numerical Methods, transl. by N. Anderson (Prentice-Hall, Englewood Cliffs, NJ, 1974)

17.44 I. Gladwell, R. Wait (eds.): A Survey of Numerical Methods for Partial Differential Equations (Clarendon Press, Oxford, UK, 1979)

17.45 A. Brandt: Multilevel adaptive solutions to boundary-value problems, Math. Comp. $\underline{31}$, 333-390 (1977)

17.46 A. Brandt: "Multi-level adaptive techniques (MLAT) for partial differential equations: ideas and software", in Mathematical Software III, ed. by J. R. Rice (Academic Press, New York, 1977), pp. 277-318

17.47 A. Brandt, N. Dinar: "Multigrid solutions to elliptic flow problems", in Numerical Methods for Partial Differential Equations, ed. by S. V. Parter (Academic Press, New York, 1979), pp. 53-147

17.48 R. V. Southwell: Relaxation Methods in Theoretical Physics (Oxford University Press, Oxford, UK, 1946)

17.49 G. Westheimer: Diffraction theory and visual hyperacuity, American J. Optometry Physiological Optics $\underline{53}$, 362-364 (1976)

17.50 G. Westheimer, S. P. McKee: Visual acuity in the presence of retinal-image motion, J. Optical Society America $\underline{65}$, 847-850 (1975)

17.51 G. Westheimer, S. P. McKee: Integration regions for visual hyperacuity, Vision Research $\underline{17}$, 89-93 (1977)

17.52 H. B. Barlow: Reconstructing the visual image in space and time, Nature $\underline{279}$, 189-190 (1979)

17.53 F. H. C. Crick, D. Marr, T. Poggio: "An information processing approach to understanding the visual cortex", in The Organization of the Cerebral Cortex, ed. by F. O. Schmitt (MIT Press, Cambridge, MA, 1981), pp. 505-533

17.54 M. Fahle, T. Poggio: Visual hyperacuity: spatiotemporal interpolation in human vision, Proc. Royal Society (London) $\underline{B213}$, 451-477 (1981)

17.55 R. Courant: Variational methods for the solution of problems of equilibrium and vibrations, Bull. American Mathematical Society $\underline{49}$, 1-23 (1943)

17.56 I. Babuska: The finite element method with penalty functions, Math. Comp. $\underline{27}$, 221-228 (1973)

17.57 O. C. Zienkiewicz: "Constrained variational principles and penalty function methods in finite element analysis", in Proc. Conf. on the Numerical Solution of Differential Equations, ed. by G. A. Watson, Lecture Notes in Mathematics Vol. 363 (Springer, Berlin, 1974), pp. 207-214

17.58 W. E. L. Grimson: A computer implementation of a theory of human stereo vision, Philosophical Trans. Royal Society (London) $\underline{B292}$, 217-253 (1981)

17.59 J. H. Ahlberg, E. N. Nilson, J. L. Walsh: The Theory of Splines and their Applications (Academic Press, New York, 1967)

17.60 J. Duchon: Interpolation des fonctions de deux variables suivant le principe de la flexion des plaques minces, R.A.I.R.O. Analyse Numerique $\underline{10}$, 5-12 (1976)

17.61 J. Duchon: "Splines minimizing rotation-invariant semi-norms in Sobolev spaces", in Constructive Theory of Functions of Several Variables, ed. by A. Dodd, B. Eckmann (Springer, Berlin, 1977), pp. 85-100

17.62 J. Meinguet: "An intrinsic approach to multivariate spline interpolation at arbitrary points", in Polynomial and Spline Approximation: Theory and Applications, ed. by B. N. Sahney (Reidel, Dordrecht, Holland, 1979), pp. 163-190

17.63 J. Meinguet: Multivariate interpolation at arbitrary points made simple, J. Applied Mathematics Physics (ZAMP) 30, 292-304 (1979)

17.64 L. Schwartz: Théorie des Distributions (Hermann, Paris, 1966)

17.65 B. K. P. Horn: Determining lightness from an image, Computer Graphics Image Processing 3, 277-299 (1974)

17.66 K. Ikeuchi, B. K. P. Horn: Numerical shape form shading and occluding boundaries, Artifical Intelligence 17, 141-184 (1981)

17.67 B. K. P. Horn, B. G. Schunck: Determining optical flow, Artificial Intelligence 17, 185-203 (1981)

17.68 K. Ikeuchi: Determining surface orientations of specular surfaces by using the photometric stereo method, IEEE Trans. Pattern Analysis Machine Intelligence PAMI-3, 661-669 (1981)

17.69 R. L. Harder, R. N. Desmarais: Interpolation using surface splines, J. Aircraft 9, 189-191 (1972)

17.70 D. Waltz: "Understanding line drawings of scenes with shadows", in The Psychology of Computer Vision, ed. by P. H. Winston (McGraw-Hill, New York, 1975), pp. 19-91

17.71 A. Rosenfeld, R. Hummel, S. W. Zucker: Scene labeling by relaxation operations, IEEE Trans. Systems, Man, Cybernetics SMC-6, 420-433 (1976)

17.72 L. S. Davis, A. Rosenfeld: Cooperating processes for low-level vision: a survey, Artificial Intelligence 17, 245-263 (1981)

17.73 O. Faugeras, M. Berthod: Improving consistency and reducing ambiguity in stochastic labeling: an optimization approach, IEEE Trans. Pattern Analysis Machine Intelligence PAMI-3, 412-424 (1981)

17.74 R. A. Hummel, S. W. Zucker: "On the Foundations of Relaxation Labeling Processes", Computer Vision and Graphics Laboratory, Technical Report 80-7, McGill University (1980)

17.75 D. M. Young: Iterative Solution of Large Linear Systems (Academic Press, New York, 1971)

17.76 J. M. Ortega, W. C. Rheinboldt: Iterative Solution of Nonlinear Equations in Several Variables (Academic Press, New York, 1970)

17.77 S. W. Zucker: "Vertical and horizontal processes in low level vision", in Computer Vision Systems, ed. by A. R. Hanson, E. M. Riseman (Academic Press, New York, 1978), pp. 187-195

17.78 S. W. Zucker, J. L. Mohammed: "A hierarchical system for line labeling and grouping", in Proc. Image Processing and Pattern Recognition Conf., Chicago, IL, 1978, pp. 410-415

17.79 D. Marr: "Analysis of occluding contour", Proc. Royal Society (London) B197, 441-475 (1977)

17.80 B. K. P. Horn: "Obtaining shape from shading information", in The Psychology of Computer Vision, ed. by P. H. Winston (McGraw-Hill, New York, 1975), 115-155

17.81 J. R. Kender: "Shape from Texture", Ph.D. dissertation, Department of Computer Science, Carnegie-Mellon University (1980)

17.82 K. A. Stevens: The visual interpretation of surface contours, Artificial Intelligence 17, 47-73 (1981)

17.83 A. P. Witkin: Recovering surface shape and orientation from texture, Artificial Intelligence 17, 17-45 (1981)

17.84 T. Kanade: Recovery of the three-dimensional shape of an object from a single view, Artifical Intelligence 17, 409-460 (1981)

17.85 E. H. Mansfield: The Bending and Stretching of Plates (Macmillan, New York, 1964)

17.86 J. T. Oden, J. N. Reddy: An Introduction to the Mathematical Theory of the Finite Element Method (Wiley, New York, 1976)

17.87 S. Agmon: Lectures on Elliptic Boundary Value Problems (Van Nostrand, New York, 1965)

17.88 R. A. Adams: Sobolev Spaces (Academic Press, New York, 1975)

17.89 J. T. Oden: Applied Functional Analysis (Prentice-Hall, Englewood Cliffs, NJ, 1979)

17.90 K. Yosida: Functional Analysis, 3rd ed. (Springer, Berlin, 1971)

17.91 B. A. Finlayson: The Method of Weighted Residuals and Variational Principles (Academic Press, New York, 1972)

17.92 S. G. Mikhlin: Variational Methods in Mathematical Physics (Pergamon Press, Oxford, UK, 1964)

17.93 W. Ritz: Ueber eine neue Methode zur Lösung gewisser Variationsprobleme der mathematischen Physik, J. Reine Angew. Math. 135 (1908)

17.94 R. S. Varga: Matrix Iterative Analysis (Prentice-Hall, Englewood Cliffs, NJ, 1962)

17.95 D. M. Young, R. T. Gregory: A Survey of Numerical Mathematics Vols. 1-2 (Addison-Wesley, Reading, MA 1972-1973)

17.96 M. R. Hestenes, E. Stiefel: Method of conjugate gradients for solving linear systems, J. Research National Bureau Standards 49, 409-436 (1952)

17.97 W. E. Milne: Numerical Solution of Differential Equations, 2nd ed. (Dover, New York, 1970)

17.98 E. Stiefel: Relaxationsmethoden bester Strategie zur Lösung linearer Gleichungssysteme, Comment. Math. Helv. 29, 157-179 (1955)

Part VI

Time-Varying Analysis

18. Multilevel Relaxation in Low-Level Computer Vision

F. Glazer

University of Massachusetts, Amherst, MA 01002, USA

Variational (cost minimization) and local constraint approaches are generally
applicable to problems in low-level vision (e.g., computation of intrinsic
images). Iterative relaxation algorithms are "natural" choices for implementation because they can be executed on highly parallel and locally connected processors. They may, however, require a very large number of iterations to attain convergence. Multilevel relaxation techniques converge
much faster and are well suited to processing in cones or pyramids. These
techniques are applied to the problem of computing optic flow from dynamic
images.

18.1 Introduction

Much work in low-level computer vision has involved the dense interpolation
or approximation of sparsely known or noisy data. A few examples are image
smoothing [18.1], surface interpolation [18.2-4], and optic flow computation
[18.5]. A recent approach to these problems has formulated them in terms of
optimization or constrained minimization. In general these techniques are
equivalent to solving elliptic partial differential equations (PDEs) with
boundary conditions and constraints.

In either formulation, these problems can be solved by a class of algorithms well suited to computer vision. It includes the GAUSS-SEIDEL iterative
method [18.6], and assorted variants. These methods are local, parallel,
and distributed, attributes which make them ideal for implementation on
locally connected parallel processors. They have one attribute, however,
that currently limits their applicability. The number of iterations required for convergence is often very high -- on the order of $O(d**n)$, where
d is the distance (in nodes) that information has to travel and n is the
order of the PDEs being solved [18.7, p. 281].

In the problem domain of elliptic PDEs this slowness has been overcome
by using multilevel relaxation algorithms [18.7,8]. In this approach, a
standard iterative algorithm is applied on grids of different resolution
all of which cover the data in registration. At each level the problem
is solved in a different spatial bandwidth. Thus, the various processing
levels cooperate to compute the final result, which is represented at the
highest resolution level. The number of iterations required is of order
$O(d)$.

Given the value of multilevel relaxation in solving elliptic PDEs with
boundary conditions, we are interested in the extension of these techniques

*This research was supported in part by the National Science Foundation under
 Grant MCS-79-18209 and by DARPA under Grant N00014-82-K-0464.

to problems of optimization, constrained minimization, and PDEs with obstruction (points through which the solution must pass). Our work in areas such as computing optic flow, interpolating sparse displacement data (for motion analysis and geometric correction), and object surface reconstruction has led us to study how multilevel methods can be applied to these more difficult problems. We will present a discussion of this along with preliminary results in the specific problem domain of computing optic flow.

Regular hierarchical structures, such as multilevel grids of varying levels of resolution, are established computational architectures in computer vision [18.9,10]. These have included processing architectures [18.11], data structures [18.12,13], and algorithms [18.14-17]. They are founded on cellular array architectures which provide high-speed efficient processing for image-oriented operations. Beyond this, they add multiple levels of spatial resolution [18.11,12,15-17] and selective attention mechanisms [18.12-14].

HANSON and RISEMAN's processing cone [18.11] is a parallel array computer hierarchically organized into layers of decreasing spatial resolution. It is designed to provide parallel processing power both locally (fine resolution) and globally to varying degrees (coarse resolutions). TANIMOTO and PAVLIDIS' pyramids [18.12] are sequences of digitizations of the same image at increasingly higher degrees of spatial resolution. KLINGER and DYER's regular decompositions [18.13] (later, quad trees) divide a picture area into successively smaller quadrants. In these last two cases, the data structures were used to provide a coarse-to-fine focus of attention which significantly speeded up recognition algorithms such as edge finding and object detection. This idea had been used earlier in KELLY's edge detection algorithm [18.14], which used edges in a coarsened image as a "plan" in locating edges in higher-resolution versions of the same image. WONG and HALL [18.15] did scene matching by correlation in a hierarchy of reduced-resolution images. Matches found in the coarse-resolution images constrained the search for matches at finer resolutions. This algorithm matched scenes which were difficult for standard correlation techniques and did so with far fewer computations. MARR and POGGIO [18.16] presented another hierarchical matching algorithm as a theory of human stereo vision based on the matching of edges between a pair of images. Edges detected in coarse-resolution channels are matched, and the matches are used to control eye vergence movements, thus allowing finer-resolution channels to match unambiguous edge pairs. Finally, BURT [18.17] has developed pyramid-based algortihms for multiresolution low-pass and bandpass filtering which are low in both cost and complexity. He has shown how these techniques can be applied to feature extraction, image compression, image merging, scene matching, and motion detection.

18.2 A Common Ground

In this section we describe a number of problems, approaches, and algorithms, covering a range of recent work in low-level computer vision. These methods are not entirely analogous in their development; hence a single, general formulation is not attempted. Instead, we try to provide a unifying framework within which various methods can be viewed. To motivate this framework we first present some specific examples of recent work.

18.2.1 Four Examples

NARAYANAN et al. [18.1] approached the problem of smoothing noisy images in the following way. Given a noisy image $F(x,y)$, find an approximation $G(x,y)$ which minimizes the total error measure

313

$$\sum_{x,y} [R^2 + a* (F - G)^2] \tag{18.1}$$

where $R(x,y)$ is a roughness measure of G, computed for a neighborhood of each point, and a is a relative weighting factor. The first term penalizes roughness of G, while the second term penalizes deviation of the approximation G from the data F. The roughness measures used were discrete approximations to 1) the Laplacian, 2) the gradient magnitude, and 3) a measure of strong corners (viz. $G_{xx}*G_{yy} - G_{xy}^2$). A steepest-descent method was used to minimize the above cost functional.[1]

In his theory of visual surface interpolation, GRIMSON formulated the problem as one of finding surfaces $S(x,y)$ having minimum total curvature and passing through (interpolation) or near (approximation) points of known depth. Approximation was formulated as minimization of the functional

$$\int \int (S_{xx}^2 + 2S_{xx}^2 + S_{yy}^2)dxdy + B* \sum_{P} [S(x,y) - C(x,y)]^2 \tag{18.2}$$

where P is the set of points with known depth $C(x,y)$. The discrete version of this minimization problem was solved using the conjugate gradient algorithm [18.18]. Interpolation was formulated as constrained minimization of the functional

$$\int \int (S_{xx}^2 + 2S_{xy}^2 + S_{yy}^2) \, dxdy \tag{18.3}$$

constrained to $S(x,y) = C(x,y)$ in P. The discrete version of this constrained minimization problem was solved using the gradient projection algorithm [18.18].

IKEUCHI approached the problem of shape from shading as follows [18.3,4]. Given a brightness image $I(x,y)$, a reflectance map $R(f,g)$, and an occluding contour dA, find the surface orientation $(F(x,y),G(x,y))$ in A which minimizes the functional

$$\sum_{x,y} [I - R(F,G)]^2 + a*[(\nabla F)^2 + (\nabla G)^2] \tag{18.4}$$

where ∇ is a discrete gradient. The first term of the functional penalizes deviation from the image irradiance/reflectance equation $I(x,y) = R(f,g)$. The second term penalizes roughness of F and G. This minimization problem was solved by setting the gradient of the functional to 0 and using GAUSS-SEIDEL iteration to solve the resulting system of linear equations.

Finally we consider HORN and SCHUNCK's method of determining optic flow given a dynamic image $E(x,y,t)$ [18.5]. Their approach is to find the optic flow vector $(U(x,y),V(x,y))$ which minimizes the functional

$$\int \int (E_x U + E_y V + E_t)^2 + a * [|\nabla U|^2 + |\nabla V|^2] \, dxdy \, . \tag{18.5}$$

The first term in the functional is the square of the rate of change of image brightness (measured in 3D space-time of the dynamic image space). When $E_x U + E_y V + E_t = 0$, spatial image brightness changes are due purely to motion. The second term is a roughness measure of U and V, where ∇ is the gradient operator and a is a relative weighting factor. The EULER equations were derived for this problem and a finite difference approximation produced a sys-

---

1. See [18.18] for a general discussion of optimization methods.

tem of linear equations that was solved using GAUSS-SEIDEL iteration. This
particular example is discussed in depth in Sect.18.4.

18.2.2 The General Framework

We will now consider a framework that makes plain the similarities and
differences among the methods described above. Figure 18.1 diagrams the major
relationships. Each box is labeled by a general technique or method. Within
each box a specific example is shown. The examples refer to the same problem
in each case, viz. the solution of LAPLACE's equation or its variational equivalent.

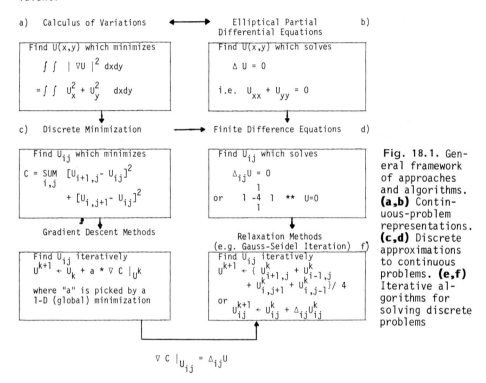

a)   Calculus of Variations ⟷ Elliptical Partial   b)
                                   Differential Equations

Find U(x,y) which minimizes

$$\int \int \; | \; \nabla U \; |^2 \; dxdy$$

$$= \int \int \; U_x^2 + U_y^2 \quad dxdy$$

Find U(x,y) which solves

$$\Delta \; U = 0$$

i.e. $U_{xx} + U_{yy} = 0$

c)   Discrete Minimization ⟶ Finite Difference Equations d)

Find U_{ij} which minimizes

$$C = \underset{i,j}{SUM} \; [U_{i+1,j} - U_{ij}]^2$$

$$+ [U_{i,j+1} - U_{ij}]^2$$

Gradient Descent Methods

Find U_{ij} iteratively
$$U^{k+1} \leftarrow U_k + a * \nabla C \; |_{U^k}$$

where "a" is picked by a
1-D (global) minimization

Find U_{ij} which solves

$$\Delta_{ij} U = 0$$

or $\begin{array}{ccc} & 1 & \\ 1 & -4 & 1 \\ & 1 & \end{array}$ ** $U=0$

Relaxation Methods
(e.g. Gauss-Seidel Iteration) f)

Find U_{ij} iteratively
$$U^{k+1}_{ij} \leftarrow \{ U^k_{i+1,j} + U^k_{i-1,j} + U^k_{i,j+1} + U^k_{i,j-1} \}/ 4$$

or $U^{k+1}_{ij} \leftarrow U^k_{ij} + \Delta_{ij} U^k_{ij}$

Fig. 18.1. Gen-
eral framework
of approaches
and algorithms.
(a,b) Contin-
uous-problem
representations.
(c,d) Discrete
approximations
to continuous
problems. **(e,f)**
Iterative al-
gorithms for
solving discrete
problems

$$\nabla C \; |_{U_{ij}} = \Delta_{ij} U$$

18.2.2.1 The Continuous Case

Variational calculus and elliptic partial differential equations (EPDEs)
represent the problem in a continuous domain. In general a variational problem can be reduced to a partial differential equation given by EULER's equation [18.19, p. 183] (Fig.18.1a,b). These PDEs are elliptic in all of the
cases we consider. Moreover, for any EPDE a corresponding variational problem can be constructed. Thus we are free to start our analysis on either
side in the top row of Fig.18.1. Both GRIMSON and HORN and SCHUNCK began
their analyses with variational problem statements.

18.2.2.2 Discrete Approximations

The introduction of finite difference approximations in place of continuous
derivatives transforms both variational problems and EPDEs into discrete

problems as shown in the middle row of Fig.18.1. The integral in a variational problem becomes a summation over a discrete set of grid points (Fig.
18.1a,c). In Fig.18.1c this gives a summation, over the 2-D grid indices i
and j, of first finite difference approximations of the horizontal and
vertical partial derivatives.

In Fig.18.1d we see that the EPDE generates a separate equation for each
grid point relating that point to its immediate neighbors. Δ_{ij} refers to a
discrete Laplacian on the i,j grid. The bottom line in that box expresses
this set of equations as a 2-D convolution with the 5-point Laplacian mask.
This system of equations can also be generated from the discrete functional
by computing its gradient (considered as a function of all the grid point
variables) and setting it equal to the 0-vector -- this being a necessary
condition for the existence of a minimum. This operation takes us from
Fig. 18.1c to Fig. 18.1d. It is analogous to using the first variation of the
continuous functional to derive the corresponding PDE. IKEUCHI takes this
path.

18.2.2.3 Algorithms

Finally, we come to specific algorithms for solving these discrete problems.
Consider first the system of finite difference equations in Fig. 18.1d. This
system is a large matrix equation Ax=b, where the vector x contains all of
the grid point variables, A is a sparse banded matrix containing the finite
difference coefficients, and b is a vector of right-hand sides which can include forcing terms, boundary conditions, or obstructions. Although many
methods exist for solving such a system of equations, the requirements of
low-level vision problems quickly narrow our choice. In particular, iterative relaxation algorithms, being local and parallel, are natural candidates
given the computational constraints of a vision system. Both IKEUCHI and
HORN and SCHUNCK uses GAUSS-SEIDEL iteration to solve their equations.

Now consider minimization of the discrete functional in Fig.18.1c. This
is a problem that can be solved using the techniques of mathematical programming (also known as nonlinear programming and cost minimization) [18.18].
These methods use an iterative scheme involving a two-step cycle: 1) pick a
"direction" to search for the minimum, and 2) perform a one-dimensional search
along that direction. Two common methods for choosing the search direction
are the steepest descent (gradient) method and the conjugate gradient method.
The former method is used by NARAYANAN et al. while GRIMSON uses the latter.
Steepest descent is shown in the box of Fig. 18.1e where the current iteration
U^k is updated by an optimal multiple of the gradient of C evaluated at U^k.

An interesting parallel can now be seen between gradient descent and relaxation methods. As the arrow joining the two lower boxes in Fig.18.1 indicates, computing the gradient of the cost functional is essentially equivalent to two-dimensional convolution with the discrete finite difference
operator (up to a scale factor). The only difference we see in the two
methods is the application of a one-dimensional minimization procedure along
the direction of the gradient in the gradient descent method. When the
functional is quadratic this minimization can be computed directly [18.1,2].
Unfortunately this computation is a global one in that it uses the full
current solution estimate and gradient images. In contrast, relaxation
methods remain strictly local. The use of a global factor does provide
faster convergence.

18.2.2.4 The Finite-Element Method

An alternative path from variational problems to relaxation on linear systems of equations is given by the finite-element method. A good example of

316

this can be found in TERZOPOULOS' extension of GRIMSON's work [18.20]. While not equivalent to finite difference methods, FEMs do produce similar systems of equations which can be solved with relaxation methods, thus providing an alternate path from (a) to (d) in Fig. 18.1.

18.2.3 An Aside on Constraints

We must distinguish between three types of constraints that determine a problem -- boundary conditions, obstructions, and inherent constraints.[2]

Inherent constraints are those that are represented in the form of the variational problem or PDE. All of the problems we have discussed involve an inherent constraint of smoothness of the solution. The order of this smoothness can be defined as the order of the partial derivatives in the functional. First-order smoothness typically uses the gradient magnitude as in [18.1,4,5] and leads to second order EPDEs (e.g., LAPLACE's equation). Second-order smoothness constraints are seen in GRIMSON's functionals where the corresponding EPDE is the biharmonic equation

$$\Delta^2 U = U_{xxxx} + 2U_{xxyy} + U_{yyyy} = 0 \; .$$

Smoothness conditions constrain the solution in local neighborhoods. The other case of inherent constraint we see is a pointwise one derived from some relationship that must hold (as well as possible) between the solution sur- face and the data. NARAYANAN's formulation requires a solution near the ini- tial data (a relationship of equality). IKEUCHI's requires surface orienta- tion and image intensity to relate according to the reflectance map. HORN and SCHUNCK require optic flow vectors to lie near the velocity constraint line in velocity space.

The second type of constraint is the boundary condition. These conditions constrain the solution along the boundary of the domain within which a solu- tion is to be found. Typical conditions include the vanishing of the func- tion and/or its derivative normal to the boundary (the DIRICHLET and NEUMANN conditions). Boundary conditions are determined both by explicit specifica- tion (essential boundary conditions) and as an implicit consequence of the particular variational problem or PDE (natural boundary conditions).

It may seem that boundary conditions are an unfortunate complication in low-level vision problems since processing should be independent of the loca- tion of the retinal boundary. We would argue that this is too limiting an idea of where boundaries occur. They should be viewed as demarcating regions within which the inherent constraints are to hold. This can be seen in IKEUCHI's work where boundaries were placed at the occluding contours in an image. What if the occluding contours are not known in advance? We are then faced with a key problem that remains to be addressed in our framework. Consider the smoothness constraints used by GRIMSON and HORN and SCHUNCK. Dependent as they are on the continuity of objects (which holds almost every- where in the image), these conditions break down across occluding boundaries. Enforcing smoothness across these boundaries corrupts the solution well into the adjacent regions. It remains to be seen whether these conditions can be detected and whether a general approach to this problem exists.

The final type of constraint is the obstruction or obstacle. We see a specific case of this in GRIMSON's interpolation where the smooth surface is constrained to pass through points of known depth. Generally, such a con-

---

2. A fourth type, the isoperimetric condition [18.19], is not listed here since it does not typically occur in the class of problems we are considering.

straint is given by a) a subdomain A_1 of the full domain A, b) a function $C(x,y)$ over the subdomain A_1, and c) an inequality between the solution $S(x,y)$ and $C(x,y)$ that must hold within A_1. Another example of this is YACHIDA's [10.21] use of exact optic flow estimates derived from prominent feature points in his variant of the HORN and SCHUNCK method. These known vectors were used as "fixed points" or seeds that did not change value during the course of iteration.

18.3 Multilevel Relaxation

We have seen how various problems in low-level computer vision can be formulated as continuous or discrete variational problems and equivalently as partial differential or finite difference equations. Iterative relaxation algorithms are then "natural" choices for solving these problems since they are local, parallel, and distributed. Unfortunately, the number of iterations necessary for convergence can be very high -- on the order of $O(d**n)$, where d is the distance (in nodes) that information has to travel and n is the order of the PDEs being solved. GRIMSON's algorithm, requiring second-order smoothness, takes thousands of iterations to approach final solutions.[3] This slowness is due to the fact that solutions which must satisfy a global condition (the variational problem) are arrived at by the local propagation of information.

Mulilevel relaxation is an algorithmic existension of iterative relaxation designed to overcome asymptotically slow convergence. By representing the spatial domain at multiple levels of resolution (in registration) these algorithms apply the basic local iterative update to a range of neighborhood sizes. Local updates on coarser grids introduce a more global propagation of information.

In the basic multilevel method the domain of definition A of the problem is represented discretely by a set of uniform square grids $G^0,...,G^K,...,G^M$ with grid sizes $h_0,...,h_k,...,h_M$. Each grid covers the full domain and we assume that $h_i:h_{i+1}=2:1$. Suppose we have a PDE we wish to solve over A, say

$$\Delta U(x,y) = 0 \quad \text{or more generally} \quad LU(\overline{x}) = F(\overline{x}) \tag{18.6}$$

where L is a general linear differential operator and U and F are vector-valued functions over R^n.

On each grid G^k we can form the finite difference approximation to these PDEs:

$$\Delta_k U_{ij} = 0 \quad \text{or} \quad L^k U^k(\overline{x}) = F(\overline{x}) \qquad k=0,...,M . \tag{18.7}$$

The discrete approximation on a coarse grid G^k approximates the same problem on the finest grid G^M. This fact was used long ago by engineers in the block relaxation method. In this method the solution on a coarse grid is used as the initial estimate for the finest resolution problem. Such an approach can be applied at multiple levels of resolution.

BRANDT [8.7,8] significantly extended the multilevel approach by showing how the coarser grid can be used in the process of improving the first approxi-

---

3. This number is based on the author's experiments. See also [18.20].

mation on G^M. He combined these ideas and developed iterative schemes that move up and down a cone of multiple grids.

If we look a little more closely at the nature of convergence in an iterative relaxation algorithm, we see that sharp (high-frequency) changes or errors are quickly smoothed. This is due to the local nature of the smoothing. It is the slow (low-frequency) error components that resist elimination. These ideas can be formalized in a local mode analysis of the particular update equation [18.7,8] whereby the error reduction is considered as a function of spatial frequency. The theory of multilevel relaxation is based on these ideas and on the fact that one grid's coarse resolution is another grid's fine. After a few iterations on a given grid, high-frequency error is considerably reduced while low-frequency error remains. At this point we can approximate the remaining problem on a coarser grid. The remaining error is at a higher frequency on the coarse grid, hence further relaxation at this level can reduce it effectively. When convergence is attained at the coarse level, that solution can be interpolated back to the fine level. This interpolation introduces some high-frequency error which is easily reduced by a few more iterations. These processes easily generalize to multilevel cyclic algorithms running on a cone of grids. Approximate solutions are sent down the cone to finer levels after they have converged. When convergence slows at finer levels they are sent up the cone for coarser processing. The role of relaxation in such a system is not to reduce the error, but to smooth it out; i.e., to reduce high-frequency components of the error. Lower frequencies are reduced on coarser grids. What is essentially happening in such a system is that different grid levels solve the problem in different spatial frequency bands.[4]

Following BRANDT's development [18.5],[5] let u^M be an approximate solution of the G^M problem and let

$$L^M u^M = F^M - f^M \qquad\qquad (18.8)$$

where the discrepancy f^M is called the residual. Assuming L is a linear operator, the exact discrete solution is $\bar{U}^M = u^M + V^M$, where the correction V^M satisfies the residual equation $L^M V^M = f^M$. If u^M is computed by some relaxation iterations on G^M then f^M has little high-frequency content (relative to the grid size h_M). This allows the residual equation to be accurately approximated on a coarser grid. The optimal time to perform this switch to a coarser grid occurs when the residual f^M is smoothed out and convergence has slowed down. Relaxation on the coarse grid produces an approximation v^k of the correction V^M. An improved level M solution is then obtained by interpolating v^k to level M and adding this interpolated correction to u^M.

A simple multilevel relaxation algorithm based on these ideas, called Cycle C [18.18], is shown in Fig.18.2. In this notation, I^k_{k-1} interpolates level k-1 data down to level k (coarse to fine), while I^k_{k+1} interpolates level k+1 data up to level k (fine to coarse). The basic rule in Cycle C is that each v^k (the function defined on the grid G^k; $k = 0,...,M-1$) is designed to serve as a correction for the approximate v^{k+1} previously obtained on the next finer grid G^{k+1}. The equation to be (approximately) satisfied by v^k is

---

4. This particular idea breaks down on nonlinear probelms. However, the multilevel approach does generalize. All of the problems we are considering are linear.

5. We will only show how the PDE approximation is handled. The equations (and algorithm) for the boundary conditions are handled in a similar manner.

```
k ← M                          ; start at finest level          Fig. 18.2. Cycle
f^k ← F^M                      ; initial RHS                    C, multilevel re-
v^k ← u^M                      ; initial solution estimate      laxation
Until v^M has converged Do
   Begin
      v^k ← Relax [ L^k . = f^k] v^k          ; a relaxation "sweep"
      If v^k has converged Then
         If k<M Then
            k ← k+1                            ; go down one level
            v^k ← v^k + I_{k-1}^k v^{k-1}      ; add interpolated correction
         Else if convergence is slow Then
            If k>0 Then
               k ← k-1                         ; go up one level
               v^k ← 0                         ; initial estimate
               f^k ♪ I_{k+1}^k(f^{k+1} - L^{k+1}v^{k+1})   ; new RHS
         End if
   End
```

$$L^k v^k = f^k \tag{18.9}$$

where f^k approximates the residual left by v^{k+1}, that is

$$f^k = I_{k+1}^k (f^{k+1} - L^{k+1} v^{k+1}) . \tag{18.10}$$

The equation on G^k is thus defined in terms of the approximate solution on G^{k+1}. On the finest grid, the equation is the original one:

$$f^M = F^M . \tag{18.11}$$

Convergence is measured using the Euclidean (L_2) norm of the residual function which we will call the residual norm. The rate of convergence is measured as the ratio of consecutive residual norms from one iteration to the next. Convergence is "slow" when this ratio rises above a threshold parameter (0.6 in our experiments and in [18.18]). Convergence at the finest level is defined by a user-supplied tolerance (threshold) below which the residual norm must fall. Convergence at an intermediate level is defined by a dynamic threshold. This coarse-level threshold is set, when we pass up the cone a level, to a fraction of the current residual norm at the fine level. This fraction is another parameter in the algorithm (0.3 in our experiments and in [18.8]). BRANDT claims robustness of such algorithms to the extent that variations of these two parameter settings produce little qualitative change in performance.

The two parameterized decisions that are used in controlling the cycles are based on global computations, i.e., they are computed from the current solution estimate over the entire grid. It will be seen later that, as BRANDT has pointed out, for some problems we can forego the computation of the residual norm and thus attain a purely local and parallel computation.

In the basic Cycle C algorithm an approximate solution only exists on the fine-level grid. All coarser levels deal only in correction surfaces which approximate solutions for changing residual equations. BRANDT also developed FAS (Full Approximation Storage) algorithms in which each grid level stores the full current approximation. This approximation u^k is the sum of the correction v^k and its base approximation u^{k+1}:

320

$$u^k = I_{k+1}^k u^{k+1} + v^k \qquad (k = 0,1,\ldots,M-1) \; . \tag{18.12}$$

Using these full-approximation functions, the correction equations can now be rewritten as

$$L^k U^k = \overline{F}^k \qquad \text{where} \tag{18.13}$$

$$\overline{F}^k = L^k(I_{k+1}^k u^{k+1}) + I_{k+1}^k(\overline{F}^{k+1} - L^{k+1} u^{k+1}) \qquad k = 0,\ldots,M-1 \tag{18.14}$$

and

$$\overline{F}^M = F^M \; . \tag{18.15}$$

For linear problems equations (18.9-11) are equivalent to (18.13-15). One advantage of the FAS method is that equations (18.13-15) apply equally well to nonlinear problems [18.8, p. 347].

A key aspect of the FAS method is that the function stored on a coarse grid G^k approximates the fine grid solution in that $u^k = I_M^k u^M$. These functions, at varying levels of resolution, provide a hierarchy of descriptions of the solution. This makes the FAS-type methods particularly appealing to problems in computer vision where structures of interest in the image can occur at many sizes. For this reason, we have chosen to work with FAS methods. The FAS generalization of the Cycle C algorithm is shown in Fig. 18.3.

```
k ← M                                    ; start at finest level
Fᵏ ← Fᴹ                                  ; initial RHS
vᵏ ← uᴹ                                  ; initial solution estimate
Until uᴹ has converged Do
  Begin
    uᵏ ← Relax [ Lᵏ . = Fᵏ] uᵏ           ; a relaxation "sweep"
    If uᵏ has converged Then

      If k<M Then
        k ← k+1                          ; go down one level
        uᵏ ← uᵏ + Iᵏ_{i-1}(uᵏ⁻¹-Iᵏ⁻¹_k uᵏ)   ; add correction

      If k>0 Then
        k ← k-1                          ; go up one level
        uᵏ ← Iᵏ_{k+1}uᵏ⁺¹                ; initial estimate
        Fᵏ ← Iᵏ_{k+1}(Fᵏ⁺¹ - Lᵏ⁺¹uᵏ⁺¹) + Lᵏuᵏ   ; new RHS
      End if
    End if
  End
```

Fig. 18.3. Cycle C/Full Approximation Storage, multilevel relaxation

18.3.1 An Example: LAPLACE's Equation

Consider the standard example problem of solving LAPLACE's equation with a fixed boundary condition: find $U(x,y)$ satisfying

$$\Delta U(x,y) = 0 \qquad \text{on the domain A} \tag{18.16}$$

and

$$U(x,y) = C(x,y) \quad \text{for } x,y \text{ in } dA \tag{18.17}$$

where dA is the boundary of A. This specific problem and its various equivalents appear in the boxes in Fig.18.1. Figure 18.4 shows the results of performing GAUSS-SEIDEL relaxation on a finite difference approximation to equation (18.16) (as formulated in the lower right-hand box of Fig.18.1). Intermediate stages in the iteration are shown in Fig.18.4a with the initial solution estimate (all zeros in the interior of A; A-dA) labeled as iteration 0. The residual norm is plotted against iteration number in Fig.18.4b. In both types of display we see an initial large reduction in error followed by a prolonged slow convergence. In the surface plot, the quick smoothing of sharp changes in the first few iterations is apparent.

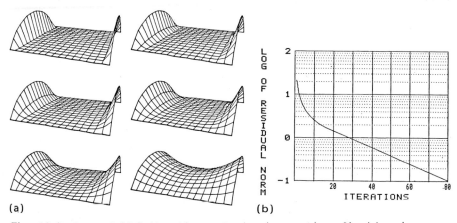

(a)   (b)

Fig. 18.4. Gauss-Seidel iteration on Laplace's equation, fixed boundary. **(a)** Initial data (iteration 0) and iterations 1, 2, 5, 10 and 100. **(b)** Semilog graph of residual norm vs. iteration number

The same problem was run under the Cycle C/FAS multilevel relaxation algorithm. Results are shown in Fig.18.5 and Fig.18.6. The surface plots show various stages of the computation at different levels. The progress of the algorithm is measured in <u>work units</u>. At the finest level one work unit is defined as one iteration. One level up it takes four work units to equal one iteration. This reflects the fact that only one-fourth as much processing is done at that level since processing is proportional to the number of nodes in the grid. In general an iteration at level k costs $(1/4)^{M-k}$ work units. The residual norm is plotted against iterations in Fig.18.6a. Each iteration is labeled with the level at which relaxation took place. Note that interpolation down the cone (increasing level number) introduces a temporary increase in error. This high-frequency interpolation error is quickly smoothed by a few relaxation iterations. Figure 18.6b also plots residual norm versus iterations but the iteration axis is labeled by work units. This gives a better indication of the work involved in reaching a given residual error.

A comparison of single and multilevel relaxation is given in Fig. 18.7. Residual norm for both experiments is plotted against iteration number. The multilevel algorithm clearly converges faster. The situation is even better than the graph indicates in that the comparison is based on iterations and not work units. In the single-grid algorithm one iteration equals one work unit while in the multigrid experiment work units accumulate much more slowly (see Fig.18.6b).

322

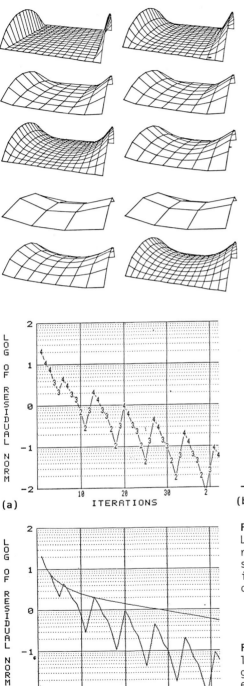

Fig. 18.5. Multilevel relaxation on Laplace's equation,
fixed boundary. Selected intermediate iterations labeled
by work number

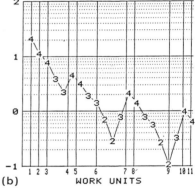

Fig. 18.6. Multilevel relaxation on
Laplace's equation. **(a)** Residual
norm vs. iteration number. **(b)** Residual norm vs. iteration with
iteration axis labeled with the
corresponding work numbers

Fig. 18.7. Multilevel vs. single-
level Gauss-Seidel relaxation. This
graph compares the results of the
experiments shown in Figs. 18.4, 5,
and 6

18.4 Multilevel Optic Flow Computation

The optic flow field is a vector field defined over the image space. It specifies the instantaneous velocity of the corresponding image component. Originally it was defined by GIBSON as the projection of the velocities of the environmental objects being imaged.

18.4.1 An Optic Flow PDE

Let us represent the optic flow field as $(U,V) = (U(x,y),V(x,y))$ where U is the x component of velocity and V is the y component. Let the dynamic image be given as $E(x,y,t)$. Consider the total derivative of E:

$$\frac{dE}{dt} = E_x U + E_y V + E_t \; . \tag{18.18}$$

This equation relates the gradient of the dynamic image E to the optic flow field (U,V). It also tells us the rate at which E is changing along the direction of motion in the (dynamic) image. Under simple viewing conditions (e.g., orthographic projection and single distant light source) we expect the projection of an environmental point to remain at a constant intensity, i.e., $dE/dt = 0$ and so

$$E_x U + E_y V + E_t = 0 \; . \tag{18.19}$$

This equation specifies a line in U,V velocity space called the <u>velocity constraint line</u>. This line is perpendicular to the spatial gradient $\overline{(E_x,E_y)}$. The vector perpendicular to this line with length equal to the distance between the line and the origin is

$$\left(\frac{-E_x E_t}{(E_x^2 + E_y^2)^{1/2}} \; , \; \frac{-E_y E_t}{(E_x^2 + E_y^2)^{1/2}} \right) \; . \tag{18.20}$$

For any (u,v) on the velocity constraint line, this vector is its component parallel to the spatial gradient (perpendicular to an edge).

   Although velocity constraint lines can be computed at all points in the image that have nonzero gradient, they do not determine an optic flow field. Other information must be brought to bear to constrain further our choice of a flow field. HORN and SCHUNCK built a variational principle to accomplish this using a first-order smoothness constraint on U and V. If in addition to this, we required equation (18.19) to be satisfied, this would lead to a problem in constrained minimization. Such a constraint is likely to prove too strong due to the presence of sensor noise and discretization (truncation) error. This consideration led HORN and SCHUNCK to include the inherent constraint of small dE/dt in their variational principle for optic flow. The resulting variational problem is to find the optic flow field satisfying equation (18.5). The equivalent PDE system (EULER's equations) is

$$a^2 \Delta u - E_x^2 U - E_x E_y V = E_x E_t \tag{18.21a}$$
$$a^2 \Delta v - E_x E_y U - E_y^2 V = E_y E_t \; . \tag{18.21b}$$

This elliptic system of PDEs generalizes LAPLACE's equation in that 1) it is a vector field equation and the component equations are coupled, 2) terms of order 0 appear, and most significantly 3) the coefficients are non-constant (they depend on x and y).

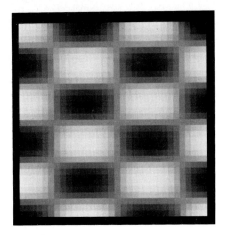

Fig. 18.8. Optic flow test data-
frame 1. Cross product of sinusoids with 1% uniform noise added

18.4.2 Iterative Relaxation

A GAUSS-SEIDEL method of iterative solution of a finite difference approximation was used:

$$u^{k+1} := \bar{u}^k - E_x*[E_x\bar{u}^k + E_y\bar{v}^k + E_t] / (a^2 + E_x^2 + E_y^2) \qquad (18.22a)$$

$$v^{k+1} := \bar{v}^k - E_y*[E_x\bar{u}^k + E_y\bar{v}^k + E_t] / (a^2 + E_x^2 + E_y^2) \qquad (18.22b)$$

where $\bar{u}$ and $\bar{v}$ are local averages.

18.4.3 Experiments

The first frame of the test data for the experiments is shown in Fig.18.8.
In the first experiment the motion is translational : 1/2 pixel to the right
and 1 pixel up. One percent uniform noise has been added to all test data
and is uncorrelated between frames. The single grid HORN and SCHUNCK algorithm is shown in Fig.18.9. Figure 18.9a shows a portion of the image plane
at various stages in the iteration. The initial estimate (iteration 0) for
the optic flow field is computed from equation (18.20). An error graph is
plotted in Fig.18.9b.

The results of the multilevel algorithm are shown in the next two figures.
In Fig.18.10 the first 14 iterations are shown for a portion of the full image
(the upper left corner). Consecutive iterations at a given level are juxta-
posed in the vector plots. In this figure and succeeding vector plots,
coarse resolution vectors have been plotted with lengths scaled to the distance between pixel centers. Figure18.11a plots residual norm vs. iteration.
Convergence is reached at the 21st iteration. In Fig.18.11b the iteration
axis also runs from 0-26 but it is labeled in work units. Convergence occurs
at 13.5 work units.

Finally we present some experiments based on other types of motion in
Figs.18.12,13. In both cases the first frame is the same as the first frame
in Fig.18.8. In Fig.18.12a the initial estimate for a rotational motion is
shown. Figure 18.12b shows later stages in the multilevel relaxation. The
iterations shown as vector plots correspond to the rightmost occurrence in
the error graph of the given level. Figure 18.13 shows similar results for
depth motion, i.e., translation perpendicular to the image plane.

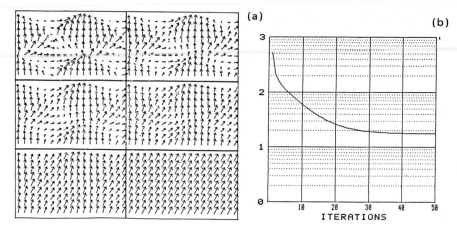

Fig. 18.9. Iterative optic flow computation, HORN & SCHUNCK algorithm. **(a)** Iterations 0, 1, 2, 5, 10. **(b)** Semilog graph of residual norm vs. iteration number

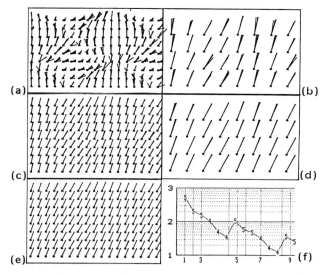

Fig. 18.10. Multilevel optic flow computation. **(a)** Iterations 1, 2, 3. **(b)** Iterations 4, 5, 6. **(c)** Iterations 7, 8, 9. **(d)** Iterations 10, 11, 12. **(e)** Iterations 13, 14. **(f)** Error Graph, iterations 0-14

In both of the above experiments the basic Cycle C/FAS algorithm fails to work. The successful runs shown in the figures were accomplished by preventing the algorithm from going higher (coarser) than the coarsest shown level (level 3) and by specifying how many iterations to perform at each level per cycle. Relaxation done at level 2 causes the estimate to diverge from the correct solution only to be corrected when back at level 3. This appears to be due to a failure to obtain an adequate finite difference approximation of the problem at level 2. Recall that the coefficients of the EPDE we are

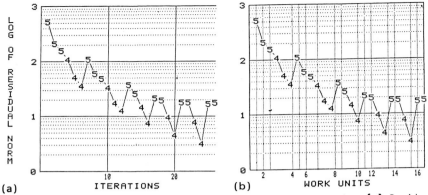

Fig. 18.11. Multilevel optic flow computation: error graphs. **(a)** Residual norm vs. iteration number. **(b)** Residual norm vs. iterations, labeled by work number

solving here (see (18.19)) are nonconstant. The level-2 grid is too coarse (low frequency) to represent the data E_x, E_y, and E_t. Merely restricting the algorithm to levels finer than level 2 is not an adequate solution, since convergence at level 3 is not soon attained. Instituting a fixed pattern of travel up and down the cone solves this problem. More importantly, it eliminates the need to measure the residual norm as iteration progresses, thus reestablishing the locality of the algorithm.

BRANDT has also suggested fixed cycling patterns to reduce computation expense, on the basis of experiments in which cycling was observed to occur in regular patterns. For some problems he has shown how to calculate optimal cycling patterns.

18.5 Summary

Variational (cost minimization) and local constraint approaches are generally applicable to problems in low-level vision (e.g., computation of intrinsic images). They provide a sound mathematical basis for ideas such as smoothness and "best possible" constraint satisfaction. Moreover, they admit computational implementations well suited to the domains of human and machine vision. These are the iterative relaxation algorithms which are "natural" choices for implementation because they can be executed on highly parallel and locally connected processors. Four examples were sketched to show both the range of problems that can be addressed and the variety of approaches that can be taken. These approaches and the corresponding algorithms were related in a general framework embodied in Fig. 18.1.

Multilevel relaxation techniques were introduced as an extension of the basic relaxation algorithms. They provide an efficient way of performing computations which at a single level may require a very large number of iterations to attain convergence. As hierarchical techniques, these algorithms are also suitable for implementation by hierarchical computational architectures. We mention specifically the cones and pyramids that have been studied extensively in computer vision (see various papers in [18.10]). The solving of LAPLACE's equation was shown as an example of the operation of multilevel relaxation and it was compared to standard (single level) relaxation.

327

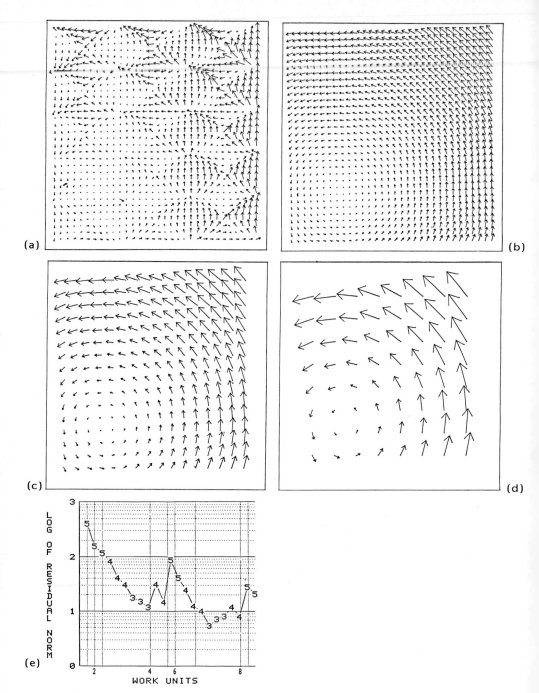

Fig. 18.12. Multilevel optic flow computation, rotational motion. **(a)** Iteration 0. **(b)** Iteration 23 at level 5. **(c)** Iteration 21 at level 4. **(d)** Iteration 19 at level 3. **(e)** Error graph

328

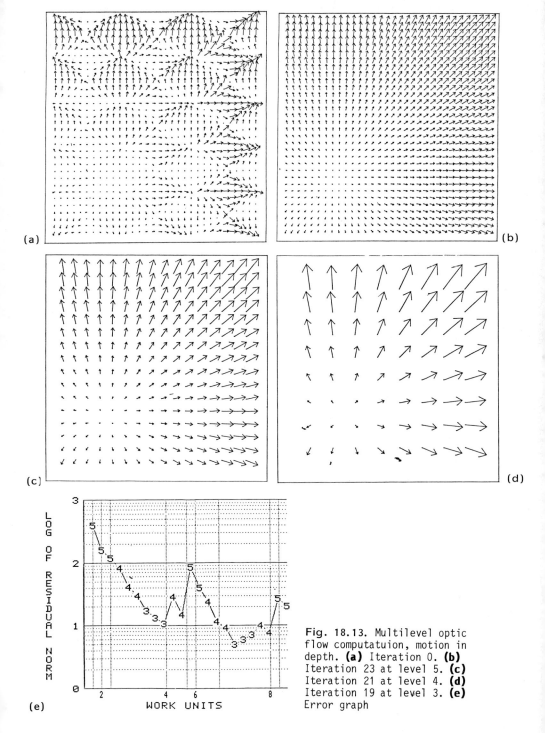

(a)

(b)

(c)

(d)

(e)

Fig. 18.13. Multilevel optic flow computatuion, motion in depth. **(a)** Iteration 0. **(b)** Iteration 23 at level 5. **(c)** Iteration 21 at level 4. **(d)** Iteration 19 at level 3. **(e)** Error graph

329

Multilevel relaxation was applied to the problem of computing optic flow
from dynamic images. Following the development of HORN and SCHUNCK [18.5],
a variational problem is established, EULER's equations are derived, and
a GAUSS-SEIDEL iterative relaxation algorithm is formulated. This algorithm
was extended to a multilevel relaxation algorithm in the style of BRANDT
[18.7,8]. Experiments exhibit the operation of this algorithm and attest to
its quick convergence.

18.1 K. A. Narayanan, D. P. O'Leary, A. Rosenfeld: Image smoothing and
      segmentation by cost minimization, IEEE Trans. Systems, Man, Cyber-
      netics SMC-12, 91-96 (1982)
18.2 W. E. L. Grimson: "A Computational Theory of Visual Surface Inter-
      polation", Artificial Intelligence Laboratory Memo 613, MIT (1981)
18.3 K. Ikeuchi: "Numerical Shape from Shading and Occluding Contour in
      a Single View", Artificial Intelligence Laboratory Memo 566, MIT (1980)
18.4 K. Ikeuchi, B. K. P. Horn: Numerical shape from shading and occluding
      boundaries, Artificial Intelligence 17, 141-184 (1981)
18.5 B. K. P. Horn, B. G. Schunck: Determining optical flow, Artificial In-
      telligence 17, 185-204 (1981)
18.6 L. A. Hageman, D. M. Young: Applied Iterative Methods (Academic Press,
      New York, 1981)
18.7 A. Brandt: "Multi-level adaptive techniques (MLAT) for partial dif-
      ferential equations: ideas and software", in Mathematical Software III,
      ed. by J. R. Rice (Academic Press, New York, 1977), pp. 277-318
18.8 A. Brandt: Multi-level adaptive solutions to boundary-value problems,
      Mathematics of Computation 31, 333-390 (1977)
18.9 S. L. Tanimoto: "Regular hierarchical image and processing structures
      in machine vision", in Computer Vision Systems, ed. by A. R. Hanson,
      E. M. Riseman (Academic Press, New York, 1978), pp. 165-174
18.10 S. Tanimoto, A. Klinger (eds.): Structured Computer Vision: Machine
      Perception through Hierarchical Computation Structures (Academic Press,
      New York, 1980)
18.11 A. R. Hanson, E. M. Riseman: "Processing cones: a computational struc-
      ture for image analysis", in Structured Computer Vision, ed. by S. Tani-
      moto, A. Klinger (Academic Press, New York, 1980), pp. 101-131
18.12 S. Tanimoto, T. Pavlidis: A hierarchical data structure for picture
      processing, Computer Graphics Image Processing 4, 104-119 (1975)
18.13 A. Klinger, C. R. Dyer: Experiments on picture representation using
      regular decomposition, Computer Graphics Image Processing 5, 68-105 (1976)
18.14 M. D. Kelly: "Edge detection in pictures by computer using planning",
      in Machine Intelligence 6, ed. by B. Meltzer, D. Michie (Edinburgh
      University Press, Edinburgh, UK, 1971), pp. 379-409
18.15 R. Y. Wong, E. L. Hall: Sequential hierarchical scene matching, IEEE
      Trans. Computers C-27, 359-366 (1978)
18.16 D. Marr, T. Poggio: A computational theory of human stereo vision,
      Proc. Royal Society (London) B204, 301-328 (1979)
18.17 P. J. Burt: "Pyramid-based extraction of local image features with
      applications to motion and texture analysis," in Proc. SPIE Conf. on
      Robotics and Industrial Inspection, San Diego, CA, 1982
18.18 D. G. Luenberger: Introduction to Linear and Nonlinear Programming
      (Addison-Wesley, Reading, MA, 1973)
18.19 R. Courant, D. Hilbert: Methods of Mathematical Physics, Vol. 1
      (Interscience, New York, 1953)
18.20 D. Terzopolous: "Multi-Level Reconstruction of Visual Surfaces: Vari-
      ational Principles and Finite Element Representation", Artificial Intel-
      ligence Laboratory Memo 671, MIT (1982)
18.21 M. Yachida: "Determining velocity map by 3-D iterative estimates", in
      Proc. 7th Intl. Joint Conf. on Artificial Intelligence, Vancouver, BC,
      1981, pp. 716-718

19. Region Matching in Pyramids for Dynamic Scene Analysis

W.I. Grosky

Department of Computer Science, Wayne State University
Detroit, MI 48202, USA

R. Jain

Computer Science Department, University of Michigan
Ann Arbor, MI 48104, USA

19.1 Introduction

Dynamic scene analysis systems extract information about surfaces and their motion characteristics from a sequence of images representing the scene, acquired using a camera which may itself be moving. Though motion helps segmentation, dynamic scene analysis systems have to work with a very large volume of data. A real-time system for the extraction of moving surfaces and the computation of the motion characteristics of the surfaces will require a special architecture and special data structures [19.1,2]. Pyramidal data structures allow the planning and computation of some properties of pictures to be performed at lower resolutions [19.3-12]. In some cases, one may use a pyramidal organization of processors to compute some properties on the fly [19.13]. In this paper, we present a scheme for pyramidal, real-time region matching in a dynamic scene analysis system, and then discuss some algorithms for the pyramid machine.

Many approaches have been proposed for the extraction of 3-D structure information from surfaces, the motion of the surfaces, and the motion of the camera [19.14-16]. Most of these approaches are based on finding the locations of feature points in the frames such that those feature points representing properties of the surfaces in the scene are obtained in more than one frame, and the correspondence problem has been solved. In fact, most existing methods for the extraction of 3-D information assume that the precise locations and correspondence of the feature points are available. As has been shown, this assumption does allow the extraction of 3-D information [19.14,16]. The problem of the determination of the feature points [19.14,17-19] has received only little attention, however. It appears that interest operators, or feature detectors based on small local neighborhoods are computationally efficient but result in too many interesting points, making the correspondence problem intractable. On the other hand, operators using large neighborhoods give a reasonably small number of points but are computationally expensive. Another, more serious problem with the large-neighborhood operators is the fact that the precise locations of the feature points are not available. Also, methods for the extraction of 3-D information usually depend on the solution of a set of equations, in many cases nonlinear equations, that is very sensitive to noise. This fact makes the extraction of 3-D information using feature points in a few frames dubious for real world scenes.

It is relatively easy to extract robust regions from images [19.20-23]. The properties of regions are less sensitive to noise as they are group properties, and noise points can affect them only to a small extent. Region-based approaches exploit surface coherence in frames. It appears that the mathematical analysis of arbitrary surfaces to compute properties that will enable extraction of 3-D information from the 2-D projections of surfaces is not easy. We are not aware of any technique which will allow extraction of precise 3-D information about the structure or motion of the surfaces from the study of properties of regions in frames.

In our system, we intend to exploit the strengths of both approaches. We extract regions representing moving surfaces in frames. Interest operators are then applied to the interesting regions, yielding feature points whose correspondence is approximately known. 3-D extraction methods are next applied to the feature points and the 3-D information thus extracted is verified by projecting it back to two dimensions and verifying it with the observed data. DRESCHLER and NAGEL [19.14] have used a similar approach.

Many approaches have been proposed for segmentation of dynamic scenes [19.20,22,23]. These approaches usually allow extraction of moving surface images in several frames. If we have moving surface images in many frames, then the next step in the analysis is to solve the correspondence problem for the regions representing the surfaces in the images. One may use cross-correlation for this purpose; but it is not reliable for surfaces undergoing rotation. Methods based on boundaries of surfaces are sensitive to noise [19.24] and require many heuristics. The success of these methods for complex scenes has yet to be demonstrated.

We interpret an image as a function $f(X,Y)$ which maps X and Y coordinates into gray levels. This allows us to consider an image, or a region representing a subimage, as a surface $Z=f(X,Y)$. A region in a frame is represented by finding a best fitting elliptical paraboloid that represents the gray-level surface corresponding to the region. Note that we are fitting the elliptical paraboloid to the intensity values of a surface extracted by other processes. It is observed that this representation allows reliable matching of regions and a by-product of the matching is the parameters describing the 2-D transformation of the surfaces. In this paper, we discuss a method of fitting an elliptical paraboloid to a region and demonstrate the efficacy of this representation. We also present an algorithm for finding connected components, regions, in pyramids. The proposed algorithm allows us to represent each region of an image at the highest possible level in the pyramid structure. It is shown that the parameters of the best-fit surfaces can be computed in the pyramid structure while forming the connected components. Thus, by using a special architecture, it is possible to compute the parameters of the gray-level surfaces very quickly, and then the matching of the surfaces may be performed without going to the raw images.

19.2 Pyramid Algorithms

Our scheme is as follows. We interpret an image as a function $f(X,Y)$ which maps X and Y coordinates into gray levels. Thus, an image can be regarded as a surface $Z=f(X,Y)$ in 3-space. Each node of the pyramid will then contain the equation of a second-order surface, an elliptic paraboloid, which is fitted through the center of mass of the level-1 subimage corresponding to this node and which minimizes the squared error between itself and the surface $Z=f(X,Y)$ over an appropriate area. This will be discussed more fully in Sect.19.2.1.

For each surface -- 4-connected region -- in the image, we now want to find the highest node in the pyramid, that is, that node closest to the apex whose corresponding level-1 subimage completely contains this surface and no other surface. If we can find such a node, the equation contained in it will convey information regarding the shape of the region, its position and its orientation. If we cannot find such a node, we change some of the links of the pyramid so that a level-k node k>1 now determines a not necessarily square region. This connected region will consist of squares of sizes $2^{k-1} \times 2^{k-1}$, $2^{k-2} \times 2^{k-2}$,..., $2^0 \times 2^0$ which are joined together across their edges. This will be discussed in Sect.19.2.2. See [19.4,8-11] for other applications of pyramid relinking.

The embedding of the above calculations in the pyramid data structure will be discussed in Sect.19.2.3.

Finally, in Sect. 19.2.4, we will discuss the matching and motion identification phase of our algorithm. This will consist of constructing pyramids for each frame. In each pyramid, we identify nodes corresponding to each surface, as above. Two nodes whose equations are equivalent after a coordinate translation and rotation will correspond to the same surface. This translation and rotation will then give information regarding the translational and rotational components of the 2-D motion, respectively, of this surface.

19.2.1 Second-Order Image Approximation

For illustration, let us assume an 8×8 grid of pixels. The coordinate origin will be placed in the exact center of the grid. Thus, the point (i,j) will be in the lower left-hand corner of the pixel in row 4-j and column i+5. This pixel will also have address (i,j). (See Fig.19.1.) Let us assume that this grid contains only one surface (4-connected region). Now, Z= $A(X-X0)^2+B(Y-y0)^2+C(X-X0)*(Y-Y0)+D$ is the equation of an elliptic paraboloid centered at point (X0,Y0). Let us find the values of A, B, C, and D which minimize the squared error between this surface and the surface Z=f(X,Y) over a circular region centered at (X0,Y0) and with radius R larger than the diameter of any possible region in our grid. For our example, any R > $8\sqrt{2}$ will suffice. (Note that f(X,Y) is assumed to be 0 outside the grid.) We are going to put X0=XCM and Y0=YCM, the coordinates of the center of mass of the surface. The reason for centering this surface at the center of mass and fitting it over a circular region is that when this is done, the position and orientation of the surface in the grid will not affect the final equation after a coordinate transformation is done which puts the origin over (XCM,YCM)

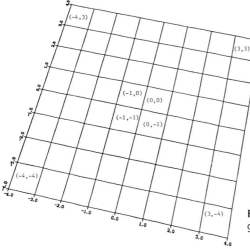

Fig. 19.1. An 8 x 8 coordinate grid

333

and the axes in such an orientation as to eliminate the cross-product term
$C(X-XCM)(Y-YCM)$.

Letting $x=X-XO$ and $y=Y-YO$, we want to minimize

$$\int_{-R}^{+R}\int_{-\sqrt{R^2-y^2}}^{+\sqrt{R^2-y^2}} [Ax +By +Cxy+D-f(x+XO,y+YO)]^2 dxdy \tag{19.1}$$

which is equivalent to

$$\int_{-R}^{+R}\int_{-\sqrt{R^2-y^2}}^{+\sqrt{R^2-y^2}} [A^2x^4+B^2y^4+C^2x^2y^2+2ABx^2y^2+2ACx^3y+2Bxy^3 \tag{19.2}$$
$$+2ADx^2+2CDxy+2BDy^2+D^2+f^2(x+XO,y+YO)-2Df(x+XO,y+YO)$$
$$-2Ax^2f(x+XO,y+YO)-2By^2f(x+XO,y+YO)-2Cxyf(x+XO,y+YO)]dxdy .$$

We finally end up minimizing

$$\int_{-R}^{+R}\int_{-\sqrt{R^2-y^2}}^{+\sqrt{R^2-y^2}} [f^2(x+XO,y+YO)-(2Ax^2+2By^2+2Cxy+2D) \tag{19.3}$$
$$f(x+XO,y+YO)]dxdy$$
$$+(\pi R^6/8)(A^2+B^2)+(\pi R^6/24)(C^2+2AB)+(\pi R^4/2)D(A+B)+R^2D^2 .$$

Setting the partial derivatives of (19.3) with respect to A, B, C, and D equal to 0, we obtain

$$(\pi R^6/4)A+(\pi R^6/12)B+(\pi R^4/2)D = 2\int_{-R}^{+R}\int_{-\sqrt{R^2-y^2}}^{+\sqrt{R^2-y^2}} x^2f(x+XO,y+YO)dxdy \tag{19.4a}$$

$$(\pi R^6/12)A+(\pi R^6/4)B+(\pi R^4/2)D = 2\int_{-R}^{+R}\int_{-\sqrt{R^2-y^2}}^{+\sqrt{R^2-y^2}} y^2f(x+XO,y+YO)dxdy \tag{19.4b}$$

$$(\pi R^6/12)C = 2\int_{-R}^{+R}\int_{-\sqrt{R^2-y^2}}^{+\sqrt{R^2-y^2}} xyf(x+XO,y+YO)dxdy \tag{19.4c}$$

$$(\pi R^4/2)A+(\pi R^4/2)B+2\pi R^2D = 2\int_{-R}^{+R}\int_{-\sqrt{R^2-y^2}}^{+\sqrt{R^2-y^2}} f(x+XO,y+YO)dxdy \tag{19.4d}$$

which has the solutions

$$A = (6/\pi R^6) \int_{-R}^{+R}\int_{-\sqrt{R^2-y^2}}^{+\sqrt{R^2-y^2}} (y^2+3x^2-R^2)f(x+XO,y+YO)dxdy \tag{19.5a}$$

$$B = (6/\pi R^6) \int_{-R}^{+R}\int_{-\sqrt{R^2-y^2}}^{+\sqrt{R^2-y^2}} (x^2+3y^2-R^2)f(x+XO,y+YO)dxdy \tag{19.5b}$$

$$C = (24/\pi R^6) \int_{-R}^{+R}\int_{-\sqrt{R^2-y^2}}^{+\sqrt{R^2-y^2}} xyf(x+XO,y+YO)dxdy \tag{19.5c}$$

$$D = \int_{-R}^{+R}\int_{-\sqrt{R^2-y^2}}^{+\sqrt{R^2-y^2}} [(4/\pi R^2)-(6/\pi R^4)(x^2+y^2)]f(x+XO,y+YO)dxdy . \tag{19.5d}$$

From Theorem 7.8 in [19.25], it may easily be verified that the above solutions do minimize (19.1).

Changing back to (X,Y) coordinates, letting $W=R^2-(Y-YCM)^2$, and putting $XO=XCM$ and $YO=YCM$, where

$$XCM = \int_{YCM-R}^{YCM+R} \int_{XCM-W}^{XCM+W} Xf(X,Y)dXdY / \int_{YCM-R}^{YCM+R} \int_{XCM-W}^{XCM+W} f(X,Y)dXdY$$

and

$$YCM = \int_{YCM-R}^{YCM+R} \int_{XCM-W}^{XCM+W} Yf(X,Y)dXdY / \int_{YCM-R}^{YCM+R} \int_{XCM-W}^{XCM+W} f(X,Y)dXdY$$

we have

$$A = (6/\pi R^6)Y2MEAN + (18/\pi R^6)X2MEAN - (6/\pi R^4)MEAN \tag{19.6a}$$

$$B = (6/\pi R^6)X2MEAN + (18/\pi R^6)Y2MEAN - (6/\pi R^4)MEAN \tag{19.6b}$$

$$C = (24/\pi R^6)XYMEAN \tag{19.6c}$$

$$D = (4/\pi R^2)MEAN - (6/\pi R^4)[X2MEAN + Y2MEAN] \tag{19.6d}$$

for

$$MEAN = \int_{YCM-R}^{YCM+R} \int_{XCM-W}^{XCM+W} f(X,Y)dXdY \tag{19.7a}$$

$$X2MEAN = \int_{YCM-R}^{YCM+R} \int_{XCM-W}^{XCM+W} X^2 f(X,Y)dXdY \tag{19.7b}$$

$$-[\int_{YCM-R}^{YCM+R} \int_{XCM-W}^{XCM+W} Xf(X,Y)dXdY]^2/MEAN$$

$$Y2MEAN = \int_{YCM-R}^{YCM+R} \int_{XCM-W}^{XCM+W} Y^2 f(X,Y)dXdY \tag{19.7c}$$

$$-[\int_{YCM-R}^{YCM+R} \int_{XCM-W}^{XCM+W} Yf(X,Y)dXdY]^2/MEAN$$

$$XYMEAN = \int_{YCM-R}^{YCM+R} \int_{XCM-W}^{XCM+W} XYf(X,Y)dXdY \tag{19.7d}$$

$$-[\int_{YCM-R}^{YCM+R} \int_{XCM-W}^{XCM+W} Xf(X,Y)dXdY][\int_{YCM-R}^{YCM+R} \int_{XCM-W}^{XCM+W} Yf(X,Y)dXdY]/MEAN .$$

Thus, to compute the appropriate minimal surface, we need only compute the zeroth, first and second moments of the image. These moments can easily be calculated in terms of the gray level at each pixel, since, for i,j integers, we have f(i,j)=f(i+a, j+b) for $0 \le a,b < 1$. Specifically, it can be shown that

$$\int_{YCM-R}^{YCM+R} \int_{XCM-W}^{XCM+W} f(X,Y)dXdY = \sum_{i,j} f(i,j) \tag{19.8a}$$

$$\int_{YCM-R}^{YCM+R} \int_{XCM-W}^{XCM+W} Xf(X,Y)dXdY = \sum_{i,j} (i+1/2)f(i,j) \tag{19.8b}$$

$$\int_{YCM-R}^{YCM+R} \int_{XCM-W}^{XCM+W} Yf(X,Y)dXdY = \sum_{i,j} (j+1/2)f(i,j) \tag{19.8c}$$

$$\int_{YCM-R}^{YCM+R} \int_{XCM-W}^{XCM+W} X^2 f(X,Y)dXdY = \sum_{i,j} (i^2+i+1/3)f(i,j) \tag{19.8d}$$

$$\int_{YCM-R}^{YCM+R} \int_{XCM-W}^{XCM+W} Y^2 f(X,Y)dXdY = \sum_{i,j} (j^2+j+1/3)f(i,j) \qquad (19.8e)$$

$$\int_{YCM-R}^{YCM+R} \int_{XCM-W}^{XCM+W} XYf(X,Y)dXdY = \sum_{i,j} (i+1/2)(j+1/2)f(i,j) . \qquad (19.8f)$$

Thus, to develop the equation of the best fitting elliptic paraboloid to a region, we need only be able to calculate efficiently

$$\sum_{i,j} f(i,j) \qquad\qquad \sum_{i,j} if(i,j) \qquad\qquad \sum_{i,j} jf(i,j) \qquad\qquad (19.9a\text{-}c)$$

$$\sum_{i,j} i^2 f(i,j) \qquad\qquad \sum_{i,j} j^2 f(i,j) \qquad\qquad \sum_{i,j} ijf(i,j) \qquad\qquad (19.9d\text{-}f)$$

for this region.

19.2.2 Segmenting an Image Via Pyramid Linking

Consider the image shown in Fig.19.2. If one constructs a standard pyramid in which each node above level 1 has precisely four sons, one cannot find any node in this pyramid whose corresponding subimage contains one and only one region. We thus relax this requirement. Each node can have as few as 1 and as many as 16 sons. The way this is done is that, as necessary, nodes are relinked to neighboring fathers. Given the 2×2 template of Fig.19.3, area 1 can be linked to either its own father or to a neighbor of this father to the west, to the north or to the northwest. Similar statements can be made for areas 2, 3, and 4.

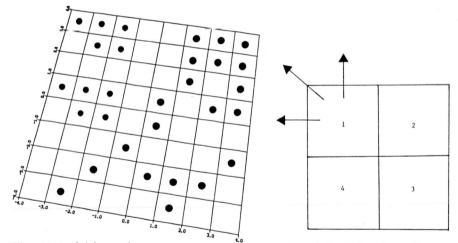

Fig. 19.2. A binary image   Fig. 19.3. A 2 x 2 template

We first label the regions on level 1. We use the standard recursive labelling scheme, but it may be done in parallel by having each pixel with a gray level above 0 pass its address to its northern, southern, eastern and western neighbors. When a pixel with gray level 0 receives inputs, it ignores them. When a pixel with a nonzero gray level receives inputs, it changes its address to the minimal address received. Thus, after a time proportional to the diameter of a region, that region is labelled by the smallest address of any pixel in that region. Then, starting at level 1 and continuing as long as necessary, we do the following. Each 2x2 subimage is examined to see how many region labels are included among its nodes. If this subimage contains nodes from at most one region, none of its nodes are relinked to another father, while if it contains nodes from two, three, or four different regions, these nodes are relinked, if possible. This relinking is done in a disciplined fashion:

1) If three nodes are from one region, while the fourth node is from a different region, this latter node is the one to be relinked.
2) If two neighboring (4-connected) nodes are from one region, these nodes are relinked to the same father.
3) Relinking is done only to a father all of whose sons are either of gray level 0 or from the same region.
4) We first try to relink nodes to a father whose sons contain the same region as the node to be relinked. If this can't be done, we then try to relink them to a father all of whose sons are of gray level 0.
5) After all the relinking is accomplished, each son of a given father has a 0 region label or an equal positive region label. The father inherits this region label.
6) Relinking is not done to a node if there is no neighboring node with the same region label. If this is the case, we have found a node in the pyramid whose corresponding subimage completely contains just one region. The information concerning this region will be kept at this node and a flag will be set indicating that this node is the root node of an individual connected region, but its region label is changed to 0, so that higher-level nodes will see it as being of gray level 0. Thus, higher-level nodes will treat this node as background for any future relinking operations, even though there is an entire connected region encompassed by this node. This latter region is called a hidden region, and all nodes with such regions are flagged appropriately.

7) Before the relinking starts on level 1, we place a border of gray level 0 around the original image. In our case, the 8×8 image is put in the center of a 16×16 image. This is done because it may be necessary to relink into this border.

Let us trace the steps taken using the image of Fig.19.2. Each of Figs.19.4-8 illustrates higher levels of the pyramid. Neighboring nodes with similar cross-hatching have the same father node. Also, nodes with an R written in them have their root flag set, while nodes with an H written in them have hidden regions included among their children.

19.2.3 Embedding the Necessary Calculations in the Pyramid

We now show how to embed the calculations of (19.9a-f) for each 4-connected region in the pyramid.

Each node of the pyramid "sees" only a single 4-connected region, aside from any hidden regions which may occur at various children of the given node. Call this region the node's primary region. We will develop a method whereby each node of the pyramid calculates (19.9a-f) for that part of its primary region which it encompasses. We will use recurrence formulas. Specifically, each node will calculate its value of (19.9a-f) in terms of the values of (19.9a-f) for its children, after all relinking has been done at that level.

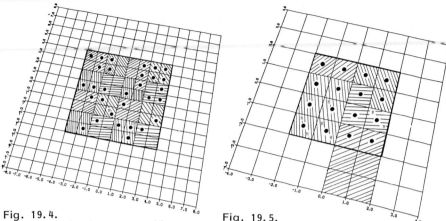

Fig. 19.4.
Level 1 of the image pyramid

Fig. 19.5.
Level 2 of the image pyramid

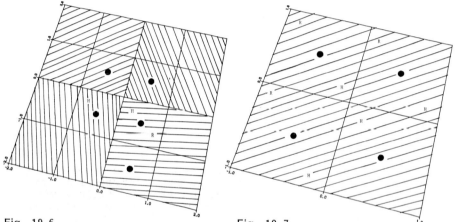

Fig. 19.6.
Level 3 of the image pyramid

Fig. 19.7.
Level 4 of the image pyramid

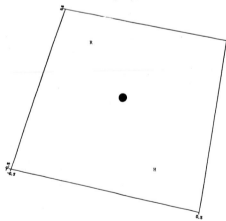

Fig. 19.8. Level 5 of the image pyramid

338

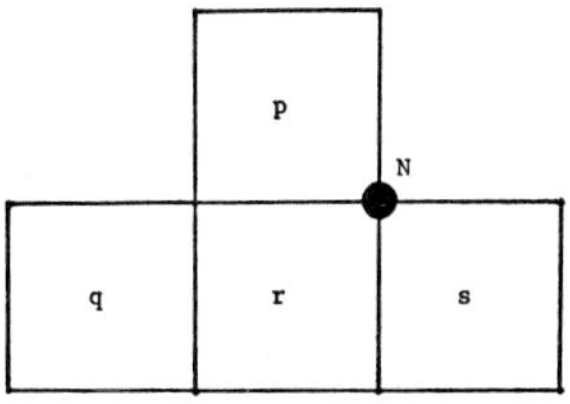

Fig. 19.9. The pyramid calculations

We will illustrate this method on level 3 of the pyramid for the calculation of (19.9f). Figure 19.9 illustrates our example. We want to calculate (19.9f) for node N. This node has four children after all the relinking has been done on level 2: its northwest, southeast and southwest children as well as the southeast child of its western neighbor. Areas p, q, r and s are the regions in the image encompassed by these children, respectively. Then (19.9f) for node N is

$$\sum_{i,j\in p}(i-2^0)(j+2^0)fp(i,j)+ \sum_{i,j\in q}(i-3*2^0)(j-2^0)fq(i,j) \qquad (19.10)$$

$$+ \sum_{i,j\in r}(i-2^0)(j-2^0)fr(i,j)+ \sum_{i,j\in s}(i+2^0)(j-2^0)fs(i,j)$$

where in each region p, q, r or s, the origin of the row, column indices i,j is the respective child. Thus, what is pixel (0,0) with respect to the northwest son of node N is pixel (-1,1) with respect to node N. The functions fp, fq, fr and fs are just the original function f with these coordinate transformations.

Now, (19.10) reduces to

$$\sum_{i,j\in p}ijfp(i,j)+ \sum_{i,j\in q}ijfq(i,j)+ \sum_{i,j\in r}ijfr(i,j)+ \sum_{i,j\in s}ijfs(i,j) \qquad (19.11)$$

$$+ 2^0(\sum_{i,j\in p}ifp(i,j)- \sum_{i,j\in q}ifq(i,j)- \sum_{i,j\in r}ifr(i,j)- \sum_{i,j\in s}ifs(i,j))$$

$$+ 2^0(\sum_{i,j\in s}jfs(i,j)- \sum_{i,j\in p}jfp(i,j)- \sum_{i,j\in r}jfr(i,j)-3\sum_{i,j\in q}jfq(i,j))$$

$$+(2^0)^2(\sum_{i,j\in r}fr(i,j)- \sum_{i,j\in p}fp(i,j)- \sum_{i,j\in s}fs(i,j)+3\sum_{i,j\in q}fq(i,j)) \; .$$

Thus, (19.9f) at node N is computed in terms of (19.9a,b,c,f) at the children of node N.

In general, in computing (19.9a-f) at a level n node, for n≥1, we use 2^{n-3} instead of 2^0 in (19.11). Also, the initializations of (19.9a-f) at pixel (i,j) of level 1 are f(i,j), -f(i,j)/2, -f(i,j)/2, f(i,j)/4, f(i,j)/4, and f(i,j)/4, respectively.

19.2.4 Matching and Motion Identification

In each node of our pyramid which completely encompasses a 4-connected region, we have the equation $Z=AX^2+BY^2+CXY+D$ of a best-fitting elliptical paraboloid through the center of mass of the region. In order to use this surface for detecting the 2-D rotational component of motion of this region through many frames, we find the angle which the major axis of the ellipse, which results from the intersection of the ellipsoid with the (X,Y) plane, makes with the positive X axis. This angle is restricted to be in the first or fourth quadrant, and is found by calculating through what angle to rotate the (X,Y) axis so that the CXY term is eliminated.

The resultant X^2, Y^2 and constant coefficients will be used in matching regions from frame to frame. Once we find similar regions in two frames, we use the center of mass and the difference in the above angles to find the 2-D translational and rotational components of motion, respectively. We assume that the rotational component is small, as this method does not give unique results for arbitrary rotations. That is, two different rotations may lead to the same answer. For example, if in frame 1, the major axis of the above ellipse makes an angle of 30 degrees with the positive X axis, while in frame 2 the angle is 60 degrees, the rotational component could be -150 degrees, 30 degrees, 210 degrees, or 330 degrees.

It is easily shown that if the axes are rotated by RAD radians, for RAD= .5*arctan(C/(A-B)), the CXY term disappears. Also, the equation of the aforementioned ellipse is $AX^2+BY^2+CXY+D=0$. Thus, dY/dX = -(2AX+CY)/(2BY+CX) or dY/dX$|_{Y=0}$=-2A/C. This implies that if sign(A)=sign(C) then its major axis is in the fourth quadrant, while if sign(A)≠sign(C), its major axis is in the first quadrant. Thus, for RAD=.5*arctan(C/(A-B)), if RAD<0 and sign(A)≠ sign(C), we add π/2 to RAD, while if RAD>0 and sign(A)=sign(C), we subtract π/2 from RAD.

19.3 Summary

The proposed approach will be part of a dynamic scene analysis system called VILI [19.26]. Here we will only discuss the planned implementation of the proposed approach. In Fig.19.10 we show an outline of the system dealing with matching and extraction of the 2-D motion parameters. The input to the pyramid comes from moving surface extraction processes such as [19.20,22,23]. The bottom level of the pyramid thus represents a segmented frame that contains only moving surface images, the stationary components of which have gray level 0. The images of the moving surfaces from two frames are available. These two frames may be consecutive frames, the reference frame and the current frame, or any other two frames. Using the scheme described in earlier sections, we will compute the parameters of the elliptical paraboloid for each surface in each frame. The matching of the regions will be based on the parameters and the spatial proximity, size, and other similar factors. Once the correspondence between different surfaces has been established, "interesting points" may be located on the surfaces. Since our approach gives the translations and the rotations of surfaces, correspondence will be simplified.

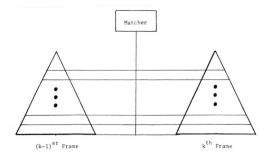

Fig. 19.10. Matching in pyramids. The lowest levels of the pyramids contain the (k-1)st and kth segmented frames of the image sequence. The matcher can look at every level of the pyramids. The matching starts at the apex of the pyramids and continues downwards as required.

The location of the interesting points will be used for the extraction of
3-D information concerning both the structure and the relative motion of the
surfaces.

References

19.1   D. P. Agrawal, R. Jain: A pipelined pseudoparallel system architec-
       ture for real-time dynamic scene analysis, IEEE Trans. Computers C-31,
       952-962 (1982)
19.2   A. Gilbert, M. K. Giles, G. M. Flachs, R. B. Rogers, Y. H. U: A real-
       time video tracking system, IEEE Trans. Pattern Analysis Machine Intel-
       ligence PAMI-2, 47-56 (1980)
19.3   E. H. Adelson, P. J. Burt: "Image data compression with the Laplacian
       pyramid", in Proc. Pattern Recognition and Image Processing Conf.,
       Dallas, TX, 1981, pp. 218-223
19.4   H. J. Antonisse: Image segmentation in pyramids, Computer Graphics
       Image Processing 19, 367-383 (1982)
19.5   P. J. Burt: "Tree and Pyramid Structures for Coding Hexagonally Sam-
       pled Binary Images," Computer Science TR-814, University of Maryland
       (1979)
19.6   C. R. Dyer, A. Rosenfeld: "Cellular Pyramids for Image Analysis",
       Computer Science TR-544, University of Maryland (1977)
19.7   C. R. Dyer, A. Rosenfeld: "Cellular Pyramids for Image Analysis, 2",
       Computer Science TR-596, University of Maryland (1977)
19.8   T. H. Hong, M. Shneier, A. Rosenfeld: Border extraction using linked
       edge pyramids, IEEE Trans. Systems, Man Cybernetics SMC-12, 660-668 (1982)
19.9   S. Kasif, A. Rosenfeld: Pyramid linking is a special case of ISODATA,
       IEEE Trans. Systems, Man, Cybernetics SMC-13, 84-85 (1983)
19.10 K. A. Narayanan, A. Rosenfeld: Approximation of waveforms and contours
       by one-dimensional pyramid linking, Pattern Recognition 15, 389-396 (1982)
19.11 M. Pietikainen, A. Rosenfeld: Image segmentation by texture using pyr-
       amid node linking, IEEE Trans. Systems, Man, Cybernetics SMC-11, 822-825
       (1981)
19.12 S. L. Tanimoto, A. Klinger (eds.): Structured Computer Vision: Machine
       Perception Through Hierarchical Computation Structures (Academic Press,
       New York, 1980)
19.13 S. L. Tanimoto: "Towards Hierarchical Cellular Logic: Design Consid-
       erations for Pyramid Machines", Computer Science TR 81-02-01, University
       of Washington (1981)
19.14 L. Dreschler, H. H. Nagel: "Volumetric model and 3-D trajectory of a
       moving car derived from monocular TV-frame sequences of a street scene",
       in Proc. 7th Intl. Joint Conf. on Artificial Intelligence, Vancouver,
       BC, 1981, pp. 692-697
19.15 T. S. Huang: Image Sequence Analysis (Springer, Berlin, 1981)
19.16 S. Ullman: The Interpretation of Visual Motion (MIT Press, Cambridge,
       MA, 1979)
19.17 D. Ballard, C. M. Brown: Computer Vision (Prentice Hall, Englewood
       Cliffs, NJ, 1982)
19.18 S. T. Barnard, W. B. Thompson: Disparity analysis of images, IEEE Trans.
       Pattern Analysis Machine Intelligence PAMI-2, 333-340 (1980)
19.19 J. M. Prager: "Segmentation of Static and Dynamic Scenes", Computer
       and Information Sciences Technical Report 79-7, University of Massa-
       chusetts (1979)
19.20 C. L. Fennema, W. B. Thompson: Velocity determination in scenes con-
       taining several moving objects, Computer Graphics Image Processing 9,
       301-315 (1979)

19.21 S. Haynes, R. Jain: Detection of moving edges, Computer Graphics Image Processing 21, 345-367 (1983)

19.22 R. Jain, H. H. Nagel: On the analysis of accumulative difference pictures from image sequences of real world scenes, IEEE Trans. Pattern Analysis Machine Intelligence PAMI-1, 206-213 (1979)

19.23 R. Jain, W. N. Martin, J. K. Aggarwal: Segmentation through the detection of changes due to motion, Computer Graphics Image Processing 11, 13-34 (1979)

19.24 J. K. Aggarwal, R. O. Duda: Computer analysis of moving polygonal images, IEEE Trans. Computers C-24, 966-976 (1975)

19.25 T. Apostol: Mathematical Analysis (Addison-Wesley, Reading, MA, 1960)

19.26 R. Jain, S. Haynes: Imprecision in computer vision, Computer 15 (8), 39-48 (1982)

20. Hierarchical Estimation of Spatial Properties from Motion

K.M. Mutch and W.B. Thompson

Computer Science Department, University of Minnesota
Minneapolis, MN 55455, USA

20.1 Introduction

20.1.1 Multiresolution Analysis of Time-Varying Imagery

Multiresolution matching techniques for motion-induced change lead naturally to a hierarchical refinement of three-dimensional properties such as edge location, surface shape, spatial layout, and motion parameters. A hierarchical representation of these relationships is useful for subsequent analysis of more symbolic properties. Aggregate information about larger surfaces is available at the coarser levels of the hierarchy. This can be used to normalize values at finer levels so that detailed, local properties are not hidden by grosser effects.

When hierarchical matching is used for further spatial analysis, it is helpful to utilize matching results at all levels of resolution. In addition to guiding the search at more detailed levels, matches at lower resolutions provide important information about dominant motion and shape parameters. Finer detail is most apparent when looking across levels in the hierarchy. Values at finer levels can then be represented as a difference from the expectations generated at coarser levels. A number of local shape properties are detectable using this formalism. Furthermore, such a system is self-normalizing, since the analysis of surface detail can ignore many of the effects caused by large object motion and/or camera geometry and optics.

20.1.2 Detail Hierarchies

Most contemporary models of computer vision are described in terms of an abstraction hierarchy. Starting with the raw two-dimensional image, information becomes more symbolic and compact at each higher level. Within levels of the abstraction hierarchy, detail hierarchies are often suggested either to guide processing in a coarse-to-fine manner or to condense the results of high resolution processing. (The term "resolution" is used here to denote a level of detail in the representation, not just the spatial resolution of a two-dimensional image function.)

Most of the work on multiresolution image analysis has focused on the development of computational processes which operate either directly on image data or on simple derived representations such as edges or regions. Detail hierarchies can exist at any level of abstraction, however. For example, MARR proposed a model of three-dimensional object representation in which coarse representations of shape are successively refined into more precisely specified components [20.1].

*Supported by the National Science Foundation under Grant MCS-81-05215.

20.1.3 Use of Detail Hierarchies

Detail hierarchies have almost always been used as a mechanism for reducing complexity and improving accuracy within a particular level of abstraction in the processing hierarchy. As such, they have been viewed primarily as a computational tool rather than as a structure for representing derived properties of the imagery. In fact, once computations using these hierarchies are completed, results at all but the finest level of detail are often discarded. In many situations, however, all levels of a detail hierarchy are important. If the hierarchy contains spatial information, then it is advantageous to represent values at a fine level of detail relative to coarser levels. Such an approach makes it easier both to determine the finer details in the first place and to separate fine detail from coarser structures. Detail hierarchies are useful representational tools for making information at different scales explicit. The existence of such a complete hierarchy at one level of abstraction can facilitate interpretive operations at other levels. For example, a procedure which estimates volumetric properties from information about surfaces can then access the surface representations at the most appropriate level of detail.

20.1.4 Motion

Motion can provide a vision system with information about spatial layout and changing spatial relationships over time. In particular, information about surface shape, object boundaries, depth, and motion parameters is available from analysis of dynamic imagery (e.g., [20.2-12]). Object and sensor motion will cause positional changes in the projection of a scene onto the image plane. These patterns of change over the image plane can be analyzed to derive three-dimensional information about the scene. However, this task is not easy. Objects can move relative to the observer with six degrees of freedom: three translational and three rotational. At each point in a sequence of images which is obtained over time, three spatial dimensions are projected onto two image dimensions in every frame. In addition, six degrees of freedom in object motion are mapped into a pattern of two-dimensional point changes across the object surface between each frame. Detail hierarchies can often aid in the analysis of such image sequences by decoupling relationships at different levels.

20.2 Multiresolution Token Matching

20.2.1 Token Matching

One necessary task in analyzing image sequences is locating corresponding structures in each frame. This is known as the correspondence problem [20.13]. One approach to this problem is matching, where a set of structures is obtained from one image and an organized search for those structures in a subsequent image is performed. The scale of the structures to be matched may vary from individual pixels or small groups of pixels to large image regions [20.14,15]. Tokens, which are derived features of an intermediate scale, have proven to be useful structures for matching [20.3,16,17]. The goal in deriving tokens is to locate distinctive object regions which will be easily detected and matched in subsequent images. The results of token matching may be represented as a sparse vector field. Each vector indicates the change in position of the token on the image plane. Borrowing from the terminology of stereo vision, we refer to this vector as the disparity. The field of disparity vectors is the discrete equivalent of the optical flow field [20.2,18], or instantaneous translational velocity of every point on the image plane.

20.2.2 Point Representation of Two-Dimensional Shape

The utility of resolution hierarchies in image interpretation can be illustrated with a simple example of two-dimensional shape representation. Consider the pattern shown in the upper left of Fig.20 .1. There are at least
three obvious levels of detail at which it makes sense to represent this
shape. At the coarsest level, it is simply a surface representable as a
single point in space. At a somewhat finer level of detail, it is a surface
with four significant "corners", perhaps representable by four points in
space. At an even finer level of detail, there are "bumps" along the otherwise straight contours of the surface, requiring a more complex representational structure. Any one (or all) of these different levels of representation may be necessary for a particular interpretation task.

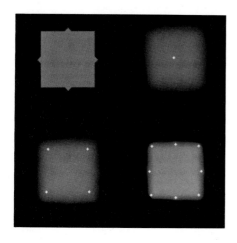

Fig. 20.1. The object in the upper
left can be represented at several
levels of detail. Three of these
levels are shown, with their corresponding tokens shown as crosses

As described above, it is often useful to be able to identify tokens corresponding to locally distinctive regions in an image. For multiresolution systems, token detectors are required which can be tuned to a particular level of
detail. In the above example, local extrema in the Laplacian of intensity
values of a blurred version of the image can be used in this manner. The
level of detail is specified by the width of the blurring kernel. Figure 20.1
shows three blurred versions of the original pattern and the tokens detected
by this method.

20.2.3 Implementing Coarse-to-Fine Token Matching

A multiresolution approach can provide increased efficiency and accuracy in
token matching. Two factors affect the difficulty of matching corresponding
points in an image pair [20.1]. When either the number of points to be matched
or the disparity range increases, the correspondence problem becomes more complex, since the number of false targets for each match increases. The need
for relatively dense disparity fields at subsequent processing steps indicates
that the number of points to be matched should be large. A desire to detect
change at a variety of scales indicates that the disparity range should be
large. A matching system operating at a single fine level of detail under
these conditions will encounter a large number of false targets for every
point it attempts to match. Such a system is computationally complex and
prone to error.

The hierarchical point representation of two-dimensional shape described
in Sect. 20.2.2 leads naturally to a multiresolution system for disparity
determination which can minimize the problems encountered by a single level
system. The points at each level in the shape description hierarchy form the
set of points to be matched at each level in the disparity determination system. Thus, at the coarsest level of detail, large surfaces which are represented by a single point are matched. Although the disparity range may be
great, there are few points, and thus few false targets. At successively
finer levels of detail, substructures within the surfaces are matched. Matches at coarser levels focus the search at finer levels. Although the total
number of points has increased, the range over which search must be performed
is narrowed, resulting in few false targets for every point. The search at
each level is performed relative to the matches at coarser levels, with a progressively narrowing search window as finer levels of detail are matched.

Several issues need to be addressed in the design of this hierarchical
matching system. It is necessary to use a token operator for each level of
detail which will repeatedly choose features at corresponding points in each
frame. It appears to be desirable to use the same form of operator at each
level of detail by adjusting the "size" of the operator appropriately. The
actual levels of detail must be chosen and described computationally [20.19-21].
At each level, matches are obtained for a sparse set of points in the image.
The resulting disparity values must be interpolated in some manner to obtain
a dense vector field for interpretation purposes and also for prediction at
the next finer level of detail. Numerical approximation techniques based on
sophisticated optimization criteria have been suggested [20.22]. Simpler
approaches to the interpolation problem include some sort of nearest-neighbor

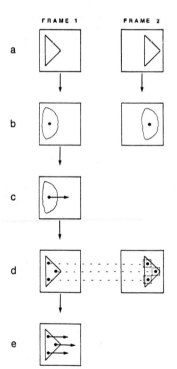

Fig. 20.2. Hierarchical token matching. **(a)**
Two frames in an image sequence. **(b)** The
two frames at a coarse level of detail,
where the object can be represented by a
single token, shown here as a dot. **(c)**
Disparity vector at the coarse level. **(d)**
Tokens obtained at a finer level of detail.
The disparity obtained at the previous
coarser level is used to center the search
window in frame. **(e)** Disparity vectors at
the finer level

scheme, or blurring (averaging). All of these approaches have problems, particularly at edges.

Figure 20.2 illustrates our technique for a triangular object. The image pair is shown in Fig. 20.2a, with the object translating to the right. In Fig.20.2b, the object is represented in both frames by a single token, as would be obtained by locating the extrema of the Laplacian at a coarse level of detail. We use a relaxation labelling technique [20.17] to obtain the matches at each level of detail. A list of potential matches in frame 2 is constructed for every token in frame 1. An initial confidence is assigned to each potential match, based upon similarity of intensity values in the areas surrounding the token points in frames 1 and 2 and upon the expectation of the true disparity provided by coarser level matches. In the iterative updating of these confidences, neighboring frame 1 tokens with potential matches of similar disparity increase the confidences that this is the true disparity for each point. The matching process for Fig. 20.2b is trivial since there is only one token per image. A single disparity vector is obtained as shown in Fig. 20.2c. By blurring this vector it is associated with every point in a region whose extent is comparable to that used to obtain the original token. The blurred representation provides expected disparities at the next level of detail. Thus, every pixel in this blurred region will have the same expected disparity vector. A confidence value which decreases with distance from the original vector is associated with the disparity at every pixel. The tokens obtained at the next finer level of detail are shown in Fig. 20.2d. In constructing the list of possible matches for each frame 1 token, the expected disparity at that point is used to center the search window for possible matches. The size of this search window varies, being smaller at finer levels of detail, and also smaller for larger confidences in expected disparity. As a result, in Fig. 20.2d each frame 1 token has only one possible match. The disparities are shown in Fig. 20.2e. Note that the process of centering the search window guides the matching process relative to the previous level of detail, and thus this scheme is both hierarchical and relative.

20.3 Multiresolution Analysis of Motion and Spatial Properties

20.3.1 A Model for Multiresolution Motion Analysis

Many approaches for obtaining motion parameters and spatial properties from image sequences assume that a dense and accurate vector field is available (e.g. [20.5,6,12]. In these approaches, the analysis is viewed as a two-step process: (a) determine disparities, and (b) analyze disparity fields to obtain three-dimensional scene properties. As these two tasks are usually considered in isolation, a discrepancy often results between the output of disparity determination techniques and the required input for three-dimensional analysis. Disparity fields obtained from realistic imagery are typically noisy and/or sparse, leading to serious problems with interpretive techniques. Although interpolation can fill the gaps to produce dense vector fields, such fields will be only an approximation of the true values. We feel that a more robust approach which integrates these two phases of motion analysis is possible by utilizing the levels of detail from the multiresolution token matching process to determine three-dimensional scene properties.

A fundamental premise in this model is that partial specifications of shape and spatial layout parameters are often sufficient for further interpretive analysis, yet are significantly easier to compute in some respects than more complete descriptions. They are typically less sensitive to noise and require the assumption of fewer constraints about scene properties and the imaging process. Subsequent sections discuss a preliminary version of a model of image understanding in which relational effects have a primary role. The model is structured to compute and represent changes in image and scene properties at different levels of detail, rather than the properties themselves. This approach leads naturally to a qualitative form of interpretation. For example, it is usually possible to determine which of two visible surfaces is farther away without first determining the depth to either surface. While this paper deals only with information arising from motion, we feel that the approach will prove to be of value when dealing with many other image cues as well.

The model structures computations through the use of <u>contextual reference frames</u>. Scene and image properties are explicitly represented at several levels of detail. The <u>value</u> of a property at a particular level is dependent on the <u>context</u> of the property at a coarser level of detail. This context is the dominant value of that property in a local neighborhood at the next coarser level. The context serves two functions. As with many other multiresolution systems, it provides expectations which can be used to guide the more detailed processing. In addition, the context acts as a base line for the representation at the finer level. At this finer level, values are represented as deviations from the expected value generated by the context. Currently, we implement these detail hierarchies using registered iconic representations which differ in effective resolution. Such an organization is convenient from a computational standpoint, but we suspect that contexts are not strictly local and are influenced by a variety of grouping effects.

The approach can be illustrated by considering the example shown in Fig. 20.3, in which the dominant motion is translation to the right. This defines a context for two other types of motion: the circular motion of the wheels and pedals and the up-and-down motion of the rider's legs. These circular and reciprocating motions are easily represented relative to the translation

Fig. 20.3. As the tricycle translates to the right, it provides the context for describing the rotation of the wheels and the pumping legs. (Art work courtesy of Jim Moen)

348

of the bicycle, but would appear as considerably more complex trajectories if represented with respect to the ground or the image plane.

Motion and spatial relationships in the world exist in a multiresolution hierarchy. The contextual reference frame approach, which is both hierarchical and relative, can enhance the recovery of such properties from image sequences by decoupling their components at different levels of detail. This approach has the additional advantage of being self-normalizing, so that effects such as camera model and observer motion need not be considered at every level of detail. The existence of detail hierarchies at one level of abstraction can lead naturally to the computation of hierarchical representations at higher levels of abstraction. Thus resolution hierarchies within levels of abstraction are useful not only as a computational tool for the efficient derivation of highly detailed information, but also as a representational tool. In particular, intermediate levels in a resolution hierarchy are valuable for their own sake, not just as a step towards computing higher resolution values.

20.3.2 Determining Motion Parameters

It is possible to obtain parameters describing the relative translational and rotational motions of the objects and sensor from the two-dimensional disparity field. Several analytic solutions have been developed which require dense and accurate disparity fields as input [20.5,6,12]. Other approaches rely upon minimizing some error function [20.10,11], thus enabling them to function on noisy and sparse fields. However, these latter techniques assume that the motion parameters are constant across the sampled field, meaning either that only the sensor is moving or that sampling must occur within the bounds of a single object. Both the analytic and error minimization approaches are of limited value in an unconstrained motion environment where only noisy and sparse vector fields are available. A hierarchical, relative approach may be more useful to obtain motion parameters.

Several distinct types of motion may occur across image sequences. These motions affect the perceived image at varying levels of detail. Observer motion, for example, causes global change across the image since the entire image plane moves. Object motions affect the image more locally. In addition, object motions of different types are manifested at different levels of detail in the sequence. The apparent motions of objects can be classified into four categories [20.23] (see Fig. 20.4). When an object translates parallel to the image plane, the vectors describing point changes between images have the same direction at every point on the object. For object translation perpendicular to the image plane and for object rotations, the vectors are different at every object point. Combinations of these motions result in more complex vector patterns which are sums of the four simple signatures.

Analysis of the vector fields at multiple levels of detail, where each level is represented relative to lower levels, simplifies the task of identifying the types of object motion. At a representational level of detail corresponding to the size of the object, the object is represented as a single token. Rotational effects are ignored. Translational effects are detectable, but three-dimensional trajectories cannot be determined. At a finer level of detail, information about the changes in the contour or surface properties of an object allow recovery of rotation and changes in depth. For example, consider the situation in which an object is translating but not rotating relative to the observation point, and knowledge about whether the object is moving toward or away from the image plane is required. This

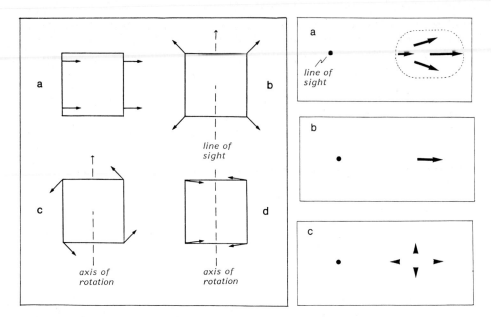

Fig. 20.4. Four vector "signatures" resulting from motion. **(a)** Translation parallel to the image plane. **(b)** Translation along the line of sight.
(c) Rotation around the line of sight. **(d)** Rotation around an axis which
lies on the object surface, parallel to the image plane

Fig. 20.5. Hierarchical analysis of vector fields can predict collisions.
(a) Disparity vectors for an object at a fine level of detail. **(b)** Aggregate translation of the object on the image plane. **(c)** Representation
of the fine-level disparity with respect to the aggregate translation.
While the vector pattern in (c) indicates that the object is moving toward the sensor, collision will not occur since the aggregate tanslation
in (b) is nonzero

may be dealt with easily in a two-step process (see Fig. 20.5). First, the
aggregate translation of the object on the image plane is determined at an
appropriately coarse level of detail. Next, the disparity over the object
with respect to this aggregate translation is found at a finer level of detail. Approaching objects have a distinctive signature: a radial pattern of
expanding flow vectors. Receding objects exhibit a similar pattern, except
that the vectors are converging. Furthermore, if all motion is in a straight
line, an approaching object will collide with the sensor if and only if the
apparent speed of translation is zero. (In practice, the nonzero spatial
extent of the sensor must also be considered.) Comparable but somewhat more
complex analysis may be useful in dealing with rotations.

20.3.3 Edge Detection [1]

In situations where an image sensor is moving through an otherwise static
environment, the directions of the optical flow vectors will vary slowly

---

1. Material in the following two sections originally appeared in [20.24].

across the entire image. At edges, discontinuities will occur in magnitude
only, and for most analytic purposes the vector field can be reduced to a
scalar field [20.2,22]. When arbitrary motion is allowed, the discontinuity
may occur in either magnitude, direction, or both. The vector field in
this case cannot be simplified to a scalar field.

Such discontinuities for two-dimensional vector fields can be detected
in a manner similar to that of MARR and HILDRETH's "zero crossings" in the
scalar case [20.20]. Discontinuity in a discrete image field means that
the variability on either side of an edge is much less than the variability
across the edge. If the edge is approximately linear and variability along
the edge is suitably constrained, the search for discontinuities can be decomposed into a separate analysis of the scalar fields corresponding to the
x and y components of the optical flow. (These constraints are generalizations of the "linear variability" assumption used in [20.20].) A discontinuity in either component corresponds to a discontinuity in the original
field. Two disparity fields from different resolution levels in the token
matching system are used. Interpolation serves not only to make the fields
dense, but also to smooth them, which reduces the effects of noise and
serves as a bandpass filter on width of the edges. A Gaussian smoothing
kernel is used, since it is optimal with respect to the condition of simultaneous locality in the space and frequency domains.

A discontinuity in either of the original scalar fields will result in a
peak in the first derivative of the smoothed field, and a zero crossing in
the second derivative. The Laplacian is a more convenient operator than
the second derivative, however, since it is invariant with respect to coordinate rotations, allowing a one-pass search for edges with arbitrary
orientations. For scalar fields that vary linearly parallel to straight

Fig. 20.6   Fig. 20.7

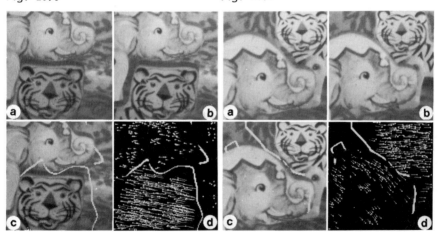

Fig. 20.6. Edge detection from disparity fields. **(a-b)** Original image pair.
(c) Edge points obtained with the method described in Sect. 20.3.3 overlaid
in white on first image. **(d)** Edge points shown with the vector field obtained by the multiresolution point matching technique

Fig. 20.7. Edge detection from disparity fields. **(a-b)** Original image pair.
(c) Edge points. **(d)** Disparity vectors and edge points

edges, the Laplacian is equal to the second derivative taken in the direction of greatest variation. The Laplacian operator applied to a smoothed function has the additional advantage of being closely approximated by the difference of two Gaussian functions [20.20].

Actual discontinuities are found by recombining the Laplacians of the two scalar components into a vector field and then searching for the vector field analog of a scalar zero crossing. At an edge, there will be a zero crossing in at least one component of this difference field, and a value of zero in the other component. Both components may have a zero crossing. In either case, adjacent vectors will reverse direction when an edge lies between them. Figures 20.6,7 show examples of this technique applied to realistic vector fields, which are noisy and sparse.

As with the zero-crossing approach to luminance edges, the Laplacian of a smoothed optical flow field can be estimated by taking the difference of two fields blurred by Gaussian kernels with the appropriate ratios of standard deviations. In terms of our contextual reference frame model, different levels in the token matching system correspond to different levels of detail. Edges are manifested by directional reversals in optical flow at a given level of detail when that flow is represented with respect to a coarser level of detail.

20.3.4 Identifying Occluding Surfaces

When analyzing the spatial organization of a scene, it is important to account for the asymmetry of occlusion edges. While edges are often described as boundaries between two image regions, occlusion edges are only the boundaries of one or the other of the corresponding surfaces. Detail hierarchies of optical flow can be used to determine which side of a discontinuity in disparity corresponds to the occluding surface. This provides information about both scene structure and relative depth.

The key to resolving this edge ambiguity is to note that, over time, the edge will have the same disparity as the surface to which it corresponds. Furthermore, only the motion components perpendicular to the edge lead to asymmetric changes in the appearance of the boundary. This observation results in a simple computational test. Once an edge has been found at a particular level of detail, a lower level of detail may be used to get an estimate of the expected image position of the edge in a subsequent frame.

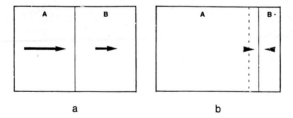

Fig. 20.8. **(a)** Disparity field obtained from initial image pair, with motion of regions A and B indicated by vectors. **(b)** Fine-level vector field from second image pair represented relative to a coarser level. A is the occluding surface. The expected edge location is shown as a dotted line. The relative vector at the expected location points toward the occluded surface

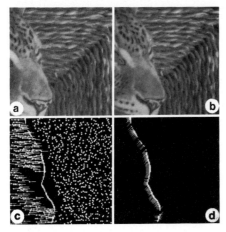

Fig. 20.9. Identifying occluding surface. **(a-b)** Original image pair. **(c)** Disparity field and edge points. **(d)** Edge elements together with associated vectors pointing towards the occluding surface

Disparity estimates at this coarser level will be affected by regions on either side of the edge and hence will be an average of the two actual values. The real edge will be translating over the image with a speed either faster or slower than the estimate. Thus, at the "expected" edge location, the fine-level vector which is represented relative to a coarser level will not exhibit a directional reversal. However, when this vector is projected onto the normal of the edge, the resulting vector points toward the occluded surface. Figure 20.8 illustrates this technique for one possible motion case, and Fig. 20.9 presents an example of the technique applied to a realistic vector field.

20.4 Summary

The use of multiple levels of detail has proven valuable in the determination of spatial properties from time-varying imagery. Particularly important is the utilization of relative representations of shape and image properties, where these properties at one level of detail are described in terms of a coarser level. In this approach, values at all levels are important for subsequent analysis. Complete detail hierarchies at one level of abstraction in a computer vision system often are useful in determining values of properties at other levels of abstraction. The approach is well suited to situations where generality is required, but only partial specifications of scene properties are needed.

Acknowedgements

The authors thank Richard Madarasz and Joseph Kearney for helpful comments, and Jim Moen for Fig. 20.3.

References

20.1 D. A. Marr: Vision: A Computational Investigation into the Human Representation and Processing of Visual Information (Freeman, San Francisco, CA, 1982)
20.2 W. F. Clocksin: Perception of surface slant and edge labels from optical flow: a computational approach, Perception 9, 253-269 (1980)
20.3 S. Ullman: The Interpretation of Visual Motion (MIT Press, Cambridge, MA, 1979)

20.4   H. H. Nagel: Representation of moving rigid objects based on visual observations, Computer 14(8), 29-39 (1981)

20.5   K. Prazdny: Egomotion and relative depth map from optical flow, Biological Cybernetics 36, 07-102 (1980)

20.6   H. C. Longuet-Higgins, K. Prazdny: The interpretation of a moving retinal image, Proc. Royal Society (London) B208, 385-397 (1980)

20.7   D. D. Hoffman: "Inferring Shape from Motion Fields", Artificial Intelligence Laboratory Memo 592, MIT (1980)

20.8   D. T. Lawton: "Constraint-based inference from image motion", in Proc. Nat'l. Conf. on Artificial Intelligence, Stanford, CA, 1980, pp. 31-34

20.9   K. Prazdny: "Relative Depth and Local Surface Orientation from Image Motion", Computer Science Technical Report TR-996, University of Maryland (1981)

20.10 A. R. Bruss, B. K. P. Horn: "Passive Navigation", Artificial Intelligence Laboratory Memo 645, MIT (1981)

20.11 K. Prazdny: Determining the instantaneous direction of motion from optical flow generated by a curvilinearly moving observer, Computer Graphics Image Processing 17, 238-248 (1981)

20.12 R. Y. Tsai, T. S. Huang: "Estimating three-dimensional motion parameters of a rigid planar patch", in Proc. Pattern Recognition and Image Processing Conf., Dallas, TX, 1981, pp. 94-97

20.13 R. O. Duda, P. E. Hart: Pattern Classification and Scene Analysis (Wiley, New York, 1973)

20.14 H. P. Moravec: "Towards automatic visual obstacle avoidance", in Proc. 5th Int'l. Joint Conf. on Artificial Intelligence, Pittsburgh, PA, 1977, p. 584

20.15 K. Price, R. Reddy: Matching segments of images, IEEE Trans. Pattern Analysis Machine Intelligence PAMI-1, 110-118 (1979)

20.16 D. Marr, T. Poggio: A theory of human stereo vision, Proc. Royal Society (London) B204, 301-328 (1979)

20.17 S. T. Barnard, W. B. Thompson: Disparity analysis of images, IEEE Trans. Pattern Analysis Machine Intelligence PAMI-2, 333-340 (1980)

20.18 J. J. Gibson, The Senses Considered as Perceptual Systems (Houghton-Mifflin, Boston, MA, 1966)

20.19 J. L. Crowley: "A Representation for Visual Information", Robotics Institute Technical Report 82-7, Carnegie-Mellon University (1982)

20.20 D. Marr, E. Hildreth: Theory of edge detection, Proc. Royal Society (London) B207, 187-217 (1980)

20.21 P. J. Burt, E. H. Adelson: The Laplacian pyramid as a compact image code, IEEE Trans. Communications COMM-31, 532-540 (1983)

20.22 W. E. L. Grimson: From Images to Surfaces: A Computational Study of the Human Early Visual System (MIT Press, Cambridge, MA, 1981)

20.23 E. Borjesson, C. Von Hofsten: A vector model for perceived object rotation and translation in space, Psychological Research 38, 209-230 (1975)

20.24 W. B. Thompson, K. M. Mutch, V. Berzins: "Edge detection in optical flow fields", Proc. Nat'l. Conf. on Artificial Intelligence, Pittsburgh, PA, 1982, pp. 26-29

Part VII

Applications

21. Multiresolution Microscopy

K. Preston, Jr.

Department of Electrical Engineering, Carnegie-Mellon University
and University of Pittsburgh, Pittsburgh, PA 15213, USA

Image processing using pyramidal methods relies on the practical recordability of the World Plane (the base of the pyramid). In many actual applications this is difficult, if not impossible. In automated microscopy for blood-cell analysis the World Plane contains data equivalent to approximately one billion bytes. The robot microscope must examine and process this data in about sixty seconds. To accomplish this a telescope is used instead of a pyramid. This paper describes telescopic methods for multiresolution image analysis with applications not only to the recognition of human blood cells but also to feature extraction from images of human tissue.

21.1 Introduction

A cash flow of between half a million to one million dollars per day is generated by the robot microscopes now in use for examining human blood cells. This represents a market penetration of from five to ten percent into the two to four billion dollar annual gross of hematology laboratories nationwide. This blood-cell analyzing business is almost as large as the entire semiconductor industry and at least an order of magnitude larger than the cash flow produced by all national companies in the robotics industry. It would therefore seem wise to examine the methodology by which these robot microscopes collectively screen and process the images of a few thousand billion objects per year.

The method of image processing employed by these microscopes is telescopic rather than pyramidal because it is not economically feasible to record the image data so as to construct the base of a pyramid. Rather than building a pyramid with its variable processing window, these machines utilize a processing window of constant dimensions containing a constant number of picture elements whose size is variable in terms of the resolution at the substrate level. Telescopic processing forms the optimal solution to multicolor, multiresolution microscopy in this case and, therefore, it is expected that it may have useful applications in other areas.

21.2 Processing Methods

The purpose of this section is to compare telescopic with pyramidal processing and to indicate the reasons for its selection as the image processing method for multiresolution microscopy. Terms are defined and block schematics are given contrasting the two methods.

21.2.1 The Pyramidal Method

Figure 21.1 is a schematic of the traditional pyramid as presented in several other papers in this volume. The image data is initially recorded as

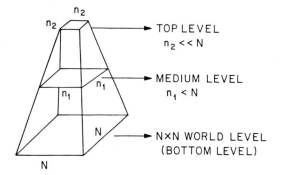

TOP LEVEL

$n_2 << N$

MEDIUM LEVEL

$n_1 < N$

N×N WORLD LEVEL
(BOTTOM LEVEL)

Fig. 21.1. Pyramidal structure for image analysis starting at the N × N World Level
and reducing to a much smaller
n_2 × n_2 Top Level

an N × N array at the bottom level of the pyramid which we refer to as the
"World Plane" or "World Level." It is also assumed that at this level the
image data has been sampled at the NYQUIST rate. Thus the highest spatial
frequency in the original image data is N/2 cycles across the N × N aperture.
Various region growing, boundary finding, feature extraction, and other techniques are then used to convert the initial data into data to be stored in a
secondary array of dimensions n_1 × n_1 which appears at one of the medium
levels of the pyramid (Fig. 21.1). Further reduction in the array size may
continue until the top level of the pyramid is reached, at which point the
resulting n_2 × n_2 array contains the final result of upward processing in
the pyramid. At this point analysis may be directed down the pyramid to
other medium levels whose contents may be modified for still further analysis
up the pyramid. This process continues until all desired intelligence has
been extracted from the original data.

21.2.2 The Telescopic Method

Pyramidal processing is based upon the assumption that the original image
data may be recorded at the NYQUIST rate in an economic and practical fashion. In practice this is seldom the case. Take, for example, the World

Fig. 21.2 a. The World Level (15000 × 15000) for the GEOS weather satellite
Fig. 21.2 b. An image data array (512 × 512) taken at the Nyquist rate

Plane of the GOES weather satellite (Fig. 21.2) where N = 15000. Each GOES satellite produces an N × N frame every thirty minutes. The data from this frame essentially fills a 300MB disk pack. It is unlikely that any method of pyramidal processing could address such a large array and complete all required processing within the time available. Instead, small sections of the entire N × N array are extracted (Fig.21.2) and operated upon as required using a more practical processing window, say 512 × 512.

When many extractions are made at various resolutions but always with the same processing window size, we call this type of processing "telescopic." This is diagrammed in Fig. 21.3. All processing arrays in the telescope are of the same N × N array size. The actual dimensions are determined by the associated dedicated image processor. Only at the highest level of the telescope are images addressed at the NYQUIST interval. This is called the "NYQUIST Level" and the pixel at this level a "NYQUIST Element." The NYQUIST Level is used only when it is absolutely necessary to extract information from the image data which appears within a bandwidth extending to the highest spatial frequencies.

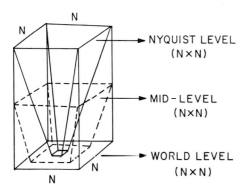

Fig. 21.3. Telescopic structure for image analysis wherein the processing window is constant at N × N while the resolution (number of Nyquist elements per pixel) is varied

Although it may appear that the telescope is simply an inverted pyramid, this is not the case. The image processor always operates upon a data array of constant size. Also the telescopic processor never requires that the World Level be recorded at full resolution. Therefore, telescopic processing implies a multiresolution input device or "scanner."

21.3 Practical Applications

This section describes two practical applications of telescopic image analysis. One is the already commercialized field of automated hematology. The other is taken from a current research project in computed tissue stereology.

21.3.1 Blood Cell Analysis

Figure 21.4 shows the image data in the World Plane used in the analysis of the blood cells of a single human subject. The field of view is approximately 2.5 × 2.5 mm which, at the NYQUIST rate of 10000 samples per millimeter, would produce almost one billion pixels. In this field of view approximately 200,000 blood cells (mostly red cells) are located which must be screened in a few tens of seconds in order to find the approximately 200 cells of interest (white cells). Screening is done using an image recorded

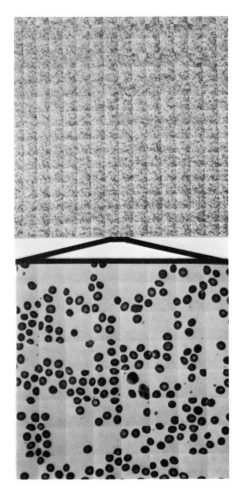

Fig. 21.4. Top: The World Level for human blood-cell analysis showing some 200,000 cells. Bottom: A higher resolution version at which level the individual white blood cells may be recognized

at a rate far below the NYQUIST rate. For example, the Coulter Electronics diff3-50 utilizes a World Level in its image processing telescope where the recording is made at 300 elements per millimeter. At this resolution the World Plane contains only 500,000 elements which are screened in the process of locating the white cells among the red cells. When the diff3-50 has located the white cells, then the resolution of the telescope switches to a medium value of 2500 elements per millimeter (Fig. 21.4). Careful study has cating the white cells among the red cells. When the diff3-50 has located the white cells, then the resolution of the telescope switches to a medium value of 2500 elements per millimeter (Fig. 21.4). Careful study has indicated that the images of white blood cells generated at this sampling rate produce satisfactory recognition criteria.

The actual processing executed per white cell is shown in Fig. 21.5 which shows gray level images of each of the five major classes of human white blood cells and the results of selected steps in the diff3-50 spatial processing cycle. In the diff3-50 processing requires a few tenths of a second per white blood cell. The output of this analysis is an estimate of the values of some 50 features (mainly spatial but also colorimetric) from which a particular cell is recognized by means of pairwise, majority voting, linear discriminant analysis. These operations are described in detail by NORGREN, KULKARNI and GRAHAM [21.1]. Technical details concerning the optics, mechanics, and electronics of the diff3-50 analyzer are provided by GRAHAM and NORGREN [21.2].

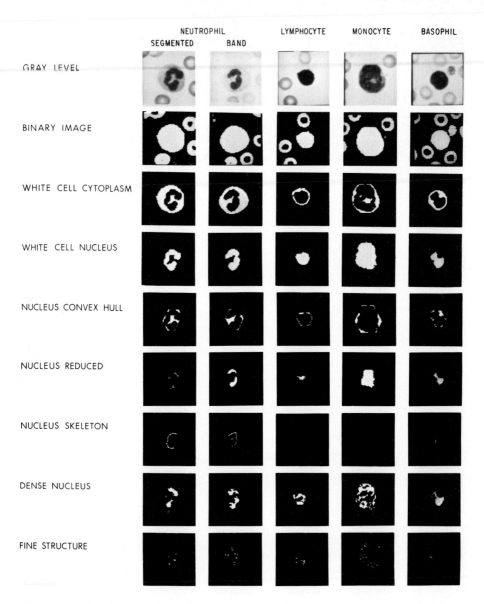

Fig. 21.5. Mosaic of 64 x 64 diff3 images with the top row showing the different classes of human white blood cells and the lower rows showing a series of binary image analyses for feature extraction

21.3.2 Computed Tissue Stereology

Telescopic processing is also being investigated in multiresolution microscopy for the analysis of images of sections of human tissue mounted on microscope slides. A still wider range of spatial frequencies is necessary in

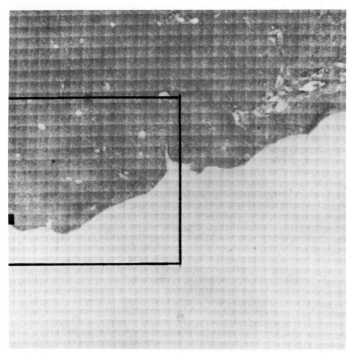

Fig. 21.6. A portion of the World Level for the analysis of human tissue samples comprised of approximately 300 billion Nyquist elements over a 5 × 5 mm field. (Small black square is a 512 × 512 array of Nyquist elements. Black border corresponds to Fig. 21.8 - top)

performing this analysis because of the wide variations in size of the various structural features of interest. Figure 21.6 shows a portion of the World Plane (5 × 5 mm) taken from the display window of a specialized research version of the diff3-50 recently produced by Coulter Electronics for Carnegie-Mellon University. This machine, as well as imaging at the World Level associated with blood cell analysis, permits a World Plane as large as 200 mm^2 (10 × 20 mm) to be addressed (Fig. 21.7). At the NYQUIST sampling rate this represents a total of 20 billion pixels or enough data to fill forty 500MB disk packs.

A telescopic sequence for processing this enormous amount of data is shown in Fig. 21.8. The upper image in Fig.21.8 shows human liver tissue imaged (in a 512 × 512 field) at the same resolution as the World Level used for human blood-cell analysis (Fig. 21.4). Moving down the column of images shown in Fig. 21.8, a line in each upper image is shown expanded by a factor of 4 to yield the corresponding line in the image below. Thus the middle image covers an area of approximately 600 × 600 micrometers and the bottom image an area of 150 × 150 micrometers. All images use a constant N × N = 512 × 512. In the upper image it is possible to recognize gross structural features such as the boundary of the tissue and the major vessels (hepatic veins and arteries). In this image the individual hepatic cells are invisible and the capillaries (thin, white lines) are visible primarily as changes in the general texture of the image. In the middle image

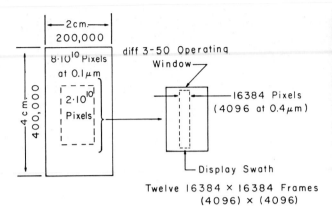

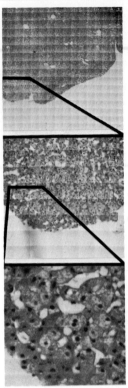

MICROSCOPE COVER SLIP

Fig. 21.7. Schematic showing the total area encompassed by a typical tissue section and the display area addressed by the Coulter Electronics diff3-50

Fig. 21.8. Progression of images produced by varying the resolution in a multiresolution microscope with the display array held constant at 512 × 512 elements. Top: 2.5 × 2.5mm. Middle: 600 × 600 µm. Bottom: 150 × 150 µm

the nuclei of the cells are just visible (small black dots) whereas the capillaries (called "sinusoids") are clearly evident. In the lower picture the hepatic nuclei are clearly defined and there is sufficient information for a differential diagnosis. The sinusoids are large and their structure is evident. The texture of the cytoplasm is also well displayed.

Research is currently underway which takes advantage of the multiresolution scanner of the research diff3-50 in order to process rapidly, by telescopic means, the data present in images of human tissue. The World Level provides an image wherein it is possible to locate the major vessels (Fig. 21.9a) The cellular architecture in the vicinity of such vessels may then be determined at one of the middle levels of the telescope (Fig. 21.9b) and, at a still higher resolution, the texture of the cytoplasm may be quantitated (Fig. 21.9c). In this way it is possible to avoid completely any attempt to address the twenty or so billion picture elements which describe a single tissue section. Instead, acting much as the human pathologist, the multiresolution scanner first provides low-resolution images in which gross structural details may be analyzed. Next selected regions are telescopically imaged for the purpose of a selective analysis employing greater detail. It has already been determined that multiresolution techniques of this kind make possible the differentiation of disease as reported by CASTILLO, YORKGITIS, and PRESTON [21.3]. Further experiments are now being conducted using tissue extracted from many different organs of the human body for the purpose of producing quantitative and useful data from computed microscopy.

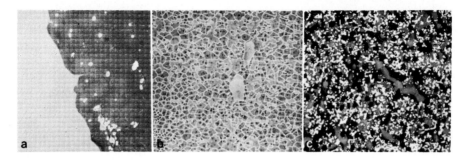

Fig. 21.9. Computer processing of a series of multiresolution images where the results at one stage guide the next. (a) Location of the major vessels at low resolution. (b) Analysis of tissue architecture neighboring a major vessel. (c) Texture measurements of the cytoplasm of cells of interest at the vessel border

21.4 Summary and Conclusions

This paper demonstrates that telescopic, multiresolution microscopy appears to solve basic-image processing problems which pyramidal processing cannot address. For example, the analysis of the blood cells of a single human individual, which must be performed in 60 seconds or less, requires that 200,000 objects be screened. At the NYQUIST rate this comprises some 600 million pixels. Clearly this is a difficult or impossible task if undertaken using a pyramid where the World Plane is initially recorded in toto. However, by recording only 500,000 elements (each comprising 1024 NYQUIST elements) it is possible to separate objects (cells) of interest from objects (cells) of no interest. The cells of interest may then be analyzed individually and recognition accomplished using a picture element size equivalent to 16 NYQUIST elements. Using this methodology microscopes such as the diff3-50 are able to screen ten million objects per hour while analyzing in detail ten thousand objects.

In effect 10^{16} NYQUIST elements are processed per year by the 500 robot microscopes now in use worldwide. However, the actual rate of extraction of elements is reduced by a factor of 1000 by means of telescopic processing. It is interesting to compare this throughput with other well-known imaging systems. For example, the earth resources satellite LANDSAT scans approximately 10^{12} NYQUIST elements per year of which only a small percentage is recorded (due to the paucity of active LANDSAT receiving stations) and an even smaller percentage is computer analyzed. Thus the throughout in NYQUIST elements of the robot microscope community is equivalent to ten thousand LANDSATs. The throughput actually extracted and analyzed is equivalent to approximately ten LANDSATs, thus demonstrating the advantages of telescopic processing.

The GEOS satellites are currently producing approximately 10^{13} NYQUIST elements per year. All of these are being recorded. This data, however, forms a World Plane so large that complete computer analysis is impossible.

Naturally, the type of analysis carried out for weather satellite data and earth resources data is considerably different from that carried out for the recognition of individual human cells, so that a direct numerical comparison may be misleading. However, it is felt that all investigators in image analysis should examine the telescopic method and take full advantage of its power.

Acknowledgments

The author wishes to acknowledge the assistance of Coulter Electronics (Concord, MA) and, particularly, of M. D. Graham of that organization, as well as J. M. Herron and the staff of the Biomedical Image Processing Unit, Department of Radiation Health, University of Pittsburgh. The research reported was supported by Grant GM28221-02 from the National Institutes of Health to the Department of Electrical Engineering at Carnegie-Mellon. Karen Schill of Executive Suite (Tucson, AZ) typed the manuscript and G. Thomas and M. Adams of the Mellon Institute assisted with the illustrations.

References

21.1 P. E. Norgren, A. V. Kulkarni, M. D. Graham: Leukocyte image analysis in the diff3 system, Pattern Recognition 13, 299-314 (1981)

21.2 M. D. Graham, P. E. Norgren: "The diff3 analyzer: a parallel/serial Golay image processor", in Real Time Medical Image Processing, ed. by M. Onoe, K. Preston, Jr., A. Rosenfeld (Plenum Press, New York, 1980), pp. 163-182

21.3 X. Castillo, D. Yorkgitis, K. Preston, Jr.: A study of multidimensional multicolor images, IEEE Trans. Biomedical Engineering BME-29, 111-121 (1982)

22. Two-Resolution Detection of Lung Tumors in Chest Radiographs

J. Sklansky and D. Petković

Department of Electrical Engineering, University of California at Irvine
Irvine, CA 92717, USA

We have developed a computer system that helps radiologists to detect the images of lung tumors in chest radiographs. The system has high sensitivity and few false detections per film. To conserve memory space and especially execution time, our system operates at both "coarse" and "fine" digitizations, corresponding to sampling apertures of 1200μm and 600μm, respectively. At the first of a series of steps at coarse digitization, our system detects on the average 47 candidate tumors per radiograph. All subsequent steps reduce the number of candidates while retaining high sensitivity. Through a sequence of feature extractions and classifications at coarse followed by fine digitization these tumor candidates are reduced to only about 5 per radiograph. The resulting miss probability is 0.10, about one-third that of an average competent radiologist.

By operating in two digitizations -- resulting in two resolutions -- rather than one, we reduce the required external memory to one-half and the execution time to one-fourth of that required in a fine-digitization-only system.

22.1 Introduction

Because lung cancer is a major cause of death in the United States, and because the early detection of lung tumors often results in increased effectiveness of preventive and therapeutic measures, we have developed a computer system that helps the radiologist to detect tumors with high sensitivity and few false detections. By designing this system to operate at two levels of digitization -- "coarse" and "fine" -- we achieved great savings in memory space and computation time. The coarse digitization is obtained at an aperture of 1200μm, and the fine digitization at 600μm.

This system consists of the following major subsystems: a preprocessor, a detector, a "Stage I" classifier operating at coarse digitization, and a "Stage II" classifier operating at fine digitization. To facilitate the processing of the image in both coarse and fine digitizations, we store the two digitizations as a two-level image pyramid [22.1]. Structurally, this pyramid is an effective match to our two-stage classifier.

In this paper we describe the design philosophy of this system, including our approach to choosing the features for each of the two stages of classification.

22.2 Overview

In this section we present a global view of the system.

22.2.1 The Data-Flow Diagram

A simplified data-flow diagram of our coarse-fine system for tumor detection is illustrated in Fig. 22.1. The system consists of two major subsystems: a Coarse Subsystem and a Fine Subsystem, corresponding to coarse and fine digitization. The Coarse Subsystem consists of a preprocessor followed by a detector, feature extractor, and classifier. The preprocessor consists of a zonal notch filter followed by a gradient operator. The detector is our recently devised "spherical spoke filter." This novel filter detects spherical nodules in the radiographic image. The detector is followed by a boundary finder which computes a simple approximate boundary for each candidate tumor. Features are extracted from the coarse image (we call these "coarse features") and entered into our Stage I classifier. This classifier sorts the candidate tumors of the coarse image into <u>Stage I candidate tumors</u> and <u>nontumors</u>. The Stage I candidate tumors are passed on to the Fine Subsystem.

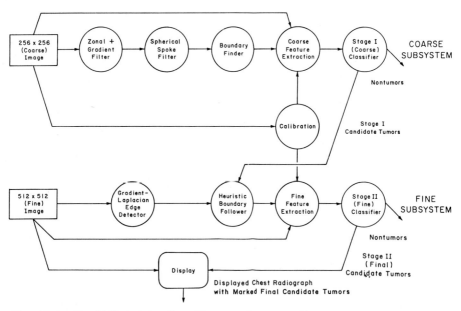

Fig. 22.1. Simplified data flow diagram of coarse-fine system for tumor detection

In the Fine Subsystem, processing takes place only in and near each of the Stage I candidate tumors. Initially the Fine Subsystem combines a 3×3 gradient with a 9×9 Laplacian to generate enhanced edge elements. These enhanced edge elements are entered into a heuristic boundary follower. After the fine digitization's boundary is formed, fine digitization features are extracted and the second stage of classification is carried out. The second and final stage of classification (Stage II) produces two classes: <u>final candidate tumors</u> and <u>nontumors</u>.

22.2.2 Matching the Structure of the Classifier to the Image Pyramid

By investigating the scatter plots of all pairs of the features that we selected for our classifier we found that the feature vectors of the true tu-

mors occupy a small subset of the space occupied by the feature vectors of
the nontumors. For simplicity we decided to use a "box classifier" -- a
piecewise linear decision surface in which each linear segment is perpendicular to a feature axis [22.2]. In such a classifier if all the features
are equally costly, i.e., if their computation requires equal amounts of time
and memory, then the classifier can be implemented as a sequential classifier in which the features are computed sequentially and in which the
order of the feature extraction does not affect the cost/benefit ratio of
the classifier. (The "cost" consists of computation time and memory size;
the "benefit" is the probability of correct classification.) On the other
hand, in practice some of the features depend for their accuracy on fine
digitization and are consequently costly to compute while other features
may be effectively and adequately computed at the coarse digitization. (For
this reason we designed the classifier in the form of two successive stages:
Stage I at coarse digitization and Stage II at fine digitization.) We refer
to these as "coarse features" and "fine features", respectively. Both the
coarse and fine features fall into three categories: contrast, shape and
texture. (Contrast and shape features are based on a spherical model of a
tumor embedded in lung tissue [22.3].)

The coarse-fine structure of the classifier is an effective match to the
data structure of a coarse-fine image pyramid. This structural match between
the classifier and the image pyramid is illustrated in Fig. 22.2.

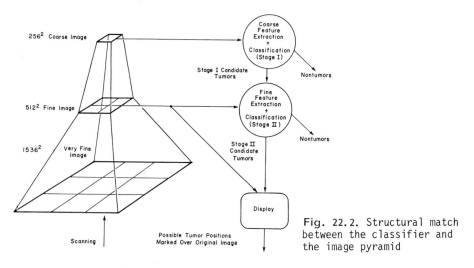

Fig. 22.2. Structural match
between the classifier and
the image pyramid

22.3 The Coarse Subsystem

In this section we describe the elements of the Coarse Subsystem.

22.3.1 Image Acquisition

Our chest radiographs are scanned on an Optronics rotating-drum microdensi-
tometer at an aperture width of 200μm and an interpixel spacing of 200μm.
This yields a 1536 × 1536 × 8-bit digital image for each chest radiograph.
This digital image is partitioned into an array of 3 × 3-pixel arrays. Each
of these arrays is replaced by its average value, yielding a "consolidated

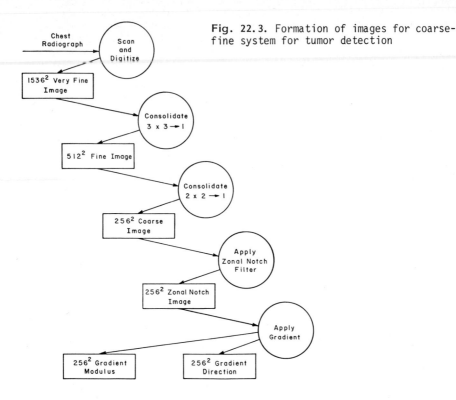

Fig. 22.3. Formation of images for coarse-fine system for tumor detection

image" at an effective aperture of 600μm. We refer to this as the fine image. A subsequent consolidation of the fine image yields a coarse image at an effective aperture of 1200μm. Both the fine and coarse images are stored on our disk for further processing.

In addition to the fine image and the coarse image, three additional 256 × 256 × 8-bit images are formed: a zonal notch image, a gradient modulus image, and a gradient direction image. (See Fig. 22.3.) Thus, for each film we obtain and store four 256 × 256 × 8-bit images and one 512 × 512 × 8-bit image.

22.3.2 Preprocessing

Our Coarse Subsystem's preprocessor consists of a zonal notch filter followed by a SOBEL gradient operator. The zonal notch filter suppresses the dynamic range of gray levels, enhances edges, and suppresses high-frequency noise with minimal distortion of edges. The SOBEL operator is applied to the image produced by the zonal notch filter, yielding a gradient modulus and a gradient direction at each pixel location [22.2,4].

22.3.3 Interfilm Calibration

A conventional approach to compensate for variations in film exposure and contrast is to perform histogram equalization [22.5]. We have found that this nonlinear process, while providing visually pleasing images, can destroy subtle information in tumor images by equalizing pixel values that are originally distinct.

A second approach is to apply a linear transformation to each image so that the transformed gray values are spread over a specified range. This transformation, unfortunately, often results in significant round-off errors; furthermore it requires additional memory space and computation time.

We devised a third approach which achieves the effect of the linear transformation in the second approach without its attendant disadvantages. In the third approach the original image is unchanged; but each extracted feature is transformed to the value it would have in an ideally linearly transformed image [22.2,6]. This interfilm calibration enables direct comparison of feature values from films with different exposures and contrasts.

In conjunction with our calibration procedure, our computer system also performs a quality check based on an analysis of spikes in the gray level histogram of the image. Errors caused by improper scanning are detected, and appropriate error messages are issued.

22.3.4 Spherical Spoke Filter

In earlier papers we introduced the "spoke filter", which successfully detected nodular tumors in medical radiographs and military vehicles in infrared scanning detectors [22.7,8].

In the present system we extended the spoke filter to detect the variations in intensities within the image of each tumor caused by the variations in thickness in the spherical model of a lung tumor. The resulting spherical spoke filter detects not only the circular shape of the boundary of a tumor image but also the hemispherical variations in intensity of such a tumor image [22.2].

Our spherical spoke filter is a very sensitive detector of nodular tumor images. Consequently, it determines the false negative rate of our entire system. This false negative rate is quite low, but the associated false positive rate is high (an average of 46 per film). Most of these false positives are removed by our two-stage classifier without additional misses, achieving a reduction in false positive rate with no change in the false negative rate.

22.3.5 Finding the Coarse Boundary

Our coarse-boundary finder examines the centers and radii of the candidate tumors detected by the spherical spoke filter. A cluster of centers that are sufficiently close to each other is presumed to be generated by a single tumor. The boundary of this tumor is formed by finding the union of the circular disks centered at these mutually close centers, with the radii computed by the spherical spoke filter [22.2]. The boundary of the union of these disks is the boundary formed by our "coarse-boundary finder". From this boundary our system computes the center and mean radius of an annular "plan" for the heuristic boundary follower in the Fine Subsystem. (See Figs. 22.4,5.) The width of the annular region is an empirically derived function of the estimated size of the tumor.

22.3.6 Coarse Features

Since textural features require a relatively large number of pixels for statistical significance, textural features are restricted to fine digitization. Thus, the coarse features in our system are restricted to contrast and shape.

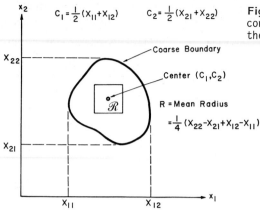

$$C_1 = \frac{1}{2}(X_{11} + X_{12})$$ $$C_2 = \frac{1}{2}(X_{21} + X_{22})$$

Fig. 22.4. R is the region for convolution; C_1, C_2, R specify the plan for the fine boundary

Coarse Boundary

Center (C_1, C_2)

R = Mean Radius

$$= \frac{1}{4}(X_{22} - X_{21} + X_{12} - X_{11})$$

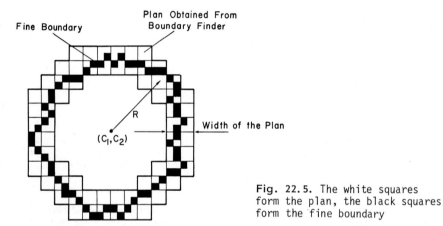

Plan Obtained From Boundary Finder

Fine Boundary

R

(C_1, C_2)

Width of the Plan

Fig. 22.5. The white squares form the plan, the black squares form the fine boundary

The following are the coarse features in our system:

F1. Contrast: The maximized difference between a) the mean of the image of those pixels whose gray-level occurrence frequencies exceed an adjustable fraction of the peak gray-level frequency within the interior and b) the mean of the image of those pixels whose gray-level frequencies exceed an adjustable fraction of the peak gray-level frequency within an adjustable-width exterior neighborhood of the candidate nodule [22.2].

F2. Absolute Brightness: The mean of the image of those pixels whose gray-level frequencies exceed an adjustable fraction of the peak gray-level frequency within the interior. (This is obtained in the computation of part (a) of feature F1.)

370

F3. Shape 1:   The maximum value of the convolution of the candidate nodule image with a variable-size circular Laplacian [22.9] matched in size to the size of the candidate nodule. The region for convolution is limited to the square region R immediately around the center of the candidate tumor, as shown in Fig. 22.4, since the maximum value of the convolution is expected to lie in that region.

F4. Shape 2:   The average value of the convolution of the above Laplacian with the candidate nodule in region R.

F5. Shape 3:

$$\frac{\text{Shape 1} - \text{Shape 2}}{\text{Shape 1}}$$

Shape 3 gives an index of the relative prominence of the peak convolution value.

F6. Shape 4:   The maximum difference of gray values between two concentric annuli in the interior of the candidate tumor image [22.2].

All of the above features are calibrated by the two constants derived from the interfilm calibration procedure (Sect.22.3.3).

22.3.7 Feature Selection and Classification

Because the feature vectors of the tumors occupy a small subset of the space occupied by the feature vectors of the nontumors, we constructed a box classifier in which each segment of the decision surface of this classifier is perpendicular to one of the feature axes.

The linear segments of the decision surface of this classifier -- two linear segments for each feature -- are determined by finding the maximum and minimum values of each feature in the population of feature vectors of the true tumors. These features were partitioned into two sets: coarse and fine.

We selected our features by a "backward sequential elimination procedure" suggested to us by M. ICHINO. In this procedure we minimized the average number of false positives per film while retaining the false negative rate of the spherical spoke filter. For each false candidate nodule a feature was labeled "essential" if the elimination of that feature resulted in acceptance of that candidate nodule by the classifier. A counter for each such labeling was incremented. The feature with the smallest count was eliminated in our selection procedure; the counting process and subsequent elimination was then repeated several times. We refer to this form of feature selection as a "guided backward sequential elimination procedure." As a result of this feature selection process we obtained the coarse and fine features described in Sects. 22.3.6 and 22.4.2.

22.4 The Fine Subsystem

In this section we describe the elements of the Fine Subsystem.

22.4.1 Heuristic Boundary Follower

Our heuristic boundary follower [22.4,10] finds a closed path which minimizes a cost function dependent on.

1. the intensity of the edge at pixel location x;
2. deviation from the annular "plan" computed by the coarse boundary finder;
3. consistency of edge direction with the annular plan;
4. the estimated size of the candidate nodule, provided by the coarse boundary finder.

Figure 22.6 illustrates the coarse and fine boundaries of a tumor image. Parts (a) and (b) of this figure show the coarse image and the boundary found by the coarse-boundary finder. Parts (c) and (d) show the fine image and the boundary found by the heuristic boundary follower.

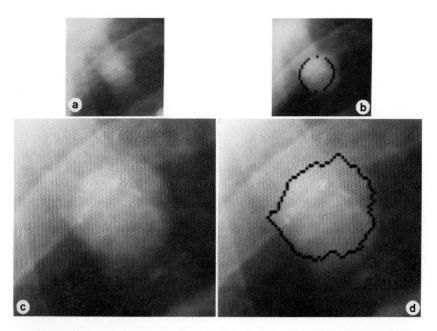

Fig. 22.6. Coarse and fine tumor images and their computed boundaries

22.4.2 Fine Features

Our fine features fall into three categories: shape features that are computed automatically in the execution of the heuristic boundary follower, texture features obtained from the histogram of gray levels in the interior of the candidate tumor, and shape features based on the distribution of edge intensities along the computed fine digitization boundary. Our fine features are as follows:

F7. <u>Shape 5</u>: The ratio of the maximum value in the histogram of edge-
element directions of the computed boundary divided by the

372

minimum nonzero value of that histogram. This feature facilitates the discrimination of piecewise linear boundaries from smoothly curved boundaries through the occurrence of spikes in the histogram of edge-element directions in piecewise linear boundaries.

F8. Standard Deviation: The standard deviation of gray levels in the interior of the candidate tumor.

F9. Skew Rate: The skew rate of the histogram of gray levels in the interior of the candidate tumor.

F10. Kurtosis: The kurtosis of the histogram of gray levels in the interior of the candidate tumor.

F11. Energy: The energy of the histogram of gray levels in the interior of the candidate tumor.

F12. Mean Edge Strength: The mean intensity of the edge elements in the computed boundary.

F13. Standard Deviation of Edge Strength: The standard deviation of the intensities of the edge elements in the computed boundary.

All of the above features are calibrated by our interfilm calibration procedure before delivering them to the Stage II classifier.

22.5 Experimental Test of Our System

In this section we describe a test of the effectiveness of our system on a carefully validated data base.

22.5.1 Our Data Base

Our data base consisted of 19 films: 16 abnormal films containing 19 tumors, and three normal films. This data base is a subset of a data base reported in [22.2]. All the tumors in this data base were proven clinically. We used just a small number of normal films, because the false positive rate for abnormal films is very close to the false positive rate for normal films.

22.5.2 Classification Performance

The sensitivity of our system is controlled by the spherical spoke filter. We set the parameters of this filter to the same operating point as reported in an earlier experiment [22.2]. In that experiment this operating point yielded three missed tumors out of 22. Thus the remaining discussion of the classification performance is concerned with the rate of false positives.

On our data base the spherical spoke filter yielded a 10% miss rate, corresponding to two missed tumors out of 19. This spherical spoke filter detected 895 candidate tumors, 17 of which were true tumors and the remainder were false. This corresponds to 47 candidate nodules per film, on the average.

Figure 22.7 shows the average rate of false positives per film produced by the Stage I classifier as a function of the number of best features used in accordance with the guided backward sequential elimination procedure. The numbers in the parentheses denote the identification numbers of the features as given in this paper.

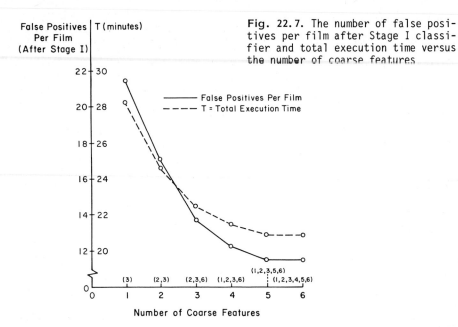

Fig. 22.7. The number of false positives per film after Stage I classifier and total execution time versus the number of coarse features

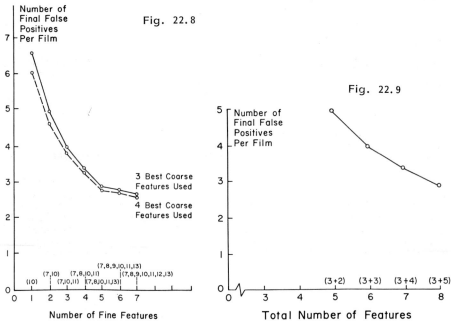

Fig. 22.8. The number of final false positives per film versus the number of fine features

Fig. 22.9. The number of final false positives per film versus the total number of coarse and fine features

We believe that the best subset of features occurs at the knee of the
curve, corresponding to three or four features. We believe this because
further reduction of the number of features raises the number of false positives substantially. The rates of false positives corresponding to three
and four features are 13.7 and 12.4 false positives per film respectively.
For these three and four features used in the Coarse Subsystem we plotted
in Fig. 22.8 the final false positive rate produced by the Stage II classifier. The dashed line corresponds to four coarse features.

Figure 22.9 shows the final false positive rate per film as a function
of the total number of features, both coarse and fine. Only the cases of
three and four coarse features are used. For example, when the total number of features is six, we consider two cases: a) four coarse and two
fine and b) three coarse and three fine. We chose the case having a smaller
false positive rate, and plotted it in Fig. 22.9. In this figure the numbers of coarse and fine features are indicated in parentheses.

Consider, for example, the case where the total number of features is
six. Here the false positive rate is 3.95 false positives per film. This
performance is comparable to that in an earlier experiment in which we used
19 features at coarse digitization [22.2]. There the miss rate was 14% and
the false positive rate was 3.1 false positives per film. Thus using a
coarse-fine classifier structure in conjunction with a two-level image pyramid we have reduced the number of features by more than a factor of 3, thereby
raising considerably the statistical reliability of our experiment [22.11,12].
(The ratio of the false-positive sample size to the number of features is
895/6 = 149, which we consider to be adequate.)

22.5.3 Execution Time

The total time T for executing our coarse-fine tumor detection algorithm
consists of the execution time C for the Coarse Subsystem and the execution
time F for the Fine Subsystem:

$$T = C + F \,.$$

In our definition of T we exclude the time required for scanning the
radiograph (approximately 20 minutes on our present equipment) and for reducing the number of pixels in the original image to 512×512 and 256×256.

The time C consists of the time Z consumed by the zonal notch filter (4
minutes), the time G for computing the gradient modulus and the gradient
direction (0.8 minute), the time S consumed by the spherical filter (4.1
minutes), the time L consumed by the calibration procedure (0.2 minute),
and the time for processing the candidate nodules at coarse digitization
T_p, where T_p is the product of the number of the candidate tumors per film
N_c and the processing time M for each candidate tumor. (In our case N_c=47,
and M=3 seconds.) Thus

$$C = Z + G + S + L + N_cM = 11.5 \text{ minutes} \,.$$

The execution time F at fine digitization is given by

$$F = N_fK$$

where N_f is the number of candidate tumors produced by the Stage I classifier,
and K is the processing time per candidate tumor at fine digitzation (45
seconds).

From this analysis it follows that T depends only upon the number of coarse features. Thus we have plotted T in Fig.22.7. This curve is represented by the dashed line. We conclude again that we should use at least three features at coarse digitization, since T rises considerably for fewer than three features at coarse digitization. For the use of three features at coarse digitization, T is 22.5 minutes.

22.5.4 Comparison Between Coarse-Only, Coarse-Fine, and Fine-Only Tumor Detection Systems

In this section we compare the performances and costs of three tumor detection systems: coarse-only, coarse-fine, and fine-only.

The performance will be described in terms of the miss rate, the number of false positives per film, and the number of features. The cost will be described in terms of computation times and the requirements for external memory.

A coarse-only system was described in an earlier report [22.2]. In that system we used 19 features. The miss rate was 13.6%, the false positive rate was 3.1 false tumors per film, the size of the external image memory was 256 K bytes, and the execution time was 12 minutes. (See Table 22.1.)

Table 22.1. Comparison of coarse-only, coarse-fine, and fine-only systems for tumor detection

Level in image pyramid	PERFORMANCE		EXECUTION TIME (excluding scanning and consolidating)	External image memory
	False negative (miss) rate	False positives per film		
COARSE				
256^2 19 features	13.6% (3 out of 22)	3.1	12 minutes	256 Kbytes
COARSE-FINE				
256^2 and 512^2 6 features	10.5% (2 out of 19)	3.95	22.5 minutes	512 Kbytes
FINE				
512^2 6 features	Expected to be similar to the coarse-fine performance		97.5 minutes (estimated)	1024 Kbytes

Since we have not implemented a fine-only system, we estimated the required memory and the computation time for this system, and we assumed that the performance of the spherical spoke filter at fine digitization is the same as at coarse digitization.

Let U denote the execution time of the fine-only system. One can show that

$$U \cong 4Z + 4G + 8S + 4L + N_c(4M+K) = 97.5 \text{ minutes} .$$

In this analysis it is assumed that the sizes of the masks for the zonal notch, the gradient and the variable-size circular Laplacian have the same

376

number of pixels at both coarse and fine digitization. Larger masks should be assumed for the fine digitization, yielding a further increase in computation time for the fine-only system. However, we did not assume these larger masks in estimating U.

We assumed that the spherical spoke filter yields the same number of candidate tumors, namely 47 per film in all three systems. In the fine-only system it is likely that the spherical spoke filter would require additional smoothing, thereby increasing the execution time U still further for the fine-only system.

The results of our comparison are displayed in Table 22.1. This table shows that the coarse-fine system is better than the coarse-only system, since by increasing the execution time and the external image memory requirement by a factor of 2 but reducing the necessary number of features by a factor of 3 we obtain the same performance as the coarse-only system. The reduction in the number of features provides additional benefit: an increase in the reliability of our estimate of the system's performance [22.11,12].

In the fine-only system the execution time U is increased more than four times over the coarse-fine system, and the external image memory is twice that required for the coarse-fine system, while both systems achieve approximately the same classification performance. (This analysis is based on an approximate scaling from coarse-fine to fine-only with no testing of the fine-only system on real data.) Thus the coarse-fine system provides an attractive cost/benefit ratio in comparison to the coarse-only and the fine-only systems for tumor detection.

22.6 Concluding Remarks

Using only six features on a data base of 19 films, our coarse-fine system achieved a false negative rate of about one-third of that of an average radiologist, while it achieved about four false positives per film. Radiologists working in a conventional manner on a data base nearly identical to the present one had a relatively small false positive rate -- about 0.2 false positive per film [22.2]. Working interactively with our tumor detection system, radiologists are likely to achieve the low false negative rate of our computer system while retaining their low false positive rates.

Since our computer system uses a relatively small number of features, we are encouraged to believe that the tuning of the system to the data base is small. To verify this belief, this tuning effect must be evaluated on an enlarged data base.

Acknowledgment

This research was supported by PHS Grant CA32847, awarded by the National Cancer Institute, Department of Health and Human Services.

References

22.1 A. Rosenfeld: "Quadtrees and pyramids for pattern recognition and image processing", in Proc. 5th Int'l. Conf. on Pattern Recognition, Miami Beach, FL, 1980, pp. 802-807

22.2 P. V. Sankar, D. Petkovic, H. Rosenberg, M. Hashimoto, K. Davila, J. Sklansky: "An experiment on computed detection of lung tumors", in Proc. Int'l. Workshop on Physics and Engineering in Medical Imaging, Pacific Grove, CA, 1982, pp. 106-114

22.3 D. Petkovic, "A Digital Data Base of Simulated Lung Tumors", Pattern
      Recognition Project Report TP-82-12, School of Engineering, University of California at Irvine (1982)
22.4 J. Sklansky, P. V. Sankar, M. Katz, F. Towfiq, D. Hassner, A. Cohen,
      W. Root: "Toward computed detection of nodules in chest radiographs",
      Proc. 6th Conf. on Computer-Aided Analysis of Radiographic Images,
      Newport Beach, CA, 1979, pp. 249-252
22.5 E. L. Hall: Computer Image Processing and Recognition (Academic Press,
      New York, 1979)
22.6 D. Petkovic: "Interfilm Calibration of Chest Radiographs", Pattern
      Recognition Project Report TP-82-11, School of Engineering, University of California at Irvine (1982)
22.7 L. G. Minor, J. Sklansky: The detection and segmentation of blobs in
      infrared images, IEEE Trans. Systems, Man, Cybernetics SMC-11, 194-201
      (1981)
22.8 C. Kimme, D. H. Ballard, J. Sklansky: Finding circles by an array of
      accumulators, Comm. ACM 18, 120-122 (1975)
22.9 M. Hashimoto, P. V. Sankar, J. Sklansky: "Detecting the edges of
      lung tumors by classification techniques", in Proc. 6th Int'l. Conf.
      on Pattern Recognition, Munich, Fed. Rep. Germany, 1982, pp. 276-279
22.10 P. V. Sankar, J. Sklansky: A Gestalt guided heuristic boundary follower for X-ray images of lung nodules, IEEE Trans. Pattern Analysis
      Machine Intelligence PAMI-4, 326-331 (1982)
22.11 D. H. Foley: Considerations of sample and feature size, IEEE Trans.
      Information Theory IT-18, 618-626 (1972)
22.12 J. Sklansky, G. N. Wassel: Pattern Classifiers and Trainable Machines
      (Springer, Berlin, 1981)

Index of Contributors

Subject Index

The numbers refer to the relevant Chapter(s)/Section(s)

Robot Vision

Editor: **A. Pugh**
1983. XI, 356 pages. (International Trends in Manufacturing Technology). In cooperataion with IFS (Publications) Ltd., U.K. ISBN 3-540-12073-4. (IFS: ISBN 0-903608-32-4)

Contents: Reviews. – Visual Processing Techniques. – Research. – Developments Weld Guidance. – Developments – Assembly/Part Presentation. – Applications. – Commercial Robot Vision Systems.

Picture Processing and Digital Filtering

Editor: **T. S. Huang**
2nd corrected and updated edition. 1979. 113 figures, 7 tables. XIII, 297 pages. (Topics in Applied Physics, Volume 6). ISBN 3-540-09339-7

Contents: *T. S. Huang:* Introduction. – *H. C. Andrews:* Two-Dimensional Transforms. – *J. G. Fiasconaro:* Two-Dimensional Nonrecursive Filters. – *R. R. Read, J. L. Shanks, S. Treitel:* Two-Dimensional Recursive Filtering. – *B. R. Frieden:* Image Enhancement and Restoration. – *F. C. Billingsley:* Noise Considerations in Digital Image Processing Hardware. – *T. S. Huang:* Recent Advances in Picture Processing and Digital Filtering. – Subject Index.

Two-Dimensional Digital Signal Processing I

Linear Filters
Editor: **T. S. Huang**
1981. 77 figures. X, 210 pages. (Topics in Applied Physics, Volume 42). ISBN 3-540-10348-1

Contents: *T. S. Huang:* Introduction. – *R. M. Mersereau:* Two-Dimensional Nonrecursive Filter Design. – *P. A. Ramamoorthy, L. T. Bruton:* Design of Two-Dimensional Recursive Filters. – *B. T. O'Connor, T. S. Huang:* Stability of General Two-Dimensional Recursive Filters. – *J. W. Woods:* Two-Dimensional Kalman Filtering.

Two-Dimensional Digital Signal Processing II

Transforms and Median Filters
Editor: **T. S. Huang**
1981. 49 figures. X, 222 pages. (Topics in Applied Physics, Volume 43). ISBN 3-540-10359-7

Contents: *T. S. Huang:* Introduction. – *J.-O. Eklundh:* Efficient Matrix Transposition. – *H. J. Nussbaumer:* Two-Dimensional Convolution and DFT Computation. – *S. Zohar:* Winograd's Discrete Fourier Transform Algorithm. – *B. I. Justusson:* Median Filtering: Statistical Properties. – *S. G. Tyan:* Median Filtering: Deterministic Properties.

Springer-Verlag
Berlin
Heidelberg
New York
Tokyo

Communication and Cybernetics

Editors: **K.S.Fu, W.D.Keidel, W.J.M.Levelt, H.Wolter**

Volume 10

Digital Pattern Recognition

Editor: **K.S.Fu**
2nd corrected and updated edition. 1980. 59 figures, 7 tables.
XI, 234 pages. ISBN 3-540-10207-8

Contents: *K.S.Fu:* Introduction. – *T.M.Cover, T.J.Wagner:* Topics in Statistical Pattern Recognition. – *E.Diday, J.C.Simon:* Clustering Analysis. – *K.S.Fu:* Syntactic (Linguistic) Pattern Recognition. – *A.Rosenfeld, J.S.Weszka:* Picture Recognition. – *J.J.Wolf:* Speech Recognition and Understanding. – *K.S.Fu, A.Rosenfeld, J.J.Wolf:* Recent Developments in Digital Pattern Recognition. – Subject Index.

The original edition of this book was enthusiastically received upon publiction in 1976. This updated and corrected paperback edition was undertaken to make the information more accessible to students. It/ contains an additional chapter (Chapter 7) which reviews recent advances in pattern recognition and image processing.

Volume 14

Syntactic Pattern Recognition, Applications

Editor: **K.S.Fu**
1977. 135 figures, 19 tables. XI, 270 pages. ISBN 3-540-07841-X

Contents: *K.S.Fu:* Introduction to Syntactic Pattern Recognition. – *S.L.Horowitz:* Peak Recognition in Waveforms. – *J.E.Albus:* Electrocardiogram Interpretation Using a Stochastic Finite State Model. – *R.DeMori:* Syntactic Recognition of Speech Patterns. – *W.W.Stallings:* Chinese Character Recognition. – *Th.Pavlidis, H.-Y.F.Feng:* Shape Discrimination. – *R.H.Anderson:* Two-Dimensional Mathematical Notation. – *B.Moayer, K.S.Fu:* Fingerprint Classification. – *J.M.Brayer, P.H.Swain, K.S.Fu:* Modeling of Earth Resources Satellite Data. – *T.Vámos:* Industrial Objects and Machine Parts Recognition.

The book deals with nine different applications of the syntactic approach to pattern recognition. They are waveform peak recognition, ECG interpretation, spoken word recognition, Chinese character recognition, shape discrimination, recognition of mathematics notation, fingerprint classification, modeling of satellite data and machine parts recognition. The syntactic approach is a new and powerful approach to pattern recognition. Its applications are certainly interesting to many different areas.
Practical applications of syntactic pattern recognition have never been systematically documented. This book, written by a group of experts in syntactic pattern recognition, gives a detailed account of each of the nine practical applications and problems for future research. Computation algorithms for implementation are also included. An introductory chapter provides the necessary background for the understanding of other chapters.

Springer-Verlag
Berlin
Heidelberg
New York
Tokyo